Parenting a preemie takes its emotional toll on mot offers practical tools to help parents take better car take better care of their baby. It's an invaluable res M.D., co-author of *The Premature Baby Book*

Deborah Davis and Mara Tesler Stein have created a gentle and safe haven for the entire family to feel through their prematurity experience. It is evident that the authors both deeply and sensitively recognize all that is lost through this experience, but much more importantly, all that is gained. —**Liza G. Cooper**, CSW, neonatal social worker

With a caring and compassionate voice, this book guides parents through the complex and ever-challenging emotional journey of parenting a premature infant. This book should be at every preemie parent's bedside from the moment they realize the possibility of the early birth of their infant. —**Dianne I. Maroney**, former NICU nurse, co-author of *Your Premature Baby and Child*

Over the past seven years I have communicated with thousands of parents coping with the intense emotions generated by the prematurity journey, and I am overjoyed that they will benefit from this invaluable resource. —**Allison Martin**, Preemie Child www.prematurity.org

With great insight, understanding, courage, and empathy, Debbie Davis and Mara Tesler Stein not only relate the story of life in and beyond the neonatal intensive care unit (NICU), they enable thousands of parents to tell their own. —**Brian S. Carter**, M.D., FAAP, associate professor of pediatrics, Vanderbilt University Medical Center

Parenting Your Premature Baby and Child: The Emotional Journey charts new ground in articulating the complex experience of premature birth and its aftermath. The overall themes of grief and healing resonate with both the authentic voices of parents and the depth of understanding and insight that the authors bring to their work. At every stage of the emotional journey there is both validation and practical advice. —**Anne Casey**, Preemie List www.preemie-l.org

Written with compassion and grounded in extensive research, *The Emotional Journey* is a comprehensive guide to the tumultuous and varied emotions that attend the birth and growth of a premature baby. I believe this book will be of enormous help to every parent caring for a baby born too early. —**Susan Madden** author of *The Preemie Parents' Companion*

In my position as Pregnancy.org's founder and owner, I meet many parents who are dealing with and preparing for premature babies. This book provides a complete and caring road map to guide parents in that preparation. I recommend it as a must-read! —**Mollee Olenick**, Pregnancy.org

As preterm birth rates rise and high-tech medicine saves ever-more-vulnerable infants, a large and growing number of families must cope with a new, traumatic form of parenthood. Davis and Stein present a comprehensive examination of the emotional and practical issues confronting these families. The wealth of wise counsel and heart-wrenching, insightful quotes from experienced mothers and fathers make this book a must for high-risk expectant couples; parents of preterm infants and children; as well as the friends, family members, and professionals who wish to help them. —**Helen Harrison**, author of *The Premature Baby Book*

Parenting Your Premature Baby and Child: The Emotional Journey is a small wonder. The voice of parents is present with great authenticity, as is the clarifying and calming but never denying or saccharine voice of the authors. Among the many aspects touched on that I most appreciated was the time devoted to listening and speaking to the father's feelings about their child, their wife and relationship, and themselves. —**Ed Tronick**, Ph.D., associate professor of pediatrics and psychiatry, Harvard Medical School; chief, Child Development Unit, Children's Hospital, Boston

Nothing can replace the dreams stolen by premature birth, but this book fills some of the aching, empty spaces. What a comfort this book will be to parents. When the world seems dark, disorienting, and full of endless suffering, hearing someone articulate, "Yes, this is crazy but you're not" is a priceless gift. —**Rochelle Barsuhn**, author of *Growing Sophia: The Story of a Premature Birth*

Invariably, upon the birth of their premature child, parents are warned that an "emotional roller-coaster" awaits them. Nothing can change the extraordinary daily dramas that unfold in a neonatal intensive care unit, subjecting parents and babies alike to a dizzying succession of devastating lows and euphoric highs. Boldly—and with remarkable depth and insight—Deborah L. Davis and Mara Tesler Stein have written a book that will help preemie parents navigate this harrowing path. What a noble accomplishment for Davis and Stein, and what an enormous asset for parents of premature babies. —**Elizabeth Mehren**, author of *Born Too Soon*

As a neonatologist who has had the privilege of caring for hundreds of premature babies and their families, as a mother who lived and survived the premature birth and death of a child, and as a teacher who will incorporate this book into the academic curriculum of the neonatology trainees in my program, I applaud and laud *Parenting Your Premature Baby and Child: The Emotional Journey*. —**Deborah Campbell**, M.D., FAAP, professor of clinical pediatrics, Albert Einstein College of Medicine; director, Neonatology, Children's Hospital at Montefiore

This book reflects both authors' experiences with the wide range of emotional reactions of parents and families when they have a premature birth. Thanks to the authors for their seven-year effort. It certainly shows up in the thorough, all encompassing, high quality of the book. —**Dr. John H. Kennell**, M.D., Rainbow Babies & Childrens Hospital, co-author of *Bonding*

An exemplary book. Drs. Davis and Stein take parents step by step through not only those first difficult weeks and months with their premature infant and child but also through the repeated developmental hurdles of the childhood years. They sensitively integrate the emotional intricacies and day-to-day realities that parents face. With wise, compassionate, and incredibly helpful suggestions, the authors give solutions to many of the challenges parents confront. Caregivers and those who support parents will also benefit by reading this book. — **Marshall Klaus**, M.D., and **Phyllis Klaus**, MFT, co-authors of *Bonding*

Parenting your Premature Baby and Child is a beautifully written, deeply felt testimony and resource for the ever-growing number of preterm parents. This book is full of knowledge, hope, wisdom, and reflection, and goes far beyond available books for preterm parents. Davis and Tesler Stein are truly gifted; they connect deeply to the reader's humanity and capacity to nurture and care. A remarkable accomplishment that will guide the field's progress for many years to come! —**Heidelise Als**, Ph.D., (psychologist), Harvard Medical School and Children's Hospital, Boston

In this comprehensive volume Drs. Davis and Stein help their readers navigate through the multifaceted and often complex journey of parenting a preemie. They provide a skillful balance of informative text and helpful aides to facilitate understanding, and help further the healing process. This fine work is destined to become a classic. —**Priscilla Hernandez Hacker**, Ph.D.

Parenting
Your
Premature
Baby
and
Child

ABOUT THE COVER

We were drawn to the image on this cover because the tandem footprints reflect the journey you are on with your baby or babies. The parent's foot next to the child's foot implies both the protectiveness and connection you experience as you walk with your child on this emotional journey. Being in the sand, the image, like the journey, includes both genders and all skin tones. Footprints are also evocative because they are usually one of the first images recorded in baby books. However, we want to assure you that we know that the baby footprint on the cover would completely engulf that of your baby at birth and for months afterward. Especially if your baby is still hospitalized, we hope that when you look at the cover you see hope for the future, when you and your growing child can make your own footprints in the sand. And just now, as we write this, it is occurring to us that this image perfectly coincides with the last heartfelt quote in Chapter 23. Like so many things about the creation and production of this book, it is synchronicity and pure magic.

Our warmest hugs and wishes,
Debbie and Mara

Parenting Your Premature Baby and Child

and

Child

The Emotional Journey

Deborah L. Davis, Ph.D. and Mara Tesler Stein, Psy.D.

•••
Fulcrum Publishing
Golden, Colorado

The information contained in this book, although based on sound medical judgment, is not intended as a substitute for medical advice or attention. Please consult your doctor or health care provider for individual professional care.

LIBRARY OF CONGRESS CATALOGING-IN-PUBLICATION DATA

Davis, Deborah L., 1955-
Parenting your premature baby and child: the emotional journey /
Deborah L. Davis & Mara Tesler Stein.
    p. cm.
Includes bibliographical references.
ISBN 1-55591-511-6
1. Infants (Premature) 2. Infants (Premature)--Care. 3. Parent and child. I. Tesler Stein, Mara. II. Title.
RJ250.D38 2004
618.92'011--dc22
                          2003020284
ISBN 1-55591-511-6
Printed in the United States of America
0 9 8 7 6 5 4 3 2 1

RJ
250
.D38
2004

Editorial: Faith Marcovecchio, Katie Raymond
Design: Ann W. Douden
Cover photo: © Joe Bator/Corbis

Fulcrum Publishing
16100 Table Mountain Parkway, Suite 300
Golden, Colorado 80403 U.S.A.
(800) 992-2908 • (303) 277-1623
www.fulcrum-books.com

DEDICATION

To all the parents who contributed to this book;
To their children;
To you and your children

CONTENTS

•••
vii

• • •
viii

• • •
xi
Contents

• • •

CHAPTER TEN

The Roller-Coaster NICU Experience 319

• • •

xiv

Parenting Your Premature Baby and Child

When a Baby Dies 359

• • •

Parenting Your Premature Baby and Child

Acknowledgments

Writing this book has been a journey for both of us. Our process of coming to understand the breadth and depth of emotion and meaning surrounding and following the birth of a premature baby has developed over a period of years. Just as for parents of preemies, our journey toward understanding and making meaning has been aided by the relationships that we had coming into this project and the ones that we have formed along the way.

Our deepest gratitude goes to Anne Casey, founder and director of Preemie-L, the premier Internet support group for parents of premature babies (www.preemie-l.org), for inviting us to involve Preemie-L subscribers as we researched the many topics in this book. This book could not have been written without her encouragement and generosity. And of course, we and many, many preemie parents are grateful for her inspired creation and gentle leadership of this group.

Special thanks to Allison Martin, leader of Preemie-Child, (www.prematurity.org), who gave us access to parents of older preemies and valuable insights into the ongoing consequences of premature birth on both children and parents.

We are eternally grateful to all the parents who contributed their voices to this book: the parents of Preemie-L and Preemie-Child, parents who filled out the Internet survey, parents who corresponded with us, and parents who were interviewed by us. Thank you for educating us with your postings and discussions, your writings and your words, and welcoming us into your virtual communities and personal lives. We have learned so much from each of you—not just about the emotional experience of giving birth prematurely, relating to a newborn in the NICU, and parenting a child after such a precarious start, but also about the powerful, transcendent bond between parent and infant, the ways that health care providers can support you and your family, and the fortitude of spirit that shows itself when you are struggling, coping, adjusting, and making the best of this unexpected and sometimes heart-wrenching path. Each of you is an inspiration to us. And whether you are directly quoted or not, your participation on Preemie-L or Preemie-Child or your correspondence or conversations with us has added immeasurably to our ability to write this supportive book. We are so grateful for your contributions, and we honor your intent to offer comfort and guidance to other parents of premature babies.

Thanks to Alaina Bacon Johnson, Psy.D., and Jane Hobard, M.A., then–graduate students at The Chicago School of Professional Psychology and Northeastern Illinois University who interviewed many parents. Your time, sensitivity, and insights during and after interviews enriched our growing understanding of the preemie journey.

Thank you to the neonatal nurses, respiratory therapists, neonatologists, obstetricians, pediatricians, and other health care providers from NICUs all over the world who openly discussed the issues that they confront with families, opening the door for us to address these issues in our research. Thank you to conference organizers who continue to invite the topic of the emotional and psychological issues in perinatal care into their professional forums.

Everlasting gratitude to Dianne Maroney, R.N., who was our match-maker, facilitating our first contact, which has grown into an amazing partnership.

Special thanks to Liza Cooper, M.S.W. with the March of Dimes, for collaborating with us to write the booklet *Parent: You and Your Baby in the NICU*, which is part of their NICU Family Support Project in hospitals nationwide, and for her continued dedication to providing emotional support to parents and families in the NICU.

Our appreciation goes to Charles Rait, R.N., and the folks at NICU Ink who supported us for five years during our research and writing process. Their faith and indulgence was key to our ability to put this book together.

We are most grateful to the folks at Fulcrum Publishing, who embraced our vision and were willing to take a chance. Faith Marcovecchio, our talented and brave editor, waded through a 1,250-page manuscript and earned our trust, awe, and appreciation.

My everlasting gratitude goes to Edward Tronick, Ph.D., and Marvin Daehler, Ph.D., who encouraged me to expand my educational horizons. Because of your leap of faith and confidence in me, I was able to find my calling.

My warmest appreciation to Marguerite Stewart, Psy.D., Peter Hulac, M.D., and Robert Harmon, M.D., who first invited me into the world of the NICU. You planted seeds.

Special thanks to all the folks associated with the Colorado Collective for Medical Decisions for giving me the opportunity to work on the important issue of medical ethics in the NICU and to hone my ability to support parents faced with agonizing decisions.

Thanks to Joyce Lung, R.N.C, for her inspiration for a part of the "A Note to Caregivers" appendix.

This book could never have happened without my husband, Ken Kirkpatrick, whose generosity, enthusiasm, and support of my writing has never wavered. To my beloved daughter, Maya Elizabeth: I'm so lucky to be your mama. You've shown me the heights and depths of motherhood. To my dear stepchildren, Faith and Jared, and Jola too: mothering you is an honor and my pleasure, and as we've woven our lives together, you have added immeasurable richness to my parenting role. All four of you have taught me a lot and deeply influence the way I write for parents.

To my family, friends, and colleagues: thank you for making circles of connection with me. These nurturing circles sustain me in the work I do. I am able to give so much because of what I receive from each of you. And finally, I am blessed to have Mara as my coauthor, partner, and friend. When she appeared in my life, I knew for certain that this book was meant to be. —DLD

Thanks to my friend Aviva Samet, Psy.D., who planted the idea for this book after my preemies were born. To my supervisors and professors at The Chicago School of Professional Psychology, thank you for helping to shape my thinking about human pain and healing.

My deepest appreciation to the nurses and doctors who cared for me antepartum during my long bed rest and who cared for my tiny preemies in the NICU and over the years afterwards. Especially to Barbara Robinson, M.D., who "held" me during six weeks of hospital bed rest and weathered the usual Thursday night crisis with me, accompanied me through my "post-preemie" pregnancy, and celebrated the birth of a baby who was "not a candidate for the NICU." To NICU nurses Barrie, Angie, and Renee who watched over my babies when I couldn't, I am forever grateful for the ways in which you sensitively and gently brought them closer to me. My experiences with you all set the stage.

I am so grateful to my colleagues and friends—you have been encouraging and supportive, asking questions and discussing our ideas. My relationships with each of you have contributed to my own healing and growth, and to the ideas and approaches in this book. To my clients who have invited me to join them on their healing journeys, your words and deepest feelings have profoundly influenced my understanding—thank you for inviting me to join you.

To my parents, your love, support, and your example taught me to always strive to be my best professionally and to work on behalf of the greater community. To my grandparents, siblings, in-laws, and extended family, you have always stood by me with love and enthusiasm. Thank you all for believing in me. My deepest love and gratitude to my husband, Richard, your staunch backing of this project made it possible and your insights and conversation always helps me to crystallize my thinking. Our partnership is truly a treasure. To my children, Gavriella Sara, Layla Chana—the babies who brought me to this journey—and Shimon Yakir, who joined them with gusto. I am blessed to be your mommy. You all continue to travel with me on this journey and never fail to inspire me.

Finally, I am blessed and so fortunate to have Debbie as my coauthor and dear friend. I could not imagine a better collaborator, catalyst, and sounding board. This book is interwoven with our partnership—truly destined and so precious.—MTS

At last, we sheepishly acknowledge the irony that this book on premature birth is long overdue. To all of the parents and health care providers who have watched this book evolve over the past seven years of gestation, thank you for your patience.

Introduction

The premature birth of your baby* is a medical crisis. But more than that, it is a family crisis. When your baby is born too soon, you must face not only the medical aspects of prematurity but also the many emotional aspects of parenting your premature baby. During your baby's hospitalization, after homecoming, and perhaps throughout childhood, there are three overarching, emotionally intense challenges you face:

- Coping with feelings
- Developing your parental identity
- Managing your relationships

Coping with feelings *includes*
- Learning to identify, express, and cope with a bewildering array of con-flicting emotions (including joy, sorrow, love, detachment, pride, guilt, gratitude, anger, confidence, helplessness, hope, fear)
- Doing grief work so that you can adjust and come to terms with your baby's premature birth and its consequences

Developing your parental identity *includes*
- Feeling connected to your baby

- Playing an indispensable role in the NICU
- Being your baby's advocate
- Acquiring new caregiving skills
- Gaining confidence
- Being protective without being overprotective
- Facing medical or developmental uncertainties or special needs
- Becoming the kind of parent you want to be

Managing your relationships *includes*
- Communicating and collaborating with your partner; your baby's health care providers; your other children (if any); and your relatives, friends, colleagues, and acquaintances
- Interacting with pregnant women and parents of full-term babies
- Acquiring a support network of other parents of preemies

This book addresses all these challenges, and more.

Indeed, this book rides on the crest of a new wave. In recent years, neonatology has become much more than medical technology. Along with providing state-of-the-art interventions, more and more NICUs are also providing developmentally supportive care to babies—and to their parents. Developmentally supportive care for a premature baby consists of close contact with the parents and being surrounded by the muted, gentle, nurturing conditions that mimic the womb. Developmentally supportive care for parents consists of honoring their need to get physically close and feel emotionally connected to their newborn and become confident in taking care of this baby. In other words, developmentally supportive care tries to give babies and parents what they've been promised.

Instead of banishing parents to waiting rooms or allowing them to merely look through a plate-glass window, modern NICU policy welcomes parents as integral members of their baby's NICU caregiving team and considers parental involvement paramount—good for the babies, good for the parents, good for the family. Indeed, when parents are given opportunities to be close to their baby and are encouraged and coached in caregiving, they can become attuned, responsive, and sure with their little one. When parents are informed about their baby's conditions and treatments, they can advocate for their baby's needs. When parents are supported emotionally, they can be more emotionally available to their baby. These positive, connective emotional experiences between parent and baby contribute to optimal infant development. This book reflects and accompanies the emerging respect for the developmental needs of the entire family and the spreading philosophy of family-centered care.

There are many good books that explain your premature baby's medical conditions, developmental diagnoses, treatments, and procedures, and that guide you in caregiving tasks. This book is different. It focuses on your experiences, feelings, and relationships around the delivery, hospitalization, homecoming, and long-term parenting of your premature baby and child. It provides suggestions and support for coping, adjusting, and finding your way. It focuses on how you can deal with the challenges you meet so you can revel in the pleasures of nurturing and cherishing your little one. With quotes from many parents, this book also strives to provide you with the comfort of knowing that your reactions make sense and that *you're not alone.*

While every family's journey is unique, you share many of the same hopes, fears, joys, sorrows, struggles, and triumphs with other parents of premature babies. It is our hope that you will find comfort, reassurance, support, and strength in these pages.

How to Use This Book

This book does not try to tell you how you should feel or what you must do. Rather, it strives to describe and affirm the wide range of experiences and emotional reactions that can follow a pregnancy crisis and premature delivery, and to offer strategies for coping with the hospitalization, homecoming, and parenting of your premature baby and child. With factual information and the words and insights of other parents, you can establish realistic expectations for yourself. You can also gain reassurance that you are not crazy; you are not the only one who feels betrayed, terrified, or guilty. You are not the only one to be wary of the tiny creature in the incubator, to wait and worry for the arrival of each new milestone, or to compare your child to both fellow premature babies and his or her full-term peers. This book is meant to help you through your experiences, at the same time encouraging you to do what *you* need to survive this journey. Whether your baby was born recently or long ago; extremely or moderately early; spent days, weeks, or months in the hospital, you will find yourself reflected in these pages. Whatever your child's outcome, you will find support.

We also encourage you to use this book as a source of information to share with others as you see fit. Certain sections may offer suggestions you'd like your friends to have or insights you'd like to share with your family's health care providers. You can also photocopy the appendices for those who are interested.

And even if your partner isn't the type to read this kind of book, try offering selected sections or chapters that are particularly relevant. Having this direction and focus can make reading more appealing and manageable, even to those who don't usually turn to books for support.

You may find yourself wondering about the parents whose quotes are used in this book. Quotes were collected over a period of six years. Parents were recruited through newsletters and word of mouth, and their interviews were videotaped. Other parents discovered our online questionnaire in their Internet searches, wrote their stories down, and sent them to us. Still more parents were participants on the leading Internet parent support group "Preemie-L" at www.preemie-l.org.

Because information for this book was gathered from many different parts of the world through e-mail, colloquial terms appear in some of the quotes. However, we standardized the various terms for NICU and incubator for consistency. For some parents, English was not their mother tongue, so you may notice some slightly atypical phrasing, which we kept in the interest of retaining their unique voices.

Some quotes were written and others were spoken, so you may detect a variation in tone. All quotes were transcribed from videotaped interviews, written questionnaires, and Internet correspondence, with minimal grammatical editing for clarity. Some parents contributed over extended periods of time, so if you detect any inconsistencies in certain parents, it's because their words offer different perspectives according to different points in their journey. All parents were quoted with their explicit consent.

You may wonder about the situational details surrounding these parents and their premature babies, or you may want to know more about what happened to them down the road. You may want to measure your circumstances, outcomes, and reactions against theirs. But each family's situation is so unique that even if you knew all those details, making comparisons with another family's journey, as tempting as they are to make, can interfere with

• • •

your appreciation of your *own* unique journey. Thus, this book does not dwell on situational details, which vary widely. Though you may hope to find yourself or your child in those details—such as specific pregnancy complications, a baby born at the same gestational age as yours, length of hospital stay, or developmental outcome—where you will actually find yourself is in the emotional nuances of other parents' experiences. This common ground is also where you will find kinship with other parents and truly know that you are not alone. And so, when you wish you knew "the rest of the story," keep in mind that you already know about the most important parts of their journeys—the emotional, wrenching, life-enriching, deeply meaningful parts, many of which may resonate for you. And what matters most "down the road" is that these parents are continuing on their journeys, and they've survived. Just as you will.

• • •

Organizing this book was very challenging. There is a time line to follow, but the three overarching themes of "coping with feelings," "developing your parental identity," and "managing your relationships" come up at every turn. At any point on your personal journey, you may feel emotionally overwhelmed, face regrets or worries, or revisit your memories. Over the years, your growth and development as a parent and a person will continue, keeping in step with your preemie's growth, development, and changing needs. All along the way, you will be dealing with your partner, your other children, your relatives, your friends, and your baby's health care providers. Since books are naturally linear and don't take well to any other arrangements, we encourage you to weave your way through this book to match the nonlinear path your experience of having a preemie takes. Some sections may feel more appropriate than others at different times, depending on your unique situation, your personality, and where you are in your journey. Use the Table of Contents and the Index to find your currently pressing concerns. For instance, you may want to check out Chapter 19, "Your Family," where you'll find information on your relationships with your partner and dealing with your other children. Even though this chapter appears later, you may want some of that insight and support from the beginning. And keep referring back to Chapter 2, "Grief and Adjustment," and Chapter 3, "Moving through Painful Emotions," as this support and information can be helpful to you all along the way.

• • •

As you weave your way through the book, you can also peek ahead into the future for preparation and reassurance, or review the past for validation, affirmation, and to make sense of where you've been and where you are. Take in whatever seems helpful and pass by whatever isn't. Return to the passages that are particularly comforting and try reading other parts later. It is not necessary to read this book through from start to finish. Even if you do read it cover to cover and then put it away, *we encourage you to revisit this book from time to time.* You'll notice that what you need will stand out every time, and what you need will always seem to be different. This book is meant to be your companion, and it will follow your lead.

If reading this book moves you to cry, try to accept this reaction. These are healing tears of grief and joy, courage and strength that mix with those of other parents. You are not alone.

Time is too slow for those who wait,

Too swift for those who fear,

Too long for those who grieve,

Too short for those who rejoice.

But for those who love,

Time is eternity.

—HENRY VAN DYKE

---

* Usually it is awkward to accommodate singleton and multiple babies in the same sentence by writing "baby or babies" or even "baby(ies)" and "child(ren)." So most of the time we will just refer to "your baby" or "your child." If you delivered twins, triplets, or more, please know that whenever applicable to your situation, "your baby" or"child" means "your babies" or "children."

CHAPTER ONE

An Unexpected Journey

When you find out you are pregnant, you are anticipating so much more than just a baby. Along with your hopes for a healthy baby, you may have many optimistic expectations for this pregnancy, the labor and delivery, and the newborn period. You may start forming a picture of the expanded family you're creating and the future you're building. Indeed, you imagine being a certain kind of parent to a certain kind of baby.

When your pregnancy ends prematurely, many of your hopes and expectations unravel. When your newborn is confined to a neonatal intensive care unit (NICU), you miss many of the early parenting experiences you were anticipating. Even after you bring your baby home, when your infant is so tiny and vulnerable, the experience may not match the one you had envisioned. Because your expectations about pregnancy, birth, and homecoming have been violated, having a premature baby can feel bewildering, frustrating, saddening, even devastating. As your baby grows, you may continue to be affected by the premature birth, whether or not your child is.

When your premature baby is born, you're not just experiencing a singular event, you're embarking on a journey. Along the way, you relinquish old dreams, adjust to what is, and dream new dreams. This process of grief and adjustment includes coping with your feelings, developing your parental identity, and managing your relationships. But this journey of parenting your preemie is a journey you probably didn't even know existed, one through uncharted territory. You may feel entirely lost and unsure.

This chapter establishes a base camp, offering you an orientation, a map, and a compass to help you make your way along your journey. First, we offer you the orientation that your baby's premature birth is a violation of your heartfelt expectations. This critical understanding gives you a context in which your emotional reactions can make sense to you, and then you can begin to grieve, cope, and adjust. Although this orientation shows you your pain, it also starts you on a journey of healing and growth.

Second, we'll provide a map of the main tasks ahead of you: coping with feelings, developing your parental identity, and managing your relationships. These tasks have always been a part of your life, but your baby's prematurity puts your emotional, parenting, and social abilities to the test. Because each parent's journey is unique, this map cannot show you precisely where you need to go or how to get there. But it can be your guide, showing you the milestones, pitfalls, and pleasures you may encounter, and offering suggestions and support as you determine your own speed, direction, transportation, and the paths you take.

Finally, since you are responsible for your own navigation, we offer you a compass to guide you on your journey and to reorient you when you're feeling lost. The needle of this compass points you toward the affirmation that parenting a premature baby is a journey that's just as legitimate, worthy, and rewarding as parenting a full-term baby, even though it's different from the experience you were counting on. Becoming a different kind of parent to a different kind of child is full of unique challenges, certainly, but also full of unique joys and opportunities for your own growth and development, as a parent and as a person.

We offer you this orientation, map, and compass so that you can go forth with faith in your ability to prevail, hope for the future, and love in your heart for your child.

Orientation

Hopes and Expectations

Being pregnant was a dream come true! We had tried for almost five years, so that positive pregnancy test was the answer to my prayers. I was thrilled beyond belief. I wanted that baby so desperately! I had every hope and dream imaginable for an idyllic pregnancy, birth, and baby. I had waited so long that everything was bound to be perfect! I immediately took on the role of "mother-to-be"—I ate well, slept, and took good care of myself and this baby of mine. —Sara

I was very happy. ... I was thrilled at the prospect of getting a big belly and having the baby kick and push at my stomach. I wanted to remember all the feelings. I was never sick. I had a great time while I was pregnant. ... I was enjoying watching my body change. —Kristina

When you are pregnant, it is natural for you to revel in the wonder and anticipation of it all. It is also natural for you to count on having all those months before the due date to prepare both psychologically and physically. If this is your first pregnancy, you expect to have time to adjust to the idea that you are about to become a parent. If you've been down this road before, you may appreciate the idea of having nine months to move through the normal mixed feelings about bringing another child into the family. Whatever your situation, you plan to finish your nesting projects, to make a place for your baby to come home to, and to be ready and welcoming when the time comes. With all of these plans and preparations, you have an enormous emotional investment in carrying the pregnancy to term.

You may also have hopes and expectations for the delivery. You may hope to be active in the birthing process, to be able to make choices that you believe will give your baby and your relationship the best possible start. You may envision gently welcoming your baby into the world. You imagine a newborn who is cute, tranquil, and fits nicely into your arms. You picture nuzzling and nursing your little one. You naturally anticipate bringing your baby home after a day or so, to the congratulations of friends and family. Picturing your healthy, robust infant, you see a bright future.

These visions are not just enjoyable daydreams, but they are also important psychological preparation for your future as a parent. Having certain expectations lets you make plans and feel some measure of control. Positive assumptions give you confidence and hope. You invest in your future as you imagine it.

I read everything I could get my hands on about pregnancy. My husband, Chris, and I wanted a natural childbirth. We practiced the Bradley method every night together. He was a wonderful coach, and I envisioned him there with me as we welcomed our new baby into the world without drugs or machines. —Rebekah

When I found out Cyndy was pregnant with twin boys, I had dreams of big, strapping football players—the first twins in the NFL. I dreamed of the things we would do together, running, biking, watching the games on Sundays. —Rich

During the pregnancy, I was not afraid of anything—I just took for granted that everything always goes smoothly. ... It never once occurred to me that things do go wrong. —Jodi

Most expectant parents have faith that their pregnancy is healthy and will go to term. They don't seriously contemplate other possibilities. Even if you feel a sense of uneasiness or if you are identified as being "high risk," it is hard to believe that bad things could really happen to *you*. You still expect relatively smooth sailing. But as events begin to unfold in unexpected ways, those assumptions start dissolving. You are confronted with the possibility that your future will be different from the one you had imagined.

I had wanted a baby for many years, and now I was finally going to have one. I imagined "she" would be perfect. I was exercising, eating well, and had already cut out all caffeine and alcohol. Still, because I was a bit on the old side, I waited to tell family and friends until I was through my first trimester. I felt like things were just too wonderful—too good to be true. —Rebekah

When the Unexpected Happens

Six weeks into my pregnancy I started to bleed. ... I was devastated. Throughout the next few weeks my doctors' appointments were not the happy events I had hoped for and dreamed of in a pregnancy. —Lauren

I was in a hospital bed with an IV in one hand, a blood pressure cuff on the other arm, and a fetal monitor around my stomach. The TV was playing ESPN's SportsCenter, and Joe was in a chair next to me. It was surreal— how did we get from one place to another, an incredible high to this frightening low? —Mindy

We'd seen the NICU on a tour when I was first pregnant, and I had thought it was for the very sick, deformed children, babies that weren't going to live. I told myself I would never be there. I'm going to have normal, healthy children. Why wouldn't I? Everybody does—except those people, those poor, poor people. So when I found myself in the NICU, I just couldn't believe it. —Vickie

The day we left the hospital without the baby, my husband and I sat on our sofa and sobbed all night long. We felt empty and exhausted. We realized we had been in shock and still were. I was feeling great loss. I rely heavily on tradition. I'm a planner. This was not how it was supposed to be, not how I had planned it. —Laura

Whether problems develop in the first, second, or third trimester of your pregnancy, your expectations for a blissful pregnancy are shaken. But even though you are shocked and distressed, you may still hold out hope for a timely, gentle delivery. When preterm birth is imminent, your hopes and wishes for the delivery crumble, but you may still hold onto your fantasies of a healthy baby. Then, when you see your baby, another layer of expectations tumbles down. When a baby is born too soon, neither the baby nor the parents are ready.

After we found out we were pregnant, the baby came five months later. ... Financially, we were unprepared. Emotionally, you can never be prepared. —Lauren

Seeing a premature baby is so very different from anything you could ever imagine! The things you have come to consider normal just aren't there! There is no fat at all on these little peanuts. Their ears are like pieces of paper, moldable to any shape, depending on how they were positioned. Their heads look monstrous in comparison to that teeny body. Could anyone possibly see their newborn baby looking like this and not be shocked, scared, and saddened? —Sara

I focused more on their baby-ness than on their medical condition. They were little and helpless, and mine. But I also had a sense that this was the beginning of a dramatic step that I couldn't undo and that would change our lives forever. —Dwight

When your tiny baby lies sick and struggling in an intensive care nursery, you can feel a shift in your expectations about parenthood and what will be asked of you as a parent. Instead of feeling well equipped to respond to your baby's needs, you feel scared, lost, and confused. As you peer at your infant, overwhelmed by the tubes, wires, and buzzing machinery, you feel helpless in the face of medical technology. You compare this surreal scene with your fantasies about holding and nursing your newborn, taking your baby home, and showing him or her off to admiring friends and relatives. You wonder how to parent this small creature; how to best stroke your baby's soft, fragile skin; how to comfort and come to know your tiny child. You wonder when you will be able to take your baby out of the hospital and somehow find your way back to the path you had planned.

I knew she had just been removed from my body, but it still seemed unreal to me. While I was in recovery, my husband saw the baby in the NICU and returned crying. My parents saw her and returned crying. I remember feeling afraid to go to the NICU. When I finally went, my reaction was still one of unreality. Of course, she did not look at all like the baby I had envisioned. My dreams met reality that night in the NICU, and I just could not reconcile the two. —Renee

It takes away the fairy tale. You know—you have a baby, everyone's happy, you pass out cigars, and the baby goes home and goes to sleep and you just give them your life. —Charlie

• • •

There is another layer of expectation that is challenged when your baby is born too early—expectations about modern medicine. At first, your faith in medical treatments and technology can lead you to assume that your baby will recover easily and come home very soon. In labor, Suzanne admits, "I thought, 'Oh, okay.' I was under the impression that you had a baby that was small, it would be in the hospital for a while, and everything would be fine. I was very naive, very uninformed."

You may believe that everything will be fine because, many times, no one is saying otherwise. Even if you know your baby is critically ill, it is hard to believe that modern medicine might not come through for your child.

When they called at 5:00 A.M. and said Travis was getting sicker, I figured I'd get there, they'd work on him a little bit, and he'd be back to normal, you know, just like on the TV shows. I didn't know what was going on.
—Charlie

As you learn more about the limits of modern medicine, you begin to realize that bad things can happen to newborns. Suddenly, illness, disability, and death challenge your assumptions about the beginning of life. Even if your baby stabilizes quickly, his or her need for intensive care is incompatible with your ideas of how newborns are supposed to be. If your baby experiences complications or doesn't fully recover, or if your baby dies, your trust in the wonders of modern medicine may be shattered.

Finally, premature birth confronts your expectations about how life is supposed to work. You may have held onto the belief that "doing all the right things" during pregnancy would guarantee a healthy baby. You may have believed that nothing bad happens to good people, and especially to their babies. You also may have held onto the hope that fervent prayer or adherence to ritual or superstition could guard you and your baby against harm. Whatever you did or believed to protect yourself, you are likely to feel alone and betrayed when crisis strikes. Most of all, you may feel cheated out of experiencing a marvel of nature—the uncomplicated birth of a healthy baby.

Things aren't supposed to happen like this. One of the tougher initial feelings was in the recovery room after the C-section. My wife was still under the anesthesia. There were four couples in the room, and the other three had babies. It was a very separating and isolating feeling. I'll never forget it. —Preston

As all of these sets of expectations are shattered, what you face is entirely different from what you imagined. The changes in your relationships, the emotions you face, your shifting identity, needs, choices, and priorities— your entire situation is transformed and nothing feels right. Your world doesn't make sense anymore, and you may worry that it never will again. It's difficult to imagine that you will ever adjust—and yet, with time and experience, eventually you will.

I think it matters a lot "where you are" in this journey. When I was in the NICU, my skin was so thin and raw that I don't really even know how I functioned. After we came home, I was better, but still, if I had to use one word, I would say I was scared. And now, I still have my moments, but after two years, I would say I am really just coming out of a fog. —Lara

In the early weeks, as you struggle to make sense of what has happened, the flood of feelings makes it necessary to cling to old, familiar dreams. As you become more comfortable with your baby, you gradually grieve for what might have been and learn to cope with what *is*. Over time, you come to accept and even appreciate the reality. Eventually, you can find the treasure in adversity.

As time passes, you realize that watching your premature baby grow brings some unexpected gifts. The joy of a smile, the appreciation of even small developmental steps, or respect for your child's individual pace makes parenting a preemie a rich experience. No matter what, you will view your child's growth and development through different eyes and with a mixture of intense, conflicting feelings. You may feel a combination of hopes and fears, disappointment, relief, and joy. You will notice that your perspective has shifted. You take nothing for granted.

I think I appreciate what I have so much more than most parents do. For example, Josh and Evan this week for the first time asked "what" and "how" questions. I literally almost started to cry. Most parents don't even notice when their kids start to ask questions. —Stephie

· · ·

14

You become wiser, too, in that you begin to realize that nothing is guaranteed. And with this growing awareness, you turn to look at your child. Each step in development, each illness, each decision you make for your growing child's welfare is colored with the knowledge that you will always do everything you can for your child, but that there are things you cannot know and cannot control.

When you have a premature baby, you must adjust your expectations. You will gradually modify some of your goals and beliefs, and redefine what it means to be a parent to this child. Premature birth sets you on a different path.

Map

A Different Path

Naturally, parenthood transforms you. Every parent experiences a wide variety of feelings that are triggered by the birth and parenting of a child. You must develop feelings of competence and confidence, along with a sense of self that includes your parenting role. And you adjust important relationships to accommodate the devotion to your new baby. But having a premature baby brings tribulations and opportunities beyond those normally faced by parents. It challenges your emotional coping abilities, your developing parental identity, and your relationship skills.

Emotional Coping Your baby's premature birth starts an avalanche of both positive and painful emotions that come together in bewildering and contradictory ways. Your newborn's hospitalization and separation from you can be supremely challenging as you deal with sadness, yearning, fear, and uncertainty. In the midst of your grief, you will also experience many moments of joy, fulfillment, hope, and love. The milestone achieved when your baby comes home is a triumph, but he or she is still recovering from the premature birth. So are you. After keeping it together during the intensity of intensive care, being at home may afford you the opportunity to fall apart and feel the brunt of your emotions. Additionally, most premature babies require special handling, and your baby's unique needs will affect you and your ongoing adjustment. And if your preemie's medical or developmental outcome holds uncertainties, or if disabilities appear, you'll continue to feel torn between your hopes and fears.

Up to this point in your life, you've probably encountered a number of painful losses and challenges, and managed to get through them. But the losses and challenges associated with a premature birth reverberate profoundly through every cell of your body and touch the deepest parts of your being. As your journey unfolds, you will most likely have to acquire new coping skills to manage the wide range and intensity of these emotions. You must learn to identify, express, and work through your pain, so that you can move through it, instead of becoming immobilized by it.

Developing Your Parental Identity When your baby arrives early, you may feel terribly unprepared for parenthood. You may need more time to finish lining the nest, to consider baby names, and to shore up your nerve. And when delivery is a medical emergency, you miss some of the classic milestones of parenthood, such as a joyful delivery and close contact with your newborn. The milestones that take their place are unfamiliar and your emotional reactions such as fear, guilt, and sorrow are not what you expected to feel. So not only are you unprepared for parenthood, you're also unprepared for this kind of introduction to parenthood. And to top it off, you're unprepared to take care of this kind of baby.

Over the years, you've absorbed much general knowledge about how to take care of a new baby, but much of this knowledge doesn't seem to apply to *your* new baby. Your baby's hospitalization and medical condition create many barriers that can keep you from feeling connected to your little one. You have to figure out your role as a parent in the NICU and learn caregiving skills that you didn't even know existed. It can take time and practice to feel confident and competent with your newborn.

> *He was so small at the beginning. You're almost scared to touch them and pick them up when they're so tiny. And then it takes you a little bit to get comfortable, and then you have to learn how to give them a bath, which is a big thing. You gave baths to your two other kids, no problem, but this is really a big thing, to feel comfortable. So I guess I had to learn how to be a mom again, a new kind of mom or a different kind of mom—to a different, new sort of baby I had never experienced before. —Gallice*

Managing Your Relationships Your baby's prematurity strains your relationships because you've embarked on a journey that most of your friends and relatives cannot relate to. The emotional roller coaster of the NICU and the fallout after homecoming heighten your need for understanding and support. And yet, most people won't understand, and some won't know how to support you. Even your relationship with your partner can become rocky as you both enter unfamiliar terrain. In addition, you will form relationships with your baby's health care providers that require a level of commitment, collaboration, and communication that you may never have practiced before. As your child grows, depending on his or her ongoing needs you may also form important relationships with therapists and teachers as you continue to be your child's best advocate.

• • •

Coping with feelings, developing your parental identity, and managing your relationships—these are the central tasks you face throughout your emotional journey of parenting your premature baby and child. All of these tasks are intertwined and you must manage them together. For example, you must process your feelings and learn effective ways of coping, so that you can come into your own as a parent who has the emotional resources to nurture and invest in your baby. If you are aware of your emotional needs, all of your other relationships benefit as well. By building closer alliances with your partner, friends, relatives, and health care providers, you can garner their emotional support and collaboration. With their support of your growing identity as a parent, you can get close to your baby, play an indispensable role in the NICU, be protective without being overprotective, face uncertainties or special needs, and become the kind of parent you want to be.

In your quest to master these tasks around feelings, identity and relationships, it would ease your journey to have a map to guide you. The map you'll find in this book consists of information, suggestions, and ideas, which can help you interpret the landscape, give you options to consider, and offer you insights to illuminate your path.

Compass

Finding Your Own Way

Just as your premature baby is beginning a new journey, so, too, are you. At first you may be overcome by grief for what might have been, but with the passage of time, you can work through those feelings and emerge with a new

• • •

appreciation for *this* journey. You can acknowledge what you've lost, yet move forward with what you've gained.

Because you're on a journey that is uniquely your own, it can help to have a compass to guide you as you learn to navigate the emotional terrain. Indeed, you can rely on different compasses, including this book, friends and family, your intuition, an insight that gives you hope, and the belief that your journey has meaning. With this book as a compass, you can get some bearings and some pointers, and figure out which way to go. Even though you may feel lost and confused at times, you can work through the emotional pain and find your way toward adjustment and healing.

With the passage of time, you will also see that you are not alone. Although each parent's journey is unique, parents of premature babies still share many common experiences, perceptions, and emotions. Parents you connect with or read about can inspire, comfort, and guide you on your journey. That feeling of camaraderie and sense of community is a compass that can give you hope.

You will discover other ways to strengthen your hope. In the beginning and with each new crisis, it is natural to believe that certain elements of the situation appear hopeless. But as time passes, you will learn to manage your fears so that they don't require more energy than they deserve, and you will find new hopes to hold on to. You will also acquire more optimism when you can look back and see that many of your deepest worries did not come to pass.

• • •

The challenges you meet, the strengths you carry, and the steps you take will be unique to your journey. From this book, your orientation is the approach, which helps you to center yourself in the midst of chaos and sends you on a healing journey; your map is the information that shows you the emotional terrain of parenting a premature baby and child. Your compass is the emotional support provided—the reassurance that your experiences and reactions are normal, the encouragement to prevail, the affirmation of your journey's value, and the comfort offered by the words of other parents who've traveled this way before you.

The Tapestry That Reflects
Your Emotional Journey

Throughout your life, you are weaving a tapestry that reflects your emotional journey—where you've been, how you've changed, and what you've learned, lost, and acquired all along the way. The threads you are weaving are the threads of feelings, the threads of your identity, and the threads of your relationships.

In your tapestry, different parts of your life are represented by woven sections of varying textures, colors, and patterns. Some parts are smooth, others are coarse. Some parts hold vibrant colors, others hold muted tones. Some parts are crisp or solid, and in other parts there is a blending of colors or textures. Some blendings are messy or clashing, and others are more harmonious.

When your baby is born prematurely, the tapestry that you've been weaving abruptly changes. The threads become rough and unwieldy, and you're not sure what to do with them. They are still the threads of feelings, the threads of your identity, the threads of your relationships, but they have become more complex, more intense, more painful, and more challenging to work with. You feel unprepared. You cannot weave the pattern you'd planned. Your tapestry is not what you thought it would be. Instead you must improvise.

Tentatively, you begin to weave with those unfamiliar strands, and you learn how to work with them. At first your weaving seems messy and discordant. But as you become more adept and at ease, you begin to appreciate the surprising and creative aspects of your weaving. What you thought was messy, ugly, or clashing is actually quite exciting. You've adjusted in ways you never dreamed of. When you step back, you can see how this weaving fits into the bigger tapestry you have been creating your whole life. In fact, your tapestry has become richer, more interesting, and more beautiful.

Along with an orientation, a map, and a compass, this book also offers you a weaving guide of sorts. It is a guide that informs, supports, and empowers you to improvise. It describes and affirms the changes in your tapestry and shows you how to value them. It encourages you to see this transformation as a reflection of your healing.

Parenting Your Premature Baby and Child

CHAPTER TWO

Grief and Adjustment

When you deliver early, you begin an emotional journey you hadn't planned. You will mourn the losses you experience, but your journey is not just about grief, it's also about joy, delight, and devotion. As such, the ebb and flow of your emotions can be perplexing and unpredictable. Sadness and happiness will mix with many other profound and sometimes disturbing emotions. You'll also experience discordant reactions—during intense situations, you may at times feel deeply involved, at other times removed; during situations that pose no threat, intense emotions may surface.

This chapter explains the reasons for this bewildering mix of positive and painful feelings, intensity, and detachment. It also offers a framework for facing these contradictions and coping with an onslaught of emotions. We look especially closely at the many painful feelings of grief that parents of preemies experience; in Chapter 3 we will elaborate on the emotions particularly challenging to work through, among them anger, guilt, and powerlessness. By beginning this book with some explanations about grief and strategies for coping, we hope to provide you with a supportive context for braving the emotional journey of parenting your premature baby and child.

Wrestling with Opposing Emotions

I saw my baby for a split second. It was the happiest and saddest moment of my life. I was the proudest mother in the world; I was also so scared for this poor, innocent little baby who needed so much more time in his mother. My husband and I glowed ... but it was a sad glow. —Misty

She was so tiny. I was just sitting there looking at her. I was thinking, "Oh, my God, that's my baby." I was just really afraid. ... She didn't look like a real baby, but like a medical experiment gone awry. She looked absolutely horrible. She wasn't moving at all, except for her chest going up and down. But she was also really beautiful. I liked the way her mouth and chin looked. It was just so cute. —Brooke

Bewilderment comes to mind. I couldn't quite get my mind around the fact that he was finally here. I couldn't quite take in that he was so fragile. I couldn't figure out the turmoil of emotions rolling around inside. I was wrung with tenderness for this little delicate creature. I wanted to hold him to my face and feel his skin and envelop him with kisses. I wanted to smell his skin and stroke his face while I studied his features. I wanted to play with his hands. I wanted to experience his presence and I couldn't. I was numb and I was on fire at the same time. I was panicked and exhilarated. I was living a paradox of emotions. —Laurie

Pregnancy and childbirth, by their very nature, stir up contradictory reactions in most expectant parents. High hopes and deep worries, joyful anticipation and pronounced ambivalence, excitement and nonchalance are common for parents, during even the easiest pregnancies. Troubles turn up both the emotional intensity and the dissonance several notches.

You get this honeymoon, the first twenty-four hours [after delivery], and the kids are coasting on all their juices from mom, and they're doing pretty good. They're intubated, but we were told that they were doing fine and there was a little while of joy. And then that wore off, and it wore off quite quickly. By that evening, things had definitely become sad. I had a cot in the room where Debbie was staying, and I'm not real big on crying, but I remember lying there

*crying because I knew—and I don't know how I knew or what I knew
exactly—that surely we were in for some serious trouble. And so it was really
hitting me at this point. So this joy we had, this joy over the excitement of
having twins, lasted for an hour before it came to an end, and then it was bad.
—Mitch*

When an expectation is violated, you may feel both surprised and
betrayed, as if the rug has been pulled out from under you. Intense feelings of
disappointment and fear may overcome your hopes and dreams. Yet your
hopes and dreams are still there, and so you vacillate between opposing
emotions. This flip-flopping can be confusing and exhausting. For instance:

- You may fear the worst, but because you are too frightened to consider
  the possibilities, you try to remain positive and hopeful.
- Your hope that everything will turn out okay gives you confidence, but
  your worries make you uncertain.
- Your feelings of joy that your baby survived are coupled with sadness
  for what you and your baby have lost.
- Proud that you carried your baby past a certain number of weeks, you
  may also feel a deep sense of failure that you weren't able to bring your
  baby closer to term.
- You may think that you must *somehow* have contributed to your baby's
  current situation, even though rationally you know you are not responsible for it.
- You may feel responsible for what happens to your baby, yet powerless
  to do anything to change the situation.
- Although you long for your baby, you may resist going to see him or her
  in the NICU because you dread what you will see.
- When you do see your baby, you may feel a surge of devotion or numb
  detachment.
- You may feel resentment toward the NICU or certain medical professionals and, at the same time, eternal gratitude for the technology and
  the skilled and dedicated staff who are working to save your baby's life.
- You may pity the families whose babies are doing worse than yours and
  envy those whose babies are doing better.
- The ups and downs of your infant's medical course during the NICU
  stay may bring on unpredictable extremes of optimism and pessimism.

- When your baby comes home, you may be eager to get out of the house or have family and friends over, but you're also terrified because of the dangers it could pose to your baby.
- As you watch your baby grow, you are grateful for every milestone achieved but always worried about the next one.

Although these competing feelings can be quite bewildering, they are naturally complex reactions to a complex situation. At times, your emotions may seem to lack rhyme or reason. If you're the mother, your postpartum hormonal fluctuations may contribute to your sense of emotional instability.

Besides experiencing opposing emotions, you may also experience varying levels of emotion, from intensity to numbness, especially early on. The numbness, especially, can be quite baffling because it doesn't match the intensity of the situation.

It all happened so fast, really, that I couldn't keep up. My thoughts, my reactions, my emotions—I just couldn't swallow it all. It almost seemed like a dream sequence. The neonatologist visited me while I was in labor, to inform me of what circumstances we would be facing. He told me there was a fifty-fifty chance she would die and, if she lived, a fifty-fifty chance she would be severely damaged in some way. I just couldn't get my mind around it. I was devastated, but it all seemed so unreal. It was so sudden and unexpected.
—Renee

I zoned out. I went numb and stayed numb for a very long time. I was dealing with the most traumatic event of my life. ... I had feelings, but looking back ... I was a zombie. —Misty

You may wonder how you can be so emotionless, especially during a crisis. Remind yourself that numbness is a necessary and normal protective mechanism. Traumatic events and frightening facts can be simply too much to take in all at once. Denial lets you hold out hope that everything will turn out okay. Detachment from the situation gives you a chance to recuperate, to build your reserves. Detachment from your baby lets you absorb difficult information at a pace that is not so overwhelming. That's why life takes on a surreal quality while you gradually grow used to your new situation, slowly understand what is happening to your baby, and begin to envision what lies ahead.

During the ultrasound, I could tell immediately something was wrong. My funny, fun-loving doctor was serious and straight-faced. I thought the worst. Then he said, "I am not finding a flow in the umbilical cord of baby A." My heart sank. I was quiet, waiting for him to say something. He just kept looking and looking. I said, "What does that mean?" He said that the flow was diminished and the baby was not getting enough nutrition. I honestly thought that no flow would have meant the baby had died and was getting no oxygen. I was being incredibly calm, now that I look back at it. —Pamela

It still hadn't quite sunk in that I'd just given birth. They put me in a wheelchair and took me down the hall to the NICU. There is no way anyone can ever be prepared for that first look at your baby in this condition. I had never seen anything so small in my life ... he looked like a tiny roast. Lying there in his big square plastic pan covered with cellophane, looking all shiny and greased up, with the heat lamps glaring above him. He honestly looked like he was being cooked. I couldn't look at him anymore. I went to my room, curled up with Jon, and cried myself to sleep. —Ami

You may look back in disbelief or embarrassment for being so naive about your situation, so in shock, so full of denial. Rest assured, your reactions were natural and to be expected. Even health care providers who are knowledgeable about warning signs or experienced in the care of premature babies have similar responses when it happens to their own babies. When it's your own life, no amount of experience and knowledge can shield you from the emotional realities. This is how Christoph, a neonatologist, describes his reactions:

At thirty-one weeks, my wife had premature labor, and reluctantly I drove her, at 4:00 A.M., to the hospital. I say reluctantly, and you may think of me as a cold, heartless jerk. But the truth is that I was in major denial. No way could we have a preemie. My wife was just being a hypochondriac. She probably had eaten something that gave her stomach cramps. And because of her hysteria, I had to get up to take her to the hospital after I had been up all night the night before. Well, it turns out she was right. She was admitted for two days, received terbutaline, and went home. If you think that this experience should have made me a little more realistic in my perception, you are wrong. When her water broke a week later, I had a hard time believing her. I was in such denial that I was ready to just drop her off at the hospital. When she started to push, I finally woke up to what was happening around me. —Christoph

Soon enough, the shock starts to wear off, and you alternate between numbness and being overcome with emotion. Sometimes you'll still feel oddly detached or far away, but at other times, something will trigger a flood, and the intensity of your reaction may surprise you. Acknowledge what a difficult time this is and remind yourself that your emotions and behaviors are common to many parents of preemies. Whatever thoughts, memories, and feelings you're having, you're entitled to them. Don't try to stifle them. Detachment helps you grasp the reality of what's happening to you, but emotional flooding gives you a chance to release and work through your feelings. Intense situations can produce intense responses.

On the third day, I was wheeled down to the NICU. I didn't notice any of the thirty other babies I passed. I was in a haze. But when I saw my son, I immediately fell in love with him. I cried, but I don't know why. I just remember being very hot and weak and woozy. —Laura

When they were born, I refused to leave the hospital. I thought they would die, so I wanted to spend every moment they were alive with them. (At least I think that's what I was feeling. I just know I couldn't leave them. They needed me, and I needed them.) After many days, my mother-in-law and mother talked me into getting some fresh air. Of course, what we saw as we walked outside were new parents videotaping taking their new baby home. I lost it at that moment, and maybe for the first time, I was really able to cry. —Stephie

The preemie experience includes lots of things I don't want to experience, and feelings that don't fit in very well with my idea of how mothers are supposed to feel. I have found that it's hard for me to accept my whole contradictory bag of feelings. —Kris

It is so important for you to recognize that these emotional waves, storms, and calms are a normal part of weathering pregnancy complications, early delivery, postpartum adjustments, the time in the NICU, the period after homecoming, and even developmental evaluations. The storms can be quite

Parenting Your Premature Baby and Child

intense and the waves quite unpredictable during a crisis, transition, or setback, but they generally smooth out over time, and you'll find respite in the calms. It is normal to feel crazy, but you won't feel this way forever. Here are some initial coping strategies to try as you begin your journey. For an in-depth discussion of these and other coping strategies, turn to later sections in this chapter, as well as Chapter 3.

- *Find out what happened.* Knowing your "story" has a tremendous healing effect. If you don't have clear memories of certain parts of the experience, ask your obstetric team and your baby's health care providers to fill in the gaps. Request medical records: the written play-by-play can illuminate what you and your baby have gone through. Knowing where you've been and how you got where you are can help you make sense of what has happened. Knowledge restores your feelings of control and mastery in the face of the unexpected.
- *Let your numbness work for you.* Detachment gives you the time you need to absorb and comprehend traumatic events. Don't fight it.
- *Give yourself permission to feel the wide range of your emotions.* In your struggle to make sense of what is happening, a number of feelings and reactions need to find a place inside you.
- *Identify your feelings.* Dealing with individual feelings is easier than confronting a huge, confusing mass of pain.
- *Accept your painful feelings.* Feelings of pessimism, dread, fear, failure, powerlessness, guilt, and sadness do not mean you're a bad parent. Good parenting has to do with facing your feelings and dealing with them constructively. Doing so frees you to be there for your baby. As Kris observes, "Accepting the hard parts and the hard feelings head on helps me be open to the joy."
- *Recognize that "feeling" and "being" are two different things.* Feeling guilty is not the same as being guilty. Feeling like a failure is not the same as being a failure. Acknowledge that you are doing the best you can—and know that your best will continually get better and better.
- *Write about your experiences and your feelings.* Putting your story and your emotions down on paper can help you gain perspective and make sense of what's going on. This can help you cope and feel less bewildered.
- *Talk about your experiences and your feelings.* Share what has happened (or is happening) and how you feel about it with someone who can be

supportive and who does not dismiss or minimize your emotions. Talking can summon the support you need.

- *Take care of yourself physically.* Eat healthy foods, exercise, and get adequate sleep. If your body is strong, your ability to cope becomes stronger, too. This is especially important for mothers recovering from pregnancy and delivery.

- *Accept your partner's reactions, whatever they may be.* Your partner's reactions and the timing of his or her emotional highs and lows may differ from your own. Accept each other's feelings and expect to be out of sync. Remember that the two of you most likely share many of the same emotions. (For more on this subject, see "You and Your Partner" in Chapter 19.)

- *Arrange support for your children.* If you have other children, you face the added challenge of supporting them while your own emotional reserves are running low. Enlist the help of all your children's secondary care-givers and other familiar people (teachers, relatives, friends, and others) in providing extra support and caring. This outside support can give you the respite you need to keep from completely draining your emotional energy stores. (For more information, see "Your Other Children" in Chapter 19.)

The remainder of this chapter focuses on the grieving process, because pivotal to your emotional calms and storms is your bereavement, or sense of loss, and how you mourn, cope, adjust, and heal.

The Grieving Process

Many parents of preemies are shocked at how deeply distressed they are by the early birth of their baby or babies. Both the intensity of their feelings and the wide range of different emotions they are experiencing can be quite bewildering. During the course of their baby's hospital stay, many parents feel as if they are on a roller coaster of hope and despair. Even after homecoming and as their preemie grows, parents may feel interminably on edge. They wait and watch their child's growth and development for signs of damage or delay. Pride and fear intermingle. If their child shows impairment, this can be a significant source of ongoing distress. Whatever the situation, grieving is a *normal and healthy* process that can continue over months and years, at varying levels of intensity and expressed in many different ways. Still, most parents are surprised that the grieving process is so powerful, complex, and extended.

The emotional side of having a premature baby can be very dark indeed. And the dark feelings (by this I mean feelings that you hesitate to speak about) come at different stages of the preemie journey. At least this has been true for me.
—*Anne*

When you deliver prematurely, grief is at the emotional core of your experience. It encompasses all of your painful feelings, including sorrow, guilt, anger, regret, and more. Love, joy, and hope are also part of this emotional core, but to appreciate or even feel the positives, it helps to get a handle on the pain. Facing your grief and your baby's difficulties head on makes it easier to cope with the wide range and complexity of your emotions. As you cope with your feelings of grief, you work through and gradually let go of your painful feelings. And by remaining open to all of your emotions, you can experience the affectionate, satisfying, and happy feelings that are also central to your journey.

Moreover, when you deal with your painful feelings, you make room in your heart for a loving relationship with your baby. Remaining open to your emotions enables you to form a strong bond with your baby, which benefits you both. You feel more confident and competent as a parent, and your baby thrives under your sensitive, nurturing attention.

If the unthinkable should happen and your baby should die, you both will have reaped the rewards of that closeness, however short your baby's life. Facing your pain frees you to have a meaningful relationship with this child. If your baby has ongoing problems, the sorrow doesn't disappear, but as you get to know and love your baby, the joy becomes more prominent. Whatever the situation, your bond with your baby can be a source of comfort and healing.

Facing your grief involves

- Acknowledging that delivering early and parenting a preemie can be a traumatic turn of events
- Recognizing the specific losses associated with your baby's premature birth
- Learning about the grieving process and ways to cope
- Figuring out ways to come to terms with your most challenging feelings and experiences

• • •
29
Grief and Adjustment

The Trauma of Premature Birth

Premature birth turns your world upside down. Instead of a joyous family experience, your baby's arrival becomes an alarming medical ordeal. Not knowing what will happen, you face an avalanche of terrible possibilities that you feel helpless to prevent. Your tiny baby, whom you love more than anything, may be very sick. Not even the doctors may know if your baby will survive or eventually be normal and healthy. Powerless to do anything to change events, you may be filled with fear and paralysis, agitation, and distress.

The shock of an early delivery can be deeply traumatic. Add to this the difficulties of adjusting to the NICU and figuring out how to have a meaningful and rewarding relationship with your sick, often unresponsive infant. Even after homecoming, parenting a preemie can be challenging. You may have extra worries and tasks associated with germs, illness, development, therapy, feeding, growth, interaction, fussiness, hypersensitivities, and possible or actual disabilities. Attending follow-up clinics, doctors' appointments, and therapies can consume much of your time and attention. You want your child to have the best possible chance to fulfill his or her potential, but you never imagined that parenting could be this hard.

Give yourself permission to acknowledge the trauma of this birth and the difficulties you and your baby face. Recognize your losses.

The Mosaic of Losses

> On the second night of my stay in the hospital, I was lying in bed, trying to sleep. On either side of me, I could hear babies crying and the enthusiastic, "Oh, he's so cute" from nurses and families. Alone in my bed, I felt my hand stray to my stomach, so recently purged of its little occupant. I felt then that I had lost on two planes: my baby was no longer inside me, but he wasn't physically near me, either. —Claire

Having a premature baby means experiencing many complicated losses. You lose the last weeks or months of your pregnancy, that time you were counting on to prepare for the arrival of your baby. You lose trust in your body's ability to carry a baby to term. You lose the kind of labor and delivery you wished for. You lose the moments after birth, which you may have fantasized about for months—the first meeting, cuddling, and nursing of your newborn. You lose the glory and celebration that normally accompany the birth of a baby. Instead, you find yourself going home with empty arms. As Gallice notes sadly, "It is *so* hard to leave without the baby. You're broken—just broken."

I felt like I had lost my pregnancy. I had just started to show and had recently bought new maternity clothes that I never got to wear. I was looking forward to looking pregnant. It was my turn to be pampered and doted on. I didn't have a baby to bring home either. Not that we were ready for a baby. There had been no shower yet. There was no baby's room. —Laura

I lost the beautiful birth at home that I had in mind. I lost the first two weeks of my son's life. I noticed one day that a nurse had clipped his fingernails. I felt angry that it wasn't me clipping his nails and that I had lost that time to do those things for my son. —Ruby

Going home was the worst. Instead of leaving the hospital in a wheelchair holding my baby—like you see in the movies, and like I saw every day when I went to visit my son in the NICU—I left in a wheelchair by myself. It was almost like I didn't have a baby, or like my baby had died. —Sally

When your heartfelt plans and fantasies dissolve, you naturally experience feelings of loss and grief. Returning to the hospital to gaze at your infant through the barriers of incubator, tubes, tape, and wires, you mourn for all that might have been. You may also grieve for what you perceive to be your baby's losses: the loss of the warmth and safety of your womb, the loss of your touch, the loss of innocence and purity that results from being poked and prodded under bright lights. You may grieve because you feel helpless to ease your baby's struggles.

After I was in the recovery room, they wheeled me into the NICU, and I saw him for the first time—I saw him the way I would come to know him. He was so tiny and frail. I started to cry. I was terrified. A nurse came over to tell the doctors or me that he was doing good, but I didn't even hear her. I was in my own little world. I just wanted him to be a "normal" baby. —Lori

Brand-new babies aren't supposed to need intensive care. Parents' arms are supposed to be enough. —Rikki

Losses may accumulate over the weeks or months your infant spends in the NICU. You may wonder how to comfort and get to know your tiny baby in this forbidding environment. This is not the way you had imagined building a relationship with your little one. Holidays, special occasions, and milestones can be painful because they aren't the way you had imagined them to be. You might feel a loss of community because most other parents are unaware of what your baby is going through and are certainly in the dark about what this experience is like for you. Even you and your partner could feel distant from each other. And homecoming is not the end of the ordeal for most parents. You will continue to deal with the emotional fallout of this experience, as well as your baby's special needs, however mild or transient they may be.

There are so many things I wish had been different for us. I still get teary when I think of all we missed out on and how hard we have had to fight to get where we are. There are so many losses associated with this whole thing that it's hard to see all of them. Every time I think about Stephen's birth and NICU days and early life, I can think of one more thing I wish I had done differently. Or I think of something I wish the doctors and nurses had done differently. None of those things can be changed now, and I will never have another chance to have a baby. —Tracy

I feel the "loss" of the visions I had for my firstborn child, and this is a never-ending emotion I imagine I will always have. —Diana

You may be overcome by grief for specific things you hadn't realized meant so much to you. You may cry whenever you see a woman ripe with pregnancy. Your heart may ache whenever you see an infant who was born at term at the time that your baby was due. That's what your baby would be like now if only—if only. You may also feel the loss of the many rites of passage into parenthood: baby showers, childbirth classes, packing the hospital bag. You might feel excluded when you hear other parents compare notes about the miracles and pains of full-term pregnancy and birth. You may cringe when you hear parents discuss the joys of those initial weeks at home,

• • •

32

cuddling with a newborn baby. You may feel awkward when others talk about the typical growth and development of their term children. It seems that you and your experiences just don't fit in, and you may feel as if you're missing out on what is supposed to be a joyful highlight of your life.

Furthermore, you've lost your innocence. This experience undermines your beliefs about life, safety, goodness, health, and power. You may struggle with feelings of vulnerability and powerlessness as you come to realize that you don't have as much control over your life as you once thought you did: your sense of confidence or grounding can be shaken as you peer into an uncertain future. You may also question your religious convictions, your faith in Western medicine, or your trust in certain medical professionals. Eventually, as you come to terms with what has happened, you will modify your philosophies and adjust your expectations. But in the beginning, losing your sense of control and safety can be most unnerving. And if you've experienced traumatic loss in the past, you may have especially strong feelings of dread ("Oh, no, not again") or hopelessness ("Bad things always happen to me").

I did not see any change in my role as a father, but what did come out of it was a recognition that the medical establishment does not necessarily do things for the benefit of the patient, nor is it as scientific as I had previously thought. —Marco

Since the birth, I have felt tremendous loss in many areas. "How it's supposed to be" is rather broad and covers all of the losses. But that's it in a nutshell. We lost "how it's supposed to be." —Cindy

Whatever your situation—if your baby is healthy and developing normally, if your infant has continuing medical or developmental problems, or especially if your baby dies—you'll have a long list of losses, big and small, that you need to acknowledge. Pinpointing those losses makes it possible to know what you are grieving. Naming your losses makes them tangible. When you name them, you assert that you are entitled to feel the way you do, that your losses are real. This can make your grief more manageable.

Understanding Grief

Because grief is so painful, some people believe that grieving is bad—something to be avoided or to be gotten over as quickly as possible. But grief isn't a problem to be solved; it's a process that unfolds. The grieving process also has great value as it provides the means for you to come to terms with your baby's prematurity. *Grieving is what enables you to heal.*

Grief is also complicated. It is more than just sorrow, and more than a set of stages that you pass through. At any time after a crisis hits, you can experience a mixture of painful, sometimes bewildering feelings. You may find it helpful to think of grief as a fluid experience of sadness, anger, guilt, regrets, failure, longing, fear, disbelief, numbness and emptiness, preoccupation, confusion, anxiety, irritability, hopelessness, depression, powerlessness, and agony.

When our baby was in the NICU, my predominant emotion was anxiety. It was hard not to worry. I felt guilty initially, wondering if I should have gone to the hospital sooner, and so on. I also felt a little angry that my doctors hadn't hospitalized me when the bleeding didn't stop. I mostly felt bad for my daughter, feeling that she had done nothing to deserve this, and here she was, put in this terrible situation. —Mary

I cried my eyes out. I felt faint, extremely scared, and guilty for bringing such a small, frail, innocent child into this situation that I really had no control over. I was so scared to love her because I truly felt that she would not make it. She was so tiny. Her skin was almost transparent. There were so many machines, tubes, IVs, beeps, and buzzes. She was so small that I thought there was absolutely no way she could survive without the grace of God. She was so helpless looking. I questioned myself about why I didn't have an abortion at the beginning of my complicated pregnancy. I felt like a complete failure. I questioned why I could not have a normal pregnancy and birth like other women. I felt cheated and very hurt, but above all I felt the greatest sense of fear I have ever felt in my whole life! —Jillian

You may also experience physical symptoms, such as fatigue, sleeplessness, sighing, breasts leaking milk, poor appetite, crying spells, shortness of breath, tightness in the throat or stomach, clenched jaw, heart palpitations—all of these are manifestations of anxiety or depression.

It can be impossible to predict how you'll feel day to day: there are no timetables. You may even begin to grieve before your baby is born.

Anticipatory grief is how you deal with the uncertainties that surround a high-risk pregnancy or a premature baby's outcome. And as each loss, anticipated or not, comes to fruition, you grieve anew. Recognize that your painful feelings will ebb and flow, and that as the initial shock wears off, you will probably feel worse rather than better. This can be disheartening. But gradually the ups will become more frequent and the downs more gentle and fewer.

As part of the ebb and flow of your emotions, you are also likely to experience "anniversary reactions." At first, you may feel most unsettled or sad at certain times of the day or week. As time passes, you may notice that you feel especially blue at certain times of the month or year. It's as if your body remembers and associates certain conditions with your pregnancy, your baby's birth, and his or her time in the NICU. Acknowledging these anniversaries helps you make sense of emotional spikes. Take advantage of these opportunities to process more layers of feelings, advancing your journey of healing. And even though you may revisit painful emotions, you are not in the same place you were the last time you felt them. This is how the threads of grieving, coping, and healing intertwine.

Indeed, over time you will visit and revisit your grief about some of your more significant losses. For example, you may find that you grieve the end of your pregnancy during preterm labor or complications, again when you deliver, and later at your due date. You may grieve for this loss when you see other women in their last trimester and again with any subsequent pregnancies and deliveries. Each time, you'll grieve in different ways, from different perspectives. It may feel like regression, but it's actually a healing progression.

Adjustment and healing happen gradually over time. Your sadness and longing will mellow, and you'll be able to move ahead into the future. Your life will never be the same, but you'll reach a point where you can accept what happened, let go of "what might have been," and acquire a sense of peace. Even if your child has ongoing problems, you can still get to this place, even though it can take a long time. (For more on grieving disabilities, see Chapter 18.)

I have good days and I have bad days. It is nice for me to know that as time goes on, the 'bad' days are fewer and farther between. I felt more numbness while it was going on than I do now. Sometimes the flashbacks and intense feelings of it happening again are more than I can handle. I am so thankful that my husband is as understanding and open about this situation as he is. I think about everything much more than we talk about it. The week after I got home was a very tough week for me. Everything hit. *Then there was a time soon after Alison was discharged that I just wanted to forget about the whole thing and for no one to talk about it. I had a desire just to go on with life. I still find myself looking at Alison and wondering how we both made it through this and saying a prayer of thanksgiving that we did. Everything took its toll, but it is getting easier as time goes on.* —Stacy

These feelings of acceptance and peace are hallmarks of adapting, coming to terms with a difficult experience. But in the beginning, you may feel that you'll never be able to accept what has happened, much less feel at peace. You may feel overwhelmed, that your grief is bottomless. How can you go on, you wonder, when healing may be months or even years away? But even in the depths of your despair, you are healing. As you mourn and cope, you are gradually coming to terms with your losses and adjusting to new realities. By shedding the tears and feeling the pain, you are engaged and actively participating in your emotional recovery. Grappling with your emotions and letting them flow through you, rather than drowning in them or pushing them away, are healing steps. Before you can see light at the end of the tunnel, you need to cry a certain number of tears or feel a certain number of pangs. You only have to shed each tear or feel each pang *once,* after which you move closer to a less painful place. *Even as you grieve, you are healing.*

There is no right or wrong way to grieve. You may experience a wide range of feelings and physical symptoms, or a narrow range. All parents of preemies experience some similar emotions and behaviors, but no two parents follow the same path. You will make your own path, find your own way, and do what *you* need to do., Your feelings are valid and natural, however and whenever you experience them, and you are not alone.

Common Feelings of Grief

I have often used the phrase "birth without joy" to describe my daughter's premature arrival. —Renee

Although situations vary widely among premature babies and their parents, there are many common emotions. The more significant or numerous your losses, the more intense and long lasting your feelings may be. You may experience glimmers or rushes of positive emotions such as love, pride, and delight, but negative feelings tend to dominate those early weeks or months when your baby is in the hospital. After discharge, your positive emotions may be more pervasive, but negative feelings can still surge or even rule while you adjust to home. Sorrow, fear, and confusion are jarring to feel at a time you'd expected to be filled with joy and confidence.

Besides struggling to understand the medical implications of premature birth for your child, you may feel overcome by some or all of the following:

- Shock and numbness
- Unexpectedly intense sadness
- Persistent worries
- Yearning to be close to your baby
- Guilt over your perceived failures and shortcomings
- Powerlessness in the face of so many uncertainties
- Isolation from others
- Anger about the situation
- Envy or resentment of others
- Fears about the future
- Longing for what might have been

Although you may feel discouraged by this long list of painful emotions, you can also feel affirmed. Having a premature baby poses a number of exceptional challenges, and your feelings are natural reactions to distressing situations. The following descriptions can help you recognize and acknowledge the emotions that make up your grief.

Shock and Numbness There will be times, particularly immediately after hearing bad news, that you may feel as though you are in shock. When you are first told the facts of your critical condition, the imminent delivery, your baby's birth, his or her fragile condition, or with each health crisis or developmental concern, the full scope of reality may not sink in for several days. This is a protective mechanism that shields you from the full impact of each emerging situation. You may appear to be taking things in stride, because the enormity of it all hasn't hit you yet.

During and shortly after your baby's birth, it is natural to experience pervasive emotional numbness. As your disbelief fades and you get a handle on the situation, the painful feelings of grief will arise. Still, throughout the following months—or longer if your baby has ongoing medical problems or emerging developmental ones—it is normal to have occasional brief periods of numbness.

My only thought was "it's too early. ... " I was in shock. I had the textbook pregnancy. I gained the correct amount of weight, tried to eat good food, exercised, was active. Until the time after I delivered, I don't remember feeling anything. I remember knowing that it was the wrong time and maybe it would all end in awaking from a dream. —Andra

I had so little time to dwell on the prospect of an early delivery. It was five days from warning to delivery. I didn't face it at all. And after the birth, I was so numb I really don't know what I felt or how I acted. —Cindy

I was on automatic, I think. People would come in, and I would laugh and joke with the nurses and the doctors. But it wasn't really me. I wasn't feeling anything. I would go down and look at my daughter, and talk to her doctor and find out information, and file it back into my brain without letting it go through any emotions first. —Brooke

I didn't know what I was supposed to do, how I was supposed to feel, or even what I felt. I wanted to hide, to run away, and yet I couldn't. I wanted to cry and scream and keen, yet the tears wouldn't come. I wanted to mourn and grieve, but no one had died, nothing was gone, except my dreams—and how could I sob for lost dreams when my baby was fighting for life? I was lost and alone. —Leanne

Sadness Sorrow is only natural—you face many losses when your baby is delivered early. You miss out on that time of eager anticipation. The birth becomes a crisis instead of a purely joyful event. You must postpone your dreams of precious snuggles, nursing, and proud showing off. Instead, you face fears about suffering, prolonged hospitalization, lifelong disability, and infant death. If any of these fears comes to fruition, your sorrow becomes that much deeper and longer lasting.

I can remember putting both hands on my pregnant belly, and I patted and stroked both my unborn babies. I told them that I was sorry, that I loved them, and then I prepared to say good-bye. All that night I waited. No matter what I tried to do, I was sure my body was going to override it and reject my babies. —Rikki

As soon as the doctor left the room, I began to cry. Not because I was scared but because I knew that my girls would literally have to fight for their lives. I knew deep down that I should have been expecting the worst. Instead, I tried to think positive and hope that nothing would go wrong. The nurse assistants kept telling me not to worry, but I wasn't worried, only sad. Sad that they would not have a good chance. —Rosa

Persistent Worries When you deliver prematurely, it seems only fitting that you should be anxious for your baby's well-being. What you may be unprepared for is the intensity of this anxiety, which may be far and above what you've experienced before. Your worries may know no bounds. When your baby's condition is perilous, fear is a constant companion. As you peer at your baby, surrounded by the wonders and coldness of medical technology, you may feel alternately grateful for what medicine can do and fearful for what it cannot.

I was afraid of death. I didn't think I could live with that. I remember being very afraid even to ask if you had a funeral for babies who died as preemies. Just to get the words out of my mouth, to even ask the question, I remember being so scared to say it. I remember walking around the mall, looking at doll clothes, and thinking what I'd have to bury my babies in. The thought that I might have to do that was just, really, really unbelievable. —Stephie

• • •

There are few guarantees in the NICU. If you tend to be a worrier or if you are uncomfortable with uncertainty or loose ends, the unknowns will be doubly hard for you to bear. If you mistrust the care your baby is receiving or modern medical technology itself, this is likely to heighten your anxiety. That's why early on, before you've come to believe in the nurses or learned about the treatments, you may feel that you must stand guard over your little one. If developmental or medical problems persist, your worries will continue as well, along with the realization that for your child, there are few guarantees in the NICU or beyond. (There are many aspects of anxiety, worries, fear, and vulnerability, and there is more specific information and support for coping throughout the book. See sections with those key words in Chapters 3–8, 10, 13, 14, and 17.)

> *I could not figure out how in the world a baby could survive being born at barely past the halfway mark. His poor little lungs were trying so hard to develop, now how could they? What about his eyes? Would I get to hear him cry? Would I end up with a C-section? He was turned properly, but what if something happened? What if my baby died? I would have to go too. I couldn't handle it. There's no way. —Ami*

If you or your partner experienced life-threatening complications before or during the birth, this is another source of worry. As a father, you are concerned about your baby, but it is natural for you to focus on your partner's recovery. As a mother, you may concentrate on your baby's condition and even feel guilty for worrying about your own health while your baby struggles to live.

Yearning For many parents, the loss of a joyful birth is a devastating disappointment. Instead of holding your slippery baby right away, you are separated. Bonding with your newborn can feel especially difficult, and you may worry about the mixed feelings you have for your baby. With parenting urges in full bloom, you may yearn to be close to your baby, yet your baby's fragile condition or your hospital's policies discouraging parents from holding their babies, even when they are stable, may thwart these desires. You might give anything to snuggle your baby close, but you may fear doing so. You may struggle with how much to invest emotionally in a baby who may die. Should you celebrate or mourn your baby's birth? You may do both, but feeling two such contradictory emotions simultaneously can be unsettling. Nevertheless, all these diverse reactions are appropriate and normal aspects of yearning for your baby. (For more support and ideas for getting close to your baby in the NICU, see Chapters 7, 8, 9, and 10.)

I didn't want more drugs [painkillers after delivery], I just wanted my baby. I spent most of the day crying and staring at the pictures of him. —Tracy

I was terrified ... and so sad. I wanted to hold him, but at the same time I didn't. But I do know that when they wheeled him out of the delivery room, it felt as if they were tearing off a piece of me as they left. —Sterling

Guilt and Failure As responsible parents, you may wonder what you did or didn't do that contributed to your baby's plight. As the mother, despite assurances to the contrary, you may feel a sense of failure that you were unable to prevent complications. Having a high-tech emergency delivery can feel like a tremendous defeat. As you watch health care professionals provide for your baby, you may feel inadequate. You may also feel guilty about how you are handling the situations connected with your baby's birth and over time. You may blame yourself for your child's suffering or outcome. (For support in coping with these painful emotions of guilt and failure, see Chapter 3.)

I had these immense feelings of guilt as if somehow I had failed her. She had to come out before she was ready, and I should have done something to stop it. Those feelings are still there. I just cannot shake the thought that maybe I could have stopped my labor. She has endured so much pain, and there was nothing that I could do to stop it. Had she been born at the right time, she would have been saved all this trauma. —Moni

You go to the hospital to have a baby, and then you come home without your child. ... All I remember is crying all the way home and feeling guilty as I left my baby behind. It seemed to me as if I was abandoning her. —Jodi

Powerlessness

I never felt as if I had control over my body with respect to the pregnancy. It controlled me. —Cindy

As pregnancy and delivery spin out of your control, you are likely to feel entirely helpless. The NICU disorients you further with its technology and confusing terminology. And there's so much you've yet to learn about your baby's condition. Even as you adjust to the NICU, you may feel powerless as a parent, unable to meet your baby's complex needs by yourself. Especially if you are struggling with feelings of incompetence, you may be reluctant to exert what little control you have. In fact, it may not even occur to you that you do have some say in your baby's care.

You may also feel powerless in the face of so many uncertainties. There is no way for you to ensure that your baby's hospital stay will be short and without crisis, and that he or she will emerge normal and healthy. If your child continues to need hospitalization, therapies, equipment, or special-education services, you pass through one foreign land after another. With each new challenge, it is natural to feel helpless initially. Mastery takes time and practice.

When you experience your newborn only through the portholes of an incubator for the first few weeks of life, it is natural to feel as if you've lost control. Even if your child's hospital course, health, growth, and development are relatively uncomplicated, this journey still didn't start out the way it was supposed to. You never expected to feel this vulnerable and unsure. (For more on powerlessness and coping, see Chapter 3.)

The worst part is that you have absolutely no control over anything. You do not make decisions about how your own child sleeps, eats, dresses, and so forth. But most of all, you cannot just wave a magic wand and make it all go away. You simply do not have that choice.

In summary, all expectations of what pregnancy and childbirth ought to be go out the window. —Jen

I had no expectations left. Every dream that I had was ruined. —Stacy

42

Isolation Adding to your stress, you may feel isolated when those around you don't fully appreciate the emotional impact of your baby's prematurity on you and your partner. While your infant lies in the hospital, relatives and friends may have little access or opportunity to welcome this new family member and share the joys and challenges with you. If your baby is critically ill, they might not understand your grief over issues seemingly unrelated to your child's survival, such as the fact that you are unable to hold your baby as much as you want. They may guard against investing emotionally in a baby who may die or who may survive with medical illnesses or disabilities.

After homecoming, your family and friends may not comprehend your ongoing sense of loss, expecting you simply to be grateful that your baby has survived. If your baby is relatively stable and comes home appearing healthy and on track, others might question why you are still upset, minimizing your losses and your fears. You may find it hard to reach out to others because you don't know what you feel or need. You may feel isolated from the community of "regular" parents. You may be coping with this crisis very differently from your partner. This can be an intensely lonely time. (For more on getting the support you need, see Chapters 19 and 20.)

> *I was very hurt and offended when so many did not acknowledge Molly's birth. It apparently did not seem appropriate to others, but I wanted pink balloons and congratulations! I wanted coming-home outfits and booties! I wonder now if what I really needed was for someone, anyone, to acknowledge that I had given birth to a baby. —Renee*

> *I'd see other moms and dads with their babies—at work, the store, the hospital—and feel completely left out of their world. —Diane*

Anger Anger naturally accompanies feelings such as isolation, powerlessness, and anxiety. You may be angry that no one understands, angry that there's nothing you can do to make it stop, angry at the uncertainties, angry that this happened at all. You may feel angry at yourself or angry at your baby. Your physical fatigue, stress, or illness can also make you more irritable. Even as you hope for the best and try to cope with this turn of events, you have every right to be hopping mad. You, your family, and your baby do not deserve this. (For more on anger and coping, see Chapter 3.)

Nothing seemed real as I lay in the bed in the labor room, waiting for Jon and my mom to get there. I was scared and nervous, and really, really mad. I couldn't figure out what the hell (sorry) I had done to deserve this happening to me, to my baby. —Ami

As it happened, I was only confined to bed for five days. But those five days were very long. I was angry that I had to submit to the rules. Perhaps I was actually angry that control had been taken away—a big issue with me. —Cindy

Envy Outside the NICU, you may feel bombarded by the sight of pregnant women and mothers with newborns and begrudge their good fortune. Inside the NICU, while your baby struggles, you may notice that other parents get to be more involved, taking care of or holding their babies. You may be green with envy, coveting their special privileges. You might even harbor fantasies that their baby will have a setback so that you can all be in the same boat. Although you may be horrified by these reactions, sure that your thoughts are signs of true evil, rest assured that you are only trying to protect your fragile condition. Making comparisons and envisioning others struggling right along with you helps you to feel less alone and afraid. Misery *needs* company.

They didn't think he would make it twenty-four hours. I went back to my room and just wept. In my room there was another mother, one who had delivered a full-term, healthy little cherub. I was so jealous, so sad. Why couldn't I be that mother? —Jayna

I could not look at a pregnant woman—even on TV—without feeling envious and hurt. Inferior. Cheated. —Shaina

A respiratory technician who cared for my boys was in the latter stages of a pregnancy, as was a nurse on the unit, and the envy I felt toward them was an ugly, wretched creature inside me. The chance to be healthy and carry a baby to term was a gift they had that I had been denied. Being around them at this time in my life brought out the very worst in me. —Susan

Fears about the Future The more precarious your baby's condition, the more you may worry about what the future holds. And contrary to what you may have hoped, homecoming does not offer instant relief from those fears. Perhaps your baby's long-term prognosis remains uncertain. Even if your preemie grows healthy and robust, you may feel that your child remains vulnerable. You are only too well aware that many premature babies are at high risk for complications, even death, from common childhood illnesses. Concerns about developmental progress can arise at any time. If your child is diagnosed with a pervasive developmental problem, you may have worries about his or her long-term care. At a time when you had hoped that things would finally settle down, you still face a new set of parenting challenges and complicated feelings. (For many parents, facing and coping with fears about the future is a recurring issue; for more support and information, see Chapters 3, 5, 8, 10, and 14–18.)

Longing for What Might Have Been Even as you adjust to what is, you may need to spend a fair amount of energy grieving and longing for that easy nine-month pregnancy, healthy term baby, and simple parenthood. Although it is painful, dwelling on what you've lost and experiencing your feelings about that loss are natural and necessary steps toward revising your original wishes and dreams. Because raising a premature baby sometimes means facing uncertain medical and developmental outcomes, you may continue longing for and letting go of layers of hopes and expectations as your child's unique needs unfold.

Longing is the essence of grieving, just as letting go is the essence of healing. The transition from grieving to healing is a gradual back-and-forth process that takes *time*. Eventually, you will also be able to let go of your hurt, regret, and resentment. This paves the way for recognizing and accepting what you've gained. Treasures arise out of your adversity, but you must discover them on your own terms, in your own time. (For more on healing, see Chapter 23.)

Coping and Healing

How do you cope with the emotions of grieving? Sometimes, especially early on, you may feel as if you can't. And that's okay. *Give yourself permission to fall apart*, to ignore responsibilities, to spend time alone with just your feelings—doing this can be key to your ability to cope.

The sections that follow suggest some ways of coping, of expressing and dealing with grief. With the benefit of hindsight, many parents point to these approaches as necessary tools to healing and surviving their emotional journey—and their baby's prematurity. The resources at the back of this book provide more information, ideas, reassurance, and support. Chapter 3 contains more information on moving through painful emotions and distressing reactions, and Chapter 23 discusses moving on.

Let Your Grief Flow

When it comes to grief, many people admire stoicism. They'll say, "She's handling it so well," meaning that she doesn't appear to be grieving—that she doesn't talk about the situation or look sad or cry. However, for mental health, coping well does *not* mean avoiding grief. Coping well means facing your loss, feeling your emotions, and getting the support you need.

When your feelings are rising, do your best to take the time to honor them. Of course, this is easier said than done. Grieving is hard work: it can make you feel broken, discouraged, and overwhelmed. Naturally, you may try to resist your deepest feelings of sorrow. But in the long run, facing your feelings is easier and healthier than habitually avoiding them. Grieving is what enables you to adjust and adapt to your baby's prematurity, whereas suppressing grief sabotages your happiness, blocking your joy along with your sorrow.

Suppressing grief can also produce negative feelings about yourself, your baby, or others close to you. When you avoid painful feelings, you may *displace* those negative feelings onto loved ones. Facing your emotions helps you uncover their true source and frees you to see your baby, yourself, your partner, and others in a positive light. (For more on the dangers of grief suppression, see "Persistent Numbness and Avoidance of Grief" in Chapter 3.)

So instead of trying to skate on the surface of your grief, submerge yourself in it. Allow your painful feelings to flow through you. You may fear that if you let go, you'll never be able to pull yourself back together. But you will. Feeling your grief doesn't mean nonstop pain. There is a natural ebb and flow to grieving, moments of intensity diffused with relief. Falling apart is always *temporary* and actually helps you to *regain* control over your life. By taking the time and energy to explore the depths of your grief, you release the powerful feelings you are holding inside: it is the brave, strong, smart thing to do. Over time, you'll discover that you can think back on your experiences and your baby's ordeal without being overcome with emotion.

Here are a few coping tips for letting your grief flow that you may find helpful:

- *Sort through your feelings and identify them individually.* Untangling your feelings makes your grief more manageable. For example, separate your feelings of anger over what you consider to be heartless hospital policies from your natural feelings of helplessness over your baby's early birth and from your frustration about your lack of experience with your preemie.

- *Give yourself time to adjust to the sights and sounds of the NICU and encourage yourself to ask questions.* The unknown is often more frightening than the known.

- *Allow yourself to voice your fears and remind yourself that you are doing the best you can to nurture and protect your baby.* Facing your fears enables you to ask pertinent questions and get the information and reassurance you need. If you feel guilty or inadequate, remember that these feelings arise from your devotion to your baby and your desire to be a nurturing parent.

- *Read about premature birth and preterm infants.* Books and articles on coping with premature birth, personal accounts by parents of preemies, and publications on medical, emotional, or spiritual issues can offer insight, opportunities to release painful feelings, and the comfort of knowing you're not the only one to go through this experience.

- *Confide in people who can be responsive and compassionate.* Get into counseling and/or join a supportive group of parents of preemies.

- *Engage in creative or athletic endeavors.* These activities encourage the expression of emotions or the release of tension, and they let you feel a sense of accomplishment.

It can also help to appreciate joy, hope, pride, delight, confidence, and love whenever and wherever you find them. Over time, as you and your baby adjust, it is those positive feelings that will govern your lives. Give yourself permission to feel overwhelmed and to fall apart—trusting that you can make it to the other side.

Have Realistic Expectations for Your Grief

Recognize that certain things can trigger your grief anew and accept that this will happen. The sight of a big pregnant belly, a newborn snuggled in a parent's arms, or the time of year when you delivered your baby can fill you with longing or sadness. Antiseptic smells, beeping sounds, or songs you heard on the radio at that time can also transport you instantly to those difficult days in the NICU. Even just driving in the direction of the hospital can give you flashbacks. This return of grief can be discouraging—but it is normal and to be expected. Reminding yourself that ups and downs are natural and sometimes unpredictable can make your journey easier.

I am so anxious about Brayden's first birthday tomorrow. I can hardly even breathe! The events around his birth are still so vivid to me, almost haunting. I've been having nightmares for the past week and having panic attacks all day long. I feel like a total mess! —Jayna

I experience flashbacks whenever the boys have wheezing incidents. I am so afraid that they will end up in the hospital again and their lives will be out of our control again. One wheeze and I'm taken back four and a half years! —Stephie

We, as parents, don't recover as quickly as we thought we did. There are lots of lingering issues—guilt, disappointment, sadness—that may take a lifetime (or half of one) to resolve. —Sue

Dwell on Your Baby

While your baby is in the hospital, it is normal for you to be preoccupied with him or her. After all, following delivery you are primed to nurture your little one. But when your access to your baby is limited, it can be supremely frustrating. Dwelling on your baby is a natural result. Your thoughts can always be with your preemie, where they belong, especially when you can't be there in person.

Others around you may encourage you to get your mind off your baby, to take advantage of your baby's confinement to get on with your "to-do" list unencumbered. But for you, your baby may be the entire list. Health care providers may also encourage you to "get away" and go do something "fun." If you honestly think you will benefit from the break, do it. A change can be renewing. However, if you feel uneasy about leaving your baby, then don't. After all, it's normal that being with your baby should provide more comfort than not being there. If the nurses criticize you for hovering, remind them that it is a parent's job to be vigilant. As long as you are fulfilling your own basic needs for nutrition, sleep, exercise, and relaxation, you aren't being *too* vigilant.

As your preemie grows, you may need to grieve repeatedly and in different ways for early losses, and also for newly found ones. Let yourself dwell periodically on your child, knowing that this focus is temporary. By giving yourself permission to tighten your focus when you need to, you free yourself up to attend to other things at other times.

If you are still struggling with grief as the months and years pass, you may worry that you are dwelling too much on your growing preemie. If you feel stuck, trust your assessment and enlist the help of a professional therapist. (For more on this, see "Professional Counseling" in Chapter 3.)

Find Ways to Feel Close to Your Baby

Early on, you may be frightened by your baby and the intensive medical technology around him or her. You may feel intimidated by the medical staff, who know so much more than you do about how to take care of your baby. It is normal to feel unsure about your role. It is natural to want to protect yourself from getting too close to a baby who may die. However, no matter what the future may bring, letting yourself feel close to your baby will help you move toward healing. Finding ways to be close to your baby also builds your confidence as a parent. Nurturing your baby is a way to do something positive in a difficult situation. (For more on building a relationship with your baby in the NICU, see Chapters 8–10. For parenting your preemie at home, see Chapters 14–19. If it fits, you might also want to read "Being with Your Baby" and "Keepsakes" in the section "Affirming Your Baby" in Chapter 11.)

Tell Your Story

Telling your story over and over can be tremendously therapeutic. You can correspond with friends and relatives, updating them with your baby's progress as well as on how you're doing. Talk about your baby and your experiences with your partner, close family, supportive friends, a therapist, and to anyone who asks and *really* wants to know what you think and how you feel. Your distress can be dramatically reduced when you receive empathy from someone who accurately understands your feelings about what you're going through.

You may find it especially comforting to turn to other parents of preemies. There is something soothing about connecting with others who know how it feels to have a premature baby. You don't have to explain yourself or hide the truth. You can talk about your baby without worrying that you'll shock these people or, worse, have to comfort *them* about your situation. You can grieve without having to fend off platitudes, embarrassment, or efforts to "fix" you. Although you may prefer to keep your emotions private, doing so can make you feel isolated and alone. Try to find at least one person (besides your partner) with whom you can vent, be honest, and fall apart. (For more about getting support, see Chapter 20.) For the most personal parts of your story, keep a journal where you can record your experiences and your deepest thoughts and feelings. (For more on journaling, see Chapter 3.)

It would've been a help to be able to sit down with somebody. I've never really sat down and really talked about all of it, because who wants to listen to it? And Bill doesn't. We don't want to dredge it all back up again. But it would've been very helpful to be able to get it out, and to talk about it with someone who either had gone through it or understood it a little bit or even just truly wanted to hear. Talking about these things is so important and so incredibly cathartic. You can talk about it ad nauseum, but now I know, it's so important to get it out and talk about it, at least in my case. So yes, I think that if I had talked to somebody and gone through the entire thing, it would've really kind of let me let go of some of this sooner than I did. —Jaimee

Keeping a journal was helpful. I had been alone a lot of those scary times so I could write about what I was thinking. Sometimes I couldn't even sort out my thoughts, but if I wrote them down, somehow they made some sense, or things came out that I didn't even know I was thinking about. It gave some sort of routine to my life when it was so chaotic. Plus, finding people to talk to who were going through the same thing at the same time. I just talked to everybody. —Stephie

You may believe, and some people will tell you, that the quicker you can forget and move on, the better off you'll be. But parents never forget and, in fact, *benefit* from taking the time to process the details of everything that happens to their baby. Dwelling on your experiences helps you to get in touch with your deepest feelings of hurt and sadness. This is the path to truly coming to terms with your baby's birth and hospitalization and to integrating those experiences into your life.

Accept the Support of Others, However Clumsy It May Seem

Friends and family generally mean well and want to be helpful, but they may not know how. There is a lot of ignorance, not only about what prematurity means for a baby, but what it means for the parents. People may make comments like these: "Lucky you, missing out on the last three months, being so big." Or "I wish my baby had been born small like that. I'll bet delivery was a snap." Or "Oh, at that weight, I bet he's so cute!" Or "She'll be home soon. She only needs to grow, right?" Or "Aren't you over this yet? Your baby is home and doing fine!" All of these comments come from ignorance, not cruelty. The speakers are trying to help by encouraging you to look on "the bright side." In our society, many people try to ignore, belittle, or erase grief in an attempt to fix it.

In the past, you too may have offered these platitudes, but now you know how isolating and hurtful they can be. Forgive your friends' and relatives' ignorance, just as those who have been through this before you have forgiven yours. Educate the people you trust and lean on most about what you need. Tell them, write them a note, or give them this book to read. After all, they *want* to know how they can support you. (See Chapter 20 for more on dealing with others.)

Accept That You and Your Partner Will Grieve Differently

Variations in personality, socialization, philosophy, coping mechanisms, and postpartum hormones affect how we grieve. Mothers and fathers also grieve differently because they usually feel differing intensities of connection with the baby. Because the mother carried the baby in her body and because her hormones are geared toward nurturing that child, it is natural for her to feel a more intense grief over the disruption of her pregnancy.

For many fathers, the worst aspect is feeling helpless, unable to "fix" the situation. A common dynamic between parents is that when the mother cries and the father can't fix it, he may struggle with a sense of failure. And, he may fear that her tears will never end. To complicate matters, it can be very difficult for a dad to acknowledge his vulnerability—his feelings of failure and fear. Instead, he may get angry or become distant to hide from his pain. At the same time, the mother may resent the father for not simply accepting and sharing her tears.

A sense of distance and isolation is also common between grieving partners. Grieving is very much a solo journey, and it is natural for parents to take turns grieving. When one partner is having an especially hard time, the other may put grief aside to "hold down the fort" and tend to life's day-to-day demands. As a result, partners may feel miles apart.

These differences make it easy to fall into the trap of judging each other: "Since he buries himself in his work, he must not care about the baby" or "She'll never get over this if she doesn't stop worrying about the baby and crying." It can help for each parent to remember that no two people grieve alike, even if they are soulmates. When you accept your partner's feelings, you acknowledge that each of you is entitled to whatever feelings you have. You may not share your partner's feelings or understand his or her reactions. You may even feel anxious or disappointed about the way he or she is feeling. But by accepting each other's silences and tears, you provide the kind of support, reassurance, and understanding that promotes healing and affirms your commitment to your partner. (See Chapter 19 for more on relationship issues and Chapter 4 for more about a father's special grief and gender differences.)

At times, I really feel like I lost the first month of our [family's] life together because we weren't able to be together twenty-four hours a day. My husband looks at it like—we were able to get her early and get to know her before she was even due! —Stacy

Seek Professional Counseling

Just as you see a doctor whenever you need help coping with physical illness, it makes sense to see a counselor when you need help coping with emotional stress. (For more on this subject, see "Professional Counseling" in Chapter 3.)

Choose to Face Your Situation and Not Let It Destroy Your Life

This memory lives on in infamy in my mind—I remember leaving the hospital, sitting at an intersection, just thinking to myself. At that point I must have realized that Debbie's fine and that these kids are about to be born, and maybe all the warnings [about the complications of prematurity] from the neonatologists were playing in my head, and I realized that these kids were at risk. And I remember sitting there thinking that if this is the hand of cards that I've been dealt, so be it, I can deal with it. It's kind of interesting that that's the kind of hand that I was dealt, but that's all right, we can do something about that. No one told me this, but I had an expectation that my kids were going to be mentally retarded and somehow physically handicapped. I just thought, "I am going to get some really sick kids who are going to live, and that was going to be my lot in life, to be a father to these kinds of kids." And I was just thinking, "Okay, that's what you're getting, and you're going to rise to the occasion, that's what you're going to do, and you're going to take care of these kids. Maybe that's not what you would have ordered, but you don't order your kids from L. L. Bean, and so that's what you're getting." They didn't turn out that way ... but I remember thinking that, and it was a pretty heavy thought. That thought has actually come back to me hundreds of times in the three years since then—seeing myself sitting in the car, I can see what the dashboard looked like, thinking, "That's the hand that I was dealt." — Mitch

Facing reality can be a significant key to survival. It's your choice whether to acknowledge what has happened or to cling to old expectations. You can decide to face your feelings and bring them out in the open or to hide from your grief. After a while, you can choose whether to integrate your baby's premature birth and its consequences into your life or be defeated by them. You can empower yourself by facing your challenges or limit yourself by hiding from them. You can move on with your present and into your future or remain stuck in your past. Many parents mention that eventually they reach a point where they realize that they have stopped wishing it hadn't happened and have started learning to live with it. When you are ready, you'll do that, too.

I think my key to surviving things with Sean is mainly the fact that he was such a little fighter himself. How could I sit there and wallow in my self-pity? If someone so tiny and helpless could fight so hard to survive, I had darn well better be fighting right along with him. —Ami

For me, I don't know that there was a key to integrating it (unless you count good old-fashioned bullheadedness). It was survived and integrated because there was no other option. It had to be. One thing that did help, though, was information. I was fortunate (or stubborn) enough to find doctors who gave me information about Stephen, and I looked up everything about him. It was as though the more I knew, the more I felt some sense of control in the completely uncontrollable situation. —Tracy

You've just got to move on and make it better for yourself and get stronger from the situation. ... What doesn't kill you makes you stronger. That's our motto. —Betsy

We survived it because we had no choice. There was nothing else to do! —Linda

On a related note, many parents find that it helps to make light of their predicaments whenever they're able, and that doing so is a reassuring marker of their positive emotional progress. As you acclimate to each new situation, you'll be able to look more often on the brighter side, perhaps finding humor among the ruins. This will help you cope by lightening your load. Laughter— even chuckling with dark humor—is good medicine.

For the longest time I was joking about being a part-time mother, because the nurses were doing this and the nurses were doing that. I'd be able to come down for a couple of hours, but then I had to go home and do other stuff. ... That is the way I deal with things. If I can't laugh about it, I can't deal with it. I had to look at the lighter side of it, because if I looked at the more negative aspects of it, I would've just been useless. I would've gotten mired down in my own mind. So I would joke around about stuff like the insurance covering the time she was in the hospital. I'm like, "Man, I've got a full-time babysitter. I don't even need to pay for it. This is great." —Brooke

When he was doing so well—and I feel very bad about saying this, but—I even said, "Why are people pregnant for nine months if you can do it in six months?" Of course, I would not say that again now after everything we've been through later. There is a reason for a nine-month pregnancy, for sure. But I was able to joke about it, which means I was able to feel better. —Gallice

Allow Yourself to Hold On to Some Hope for the Future

Whether your baby becomes healthy or has ongoing health or developmental problems, your life can have meaning beyond being a "preemie parent." As you work through your painful feelings, you begin to discover the joys that await you. As you adjust, you can learn to accept this different journey. Healing and surviving your baby's premature birth, hospitalization, and outcome can convince you that you can survive almost anything. Recognize your own resilience. (Take a look at Chapter 23 to see what that healing might look like.)

I feel I got to the other side after that first birthday—that was the big step. ... I still get emotional about it, but it's in the past now. We're over it, but it's still a big part of our lives and always will be. It's just not as devastating as it was. We've gotten past the pain, past the anger, and past the "why me?"
—Marcia

Now there are so many things every day that they do that make us laugh, and we just think, "Gosh, we're so lucky." We've been just really lucky with them. ... If you stay on the positive side of it, you don't get bogged down with the negative details. —Betsy

Look for the Treasure in Adversity

As you heal, you will adjust to this experience and integrate it into your life. You will claim it and own it as a part of what makes you *you*. You may look back and say things like, "Before this happened, I was so shy. Now, I'll stand up to anybody to get what I need." Or "I used to take so much for granted. Because of what we've been through, I can appreciate what is truly important." Or "If I hadn't been through this, I wouldn't have the friendships, the job, the interests, the special joys that I so value now." Recognizing the positives can be key to finding meaning in this experience and integrating it into your life.

Three years later, I am less consumed, more able to concentrate, and once again an effective businessperson. But I will never be able to lose myself in my job, in my company, in my own life as completely as I once did. There is so much more in my life, so much more in my heart, so much more, both wonderful and painful, that none of it can ever be as important to me as it once was. I do my job well, but no business deal can ever mean as much now that I truly understand the blessings that we have and the risks that we face each day. I am better for my experiences. My priorities are based on what is truly significant, and I appreciate life's tenuous gifts so much more. —Susan

Finding the positives does not mean forgetting the negatives, but it can soften them. Finding the positives is also something you must do for yourself, when you are ready. It can't be rushed—and try as they might, others cannot do it for you. When you are ready, you can find the treasure in adversity. (For more on this, see Chapter 23.)

Multiple Birth and Multiple Realities

Those of you who found out you were pregnant with twins, triplets, or more may have felt especially excited, blessed, and proud. Even as you worried about your pregnancy and how you would manage so many babies at once, your joy multiplied. But when your babies were born prematurely, your worries, your losses, and your grief multiplied as well.

As a parent of multiples, you have more than one baby struggling in the NICU instead of being cradled in your arms. Will your babies be okay? How will you take care of more than one fragile infant? You may also mourn for your babies' lost time together, as they lie in separate places, away from each other's warmth. Plus, it is the rare set of multiple babies who have identical hospital courses. You may have more than one series of complications to deal with. Your babies may not be able to come home at the same time. *This is not what you were wishing for.*

Your babies' differences in the NICU and beyond give you more to deal with as you raise twins, triplets, quads, or more. When you are facing multiple realities, you will react and respond to each one differently than if you had to cope with only one reality. You need to find people who can understand and listen to all of your experiences with each baby. This will help you celebrate each triumph and mourn each defeat. Remember that the realities you are enduring would be considered overwhelming for a family to deal with over a number of pregnancies and several years. You are experiencing them *simultaneously*.

Recognizing the special rewards *and* difficulties of having multiple preemies validates your struggle. Both your joy and your grief are magnified. With multiples, you also have the added challenge of finding the time and energy to attend to your own needs. Particularly if you experience the death or disability of one or more of your babies, you may not have the luxury of attending to your grief enough. It may take you many years to adjust and heal. It is especially important that you be patient with yourself and your feelings.

What I've come to realize is that I haven't ever had a time to indulge (I don't mean indulge in a patronizing way, I really mean indulge) in grief or the grieving process. Through each situation, there have always been so many other demands on my time, that I am never able to focus on grieving. Now I am a busy mom of two preschoolers, working more than full time and not able to just pull the covers over my head for a few days, which I think would do me good. This isn't making me feel sorry for myself, though. I am glad to have my kids and my company and my life now. It does make me feel a little kinder toward myself, a little more patient that I am still slogging through all this even five years down the road. It helps me to understand that I wasn't able to properly grieve, and though that wasn't my fault, the outcome is definitely my reality. —Susan

If more than one of your babies dies, you have more than one bereavement to bear. If some survive, you may feel especially isolated in your grief for the baby or babies you are missing if others encourage you to forget about your bereavement and focus on the living. You may wonder how to help your surviving child(ren) deal with the loss of that special relationship as well. You may always long for the chance to hold your babies together in your arms.

I hated not being able to be in two places at the same time. I had two beautiful twin girls, and yet I was never able to enjoy the two of them at the same time. How I wish I could have had them, at least for a couple of months, even days, at home together all to myself. —Rosa

If you used selective reduction, you have the added burden of wondering whether the procedure increased your risk of premature delivery. Remember that trying to carry more babies would have raised the risk even higher. In any case, you feel bereft and excited at the same time. (See Chapter 11 for coping with the death of a baby.)

Respect Your Own Needs

As you grieve, be gentle with yourself. Remember that you deserve to get what you need.

Because your grief belongs to you, *you* are the best one to figure out what you need to do to get through it. You may read or hear a lot of advice. Some suggestions may seem more appropriate than others, depending on your situation, your personality, and where you are in your grief. Keep what fits, discard what doesn't. Even as you consult this book, embrace only the things that feel right for you. No one can tell you how you *should* feel or what you *must* do. You will discover these answers for yourself.

> *I remember that the social workers would come and talk, even if just to ask how the girls were doing and whatever I would want to talk about. They kept asking me, "Are you doing okay?" Then I started to feel really bad for doing okay. I thought, "Why? Shouldn't I be?" I began to question myself. Should I be feeling bad? I almost felt guilty. Then I realized that I was okay and that I was strong enough to deal with life's challenges. I had been so prepared with the possibilities of things that could go wrong that when they did, I was ready. I have always told myself, "Why cry over spilled milk? Instead, clean it up and move on." I am not the type of person who worries over things that are out of my control. —Rosa*

Points to Remember

- You may wrestle with many opposing emotions that come together in confusing ways. It is important to give yourself permission to experience your feelings without censoring them. Identifying your wide range of feelings and making room for them help you make sense of what's happening to you.
- After your baby is born, grieving, coping, adjusting, and healing are intertwined. To grieve is to heal.
- Trying to ignore or hide your grief won't make it go away. Grief is patient—it will stay with you until you face it and work through it.
- When you are ready, expressing your painful feelings is what enables you to move through them and let go of them. By releasing emotions such as guilt, anger, and despair, you *unburden* yourself and make way for peace and healing.
- Grieving is not a sign of weakness. Rather, it is the healthy, smart, necessary, and brave thing to do.
- Try to give yourself permission to fall apart, to reduce your responsibilities, to withdraw at times and be alone with your deepest feelings and your memories.
- Tell your story: write in a journal or correspondence; talk to your friends and family; connect with other parents of preemies. Rely on those people who can listen without trying to "fix" you.
- Do the things that help you feel close to your baby or babies.
- Let yourself take breaks from your grief and find respite in things you might enjoy.
- Be kind to yourself. Cry every tear. Take all the time you need.
- You will survive.

CHAPTER THREE

Moving through Painful Emotions

*A*s you grieve over the losses associated with your baby's premature birth, you are likely to encounter some particularly painful emotions that can be difficult to express, cope with, and work through. Many of these emotions have to do with feelings of responsibility and loss of control, which are opposite sides of the same coin and arise from the belief that you should be in charge of your own destiny.*

As you struggle to come to terms with this situation, you may go over and over the events preceding your baby's early delivery, wondering what you could have done differently to prevent it. Even if medical experts tell you that your baby's premature birth was inevitable and unavoidable, you may be reluctant to accept their assessment. You may rail at the unfairness of having to deal with a complicated pregnancy and a preterm delivery, and with a child who perhaps bears the costs of such an early birth. You may also struggle with your religious faith or your beliefs about life, goodness, and destiny.

This chapter takes a closer look at the more painful and challenging aspects of grief and adjustment, including feelings of anger, guilt, incompetence, powerlessness, failure, fear, vulnerability, and numbness that many parents of premature babies experience. These emotions tend to come up around different issues at different points on your journey, so throughout the book, you'll find even more information and support as it applies specifically to your time in the NICU, homecoming, parenting, your child's development, your family, social support, and future pregnancies. This chapter provides an overview that identifies and touches on the many aspects of these emotions, so that you can see how your feelings and reactions make sense and fit into the larger picture of your grieving process. We also offer some basic tools that are especially helpful for acknowledging and working through these painful emotions, including getting to the bottom of your grief, counseling, journaling, and spiritual support. Also remember to refer back to Chapter 2 for more general information, support, and suggestions for coping and moving through your grief.

Moving through Feelings of Failure, Incompetence, and Powerlessness

I felt like such a failure as a mother. I had failed to protect them. I also had two other children who were crying at home for me as well. I felt so torn. I didn't want to leave either place. —Miriam

I felt like I hated everyone, but mostly myself. I had let this happen to my baby. How could I be so helpless? —Jenny

Feelings of failure, incompetence, and powerlessness are interrelated. These feelings come from the belief that there was something that you could have done better or differently.

If you're the father, you may have expected that your newborn's robustness would be a testament to your paternal abilities. When your baby arrives so fragile and tiny, your fatherly pride and confidence may feel deeply wounded. You may feel that you failed to safeguard your family, adding to this perception of "second-rate" fatherhood. (For more on this subject, see Chapter 4, "Especially for Fathers.")

If you're the mother, you may feel like a reproductive failure. You may agonize that you were powerless to keep and protect your infant inside your womb until the due date. You may worry that these difficulties are signs of your incompetence or that you don't deserve to be a mother. With your baby in the NICU, you may also feel as if you have no useful role. This increases your feelings of failure and incompetence, and can contribute to feeling disconnected from your baby.

> *[At the company where I work] we print a lot of the baby and parenting magazines ... and it seemed like for the longest time, I would be the one who would have to shoot those jobs ... and I would be reading these articles and I'd be like, "I can't relate to this whatsoever. I don't have a clue what any of this means." It was almost a form of masochism. I would read them, and I would know that I was reading them, and I knew why I was reading them—because I wanted to find out what I had missed—and it was like I was beating myself for not having a "correct" pregnancy. —Brooke*

> *I felt like my job was done, and so I was just tossed. "OK, your job is done, you didn't do a great job at it, but you did it. So thank you and we'll see you later." I didn't feel like a parent at all. Even touching her that one time, I don't think I comprehended that that was what was inside of me. —Michelle*

Some couples feel an intensified sense of failure because they have experienced infertility, more than one complicated pregnancy, and/or the disability or death of one or more babies. If you struggled with infertility or used reproductive technology, you may agonize that after all that effort, you still couldn't deliver a healthy baby or babies. If you have a pattern of high-risk pregnancies, you may feel particularly discouraged. If your baby has a complicated hospital course, you may see it as a reflection of your own inadequacy. If your baby dies or if your child develops chronic health problems or developmental delays, this generates a whole new level of feelings of deficiency and defeat.

> *I felt like I had failed, like I was a failure. I'd tried so hard, but I didn't get it right; I didn't get to finish it. The sense of loss and incompletion was overwhelming. I didn't think I could become pregnant again, knew that I would never undergo infertility treatments again, knew I would never have the joy of telling people I was carrying twins again. I was mourning all of this at the same time that I was mourning for my tiny, wounded boys. I can't possibly explain the grief and guilt I felt—I still feel—at not being able to protect them, to keep them inside and away from the incredible pain they were*

suffering because I wasn't strong enough, because my body failed them. I desperately wanted to have another chance to get it right. —Susan

Feelings of failure also arise in the NICU as you struggle to find your place as your baby's parent. Stacy recalls, "It hurt having to go see Alison in the hospital and watch others taking care of her. That was supposed to be my job. I almost felt as if she were not even my baby—as if I was just her babysitter, going in to hold her every once in a while."

Feelings of failure and fears of incompetence can be immensely uncomfortable because they rob you of your faith in yourself. You may become paralyzed and fearful of taking risks or trying to figure things out for yourself. You may feel powerless to control the situation and vulnerable to even more disappointment or tragedy.

There are a number of ways you can cope with and work through these feelings of defeat:

- *Write in a journal.* Just putting your feelings down on paper can help unburden you as well as give you the insights you need to feel better about yourself.
- *Renew hobbies and other interests.* Engaging in activities at which you feel competent helps you regain feelings of self-worth.
- *Talk to someone supportive.* Your partner, a good friend, a member of the clergy, a counselor, your baby's primary nurse—any of these individuals may be able both to accept your feelings and to reassure you that you are a good parent and a good person.
- *Gather information about the situation.* Learn all you can about your pregnancy complications, your delivery, and your baby's condition. Ask questions—your baby's health care professionals are full of medical insights. Research the issues that worry you the most. Knowledge is empowering. (See Chapter 7 for more about information gathering.)
- *Practice doing what you can for your baby.* Don't fall into the trap of thinking you can't learn how to take care of your baby. Like any skill, taking care of a preterm baby requires experience and time to acquire. Practice builds confidence. (See Chapters 8–10, and 12–16 for more information on infant caregiving.)
- *Work toward accepting yourself (and if you're the mother, accepting your body) with your imperfections.* Everybody has strengths and weaknesses. It is healthier

to realize you are imperfect than to continue striving for impossible perfection.

* *Acknowledge your own needs.* Remember that no matter what happens, you are a person of worth who deserves the best. Reach for what you need to make your life fulfilling.

Because you've been through a traumatic experience, it can take a while to feel as if you can reclaim some measure of control over what happens to you. As you recuperate, your feelings of confidence and self-worth will return. In fact, many parents report that they come through this experience feeling more confident and worthy than before. You can create something to be proud of, you can strengthen your family or yourself, and you can find things to be grateful for in places you never imagined. Although feelings of powerlessness and vulnerability are frightening at first, it is also quite freeing to learn that you don't have to try to control everything that occurs around you. (For more on this subject, see "Moving through Vulnerability and Fear" later in this chapter.)

Moving through Feelings of Anger

Having a preemie ended the fairy tale. The fairy tale is over. I walk around in anger because this is not what I "signed up" for. —Raquel

I remember feeling really mad at my cervix for failing me, just really mad at it. But it was like it was not part of me. It wasn't me that I was mad at, it was this part that had failed and had done something really bad, and I was mad at it. —Stephie

Anger is a powerful and compelling emotion that may consume you at times. You may feel angry at bed rest, at your contractions, at invasive medical technology, or at the doctors and nurses who keep you from your baby. You may be furious with the injustice of the world, fate, God, or Mother Nature. You may feel as if you paid your dues and yet you were cheated of a healthy baby. You may resent other parents in the nursery whose preemies are doing better than yours or feel jealous of friends who have uncomplicated deliveries and newborns in their arms. It's all so unfair.

I was thinking, "If you have one problem, that should protect you from having one of the other possible problems." I know, of course, that this isn't true, but I had gone through all that infertility stuff and then how cruel that I should also have to have a preemie! I felt as if I had spent all that time and money and I wasn't getting what I had paid for, as if there was a contract or something! —Nola

I felt this jealousy when I was on bed rest and knew I wasn't going to have a natural delivery, and my best friend would visit me with her son, who I saw born into the world. My loss was already potent, not being able to look forward to this [gentle birth]. I felt this jealousy when I was in the NICU with my son, and the little girl next to him, who was also born at the same gestation, was off the vent and growing. Or when the woman next to me was pumping full bottles of breast milk and I couldn't get even a half ounce after two months of pumping, so my son was now on formula. I felt this jealousy when my friend had her home birth and, as much as I wanted to be there, I couldn't handle it. I was overjoyed with her, even though it killed me to think of her little boy being cuddled in her arms in bed for twenty-four hours after his birth, just nursing and sleeping peacefully. —Maren

If you believe you received inadequate care, you likely feel angry about the circumstances that surrounded your early labor and delivery. You may be furious at the doctors who discounted the severity of your symptoms or minimized your concerns. Someone may suggest that you bring a lawsuit against the hospital or the doctors, but most parents can see that this won't get them what they really want—a term pregnancy and a healthy newborn.

In the NICU, you might feel aggravated by the lack of information, the inability of the medical caregivers to be forthright, or their failure to include you in decision making for your baby. Your desire to pump and provide breast milk, to be more involved in caregiving, or to have adequate opportunities for privacy or holding your baby close may not have been supported.

After homecoming, you may loathe the multitude of doctors' appointments and therapies—even effective ones. If your child has ongoing special needs, there might be aggravating medical complications, misdiagnoses, or attempts to label your child. You may feel exasperated with a child who is more sensitive, more frail, more finicky, or more challenging to raise due to complications of prematurity. Any rehospitalizations are not just depressing; they can fan the flames of your anger. Life is not supposed to be this difficult. (For more on this subject, see the sections dealing with anger in Chapters 15, 16, and 18.)

Most likely you wish you could show off your new baby without having to worry about germs or questions about size or age. People's ignorant comments and suggestions might be infuriating. You may find it intolerable to be around parents and their term infants or hesitate to join their conversations about their babies' development because your baby hasn't "caught up." Even if you try to avoid these "normal" parents and babies, they seem to be everywhere.

Particularly if you have multiple preemies or other children at home, you may feel irritated by the fact that there just aren't enough hours in the day to tend to everyone's needs or to have much time to yourself.

Venting Anger Constructively

One way to move through anger is to find constructive ways to express it. But some people are under the mistaken impression that expressing anger means being aggressive or hurtful. Although you are entitled to nasty, angry feelings, you can behave in ways that will not hurt you, other people, or items that you value. The goal is to maintain control over your behavior, stay aware of your thoughts, and accept that your emotions are what they are. Sometimes, just acknowledging your anger can help you to move through it and let it go.

> *I had been cheated. That's why I couldn't go to see him. Because he was still supposed to be mine. He was still supposed to be inside of me. He was supposed to be getting everything those machines were giving him from me. And so although I couldn't put it into those words at the time, that's why I was being resentful toward my baby and then hating myself for being resentful toward my baby. But now I know that [resentment] was just [from] what had happened.* —Kathy

Here are a number of nondestructive ways to vent, work through, and let go of your anger:

- *Engage in vigorous exercise.* Even a brisk walk can reduce tension.
- *Make use of your anger's energy.* Remember that anger can be an energy to be mined. Turn your energy toward advocating for your baby's needs,

hunting down resources, finding support, making institutional changes, or working for other worthy causes for which you have a passion.

- *Write an angry letter.* If you're aggravated with someone or something—the doctors, God, fate—put your anger into words on paper. This letter isn't for sending, it's for articulating your anger and despair.
- *Write in your journal.* Describe your angry feelings and their sources.
- *Create something.* Draw a picture or create a clay sculpture that shows your distress.
- *Air your grievances.* Tell people (or the hospital) what you need or want.
- *Talk to someone.* Make sure the person(s) you choose can listen and accept your anger without increasing your agitation.
- *Talk to other parents of preemies.* These parents share situations similar to yours and are likely to understand your anger.

Recognizing Your Anger's Triggers

Another approach to managing anger is to become more aware of the thoughts and situations that trigger and maintain your anger. Anger has its place in the emotional landscape, but it can be problematic if it becomes a reflexive or overwhelming response. To keep your anger from becoming destructive, keep in mind that some of the assumptions triggering your anger may not be based in reality and that you may misunderstand others' intentions. For example:

- *Do you feel entitled to be treated in a certain way?* Instead of blaming others for not treating you as you want to be treated, practice asking for what you need or find ways to satisfy your own needs. Also practice treating others the way you want to be treated.
- *Do you assume that your baby's health care providers are trying to thwart your attempts to be close to your little one?* Instead of attacking the staff, ask them to teach you how to do things for your baby. You may discover that by giving these people the benefit of the doubt—and letting them know what you need—you become more aware of and open to their ongoing attempts to encourage and include you.
- *Do you continue to rail against the unfairness of the situation?* Try letting go of the belief that life should be fair or that you should have gotten a better deal. Understand that although you do not deserve this, bad stuff does happen to good people.

- *Do you assume that you are in control and that your expectations will be fulfilled?* When life doesn't go as you planned, you can prevent needless suffering by letting go of your expectations. Instead of wishing for a specific outcome, hold onto a "wondering" frame of mind. Trust that you can find meaning in whatever happens.
- *Do you continue to think about an infuriating incident long after it has passed?* Instead of going over and over what happened, be angry and be done with it. By reviewing it repeatedly, you continue to feed the fire of your anger. Give yourself permission to let it go. What has passed has passed—focus on living in the present. You can express your feelings, you can learn from an experience, but then you *can* move on without giving in or betraying your principles.

If you're having an especially difficult time managing your anger, consider the possibility that this situation is tapping into an old well of rage and helplessness. Consider professional counseling to help you work through old hurts so they can stop contaminating your reactions to current situations.

Whatever the source of your anger, you are entitled to professional support to help you get through this time. Your anger is valid, but you also deserve the peace that comes as you work through your anger and move forward. (For more on counseling, see the "Professional Counseling" section later in this chapter.)

Moving through Guilt

There's this guilt that will probably never leave me. That's so big at the beginning. You just can't help feeling guilty, so guilty. This guilt that you're the mother and you weren't able to keep him inside. You're the only one to blame because—well, actually you're not the only one to blame, but at that point, you think you are the only one to blame. It takes a long time to get over that.
—*Gallice*

Feelings of guilt arise from normal parental feelings of responsibility. But feeling personally responsible for your baby's plight can be a horrifying burden.

Because the mother carries her baby in her womb, it is natural that she feels responsible on some level when her baby is born early. If you are the mother, you may feel guilty because the pregnancy couldn't be maintained. If you had a condition that made continuing the pregnancy unsafe for you or your baby, or if you were in preterm labor, you may wonder, "What kind of a mother would provide a hostile or rejecting womb?"

If you believe that you failed to get adequate medical care or that you ignored signs that were ominous, you will agonize over what you could have done differently, and it can be harder to come to terms with your child's premature birth. Even if you know in your heart that you took the best actions and made the best decisions you could, you may still blame yourself. And even when you know your baby's delivery was beyond your control, lingering feelings of responsibility can spawn feelings of guilt. Guilt is the agony of anger and blame turned inward. Guilt is a way to hold onto the illusion of control over the uncontrollable. It's a way to try to make sense of the senseless.

I felt extremely guilty. I had no one to blame, so I blamed myself. Then I blamed the doctors, my husband, even God. I just couldn't make sense of any of it. —Jayna

I felt a lot of guilt that my children were born so early. Intellectually, I knew I had done everything possible to give the girls a chance, but emotionally, I still felt the guilt. —Kimberly

I felt both guilty and like a failure. What did I do to cause my baby's early birth? He has to go through so much, and I didn't even feel pain from delivering. I still wonder if I did something wrong. —Cynthia

We both lived in guilt. [My husband] for being a doctor and not seeing that my pregnancy was in trouble and not getting me help when I needed it (even though he is not an ob-gyn and could not have known). Mine for "allowing" myself to give birth so early. —Raquel

Many parents also feel directly responsible for exposing their baby to the harsh conditions of the NICU. There's just no comparison between where your baby is and where your baby is supposed to be. At times, your infant's medical care might feel like a runaway train, particularly if there is one complication after another. If the prognosis is poor or uncertain, you may face decisions about aggressive medical intervention. If you had to make life-and-death decisions, you may feel especially responsible for the outcome. Guilt may accompany any regrets you have. (For more on guilt about difficult decisions, see Chapters 10 and 11.)

I often wondered if I had wished too hard for a son. I had gotten my wish, yes, but look at the situation he was in. I felt guilty about that. —Shaw

Some parents also feel guilty about not being with their sick baby at certain points. You may berate yourself for not spending more time or doing certain things with your baby in the NICU. Or maybe you misjudged your baby's needs and regret that you didn't or couldn't fulfill them. If you couldn't be with your baby during some painful procedures, you may deeply regret missing those opportunities to try to soothe him or her. (For more support on these topics, see "Being There for Medical Procedures" in Chapter 7 and "Managing Your Regrets" in Chapter 8.)

Feelings of guilt can arise from other feelings of inadequacy. If your child continues to show negative effects from prematurity, you may feel particularly guilty over your failure to protect him from this fate. When it takes a while to find the right diagnosis, the right medication or dosage, or the right treatment, school placement, or therapist, you may feel guilty for the time and energy wasted on pursuing options that in hindsight brought little or no benefit. These are all difficult sorrows to bear. (For more on this, see "Guilt" in Chapter 18.)

For many parents, becoming pregnant is like a promise. Your wishes, hopes, and dreams for this child become loving promises to your baby. And when your beloved child doesn't have the life that you had envisioned and hoped, you may feel that you have betrayed him or her.

What an awful feeling for a parent to have—to love and treasure a baby and then, in the NICU or beyond, to feel as if you've betrayed your little one. You may wonder if your child feels betrayed by you. Rest assured, children do not blame their parents for their prematurity or the consequences. You needn't blame yourself either.

Feelings of guilt trail many parents throughout their journey. Even though guilt is a common reaction, there are ways you can moderate, work through, and even let go of it.

Tips for Letting Go of Guilt

Consider the Circumstances As you wrestle with feelings of guilt, it is important to remember what your emotional or physical condition was during the times you feel guilty about. Continuing your pregnancy was not an advisable option—or even a choice. During those times you avoided going to the NICU to be with your baby, the feelings that threatened to flood you may have been too much for you to bear. Recall what difficult times those were. How could you have done better when you were already doing the best you could under the circumstances?

Perhaps you wish could have been a better advocate for your baby in the NICU, standing up to the medical team and making them see what you were seeing. But how could you have insisted on changing the standards of medical care?

It may help to remember that hindsight is twenty-twenty—and foresight can be blind. Without a crystal ball, how could you have known the best path to take? How could you have done more or been any better, given the support, resources, information, and options you had at the time? It is easy to kick yourself in retrospect, but you never planned or wished for your baby to struggle in the womb or in a NICU. You certainly didn't intend for this to happen.

Particularly if you were carrying multiples or if you experienced maternal complications, your body may have been seriously taxed. If the doctors let the delivery happen after you told them that you couldn't bear another day, *trust your intuition about this.* Looking back, you may wonder why you didn't hold on or what the big deal was, but this is the result of your amnesia about physical suffering, not your misjudgment. Respect your perception that your pregnancy had reached the point of diminishing returns. It is truly possible that had you carried your baby or babies one more week, their outcomes (or yours) might have been worse. When placental failure, infection, or serious maternal complications are present, the baby is safer in the NICU than in the womb.

Recognize the Limits of Your Control Another way to let yourself off guilt's hook is to identify those things that were beyond your control. You may have made heartfelt promises to your unborn child, but no parent can guarantee that all their promises will come true. You can still have your wishes, hopes, and dreams. You can still try to protect your children. But when those wishes don't come true and when you're unable to protect your children from harm or even death, you cannot possibly carry all the blame. Plenty, if not all, of the responsibility belongs to the limits of medical intervention, fate, Mother Nature, or whatever higher being you subscribe to.

No mother should feel responsible for the preterm birth of her child because, despite the "medical full court press," babies are born too early. Bottom line, doctors don't fully understand the labor process: they don't really understand why some women will contract for months with little or no change and others will contract for minutes and wind up with a preemie. —Sheila

If you are painfully struggling with the emotion of guilt, try the following:

- Recognize that you cannot always avoid tragedy or know the right course of action. No one can.
- Instead of being angry with yourself for things you did or didn't do, remember that you never intended for your baby to be born prematurely.
- Instead of being disappointed in yourself, be disappointed that medical science doesn't fully understand pregnancy complications and cannot predictably prevent or stop them.
- Instead of regretting decisions you made, regret that you had to choose without benefit of sufficient information or support.
- If you had to choose between death and suffering, acknowledge that your options were "terrible" and "horrible."
- If you fear that you didn't speak up enough, be aggravated that the system or your doctors didn't encourage parental input.
- Accept that you did the best you could in an impossible situation.
- Recognize that guilt is a normal and natural parental reaction that subsides over time as you let go of what might have been and embrace what is.

Reframe Your Feelings of Responsibility When you are feeling responsible for your baby's condition and fate, try casting your feelings of guilt in a more positive and *realistic* light, so that you can reframe your thinking when these feelings arise. Some of these approaches can help:

- Recognize that feelings of guilt arise out of your devotion to your child.

- Consider that "feeling" guilty is not the same as "being" guilty.
- Accept that you did the best you could.
- Don't blame yourself for not knowing everything.
- Remember that you made the best decisions you could based on the information and support available.
- Accept that being a perfect parent is an impossible standard to uphold.
- Don't expect yourself to make sacrifices at the expense of your own basic needs. Depleting yourself also depletes your ability to be an effective parent—you can't nurture your children if you don't nurture yourself.
- Understand that when others criticize your parenting, they are really saying what they believe they would do. That isn't necessarily what you want to or should do.
- Give yourself permission to make mistakes and accept that you are learning "on the job."
- Realize that you cannot always keep bad things from happening.
- Talk to others who can reassure you that you are not to blame.
- If this appeals to you, embrace the idea that your child's fate is determined not by you, but by what is in his or her higher good.

I felt helpless. My first thought was, "Why us? What had I done wrong?" I now know that it is not me that did anything wrong—it just happened. —Jodi

I do still go over the whole sequence of events in my mind. What did I do? What could I have done? Should I have told them to wait and not do an amnio with such low fluids? So many questions! Someone told me of the amnio risks later, and I almost cried. I didn't know! *... I hope that in writing all this, I am able to have some peace from it all. I really did do the best that I could, given the circumstances. —Linda*

There was a time when I really wanted to know exactly what had caused Vincent's IVH [intraventricular hemorrhage], and whether there was anything else I should be blaming myself for. As time goes on, the reason seems to matter less. —Anne

Parenting Your Premature Baby and Child

Accept and Learn from Your Mistakes Even if you are convinced that you fell short, you can still get to the point where you accept the fact that you made an error in judgment and forgive yourself. To do this, find a way to express and let go of your pain. One way is to write down your thoughts and feelings of doubt and recrimination. Try writing every day, for as many days as it takes to forgive yourself. Write until you can look in the mirror and say, "My child is fortunate to have me for a mother/father." This may seem like an insurmountable task, but the reward is great.

You can also make your guilt productive by learning from your mistakes. If your guilt spurs a positive change in your behavior, perspective, or parenting style, then you are using it wisely. You might also want to consider the philosophy that there are higher spiritual reasons for this child to be on this particular journey. Your child's journey may be unaffected *or even made easier* by the very decisions or behaviors for which you fault yourself.

Ask for Forgiveness If you just can't let yourself off the hook, you can write your child a letter and ask for forgiveness. Keep this letter to yourself—writing it is a good way for you to pour out your feelings and let them go. Although you are entitled to your guilt, working through it lets you live peacefully with yourself and honorably with your child's birth. The goal is to shape your crushing burden of guilt into more manageable feelings of parental responsibility. Although a part of you may always wonder about your responsibility for past events, use those feelings to inspire a renewed sense of responsibility toward parenting your child into the future.

I think most of us, if we are honest with ourselves, have confessions relating to guilt and our little ones. Please know that you are not alone. I don't think any of us made choices out of a malicious intent to bring on premature delivery but rather out of a desire to try to maintain a somewhat normal balance in a totally unbalanced time.

When I was placed on home bed rest, I was told to stay down absolutely as much as possible, but that I could get up to grab a very fast snack or to use the washroom. I remember standing at the stove making pasta for pasta salad over and over (it was my craving at that time), and even now I feel guilty and even embarrassed that I may have brought on my full-blown labor because of my insatiable need for rotini. What was I thinking, hanging out in the kitchen for twenty minutes at a stretch with a cervix that was soon halfway to delivery? I just didn't know the consequences, and I was all alone.

Then, in the four days I was hospitalized before Cailean was born, I was given medication to help prevent his birth. He suffered complications at two days of life that studies later "potentially" linked to the prenatal use of that medication. Oh my. Now I had not only brought on his preterm labor/delivery, but because of the meds they offered and I accepted, I had perhaps caused his neonatal crises as well. Years later, two years after my younger preemie was born, diagnostic studies revealed I had a condition that became the attributable cause of my obstetric complications. Sigh. Now I knew with some certainty that my body had been engineered all along to basically reject these little loved ones of mine. ...

Now that my boys are four and six years old, much of that guilt has eased, and when I think back, I'm more inclined to be proud of all that I did do to help continue, support, and prolong my pregnancies. What does remain is an enormous sense of responsibility, and it helps me raise my sons with great care and vision for what they can become. —Maureen

Knowing with some degree of certainty that most of the difficulties facing our children stem from prematurity adds a layer that simply can't be dismissed. If not for prematurity ... so much would be different. It's not at all beneficial that a certain amount of guilt remains unshakable whenever we see our children struggle ... but it's the pure essence of humanity. —Sheila

Moving through Vulnerability and Fear

It's as if I am walking through my life and the path I am on and all I can see to my left contains all the blessings and wonderful possibilities for my family and our lives and our future. When I look to the right, I see a terrible cliff dropping off into disaster. The cliff was always there, is always there for everyone. Anything can happen. But before the losses we have experienced, I was able to concentrate on the path I was on and all that lies to the left. Since my experiences, I spend a lot more time conscious of and worrying about the abyss. I don't feel safe anymore, even though that safety was always at least potentially an illusion. I really miss the ability to live with that illusion. —Susan

• • •

During your pregnancy, like many expectant parents, you probably thought that with enough good judgment, good habits, and foresight, you could avoid misfortune. You may have believed that bad things only happen to bad people. When your baby was born early, you might have asked, "How could this have happened to us?" But as the futility of the question sinks in, you realize that you can't control every aspect of your life. This can be quite unsettling and aggravating. Even if, in hindsight, there are things you would do differently, it can be unnerving to admit that no one can have twenty-twenty foresight.

When you grasp that you are vulnerable to misfortune, you may feel betrayed, helpless, or fearful. The premature birth of your baby can make you question your assumptions about life. Life may seem so unpredictable now. But eventually, you *can* find a balance between feeling powerless and maintaining some control over your life. You can also acquire the sense of peace that accompanies "surrender," casting off the belief that you have to be on guard, cover all your bases, and be in charge of everything around you. You learn to take each day as it comes and to cherish what you have. You stop striving for perfection and learn to accept yourself and your child for who you are. Surrendering also means no longer regretting the past and fearing less for the future. What will be, will be. You can learn to worry less, not more.

But how can you trust the world again? Many parents simply come to accept that difficulties are a part of life. Then they realize they can manage. Even if you must deal with continuing setbacks, labels, and challenges with your child's health and development, you learn the drill of dealing with your feelings of shock or foreboding, gathering information and options, grieving for your child and yourself, and trying to maintain hope in the face of loss. Life won't always go the way you'd hoped or planned, but you know that you can prevail, whatever happens.

Some parents find comfort in the philosophy that each of their children has his or her own destiny to follow, and that they cannot exert total control over what that path might be. Of course, you probably expected to have a lot of control, at least through your child's adolescence when "letting go" becomes a skill most parents work to master. Little did you know that your premature baby would require you to learn about letting go so soon. (For more on letting go, see "Balancing Hopes and Fears" in Chapter 10, "Coping with Feelings of Vulnerability" in Chapter 14, and "Understanding and Managing Heightened Vigilance" in Chapter 17.)

• • •

Moving through Painful Emotions

Post-Traumatic Stress Disorder

Periodically, I resolve to meet my challenges from a positive, upbeat point of view. Intellectually, cognitively, I understand that's the right way, the best way to look at things. But there is something else at a darker, deeper emotional level that won't cooperate with my resolve. I wake up in the middle of the night aware of terrible danger. I don't know what will happen or when, I just sense it out there. And I lie awake, trying to think of how to keep it from coming, what to do, how to protect.

In the cold morning light, I think I understand that somehow I am trying to relive, to correct, what happened to us all nearly five years ago. But that understanding doesn't stop the terror resting just underneath, the terror that wakes me alone and unequal to its terrible force. —Susan

Some parents experience a hypervigilance that may indicate post-traumatic stress disorder (PTSD). PTSD is a result of enduring severe stress that is tremendously overwhelming, wherein a person experiences or witnesses threats to the safety or physical integrity of him- or herself or others. During this time, the person's response includes intense helplessness, fear, and/or horror. Having a premature infant struggling for survival in the NICU certainly qualifies as such an experience.

The essential, persistent features of PTSD include

* Re-experiencing the trauma through recurrent, painful, and intrusive recollections; dreams or nightmares; and even dissociative states in which one relives aspects of the trauma. It's as if the person is transported back in time and is again experiencing the original trauma. The PTSD sufferer can experience flashbacks and intense memories triggered by smells, sights, sounds, or other situations that resemble or symbolize the trauma.

* Unwillingness to think or talk about the experience and avoidance of those reminders that trigger memories or feelings. PTSD sufferers often experience diminished responsiveness, including detachment from others, reduced interest in previously enjoyed activities, and decreased ability to feel emotions. They may also feel numb and detached from the original traumatic experience, not even remembering certain parts of it; this lack of memory cannot be attributed to the effects of medication or illness.

- Physical hyperarousal as a result of visceral terror. A hallmark of PTSD, the symptoms of physical hyperarousal include outbursts of anger, difficulty concentrating, insomnia, and excessive vigilance, including hyperalertness and an exaggerated startle response.

One way of understanding the phenomenon of PTSD is that it originates in the need to gain mastery over a terrifying trauma experienced while in a passive and helpless state. It is possible that by reliving the event, a person is attempting to come to terms with it—that is, to make sense of it, to not feel responsible for it, and to accept that it was unavoidable. Nowadays, with growing knowledge about brain chemistry, PTSD is also considered to have a strong biological component. Treatment options include psychotherapy, medication, group therapy, and a unique treatment called EMDR (eye movement desensitization and reprocessing, which utilizes a person's own innate ability to process information and transform the memory of disturbing and traumatic experiences to a more adaptive, healthy recollection). If you are interested in pursuing EMDR, be sure that you find a practitioner who has received specific training in this technique.

Lots of numbness through the whole thing, except for a few "breakdowns." The big breakdown hit about two years after my son was released, and I was temporarily placed on Paxil to combat my bout with mild depression. The doctors told me I was going through something similar to post-traumatic stress disorder and was at a point where I couldn't handle the stress any longer. I asked to be taken off the medicine after fifteen months or so because I felt I could handle things on my own. I've done well, without any major bouts with depression and definitely no feelings like I had prior to the medication. —Andrea

Having some or even many of these symptoms doesn't necessarily mean that you have a full-blown case of PTSD. You can be traumatized by an experience without being disabled by it. But whether you are clinically experiencing PTSD or not doesn't matter. What is important is that *your symptoms count*, however mild or severe they are. You have been through a traumatic experience, and your symptoms are related to that trauma. Knowing the source of your bewildering reactions can help you make sense of them. If you feel unable to function, definitely seek help. But you needn't be diagnosed with PTSD to benefit from assistance coping with your symptoms—learning ways to calm your body, reprocess your memories, and heal the trauma.

Persistent Numbness and Avoidance of Grief

Grief that is continually avoided will appear indirectly, in ways that can severely compromise your health and happiness. Avoiding grief, whether intentionally or unintentionally, may result in any of the following physical manifestations:

- *Physical illness,* such as recurring fatigue, headaches, infections, heightened allergy sensitivity, aching muscles or joints
- *Overactivity,* such as workaholism, routine multitasking, filling up the calendar with commitments, restlessness
- *Anxiety,* a vague, uncomfortable feeling of fear or dread that may be accompanied by rapid breathing and heartbeat, nausea, diarrhea, headaches, sweating, irritability, insomnia, trembling, nightmares
- *Depression,* including vague feelings of dissatisfaction, unhappiness, boredom, loss of interest in life, excessive sleeping or insomnia, difficulty concentrating or making decisions, intense guilt, irritability, unfocused crying spells
- *Disrupted relationships,* such as negative or detached feelings toward your preemie, marriage troubles, broken friendships, intense conflict in family relationships, persistent feelings of isolation
- *Drug abuse,* including abuse of alcohol, cigarettes, tranquilizers, pain killers, and other drugs
- Other compulsive or *addictive behaviors,* such as engaging excessively in eating, exercise, shopping, gambling, cleaning, sleeping, television watching, computer use, fervent religion, sexual activity or infidelities. (For more on addictions and compulsions see "Avoiding Grief" in Chapter 4.)
- *Violence,* such as getting into physical or abusive verbal fights with others, including family members; car accidents
- Other self-destructive behaviors, such as *failure* to use good judgment, accidents that might have been avoided with normal caution or alertness

Occasional avoidance can help you cope with the situation by alleviating intensely painful feelings and allowing you to catch your breath. But a prevailing or continuing feeling of numbness or detachment accompanied by any of the symptoms just listed may indicate that you are avoiding grief to your detriment. If you are experiencing any of the difficulties just described or if others are expressing their concern about your health, behavior, or functioning, you may benefit from counseling with a therapist who can help you face and cope with your pain and adjust to your losses. (Look under "Professional Counseling" later in this chapter.)

For some parents, numbness can also result from relentless uncertainty about their baby's condition or prognosis. It is exhausting to alternate between hope and hopelessness. When your hopes are raised and then shattered so many times, emotionally you may no longer react. This kind of numbness can be longer lasting and more debilitating than the initial shock you feel at your baby's birth or when you hear about a medical crisis or receive a diagnosis. If you think you've become too detached from your feelings, you may benefit from counseling, writing a journal, or telling your story to someone who can listen and help you make sense of this roller-coaster ride. Getting back in touch with your emotions can help you move forward in your grieving process. (For more on grief and coping, see Chapters 2 and 4. For more on dealing with uncertainty, see "Waiting" in Chapter 10, "Coping with Feelings of Vulnerability" in Chapter 14, "Perspectives on Parenting Your Preemie" in Chapter 15, and "Living with Uncertainty and Ambiguity" in Chapter 17.)

Getting to the Bottom of Your Grief

Feelings such as anger, guilt, failure, and anxiety can arise from the belief that you are in charge of your own destiny. You make plans, you fulfill them. You have goals, you attain them. You may put your faith in medical technology, health care professionals, God, fate, Mother Nature, or universal justice.

When your baby is born prematurely, you may feel angry that your plans and goals were thwarted, and you may feel betrayed by your faith. You may feel guilty that you couldn't prevent your baby's burdens or regret that you cannot fully protect your little one. If you had to induce labor early or if you made decisions about whether to pursue medical intervention, you may feel even more responsible for what happened. You may agonize: "What happened? Why me? Why my baby?" You want answers to ensure more control in the future.

I did find myself going over the day before his birth, over and over again. I tore myself apart wondering what I could have done differently. If only I hadn't done this, if only I had done this ... that sort of thing. —Claire

A more realistic perspective is that you don't always have the power to prevent bad things from happening and that misfortune can strike even when you least expect it. But feeling vulnerable to misfortune and hardship can be a terrifying feeling to face. To avoid the fear and powerlessness that come with vulnerability, you may hold onto anger, guilt, regret, anxiety, and failure for a while. These emotions protect that comfortable illusion of being in total control. Later, as you adjust, you come to the painful realization that you don't have control over everything that happens in your life. Sometimes, as hard as you try, you cannot even protect your children.

You may also hold on to your anger or guilt as a way to avoid sadness, hurt, and despair. These feelings are at the bottom of your grief. They are so painful that you may try to cling to edges of this pit of despair, so that you don't hit bottom. Anger, guilt, anxiety, and failure can serve as fingerholds. One mother describes not having really grieved her losses and seeing that anger as her primary response:

I guess until recently I had never really thought about the grief caused by the loss of rites we go through as our tiny babies are cared for by the medical system. I was too busy doing what needed to be done to get myself and my family through the whole ordeal of having Rowan so early.

Now it has hit with a vengeance. I find myself always on the defensive when it comes to general parenting and health issues. I am not as tolerant of "well-meaning" people and their advice as I was with my other two babies. I will often fly off the handle at simple things like my father-in-law's commenting on how Rowan is holding his arms out to the side or the sterilizer still being used for bottles. I know that mostly the intentions are good and often it is just a way to find a topic of conversation meaningful to both of us, but I can't stop my defenses from stepping in and taking over in situations like this. My intellect goes onto the back burner. —Bess

It is common for parents to hang on to these feelings and avoid the depths of despair. Unfortunately, continuously holding on to feelings of guilt, failure, anger, and anxiety can be incapacitating. You may feel moody and irritable, held hostage by your intense emotions. Guilt and failure can diminish your feelings of self-worth. Anger and anxiety can interfere with your enjoyment of life. For now, you may claim that you deserve to feel bad about yourself and miserable about life. But as time goes on, you may become weary of being angry or guilty and want to move on. This can be a sign that you are ready to tackle your deepest feelings of sorrow and relieve yourself of that burden.

One way you might try to get in touch with your sadness is this exercise: Begin by recognizing that your grief hides beneath your layered defenses of anxiety, guilt, failure, and anger. You might say to yourself, "I feel so anxious about not being able to protect my baby from invasive medical procedures." Try replacing "anxious" with "guilty" or "failure" (or start wherever you are), as in "I feel so guilty (or like such a failure) for not being able to protect my baby." After you immerse yourself in guilt or failure for a while, say, "I feel so angry that this terrible thing happened and I couldn't protect my baby." Finally, when you've let yourself feel really angry, replace "angry" with "sad": "I feel sad that I couldn't protect my baby." Then let yourself express those painful feelings of sadness.

> *I found myself getting angry that people actually lead "normal" lives. I was so wrapped up in our day-to-day crisis that I felt cheated of all the things we were supposed to have. I'm not angry any longer, just sad that I'll never experience some of the most common experiences a parent expects. —Cindy*

Parents have other ways of getting in touch with sadness. You might try dwelling on painful memories, writing or talking about them, or listing the wishes and dreams you've had to let go of. If you have a box, book, or envelope of keepsakes and photographs, going over them and tearfully reliving your experiences can help, too. When you are especially stressed, anxious, irritable, or depressed, finding ways to express emotions can help you to release tension. Although doing this is painful, you may discover that it helps you to get through a tough day or week more easily.

While some parents immerse themselves in grief, others bury themselves in work, parenting, or other activities. But avoidance can produce quite a different outcome than immersion. Parents who give themselves time and permission to grieve deeply are more likely to feel they are on the road to coping and healing. Those who hold back may eventually recognize that their lives continue to be compromised by the grief they have tried to avoid.

If your baby is experiencing a complicated hospital course or delays and impairments are being discovered, you may feel that your hopes are being dashed over and over again. Sometimes parents feel as if they are getting repeatedly sucker punched. This can be extremely stressful, and it adds to your losses and your grief. Each time your grief is renewed, you have to return to the pit of despair before you can climb out again. It's either that or stay perched on a precarious ledge. Neither one is easy, but at least the pit of despair is temporary.

As you are immersed in your most painful feelings in the pit of despair, you begin to grasp how truly vulnerable you are to the twists and turns of fate. Feelings of fear are natural. Indeed, fear often underlies your most painful feelings, including anger, guilt, anxiety, failure, and depression. Many people find it easier to get mad, blame themselves, run around in a panic, or withdraw than to face feelings of vulnerability and fear.

Professional Counseling

If I could relive that time, there are things I would do differently. Besides being more assertive with the hospital staff, I would have sought help for myself. I believe I could have served Molly better if I had had a grip on my feelings. —Renee

Many parents benefit both from individual counseling and from attending a parent support group. A support group can help you feel less isolated, give you opportunities to develop supportive friendships, and offer hope for the future as you observe how others have managed. Individual counseling has the added benefit of letting you air your feelings at greater length and helping you work through other personal issues that may be affecting your adjustment. One mother talks about her need for help:

Some things are too big to work out on my own. ... Is it uncommon to feel this way, to realize that years later, there's all this "stuff" that's still there, still unresolved? When does it end? ... How many more layers of pain are there?

Why is it that James has come out of this so much more whole than me? I'm sure that I was normal once. Now I wonder if I ever will be again. —Leanne

If you have overwhelming feelings of anxiety, fear, guilt, anger, or depression, professional counseling can give you the extra support you deserve. Family therapy can benefit your other children and your relationship with your partner. You may feel the need for counseling at any time, even years later, and at more than one point along your journey, particularly when you encounter situations that spark your grief anew.

All of your feelings and behaviors may be a natural part of grief and a normal response to trauma. Even so, you are entitled to professional support to help you get through it all. Also remember that it is normal for this kind of crisis to push you to examine coping techniques that may have worked well enough in the past, but that may now be causing you additional pain and getting in the way of your ability to grieve and heal. Your old ways may no longer work. This crisis is too big for you to blunder, muscle, or sidestep your way through it. Your baby's preterm birth can act as a catalyst for growth by compelling you to adopt healthier ways of dealing with crises and emotions. A skilled therapist can support you through this process of change and adaptation.

Kris talks about the benefits of counseling and about how she and her husband turned their baby's prematurity into an opportunity for growth:

The stress of Lars's early birth and ongoing issues has brought new issues as well as preexisting things to the front. It's easy to blame problems on our situation, but recognizing that many of the things that are driving us crazy are old patterns has been very illuminating for us. And my husband, especially, is now dealing with issues like letting fear dominate his life, mild depression, and anger management that have been with him for a long time but that he has been able to deny in the past. I really feel that our relationship has been strengthened and deepened by our experiences with prematurity—not that I would recommend it [as the way to go about it]. —Kris

You may benefit from seeing a counselor if any one of the following is true:
- You think it might help.
- You are worried about any of your feelings or behaviors.

- You feel "stuck."
- You feel prolonged numbness or detachment.
- You feel extremely anxious or obsessive.
- You feel a visceral terror at times.
- You consider committing suicide. **THIS IS A MEDICAL EMER-GENCY. Seek help immediately.**
- You feel unable to function or cope.
- You have trouble getting out of bed or starting your day.
- You are often unable to advocate for your baby, in the NICU or beyond.
- You fear you might not be able to take care of yourself or your baby.
- You don't feel connected to your baby.
- You find little joy in other parts of your life even after some time has passed.
- Your relationships are deteriorating.
- You feel a parent support group isn't "quite enough."
- You want someone outside your circle of friends and family who can listen, understand, and support you.

Some people hesitate to enter counseling for fear they will never stop needing it. For many people, getting into therapy implies weakness, mental illness, or character flaws. Actually, the reverse is true. Recognizing the need for counseling indicates personal strength, health, and courage because being successful in therapy means facing your feelings and problems and gaining trust in yourself. Therapy also implies a commitment to your children and your partner: those relationships will thrive as you become healthier emotionally. Therapy can help you to:

- Feel and express a wide range of emotions
- Understand your reactions
- Learn new ways of coping
- Acquire more skills for working through problems
- Feel nurtured and understood in a deep and complete way by a skilled listener
- Feel better about yourself, more aware of your strengths, competence, flexibility, and resilience

Ultimately, through the process of therapy you gain the ability to help yourself. When you stop going regularly, your counselor can remain available for occasional consultation if the need arises.

At the very least, a supportive counselor can help you express and cope with your feelings of loss and regret. Counseling can help you face and manage those worries and concerns that you feel uncomfortable discussing with others. With that special support, you will find it easier to come to terms with your baby's premature birth and its consequences. Even just a couple of visits with a counselor might give you reassurance and the boost you need. You might also want to explore other emotionally healing avenues, such as art therapy, yoga, meditation, journaling, acupuncture, homeopathy, naturopathy, and massage.

If you decide to try counseling, look for a licensed professional who understands your needs and the grief and trauma of having a premature baby. A reputable counselor can be a psychologist, a clinical social worker, a psychiatrist, a psychiatric nurse, or a member of the clergy. To locate specialists in your area, contact professional organizations or check the Yellow Pages listings under "Psychologist," "Psychiatrist," "Social Worker," "Counselor," or "Mental Health Services." Recommendations from people you know can be the most valuable way to find the best therapist for you. You might ask

- Other parents of preemies
- Your doctor or midwife
- Parent support-group facilitators
- The social worker or psychological support services at your local hospital
- Your NICU social worker
- Your community mental health clinic
- Your place of worship
- The local college, university, or medical school counseling center
- A family services agency
- Your child's physical or rehabilitative therapists, pediatrician, or school

If cost is a concern, community and university mental health clinics operate on sliding fee scales, so you pay what you can afford. Many private counselors will negotiate their fees. Most health insurance or employee assistance programs will pay some or all of the cost. Tell yourself that you are *worth* it and that your children will benefit from your improved responsiveness.

I didn't start to feel really depressed until past James's first birthday. Those first twelve months I was too busy to feel anything. I had friends ask me the old "How do you do it?" question time and time again, and I'd just smile and shrug and keep on going and going and going and going. Back then I didn't stop. My coping skills, which seemed admirable at the time to friends and family, were in reality almost nil. (My way of coping with stressful situations has been to avoid thinking about them—and then eventually they go away. Or pretending that everything was fine and not confronting my feelings, turning everything inward and hiding it all.) So, I wasn't coping, but I was moving so damn fast that no one realized that I was avoiding the whole thing. Everyone raved at how well I was doing. I have great masks and have many and varied versions for every occasion. It was like I had a split personality: the outside me walked the walk and talked the talk, and the inside me cried the whole time and no one really heard.

Then I became pregnant with Hannah, and I was bedridden for the last eight to ten weeks of my pregnancy. I had to STOP, and I had time to THINK, and the past two and a half years came crashing down on top of me. About six months after Hannah's birth, I became suicidal and had horrible nightmares and daydreams and thoughts. I eventually felt that I was tumbling down a deep, dark hole and the rope that connected me to the daylight was quickly running out, so I rang a help line and got counseling very quickly. When it became obvious to me that counseling alone wasn't helping, I told my psychologist that we needed to be more aggressive, and I started taking antidepressants.

Two weeks after starting on them, my world went from black and white to color. About six months later I found this Internet list [Preemie-L] and the colors became more vivid, and I decided finally that living was a great thing.

There are plenty of reasons why you feel the way you do, hundreds and thousands of them. But don't wait to get help. There is no reason that you should get to the point where I was. You are a person worthy of help, and you deserve the best help that you can find. —Leanne

If you are ever so distressed that you find yourself making plans to commit suicide, THIS IS A MEDICAL EMERGENCY. Call a friend to help you. Or call your doctor, go to the emergency room of your local hospital, call a twenty-four-hour crisis number (look in

the Yellow Pages under "Mental Health Services" or "Hospitals"), or dial your local emergency assistance number (911 in most areas). *It is essential for you to get the care you need immediately.*

Journaling

Journaling is simply writing down your thoughts, feelings, and observations. It is a key coping mechanism that has many benefits.

- Putting your emotional experiences on paper helps you to identify and express your deepest feelings and frees you from the burden of holding them inside.
- If you are having trouble sleeping, writing can help you unload the thoughts and fears that are incessantly circling in your mind.
- Jotting down your observations can help you formulate your questions.
- Recording answers and insights enables you to absorb and keep track of them.
- Listing your hopes can make them seem more real.
- Chronicling your baby's development can help you recognize your baby's progress.
- Writing also helps you make sense of what you're going through. You can zero in on your pain, put your feelings into perspective, and discover solutions. Reading your journal is a way to acknowledge what you've been through and to affirm your love for your child. Your dated entries can provide reassuring evidence of your own healing.
- In your journal, you can include poems, sketches, and important mementos. You can also write "letters" to your rude neighbor, a kind stranger, your doctor, the hospital administrator, Mother Nature, God, fate. These letters aren't to be sent. Writing them is simply your opportunity to vent, especially angry feelings. Particularly if you have regrets, write a letter to your baby. Then if you wish, imagine or write your baby's reply.
- For some people, participation in an online Listserv feels like a form of journaling, but with the benefit of getting supportive responses.
- You can keep a journal in anything—a fancy leather-bound diary, a spiral notebook, a plain sketch pad, or a book especially published for that purpose. (See the Appendix C, "Books for Parents of Preemies.") If you have private time and space on a computer, this can be a good

option, especially if you can print your file onto paper for reading and safekeeping.

I am so glad I found the words. Watching my family unfold in the starkness of the alphabet, letters black and white, in sometimes anguish-filled and explosive as well as often dreamy and passionate words, gave me a chance to live outside the desperation that sometimes tried, and succeeded, in fencing me in. —Maureen

Keeping a journal is something you do for yourself. You are the writer and the only reader. It is private, a place where you can be honest and uncensored. If done regularly and sincerely, journaling can be very therapeutic. Some parents find it a helpful adjunct to counseling.

With the boys, Cailean and Devon, writing was my sustenance, my sanity. I began their individual journals the moment I conceived and chronicled emotions, practicalities, plans, dreams, nightmares. Though they are six and four years old, I continue to write, record, remember. The journals have become an enormous part of how I care for them and the family. ...

It's been amazing to be able to go back and revisit my mind-set and heart-set from when I first carried them so hopefully within me. It's beyond enlightening to read about their birth crises, their NICU stays, their milestones (which have included everything from first breath off a ventilator to first day of kindergarten), their funny moments, their silly songs and comments and jokes, their tender expressions of love for me, their dad, each other, the sister they never knew, the brother they are expecting. Sometimes I read through some of the early pages and I am astounded that the lanky, vibrant boys I have to shush at night because they are so giggly and talkative together long past bedtime are the same creatures who once fought so valiantly for each breath, splayed out on open warming tables. I often just sit in front of my computer screen humbled by the depth of my love for them, along with the recognition that I have been overwhelmingly privileged to witness the growth of these miracles I proudly call my sons. —Maureen

Spirituality and Religion

Your spiritual and religious beliefs may help you cope with your grief, or they may make you more confused or angry. Especially if you consider yourself devout, you may be surprised at your doubts. You may feel angry with God or disappointed in your religion. You may even reject some of the concepts you formerly embraced without hesitation. When life turns down any unexpected, challenging path, it is natural to question your assumptions. Whether you subscribe to a religious tradition or your own unique blend of philosophies about life, destiny, goodness, and higher powers, it is normal to reassess your beliefs and even to modify them based on the lessons you are learning.

> *Everybody's put here for a reason. It's for a reason. There are a lot of times when I question my faith and I think that something like this shouldn't have happened, that I don't understand why, but I don't think it's for me to understand. —Betsy*

If you have been taught that faith means unquestioning acceptance, you may worry that your current state of doubt and inquiry dooms your chances for righteousness or heavenly reward. You may wonder if your baby's premature birth is a test of faith and worry that you've "failed" that test. You may even fear that this "lack of faith" you are feeling now was lurking inside you all along and that your baby's prematurity is your "punishment."

If you are questioning your faith or feel guilty about your fears or doubts, here are a few ideas to ponder. As always, select the ones that feel right for you.

- Whether or not you consider yourself to be religious, you can adopt spiritual philosophies that give you answers and help you cope. Look for deeper meaning, and you will find it.
- You can make choices. Whatever your beliefs, even if your religious tradition emphasizes judgment, remember to find and trust the compassionate qualities of your God or higher power. Look for and hold onto the spiritual relationships and meanings that nurture, comfort, and empower you.
- You can choose to follow the teachings of those you would like to emulate in word *and* deed. Some of the most respected, beloved religious leaders and teachers are those who not only encourage spiritual behavior but also lead by example.
- If your community of worship or your clergyperson cannot tolerate

your questions or emotions, you are not getting the guidance and support you deserve. As you search for fellowship or direction on your spiritual quest, look for and associate with spiritual sources, including people, books and media, activities, and places. Open yourself to the possibilities, and they will come to you.

- If being religious is important to you, your devotion is measured not by the blindness of your faith but by the honesty of your questions and the openness of your mind and heart toward different answers. It is far more meaningful to be a conscious follower than an obedient one.

- If you feel tormented by your religion, explore other denominations or philosophies within it and even other belief systems. Learn about other values and ways of viewing life, purpose, and the big picture. Look for a spiritual path that feels right to you—not convenient, easy, or simple, but honest and heartfelt.

- If you are struggling to understand what's happening to you within your religious framework, try finding a spiritual mentor who can help you make sense of your experiences.

- Don't use religion to hide from your grief or your imperfections. Religion cannot make up for the hidden parts of yourself or your life. Be your authentic self—and subscribe to a set of beliefs that celebrates that self.

- Recognize that you can embrace a spiritual life without embracing religion. To be spiritual is to marvel at the wonder and mysteries of life (and death), to appreciate and respect the blessedness of nature and all living things, to ponder a greater power and knowledge, to seek, to question, to contemplate, to be willing to not understand. To be spiritual is to be conscious of the values you hold and to live your life consistent with those values. To be spiritual is to welcome the different beliefs of others because you know that each person's reality belongs to him or her, just as yours belongs to you. Of course, a religious person can be spiritual, too, but there are plenty of people who profess religious belief without embracing much in the way of spirituality. You can strive to be spiritual whether or not you are religious.

Points to Remember

- Feelings of guilt, anger, failure, incompetence, and powerlessness are all related. These feelings arise because you couldn't prevent your plans and dreams from turning into a nightmare. These emotions can make you feel as if you're out of control and vulnerable to even more tragedy.

- You can find healthy, constructive ways to express these feelings. By forgiving yourself and turning your anger outward, you can let go of self-destructive guilt. By acknowledging your anger and identifying its triggers, you can loosen its grip on you. By recognizing your worth as a parent to your baby, you can regain feelings of competence.

- For a while, feelings of guilt, anger, and failure can shield you from your deeper feelings of sorrow and vulnerability, but over the long run, using those feelings as buffers can become incapacitating.

- Getting in touch with your deeper feelings of grief can free you from the destructive clutches of guilt, anger, and failure. Of course, being in despair can be incapacitating, too, but it's only temporary. Getting to the bottom of your grief can help you move toward healing. Holding onto destructive feelings will make you feel worse over time.

- Do whatever helps you to move your grieving—and therefore, your healing—to deeper levels.

- Accept your vulnerability to tragedy. Although feelings of powerlessness and vulnerability are frightening at first, it is also quite freeing to learn to live with the knowledge that you don't have to try to control everything that occurs around you.

- If you are feeling stuck, you may benefit from counseling. Seeking professional help is a sign of your courage and willingness to face yourself.

- Journaling can help you make sense of your reactions and find meaning in your experiences. Writing is also a way to affirm your love for your baby, and your dated entries are evidence of your adjustment and your baby's progress.

- Whether or not you consider yourself to be religious, you can adopt spiritual philosophies that give you answers and help you cope. Look for deeper meaning, and you will find it.

CHAPTER FOUR

Especially for Fathers

Fathers and mothers experience many of the same perceptions and feelings after the premature birth of a baby. But just as moms have their own unique roles and burdens, so do dads. As a father, you act as the go-between when your partner is still unable to go to the NICU. In this role, you are linking your family together, but it is also natural to feel torn between staying with your partner and going to your baby. You also may feel helpless to shelter your partner and your baby, feeling that you have failed as "protector" of your family. You may struggle with feelings of uselessness and frustration at not being able to control or "fix" your baby's premature arrival, hospitalization, or condition.

> *I was not aware of the experimental nature of care for premature children, and also mothers who might deliver prematurely. In our case, it appeared that everything was under control until the last moment. In fact, the very day that Luke was delivered (by C-section) the hospital staff was coaching me on how to care for my wife when she came home. That has left a lasting impression on me because I was never told why the decision [to deliver] was made, nor what the alternatives were. I was only told to come in at 4:00 A.M. or else I'd miss my son's birth. I was also surprised at how little say parents have in some*

decisions. In the NICU that authority is given over to the doctors, and the parents seem secondary. —Marco

I'd always been a pretty optimistic person before this. If I got in a bind, I always figured I could find a way out or work my way out of it. But this was something totally different, you know? Nobody knew—and that was probably the most upsetting thing, that nobody knew and nobody could tell you what you could do, what I could do or what anybody could do, to fix it. And as it turned out, there was no fix. —Tim

Perhaps for the first time ever, you are in a situation over which you have very little control—and the stakes are high. There's no doubt about it—having a premature baby can bring a dad to his knees.

We were having a little boy. I was a proud papa to be. A son at last. Well, the night Linda went in to premature labor I thought that pride would be dashed. I knew the chance of survival was slim. ... small and so frail, he fought with everything he had. To see him all hooked up—translucent skin, so tiny—it really hurt. —Shaw

Your pride takes a hit as well. You may be hurt by the way the NICU limits your access to your baby. You may resent being expected to "ask permission" to do even those things you might already feel competent doing, such as bathing and diapering the baby, or changing the dressings. You might experience an acute sense of loneliness and a hesitancy to talk about certain issues. For instance, you may feel embarrassed by how frail your infant appears to friends and relatives. Or you may feel unsure about critical decisions to pursue aggressive intervention for your baby, because you want to protect your family from financial, emotional, and physical burdens. You may worry about appearing selfish, weak, or unable to provide for your family if you share these kinds of concerns, even though you're quite entitled to have them.

Fathers can be especially affected by these feelings of frustration, failure, vulnerability, and powerlessness, but because of the pressures and expectations our culture places on men, many fathers feel alone in their efforts to deal with these emotions. This chapter acknowledges the distinctive aspects of a father's grief.

I can remember the day, going in to see him all hooked up to the vent. My wife about passed out and I just fought it back, but the tears welled up inside me. Geoffrey recovered and was out a few months later, but every time I think back I realize just how he almost did not make it and how short his life could have been. ... One thinks of our children as being invincible and to see a young baby who has so much of his life to look forward to teetering on the edge of life was very difficult for me. —Shaw

Gender and Grief

I found it tough at times to balance the expected strength of being male and the sadness and fear of being the father to a baby who was struggling for life in the NICU. —Shaw

In many cultures, people value the ability to show emotional restraint in the face of adversity. To "handle it really well" means you are unemotional, brave, rational, independent, and productive, even when your world is falling apart. This measure of "strength" is particularly valued in men. Indeed, many men resist grief because even as young boys, they were taught to be ashamed of expressing need, crying openly, being weak or afraid, or showing affection for other males. "Real men" aren't supposed to feel diminished, out of control, or be in emotional pain. "Real men" aren't supposed to weep or lean on others. These cultural pressures create unique hurdles for men, discouraging them from many of the emotional expressions and behaviors that can be beneficial for working through grief. A father who appears unaffected may harbor many painful emotions that he either avoids or keeps hidden. He may be profoundly bereft but subdued as he conforms to social expectations.

You know us men, I had to be the big tough one, the alpha male, if you will. I fought it back and fought it back. So that my wife would not see, often after she went to bed, leaving me alone at my computer screen or in front of the TV, I would just lose it. Particularly on those tough days when Geoffrey was fighting for life. I would sob and cry and would just sit there until weariness would take over and I would be falling asleep. Then and only then would I wander off to bed. —Shaw

Many men also find it difficult or unnatural to verbalize their thoughts and feelings. As Charlie said during his interview, "I'm not much of a sharer." For many fathers, it's hard to find the words, and many men exhibit a narrow range of emotions, seek and accept little support, and are not eager to express painful feelings and talk about their babies. Is this reticence due to living in a society that values male stoicism or due to the fact that males are neurologically different from females? Culture or biology? It's undoubtedly both.

I think the experience of the NICU really does impact us, but I think it's tough to put into words and it's tough to go back to and look at. Sometimes you're just trying to get through another day of supporting your family. —Ed

Jill asked me if I was mad, and I told her no. I walk and walk and walk, and I know that I'm pretty sure I lied. —Jeff

Our individual propensities are influenced by cultural expectations, biological gender differences, as well as gender stereotypes. Grieving mothers tend to allow themselves certain behaviors and benefit from certain coping skills; fathers don't necessarily feel the same urges or find the same benefits. But if you are a mom, you don't have to interpret your emotionality to mean that you are an irrational, hysterical, weak, emotional mess; if you are a dad, you don't have to think of your desire to hold it together in order to support your partner to mean that you are a hyperrational, unemotional, stoic fortress. Pay attention to social pressures and cultural expectations. Be aware of them so that you can claim your own coping style, instead of adopting the response you think is expected of you. You can allow your emotional and intellectual reactions to ebb and flow. Sometimes you'll feel more emotionally inundated and other times more rational or deliberate; there is no need to simply conform to the stereotypical roles of "mom" and "dad." Yet if your natural tendencies are similar to what you perceive as stereotypical reactions, feel free to let them flow in ways that feel right for each of you.

Whether you're a mother or a father, do what *you* need to do to face and adjust to your losses. Know that it's okay to cry and also okay not to. It's important to remember that the quality of a man's grief work is indicated by his healthy adjustment to loss, not by how closely he conforms to cultural expectations or to an ideal of grief expression and coping style. The following sections examine the healthy ways that men tend to approach grief, as well as some of the pitfalls of cultural conditioning. These approaches and pitfalls are described in three different, but compatible, frameworks. These frameworks are useful because they can help you make sense of your emotional experiences, giving you the words and means to get a handle on what you're going through. If you see yourself in any of the following descriptions, you can feel validated in the way you are dealing with your baby's early delivery and hospitalization, and the challenges of parenting your baby in the NICU and after homecoming. If you are feeling overwhelmed, adrift, detached, or immersed in chaos, these frameworks can help you understand and accept your reactions. They can also help you recognize and mobilize your coping strategies. You can even construct your own framework, combining the approaches that resonate for you.

Intuitive Grievers, Instrumental Grievers

In the book *Men Don't Cry, Women Do* Terry Martin and Kenneth Doka look at styles of grieving. They describe grievers as "intuitive" or "instrumental," with subcategories of "blended" or "dissonant."

Intuitive grievers tend to feel emotions intensely and be emotionally expressive. They often share and talk with others, focusing on their internal experience—on how it felt as well as what happened. They tend to feel flooded with emotion, depleted, distracted, and depressed. They are inclined to turn inward and "work through grief," letting feelings flow to restore a sense of normalcy and balance. For parents coping with their baby's premature birth, examples of an intuitive style might include reading books on prematurity, parenting, emotions, or related issues; journaling; talking with others; dwelling on feelings and experiences or spending hours at the baby's bedside. Intuitive grievers are typically, but not always, female.

Instrumental grievers don't feel emotions as intensely and are less likely to be flooded with emotion, cry, or express feelings. They tend to focus less on how they feel and more on what happened, what they think about it, and how they will adapt and adjust. They often express and discharge grief through activity: hobbies, sports, problem solving, addressing issues, and figuring out what they're going to do about what happened. Engaging in these activities is an indirect, symbolic way of working through grief and restoring a sense of normalcy and balance. For parents coping with their baby's premature birth, examples of an instrumental style might include

- Putting energy into a new hobby, sport, or other recreational activity that restores feelings of competence
- Building a baby cradle or creating a comfortable home for your baby, which fuels feelings of connection and caregiving, even though you cannot be at the hospital every hour of every day
- Researching the baby's medical conditions and treatments to gain mastery of the situation
- Organizing a support group to fill a need for yourself and other parents
- Staying on top of medical insurance paperwork so as not to be over-whelmed

Instrumental grievers are typically, but not always, male.

Things were much more cognitive to him than emotional. He reacted more like someone watching a movie than as [to] reality. I definitely lived the reality. I know that he has never let himself feel the reality of what we all went through. I wish he could, but he doesn't see the point in being sad about something that happened four years ago. —Stephie

If you are an intuitive griever, you may look at your physically ener-gized partner and assume that she or he is either uncaring or suppressing emotions. Recognize that she or he is simply an instrumental griever who in turn may be concerned that your emotional reactions are an unreasonable and unnecessary drain on your well-being. It can help you both to embrace your own style of grieving and accept your differences. Whatever your style, you are on a valid and healthy path.

Of course, you may not always fit neatly into one category or the other. Most people fit along the continuum between intuitive and instrumental grieving. **Blended grievers** may flip back and forth between feeling versus thinking, focusing on how they feel versus what happened, feeling depleted versus energized, feeling flooded versus getting busy. Or they may start out their grieving process at one end of the spectrum and after a time, shift to the other end. They may also react differently to different kinds of losses. In any case, blended grievers experience elements of both grieving styles.

Finally, there are **dissonant grievers**. These folks grieve according to what they believe is expected of them, rather than what comes naturally. They are concerned about managing their image and reacting the "right" way, and they screen behaviors and suppress emotions in order to control the impression they give. They run the risk of complicating their grief, because they are fighting their natural tendencies and avoiding grief, rather than working through it.

To avoid becoming a dissonant griever, allow yourself to feel what you are feeling and do what you feel like doing. If your reactions feel real and natural and are flowing, then most likely you're being true to your style of grieving. But if you are worried about what others might think of you, or if you feel embarrassed or ashamed of your reactions, you may try to behave unnaturally or according to a script. If you routinely disrupt your authentic flow, you run the risk of complicating your grief.

Of course, in the beginning, many grievers feel disorganized, disoriented, and shut down. But if you continue to control your emotions in order to take care of everyone else, or if you feel ashamed of your emotional flooding, you may be an intuitive griever who is trying to fit the mold of an instrumental griever. If you feel guilty for being unemotional, or worry that you're "a bad parent" whose calm indicates a lack of investment, you may be an instrumental griever who is trying to fit the mold of an intuitive griever.

In general, if you feel overly self-conscious, tend to second-guess yourself, are concerned about how you're "supposed to" react or worried about "doing it right," you may be undermining your own authenticity, tendencies, and strengths. Instead, embrace your style of mastering loss and grief, and know that wherever you truly are, that's truly where you should be.

Also, keep in mind that the advice you may read or hear from others may or may not fit you, according to whether it complements your style of grieving. Simply try the advice that feels right and works for you, and pass by the advice that doesn't.

Whatever your style, there is no easy fix to your grief. Whether you experience emotions that are more vivid or more subdued, you still have to gain mastery over what happened, move through your grief, make meaning, and adjust. Whether you do that by talking to friends about your painful emotions, founding an international organization that funds research in neonatology, or engaging in anything in between, you're on the right track as long as you are engaged in your own true process.

• • •

101

Especially for Fathers

Dashers, Delayers, Displayers, and Doers

For his book *FatherLoss*, Neil Chethik interviewed men about dealing with the death of their fathers. He describes four types of male grievers: dashers, delayers, displayers, and doers. Many men fit more than one profile, moving through different styles of grieving according to their unique process. While your baby's premature birth is not the same as the death of a father, you do have profound losses to mourn that center on your role as a dad.

As you read the following descriptions, you'll see how the "intuitive" and "instrumental" styles of grieving run through them (see previous section). Displayers have intuitive grieving tendencies; dashers and doers have instrumental tendencies; delayers are blended grievers, or if they've paid a toll for their avoidance, they can be considered dissonant.

Dashers are men who dash through the grieving process. Many are thinkers, creating an intellectual framework to cope with what has happened. Some of these men have had previous experience dealing with difficult losses; others rely on their spiritual beliefs to make sense of events. Some dashers experience less of an emotional reaction because they had plenty of forewarning and the attendant anticipatory grief; others were not affected much because they felt disconnected from the situation. Dashers simply accept what has happened and spare themselves the suffering that occurs when one greets reality with protest or resistance. They tend to skip deep or prolonged despair and come to terms with their loss quickly or without much struggle.

Delayers experience a delayed reaction to loss, sometimes months or years later. Some of these men might appear to be dashers, but they aren't able to accept their loss and are actually filing away their despair. These men finally grieve when they can better afford to: after the chaos subsides, after others in the family have moved through their grief, or after a strong social network is in place. Other delayers finally grieve when they are overpowered: after they experience another loss or some other catalyst that opens the floodgates; after the burden of avoiding their grief becomes unbearable, compelling them to face it; or after they hit bottom and are forced to step away from a grief-numbing addiction that has impaired or destroyed their health, relationships, employment, finances, or their ability to live a life that honors their authentic self.

Displayers tend to open the floodgates right away, experiencing intense emotions as events unfold. They tend to be sensitive and expressive, feeling a range of powerful emotions that feels erratic and draining. Unlike delayers, displayers have feelings that are close to the surface and easily find expression. Unlike dashers, they experience deep despair and struggle to find meaning or come to terms with their loss.

Doers are action oriented. They are deeply affected, but tend not to be overwhelmed by their emotions. They cope by taking action. They may engage in activities that help them feel a sense of accomplishment, that calm or distract them from overwhelming emotion, or that connect them with what they are missing. For many men, going to work is a way to regain some semblance of control and feelings of accomplishment. Just being at work can be a welcome distraction, a calming, familiar routine. A doer may spend long hours researching his baby's medical conditions and treatments, preparing the house for the baby's eventual homecoming, collecting or creating mementos of special times, or taking charge of the insurance filings.

Any combination of these four styles can make up your unique grieving process. You may see yourself primarily in one style, with a mixture of certain aspects of the others. Each style offers ways to successfully deal with loss. However, taken to extremes, any of these four styles can become maladaptive. A dasher can dash too quickly or superficially. A delayer can delay too long. A displayer can get stuck in a destructive rut of anger. A doer can be too busy to feel. However he does it, when a man avoids his genuine emotions, he derails his ability to come to terms with his loss and move on.

Avoiding Grief

As an intermittent coping method or a temporary phase, avoidance can be a valid part of the grieving process. Filing grief away can be a way to manage the pain, but if habitual, it actually interferes with coping, adjusting, and healing. In the book *Men and Grief: A Guide for Men Surviving the Death of a Loved One*, Carol Staudacher identifies five common styles of filing grief away: silence, secrecy, action, anger, and addiction. Two or more of these styles often accompany each other.

Incidentally, these ways of handling grief are not exclusive to men. Both men and women are influenced by a culture that values emotional restraint in the face of adversity. However, the focus of this section is men and the social conditioning that can push fathers away from their feelings and toward these harmful responses to loss and uncertainty. The definitions that follow may help fathers in particular to question social expectations and claim their grief. Knowing about these traps can help you avoid falling into them—or help you climb out of them in order to get on with your life. For specific ideas and support for reclaiming your emotions, see Chapters 2 and 3.

Common Styles of Filing Grief Away

Silence: From childhood, many boys are shamed when they express needs, want affection, or show emotion, and as men, they've learned to avoid their feelings to avoid the shame. By withdrawing into silence, you protect yourself from the "shameful" feelings associated with grief. Since family and friends may not ask how you're doing, *really* doing, your silence is reinforced. Unfortunately, if you're unaware of your painful emotions, you are at risk for the health and emotional problems associated with repressed grief. (See "Persistent Numbness and Avoidance of Grief" in Chapter 3.)

Secrecy: When you were young, your family may have allowed expression of emotions, but you may have quickly learned that your peers were not so accepting. Also, you may have noticed how other men in your family tended to keep feelings private. Or perhaps your family denied emotions, but you bravely acknowledge your feelings, keeping them to yourself. While this is much healthier than silence, you miss out on the benefits of social support, recognition, and validation.

Anger: If you use anger to push away despair, you also push away healing; instead of coming to terms and letting go, you hold on—to condemnation, to revenge, to resentment, to bitterness, and ultimately, to your grief. Or if you are acknowledging your feelings privately but keeping your feelings a secret from others, you miss out on the benefits of social support, recognition, and validation. (See "Moving through Feelings of Anger" in Chapter 3.)

Action: If activity becomes compulsive or you become overextended, then your actions don't contribute to your well-being or to your family's welfare. Distracted from your responsibilities, you're exacerbating feelings of helplessness associated with your baby's birth and condition, and your role as a father. And if action displaces grief indefinitely, you never handle or resolve those feelings. Instead, you bury them, and it takes vast amounts of your energy and perseverance to keep them at bay.

Addiction: Abuse of substances such as alcohol or drugs, or engaging compulsively in behaviors such as eating, exercise, gambling, or sex can alter emotions by altering brain chemistry. Engaging excessively in certain behaviors can also provide an emotional fix by immersing you in an activity that distracts you from other parts of your life. Some addictions or compulsions look good, even admirable, from the outside. Long-distance running, working overtime, getting a charitable organization off the ground, or becoming an expert at something can enhance your life when done in moderation. But anything can become destructive when it takes you away from your relationships, responsibilities, health, and feelings. If you feel obsessed with any activity or with acquiring any substance, if your behavior worsens or threatens to injure your health or your finances, if you are neglecting family or friends, there is probably an addiction at work. Addiction is a sign that you are hiding from pain—pain that won't heal until you face it and cope with it. Of course, everyone needs diversion, and excelling at something can build feelings of confidence. But you only reap these benefits if all the important areas in your life are getting the attention they deserve. Addiction helps you hide; it does not help you cope.

Father as Protector and the Utility and Cost of Filing Grief Away Putting grief aside can be adaptive to a certain extent, especially early on, when reality is so overwhelming, or occasionally as time goes on—*if it is balanced with the ability to deal with your emotions.* If you're constantly filing away your grief and cutting off access to your feelings, it can become maladaptive and compromise the quality of your life.

Unfortunately, most fathers feel that they cannot grieve for long. While the mother recovers from pregnancy complications and delivery, the father typically takes on the role of protector and caretaker. As Charlie says, "There was just no way I could curl up in a corner somewhere. I had two other kids who needed me." Especially in the early days, you may be the one who makes the hard decisions, keeps the household running, and protects your partner from too much responsibility or insensitive people—all this while also continuing to work at your job outside the home. Whenever a new crisis arises, you may put your feelings on hold because you cannot afford to be emotionally overwhelmed. And if you do find emotional release, you may try to protect your partner by keeping your feelings to yourself.

Not only was my son in the hospital, but she was too. I had to hold it together for all of us. Aside from the obvious fear that I would lose my wife and son, after the initial shock I couldn't dwell on his prematurity. It may sound cold but I looked at it as either he'll make it or he won't. I kept hoping that he would make it, but felt that if he didn't, I'd cross that bridge when I came to it. … I had to keep it together so it wouldn't affect my judgement while at work as well. —Hugh

Throughout the hospitalization and even after homecoming, you may continue this protector role and diligently avoid becoming caught up in the emotional drama that surrounds the baby. Especially if the baby is very sick, the mother may be the one who most keenly feels the stress of caregiving and vigilant about their child's health and development. The father may be removed from those details and just appreciate the big picture. But maintaining distance makes it difficult to accept or come to terms with harsh reality.

In the past few weeks there have been some concerns about James's growth and development. These are things that I have worried about for a while, but now the doctors are taking some notice also. Whenever I bring these concerns up with my husband, he gets defensive, as if the doctors are picking on James, when they're only stating medical facts. My husband loves his son very much, as of course do I, but I think I worry about James more openly than he does. —Marina

As a father, you may conceal or hide from your emotions in an attempt to avoid, fix, or smooth over your partner's feelings so that she won't dwell on them. You may resist talking about your shared disappointment and fears, thinking that your silence will lessen your partner's grief and worries. Your avoidance only serves to isolate her. She will grieve and worry intensely regardless of your protective efforts. In addition, putting a lid on your own emotions can undermine your health and healing. It can also push you and your partner apart.

I have a few appointments set up to assess James's growth and development, and in a way, I wish my husband wouldn't accompany us. I guess I want to be able to talk to the doctor about all of my fears without my husband

thinking I'm nuts and telling me that "James is fine, just look at him!"
—Marina

My husband told me about a month before Emma was discharged that he wanted a divorce. He doesn't quite acknowledge how stressful Emma's pregnancy, birth, and recovery have been on our relationship, though. He never talked much to me while Emma was in the NICU. When he did, he basically told me to "get over it" and that I "wasn't coping well" with everything.
—Diane

In particular, you may be conditioned to shut down the natural feelings of fear, helplessness, and vulnerability that occur with crisis and grief. Ironically, by wearing a mask of invulnerability, you close off the opportunity to face and conquer your fears. You also dampen *all* your feelings, including joy, affection, and generosity. Although you appear strong, you might feel like a hollow shell, held hostage by your fears. Although you may think you are controlling your grief, in reality, when you're spending so much energy to remain detached, tough, or in denial, your grief is controlling you.

Getting in Touch with Fear, Powerlessness, and Vulnerability

I wonder what kind of father would allow this to happen to his family.
—Jeff

Mothers tend to feel responsible and guilty when a baby is born early, and fathers tend to feel powerless. You may be very hard on yourself, not just as a father, but as a man. You may believe you should be able to shield your family from any harm. You may feel embarrassed or ashamed that you are the father of a baby born too soon. You may feel like less of a man because you were unable to steer your family clear of this crisis. When your baby struggles in the hospital, you may question all the assumptions you have about control and power. During the roller-coaster NICU ride, you *know* that there are no guarantees that this baby will be safe.

The worst day in my entire life occurred in my daughter's second week, when she had a collapsed lung, and we thought we might lose her. ... By this point I

*had totally bonded with her, and would have been in incredible pain if we had
lost her then.* —David

Complicating paternal feelings of helplessness is the fact that during
pregnancy, delivery, postpartum adjustment, and breast-feeding or pumping,
the mother is physically involved in whatever happens to the baby. She is the
one who feels the symptoms, discomforts, and pleasures of nurturing new life.
She is the one who feels the contractions of labor, endures bed rest, takes the
labor-stopping drugs, and produces breast milk. She is the one who may very
well put her own health and life on the line. The father, in contrast, may feel
physically removed from the situation—and powerless to help in so many
ways. In fact, as the father, you may feel that enduring the pain yourself would
be more bearable than witnessing it happen to your partner.

Feelings of vulnerability and powerlessness can be extremely distressing
and confusing. Because men generally are expected to take charge and to be
the masters of their destiny, you may find it difficult to accept the idea that
you cannot always have control over what happens. You may consistently try
to cover up your feelings of helplessness, but doing so only adds to your inner
turmoil and generalized anxiety.

*For many months after Christopher was home and doing beautifully, I was
still very afraid that he would die. I woke up repeatedly at night hallucinating
that he was crying, and then I got angry at myself for waking up, especially
since I was exhausted from doing 4:00 A.M. feedings. The more I tried to
control and suppress my fear, the more control it had over me.* —Michael

It is far easier and healthier to get in touch with feelings of fear and vulnerability. Although doing so is painful and humbling, it can enable you to let
go of the feelings of anger, guilt, failure, blame, and responsibility that come
from trying to control the uncontrollable. You learn to identify and let go of
those challenges that can't be fixed. For instance, you cannot put your baby
back in the womb or undo the complications of prematurity or ease your
partner's grief. This is frustrating, but it's not a mark of failure on your part.
You can accept that your baby's birth and hospitalization are out of your
hands, that your partner is blameless, and that sometimes, bad things happen.
Recognizing that your baby's destiny is not under anyone's complete control

can enable you to accept what you cannot change. Try to accept the feelings of helplessness that come with being a father.

And remember, just because you're powerless to fix the unfixable doesn't mean that you are useless or have lost all control of the situation. You are still capable of fixing the fixable. You are a competent man, a helpful partner, and a good father.

When I left the hospital the first night of the boys' life in the NICU, I was confident that they would be fine. They were small, to be sure, but I was reassured by the feeling that they were in very good hands. That night, at around midnight, the phone at my home rang, with the caller ID showing the name of the hospital. I was informed that Justin (the two-pounder) had low platelet levels and would probably need a blood transfusion. I was further told that it was a fairly routine thing, and not to worry. However, given that they needed my authorization to perform it, I inferred that it was anything but a routine procedure. I hopped in the car, and drove the thirty miles to the hospital at 1:00 A.M. Although I was told to remain home, there was no way I was going to let my poor little boy go through this thing alone. During the ride, I kept repeating to myself "You'll be okay, buddy, you're a fighter, my boy's gonna make it," through tears. I don't think I will forget that ride—it is the moment in which I most feared that perhaps Justin would not make it. As it turned out, when I arrived, they informed me that they did not need to do the transfusion after all (although they would do two of them in later days). The NICU nurses also told me that they had a bet going with each other over whether or not "Dad" would come down to the NICU after that phone call, even after being told not to bother, for such a routine procedure. I won somebody some money, and, in the process, realized for the first time just how much I cared for my boys. —Craig

Keeping Roles Flexible

There is nothing wrong with dads taking on a protector role—it can help your partner and entire family immensely. But if you have no respite from that role, you don't get the chance to face your emotions—and you won't be able to tolerate those emotions in your partner. This can create impenetrable barriers between you. And if you put your emotions on hold, you may also put barriers between you and your baby. One mother talks about how her husband switched into protector mode when pregnancy complications arose and how this initially diminished his connection with their unborn son.

My husband wasn't even sure he wanted to have a child, was terrified throughout the pregnancy that something would happen to me, and when all of his nightmares came true (true enough, anyway), he was wonderful. He was wonderful and so there for me through all the rough spots in the pregnancy. What he had trouble with was the joy. He never wanted to feel the baby move or talk about names—until I gave him a taste of what the "terrible twos" would be like if toddlers had hormones. What turned out to be just two or three weeks before our son's birth, he finally allowed himself to connect to the life growing inside me, and we spent the two nights we were waiting in Labor and Delivery to get serious about names. —Kris

If, as a father, you feel trapped in or obligated to continue the role of protector, try to include your partner in decision making and in dealing with day-to-day situations. When you and your partner share the burden, your partner can participate in decisions and responsibilities that are meaningful to both of you, which is far healthier for her than enforced helplessness. *Being protective is not always the same as being supportive of your partner or connected to your baby.* Instead, share involvement in the things that matter. When you get some relief from carrying all the burdens of those responsibilities, you'll have more room to be emotionally present and emotionally available.

Also recognize that your partner will have her feelings whether or not you acknowledge them. If you can listen, and resist the urge to fix or judge, you are providing immeasurable support. A simple statement of understanding, such as, "It sounds as if you're really feeling discouraged about that" is far more helpful than saying, "If you would try to do this or that, then you wouldn't feel so discouraged." Also try to share what you're thinking and feeling. It will gladden your partner to hear from you, and you'll benefit when she listens openly and supportively to your feelings. Talking builds bridges across the gap between you, and you may both find it easier to cope as you reap the healing power of shared experience—and of flexible roles.

My husband and I talked all the time. If I was getting too aggressive, he would pull me back a little bit; if he was getting too passive, I would poke him a little bit. And we know each other's capabilities. I'm more of the person to be there and hands on. And he felt that he needed to be home and help [our older son] Cody stabilize, do the dad-son thing together, and keep the home as mellow as possible and we'll let mom deal with what's happening at the hospital. ... Good balance and good communication. —Pam

As you learn to become less protective and more supportive of your partner, don't fall into being "the supporter" all the time either. Let yourself receive support sometimes—valuable support can come from friends, family, work colleagues, and your health care team, as well as your partner. Accepting any kind of emotional support and help with burdensome tasks will enhance your ability to cope as well as your ability to support your partner and your ability to form a close relationship with your baby. (For more on social support for fathers, see that section in Chapter 20.)

Mat had a really hard time being in the NICU. It was very overwhelming to him. His focus in the early days was taking care of me, and I was totally focused on Lars. We were lucky to be surrounded by family, and I asked them to please take care of Mat. Also, having a special relationship with Lars's primary nurse made time at the hospital much easier for Mat. I dealt with all the insurance B.S. and learned everything I could about Lars's condition and care, and supported Mat in caring for and about Lars when he was there. Mat did kangaroo care, bathed and diapered, and was amazing in the way he was able to go back and forth between work and the hospital, managing to be truly present in each place most of the time. —Kris

If you are a novice at dealing with your emotions, before you can shed your old ways, you must have the chance to acquire some new ways of doing so, to manage the feelings that arise. It's like moving a household—you need to commit to a new house before you can move out of the old one. You may decide to hold onto both houses for a while so you can check out the new place and take your time figuring out which stuff fits there and which stuff goes to the dump. So it is with your emotional life: to protect yourself and what's important to you, you can expect to hold onto some old ways while you figure out and practice the new ways. But take heart. When you make the decision to change, you are well on your way.

• • •

Review Chapters 2 and 3 for tips on feeling your grief, coping with it, adjusting, and healing. And remember, facing your grief and your fears frees you to experience other feelings, such as the joy of holding your baby in your arms.

Talk to someone. Talk about what it feels like. Granted, that works for me. It may not for others. But I wouldn't suggest clamming up. However, I suspect that many fathers don't talk about the pain because they think they're the only one who wasn't strong enough to make it through. I think most men are "walking wounded" in the NICU. They just don't know where to report and don't want to draw attention from the rest of their family. But I also believe that if fathers take care of themselves, they will be better able to take care of their family. —Ed

Couples and Grief

You and your partner may experience many differences between you, but rather than feeling like you do it right and your partner does an inferior job, know that every style of coping is valid. The key word here is *coping*. If you are aware of your feelings and able to identify them, even if they don't make sense to you at times, you are coping. If you feel overwhelmed at times but not *continually* overwhelmed by physical or emotional distress, you are coping. If you are able to be present in the moment, rather than constantly reliving the past or worrying about the future, you are coping. If you are *gradually* letting go of what might have been and adjusting to what is, you are coping. If you feel like you are learning and growing, and reframing the situation in ways that give you hope, even as you are grieving, you are coping. Whether you talk about your feelings or keep them to yourself, whether you set aside time to reflect or keep a busy schedule, whether you can find the words or not, be true to your process and your needs. Know that the bottom line is that you face the situation and your feelings and find ways to cope that work for you. Don't try to measure yourself against what you think you "should" be feeling and doing. Just be.

Indeed, no two parents grieve or cope alike, and every couple will notice the differences between them. Some of their differences are a natural result of cultural expectations, some are due to the biological differences between fathers and mothers, and some are due to the dynamics of the relationship. But many differences arise simply because each parent is a unique individual. Each has a unique personality, a unique inborn temperament, a unique personal history, and a unique interaction with cultural, social, and familial norms. Each parent will assign a particular meaning and framework to his or her experiences. The losses associated with pregnancy, childbirth, and the newborn period will hit each parent in a singular way. Each parent will follow his or her own process of grieving, coping, adjusting, and healing.

> *I never felt guilt or pained by the fact that my daughter was there [at the hospital] instead of at home, because I felt confident that the nurses were giving her good care. Whereas, my wife definitely felt a sense of loss that my daughter would not breast-feed, and needed to be bottle-fed; as a man that was never part of my expectation. I expected to be able to hold, hug, clean, caress, play with, and talk to my daughter, and I could do all of those things on a daily basis. That I did these things in the hospital instead of at home really didn't make a big difference to me. —David*

> *I would say—and this is coming from a guy's perspective—that the delivery was relatively uneventful because, after all, these kids weren't much bigger than a sandwich. Even though they were twins, it was not such a big deal. —Mitch*

Additionally, parents naturally vary on how they respond to different types of interpersonal support. Some parents will eagerly talk at length about their feelings face-to-face with an empathic listener. Other parents are uncomfortable talking about how they feel, but can talk at length about *what happened*. Still others feel invaded, judged, and pressured when they hear, "We should talk," but they may open up to the more inviting, "I will listen if you need to talk." And some parents find it easier to relate side-to-side than face-to-face, perhaps in the car, on a hike, on the golf course, or while working on a project. Still other parents would rather go it alone than share with someone else, or participate on an online support group rather than communicate face-to-face.

> *I would say that I tend to hold things in more, while my wife would want to talk about them right away. I feel like there are some things I can bring up and talk about but other things are too touchy and would cause a rift, however temporary. —Hugh*

My husband and I are very different in how we deal with things. Most of the time our styles complement each other. Under stress, it's more difficult. I tend to need to talk and express my feelings, [and to] research and explore everything that's happening or may happen with our baby. He is optimistic she will be fine and tries to bury the fears. When I'm stressed about the whole situation, I cry and need to talk. When he's stressed about it, he gets irritable and withdrawn and needs to be left alone. If we're both upset at the same time, it's really, really hard because we need exactly opposite things. —Balbir

Parents also vary on how they approach their grief. Some parents dive into the core of their pain, while others skim over it, taking in small doses so that it feels more manageable. And some people are more adept at compartmentalizing their grief, putting it away so they can accomplish other things. That's why some parents' grieving process may seem delayed or take longer or be more roundabout than another's grief. And some parents, being instrumental grievers, tend to be action oriented, preferring to get something done rather than sitting with their feelings.

He's never cried over this, never once, which I wish he would do. He looks at me now and says things like, "It's over with, they're fine, why should I cry about it?" I still don't completely know how he dealt with it or how he felt. Like the first week after they were born, his dad and his brothers took him golfing—like okay, let's get his stress out. And I was kind of ticked because I was left visiting the babies and dealing with all the people coming back and forth, and I was like, how could he be golfing? We have these sick little babies. But I guess his family was thinking, "Let's get his mind off it. This will help him feel better." —Stephie

Although there are certainly NICU babies that have things much tougher than the boys did, this does not mean they had an easy ride. ... I was never quite at ease with their continued progression and health—I always kept a thought, tucked away in the back of mind, that things could suddenly go really bad. Each time this thought crept into my consciousness, I made a distinct effort to resist even allowing the concept to remain in my thoughts for very long. I would think "no, no, no, just don't think of it ... so what football games are on this weekend?" or something else to immediately divert my mind to other things.

• • •

This occurred about threee or four times a week, for the eight weeks they were in the NICU. —Craig

Don't fall into the trap of dismissing your partner's style as "just like a man" or "just like a woman". This attitude widens the gap between you. It is hard enough to find each other as it is. Instead, focus on the fact that you are different individuals and you'll find it easier to tolerate and respect the differences between you. You'll also be more likely to find that you have plenty in common. (For ideas on coping with differences between you and your partner, also turn to "You and Your Partner" in Chapter 19 and "Social Support for Fathers" in Chapter 20.)

I would suggest more wives and moms ask their husbands and partners what it was like for them and just listen. Don't compare, don't judge, just listen to what it was like. And it may take more than once. That's just my buck twenty-five. —Ed

Points to Remember

- Perhaps for the first time ever, you are in a situation over which you have very little control—and the stakes are high. There's no doubt about it—having a premature baby can bring a dad to his knees.
- Fathers can be especially affected by feelings of frustration, failure, vulnerability, and powerlessness, but because of the pressures and expectations our culture places on men, many fathers feel alone in their efforts to deal with these emotions.
- As a father, you may feel isolated, misunderstood, and compelled to file your grief away. Be aware that your grief can be different from a mother's, but just as deep.
- There are many different ways that men can successfully deal with loss. Whatever your style, when you face your genuine emotions and go with your natural, healthy flow, you enhance your ability to grieve, come to terms with your losses, and move on. Honor your own style of grieving.
- When you take on a protector role, it can help your partner and entire family immensely. But if you have no respite from that role, you don't get the chance to face your emotions—and you won't be able to tolerate

those emotions in your partner.

- Face your feelings of fear and vulnerability. Although doing so is painful and humbling, it can enable you to let go of the feelings of anger, guilt, failure, blame, and responsibility that come from trying to control the uncontrollable.
- Eventually you can find a balance between maintaining control over your life and accepting the limitations on your control. Focus on fixing the fixable.
- Even if you have felt unable to grieve because of lack of permission or practice, you can try to do things differently, to face and cope with your feelings.
- If you are feeling stuck, you may benefit from counseling. Seeking professional help is a sign of your courage and willingness to face yourself.
- Although you and your partner may hold different perspectives and can be expected to grieve differently, you can tolerate, accept, and not be threatened by these differences. They are normal and necessary.

CHAPTER FIVE

Delivering Too Early

*T*he *preceding chapters give you information for understanding and coping with the discordant emotions that surround the preterm arrival of a baby. This chapter focuses on the beginning of your parenting journey: pregnancy complications and your baby's birth and admission to the NICU. It describes and affirms the common ground that parents of preemies share: their emotional reactions to the unexpected events surrounding the delivery and their responses to being separated from their newborns. Reading this chapter can help you to organize thoughts and feelings into your own coherent narrative. "Getting your story together" can be healing. It helps you make sense of your experiences and your reactions, and it can illuminate the path you're now on.*

Pregnancy Complications

If your pregnancy is identified early on as high risk because of known physical conditions, maternal age, multiple babies, or a previous, difficult pregnancy, there is a sharp edge to all your dreams, hopes, and fears from the beginning. It's hard to walk the fine line between enjoying the pregnancy and being aware of every ache or twinge. It is a challenge to be blissful *and* vigilant.

If your pregnancy is identified later on as high risk, you may have difficulty grasping what "high risk" really means. It's hard to believe that frightening and life-threatening events could really happen to *you*.

I cried and cried at the appointment because I was embarrassed to have something wrong with me. I was supposed to have a perfect pregnancy and delivery. I thought, "Okay, we can turn it around then." —Ruby

I'll never forget that first night in the hospital, being poked by those interns. I couldn't sleep at all. I kept thinking it was just a mistake and that when the "real doctors" came to examine me, they would set it all straight and send me home. But, of course, that didn't happen. —Rebekah

When all the doctors would talk about prematurity and how I had to take it easy for the baby, I must say "the baby" seemed so abstract. I was in serious denial, plus I had had such a boring pregnancy with my first that I did not think this could happen to me. —Kimi

There I was, flat on my backside. How was I going to make it through the next three months? Of course, I was sure I'd carry the baby at least close to term. I had no sense of urgency, as I should have had. I still feel guilty about that. —Cindy

When serious pregnancy complications occur, the denial you feel in the midst of this medical emergency is a normal first response to a frightening turn of events. You cannot take in the gravity of the situation right away. First you protest: this cannot be happening. Then you disappear into a fog, as your mind protects you from entertaining the most frightening possibilities.

In retrospect, you may feel sheepish or guilty about your initial denial. If your clothes or the bedding is suddenly soaked, it's easier to assume you've urinated accidentally than that you are leaking amniotic fluid, because the consequences of the former don't threaten the baby. Or you may assume that after some monitoring, you'll resume your schedule for the day.

It takes time to fully comprehend both the factual and the emotional implications of what is happening to you and your baby, particularly if the situation becomes serious suddenly. You may feel stunned, distant, confused, or inept, and struggle to comprehend what the doctors and nurses are telling you. Especially if you are used to being in control and in charge, you won't feel like yourself in the midst of this crisis. And even if you were *expecting* complications, there is still no way to prepare yourself emotionally.

In forty-five minutes we went from "We're having twins. Isn't that great?" to a shocked, crying, sad, and frightened "We're having them now—we're going to the hospital." So here we are, scared. We have no idea. We know squat about what's going on. I'm in my own world, and Debbie's in her world. —Mitch

When I called the doctor that morning at 2:00 A.M., he said to bring Lauren to Labor and Delivery. I was so upset driving the twenty miles to the hospital that I could hardly keep the car on the road trying to see through my tears. When I got to the hospital, I drove up and down the street three times looking for a "Delivery" sign. I'm lucky that they didn't have a delivery sign, or I would have left Lauren at an empty loading dock while I went to park the car. After I had circled the hospital one more time, Lauren had sense enough to tell me to just go to the Emergency Room and they would get her up to Labor and Delivery on the third floor. Actually, I'm glad that the doctor did not tell me on the phone that Labor and Delivery was on the third floor, or I might have tried to drive my car up the stairs. —Michael

I assumed that the hospital staff would check the condition of the baby or conduct some test and send me home. I was shocked and devastated when I was finally told that I would be staying in the hospital, hopefully for weeks, until the baby grew larger. It took me several hours to digest this sudden turn of events. —Renee

The prospect of labor and delivery, or possibly a C-section, so soon and without psychological preparation can be devastating. If you are given drugs to try to stop your labor, the awful side effects only add to your feelings of disequilibrium. If this is your first delivery, you may feel especially unready. Without benefit of childbirth classes, you may feel unqualified and overwhelmed with what's happening inside your body.

Besides the shock value of discovering that there are complications, events may be happening with such speed that it can be difficult to take in all

•••
119
Delivering Too Early

the information about what this situation means for the rest of your pregnancy and your baby's future. You may feel uninformed, either because you can't absorb the information you're receiving or because people are shielding you from the hard realities. If you are in serious condition yourself, it is terrifying to realize your own life is at risk, even if you only recognize it in hindsight. Unfortunately, fathers may be only too well aware of the dangers to the mother and the baby and may struggle with how much to share with their partner.

I was left with the much-dreaded feeling that I was not being told all that was going on with me and with the babies. The doctor talked to my husband, and they felt that "sparing me" was best for me—when, in reality, it left me feeling insecure and not able to trust anyone. —Sara

Joe shared with me recently that during one particularly bad hemorrhaging episode, I blacked out and he carried me to the car. He thought that was "it"—that this pregnancy was over and that the baby had died. He felt that he could easily lose his baby son and his wife. —Angela

Complications don't necessarily lead to immediate delivery. If you have weeks or months of monitoring and bed rest after problems are detected, you have time to recognize both the dangers of the situation and its maddening uncertainties. It can be a very difficult time.

I lay in the bed, knowing all too well what each contraction meant. The nurse gave me wet washcloths, and I cried silently. I felt defeated and indescribably sad. —Renee

Bed Rest

Mostly I cried. And stayed very still. Even when I wasn't on "bed rest," I was. I didn't move any more than was absolutely necessary and would find myself holding tightly to the underside of my (very small) stomach as if to hold the baby in there. —Sterling

Entirely unlike "rest," bed rest is very difficult work for both parents. The mother must work at maintaining a troubled pregnancy. The lack of activity can lead to her physical debilitation. The father must take on most of the mother's day-to-day physical tasks, in addition to his own responsibilities. If the mother must be hospitalized, this can further strain the family's emotional and financial reserves. But even from a dad's perspective, tending to a bed-resting mother is easier than having a struggling infant in the NICU.

Shortly after that [first crisis in the NICU], in retrospect, I was able to realize that those ten days of Debbie lying on her head [on bed rest] with all of that ugliness, that was a picnic compared with what was to come afterward. Because there was no danger—it was just using a whole bottle of "No More Tangles" and the discomfort of putting in contact lenses while upside down, compared with someone [the babies] [experiencing] pulmonary hemorrhaging. —Mitch

Another challenge of bed rest is that you view the passage of time differently. Instead of simply waiting for the requisite forty weeks to pass, you begin to count with urgency not weeks, but days, and after the administration of antenatal steroids, hours. You begin to envision your baby's growth during each week of gestation with a new urgency.

You also may feel as if you're in a time warp and out of sync with the natural pace of pregnancy. Confined indoors, you may feel oddly disconnected from shifting weather and changing seasons. Instead of routine prenatal checkups, you need intensive medical intervention. Instead of gradual preparation for childbirth, you face the threat of imminent delivery. Instead of receiving reassurances, you get furrowed brows and endless warnings to lie down. Questions that you might have asked before out of simple curiosity take on a new intensity, and the answers you receive often are not definitive.

I think I asked every medical professional who entered my room the same questions: "Why is this happening?" "Does it usually take this long for magnesium to stop the contractions?" and, most important, "Do you think the contractions are spreading out?" I learned quickly that there are few answers in situations like these. For a long time, I was afraid to ask what I could expect from babies at this gestation. —Rikki

...

121

Bed rest gives you a lot of time to be alone with your thoughts and fears. Even if you try to keep your hopes up, your worries loom large, multiply, and grow more palpable. You may go from hoping that your baby will be cute and easygoing to hoping that your baby will stay alive. And you face the terrible realization that there is so much that cannot be predicted and more that cannot be controlled.

I can remember sitting on the bed in the triage room, staring at the monitor. I absolutely couldn't believe that I was having contractions—and I couldn't wrap my head around what that really meant. The nurse tried to turn the monitor away from me, and I kept turning it back so that I could see it. The nurse was afraid that the monitor would make me anxious. The truth is that everything made me anxious—I was terrified. —Rikki

The worst thing I pictured was giving birth to a very small baby, smaller than I could ever imagine, and being able to share only a few minutes with my newborn before he or she died. That terrified me, and I went through it over and over again in my head because when it happened, I wanted to be able to be there with the baby at 100 percent. I wanted to be prepared to say "hello and good-bye," not so upset that I would miss the entire life of my child.

My second worst fear was to give birth to a baby who would be a living "vegetable" for the rest of his life. I was unable to get any information that first week at the hospital, and I thought that premature babies had much worse outcomes than they really have. Sometimes that fear made me think of "ending" the pregnancy by getting up and walking around, to get it over with and move on with my life, trying to be pregnant again. I am so glad that I didn't do that—and I really don't think I was serious, but the thought did hit me. —Inkan

Holding On to Your Sanity

The delicate dance of sustaining the pregnancy without compromising yourself or your baby may consume much of your emotional energy and attention when there are complications. For some mothers, as soon as they adjust to the current medical situation, it changes. This constant unpredictability, this cycle between optimism and pessimism, can be exhausting. You may wish that someone would just knock you out and wake you up when it's over. You are willing to do what it takes—but do you have to live through every minute of it?

> *I just felt as if there were so many emotional ups and downs. That was perhaps the hardest thing. One day they talk about sending me home, and the next there's a fetal monitor strapped around my belly indefinitely. —Rebekah*

> *How I got as far as I did, I will never know. It was pretty awful. But every day I said, "Every day gets me one day closer to another week, and every week gets me closer to forty." And that's how I got through it. ... I lived every day of the first twenty-four weeks of the pregnancy terrified of losing Yoni. At twenty-four weeks, which is the age of viability, I didn't cheer, but I breathed a major sigh of relief, thinking now, at least theoretically, he was viable. —Micki*

Reaching for protection, you may turn to your religious faith or other spiritual grounding. You may make bargains with God, fate, or Mother Nature. You may also feel that your faith or patience is being sorely tested.

The more unpredictable your situation, the more desperate you may be for some measure of control over your baby's fate. You may engage in superstitious behaviors, avoiding jinxes, surrounding yourself with lucky charms, and looking for good omens.

Walking that fine line between hope and despair, you may try to deny the horrible possibilities and at the same time try not to get your hopes up too high. Or you may hedge your bets and try to protect yourself from the worst by withdrawing emotionally from this baby. On some level, you have the awful awareness that these pregnancy complications could lead to the delivery of a seriously compromised baby—or one who might die. Denial and detachment mixed with terrible fear and dread make for a bewildering roller coaster of emotions.

> *During the two months between the first hospitalization and the delivery, I was very worried that I would lose the baby. I had been very excited about the baby and had begun preparing for the arrival from the start of this pregnancy. Now, I wouldn't let myself get my hopes up. I imagined frequently what it would be like for the pregnancy to end without a baby. —Shaina*

I feel at this point I began preparing myself, subconsciously, for what might be the death of both my babies. I guess I thought that if I detached myself from my feelings for them, it wouldn't hurt so much if I lost them. —Sara

Not knowing what will happen and facing continual uncertainties about your baby's condition after birth is enough to make anybody feel crazy. If you are lucky enough to join a support network of other parents of preemies (perhaps through the Internet), you can benefit emotionally. You'll learn that bed rest doesn't last an eternity, and you'll benefit from these parents' different perspectives of what's on the other side of delivery. (If you are currently on bed rest, see Chapter 22 for more information and tips for coping.)

After being "educated" by other preemie parents for six weeks through the Preemie-L mailing list, I was so thankful for every day passing by with no problems. It was like climbing up a long ladder, not knowing how long, but I got a better view as time went by, and I knew that we were about to reach the end of it, even if it felt like ages sometimes. —Inkan

Holding On to Yourself

As you fight to hold on to your sanity, you also may strive to hang on to your sense of spirit. The world can seem surreal when you are lying in bed, perhaps at an uncomfortable tilt, on medications, counting the hours, with restrictions on activity and a flurry of medical people keeping track of all sorts of bodily functions. You may find any sense of confidence and competence slipping away. You may worry that, in the process of maintaining your pregnancy, you may lose yourself.

My husband kept telling me the lives of the babies depended on my "hanging in there," and the nurses touted my ability to incubate—but what about me? I felt very self-absorbed—concerned about my mental state. —Sara

You may struggle to remember what you know about yourself, your limits, and your strengths. You have to submit to medical technology, and although you know it's necessary, it may go against your grain. You might not be used to relying on others for help and may find it difficult to "impose." You might wonder why you find small surprises too much to handle when normally you take things in stride. Even changes in nursing staff or shift changes can be hard to tolerate when you are already overwhelmed with uncertainties.

You may have worries about your own medical condition, your future health, your very life. Knowing that the physical consequences of this pregnancy could be devastating for you is quite sobering. If you are reaching your limits of endurance or if you physically cannot tolerate being pregnant any longer, you may agonize over secretly wishing that the pregnancy would end, but hesitate to express your concerns for fear of appearing to be "selfish" or a "bad mother." You may have trouble finding a safe time to talk about your fears for yourself.

The night I became so sick, I just spent the night praying that if it was time to take the baby, God would let me know. The next morning my doctor came in, and I just remember telling him, "Help me" because I felt as if my body was giving out. —Leah

I didn't feel as if I was going to die until after the birth—and then it was with such paranoia that there is not much I can pinpoint about it emotionally. I remember being very afraid to go to sleep because I didn't think I would wake up, and then I remember feeling as if I was being selfish worrying about my own life when my son was on a ventilator. —Terri

It can be a struggle to feel competent and to hang on to some shred of control over your body during this time. Having people around you who listen to you and encourage you to advocate for yourself, not just for your baby, can be very helpful. It can be even better when they do some of the advocating for you. But when they don't, it can add to your distress.

I was undoubtedly my nurse's worst nightmare, but I felt I was responsible for all that was being done to me and to my babies. I knew me best; I knew where to best find the babies for the twice-daily monitoring. It irritated me no end to have a nurse come in and "take over" and not listen to me! —Sara

When Delivery Is Inevitable

In spite of the mother's best efforts and intensive medical management, sometimes early delivery is unavoidable or the better option. Because pregnancy complications and bed rest are so challenging, the thought of impending delivery can bring on contradictory reactions. You may both welcome and dread the approaching birth. You may feel torn between wanting your baby to be safe and wanting your baby to be safe *inside you*.

You may be glad that your ordeal is about to be over but sad and distressed that your baby will now need to struggle outside your body. You may be proud of making it as far as you did but still feel a sense of failure for having such a hard time. You may feel grateful that the limbo of bed rest is done and yet fearful of the continuing uncertainties for your baby. Or you may be desperate to deliver, so focused on your own misery that you can't think about your baby.

> *During the ten days I was on bed rest, I became more and more depressed. The absolute lack of stimulation really got to me. I quickly became teary, very belligerent, and began to feel ambivalent about the babies. I wanted this ordeal to be over—regardless of the outcome. —Sara*

> *It just went from bad to worse. And all I could think of was, "I just want this to be over." So I had two sides of the coin—the side where I'm fighting for the life of this baby and the other side where I just wanted to give up. I was so tired of all of this. It had already been a very long pregnancy. —Vickie*

Sometimes, delivery is induced or allowed to proceed because continuing the pregnancy poses a threat to the baby. If the doctors determine that your baby would fare better outside rather than inside your womb, you may be anxious for your baby to be born, to improve his or her chances for survival.

> *I remember the feeling of profound relief that washed over me when they decided to do my emergency C-section! Leah had died in utero a few days earlier, and I had been told that we would try to prolong my pregnancy as long*

as possible, but Naomi could, of course, die in utero also, go into distress at any time, or maybe even go close to term. It was a psychologically untenable place to be. I wanted Naomi to be as healthy as possible, but in truth each moment I continued to be pregnant was filled with horror as well. I felt like I defined a walking time bomb. ... I felt relief at having her in the NICU's hands and out of my womb. —Shoshana

When the doctor said "emergency C-section," I felt as if the wind was being knocked out of me. All I could think was: "Just get that baby out. I don't care how you do it, just get him out!" I felt very sick. I didn't know if it was from pain or fear, or both. I was most afraid of whatever unknown complication was threatening the baby from inside, where we could not deal with it. I felt that if we could just get the baby out, he would be okay. —Shaina

After doing all you could to remain pregnant, you may feel a sense of release when staying pregnant is no longer an option. You now turn down a new path toward your baby's early birth.

When the doctors finally prepped me for my cesarean, I felt some relief. My five weeks in the hospital had been full of close calls, and I was exhausted— emotionally and physically. I wanted it all to be over. —Rebekah

As the epidural was administered, I felt a calmness come over me. This was indeed "it," and there was nothing more I could do. I couldn't fight any longer. It was in God's hands now. —Sara

I tie on my papery surgical mask and wonder how life is about to change. Wondering how I'm going to screw up this kid. Wondering if I'll get the chance. Wondering. —Jeff

Delivery

I had such hopes and dreams when I was pregnant with my first child. I'd lie in bed and wonder what my baby would be like. Would the last few months of this pregnancy be as uncomfortable as I'd heard? I thought about the birth, the first cuddle, hearing that first cry, the first breast-feed, first bath, all of these things, and more. And then in the space of a day they were all gone—all my dreams, all my hopes, my desires, gone, changed, forever different. There was no celebratory champagne, no moments of rapture as we gazed upon this wondrous child snuggled at my breast, marveling at what we'd created, no quiet kisses, no tears of joy, no laughter, no counting of toes and fingers, nothing. There was instead pain and fear, tears and confusion, anger and shame, panic and agony, emptiness and terror, dread and heartache. Instead of trying to grapple with nappy pins and grow suits, night feeds and burping, I quickly learned about ventilators and oxygen, CPAP and IVs. Questions about NEC, ROP, and IVH, blood transfusions, and lung damage replaced those normal newborn thoughts. Instead of wondering whom he looked like, I wondered if he would live. Of course, mere words on clean white paper can never convey the absolute hopelessness of that day. Nor can words ever accurately describe the feelings as you are wheeled into an operating theater, to have your baby ripped from you, months before he should be, begging the staff surrounding you to save him and seeing the look of pity in their eyes as you realize that it might already be too late. There is no way to explain the feeling of having a mask placed over your face and feeling your baby move and wondering if that might be the last time you feel him alive. My dream had become a nightmare and there was nothing that I could do. Part of me wanted to run, run far, far away, and keep on running until it didn't hurt anymore, and then another part of me demanded that I stay by this scrap of humanity, this tiny, bruised boy that my body had failed to keep safe. I wanted to scream, but what could I say? —Leanne

Delivery gives rise to a new mix of emotions and reactions. You may feel worried but also excited about meeting your baby. Particularly if delivery is sudden, feelings of shock and numbness may surround the event. If the delivery is an emergency, you may not even be aware of what has happened, and when you come out of the anesthesia, you may not know your baby has been born until someone tells you, perhaps many hours (or days) later. Even if you're awake during delivery, you are likely scared and filled with anticipation, but perhaps also feel removed. Your shock can protect you from entertaining the terrible possibilities and let you focus on the joy of your baby's arrival.

Parenting Your Premature Baby and Child

I felt my insides were writhing—it was a strange sensation to have my uterus contracting. This was not at all what I imagined our birthing experience would be. Jeff and I had signed up for parenting, breast-feeding, and child-birth classes. None had started. We were not prepared. I really felt I was apart from my emotions and this experience. —Sandy

It was a mixed bag of emotions. We were worried and shocked that this was happening, but we were excited about meeting our new little babies. At this point I remember even feeling thrilled that the doctor said we would deliver the next day. He went on and on about the risks and the chances for success for the babies. I just knew, though, that everything would be okay. I was about to have children after seven long years of waiting. —Pamela

When things happen quickly, there is little time to process major decisions or get used to the idea of delivering so soon. There may be resuscitation issues to consider but no opportunity for discussion. Sometimes, the doctors aren't even sure if the mother will survive the birth. It is awful to suddenly confront the possibility of losing not only your baby but also perhaps your own life or the life of your partner.

I couldn't move. I couldn't talk. I just sat and sobbed. My worst fear had just come true in my head. I had come to love this baby growing inside of me, and now he was going to die. I couldn't take it. —Ami

The doctor said, "I truthfully don't know what's going to happen. I don't know. You could bleed out on the table. You might want to say something to your husband." So I said good-bye to John and good-bye to my mom because I didn't know what was going to happen.—Nettie

I went to the hospital to have my blood pressure checked, and as I walked into OB admitting, I had a grand mal seizure. I apparently had a condition known as eclampsia and was later advised that the only way to save my life was to remove the baby. Apparently the baby was not in any distress. I was in extreme physical pain from an enlarging liver and severe headache, and I don't remember much of what transpired. My husband had to make all of the decisions alone.—Victoria

Delivering Too Early

Even if you and your medical team have the chance to talk about difficult decisions, this doesn't make them any easier. In some cases it can be impossible to know what decisions need to be made until the baby is born, leaving you in a wait-and-see situation. The worries can be overwhelming and the uncertainties frightening. But even if the doctors aren't questioning your baby's survival, you can never be fully confident or fully prepared going into delivery.

The first feeling when the doctor said that I was going to have a C-section right away was, "No—I'm not ready!" I wanted to be pregnant for a couple more weeks! Then I was afraid to face my son, to really see how he was. … I wasn't ready to face the truth if it wasn't a happy one. —Inkan

The whole time they were prepping me and doing the C-section I was crying. They told me to stay calm—like that was possible! I just kept thinking, "If I lose my baby, I will die." —Dusti

Whatever the situation, the moment of delivery is an intense and watchful period. Everybody holds a collective breath, hoping for the best and wondering how the baby will respond to being born. Tracy remembers, "The silence that followed his birth was the loudest thing I have ever heard."

When I saw [the babies] for the first time, it was a relief that the trials and tribulations of trying to hold on to the pregnancy were over. Now we had new trials and tribulations to work on, and that was Riley and Banning. —Pam

In spite of your worries, there are often glimmers of hope. As you watch the doctors and nurses work on your newborn, you may anxiously look for signs of survival and spunk from the baby. For many parents, hearing the baby cry is a powerfully welcome and reassuring sound. As Sharon remembers, "I was afraid that he would die, but once I heard his little squeak of a cry, I knew he had the will to survive." Encouraged, you may be able to rejoice in the moment.

There were so many people in the room, it was like a minyan—that means ten adult male Jews, enough to have full prayers. There was a neonatal team for each kid. An awful lot of people. And then Daniel was born, and he was cute—I remember seeing his little hand—and he was whisked away immediately and intubated, and that was the last I saw of him for a while. After some manipulating, Shayna was born, too, and it was a little exciting—there was actually some happiness. We'd just became the parents of twins, and for a little bit, it was kind of okay. —Mitch

You may also look for signals from the medical team. They might try to bridge the gap between you and your critically ill newborn by bringing the baby to you for a peek and maybe a kiss before the move to the NICU. You may struggle to figure out how to relate to your little one during this first but fleeting moment. Dare you touch such a fragile infant? Indeed, some parents fear that they are being asked to say good-bye to a baby who may die.

After three pushes he was out, and he didn't look good. He was purple. When they went to clean his nose and his throat, there was so much blood, it was scary. ... I was afraid. My husband lost control. He had to leave the operating room, and I could hear him in the hallway, punching the walls. And the baby didn't cry. They were doing CPR on him, resuscitating him. And finally, the neonatal resident went out in the hall and got Tom, and at that point I had just about convinced myself that the baby was dead. And they brought Tom back and said, "Here, you can see your son." And Tom looked down and said, "Oh, wow, he's pink, he's pink, he's pink." After being born so blue and purple and scary, he was pink, and he was okay. Then the nurse brought him over to me and said, "Here, you can hold him." And I held him for just a little minute, kissed him, told him I loved him, and she took him back and he was on his way. But I wasn't sure why she had handed me him and not my daughter. I was convinced that they thought he wouldn't make it and wanted me to be able to see him.

After all this time and a happy outcome, I'm sitting here bawling about it. —Pam

The nurse brought Ryan over, hurriedly, telling me to give my son a kiss. I took this to mean, "You may never have another chance. Better kiss him now," and I was resistant. I brushed the top of his little head and said I'd see him soon. They brought Elizabeth over and put her head next to mine for a picture. I felt "removed" still, and I wavered between "How dare you think my baby will die" and "I can't love them, they might die." —Sara

When your preemie is born, you may feel a profound sense of detachment from your child. You may encounter isolated moments of wonder and joy, but looking back, you may remember just going through the motions, without much feeling at all. There are several reasons for this. They include shock and fear and, especially for the mother, exhaustion, shifting focus, and the emptiness both around and in you.

Shock and Fear

I don't think anything in the world can prepare you for the sight of your premature baby. I only saw her for a moment before she was whisked away to the NICU. She did not appear in any way to be human. —Renee

After being preoccupied with pregnancy complications, perhaps undergoing bed rest and monitoring, and then getting through labor, it can be difficult to change gears rapidly enough to absorb the details—even the reality—of your baby's birth. There may have been precious little time to prepare yourself for the delivery. It is a terrifying time. Many mothers report feeling disoriented or, as Sandy remembers it, "feeling as if this was an out-of-body experience. How could this be happening?" It may seem as if you have been dropped in the middle of the ocean without a boat. Your baby is here, and you can't believe it. It takes time to grasp this new and difficult reality.

The first time I saw Jake, I was being wheeled back from the recovery room. I was still somewhat in shock from how quickly everything had happened. I was about as frightened as I had ever been in my life. I couldn't believe that was my baby. —Susie

They called me and said it was a boy, and I could see him through the window. He wasn't crying or anything, just kind of lying there, very small. It was like I was in a dream—this really wasn't happening, my wife's still pregnant in another room somewhere—and here, my son's lying here all hooked up to wires and stuff like that. That was a real, real drag. —Charlie

All I remember is the activity in the operating room and the calm reports from the doctors. ... Numbness set in quickly as I looked at the two tiniest faces I had ever seen gazing out at me as if in confusion. "Show her the baby," my doctor said as each one was examined and prepared for transport to the NICU. "Kiss her," she said each time to me, the stunned and paralyzed mother. That was the last I saw of them until 2:30 that morning, when I finally thought to ask if I could go to see my babies. —Rikki

Shock can keep fear at bay. Despite the frightening realities surrounding you, shock lets you see only one small detail at a time, which is about all you can handle. Looking back, you may wonder how you could have acted so calmly, yet felt so crazed. Even if you were medically stable, it may not have occurred to you that you could touch or even go to see your baby in the NICU. You were simply out of it. This calm before the storm is normal.

I was totally shocked. He was so tiny and fragile. I was afraid to touch him at first. I cried for days after my first visit. ... To tell you the truth, he was the most beautiful baby I'd ever seen and yet he looked like an alien. My first thought was, "This can't be my baby. They must have given me someone else's baby." —Jonette

Exhaustion

When your body has been through the wringer of pregnancy and delivery complications, it naturally diverts a lot of energy toward physical recovery. The pain and exhaustion of the ordeal can leave you numb and depleted. Diana recalls, "I was very tired and didn't want to deal with the situation." Particularly if you required invasive procedures or medications, your body doesn't have many spare resources. As a result, you may feel as if you are in a fog. You might have trouble absorbing the complex information about your baby's condition. And while you know intellectually that the creature in those fuzzy photographs is *your baby*, you might feel distant and detached. When you finally do go to the NICU, you may feel nothing or very little.

When I finally heard the baby cry, it hit me that he was alive and that I should have been worried about him, although I hadn't been for the last few hours. I felt so detached from everything that I pointed to a spot of blood on my arm and said, "Look, there is some blood," as if it were some sort of interesting fact. I didn't realize that my placenta had abrupted. —Ruby

Your body must recover without a baby in your arms, and your exhaustion makes you care less about your detachment.

Shifting Focus

Before delivery, particularly with prolonged attempts to stop labor or manage complications, the mother and the baby inside her are the center of attention. But after delivery, attention turns to the baby, and the silence surrounding you can be deafening. This abandonment can feel quite surreal, reinforcing your feelings of detachment.

Once the afterbirth was taken care of, I was left alone—I mean, alone in the room. That was the worst part. I didn't know anything. No one was there to calm my fears and hold my hand. Of course, everyone was concentrating on the baby—rightly so. Thankfully, they drugged me heavily. I had three transfusions as a result of blood loss. I don't remember a lot about the next few hours. Actually that's about the time I began blocking a lot of things. —Cindy

Then everyone was gone. I wanted to go too and was very frustrated when the nurses wouldn't let me get up to go to the nursery. I felt fine. Looking back on it now, I wasn't all right, I was in physical shock from the delivery and emotional denial from the whole event. —Andra

Because you still require a lot of medical support, you may resent the focus turning away from you. Now all the action seems to be in the NICU. Although you want the medical team to do all it can to care for your baby, it is normal to feel angry and neglected.

The shift in focus also highlights the fact that you and your baby are apart now. Strangers are tending to your little one, the father may be with the baby (or is torn about where to be), and you feel bereft and left behind.

The nurse let me kiss them. Then they asked my husband to accompany the twins to the NICU. At that point, I felt alone and jealous that I couldn't get up and go too. —Pamela

You might also feel disoriented and afraid because you aren't present in the NICU to protect your child. After months of being intensely connected and in tune with the child in your womb, all of a sudden you are disconnected and barred from being involved or knowing what's happening. In all, this shift of attention can add to the feeling that you've been cheated—of your pregnancy, your delivery, your baby, your role.

We glanced at him really quickly, my husband took a couple of pictures, and then he was gone. It's so strange because you just lie there and the room is so quiet and you're wondering what's happening, what's going on? It's a huge letdown because you're expecting more from the delivery of your baby. —Vickie

Emptiness

Your precious baby has been taken from your womb; your body feels empty and bereft. You may envision your baby surrounded by doctors and nurses working feverishly. Will they be able to stabilize your baby's condition? Alone, your imagination can run wild. Your worst fears are your only companions. Your fears and longing for your child may be so overwhelming that you begin to protect yourself by filtering information about your baby and numbing yourself to intense feelings, leading to an even greater sense of disconnect from your little one. Forced separation from your baby only intensifies your emptiness, detachment, and denial.

It took me about a week to get a grip on the fact that I had actually had a baby. I kept feeling as if I'd never been pregnant—or as if my baby had died. It just wasn't right to come home without your baby after giving birth. It probably wouldn't have been so bad if I'd been able to hold him. —Ami

I was in denial of the whole experience, so I thought that the staff was out to make my baby look sicker than he actually was. I just laid there and told myself that he was going home in the morning. I told myself that every day for the next thirty-two days. I felt as if someone had ripped out my heart and given me a piece of paper with some baby's footprints on it in return. —Jenny

Longing to recapture your pregnant state may be another way of expressing your emptiness. You may focus on being pregnant again in the future.

The minute I was conscious after my twins were born, I wanted to be pregnant again. Even though I'd been sick beyond all imagining, even though I'd nearly died on more than one occasion, I wanted desperately to be pregnant again. The state of pregnancy had come so hard to me, it was so precious, so incredible. I couldn't believe it was over. I felt so empty, so ordinary. —Susan

Separation from Your Baby

I felt like saying, "I want to hold and cuddle him! Please let me!" But at the same time I knew full well that that was not the best for him, and I wanted him to get the best care possible. —Lori

The neonatologist said, "We have to transport. We have no equipment to deal with this here." And I'm just saying, "But I want to see my baby again, I want to see my baby again, I want to see my baby again." And they said, "You can't." —Beth

I was terrified ... and so sad. I wanted to hold him, but at the same time I didn't. But I do know that when they wheeled him out of the delivery room, it felt as if they were tearing off a piece of me as they left. —Sterling

You may resent the medical team's presence even as you appreciate their efforts to stabilize your newborn. And now they are the ones determining when and how you will have contact with your baby. Instead of having long moments in which to get to know your infant, you may have only a quick look, a rushed touch, perhaps a kiss before he or she is whisked away to the NICU. The physical separation adds to feelings of emotional distance from your baby. Helpless to prevent your baby's early arrival, you may also feel helpless to mobilize yourself as a new parent, and your feelings of disengagement might make you doubt your devotion. Overwhelming feelings of sadness, anger, guilt, and fear can paralyze you for a while.

How could I have these negative feelings? How could I not want to see my baby? How could I be upset with my husband for wanting to see his baby when just two days ago I was upset with him for saying, "Take care of my wife and forget the baby." There were a lot of feelings of being cheated, and I stared at that picture [of the baby] a lot. —Kathy

The next few days were horrible. I went into a deep depression. I didn't see my son for a week after he was born. I had to stay in the hospital because my blood pressure was still up and I was very swollen. ... When I finally got to see my son, he was off the oxygen and breathing on his own, and I got to hold him the first time I saw him. That was when it was all worth it—it didn't seem real until then. —Dena

Some babies are in good enough condition for their parents to touch or even hold them before they are taken away to intensive care. But even if you're able to hold your newborn, you may not be able to enjoy doing so because of your own condition. And, too soon, your baby is moved to the NICU, leaving you with a confusing mixture of reactions.

After T. J. was born, he was quickly whisked off to the NICU. The respiratory team did stop by my bedside so that I could peer into his incubator and offer him my finger. He wrapped his little hand around my finger and squeezed. That was precious, but I longed to hold him and touch him. I remember feeling an incredible sense of loneliness when he left my womb and was immediately taken to the NICU. Most of all, I was exhausted both physically and emotionally. —Claire

This transition from expectant family to parents of a critically ill newborn is painfully abrupt. Some mothers are awake following delivery and are acutely aware of the distance between them and their newborns. Being confined to bed can make the situation even worse. Michele recalls: "Plenty of times I wanted to pull out the IV and run to their side. I didn't have the strength to do that, or I would have!" Mothers who wake up long after the delivery become aware of an emptiness and a feeling of distance. If you delivered in a hospital that did not have the level of intensive care your baby needed, he or she may have been transported miles away, another surreal and painful aspect of your experience. If you're surrounded by term babies and their cooing families, the contrast between their circumstances and yours can feel unbearable.

It is a moment I'll never forget, lying in my hospital bed with Joe standing nearby listening to the helicopter taking Leo away. Joe and I just looked at each other and said, "What just happened? Are we really parents? Do we really have a son?" It was all very unreal. —Mindy

The transport nurse explained to me what they were doing with him and basically what I could expect over the next day or two. I don't remember a word she said … but I do remember her telling me to feel free to call anytime to check on him and making sure I had a couple of pictures of him to keep with me. Then he was gone, and I was left in a room across from the nursery listening to newborn cries and knowing that my baby's was not among them. —Tracy

Left behind to recover, the mother may agonize over the separation while the father shuttles between mother and baby. As the father, able to come and go, your first impulse may be to stay with the mother. You may assume that she'll recognize and appreciate your presence, whereas your baby won't know the difference. You may be more worried about your partner than about your infant, even if the baby's condition is more serious. It is common for the father to worry more about the mother than the baby, and for the mother to worry more about the baby than about herself, even if she herself is in critical condition. (See "A Father's Special Worries" at the end of this chapter.)

Fathers want to be everywhere at once, but they can't be. Your partner may insist that you go with the baby instead of staying with her, but this may be difficult for you to do. And yet, going with the baby lets you play a singular and vital role. Many times, the mother really does need and want you to be with your baby, so that at least one of you is watching over your little one. Even if she envies your ability to be with your newborn, she longs for the news you bring and is grateful that you're brave and willing to make those solitary treks to the NICU. Taking on this "job" can also help you cope with and orient to the situation and strengthen your feelings of fatherly pride.

The first day I visited Chris in the NICU I was lucky enough to get some advice from a neonatologist, who told me that I had a unique opportunity in this crisis as a father. I could do something better than anyone else could. I could be the link between Chris and my wife, Lauren, who was in a different hospital. I could help Lauren believe that she really had a baby, and I could help her to get to know Chris despite the ten miles between them. —Michael

The first day Laurel wasn't going anywhere, so I was the one to describe Buddy, take pictures, relay weight and length, make phone calls, and so on. But that also gave me a purpose and something to do. —Ed

It was amazing to me how they all responded to Tom. They were just incredible with him (even turning to his voice). It was almost twenty-four hours later that I got to see them, and he was down there every two to three hours with them so they knew him. —Betsy

Whether your preemie is in a NICU down the hall, across town, or in another city, separation from your baby immediately after delivery can be tormenting. Many parents recognize their feelings about this separation only later, after the shock of delivery wears off and the mother recovers from the birth. Over time, you will grieve the loss of those first precious newborn moments with your baby.

Seeing Your Baby
for the First Time in the NICU

Other than a quick glance in the delivery room, many mothers of preemies don't meet their baby for the first time until hours (or even days) after delivery. Until then, all you may have is a photograph of your little one taken in the NICU. This tantalizing glimpse of your baby may leave you with mixed feelings. You may treasure this image, and also be put off by it. Laura remembers: "The picture was dark and fuzzy. He looked like a sick monkey. But suddenly I was less fearful of seeing him." Yet it can also be very difficult to feel devoted to a blurry image.

I got the proverbial Polaroid photos the next morning from our social worker and was completely ambivalent. I played the role I thought I was supposed to—the doting mother telling this stranger how cute my babies were—but as soon as she left, the photos went in my drawer, and I didn't look at them again. —Sara

If more than a few hours pass before you can see your baby, feeling like a mother can be almost impossible. You may, in fact, feel as if you do not have a baby at all. It may not occur to you that you can go to the NICU or you may hesitate, fearing what you will see there. Medication side effects, your own recovery from pregnancy, or delivery complications can also compromise your ability to be with your newborn. When you finally do see your infant, it can be hard to believe that this little stranger is your child. You may find it difficult to envision this tiny, vulnerable being's growth or future. You may not let yourself feel connected to this baby.

He looked like a little old man. I couldn't believe this was a living human being. I couldn't imagine how they put so many tubes in such a small baby.—Susie

The first time I saw James he was lying in his Glad-Wrapped warmer bed, splayed like a frog, surrounded by machinery, and covered in tubes and monitors and leads. My only feelings for him at that time were that he was going to die. I turned and left that NICU ward and returned to my room convinced that my son was as good as dead. I will never forget those feelings. —Leanne

He was lying on a flat sort of raised crib, and his little chest was all depressed, and he was sort of panting. It was really strange, but I had no emotion at that time. I was glad it was finally all over. I really didn't care if I saw him or not, which was really sad, especially when the neonatal nurse told me he wouldn't last the night. The next couple of days were a blur of pain-relieving drugs. —Amber

Some mothers of preemies are in such a fog that they cannot recall their first sight of their baby. Cindy says: "I remember the trip to the neonatal unit, but I don't remember the first time I saw her. I felt numb—like I was there physically but not mentally. I felt as if I was having a continual out-of-body experience." For others, the image is burned into their minds.

She looked like (and please don't take this the wrong way) one of those aborted, late-term fetuses that you see in literature! She had no eyelashes, eyebrows, fingernails. Her chest was concave, and you could see every vein in her tiny little body. She also had no nipples on her chest—we watched them come from the inside out as she developed! I was terrified of her and for her! I never thought something so tiny could possibly live, and I kept apologizing to her. It still, after nineteen years, brings tears to my eyes to remember looking at her in that incubator. —Janet

I was in love and in shock all at once. I saw this beautiful, tiny little infant who looked like a baby bird who had fallen out of his nest too soon. He was hooked up to all sorts of machines, had a vent tube, numerous IVs, and an umbilical catheter. He was red and wrinkly. His head was very large for his short body. He reminded me of what Frankenstein must have looked like! I cried, and all I could think was "What did I do wrong? Why is my baby suffering so?" —Jayna

My first feeling was that I wanted to rip all of those machines off him and hold him and make everything all right. —Jennifer

When you are finally able to see your preemie, you may be struck by the miniature body, complete yet so fragile looking. You may stare in awe at the transparent skin, the lack of body fat, the tiny limbs, the strangely shaped head. As Rosa says, "I still can't picture them that small." If your baby is extremely premature, you may be surprised that your baby's eyes are sealed shut, fingernails are unformed, and downy hair covers the body. Some mothers imagine something grotesque and are quite relieved at how "babyish" their baby looks. Others imagine a small version of a plump Gerber baby and are quite shocked at their baby's actual appearance. Still others are both attracted and repulsed by this tiny creature.

When I saw them, I thought they were so beautiful. They had hair, and they were really little, but everything was there. They didn't have tushes, and they didn't have belly buttons. Those were the only two things that were missing. Other than that, they had everything. —Stephie

I think he looked better than I expected him to look because, of course, I was very scared of what the baby would look like. I was really scared of finding him disgusting and repulsive, and of not being able to get attached to him.

• • •

The first time I saw him, I thought he looked so tiny and skinny, but he was not repulsive, not at all. The first day, I already found him cute and good-looking, and I was in love with him right away. —Gallice

The first thing I said when I saw him was "What is wrong with his head?" I feel horrible about that now, but it was so misshapen that I thought something was terribly wrong with him. Then he let out a little wail, and I broke down. The doctors assured me that that little noise was a very good sign—but it was so hard to believe. —Sterling

I will never forget the first time I saw him. ... It was the most horrifying, pathetic sight I had ever seen. He lay there covered in tubes and wires and was fully ventilated. I almost screamed, and I vividly recall putting my hand over my mouth to stop myself. I'd had a "perfect" baby just two years earlier, and now this. I kept on thinking what a terrible introduction to life—he had come from a nice, warm, harm-free environment to this. It really hurt me. —Amber

At first sight, many parents of preemies ascribe alien qualities to their newborn. But whether the baby looks beautiful or strange (or both) to you, seeing your tiny newborn covered with wires and tubes and surrounded by beeping equipment can be overwhelming. Mothers, in particular, often find it painful to think about how their baby, who should be encircled in their soft, watery womb, is now being surrounded by specialized technology administered by strangers in scrubs. In fact, these feelings may be so painful that you may keep yourself from feeling much of anything.

The first time I saw [the babies], I just cried and cried. The outcome did not look good. I was told that they had about a 25–30 percent chance of survival. The NICU nurses didn't say too much. They were just too tiny. It was very quiet in the NICU that day. —Tamara

We went together to see her in the NICU. She was on her stomach, and all I can remember is the image of her bottom, with virtually no fat on it at all, pointing up at us. She was very red and had wires all around. I think I've repressed many of the emotions of that time. —Diana

Whether you're the mom or the dad, there is a surreal quality to seeing your baby for the first time on a warming table or in an incubator. As you grapple with overwhelming emotions in the alien world of the NICU, you may ignore the tubes and wires and block out the risks that lie ahead. You may focus instead on your hopes and on what you *do* have to celebrate.

I wasn't thinking about the fact that my girls were on life support or that I had no idea what condition they were in, only that I was finally going to meet my girls and they were going to meet their mother. I wasn't scared once I saw their small, fragile bodies or the fact that they were hooked up to so many monitors. I was so excited to finally have two girls. —Rosa

As reality sinks in, though, your feelings of detachment or celebration soon turn to sadness and fear. Grateful for the medical care that sustains your baby, you also may be concerned about the emotional and physical suffering that intensive care may inflict. You may begin to mourn the loss of a trouble-free start to life. And as you think about the future consequences of prematurity and its complications, you may also begin to grieve anticipated losses. When you can look at your infant and begin to realize that this is *your baby* and that your baby was born too early, you can also begin to absorb the fact that your child is at risk.

I was very afraid that the split-second glimpse I had had of my baby alive would have to last a lifetime. I was afraid my baby would not make it to the first time I would be able to visit him in the NICU. I was happy about being a mom ... but I was not happy with how quickly and unexpectedly it had happened. I hurt. I ached for my baby. —Misty

I would stand by their warming beds looking down at their limp, still bodies and sob. The only thing I could think to say was that I was so, so sorry. I felt as if I had failed them on the most fundamental level. —Rikki

If you deliver multiple babies, you may be extra-anxious to see and compare them. If their medical conditions vary, your emotions will be a mixed bag. It can be confusing as well as exhausting to feel distressed and relieved at the same time. And you may worry about their separation, not only from you but also from each other. If one or more of your babies die, these feelings deepen. (See Chapter 11 for more on this subject.)

I hated the fact that they were about three feet away from each other and not together. For their short life in the womb, they had been together and were probably wondering what had happened to their other half. —Rosa

As you become accustomed to the NICU and your baby, you'll also experience feelings of devotion and pleasure. You can begin to recognize this little personality as the same one you carried in utero. This is the first step in relating to your baby. As you learn to look past the equipment, you may begin to recognize familiar features—family resemblances that bring you joy. Noticing these things brings a touch of normalcy to life. Getting to know your baby strengthens your connection. (See Chapters 7–9 for more on adjusting to the NICU and feeling close to your baby.)

I was happy to finally be going to where my baby was. The first time I was watching him, I recognized all the little baby movements that were inside of me just a short while ago, and I got excited because I could tell he was my baby. —Ruby

We didn't get to hold him for a few days, but I remember sticking my hand under that plastic wrap and stroking him and touching him and just seeing how beautiful he was. And just—he was mine. That's what I couldn't believe, mostly. I felt like a parent when I could see him—not after I delivered and not being in that hospital room. That's the most empty thing, when you can't see that baby. It's going to the baby and sitting by that baby's bedside. You just want to tell all the other parents, "This is my baby!" —Vickie

Mother's Hospital Discharge

Going home without her was about the toughest thing of all. ... You get this disconnected feeling, as if part of you isn't fully there. It's hard to describe. —Linda

It was weird to return home without my baby. I felt as if everything had changed, but when I returned to my apartment, it seemed as if everything was the same. I was at a loss. It was painful to look at the empty crib—I so longed to have it full. —Claire

Coming home was especially difficult. I knew I was leaving the most important piece of my life in the hospital. Some friends had decorated our house with "It's a boy" decorations. ... I don't know if that made it easier or harder. It was very depressing. —Misty

I can't even begin to tell you how terrible it is to have to go home without your child, not knowing if you'll ever see him again. —Dawn

Being discharged without your baby may feel like the most devastating separation. Even if you knew you were likely to deliver prematurely, you probably didn't envision leaving the hospital with empty arms. Seeing other mothers being discharged with their healthy newborns presents an unbearably cruel contrast with your situation. As Jayna recalls: "This new mom had her baby with her. They were going home together. *My* baby would have to stay in the hospital for months, fighting for his life."

It can feel strange to enter your home, knowing your due date is still weeks or months away but that you are no longer pregnant. Instead of carrying a baby in your womb, you are carrying a heavy emotional burden.

I firmly believe that leaving the hospital that day (and I stayed as many days as they would allow me) was the hardest thing I had to do. I was discharged with three other mothers, all of whom had their babies with them—big, healthy, fat newborns—and mine was still upstairs hooked up to machines that he couldn't live without. And I was being forced to leave him. I can't think of anything that was as hard. —Sterling

Even though I knew my chances of having the babies in the NICU were about 95 percent, I hoped throughout my pregnancy that I would take them home with me. When I went home without them, I didn't feel like a good parent. I felt like I was leaving them behind. I felt great guilt, rather than the joy I had anticipated. —Jill

• • •

145

Delivering Too Early

Debbie was being discharged the day after the kids were born, and it was very ugly because here, you're carrying twins, you give birth to your twins, and you come home with nothing. ... We had the feeling of, like, a close family member had died—it was like coming home after a funeral instead of coming home after giving birth. —Mitch

Your discharge may also bring you some relief. After all, your home is more comfortable than a hospital room. Especially early on, when the NICU is so overwhelming and you don't feel at ease with your baby, being able to retreat to your home for rest and respite may not be all bad. It is normal both to wish for more closeness with your baby and to appreciate your freedom to leave the hospital. Separation can be both an agony and a relief.

I was discharged just thirty-six hours after his birth. It was so hard to tear myself away from that warming table. I knew that as soon as I left, he would go downhill again. I didn't want to leave, but I didn't want to stay. —Jayna

Going home was almost okay because I had spent about ten days in the hospital. I couldn't stand to see mothers and babies going home together. It hurt. So I yearned [for the babies] from the safety of my home. I was still too emotionally drained to think too much about anything else. I only rolled with what life was throwing my way. —Rosa

And so you struggle between these two worlds—home and the NICU. As the numbness wears off, you may begin to feel obsessed with your baby. This obsession can seem odd since your infant is confined to the hospital and not completely under your care. But although your little one isn't home with you, your obsession is a natural expression of your devotion. Your heart is exactly where it should be—with your baby.

I got in the car and cried all the way home. My husband tried to console me, but all I could think of was that I had just left my only son in the hands of strangers and he was less than one day old. We got home, and I greeted my two daughters with little enthusiasm, even though I hadn't been home with them in almost a month. All I could think of was getting Ricky home with us. It consumed my every moment, even the few that I slept. —Jenny

Tips for Coping with Separation from Your Baby

To cope with being separated from your baby, try any of the following ideas that feel right to you:

- Acknowledge your baby's birth in ways that comfort you. It may help to decorate the nursery; shop for baby clothes, toys, or supplies; or start a photo album or baby book.
- Send out birth announcements. Notify people of your baby's birth, sharing whatever details you choose in order to let them know that this is neither easy nor routine for you. This process also gives you a chance to welcome and show your love for your newborn.
- Write down your observations about your baby: preferences, features, resemblances, expressions.
- Learn more about your baby's delivery. Talk with your partner. Ask the attending nurses and doctors about the details. It may also help to ask why things were done the way they were. This information helps you reclaim memories, satisfies your need to know, and fills in the gaps of your story.
- Tell those who want to listen about the delivery and your baby. Telling your story over and over can be tremendously therapeutic. You can also write your story in a keepsake journal or baby book.
- Place breast pads or a cotton shirt you've slept in for several nights in your baby's incubator. Your scent may be a comforting reminder of your presence to your baby.
- Ask the nurse if you can have something with your baby's scent on it to take home with you. Smelling this item may help you feel close to your baby.
- Record yourself reading a story or poem, singing, or talking, and leave the tape in the NICU with your baby so it can be played at low volume when your baby is fussy.
- Spend as much time as you can or want with your baby. Don't let others discourage you or urge you to take breaks or to "get away" if you want to stay. Also, don't let others make you feel guilty if you do want to take time away.
- Take photographs of your baby and look at them regularly. It is especially important to keep updating the photos as your baby's appearance and condition change.

- Write notes to your baby about your thoughts, wishes, and devotion.
- Write notes "from" your baby to post at the bedside, to remind caregivers about special needs, sensitivities, or preferences.
- Post notes at your baby's bedside to remind caregivers to wait for you to arrive if you plan to be there for feedings, caregiving, or tests.
- Ask your baby's primary nurse to write short notes to you "from" your baby, reporting on his or her condition and new developments from your preemie's perspective. (For more on "baby diaries," see Chapter 8.)
- Don't underestimate the power of breast milk. If you can do it, pumping can make you feel that you are doing something motherly. Even if your baby isn't ready for breast milk yet, pumping and storing the milk is a way to bank on the future.
- If you decide not to breast-feed or if milk production is not possible or too stressful for you, tell others not to second-guess you. You can give gentle hints, such as, "I really value the friends I have who can accept this without trying to change my mind, scold me, or lecture me about how to relax."
- Buy a special piece of jewelry or other commemorative object to represent your baby's presence in your family.
- Turn to religious or spiritual icons to mark the birth of your baby. Welcome and shelter your little one in ways that feel meaningful to you and your family and community.

(For more on coping and parenting in the NICU, see Chapters 7–10.)

A Father's Special Worries

I'm sure Debbie wasn't thinking about herself, I'm sure she was thinking only about these unborn children. Not to sound too terribly callous, but I didn't know these unborn kids, nor did I have any understanding of what was really going on. All I knew was that my wife was in the hospital, and I was not thinking about any unborn children, I was thinking about my wife's health. In retrospect, I guess it's kind of silly. Debbie wasn't at risk for anything. The only risk was losing the kids, but I didn't realize that. I was thinking, "My wife is in some sort of trauma right now," and I was very concerned about her. —Mitch

During pregnancy complications and the first days following delivery, many fathers of preemies fear more for their partner than for their baby. Particularly if your partner was on bed rest or seriously ill during the pregnancy, her safety can be foremost on your mind. This is normal and natural.

Even if the mother was never in any physical danger, her emotional turmoil can make it seem as if she will never be the same again, that she will be this way forever. If she seems anxious, depressed, withdrawn, or apathetic, you may worry that she'll be unable to love and care for this baby. Especially if the depth of her grief seems so much greater than the feelings you are experiencing, you may be concerned that she has lost her connection to reality. Her anguish may seem endless.

Leaving the babies behind in the hospital was uglier for Debbie than it was for me. ... I suspect that's a typical dad response. I was much more concerned about Debbie's state of welfare than I was, certainly, about my state of welfare—and also I sort of felt as if the kids were in the best possible hands. Whatever happens, happens. I'm an eternal optimist, and I figured that they'd kind of be fine. But Debbie was in horrible shape, and I was concerned. I was preoccupied mostly with her distress. I was completely on call to calm her.—Mitch

It *is* great if the father can be a calming influence without trying to "fix" the mother's feelings. Rest assured that it is normal for the mother to worry, feel crazy, act different, and grieve deeply. Naturally, if you are concerned that she may need outside help, suggest that she accompany you to a support group, counselor, or her physician. If she won't go, you can go alone. But nothing, even having a healthy baby at home eventually, can erase her grief. This is something she must go through, just as you must.

With the opportunity to actively mourn her losses and make some sense out of all of this, the mother *will* eventually come out of it (as will you). Indeed, the more in touch with your painful feelings you can be, the easier you may find it to tolerate hers. And although it is true that she will never be exactly the same person after this, neither will you. Recognizing each other's personal growth as a result of this experience can inspire heightened respect and endear you to each other even more.

• • •

Delivering a tiny preemie is a life-jarring experience. This is a serious medical event, affecting mother and child with emotional ramifications for the father and the entire family. As you grieve, try to remember that all expectant and postpartum parents grieve for one thing or another. Even a routine pregnancy and delivery is never "perfect." All parents must adjust their fantasies of the "perfect" child to accommodate the real child. It may help to keep in mind that you are still having a meaningful reproductive experience that happens to be quite a bit more intense, frightening, and demanding than the average birth.

This perspective emphasizes that although your journey can be very difficult, it can also be every bit as meaningful as having a term pregnancy and baby. Facing your grief is what moves you toward healing and realizing those rewards.

Points to Remember

- The medical emergencies of pregnancy complications and premature delivery are accompanied by intense emotions, as well as by numbness and detachment.
- Numbness protects you from the overwhelming nature of this crisis. When it wears off, emotional flooding follows. This emotional unburdening is a natural process. Go with the flow.
- Your extraordinary feelings, or lack thereof, do not make you "bad" parents. You are good parents who are responding to an extraordinary situation.
- As you get used to the appearance of your new baby and adjust to the sights and sounds of the NICU, you will be able to start to get to know your little one. Despite your worries and fears, you can form a meaningful connection.
- Do those things that help you acknowledge your baby's birth and feel close to your baby.
- It is normal for the father to worry more about the mother than about the baby. You may be concerned that the mother will never recover from this trauma, but in time she will—as will you.

CHAPTER SIX

Physical Recovery

For the mother, physical and emotional recovery are tied together. When your baby is born too soon, medical complications and emotional devastation can feed into each other, confounding your recuperation on both levels.

The first day, I was on so many medications that I was not sure that I wanted to see or hold Alison. Looking back at it, I can hardly believe that my physical sickness was affecting me in such a strong way. I was very weak. I remember trying to give myself ice with a spoon out of a cup. I had no coordination at all. I felt almost like a failure. Here I had a baby, my husband was able to spend some time holding her, and I had not even seen her yet. —Stacy

If your pregnancy was complicated, you may have a difficult recovery, not just from the pregnancy, but from the harm it caused to your overall health. The amount of time it takes to recuperate can be frustrating, especially if you long to spend more time at your baby's bedside. If you need a lot of medical support, you might even feel indifferent toward your baby.

The truth is, I felt very detached from Josie at first. I would visit her in the NICU, but the pain from the C-section made it hard to concentrate on her. The pain medicine I took made me very groggy. All I wanted to do was sleep and recover, but I knew there was someone in the world who needed her mother very much. —Rebekah

I lay there feeling completely numb and shaking uncontrollably. I knew the shaking was a physical reaction of some sort, but I couldn't figure out the emotional numbness. I tried to get it in my mind that I had just become a mother and to experience some emotion about that, but I couldn't access anything. I remember wondering when I would. —Laurie

As you recover physically, your concerns about your body may go beyond the requirements for simple postpartum healing. If your pregnancy was complicated by infertility treatments, anomalies in your reproductive organs, placental problems, birth defects in your baby, or by unknown factors, you may wonder about your body's contribution to your baby's difficulties and premature delivery. You might feel betrayed by your body, not trusting its ability to carry and deliver a healthy baby. You might feel asexual, not at home in your body, and you may not want to be touched. You may worry about the possibilities for future pregnancies. Particularly if you had complications during or after delivery, physical—and emotional—healing from your baby's traumatic preterm birth will take some time.

You have a heart, a mind, and a body. All three need your attention and care in this critical period. As discussed in Chapter 2, if you neglect your emotional needs, your physical health can suffer. Likewise, neglecting your physical needs can have a detrimental effect on your emotional well-being, which in turn can hamper your ability to be there for your baby. Both you and your baby will benefit from you taking care of yourself inside and out. With time and your own good care of your body, you will recover physically. Good nutrition, rest, and emotional support can lessen some of the fatigue, sadness, and anxiety normally associated with postpartum recovery. As you begin to feel better physically, you will be better able to cope emotionally.

I don't remember thinking too much about how I felt, only that the longer I slept, the faster I would get better and the sooner I could start being a mother to my girls. —Rosa

Because your physical recovery is an important component of your parenting journey, this chapter contains the facts about physical postpartum adjustment as they apply to mothers of preemies. It may be difficult for you to read "regular" pregnancy books that approach postpartum recovery with the assumption of a term pregnancy and a healthy baby at home. If you need or want more information than you find here, the other books can be good resources, and you can rely on this chapter to validate your special situation. (For recommended books, see "Health, Pregnancy, Fertility" in Appendix C.)

Both parents should find useful information in this chapter's sections on sex and contraception, fatigue, sleep, nutrition and exercise, and relaxation. If you are the father and your partner is breast-feeding, it's important that you read about breast care so that you can support her and contribute to your baby's sustenance. It is important that *both partners* read the section on postpartum adjustment to understand what is "normal" and what may signal trouble. **If the mother is having difficulty in the postpartum period, especially if she seems not to be quite "herself," she maynot be able to seek help on her own. As her partner (or family or friend), do seek medical attention for her.**

Use the information in this chapter along with the advice you receive from your doctor or midwife, as well as your own common sense. Your unique condition and special needs may call for more specific recommendations. Always consult your doctor or midwife if you have any symptoms that seem worrisome or if you just feel as if something isn't quite right. Note any pain, discomfort, fever, or other unusual symptoms. Although you may be focusing intently on your baby's physical condition, also stay mindful of your own. Be your own best advocate.

Phantom Feelings of Pregnancy

It felt a little strange to not be pregnant anymore and to not have anything to show for it but frozen cups of milk. —Ruby

After you deliver, one of the first things you may notice is a physical, aching emptiness. For months, a growing baby has been an integral part of you. Then suddenly, your baby is out of your womb—and out of your sight. Instead of being able to close your eyes and place your hands on your belly to feel movement, you feel your empty uterus contract. The fetus's kicking and uterine contractions can be so similar that sometimes, for a moment, you may feel and even believe you are still pregnant. Although this experience is familiar to anyone who has delivered a baby, the difference in your situation is that you are still *supposed to be* pregnant. In fact, if you missed out on the opportunity to savor much fetal movement during your pregnancy, these strong uterine sensations after the birth can represent one more deeply felt loss. These contractions may feel stronger than any kicks your tiny baby ever gave you.

Although such phantom feelings of pregnancy can be agonizing, they can also help you comprehend that your baby is outside your womb now, rather than inside it. Accepting this reality can be a tremendous challenge to a new mom of a preemie. After all, your due date may be weeks or months away, yet you do not have your newborn at your bedside or in your arms to confirm that you're no longer pregnant. Even though you're in shock and disbelief, your uterus is reminding you that it's no longer cradling a baby. Your body will not allow you to detach fully. You can rely on it to try to keep you grounded, anchored in reality, in the midst of your denial.

> *I can remember laying in my room after delivery and feeling the uterine contractions, and thinking, "Oh someone's kicking," and then thinking, "No, no one is kicking." And over the next few hours, with every contraction, I had to remember it wasn't contractions of labor and it wasn't babies kicking me. It was my body adjusting to being empty. —Rikki*

Postpartum Adjustment

For any new mother, physical and hormonal changes normally contribute to emotional upheaval during the postpartum period. After delivery, hormone levels plummet, contributing to negative feelings that can continue for several months. Along with the need to recover physically and hormonally from childbirth, caring for a tiny, helpless infant is quite demanding. New mothers are typically sleep deprived and overwhelmed. Unrealistic expectations about motherhood as a time of unchallenged joy can add to feelings of self-doubt or anger.

Being surrounded by a support network and having realistic expectations make postpartum adjustment easier for new mothers. But in the unanticipated and unfamiliar circumstances of a preterm birth, your support network may not come through, and it's hard to know what expectations are realistic. Suddenly, *all* of your expectations need to be revised. Feelings of isolation and disappointment are central to the challenge of the postpartum period for mothers of preemies.

It just wasn't right. It's not the way it's supposed to happen. Here I am, recovering from pregnancy, but I don't have my baby with me. —Marsha

Later, about the time you've learned to negotiate the NICU and have adapted to having a hospitalized infant, you face your baby's discharge, when you become the primary, round-the-clock caregiver. You may think that, finally, your original expectations will be fulfilled; but for most families, life with a premature baby means constructing a *new* set of realistic expectations. Your fragile infant may require special monitoring and need to avoid family gatherings and public outings. Figuring out how to cope with this imposed isolation—for yourself and for your child—and adjust to parenting a preemie at home can take time and practice, and it naturally extends the difficulties of the postpartum period. (For more on this extended adjustment period, see Chapters 12–14.)

Baby Blues

"Baby blues," which most mothers experience to some extent after delivery, are influenced by the natural readjustment of your hormones to nonpregnant levels, and they can increase your emotional load. This readjustment period can last about two weeks and accounts to some extent for your mood swings, tearfulness, and longing for your baby. Your readjustment period is made more complicated and bewildering because these early weeks coincide with your orientation to your baby and the NICU. Fatigue, insomnia, or heavy, aching arms are common symptoms after premature delivery and can have both physical and emotional roots—adding to the baby blues you may already be experiencing due to hormonal recovery.

The weeks after delivery are thought to be a time when mothers are physiologically primed to focus and dote on their babies. Of course, in mothering your preemie, these natural feelings of devotion are met with barriers in the form of your baby's condition and hospitalization, plus your own grief, anxiety, and feelings of numbness and detachment. So while you are physiologically primed, neither the situation nor your emotions are in sync, and this can feel very confusing and frustrating. It's no wonder that many mothers of preemies experience a difficult postpartum adjustment.

> *I felt torn in half. Like there was a part of me that wanted to be in bed with them, taking them back in, but at the same time I was so incredibly knotted up with terror and sadness at their condition, that it got in the way of any natural instincts I might have had to know what each of them needed. [For instance] I didn't feel confident picking up Hannah after a blood draw when she was screaming. I couldn't push past the anxiety, fear, and sadness, to "Yes, you pick up a crying baby. I know this." It's like it was an effort to remember that it was loving and a good thing to pick up a crying baby, that it was allowed, that's what mothers do, and to not be looking over my shoulder, wondering if I'd get in trouble, or hurt her. —Rikki*

Risk Factors for a Difficult Postpartum Adjustment

Biological, psychological, and social factors all contribute to how a woman copes with having a baby, whether the birth is uneventful or complicated. Here are some questions that help determine if a mother is at risk for a difficult postpartum adjustment. The more your answers lean toward stress, conflict, or deprivation, the more elevated your risk. As you read this list, note how many of the factors are applicable to mothers of premature babies.

- *Biological factors.* To what degree is the mother affected by the hormonal changes and physical demands that accompany childbirth and breastfeeding? Were there complications with the pregnancy or delivery? Is there a history of depression or anxiety in the mother's own history or in her family? Does the mother have a thyroid imbalance?
- *Psychological factors.* Is this the mother's first baby? Do her expectations for motherhood fit with reality? Does she have perfectionist tendencies or a need for control? Is she pessimistic, worried, or self-critical? How has she coped with major life changes in the past? Does she have unresolved losses, particularly with regard to infertility or childbearing? Does she feel trapped or as if she is losing control over her life?
- *Social factors.* What is the quality of the mother's relationship with her partner? Were there problems in the relationship before the birth? Is the

mother a single mom? Does she have an emotionally supportive network of friends and relatives? Is her employer accommodating her needs? Is her baby high need, unresponsive, fussy, or a temperamental mismatch with the mother?

As you can see, giving birth prematurely automatically raises your risk of having a difficult postpartum period.

"Normal" postpartum adjustment, or baby blues, include such symptoms as tearfulness, fatigue, insomnia, exhaustion, anxiety, irritability, anger, and mood swings that are especially noticeable during the first week or two after the birth.

Any mother can develop a more serious postpartum reaction, which may occur at any time during the first year after delivery. The postpartum reactions described in the following section are commonly grouped under the term postpartum depression (PPD) and are more serious than a "normal" postpartum adjustment.

Types of Postpartum Reaction

Postpartum Mood Reactions Commonly known as "postpartum depression," the mother's mood swings and negative feelings about herself and the baby are more pronounced, longer lasting, and interfere more with everyday functioning than do symptoms typical of the "baby blues." These intense mood reactions include frequent crying; feelings of helplessness or hopelessness; and lack of energy, interest, or motivation. For those mothers with an underlying bipolar disorder, there may also be episodes of mania during which the mother has periods of excessive energy, insomnia, and irritability.

Postpartum Anxiety Reactions Postpartum anxiety is marked by exaggerated shifts between feeling safe and feeling in danger. Generalized anxiety, worry, and panic are pronounced. The mother may experience obsessive and intrusive scary thoughts that she can't seem to control. She may have panic attacks, complete with buzzing ears, tingling limbs, shortness of breath, dizziness, flushed skin, or pounding heart. She may also carry out compulsive rituals in an attempt to quiet her anxiety. The symptoms are so bothersome or distracting that the new mother has trouble accomplishing her daily tasks.

Postpartum Thought Reactions A type of psychosis, postpartum thought reactions are rare but very serious. In addition to the anxiety and depression symptoms just described, the mother may experience life-threatening confusion, hallucinations, or delusions that interfere with her normal functioning. She may see or hear things that are not there, and no amount of convincing will persuade her that these are not real. She loses touch with reality and poses a great danger to herself and her baby. **Postpartum thought reactions are A MEDICAL EMERGENCY. Seek immediate medical attention for the mother.**

Postpartum Adjustment: The Bottom Line

For mothers of preemies, adjustment to parenthood is very complex. It is often difficult to discern whether your reactions stem from postpartum physical and emotional changes or from your response to the preterm birth—you can assume that it is an interaction of many factors. The bottom line is whether you (or others) believe that your emotional state is interfering with your ability to function. If you are sensitive and cry easily in many situations, your tears aren't necessarily a sign that you have a serious hormonal imbalance or postpartum depression. You have a lot of stress to handle and many strong feelings about your situation. But if your behavior or emotions are compromising your ability to manage everyday life, get along with others, feel good about yourself, or take care of your baby, then you deserve to get the assistance, support, counseling, and medication you need. You can talk to your doctor or midwife about a referral for counseling. Your therapist may recommend medication to aid your healing. Check Appendix C under "Health, Pregnancy, and Fertility" for further reading or to contact a support organization. Also see "Professional Counseling" in Chapter 3.

Tips for Coping in the Postpartum Period

- *Adjust your expectations.* Recognize that all new mothers feel overwhelmed in the beginning and that most mothers must adjust their expectations about motherhood. Having a baby is not the same as having a job. Being inefficient and feeling incompetent are natural aspects of taking care of an infant. In general, especially during the first year, *if you're brushing your teeth, you're overachieving.*
- *Expect strong emotions.* Parenting a preemie coupled with postpartum adjustment is likely to intensify the emotional consequences of this time for you. It is unfair to compare this adjustment to previous childbirths or to other mothers you know with term babies.

- *Plan for a lengthy adjustment.* Your postpartum adjustment will likely continue well after your baby comes home. Homecoming can be physically and emotionally stressful. And when the excitement dies down after the first few weeks of your baby's arrival home, exhaustion may set in.

- *Accept your reactions, whatever they are.* You may feel embarrassed about your inability to cope in the postpartum period, but just as delivering prematurely is not a reflection of your fitness as a mother, neither is suffering from a postpartum reaction. Having trouble adjusting after childbirth, whatever the circumstances, is very common. As researchers learn more about the postpartum period, they are discovering that most women experience some depression, with 10 to 20 percent experiencing significant depression. Having an easy postpartum adjustment is not a measure of a woman's worth, mothering capabilities, or moral fiber, and neither is having a difficult time. If you are having difficulty adjusting, it's not your fault. You did not cause this or ask for it.

- *Recognize the source of your feelings.* The distorted thinking that accompanies postpartum reactions can exacerbate feelings of self-blame or self-criticism and anxiety about your baby, even if you are not usually a negative thinker. These negative feelings are not about being a bad mother or having character flaws—your brain is reacting to postpartum chemical and hormonal adjustments. Recognize that *any* mother in your shoes would be affected by this combination of complex biological, physical, hormonal, social, and psychological factors.

- *Talk to someone who can listen.* An important first step to finding relief from painful postpartum feelings is being able to talk about them and have them understood and validated by someone who can listen empathetically. Just being reassured that you are not crazy and that this is a treatable condition can be immensely helpful.

- *Consider medication.* Sometimes medication can be a useful aid to get you back on track. Your doctor might prescribe an antidepressant, antianxiety medication, or hormonal therapy. If you are providing breast milk for your baby, ask about any effects the drug might have on your production or the quality of your milk. If you decide to try alternative or herbal treatments, check on their effects as well. Keep in mind that even if you're breast-feeding, medication may be recommended. Selective serotonin reuptake inhibitors (SSRIs), in particular, are transmitted only in trace amounts through breast milk, and the risks to your baby are far less than the risks of untreated anxiety and depression are to you and to your child.

- *Make a plan.* Find ways to structure your days, devote more time to yourself, set priorities, acquire realistic expectations for yourself and your baby, and learn methods for relaxing and reducing stress.
- *Arrange for help.* Recognize that it's normal to be preoccupied with and devoted to your baby and let other responsibilities slide. Particularly right after your baby is discharged from the hospital, it is important that you have assistance. Enlist the help and support of others, including but not limited to your partner (who is also under stress). Hire someone, maybe just a teenager, to help with errands, chores, and child care, even if it's only for a few hours a couple of times a week.
- *Experience a fourth trimester.* The "fourth trimester" is the normal period of absorption that mothers experience with their newborns. During this time, mothers need to be sheltered and supported so they can recuperate from pregnancy and childbirth, establish a feeding schedule, and devote attention to learning about and meeting the needs of their newborn. Even though you may have spent some time getting to know your baby during his or her hospitalization, give yourself permission to have an extended "lying-in" period of nesting, learning, and bonding when your baby comes home. Even if homecoming is months after delivery, you deserve to have this experience. It's important that you and your infant get acquainted on your home turf. If it feels right, have a close relative or friend stay with you so that you can immerse yourself in your infant, just as you would have if you had delivered on your due date. (Even if you've been home for a while, try a modified version of this with your baby.)
- *Ask for support.* If you are having trouble summoning up the courage to get help or the energy to do what you need (that is, if you are having difficulty being your own advocate), tell someone close to you—your partner, a friend, a family member—that you are having a difficult postpartum adjustment and you need them to advocate for you. Let them help you figure out what you need *and* help you get it, including an appointment with a health care provider *who takes your symptoms seriously.*

Parenting Your Premature Baby and Child

- *Recognize that you deserve help.* Most important, whatever form your adjustment takes, know that you *deserve* to have help and support during this time.

Breast Care for
Breast-Feeding Mothers

This section contains basic information for breast-feeding mothers and their partners. Most mothers of preemies will pump milk for their infants, particularly at the beginning, and some mothers will continue to pump for babies who will take only the bottle or who must be tube-fed. This section is addressed to mothers who are producing breast milk, whether they are pumping, putting the baby to the breast, or both. We'll look at the advantages of breast-feeding for both mother and baby, as well as at the mechanics, establishing your milk supply, overcoming challenges, and ways to enhance supply. For information about any aspects of breast-feeding not covered here, consult "Resources" in Appendix C at the back of this book. If you want more information or support with the emotional aspects of feeding in general, turn to the "Feeding Issues" sections in Chapters 9, 14, and 16.

Advantages of Breast Milk and Breast-Feeding

I kept myself going by pumping milk for my son and telling myself that this was one way I could help him. —Sarah

Milk is a gift of nature, and providing it to your baby is one of the few things that only you, the mother, can do. Indeed, if you were not planning to breast-feed your baby, the premature birth may cause you to reconsider. And if you were planning on or leaning toward breast-feeding, your baby's prematurity may strengthen your resolve.

Although many people associate breasts with sex, every nursing mother knows that breasts are all about providing key nourishment for babies. Breast milk has unique properties and essential nutrients that help babies digest, grow, develop, and fight off disease and infection. No formula offers so many benefits. In fact, your body knows that you delivered early, and so it produces a milk that is ideally suited to your premature infant, one that contains more protein, fat, and minerals than the milk term-moms produce. If you can provide breast milk and your tiny baby can tolerate it, he or she will benefit greatly.

> *It was very gratifying, from very early on, to know that Charlotte was being fed my breast milk, because I knew this would be the best thing for her, and in a way it made me feel closer to her. —Kate*

When your baby can be put to the breast, breast-feeding is *less* stressful for him or her than bottle-feeding because your baby can pace the flow of milk, pausing when necessary without choking on the unobstructed flow from a rubber nipple. The benefits of breast-feeding to you include

- Skin-to-skin contact with your infant, which can help you feel close and attuned to your baby
- A sense of normalcy around the birth and your baby
- Increased confidence in your mothering abilities
- A feeling that you are indispensable to your baby's health and well-being
- Hormonal benefits that aid in postpartum healing

The Mechanics

If you were planning to breast-feed your baby, you may fear that you can't because you gave birth prematurely. But even if you didn't make it to the third trimester, hormonal changes that cause your breasts to start producing milk accompany your baby's birth. For the first few days, your breasts secrete colostrum, a substance high in antibodies and extremely beneficial to babies. Within two to five days, your milk will come in. The engorgement period lasts about forty-eight hours, and your breasts may be uncomfortably full. By pumping, you can establish your supply. Even if you are too ill at first to pump or if you decide not to breast-feed and then change your mind, hourly pumping for a day can reestablish a supply that is dwindling after the engorgement period passes.

When a pump exerts suction (or when a baby sucks) on your nipple, this tells your brain to release two hormones. Prolactin makes your milk glands produce milk. Oxytocin (which also plays a role in uterine contractions during labor) contracts the tiny muscles that surround the milk glands, squeezing the milk down into small reservoirs just behind the nipple. This is known as the milk-ejection, or "let down," reflex. When you sit down to pump, signs of let down may include a sudden thirst, tingling sensations in your breast, leaking nipples, or a feeling of deep relaxation.

Even though you may not be able to put your preemie to your breast for many weeks yet, when you provide breast milk by pumping, this is a form of breast-feeding. Even if your baby is too sick or unable to drink yet, your milk can be fed to your baby through a tube going directly to his or her stomach. If your baby's digestive system cannot tolerate breast milk for now, your milk will be saved for your baby's use down the road. By building up and maintaining your milk supply by pumping, you ensure that your baby will have your breast milk—and that you will be able to try to nurse your baby when she or he is strong enough and can coordinate the suck-swallow-breathe skills that mark efficient nursing.

Establishing Your Milk Supply

Start Pumping as Soon as You Can If you are well enough, you can start pumping your breasts within hours after delivery to build up and maintain your milk supply. Tell your nurse and your baby's nurse that you want to breast-feed, and they will give you the equipment, training, and encouragement to do it. If the hospital has a good lactation consultant, use this resource. You can also ask your doctor, midwife, or nurses if they can refer you to a lactation consultant outside the hospital. Speak up if you are not happy with the information or support you are receiving for breast-feeding. You deserve to get what you need.

> *The nurses brought me an electric pump and suggested that I start right away. At that point I really wasn't into it. I didn't feel like a new mother at all, yet they expected me to pump my breasts and start making milk. I hated having to do that. It felt weird. But as soon as I was able to spend a couple of minutes with these beautiful little very premature girls, I decided anything I needed to do to help ensure they would be okay I had to do right away. —Rosa*

Expect Small Amounts, Especially at First When you first start pumping, don't be discouraged by the small amounts. First feedings can be as small as one-quarter of a teaspoon. Practice pumping for five to ten minutes every three hours and save every priceless drop. Use a hospital-grade, double electric pump so that you can pump both breasts simultaneously.

> *At first it was hard. I really had to force myself to begin the milk-production process. Once I got home, it was much easier. I decided to go out and purchase a new electric pump to make things much easier for me. It got easier and easier as the days went on.* —Rosa

Understand Engorgement—or Lack of It Take advantage of the engorgement that may occur when your milk comes in. Pumping provides physical relief from the pressure of the milk building up and reassures you of your supply. Feeling able to produce enough milk can be especially comforting if you have multiple babies.

On the other hand, some moms do not experience engorgement. It's not clear why, although some speculate that it might be related to the incredible stress of early delivery, emergency cesarean section, having a struggling baby in the NICU, and/or the medications that are used to induce labor or stave off eclampsia. You are not alone if you do not experience engorgement or if you find that, no matter how well you follow the guidelines set out by the lactation consultants for pumping, your milk supply doesn't seem to increase. Many moms who find the initial weeks of pumping difficult and unproductive go on to successfully supply breast milk for their preemies. Other moms pump what they can for as long as they can. Struggling to find a balance between your baby's needs and your own physical abilities is natural.

Pump Frequently and Completely Don't be afraid of pumping too often: it is easier to taper an abundant supply than to build up a dwindling one. To establish your milk supply or to build it up, try pumping every two to two-and-a-half hours around the clock for a couple of days and nights (or eight to twelve times during the day, if sleeping at night is paramount). After your milk supply is established, it's a good idea to pump at least once in the middle of the night. If getting an uninterrupted night's sleep is important, though, go no more than eight hours (give or take) at night without pumping and then pump at least eight times throughout the day. Whenever you pump, be sure to "empty" your breasts. Doing so extracts the hindmilk, which is highest in fat— these are calories your preemie needs. Pump for a minute or two after the flow of milk stops or after it slows to drips.

Parenting Your Premature Baby and Child

Keep in mind that pumping frequency (how often you pump) is more important than pumping duration (how long you pump). As a rule, it's more effective to pump for ten to fifteen minutes every three hours than to pump for twenty to thirty minutes less often. Pumping less often is less effective in establishing a milk supply because when the milk sits in the breasts too long, they become engorged and the pressure signals your body to cut back on milk production. Continuing to pump after the ducts are drained does little to step up milk production. *Frequently* reducing the pressure in your breasts signals your body to continue to make milk. To establish or increase your supply, simply pump at shorter intervals for no longer than is necessary to empty your breasts.

Learn the Procedures for Sterilizing Equipment and Storing Your Milk
Ask your baby's doctor what procedures you should follow to sterilize your breast pump parts and bottles and to freeze and store your breast milk. See Appendix C, the "Resources" section, for information on contacting La Leche League to obtain the organization's most current guidelines. Also practice good hygiene. Shower daily and wear a clean nursing bra. Wash your hands before pumping and keep them clean until you seal the container that holds your milk. After each use, wash all the breast pump parts that come into contact with your milk using hot, soapy water.

Overcoming Challenges to Breast-Feeding

Although breast-feeding is one of the most natural things in the world, you're not born knowing how to do it. Like most mothering skills, you need to learn it and practice it. And breast-feeding has its challenges, especially with a baby in the NICU. Keep the following tips in mind as you work to master this important skill.

Be Persistent You may notice that your milk supply fluctuates with your baby's medical condition. For some mothers, the better their baby is doing, the better their milk supply. If your baby encounters an extended bad patch, it is important to keep pumping for five minutes at a time, even if you only extract a few drops. When your baby's condition improves, your persistence may pay off: some mothers' breasts begin to produce milk again after a period of stress-related depletion. If your supply is dropping off, it does not necessarily mean that your breast-feeding days are over. You can decide to hang in there and see what happens.

Use the Best Pump You Can To make pumping easier and more efficient and effective, use a hospital-quality electric pump in good working order with a double pumping kit. Most hospitals will help you obtain one.

Find the Routine and Rituals That Work for You To enhance your milk-ejection reflex, establish a ritual that conditions your breasts to "let down" when it's time to pump or feed. If you have other children, get them occupied with something or hand them off to your partner so that you won't be disturbed. You might sit in the same comfortable chair or position, sip water out of the same container, or apply a warm washcloth to your breasts and massage them. Provide whatever breast or nipple stimulation is comfortable and works for you. Listen to relaxing music, read, or watch television. Take deep, cleansing breaths and imagine being in a beautiful place, perhaps with a waterfall of milk.

Pumping advice often includes the suggestion to look at a picture of your baby or to think about holding your baby against your skin or putting your baby to the breast. But when you're just getting started, you don't have those photos and experiences to rely on. Advice of this sort can be both aggravating and depressing. Stacy remembers: "One of the things that irritated me the most was when a lady came in to show me how to pump. She told me to think about the first time I had held my daughter and how well she was doing. All I had seen of my daughter was two very cloudy Polaroid pictures."

If looking at or thinking about your baby brings up too many anxieties or feelings of grief, this approach may not help. While some moms find that smelling a blanket that their baby has slept on helps when pumping, others find that detaching entirely from thinking about the baby is most helpful. Many moms talk on the phone, read, or relax in other ways while pumping. Others use pumping as a way to structure their time or to take a break from the chaos of the day. You may find it helps to think of pumping as just a task to accomplish. If thinking of your baby helps, you might want to form images of your little one feeding and growing. Find the ritual or routine that works for you.

Seek Help for Nipple or Breast Pain Pumping and breast-feeding have potential complications and hurdles. Breast and nipple pain may occur for several reasons. See your doctor or midwife for an exam and advice. Many times, normal adjustment takes care of the problem, or there is a relatively easy remedy for it. Still, it can be hard to persevere with pumping or breast-feeding when doing so is yet another painful struggle.

Causes of Nipple or Breast Pain Seek out as much information and support as you need if you are having nipple or breast pain. Some reasons for sore nipples or breast pain include pumping suction, the need to adapt to your baby's suck, a yeast infection, a clogged milk duct, and a breast infection. Here is some information about each of these.

- *Pump suction.* If your nipples become sore from pumping, try turning the pump's suction down and temporarily limiting pumping time to less than ten minutes until you're not so sore. It may help to put lanolin around the areola before pumping. Ask your lactation consultant or pump supplier for a flexible insert that you can use to take the pressure off your tender spots.

- *Adjustment period.* During the first couple of weeks after you start putting a baby to your breast, it is normal for your nipples to be sore for that first half-minute after the baby latches on. Some babies have very strong sucks, and some mothers have very tender nipples. If the pain subsides within thirty seconds and your baby is swallowing, you're doing just fine. Your nipples need time and experience to adapt to their new job.

- *Yeast infection.* If you develop a yeast infection, your nipples may look normal or be bright pink. You may feel burning or stabbing pains in your breasts. You'll need a prescription topical antifungal cream for your nipples, and if you are breast-feeding, your baby will need to be treated at the same time with an oral medication. To avoid reinfection, sterilize *anything* that comes into contact with your baby's mouth or your nipples, such as pacifiers, bottle nipples, or breast pump parts, in simmering water for twenty minutes. You can continue to breast-feed or pump during treatment.

- *Clogged milk duct.* A clogged duct will cause a red, hot, tender area on your breast and can be a precursor to a breast infection, medically called *mastitis.* You may be able to keep the infection from developing by taking it easy for several days, resting in bed, and drinking extra fluids. Also soak your breast several times a day in a tub of warm water, massage it gently, and pump more frequently. A clogged duct can take two to three days to resolve, and as the clog moves down the duct, you may notice a painful white spot on the tip of your nipple. Because a mechanical obstruction can sometimes cause a clogged duct, avoid underwire bras that press on your breast and don't sleep on your stomach. Consult a lactation specialist if you repeatedly get clogged ducts.

- *Breast infection (mastitis).* Signs of breast infection include the following:
    - ▲ Any red, warm, hard, or tender areas in your breasts
    - ▲ Fever (oral temperature above 100° F)
    - ▲ General ill feeling
    - ▲ Tender lymph glands in the underarm area
    - ▲ If you develop fever, chills, or flulike symptoms before or after you notice a clogged duct, you may have mastitis. Call your doctor or midwife so that you can receive an antibiotic to treat the infection. If your baby is feeding at your breast, it's safe to continue to breast-feed because your baby probably has the germ already and the milk is rarely infected. If your baby has not yet nursed at your breast, you may be told to discard the milk from the infected breast(s) until the antibiotic has cleared the infection.

Recognize the Effects of Diet on Your Breast Milk Breast milk is affected by the foods you eat. If your baby is irritable or gassy after feedings, he or she may be sensitive to something you ate before you pumped that milk. Common culprits are

- "Gassy" vegetables, including cabbage, onions, garlic, broccoli, cauliflower, turnips, beans, sweet peppers
- Strong spices, including chili peppers, curry, pepper, ginger, cinnamon
- Caffeine, found in coffee, black teas, chocolate, some soft drinks (caffeine accumulates in the newborn and causes night irritability)
- Foods that are at least 90 percent dairy products, such as milk, ice cream, cheese, yogurt, pudding
- Common allergens, such as peanuts, eggs, corn, and wheat. In fact, *all* pregnant and lactating mothers are advised to avoid eating foods containing peanuts.

Your baby's discomfort or irritability can be caused by food intolerances even if symptoms don't surface until weeks or months after birth. To find out what is causing your baby distress if your baby is receiving fresh milk, you can eliminate all the foods on the list from your diet for a week. If your baby is receiving frozen milk, try dipping into a different week's supply or provide as much fresh milk as you can. If you notice an improvement in your baby, you'll know that what you are eating is affecting him or her. Reintroduce the foods one at a time to figure out which are the offending ones. Because dairy products are particularly associated with colic, you could eliminate that food group first and see if doing so brings your baby relief.

Call your doctor, midwife, or lactation consultant if you have any concerns about your breasts, your nipples, your milk, your milk supply, pumping, or your baby's feeding—or if you notice any signs of breast infection.

Enhancing Your Milk Supply

To enable their bodies to supply milk, breast-feeding moms are encouraged to get adequate rest, relaxation, exercise, and nutrition. (See the discussions at the end of this chapter for more about these elements of good health.) It seems unfair to add these requirements to an already-stressed NICU mom's to-do list—but exhaustion and poor nourishment drain a mother's often-sparse reserves for making good milk for her baby. Here are some suggestions for enhancing your milk supply.

Stay Hydrated Not drinking enough fluids can cause dehydration, which can make it difficult to produce enough milk for your baby. To stay hydrated, just remember to drink a glass of water every time you pump. And since NICUs are warm, take a full water bottle with you when you are with your baby, so you'll have easy access to what you need.

Avoid Milk-Tainting Substances Some oral contraceptives, antihistamines, and diuretics can affect your milk, so it's best not to use them while pumping or breast-feeding. Do your best to eliminate caffeine (found in coffee, some teas, many soft drinks, and chocolate) and give up nicotine. Both of these not only taint your milk but also can diminish your milk supply.

Eat Well, Exercise, Rest, and Relax Eat a well-balanced diet to maintain your health. Get appropriate exercise as well as plenty of rest to build your stamina and reserves. Do things that relax you. This may include exercise, such as going for a walk, or it may mean taking a daily shower or reading for fun. Look at it this way: healthy habits benefit your milk supply, so you are doing these things not just for yourself but also for your baby.

Whenever you feel discouraged about how much you can't seem to accomplish (household projects, chores, errands), remember that your *main job* right now is to be a mother. Eating, drinking water, resting, relaxing, exercising, and, especially, pumping and spending time with your baby are all *essential tasks*. Put them all on your to-do list, in the "top priority" section. Throw away the old list with all that stuff you thought you'd accomplish back when you were naive about what motherhood would be like for you. And remember, if you accomplish just one household task a day, you qualify for a medal of honor *and* a standing ovation. (The same is true of mothers who are not sup-plying breast milk!)

With rest, good nutrition, encouragement, and support, most mothers are able to provide at least some milk for their premature babies. Still, when your baby is in the NICU, providing breast milk by pumping and then trying to teach a tiny baby to nurse can be frustrating. You may feel ambivalent about breast-feeding in ways that you did not expect. For more on the emo-tional aspects of breast-feeding your baby, see Chapters 9 and 14.

Breast Care When You Aren't Breast-Feeding

If you cannot breast-feed, decide not to do so, or stop after doing so for a while, your body may still produce milk because of the hormones in your bloodstream after delivery. Your breasts may become engorged with milk several days after delivery or when you stop pumping. This can be quite uncomfortable, but the presence and pressure of milk are what signal your body to slow and ultimately shut down the milk supply. You can lessen the pain by pumping just enough to reduce the pressure. This will enable you to taper your milk supply. Don't pump more than you have to, or your breasts will step up production again.

Some mothers find pumping too emotionally distressing and prefer to put up with the discomfort. If you don't pump, your body absorbs the milk and your breasts soften gradually. Binding your breasts tightly or wearing a snug bra can reduce discomfort. You might also try putting green cabbage leaves over your breasts (inside your bra). Taking over-the-counter pain reliev-ers or placing cold packs (such as a bag of frozen peas) on your breasts may help relieve pain. A five-day regimen of vitamin B_6 (200 mg per day) may also reduce engorgement. You can also try suspending your breasts in hot water (by kneeling over a bathtub or large pan filled with hot water). The heat may cause the milk to flow out without stimulating milk production. Call your doctor or midwife if you notice any signs of breast infection:

- Red, warm, hard, or tender areas in your breasts

- Fever (oral temperature above 100° F)
- General ill feeling
- Tender lymph glands in the underarm area

Recovery from Cesarean Delivery

If you had an uncomplicated cesarean delivery, you can expect to be discharged three days after delivery. Your body will need about six weeks to heal completely. If your cesarean was an emergency procedure or you had a classical (vertical) incision, you may need even more time to heal. If you have other complications, you can expect to remain hospitalized for many days.

It is important to remember that following a C-section you are recovering from major surgery. You may tire easily for several months after delivery. Walking or standing for long periods can be exhausting. Give yourself time to heal before resuming your normal activities. Ask your doctor or midwife about special restrictions. You may be instructed not to lift anything heavy and to refrain from activities that put stress on the abdominal muscles, such as mopping or vacuuming. Do not drive during the first one or two weeks after the cesarean because your reaction time is slowed. If you had a classical incision or an emergency cesarean, ask your doctor or midwife for more information about your recovery process.

Examine your incision daily to make sure that it is healing properly. Check with your doctor or midwife about bathing and removal of bandages. Call your doctor or midwife if the edges of the incision come apart or if you notice any signs of complications or infection. These include
- Increased pain or tenderness in the abdomen
- Increased swelling, tenderness, or reddened skin around the incision
- Fluid or discharge from the incision
- Fever (oral temperature above 100° F)
- Continual urge to urinate or frequent urination

Also see the information that follows on uterine healing.

Uterine Healing

It takes four to six weeks for your uterus to return to its prepregnant size and position and for your cervix to close. To help maintain uterine firmness and prevent heavy blood loss, you or your nurse can massage the uterus, stimulating it to contract. Pumping your breasts can also encourage your uterus to contract.

For up to eight weeks after delivery, a bloody discharge called *lochia* flows from the uterus through the vagina. Lochia is made up of the uterine lining as well as blood from the site where the placenta was attached. Over time, the color of the lochia changes from red to pink or brown to whitish-yellow. Occasionally you may notice clots up to the size of a quarter. You may also notice an increase in flow when you stand up or engage in physical activity. Within one to three weeks after delivery, the clotted area at the placental site loosens, and you may notice increased bleeding for a few days. In general, increased bleeding means that you need to lessen or slow your activity, get more rest, and drink more fluids. To reduce chances of infection during this period, avoid vaginal penetration, including intercourse, tampons, menstrual cups, or douches—ask your doctor or midwife how long you should avoid these intrusions. If you had severe uterine bleeding during your pregnancy or delivery or a uterine infection before or after your baby's delivery, ask your doctor or midwife for more information about what to expect.

Call your doctor or midwife if you notice any signs of complications or infection. These include

- Pain or burning with urination
- Headache, muscle aches, dizziness, or general ill feeling
- Nausea, vomiting, constipation, or abdominal swelling
- Unpleasant-smelling vaginal flow or discharge
- Vaginal bleeding that saturates one or more sanitary pads in one hour
- Lightheadedness, particularly with heavy bleeding
- Fever (oral temperature above 100° F)

Perineal Care

The perineum is the area between the vaginal opening and the anus, which must stretch when a baby in born. Sometimes the perineum will tear during childbirth, for which you may or may not need stitches. Sometimes an episiotomy, a surgical incision that makes the vaginal opening larger, is performed. Although routine episiotomies have fallen out of favor for normal deliveries in recent years, if your baby was in distress, you may have received an episiotomy so that the baby could emerge more quickly.

If you had to have an episiotomy because of the emergency nature of your delivery, you may feel cheated of the chance to try to deliver without being cut. It may seem a cruel irony that you needed to be sliced open so that such a tiny head could emerge. This is another loss you must grieve.

If you received stitches, they will dissolve and your perineum will heal in about three to six weeks. You may feel discomfort, especially during intercourse, for several months. Talk to your doctor or midwife if the discomfort persists.

Whether or not you received stitches, your perineum needs special care to prevent infection, relieve pain, and promote healing.

To prevent infection, keep the area clean by rinsing it with warm water after urinating. Always wipe from front to back to avoid spreading organisms from the rectal area. Change your pad or panty liner at least every two hours. Take showers rather than baths so that your perineum doesn't sit in unsanitary water.

To relieve pain and promote healing, sit in a *clean* tub of shallow water several times a day for fifteen to twenty minutes. Use warm or cold water, whichever feels more soothing to you. If you use warm water, lie down and relax for fifteen minutes afterwards, to reduce the swelling caused by the water's warmth.

To relieve pain, you can also place cold or hot packs on your perineum for twenty to thirty minutes. Ice is recommended right after delivery and intermittently for up to twenty-four hours. At first, cold reduces swelling and inflammation. As you recover, heat may feel better and promotes healing. Always place a layer of cloth between your body and the pack to protect your skin from excessive heat or cold. Make sure the temperature feels comfortable at all times, not too hot or too cold.

•••

To relieve soreness, you can also soak a cotton ball in witch hazel (available in drugstores) and pat it on your perineum, or you can buy commercial pads containing witch hazel (Tucks) and put them on your sanitary pad. Witch hazel also soothes the pain of hemorrhoids. To ease pain when you sit, try sitting on a donut-shaped pillow or squeezing your buttocks together before sitting.

Do not insert anything into the vagina before your postpartum checkup. Call your doctor or midwife if you notice any signs of complications or infection. These include

- An increase in pain, swelling, redness, drainage, or bleeding around the incision or tear
- Headache, muscle aches, dizziness, or general ill feeling
- Nausea, vomiting, constipation, or abdominal swelling
- Fever (oral temperature above 100° F)

The Postpartum Checkup

About six weeks after delivery, your doctor or midwife will want to give you a pelvic exam and check your general physical condition, your urine, your breasts, and your abdominal wall. This postpartum exam can reassure you that your body is healing properly. If you had complications before, during, or after delivery, your doctor or midwife may want to see you less than six weeks after delivery. If you have questions, want to learn more about what happened during delivery, or need reassurance that you are recovering physically, you may want to make an appointment with your care provider before the six-week checkup.

This postpartum checkup may be the first time you have seen your obstetrician since the early hours after delivery. Depending on the circumstances of your delivery, you may have some strong feelings about how your doctor or midwife handled your baby's birth. This is a time when you can begin to talk over what happened. It can be helpful to fill in your memory or knowledge of the details surrounding the birth. The more you know, the more cohesive your experiences will be. This can make them easier to cope with. Even painful knowledge can be empowering, and empowerment can help you heal.

Because obstetricians' offices are generally full of pregnant women and mothers with infants, you may want to ask for the first or last appointment of the day, or for one just before or after lunch. Many mothers of preemies find it too painful to be around women with blooming bellies or blossoming babies. If sitting in the waiting room feels uncomfortable, explain your situation to the receptionist when you arrive and ask to be seated in an exam room.

Sex and Contraception

Parents vary in their interest in sex after their premature baby is born. For some, sex provides the intimacy they crave; for others, it is too physically or emotionally draining. If you associate sex with getting pregnant, it can be a painful reminder of what you've lost.

Fatigue, soreness, and hormonal changes may also affect your interest in sex. You may be told to avoid vaginal penetration until your healing is checked at the six-week postpartum exam. Physically, you can resume intercourse when your bleeding stops and when you feel comfortable with penetration. It is important that intercourse be gentle. A water-soluble lubricant (such as Astroglide or K-Y Jelly) may be helpful in reducing discomfort. You can also substitute other ways of expressing intimacy and physical affection for intercourse for a time. (See Chapter 19 for more information on couples and sex.)

For some, the interval after a preterm birth is filled with longing for pregnancy. This longing can be confusing: are you longing for the remainder of the pregnancy you lost, or are you wishing for another pregnancy that you can complete? Some moms describe feeling terrified of ever being pregnant again. Others refuse contraception because they want to get pregnant again as quickly as possible. Still others can't even imagine being pregnant but also cannot tolerate the idea of using birth control.

If you are still recovering from pregnancy, you need time to heal physically before attempting another conception. Many parents also cite the burdens of caring for a preemie as a reason to wait. If you want to be certain not to conceive, you need to use birth control the first time you resume intercourse. You can get pregnant before your menstrual periods begin again; the first ovulation can happen at any time.

Contrary to popular myth, pumping and breast-feeding are not foolproof contraceptives. Additionally, your diaphragm will need to be refitted after each pregnancy to accommodate changes in the size of your cervix. This can be done at your six-week checkup, when your uterus and cervix have returned to their normal size and position. You will need to use other birth control methods in the meantime, such as condoms and foam. If you would prefer an oral contraceptive but are worried about contaminating your breast milk, ask your care provider about a brand considered compatible with breast-feeding. Discuss birth control with your doctor or midwife to find the method that is right for you. Take the time you need to make the decision about whether or when to pursue another pregnancy. (See Chapters 21 and 22 for more on subsequent pregnancy.)

Fatigue

Term mothers with uncomplicated deliveries experience fatigue during the postpartum period. It's a normal part of recovery. Mothers who deliver early have the same hormonal and physical readjustments. Plus, both parents also have the fatigue that accompanies dashed expectations and the grief and fear that come with having a hospitalized newborn. Health or delivery complications multiply the readjustment challenges, as do the physical demands of traveling back and forth to the hospital at a time when you should be in your cocoon at home.

Causes of Fatigue

Other factors can contribute to the fatigue you may feel. They include

- *Prenatal bed rest.* If you were on complete bed rest, your body is unaccustomed to much physical activity. You may be surprised at how long it can take for your muscles and your cardiovascular system to get back in shape. If you were tilted backward (Trendelenburg position) during your bed rest, you may also experience persistent backache.
- *Being an older parent.* If you're not in your early twenties any more, don't expect to be as energetic as the young parents you may see in the NICU. The older you are, the more tired you may be.
- *Adjusting to first-time parenthood.* Adjusting to both first-time parenthood and to parenting a preemie is a bigger adjustment than you'd planned. Expect to be more tired than you thought you would be. The uncertainty that may have replaced your predelivery confidence contributes

to this fatigue, as does feeling overwhelmed.

- *Adjusting to parenting a preemie.* If you're an experienced parent, you probably assumed you would know how to parent this baby. Now you recognize that you will have to learn to be a different kind of parent to a different kind of child. You probably didn't expect the additional stresses, lessons, and complicated logistics that accompany this baby. All of these produce more fatigue than you may have experienced with previous newborns.
- *Meeting the needs of your older children.* If you have older children, you may have assumed that this baby would fit right in to your family. Instead, your baby is in the NICU. This is not the kind of sibling adjustment you'd planned on. (See Chapter 19 for more on this subject.)
- *Adjusting to parenting multiples.* Although you may have had a number of weeks to adjust to the idea of more than one baby, your preparation time was cut short. Not only are you dealing with multiple babies, but with multiple hospitalized preemies, each with his or her own individual and perhaps complicated medical course. It's hard enough to deal with multiple babies; you may also have to deal with multiple medical realities.
- *Sliding from control to chaos.* Your life may have been humming along with everything fitting together and flowing smoothly. Now a monkey wrench has been thrown into the works. Dealing with chaos can be extremely tiring.
- *Worries about your baby.* The more complicated your baby's hospital course, the more drained of physical and emotional energy you'll feel. There is so much information to absorb and so many possibilities to consider. If your baby's prognosis is not good, you may feel overwhelmed by what lies ahead.
- *Dealing with uncertainty.* Those who like closure and hate suspense or loose ends may feel totally undone by the uncertainties presented by their preemie. When will your baby start gaining weight? Get off the ventilator? Be able to be held? Start feeding by mouth? Come home? Will your baby come through this without lasting medical problems or disabilities? When will he or she receive a clean bill of health and development? Uncertainty can be very exhausting.
- *Sleep deprivation.* Parents of preemies may think they're safe from sleep

deprivation because their baby is still in the hospital. But even though your baby isn't home yet, he or she can still keep you up at night with worry, pumping, and midnight calls to or from the NICU. (See the next section, "Sleep," for ways to deal with this.)

- *Worries about finances.* You may start receiving bills for NICU treatment even while your baby remains hospitalized. The stress of dealing with insurance companies, managing deductibles, and figuring out what parts of these bills are your responsibility can be crushing. If the mother was working before the birth, the loss of her income can add to the financial pressure. Stress over money coupled with worry about your baby can be unbearably exhausting. (See "Work and Home" in Chapter 20 for more on managing financial stress.)

Tips for Reducing Fatigue

Your fatigue is very real, so it's important to take it easy. Trying to take on too much too soon can exhaust you and prevent your physical and emotional healing. You'll get back on track more quickly by taking it slowly when you need to. The following suggestions may help reduce fatigue, which will increase your ability to cope with your emotions and to be with your baby, as well as to manage the activities of everyday life.

- *Reexamine your priorities.* Cut out all but the most essential of the essentials. Prioritize. Expend energy only on what *you* consider most important.
- *Make parenting number one.* Postpartum, your main job is to be a parent to your preemie. If you accomplish anything beyond that, you're over-achieving.
- *Learn to say no.* Don't take on any responsibilities that aren't key to your health and to your job as a parent.
- *Let others help.* Make a list of the things you need to have done, so that when friends ask how they can help, you can tell them on the spot. By letting friends help, you reduce their feelings of helplessness. Think of your chores as "therapy" for your friends and relatives. This might make assigning them easier. As an alternative, hire someone to do the household chores, the cooking, and to care for your other children.
- *Limit housekeeping.* Unless you have help, keep housekeeping to a minimum. Do *essential* housework and errands during the part of the

day when you feel most energetic.

- *Keep meals simple.* Takeout and paper plates were invented for a reason. Use them.
- *Sleep or rest whenever you find the opportunity.* Don't limit sleeping or relaxing to nighttime. You may not get enough sleep during the night if you are getting up to pump. Rest, sitting or lying down, whenever you can. Your body needs to use most of its energy reserve to heal itself. Help it do that by not taxing your system unnecessarily. Even if you can't sleep, staying in bed at night benefits your body.

Sleep

When I was up in the middle of the night—I had such bad insomnia during that time, I just couldn't sleep—I never knew if it would make me feel better to call the hospital. I didn't know if I was going to get good news or if it was going to be bad news. And if I got good news I still didn't know if it was going to make me feel good enough that I could go back to sleep. And usually the news was that there was no change. But I'd sit there for a half an hour, just debating about whether to call or not, being terrified to pick up the telephone, not knowing what the report would be. —Stephie

To parents of a preemie, the typical postpartum advice to get plenty of rest and sleep when your baby sleeps is meaningless or even callous. It is very common for parents of preemies to experience sleep disturbances. Your baby may sleep through most of the NICU stay, but you will most likely be wide-awake with worry. Getting up in the middle of the night to pump breast milk or to call the hospital to check on your baby definitely disrupts your sleep. Sleep deprivation is a natural part of parenthood, but it is usually more severe for parents of a preemie. These approaches can help you get the sleep you need:

- *Accept the inevitable.* While your baby is hospitalized, you may feel pressured to stock up on sleep in preparation for his or her homecoming. That can make it all the more disconcerting if you find you have trouble sleeping. Keep in mind that new parents are supposed to be up in the middle of the night. It's normal for thoughts and feelings about your baby to keep you awake, even though your baby isn't home yet.

Even getting up to pump your breasts is reassuring evidence that you are the mother of a new baby. Instead of resenting your lack of sleep, use the time to do restful things that help you feel close to your baby. Remind yourself that your sleeplessness links you with new parents everywhere. If it makes you feel closer to your baby, try sleeping in the nursery, cuddling a stuffed animal, or sleeping with a blanket that has your baby's smell. If you are wide-awake in the middle of the night, you might try calling the NICU to check on your baby. Somebody is there—and awake—around the clock. Staff are quite used to 3:00 A.M. calls from parents missing their little one. Even if you're afraid of what you might hear, getting a bad report may be less distressing than sitting in the dark with your imagination.

- *Clear your mind before bed.* Your mind needs time to think and to grieve. When you are very busy during the day, nighttime may be the only time you have for these activities. If this is the case, try setting aside time during the day to deal with your feelings. Riding the bus to work, writing in your journal, or going for a walk alone can give you time for your inner self. Writing down your emotions, thoughts, hopes, and wishes can release them from circulating in your mind. Doing this during the day can free your mind to relax and sleep at night. Writing may also help you get to sleep if you're having a restless night.

- *Sleep as long as you need to.* Don't be surprised if you need more hours of sleep than you did before the baby arrived. During the postpartum period, your physical healing may increase your requirements. Staying with your baby in the hospital, keeping aware of his or her medical conditions, learning how to meet your baby's needs, and caring for a preemie in the hospital or at home are all very strenuous.

- *Sleep when your body calls for it.* If you feel like napping during the day, do it. At night, as soon as you feel sleepy, get into bed and turn off the lights. If you put off sleep, you may get a second wind—and this may keep you from falling asleep later. By going to sleep when your body feels primed for it, you'll get a better quality sleep.

- *Don't worry too much about the occasional sleepless night.* Sleep research has shown that even if you awaken often during the night, you still get some sleep. Even if you believe that you "hardly slept a wink last night," you probably slept in short bouts if you stayed in bed with your eyes closed.

• • •

You may feel more tired than usual because you missed out on some needed *deep* sleep, but don't let the occasional restless night discourage you. You're probably getting more sleep than you realize.

- *Look for causes of ongoing sleeplessness.* If you feel as if you are hardly sleeping at all *night after night*, ask your doctor to prescribe a sleep study. This involves spending a night in a sleep lab, where you are hooked up to monitors and observed. There may be an underlying physical cause for your disrupted sleep that can be treated if it is identified.
- *Exercise during the day.* Physical exercise flushes your body with healthful biochemicals that can help you to feel more relaxed at bedtime and sleep more soundly.
- *Wind down at night.* Set aside time in the evening to wind down with a warm bath or shower, or some other quiet activity. Go to bed early and read. Then when you're ready to nod off, you can just do it. Establishing a familiar bedtime routine or ritual can calm you. Drink warm milk if that appeals to you. Avoid caffeine, which is found in many soft drinks, chocolate, coffee, and tea. Nicotine is another stimulant to avoid. Alcohol can also interfere with normal sleep patterns.
- *Arrange for quiet.* Research shows that people sleep more deeply in silence. If your partner wants to watch TV or listen to music, suggest that he or she use earphones. If you like to fall asleep to music, put it on an automatic timer that will turn it off. Use your storm windows year-round to block out street noise if possible. You can also buy foam earplugs at the drugstore.
- *Learn techniques to help you relax.* Practice relaxation techniques at bedtime or when you are awake in the night. For instance, close your eyes and think of gentle downward movement. Picture yourself floating down like a feather from the sky. (For more techniques, see the section on "Relaxation" later in this chapter.)

Nutrition and Exercise

After your baby's birth, life can be quite hectic. You may not have much of an appetite, or you may reach for foods that aren't particularly healthy just because they are quick and available. Especially if you are recovering from a difficult pregnancy or delivery, or if you are providing breast milk, it is important that you eat a well-balanced diet containing adequate protein, vitamins, and minerals. Ask your doctor or midwife about any special dietary needs or restrictions. Because you are under stress, it is important that you get enough B and C vitamins, iron, and zinc. You can continue to take prenatal vitamins, especially if you are breast-feeding. Drink plenty of water to keep your body functioning smoothly. If you are breast-feeding multiples, it is especially important that you choose highly nutritious foods and consume the extra calories you require.

Recognize the Pitfalls of Dieting

Like many postpartum moms, you may be concerned about getting your body back into its prepregnancy shape. You may feel impatient about losing weight and be tempted to go on a diet. But restricting your eating will merely add to the deprivation you already feel over your baby's early birth. Both physically and emotionally, your recovery will benefit from balance, not restriction. Instead of trying to achieve the "perfect" body, go after what you're really seeking—a sense of well-being and wellness.

Learn New Eating Patterns

To achieve a sense of well-being and wellness, replace dieting with natural eating patterns. Stop thinking of foods as "good" or "bad." All foods are good; some are just more healthful than others. The only forbidden foods should be those you find distasteful. When you stop forbidding yourself food, you take away its power over you. Give yourself permission to eat whatever you want, whenever you want. Stop thinking, "This is my last chance to indulge—the deprivation starts Monday." As you establish more-balanced eating patterns in which you reach for healthy foods because they are the ones your body needs, junk food won't need to be banned. It just won't be very appealing. You will learn to associate healthy eating with feeling well nourished.

Substitute Exercise for Dieting

Exercise is far more beneficial to overall health and fitness than cutting calories. It keeps your body strong and your metabolism humming.

Of course, during the first few weeks after delivery, you may be too tired, weak, sore, or vulnerable for exercise. Many obstetricians suggest waiting three to six weeks following an uncomplicated vaginal delivery before beginning physical exercise (often until bleeding stops). If you had complications, a cesarean delivery, or especially if you were on extended bed rest, you may need to resume activity very gradually. Physical therapy can be very helpful for mothers whose muscles atrophied while they were on bed rest. Ask your doctor or midwife if you have any special exercise requirements or restrictions. Also listen to your body and respect its limitations. For a while, you may need rest far more than you need physical activity.

Fit Exercise into Your Everyday Life

As your body recuperates, it will be able to benefit from exercise. Engage in activities that are fun and relaxing for you, at a pace that is enjoyable. Forcing yourself to do tedious or punishing workouts can cost both your body and your spirit much more than they gain.

You may feel that you don't have the time or the energy for exercise, but even a walk around the block can clear your mind and benefit your body. If you are feeling pressed for time—after all, you want to spend every spare minute you can with your baby in the NICU—make exercise a part of your hospital routine. Park the car a little farther away from the hospital entrance each day until you're at least a ten-minute walk away. Or get off a few bus stops earlier. Find the stairs and use them instead of the elevator. Park at the far end of the shopping center or mall lot. Make walking a way to spend time with friends or your partner. If you weave exercise into your everyday life, it won't seem like just another time-eating chore.

Recognize the Emotional Benefits of Exercise

After postpartum recovery, many mothers notice that physical activity helps reduce stress and helps them cope with their feelings. A bicycle ride can lift depression. Hitting a tennis ball can be a good outlet for tension. Dancing or exercising to music can reduce anxiety. Playing golf, basketball, or volleyball is a way to spend fun time with others. Gardening or vacuuming the whole house can give you a feeling of accomplishment. Once you discover that exercise adds to your sense of well-being, it becomes more appealing and rates a place on your list of priorities.

Accept Your Body

You just had a baby. As a new mother (especially if you're breast-feeding), enjoy the motherly softness of your body that follows childbirth. With time, good nutrition, and gentle exercise, you will feel better physically and emotionally, and your body will return to what is normal for you. Find ways to nurture yourself and your body. Sleeping, resting, taking a long bath, spending time alone just thinking, doing something creative or artistic, talking to a friend, and getting massages are all ways to feed yourself, body and soul.

Relaxation

Along with nutrition and exercise, relaxation can help reduce fatigue, anxiety, and insomnia. A relaxed body can put its resources into healing.

There are a number of good audiotapes and videotapes on progressive relaxation techniques, including yoga and meditation. Other approaches to body relaxation include consciously releasing muscle tension, using imagery, listening to music, humor, and simply breathing deeply.

Releasing Muscle Tension

To release muscle tension, lie down in a comfortable position with your body weight supported. Relax your facial muscles—your jaw, your eyes, your brow. Then, starting with your toes (and then your feet, ankles, calves, and so on), slowly relax each body part, working your way up to your scalp. Some people find it helpful to clench each muscle or part before relaxing it. Breathe deeply and completely. As you relax, you may find that your tears start to flow. This emotional release deepens your ability to relax.

Imagery

To use imagery to relax, close your eyes and imagine a place that makes you feel peaceful: a sun-drenched sandy beach on a turquoise sea; a clear, cool mountain lake nestled beneath snowy peaks; the shimmering heat of rose-colored canyons. Picture the details of your scene—the sights, sounds, smells, and textures that please and relax you. This is a place you can always go to feel relaxed and at peace. Practice going to your place when you are calm so that you'll be able to retreat there easily when you are in crisis mode and need a break.

Parenting Your Premature Baby and Child

Music

Listening to music you enjoy can also have a calming effect. Gregorian chants, a cappella pieces, New Age recordings, and Native American flute music have very soothing qualities. Recordings of nature sounds can also be quite restful.

Laughter

Humor sets off beneficial biochemical reactions in your body and brain, making it very therapeutic. Appreciate the funny things you see and hear. Find humor in daily living—in the situations you find yourself in or in the interactions you have with others. Even dark humor can reduce tension. Set aside time to read humorous books or to watch a TV show that tickles your funny bone. If you have e-mail, tell your correspondents to forward the funny stuff your way.

Other Relaxing Activities

Try making a list of the friends and activities you find relaxing. Refer to the list when you are looking for a break or if you need a reminder that life still has its rewards. Make time for something pleasurable every day. Recognize that you deserve to take time out to relax. Socializing, recreation, and hobbies are as important as good food, exercise, and sleep to your recovery.

If it helps, include relaxing activities on your priority list. If you feel that you don't have time to relax, try making a list of *everything* you did today, including all the things you did for your baby. Seeing how much you are doing can help you get a handle on where the hours in the day are going. Looking over that long list can give you a sense of achievement *and* permission to relax.

Complementary Medicine

If you have physical or emotional complaints that are not being adequately addressed or treated by Western medicine, you may want to look into alternatives. Although traditional medicine tends to have success treating acute infections and traumatic injuries, there are many problems (such as migraines, asthma, sinusitis, yeast infections, depression, infertility, arthritis, back pain, and allergies) that may respond to alternative therapies. Alternatives sometimes offer fewer side effects and may address underlying causes rather than just alleviate symptoms. Some alternative therapies complement Western medicine, and your physicians may recommend that you try them.

Among these alternative approaches are "lifestyle" programs that focus on healthful eating—macrobiotic or vegetarian diets, natural and organically grown foods, food supplements—and managing stress—yoga, meditation, and other relaxation techniques (see the previous section). Other approaches focus on the mind-body connection, including biofeedback, visualization, art or music therapy, hypnotherapy, and prayer. There are "touch" therapies, such as chiropractic and massage. Finally, there are therapies traditionally used in other cultures, including acupuncture and herbs from China; Ayur Veda, an ancient healing system from India; homeopathy, a microdose pharmacology from Europe; and Native American healing practices, such as the sweat lodge. Exploring alternatives that appeal to you can be worthwhile.

To protect yourself from quackery, use the following guidelines:

- Get referrals from people you trust who've had experience with the alternative you are considering.
- If you don't feel comfortable with a certain practitioner (the pairing is not a "good fit"), look for someone else.
- Be skeptical of unrealistic claims or cures that require little effort, especially on the practitioner's part.
- Have realistic expectations. No therapy helps everyone, all the time. Otherwise, everyone would be flocking to it.
- Avoid practitioners who tell you that the medical establishment wants to keep its remedies secret. Besides displaying their own paranoia and preying on others', their intent may be to discourage you from getting other opinions.
- Work with people who are willing and able to explain the rationale behind the treatments they recommend. Good medicine arises from a coherent and consistent system of ideas and observations. If a cure is "magic" or "miraculous" or if its practitioner can't explain it in a way that makes sense to you, it means that the practitioner is deceiving you or doesn't understand what he or she is doing.
- Demand credentials, such as rigorous education from accredited schools and certification or licensing from accrediting bodies.
- Keep in mind that even though an herb is "natural," it can be just as potent as a prescription drug, can have side effects, and can interact in a negative way with other medications you may be taking. Always consult

your health care provider for advice on using herbal or other "natural" or unregulated remedies that you can purchase over the counter.

Points to Remember

- Expect the combination of postpartum adjustment and adjustment to parenting a preemie to intensify the emotional consequences of each.
- If your behaviors or emotions are compromising your ability to function, you deserve to get the assistance, support, counseling, and medical attention you need.
- Take care of your body as a way to help you cope with your emotions. Nurturing yourself is the first step in being able to nurture your baby.
- As a mother, if you feel disappointed with how much you can't seem to accomplish, remember that your main job right now is to be a mommy. Eating, drinking water, resting, relaxing, exercising, and, especially, pumping and spending time with your baby are all *essential tasks* that you are completing. If you accomplish anything else, you are overachieving.
- Practice relaxation techniques; eat healthy foods; and do some gentle, fun exercise to help you cope with fatigue, insomnia, and anxiety, and reach for a sense of well-being.
- Find the time to grieve and to think, talk, and write about your baby, especially during the day.
- Honor your unique needs for sleep, physical recovery, nutrition, exercise, relaxation, and sexual intimacy.
- Explore complementary medicine or alternative treatments if you believe that Western medicine is not meeting all your health care needs.

Parenting Your Premature Baby and Child

CHAPTER SEVEN

Acclimating to the NICU

Generally, a premature baby is not fully prepared for life outside the mother's body, and premature parents are not fully prepared for life inside their baby's new quarters: the neonatal intensive care unit, or NICU.

When your baby is first whisked away to the NICU, you may feel both fearful and lost, left behind and out of the loop. The doctors and nurses providing your baby with skilled care speak in an alien language about stuff you've never heard of. Even if you toured the NICU before your baby's delivery, the sights, sounds, smells, technology, and activity of intensive care are still unfamiliar. Seeing all the tiny babies, some of whom may die, can be very distressing. What about *your* tiny baby, you wonder.

They moved me to the maternity floor, and we waited for the call from the NICU that would say we could go see the baby that we had just had. The longer the time stretched, the more anxious we became. We had been told that it would take time to get Thaddeus set up and evaluated, but we became afraid that something was wrong. I tried to make conversation, but half my mind was up three floors with the baby I didn't yet know. Finally, we got the call saying we could go up and see our son. I was put in a wheelchair, and we entered the NICU, the artificial womb that we all would live in for a while.
—*Laurie*

Mothers who are still recuperating from delivery may be unable or reluctant to go to the NICU. As much as you long to be with your baby, you may feel too overwhelmed, too afraid to follow through on that longing.

He was so small. How could a person so small hold on to life? I remember wondering if he was in pain because of all the equipment he was hooked up to. ... I felt so bad because my new baby was all alone in the big world. His mommy was only able to spend short amounts of time with him. —Cynthia

I wanted to be there, but—and I don't know if I was finding excuses not to be there or if I had to go back to pump in my room—there was always something that made me not be there. It was too much to handle in the beginning. —Gallice

I was on morphine for the next two days and was very foggy about a lot of things. I had a fever and was not allowed to go see the baby. Privately I was thankful. I was terrified of seeing him. I had no idea what to expect. At the same time, I was terrified that he would die before I got to see him. —Laura

Early on, it's natural to be frightened by the technology and equipment that surrounds your baby, and you may be startled by every alarm that sounds. But as you learn your way around the equipment, you'll soon be able to interpret the lights and noise, and the NICU will seem less overwhelming. For instance, many machines are monitoring devices: all they do is measure your baby's heartbeat, temperature, or breathing rate. The sound of an alarm doesn't necessarily mean that your baby is in serious trouble. The alarms are set to go off *before* the situation is critical. They indicate that your baby needs attention or some corrective action to *avoid* a serious problem. So, when you hear an alarm, look at your baby before panicking. Be reassured by regular breathing, quiet resting, and good color.

You can also expect to be overwhelmed by the intense climate inside the NICU. Tim recalls, "You could tell when things were upbeat, and you could tell when things were going bad because people would talk in whispers or quieter tones or there'd be times when the nurses would be crying."

Finally, it is normal to be intimidated by the complex terms and unfamiliar words, as well as by the busy, knowledgeable medical staff. Every diagnosis sounds so frightening and so serious. You wonder how you'll ever understand your baby's conditions, master the medical language, and most of all, trust these strangers with your precious newborn.

I felt constantly overwhelmed, not only with intense feelings, but also with information. At times I felt as if I would never understand everything that was happening. —Claire

On my discharge day, it was so hard to leave. I was afraid to leave him. You've just started to bond, and with all your anxieties and fears, now you're going away from him. It really hurts because you don't trust anything at that point. You don't know he's in loving hands yet. You think you have to be there all the time to protect him. —Gallice

Our 100 days in the NICU were 100 days on another planet. My son's life depended on these people. My life depended on those people. Would they be kind to him, listen, respond, care, make good decisions? —Susan

When your baby is first admitted to intensive care, all you may hear is "intensive." As you acclimate, though, you'll begin to see and appreciate the "care" part of the term. While you regain your strength and can spend more time with your baby, the NICU will begin to feel familiar to you. When you start to understand what is going on around your little one, you begin to find your place in the NICU *and* as your baby's parent.

Warming Up

For the next two days, I visited the nursery often, but only with my husband. I was still afraid to do much by myself. I was still overwhelmed by everything. Once I was released from the hospital, I quickly adjusted to visiting by myself. After my first solo visit, I began to relax and rely on the nurses for help when I didn't know what to do. —Kimberly

It took me a few days to be comfortable. It's hard to cope with. I didn't want to be there. In my mind, I was still pregnant, even though he wasn't in my tummy any more ... so it took me a couple of days to adjust. The third day was better. And then I wanted to be there most of the time. —Gallice

Most parents don't jump eagerly and fully into the NICU experience. Instead, they stick a hesitant foot in the door, one toe at a time. Those who are cautious or reserved by nature may take more time to adjust than those who are more confident or extroverted. Give yourself the time you need to acclimate—to the NICU, the technology, the language, and the medical staff. Soon you will become familiar with the policies, knowledgeable about treatments and equipment, fluent in the terminology, and friendly with the staff.

In addition to the challenge the NICU itself presents, you must also figure out a different parenting role, one that will work for you and your premature baby. This can be the most important part of acclimating to this place. It is also a painful challenge because you feel robbed of so many precious moments. It may seem that you and your baby are missing out on something critical and fun: the joys of bonding and early parenthood.

Getting Oriented

To adapt to the realities of parenthood in the NICU, a look back at history may help put your situation into perspective. Childbirth and infancy have always held a degree of peril. In the past, throughout the world, maternal and infant mortality were shockingly high as a result of infections and other complications of pregnancy and childbirth. By the early 1900s, most prospective parents in Western cultures welcomed medicine's efforts to tame labor, delivery, and infant care with "modern, civilized" methods.

With advances in medicine, science, and industry, "natural" childbirth fell out of favor. By the 1950s, childbirth had moved out of the home and into the hospital. Labor and delivery were managed by doctors and became a passive medical experience for the mother. Newborns were kept in sterile isolation. Breast milk was considered inferior to scientifically developed formula, and breast-feeding was seen as crude. Mothers were told that cuddling might endanger their babies' well-being. Fathers were an afterthought. In short, the joys of bonding and early parenthood were dismissed.

In recent decades, however, routine obstetric and newborn care has again changed dramatically for term babies and their parents. Cultural values have shifted back toward honoring the ways and balance of nature, including the instincts and preferences of parents. Childbirth and breast-feeding are now viewed as natural processes. Parents are requesting less-invasive medical options, and hospitals are adopting the attitudes and methods developed by birthing centers, where mothers and their partners take an active role in labor and delivery. In addition, scientists have "discovered" the existence and importance of parent-infant bonding, and this has changed newborn nursery practices around the world. As mothers and fathers have reclaimed their right to be close to their babies after delivery, the interior decor of many maternity wards has become more homelike. Childbirth and postpartum care have again become family centered.

But during preterm delivery and in the NICU, family-centered care can be slightly behind the curve. Due to the technology involved and the emergency situations that often arise, the environment is often less family friendly. Parents of preemies can't help but compare their distressing, hospital-centered experiences to the "good," family-centered experiences that many parents of term infants have. The whole preemie experience mirrors the hospital experience of the past: medical delivery, newborn isolation, mechanical feeding, prohibited cuddling. Of course, this medical management and focus on technology can save lives.

You may embrace this focus because it can do wonders for your tiny baby. You may feel fortunate that your baby is in such a "safe" place, and your concerns for your infant's well-being may override your wishes to get close to your little one. At the same time, though, you may resent your exclusion from the "new" approach to newborn care and early parenting. With all the technology surrounding your newborn, it looks like there's no room for you to take an active parenting role with your fragile baby.

But as you settle into the NICU, you will discover that another revolution is happening right now, one focused on the care and parenting of premature babies. NICU medical specialists are increasingly addressing such issues as emotional support for parents and developmental care for premature babies. New ideas about involving parents in their baby's care are sprouting from the research and experiences of farsighted neonatologists and other professionals. Some hospitals are just beginning to learn that instead of requiring families to adjust to the NICU, the NICU should adjust to families. Other hospitals are actively implementing this approach. (See the next section, "The

Growth of Developmentally Supportive Care," for more on this subject.)

Given that newborn intensive care is still in the midst of a revolution, you may be frustrated sometimes by the lack of sensitivity or responsiveness to your emotional or parenting needs. It may help to keep in mind that policies and attitudes are the way they are *not* because of hostile intent. The first step in saving babies was the invention and installation of the technology; without it, few preemies would survive. Now, as attention turns toward the holistic needs of babies and parents, the system is gradually evolving beyond the technology to address emotional and familial needs. Just as you and your baby need time and experience to develop and grow, so does the world of high-risk pregnancy management and NICU care. Your medical teams are on the cutting edge and face a steep learning curve as they figure out how to balance and integrate medical and emotional needs.

With that in mind, you *should* make your needs known in the NICU. As modern-day health care consumers, most of us have absorbed the need to be in charge of our medical care and ask questions. However, we are still learning how to take charge of our *emotional* care and voice our emotional needs and concerns. As we are becoming more aware and skilled in the emotional arena, health care providers are becoming more responsive and able to work with patients in that regard. Just as you expect specialists to guide you through the medical experiences that face you and your baby, remember that you can guide *them* through the emotional side of this equation. By practicing emotional advocacy for our babies and ourselves, each of us can contribute to improving family-centered care for those who come after us.

The Growth of Developmentally Supportive Care

Most parents are unsure of how they fit into the NICU, especially at first, when their access to their baby may be most limited. Sometimes, the medical staff will hesitate to let parents touch or hold babies who are ventilated or recovering from surgery. You may deeply resent the fact that your baby has "gatekeepers" who may tell you to back off. You may not see these people as your allies, your teammates, and your advisors—yet.

In the beginning I didn't even try to ask too many questions. I didn't try to learn the nurses' names. I wasn't there for social hour. It was pretty much just trying to sit at their bedsides and talk to them. Then the nurses taught me how

to touch them—like, you're not supposed to stroke them but kind of cup them.
Their skin was so paper thin that it would rip, so we had to be very careful.
When I was shown that, I was so grateful. Some of the nurses wouldn't let
you even do that, but the ones who would, I was grateful. —Stephie

A question that kept running through my mind was "Why do they get to know
more about my daughter than I do?" And at first the nurses and the neonatolo-
gists kind of intimidated me, but after I had a chance to get to know them,
they were not so bad. —Stacy

Fortunately, the best state-of-the-art NICU policy and practice involves
parents and encourages them to get close to their babies. Rikki recalls asking
to go see her babies a few hours after delivery, in the middle of the night: "I
expected an argument but was given a wheelchair instead." The focus today is
on gentle, responsive, supportive care for babies who need intensive care. But
it wasn't always this way.

A Short History of NICU Care
In the late 1960s and early 1970s, when neonatology was a brand-new
specialty, it was standard practice to keep babies distant, untouchable, and
surrounded by technology under the assumption that this would speed their
recovery. Unfortunately, as it turns out, many of these practices were bad for
babies. Deprived of their parents' presence and touch, babies were stressed
further. Bombarded by lights and noises, preemies' immature nervous systems
were often overwhelmed. As a result, healthy development and immune
function were inhibited.

Technology-centered NICU policies also had a devastating effect on
many parents. Parents were often treated like intruders, making it difficult for
them to form close connections with their babies. Discouraged from asking
questions and communicating their concerns, parents felt powerless, alone,
and incompetent.

As survival rates climbed, so did the population of NICU babies—
and the number of vocal parents who wanted, *needed,* to be more involved and
close to their infants. These parents also pressed for certain issues to be
addressed, such as a gentler, more nurturing environment for their babies;
adequate pain control; parental decision-making power; and closer attention

to long-range outcomes, not just survival statistics. So, in the 1980s and especially the 1990s, neonatology hit its stride. By that time it could afford to turn its focus from the remarkable technology that was saving lives to the *quality* of those lives, both during hospitalization and after discharge.

Today an important feature of the most modern NICU practice is *developmentally supportive care,* care that promotes, sustains, and enhances the physical, emotional, and intellectual development of preemies while they are in the NICU. More specifically, developmentally supportive care respects the infant's immature nervous system and includes low lights, hushed sounds, warmth, swaddling, nesting, gentle touch, and adequate pain control. The goal is treating each baby as an individual and determining what his or her special sensitivities and thresholds are. That way, medical staff can tailor their handling to your baby's unique needs. Indeed, your baby may grow faster and fight infection better when not taxed by unnecessary stimulation. Other examples of supportive care include proper body containment (swaddling, nesting) and careful positioning to improve posture and muscle tone development, better oxygenation techniques, and protection from constant or bright lights to avoid damage to the eyes.

These developmentally supportive practices improve preemies' quality of life during their NICU stay and can result in better outcomes beyond the NICU. It makes sense that gentle, supportive care would improve health and development, and it is certainly the most humane way to treat tiny babies. It is also less distressing to witness and helps parents feel better about entrusting their baby to the NICU.

Because developmentally supportive care is responsive to the infant's needs, this type of care reinforces the parents' own nurturing urges. And as parents have been invited into the NICU and encouraged to participate in their infant's care, researchers have noted that this participation seems to benefit not only the baby, but also the parents and family. Instead of feeling at odds with NICU policies, parents feel comfortable with them and see that their instincts are valued. When the care plan includes breast-feeding and/or kangaroo care (holding of a diapered infant, covered with a blanket, against the parent's bare chest), the mother and father can experience that they are intimately necessary to their baby's health. And in spite of the trials of hospitalization and separation, they can feel their role as parents.

Indeed, involving parents in their infant's developmentally supportive care is *developmentally supportive for the parents* as well. Your presence, questions, advocacy, and involvement in your baby's care should be an integral part of your NICU experience, because these promote

- Your developing identity as a parent
- Your developing competence as you become a different kind of parent to a different kind of child
- Your developing collaborative abilities with NICU staff
- Your developing ability to cope with intense, often painful emotions

For instance, at a time when your relationship with your baby is the most fragile, participating in his or her care helps you feel competent and connected to your newborn. You practice being attuned to your baby. You learn new skills in relating to and collaborating with your baby's medical caregivers. The emotional support you receive from these caregivers shows you that your feelings are normal, puts you in touch with your needs, and offers guidance in how to cope. In short, this close contact is not just important to your baby, it's important to *you.*

I gained confidence in myself as a parent, especially because the NICU allowed us and taught us how to be active in our son's care (taking temps, swabbing his mouth, sponge-bathing him, and so on). Being allowed to do these things brought home the fact that this was my living baby and I was a very active and good parent. Without realizing it, I became very comfortable with touching/handling my son and grew to love him very deeply. —Andrea

NICU policies and practices are finally reflecting what parents have known all along: medical technology is important for preemies, but so is nurturing and a parent's touch. Providing a developmentally supportive environment for the whole family can have beneficial effects on the medical status and developmental outcomes of babies—and their parents.

The nurse who was his primary was on, and she put us right into that role of parent. She oriented us to the systems there and told us we had access to every scrap of information about him. She also helped us learn immediately how to touch him and what would be soothing to him. She got us in touch with him right away, and that helped a lot. —Laurie

There was one nurse (isn't there always) who seemed more concerned with being in charge than with being helpful. Other than that, I was so pleased with the way the NICU was handled. —Jill

Coping with the Technology-Centered NICU

NICUs vary in how much they encourage mothers and fathers to take an active role in parenting their babies. Some hospitals provide tremendous support, inclusion, access to information, and emotional space for parents to learn and grow at their own pace. Other hospitals hesitate to make room for parents on the care team or fail to provide adequate support for emotional and parenting issues. Many times, the baby's medical condition at a given time governs how much parents are encouraged to interact with their preemies. In some hospitals that are still in the process of instituting a more family-centered approach, the climate is determined by the staff on duty.

I was grateful for anything that I could do that was somewhat of a normal experience because I knew [the babies] needed to be held and touched and I felt so bad that I couldn't. If it were up to me, I would have taken them home and had private care so that I could have had some say in what was happening. The technology and stuff didn't scare me—it was the "unlovingness" of it that scared me. That they needed the nurturing and they weren't getting it, that's the part that bothered me. If anybody needed it, they needed it—more than any healthy baby did. —Stephie

I was his mother, and that was it, although sometimes I had to remind the staff to let me know of things that were happening because sometimes they sort of forgot that the child had parents. —Pascale

Each twelve hours someone new took control of my child. Some were warm and inclusive and opened the door to me and my ability to begin to learn to be a mommy. Some were cold and controlling and kept me firmly on the fringes of my child's care. A few have become lifelong friends; a few have become enduring bad memories. Most fell somewhere in between. But when we were there, when I was waiting to see who would live, who would die, what would happen next, I was completely at their mercy. —Susan

Understandably, how the hospital staff welcomes you has an effect on your adjustment to parenting in the NICU. Your ways of coping and your efforts to parent your baby may or may not fit with the culture of the unit. If the fit is good, you are likely to feel comfortable while your baby is hospitalized. If the fit is not good, though, or if the fit does not accommodate your growing and changing needs, you may struggle to feel accepted and appreciated in the NICU and feel thwarted in your attempts to be an active parent.

One of the doctors yelled across the room for me not to touch my child one morning. He said, "I just told you that he needs his sleep." Now this doctor didn't know that I sat at the end of Casey's bed for sixteen hours a day and left his blanket over his bed so he could sleep. Part of our ritual was that first thing (when I was sure my hands were cleanest) I would reach in and touch him and say good morning. That day I had to leave feeling that he wasn't even my baby! —Kelly

I had to worry that he would desat while I was holding him. That used to piss me off, because the nurses could do all their stuff to him and do whatever they were going to do, and then you go to hold your baby and they think you've ruined him for the day. That used to make me mad! —Stephie

You have no control. I was like, "Could you please just listen to me? Maybe I know a little bit. Please, just listen to me. Just listen to me. How much can it hurt to listen to me? I'm not going to try to cause her any harm!" —Michelle

Asking for a more active role and being given it can make you an agent for change in your NICU. Jo explains how that happened in her NICU.

We refused to leave during rounds. Our rationale was that it was our child and we were going to be involved in her care. We also spent long hours in the medical library and on the Net looking for information. In fact, it got to such a stage that our neonatologist would ask us what our thoughts were during rounds. What really gave us confidence was the spirited debates that would be conducted by Ngioka's bedside during rounds. Our neonatologist, Scott, was willing to accept input from everyone—nurses, residents, and parents—everyone who had a stake in Ngioka. This made us feel that (a) her carers were willing to get the latest and best information available in relation to Ngioka's situation and (b) her neonatologist didn't have the "I am God … and therefore my word is law" complex and was willing to accept input.

Later on, when she was in Bay 3, a couple of the nurses tried to enforce the "no parents during rounds" rule. The neonatologists actually asked where we were and said we could be there for rounds. They also started to ask what we had been observing, and a "parent sheet" was placed by all babies' bedsides for the parents to write on. The rationale for this was that the parents were sitting by the baby's bedside watching. A nurse was responsible for two or three babies, and therefore not in a position to notice everything.

While we were in a situation that made us feel hopeless, this small gesture from our neonatologist empowered us. In some very small way, he made us feel as if we were an integral part of Ngioka's care team. —Jo

If you ask for a more active role but are refused, you may wonder what impact these limitations will have (or did have) on your growing relationship with your baby. Try to remember that parents and babies are resilient. Forming a relationship is a flexible process. However, you do need to grieve for what you feel you are missing or have missed. Doing so will free you to find meaningful ways to be with your baby during and after hospitalization. (For more on this topic, see Chapters 8, 9, and 13.)

Certainly, the more family-centered your NICU's approach, the more effective you'll feel as a parent. But even if your NICU is more technology centered, you can still parent successfully. Chapters 8 and 9 look at the process of developing a parenting relationship with your baby in the NICU.

The remainder of this chapter examines three skills you can learn as you grow familiar with your baby's NICU:

- Becoming a member of your baby's health care team
- Being informed
- Advocating for your baby

Joining Your Baby's Health Care Team

It is very important that you form good working relationships with the medical staff in your baby's NICU. You benefit because you are more likely to be kept informed and given the chance to do some real caregiving, and your baby benefits from your presence and involvement. Family-centered NICU medical professionals recognize the valuable role parents play and embrace them as members of the health care team.

I distinctly remember during Buddy's last week, having a nurse ask me if I would like to help change his central line dressing. I remember this incredible excitement and anticipation as I put on a gown, a mask, and some gloves. All I really did was make sure that Buddy's arms didn't get in the way, but to me it represented a few things. First, I was able to help in the care of my son. I can't [overstate] the importance of that. Second, there was a sense that the staff saw me as competent because they had asked me to help, and in a way, I thought, "They wouldn't ask me to help unless they thought I was good enough and capable of doing it." Third, I felt like I could—and would—do a "better" job than anyone else. I believed I could read my son's behavioral signs of discomfort or irritation, and that I was uniquely qualified to do something about it. I could talk to him softly. I could gently move his arms. I could reposition him if it looked awkward. I wasn't real concerned about the central line site. I was concerned about how "the patient," my child, was doing. —Ed

As you consider what it means to become an integral part of your baby's health care team, you may protest, "But I'm not a doctor, I'm just a parent." Especially if you tend to place medical professionals on a pedestal, you may feel inferior to these people who are looking after your baby—and you may believe that your baby's health care providers see you that way too. But you're not inferior, you're simply *different:* you bring another perspective, a different orientation, and an extra level of dedication to the team. Rest assured that these health care professionals *expect* you to ask questions. They know that you need to learn how to take care of your baby.

You may envy the parent of a preemie who happens to be a nurse or a physician, but unless the parent's specialty is neonatology, he or she is most likely as uninformed about premature babies as you are. These parents often feel doubly incompetent, both as parents and as medical professionals. They need information as much as any other parent but may feel especially awkward about asking questions, afraid to show their lack of medical knowledge. One mother talks about how this physician-as-parent dynamic endangered her son's life after he was discharged:

What I'm really sad about is that no one ever mentioned RSV to us. They said, "Be careful, wash your hands." And that's another thing I feel bad about: because we are physicians, people expect you to know about your baby, and they forget that you're a normal parent. That's really hard because you feel embarrassed to ask certain things that a normal parent would be allowed to ask. They expect you to know things, or maybe they don't even think of telling you something. You may be a physician, but it's a completely different field, so I feel bad that nobody mentioned RSV to us. —Gallice

Consider this: you *want* your baby's health care providers to assume you are an ignorant parent, so they'll teach you everything they can. Whether you work in a health profession or not, ask questions, and let yourself be tutored and coached.

If your specialty happens to be neonatology, you can expect to feel extraordinarily powerless as you are asked to step aside. You also probably know what it's like to take care of an infant born to an NICU professional—it can be nerve-wracking because they are qualified to scrutinize every detail of your caregiving. Now that *you* are in the position of being a vigilant parent, you don't want to intimidate the staff taking care of your baby.

As neonatologists, we expect parents of babies to let us do the "doctoring" while they sit back and are parents. Especially when parents are health care providers, we tell them that they are not doctors or nurses or physical therapists but that they are the father or the mother of the baby. Now, all of a sudden, I realized how hard and unrealistic these expectations were. ... All of a sudden, I found myself in the role of a wild animal trying to fight off any harm that might befall its young. I fought very hard the impulse to push the staff away so that I could do the job myself, and I was only successful because our baby started to do well shortly into her life. —Christoph

Forming Relationships with Medical Staff

Forming relationships with medical staff can be an intimidating task. You become acquainted under duress, and you may resent the amount of power they seemingly have over your baby and your life. You may feel that nobody can give your baby the kind of sensitive, loving care you can.

I hated seeing him so lonely in his incubator and with his bandages and wires everywhere. I wished that the nurses would hold him more, especially when I was too sick to. —Ruby

I learned quickly in the NICU that nurses wield incredible power. My children were dependent on a nurse to recognize the symptoms that required a physician's intervention. [The nurse's] attentiveness and reactions can literally have life-and-death implications for a critically ill child. And [the nurses] set the tone for my life when I was there. —Susan

We didn't completely trust that everybody there was doing their best to take care of our kids. Even though they're professionals and are good at what they're doing, I guess I felt that nobody cared about [our babies] as much as I did. So I was very watchful of the nurses and quickly came to appreciate some nurses over others. —Debbie

At first, you may feel wary of *all* the doctors and nurses because you don't really know them. And there are so many of them. It may seem as if there is an endless parade of new faces at your baby's bedside, particularly if your baby is in the NICU of a medical center or a teaching hospital. You may wonder how your baby can possibly receive any consistent care. Is anybody really keeping a close eye on your child?

The nursing staff are the key to your baby's care. Neonatal nurses are highly trained specialists. Many hospitals assign a primary nursing rotation for each baby so that twenty-four hours a day, seven days a week, one of your baby's primary nurses will be on duty. Your baby's nurses become familiar with you and devoted to understanding and meeting your baby's individual needs. Depending on the unit, your baby's primary nurses may be responsible for:

- Assessing your baby's condition and progress
- Notifying the doctors of any changes
- Making recommendations to the doctors and other members of the health care team
- Carrying out doctors' orders
- Planning and implementing all nursing care, such as feeding, bathing, positioning, administering prescribed medicines, and managing IVs
- Being involved in parent education

- Supervising the care your baby receives from other specialists and assistants
- Being involved in discharge planning

The doctors are experts in neonatal medicine, but the primary nurses become experts on your baby's unique, broad, hour-to-hour profile. Therefore, if you have questions about how your baby is doing today, ask your baby's primary nurses. Nurses can be your main source of information and insights about your baby's medical status, as well as his or her temperament, behavior, sensitivities, communication, feedings, triumphs, and challenges. In time, as you all take care of your baby, you can form close relationships with your baby's primary nurses.

> *The nurses became our family for the three months we were there. We shared our day-to-day lives with them. They knew the babies as well as, if not better than, we did! They were the people we entrusted with our babies' lives—the ones we left them with when we left the hospital. Had I not had the relationship I did with the nurses, I never could have left every day. —Sara*

Of course, nurses work closely with doctors. Compared with the nursing staff, whose scheduling tends to be consistent and predictable, the group of doctors on your NICU may change often. In a teaching hospital, the doctors you encounter will have varying amounts of experience, depending on what year of training they're in. Even though all these doctors have graduated from medical school, you may cringe at the thought of an intern (first year out) or a resident (second or third year out) taking care of your baby. Keep in mind that interns work with residents, fellows, or neonatal nurse practitioners (nurses with advanced degrees and training in caring for critically ill newborns), and residents are closely supervised by a team of neonatologists.

Having a team of doctors means that at least one neonatologist is available in the hospital around the clock, every day of the year. *When your baby is unstable or needs critical medical attention, a neonatologist is called in.* The attending neonatologist may call in other physicians who specialize in cardiology (heart), neurology (nervous system), pulmonology (lungs), or other areas. Remember that everyone's number one priority in the NICU is discovering and meeting babies' medical needs. If you are uncomfortable with the care your baby is receiving from any of the doctors, ask your nurse to contact the attending neonatologist for a consultation—*immediately* if necessary—or make the contact yourself.

Because there are so many people on your baby's health care team, you may feel lost. When you have questions, who should you ask? How can you contact a neonatologist or a specialist? How will you understand and remember the information these care providers give you? Here are some suggestions:

- *Recognize that you are an integral member of the health care team.* Even when you still have so much to learn, your presence, input, and questions are critical to your baby's care. The doctors and nurses know that when you are involved and understand what's going on, you can be a better advocate for your baby. As you grow more confident and look toward discharge, consider yourself to be in training to become the *leader* of your baby's team—because after your baby is discharged, you will be.
- *Identify your contacts.* Ask your baby's doctor whom you should contact when you want to check on your baby from home, and whom you should talk to when you have questions or concerns. Write down the names, phone numbers, and pager numbers that you get from your baby's doctor and nurse, and carry this list with you at all times.
- *Take notes.* To help you absorb information, take notes during conversations and meetings so that you can refer to them later. Ask your baby's nurse or doctor to write out unfamiliar terms so that you know how to spell and pronounce them. This information will make it possible to ask others for information and to search for facts in books, medical journals, and on the Internet.
- *Repeat the facts as you understand them.* Repeat back to the doctors and nurses what you hear and understand them to be saying. This will enable them to clarify as needed, and it will also help you absorb and remember the information.
- *Consider taping meetings.* Ask permission to audiotape discussions and care conferences, if you think this will help you absorb the vast quantities of information you're expected to digest. A tape will enable you to listen to the explanations more than once, and it's a useful tool for keeping other family members informed.
- *Learn to read your baby's chart.* At first, it will be a challenge to decipher your baby's chart, but as you become fluent in the language and abbreviations it contains, your baby's chart can help you keep abreast of his

or her condition. Chart reading can complement open communication with your baby's care providers. Consider the chart a tool for *enhancing* discussions with your baby's nurses and doctors, not *replacing* them.

- *Welcome all support you are offered.* Because they recognize that having a preemie is very stressful, many NICUs employ a variety of professionals to assist the doctors and nurses in providing psychosocial support to parents as a matter of course. If a social worker, a psychologist, a psychiatrist, or a member of the clergy approaches you, don't assume that the staff has "reported" you or that they believe you are not coping well. Instead, appreciate your NICU's devotion to parent care.

Valuing Your Own Contributions

While your baby is surrounded by highly trained medical professionals and high-tech equipment, you may wonder, "How can I possibly contribute to my baby's medical care?" Especially when your baby is being closely monitored by machines, you may feel that there is no need for your observations and input.

It's important to keep in mind that monitors tell only part of your baby's story. As a parent, don't watch the monitors—watch your baby. Your eyes and ears will tell you more about your newborn than the machines will. By keeping close watch over your baby, you will learn to recognize the tiniest details *and* the big picture, things that machines—and even doctors and nurses—can miss. Many parents can recall a time when they knew something was up before anyone or anything else detected it. Despite its many strengths, modern medicine still has its limitations. A parent's observations can sometimes be the most keen, and parental intuition is very powerful. Feel proud that you can play this unique role in your baby's medical monitoring.

The nurses and residents just didn't share my concern. Finally, when Spencer's blood sats continued dropping without explanation, a very good nurse went over a resident's head and insisted on a visit from an attending physician. I know that I presented that medical team with a critically ill infant facing a number of life-threatening conditions. I also know that I recognized trouble long before the professionals did. And knowing what I know now about NEC (things I didn't know then), I am at a loss to explain how those who should have seen the symptoms missed them. —Susan

They were considering amputating her left leg because the burn [from a tempo-
rary loss of circulation] on that leg was not healing as quickly as they would
have liked. I pleaded with them to wait, prayed a lot, and she did finally heal
to their liking. It felt great to be right! It was a hard decision, but I knew it was
the right one. I knew in my heart of hearts that she would heal up, and they
were not going to ever again make up my mind on anything. I learned the hard
way from the pregnancy itself that my instincts are usually right. —Janet

Valuing the Staff's Contributions—
and Knowing They Value Yours

To form an effective partnership, it is important for parents and health care
providers to understand and value each other's roles and responsibilities. For
instance, some parents blame the doctors for overlooked clues, belated or
mistaken diagnoses, ineffective treatments, or a lack of definitive answers.
But sometimes the diagnosis, the best treatment, or the outcome is not
obvious, and it's the doctors' job to explore possibilities. Sometimes tests have
to be run and treatments tried before the doctors can rule out possibilities and
move on to the next set of options. Treatments may take longer than expected
to be effective for your baby. Some babies defy logic or the odds. Sometimes,
the outcome is uncertain. Often, only time will tell.

On the other side, some health care providers criticize parents for
having unrealistic expectations, being emotional and hypervigilant, and asking
too many questions. But it's your job to hold on to hope—to want your child
to get better faster and to do normal baby things. Additionally, you have a
right to your intense emotions. The NICU is an intense place to be. It's also
your job to watch your little one like a hawk and to become attuned to your
baby. And you need to ask questions to ensure that your baby's best interests
are being served.

Sometimes a parent's questions are pointed. As part of being your
child's advocate, it is your job to question the doctors when they seem to be
off the mark. Other questions will come from your need for clarification or
more information so that you can understand what the doctors are attempting.
Additional questions may prod the doctors to examine your baby or interpret
test results from a more helpful perspective.

When parents and doctors remember that they share the same goal—
that is, getting the baby healthy and homeward bound—it is easier for each to

appreciate the other's unique contributions to the partnership. As a parent, you can do your part by doing your job assertively and proudly—and having faith that the doctors are doing the best they can. Be mindful of the demands you place on them and be fair in your assessments. You always have a right to a second opinion, and responsible doctors will honor that right.

I understand, now, that medicine is at least equal parts art and science. I don't believe that anyone caring for my son intended any harm. I think that they most likely all did their best. I understand, though, that their "best" was highly dependent on individual levels of skill, experience, dedication, burnout, overwork, distraction, desire. ... They were people just like me, people with a little more knowledge, maybe, but no more power. —Susan

Being Informed

As your baby's concerned parent, it is normal for you to want information about what's happening to him or her and why. Part of getting to know your baby is seeing past the medical conditions. But you also need to know what's going on medically. Being informed is your responsibility as your baby's advocate.

About a week after the birth, the haze started to lift. I began to ask many questions. I was determined to be as involved in my son's medical care as possible. I got a book about premature babies so I would know what to expect. —Laura

Besides the NICU, I spent most of my time at the library trying to find information about prematurity. I believe the more you know about what you are facing, the better off you will be. —Kimberly

Being informed is not easy. A million half-formed questions may be swirling around in your head. Exhausted by the delivery and yet full of adrenaline, thoughts may flood your mind. You may be asked to agree to treatments that you don't fully understand. You are challenged to absorb an overload of medical information, to sort through it, and to make the best choices for your baby. Being informed can be a monumental task when your mind is reeling from the shock of your baby's birth or condition.

The attending neonatologist and the nurse both tried to orient us to the most important details about [our baby's] condition and about how long to expect he would be in the NICU—the standard "until his due date" warning. We were both so shell-shocked that not much sunk in. The only thing I think we both got was that we could come in any time and that we were in for a long haul.
—Laurie

Ease of access to information can be equally important to many parents. Being told by a nurse, "You'll have to talk to the doctor about that" in response to a request for even the most mundane information can be very aggravating. Some caregivers hesitate to reveal much about a baby's status because they don't want to overwhelm the parents or cause unnecessary anxiety. You may appreciate their caution, but more likely you will feel exasperated by it or excluded from your place on your baby's medical team. It is easier to cope with this difficult situation when you have full access to the information you want and when all caregivers respond fully, honestly, and respectfully to your questions.

When they share their knowledge with you, your baby's health care providers promote your empowerment and support your efforts to gain some control of the situation, in spite of the uncertainties. If they deflect your questions or tell you "not to worry about that," you may begin to see acquiring information as a battle, one with desperate overtones. When health care providers withhold information, your feelings of incompetence, anxiety, and lack of control are heightened, and it can be difficult for you to trust the medical team. You may find yourself insisting on information that you don't really need or want—simply to establish your right to have it.

The topics involved—critical illness, reproductive physiology, and perhaps even disability or death—are difficult topics to contemplate. Yet learning the details can help you come to terms with what's happening. Filling in the blanks about areas that you don't understand or don't clearly remember can help you to establish a coherent picture of what has already occurred and what is happening now. Having a clear picture of the situation is a crucial part of parenting your baby.

The Benefits of Being Informed

How can being informed help you and your baby? There are many ways.

Empowerment Information is empowering. Knowledge about your baby's conditions and treatments makes you feel involved and proficient. Researching prognoses and looking into various possible outcomes (even the worst ones) can help you feel prepared and give you some sense of control. It's easier to cope when you have the information you need.

Information also prepares you to make the important choices that may need to be made and to oversee the quality of your baby's care. The best advocate is an informed advocate. (For more on advocacy, see the final section of this chapter.)

Reassurance Information can be reassuring. When you know what is happening, your imagination doesn't run wild. When you learn what all the leads and lines and machines are for, it is easier to be relaxed around them. Even if your baby is on a ventilator, knowing what the vent is doing for your baby and how it is doing it can help you view it as a friendly beast.

Mastery Reading about your baby's condition can give you a sense of mastery over the trials you've experienced, even after your baby is discharged from the NICU. Gaining a better understanding of what happened and the possible causes can help you as you work to heal your sorrow and move on. Even if there is no clear-cut answer to what caused the pregnancy complications, the premature birth, or your baby's current condition, you can benefit from learning as much as you can. Knowledge lets you settle on an explanation that makes sense to you, whether it can be proved conclusively or not. Alternatively, the information you gather may help you accept that the reasons remain a mystery.

Teamwork Information makes it possible to collaborate more effectively with your baby's medical team. Even when there are no clear answers, the interpersonal relationships you establish with the medical staff and your mutual effort to make sense of what has happened can be profoundly comforting. Your health care teammates can provide a "holding" environment that reassures, steadies, and calms you, making you less likely to panic.

> *The NICU staff was great about letting me help out with T. J.'s care. Still, the major decisions about his health were in the hands of the doctors and nurses. In this instance, I was grateful to give them control because I felt very overwhelmed. I had faith in them. —Claire*

Uncertainty and Fear Management The simple act of seeking information can ease the stress of living with uncertainty. Even when the facts are scant or unavailable, you can reassure yourself that you know as much as you can. Organizing and accumulating information can help you feel more in charge and reduce your anxiety about the unknown. And when you know that your requests for information will be met, you feel less urgency about acquiring it. If your baby is critically ill or if you have gnawing fears about the possible death of your baby, you may want information about chronic illness, disability, or even refusing aggressive medical intervention and letting nature take its course. Information can empower you and give you some feeling of control. It can be scary to delve into some topics, but it can be even more frightening to stay in the dark and not know what you want and need to know. For instance, reading about parents' reactions to the death of their baby can't tell you how you would react in the same situation, but it may give you some reassurance that you would be able to find a way to cope, as they did. And that feeling— that you would be able to get through it—can give you some peace of mind. (For more on this subject, see "Facing Your Fears" in Chapter 8.)

> On the second day, when another baby died in the NICU, that's when I realized I had to know and understand exactly what we were going to be going through in order for me to survive. I didn't want anything blind. So that's what made me start reading, asking questions, talking to people. —Vickie

> According to the books, my girls had a slim chance of survival. Oddly enough, the information from those books gave me strength. I at least had some idea of what I was facing. It was overwhelming and very upsetting, but at least I knew. —Kimberly

Confidence Building Grappling with your preemie's medical problems and your anxieties can help you adjust to parenting in the NICU and build your confidence in your ability to take care of your baby. In fact, health care professionals are wary of overly optimistic parents who do not ask questions or voice concerns. Some of those parents are not tuned in to their baby's needs and can miss signs of real trouble. Others lack the confidence built from asking questions and practicing caregiving in the NICU, where they can receive round-the-clock staff instruction and support. Many of these parents become extra-anxious after they take their baby home. They postpone all their adjusting to the time after discharge, making many frantic phone calls to the NICU and more than one emergency room visit with a healthy baby. Being informed builds your confidence to handle caregiving challenges in the NICU and beyond.

The Challenges of Being Informed

Information can be empowering, but it can also be overwhelming. Every parent has unique needs for information. You may want to know all there is to know about everything that has happened, is happening, and might happen—or you may want to know only the abridged version. And naturally, the type of information you want and need can fluctuate. You may want all the details right away, or it may be a while before you are emotionally ready for them. Depending on what else is going on with your baby or with you emotionally, there may be times when you want to know more and times when you want to know less. Stephie points out, "Being ignorant can sometimes be the best thing for getting through it." Stay aware of your questions, even the ones you're afraid to ask. Let those questions guide you to the amount and kinds of information you need to help you cope at various stages.

It can take time to be able to put your questions into words, even if you want answers now: you need time to absorb what you've been told so that you can figure out what more you want to know. And, it can take a while for your hidden fears to surface, enabling you to ask the questions that are tor-menting you; then you may hesitate, afraid that the doctors will tell you something you aren't ready to hear.

What you most hope to hear is reassurance, and it can be difficult to obtain or even accept once you do obtain it. You can't help but look around you and notice all the complications that befall babies as tiny as yours, making positive news hard to believe. On the other hand, if the medical professionals hesitate to predict your baby's outcome or if their forecasts are less than opti-mistic, their pronouncements feed your fears.

I learned to not ask questions that would upset me, like "When am I going to get to hold my baby?" I was afraid I was going to get an answer I didn't want to hear. ... Another thing I learned was that I could only deal with what was happening in the present. I didn't want to know what was happening tomorrow or in the future. I didn't want to know because I was so overloaded with what was happening right there ... although that could have been something positive to hold on to. But I think I already felt as if my hopes had been hurt about other things, that I just didn't even want to be told, "It'll be fine months from now," or whatever. I just didn't even want to think about the future. —Stephie

Sometimes, you won't know what kinds of information you need. When you feel anxious or desperate for reassurance, it can be hard to put your finger on exactly what would help. You may think more information will help, but sometimes it doesn't. If you are someone who wants not just to know but also to *do* something, having information can be a double-edged sword. You may feel more informed but not necessarily any more powerful to do anything about the situation than before.

Finally, you need more than just simple information from your teammates. You need to understand how the information you're being given applies to *your* baby. And that information needs to be given to you in caring ways that recognize how emotional and difficult it is for you to hear and absorb much of it. A spirit of sharing and collaboration needs to mark these exchanges. You need to feel that your teammates consider your questions important, not an imposition.

Sources of Information

Your list of questions about the premature birth of your baby is probably quite long. You may need to know more about the physiological events that took place in your body or your baby's body before the delivery, the causes of and treatments for your pregnancy complications, or details about your baby's delivery. You may want observations about your baby; information about the interventions that have taken place; details about your baby's current diagnoses, tests, treatments, uncertainties, possibilities, and prognoses. You may desire information on the origins and physiology of your baby's conditions, graphic photographs from medical books, or vivid color photos of your baby so that you can look at them when you're away from the NICU. Although vocabulary regarding ventilator settings, oxygen levels, and preemie growth curves have only recently become part of your lexicon, you may be amazed at how your world suddenly revolves around these measures.

Your teammates—the doctors and nurses—will be your most important sources of information, especially about your baby. You can also consult other sources. A number of books have been written for parents of preemies about the medical equipment, diagnoses, tests, treatments, and terms that they may encounter during their baby's hospital course (for a listing, see "Books for Parents of Preemies" in Appendix C). If it helps, keep one of these books handy so that you can look things up and read them over and over. Ask your doctor or your baby's doctors and nurses to refer you to resources or to give you copies of pertinent articles and books. As you get to know other parents of preemies, ask them for guidance on how to find information on various topics. If you live near a medical school, you can use its library, or your local public library may be able to arrange interlibrary loans with medical school libraries. You also have access to many libraries on the Internet. Use the resource librarians—they are familiar with requests for all types of information.

I think that parents have to ask or tell somebody what they need—because, obviously, these doctors and nurses aren't mind readers, and everybody has got a different level of experience. Now, I went to the library and took out every book I could find, and I read everything and I knew every term and understood every phrase that they were saying, and if I didn't, I would ask. —Pam

There are many organizations that you can call or write to for specific information on the condition(s) you are researching. Many of these groups publish excellent sources of information, including newsletters, magazines, Web sites, and other materials. Many national organizations network with each other, so you can contact a more general group and ask if they know of any group that might meet your specific needs. (See Appendix C.)

Over time, you'll be amazed at how much information you can absorb, especially when you're no longer in shock or overwhelmed with anxiety. You will become fluent in the language and vocabulary of the NICU and in deciphering the sights and sounds of the high-tech medical equipment.

Don't be surprised if your interest in obstetrics and/or neonatology lasts for quite a while, if not for a lifetime. Medical science is ever changing: you may want to stay current with a particular condition and its treatments. Keep in mind, though, that more information can raise more questions or regrets. If you uncover information that was not given to you or if you find out about treatments (or risks of treatments) that you didn't inquire about earlier, you may wish you had asked more questions at the time. Or if a "cure" is found, particularly if this happens within a year or so of your baby's birth, you may berate yourself for not pursuing that option during the window of opportunity. It is important to remember that *at the time*, you didn't have access to that information. Recognize that you are not to blame when information is withheld from you or unavailable to you. You can't be expected to know the unknowable. Aim your anger away from yourself—and toward medical science, an obstructive member of the medical team, or a medical system that often minimizes parents' need for information.

Communicating with Medical Staff

Parents vary in their styles of information gathering. Some parents want just the basic facts about what is happening right now; others want to know every detail. Information-sharing styles can vary among doctors and nurses, too. Some parents' styles may be a better match with the styles of some staff members than with those of others. For instance, if you just want to know what is certain or the bottom line, you may feel more comfortable with teammates who don't mention all the details, uncertainties, possibilities, and worries. If teammates want to give you that information or share their intuitions or guesses, you can explain that you appreciate their candidness, but that to cope, you need to know only what they are *certain* is happening today and what it means.

If, on the other hand, you want to be fully informed of all the details and possibilities, you may feel more comfortable with teammates who believe parents should know everything the medical staff know. If a doctor is reticent about sharing information, explain that you need and want to be fully informed, to know all that's going on and what staff are thinking, because it helps you cope. Vickie remembers: "The doctor went through all of the problems. And he really prepared me, as opposed to making promises that he could not keep. And I preferred that. I'm more like, 'Give it to me straight so that I know what I'm dealing with.'" Having the details you need also lets you feel more involved and that you are an important member of your baby's health care team.

Working with medical caregivers who share your communication style may feel easy. Once caregivers with differing styles know what you need, most will also be responsive to your style and pace. Still, dissimilar styles can make communication challenging at times.

Bridging Communication Barriers

The first doctor we had, I called him Dr. Gloom-and-Doom because every-thing that came out of his mouth was just horrible. I'm sure he probably had reason to be pessimistic, but maybe some doctors would have said it a little dif-ferently. Everything he said scared the hell out of me. If I didn't understand something, I might ask him, but I learned not to ask him for information because it was just too scary. —Stephie

I came to hate the word stable. *As a mother, I wanted to know details, facts, incidents, things that happened—not just, "She's stable." That puts you out of the loop so fast. You feel, "Okay, they don't want to tell me anything. I have no part in this." —Beth*

Communication barriers are practically inevitable in the busy, highly charged NICU setting. Naturally, parents cannot absorb information as quickly and efficiently as their health care teammates might like. Sometimes, personalities clash. Parents and medical staff also have different perspectives, which can sometimes hamper communication. And some parents simply want more information than they are being given. To overcome these barriers, it is especially important for parents and medical staff to work together, to appreciate each other's contribution to the problems *and* the solutions.

Information Overload

What would I do differently? I would have tape-recorded everything. I cannot remember most of what I was told for about three months. That is a frighten-ing feeling. —Cindy

When you are under tremendous pressure, you may be too shocked to take in all the information that is given to you. Overwhelmed, you may unknowingly shield yourself from the grim realities while you get your bearings. Sometimes, parents are so dazed that they don't recall having a conversation with a doctor or a nurse about a particular issue. The exchange is documented in the chart, and the doctor is saying, "We discussed this yesterday," but you are convinced that you didn't. If you find yourself in this situation, don't assume that the medical staff is trying to put one over on you. Also, try not to be embarrassed about your inability to remember everything. Forgetfulness is normal, especially when your baby is having a tough time in the NICU. It takes time to integrate complex and painful information.

> *The first night the boys were born, we were told by Doctor Gloom-and-Doom that there were fifty ways the boys could die or have brain damage. Those weren't his words, but they are a summary of what we were told. So, when the boys encountered anything the doctor had mentioned, I thought they would die. I never heard the doctor talk about treatments. Either he never did, or after he told us so many horrible things, I couldn't listen anymore. So, each time the boys developed something on the list and a new medicine or intervention was tried, I was ecstatic. —Stephie*

When the news is bad, parents can't always—and sometimes don't want to—hear what is being said to them. If you need to hold on to the hope that your baby's prognosis is good, you may resist the staff's efforts to inform you of a poor prognosis. If your child's medical team is not direct or open with you, it can be even more difficult to understand that the outlook is not good.

> *It was hard to get information out of the doctors. I was often met with responses like "Why would you want to worry yourself about that?" when I asked about the long-term outlook. Looking back now, I realize that the doctors didn't have much hope for my son. I, on the other hand, had nothing but hope. —Laura*

It can also take time to make sense of the information that you are given. You have no context for organizing the information you're receiving so rapidly. You can only grab on to bits and pieces of the words, concepts, and possibilities you are being flooded with.

If you find yourself asking the same questions repeatedly, it can take courage to ask them again. When you find yourself in this situation, request that the person answering your question use simple, concise language. Bring paper and pen, and invite the doctor to write down key terms and draw

Acclimating to the NICU

pictures. Slowly, with repetition and time, you will make sense of what the doctors are telling you. That's why it can be so beneficial to ask for repeated explanations, to request drawings, descriptions, or treatment options in writing, or to tape-record important discussions. These approaches help you to retain information so that you can organize it later.

Some professionals worry that parents under tremendous stress cannot make decisions about their critically ill baby—after all, didn't they forget what they were told just hours ago? But the belief that "stressed parents can't think" is a misconception. The real problem is that parents need time and several different presentations of the same information to begin to create organizational schemes for everything they are learning. When provided with appropriate support, including a variety of approaches to relaying information and clear, accurate explanations, even overwhelmed parents are capable of understanding and being active in decision making and in their baby's care.

Interpersonal Conflicts Not every parent will get along with every health care provider—it's simply human nature. The reasons are many: personality conflicts, stress, bad timing, cultural differences, an unfortunate incident. On the flip side, most parents also form intense connections with certain caregivers, to whom they look for comfort and advice. As a parent, it can help to focus on the care providers who are supportive and try not to hold grudges against or fear those who are less than helpful.

I tried to breast-feed, but Ricky was using more calories than he was taking in. One night, I was particularly frustrated, and I remembered what one of the nurses had told me. "When you can't get him to eat, just hold him and let him know how much you love him. Both the food and the love make him grow and mature." So I was holding him and sobbing and talking to him when one rude nurse came over and told me that he had to be fed now and then returned to bed immediately, so as not to tire him out completely. I told her that I would like a few more minutes, just to hold him and love him. She said that I was too upset and should leave and come back another time to "visit." I just looked at her and told her to butt out and leave us alone, because Ricky was still my son and I was his mother and I should be able to hold and love my son. The overall feeling I got was that I was in the way. I will never forget the way I was degraded and belittled by that nurse. —Jenny

Even parents who are neonatal health care providers whose babies are in the NICU experience feelings of powerlessness and communication challenges familiar to all parents of preemies. Christoph, a neonatologist whose premature baby spent time in the NICU, remembers many uncomfortable moments: feeling hurt by the insensitive comments of nurses, having to resist the urge to take charge of his baby's care, feeling like an incompetent parent next to the doctors, and feeling frustrated that the health care providers did not listen to his concerns. These are, unfortunately, all common NICU parenting experiences.

Differing Perspectives As a parent, it is important to recognize that your frame of reference differs from that of your health care teammates. For example, some medical staff may share their hunches about diagnoses or prognoses without giving you any background or framework for those thoughts. Future possibilities can be startling or frightening to hear when all you have is partial information or information that you can't make sense of. You may take a comment as gospel when you hear a doctor or a nurse mutter something such as, "This looks like seizures" or "I'll be surprised if he makes it through the night" or "I've rarely seen such a severe infection." The caregiver, meanwhile, may merely have been thinking out loud. Unfortunately, before you have time to react, the caregiver may be gone, and there's no one to answer your questions! So, if you overhear something that bothers you, try to ask for clarification on the spot—for example, "What did you just say? I want to make sure I understand what you just said." Asking for clarification may not erase your fears, but it can give caregivers a chance to explain offhand remarks, to retract guesses, and to tone down exaggerations.

> *With Evan's blood fungus, the doctor literally said to me, "I wouldn't be surprised if he was dead in two days." He actually said "dead." Up until that time, everybody had used euphemisms, like "We'll have to wait and see" or "Let nature take its course." No one had said "die." When the doctor said that, of course, I sat there for the next forty-eight hours at my baby's bedside because if he was going to die, I wanted to be with him for the time I had left with him. And then forty-eight hours later, I'm sitting there at the bedside, and the doctor comes over and he says, "He looks great today, doesn't he?!" And I'm, "Huh?" and he says, "Oh yeah, his fungus is still there and stuff, but he's doing okay." And I'm like, "You mean he's not going to die?" And he*

• • •

219

Acclimating to the NICU

shrugs it off, "What are you talking about?" And I'm like, "Hello??!!"
—Stephie

There are other differences in perspective between parents and health care providers. When your teammates talk about your "sick" baby, you may wonder what they mean by "sick." Isn't your baby just "immature"? Isn't he or she *supposed* to have trouble breathing or eating at this gestational age? That's not sick, that's normal! On the other hand, the fact that your child may have "lost a few grams" or be "a little jaundiced" or have "a few periods of apnea" may seem to the nurses like no big deal, just a "preemie thing." But for you, the news may seem ominous or be the straw that breaks the camel's back. Vents, shunts, central lines, scalp IVs, cannulas, gavage feedings, and splint boards may be everyday sights to doctors, nurses, and therapists; they may be horrifying to you.

> *Daniel started to do stuff that was scary. He got his first apnea attack, and he stopped breathing and his oxygen level in the blood was not what it should have been and his heartbeats were inappropriate and all this kind of stuff. We later found out that these little things were exceptionally routine and that these nurses do this day in and day out, but at the time, the way I looked at it was that this one nurse basically had just saved Daniel's life. I mean, he was going down, he'd stopped breathing. She bagged him and brought him back. So it was a very tense moment. —Mitch*

When you are concerned but no one else makes a fuss or says, "Hey, this is really bad," you may wonder if your child is receiving adequate care. When you're the only one who perceives the situation as dangerous and your fears are dismissed without explanation, you may wonder if you are a weak person or crazy for thinking such thoughts. Or even more disturbing, you may feel that you can't advocate for your baby because you don't know when to sound the alarm.

Because the perspectives of parents and health care providers differ, it is very important that your health care teammates

- Have care conferences at which they allow ample time to talk to you about what is going on *and* stay with you as you formulate questions
- Respond to your questions directly and honestly

- Recognize, based on your questions, what you want to be told; provide the hard answers openly and compassionately; and most important, stay with you as you face those answers
- Remain open to questions, even ones you've asked before
- Keep the lines of communication open over time to give you the chance to work through your disorganized thoughts and crystallize your unformed questions
- Recognize that you may need to hear things more than once to absorb them and their implications
- Say what they mean
- Avoid exaggerations or representing guesses as facts
- Watch for your reactions and encourage you to seek clarification when you need it
- Reassure you when, in the context of the NICU, your baby's condition is considered normal or even mild, or if your baby's medical course is common
- Respect your role as loving parents who are involved and advocating for their baby. (For more on caregivers, see Appendix A, "A Note to Caregivers.")

Likewise, it is important for you, the parent, to
- Realize that your teammates cannot read your mind—you must ask for what you need
- Keep track of your questions, so that you can make the most of your meetings and conversations
- Ask the questions that most trouble or embarrass you, or that you fear are "too stupid"; doing so lets your teammates know what reassurance you need, and their responses can also help you trust their ability to take care of your newborn
- Stay informed about topics of concern by other means (videos, books, the Internet)
- Make it clear (especially if you feel you aren't getting straight answers) that for you, coping with the truth is easier than being patronized and "protected"
- Seek out multiple ways of meeting your emotional needs; don't rely only on the medical team. Talk to a counselor, social worker, or

member of the clergy; go online or join a support group.

- Consider yourself the most important person in your baby's life. Looking at your role from that perspective should reduce feelings of suspicion, competitiveness, or timidity, and you'll be less likely to project unkind motives onto your teammates.

Limits on Information Sometimes parents become frustrated because they aren't getting all the information they feel they should have. Knowledge can relieve anxiety about conditions or issues. Instead of assuming that your teammates are withholding the information from you, assume that it's an oversight and ask them to tell you what you need to know.

I wished that the doctors and/or nurses had explained more about what feeding complications could arise, so that when feeds were stopped or started, I felt like I understood more of what was going on. Once it was explained to me about such complications as NEC [bowel disorder], I dealt much better with the feedings being stopped because I understood that this was protecting her rather than hurting her. I think it's a parent's instinct to feed their child, but preemies aren't necessarily ready for actual food, and it needs to be introduced slowly. It was very frustrating for me when I didn't understand that. —Nola

Some gaps in information may be inevitable because your health care team doesn't always have the answers you crave. For instance, if your baby is critically ill, the doctors and nurses may not be able to say what will happen next, how your baby will respond to a certain treatment, or what the outcome will be. When they answer, "I don't know," you can still ask them for the range of patterns, responses, or outcomes they expect. In the face of uncertainty, you can also ask various staff members for their opinions. You may find it helpful to collect and rely on the educated guesses, considered opinions, and breadth of experiences of your NICU staff.

If you feel that the doctors or nurses are keeping information from you, they may be trying to shield you from knowledge that they believe would overwhelm or unnecessarily frighten you. If you are the type of parent who doesn't want to know all the "gory details," this may work for you. But if you want to know everything the doctors and nurses know or even think about your baby, this protectiveness may feel patronizing. For you, not knowing what is *really* going on is far worse than confronting even the scary details.

Information is empowering to you, knowledge helps you master your fears, and inclusion by the medical team helps you cope with the uncertainties. The bottom line is that, for you, feeling disempowered, patronized, and excluded is worse than feeling overwhelmed and scared. You appreciate and expect openness and honesty from your baby's caregivers.

Unfortunately, some doctors and nurses are very uncomfortable with scared parents. If you sense this to be the case, you can remind them that it's not the information itself that is scary—it's the situation and all the unknowns surrounding it. Remind them that when you are feeling overwhelmed or scared, you simply need to have your fears acknowledged—not erased, fixed, or ignored. You are competent and able to cope with your own sadness, anger, and anxiety.

When you are in the NICU, you need support from staff, not protection. With support, you can face the reality presented by your baby, which may include challenges, uncertainties, hopes, and possibilities. With support, you can cope with the attendant fears and sorrows—and thereby experience the joys of parenting this tiny, precarious life.

Advocating for Your Baby

I broke all the hospital rules—I took one baby and then took the other and sat in a neutral spot with both of them together. Heck yeah, I did! And the hospital didn't like it, but they lived with it. Because, I thought, these babies had been inside me, together, for as long as they were, and I'm sure, when they were born and separated, they were like, "What happened, and why am I here, and where is my counterpart?" You know? And that's probably what I felt worst about: having to have them separated and not be together and have that bonding thing. I was worried about that for a long time. —Pam

Many parents feel a surge of parental devotion when they realize that they are their baby's best advocates. But it can take a while for you to realize that the doctors aren't the ones who have ultimate authority over your baby— *you* are the one. The true nature of the doctor's authority is medical expertise. Your baby's doctors are responsible for having the latest medical knowledge about neonatal conditions, complications, diagnostics, and treatments (including their risks and benefits). They are also responsible for carefully and compassionately applying their knowledge and wisely advising parents. The doctor is someone you've hired, a valued consultant who helps your baby try to get healthy and who helps you navigate neonatology so that you can do your job as a loving, protective parent.

Because of a lot of things that happened in the NICU and after, I really realized that I had to be an advocate for my child, because nobody else would. Just because a doctor says something, doctors are not god. It's an opinion; it's an idea. Doctors can have a bad day, too. And they're not going to see every- thing a parent sees. Parents have to realize that their instincts are really good and to believe and trust those instincts. Not only trust those instincts, but then be an advocate for your child based on them. —Vickie

Serving the Best Interests of Your Child

I advocate strongly for my children because they don't have a voice, they can't talk for themselves. A lot of times people in the medical professions think they have a job to do and they do it in any way they can, without considering that it's a baby with feelings. Even though babies can't talk, they still have all the feelings you would have if someone was sticking four needles into your head at one time. —Betsy

If your baby is still in the NICU, you can be as active as you want in seeing that your baby receives appropriate, sensitive care. Remember that your baby is a member of your family, and you are the parent. As long as your goal is the "best interests" of your child, it is your right to be as involved as you want.

Of course, when the benefits of a medical treatment clearly outweigh the risks, you'll want to (and be expected to) agree to it. But when the benefits don't clearly outweigh the risks, or when the outcome is uncertain or the prog- nosis is poor, you should be included in the decision-making process. In any case, your informed consent is required for all major or experimental proce- dures. Aside from life-threatening emergencies, you may be involved in many decisions. You can also request that even the simplest changes in routine care plans be run past you before they are carried out. As an emotionally invested parent, part of your job is to scrutinize your baby's care.

I was worried about the effect that [the medication] would have on him long term. When I was pregnant, I don't think I took regular-strength Tylenol more than five times, and here they were pumping all this stuff into him. —Micki

They had a lot of X rays. I didn't like that. My mom never wanted us to even get dental X rays. So here were my babies, who weren't even supposed to be born yet, getting X rays every day. I was not very happy about that. But it couldn't be helped. It had to be done. —Debbie

When giving informed consent for a treatment or procedure, there is so much to scrutinize. In fact, you may feel overly informed because the hospital has a legal obligation to disclose every possible risk, no matter how unlikely. Reading the long list of dangers, you may feel terrified about permitting your little one to undergo a treatment or procedure. Ask about the likelihood of a particular danger befalling your baby and how the risk relates to the potential benefits. Also ask what is likely to happen if you refuse consent. For instance, transfusions pose potential risks, but if your baby will die without one, then the scale would clearly tip in favor of the transfusion. If, on the other hand, your baby will probably do okay without the transfusion, then you might safely opt to refuse permission.

Your advocacy and assertiveness are essential to your baby's care, but some parents fear the effects of advocacy on the quality of their baby's care. You may wonder if being assertive, expressing feelings, posing too many questions, or making demands will cause you to be labeled "difficult"—and as a result, cause your baby to receive inferior care. But babies are not held responsible for their parents' behavior—and health care professionals don't perform less competently or lower their standards to "get even." Babies are *never* denied the best care possible, no matter how assertive, emotive, questioning, demanding, or challenging their parents are perceived to be. In fact, *constructive* assertiveness can be a benefit to your relationships with NICU staff, and advocacy can improve the care your baby receives.

I think that I had a pretty good relationship with the doctors and the nurses because I was there and I was on them, in their faces, all the time, asking "Why? Fine, you're going to do this blood test. What is the blood test? What is it going to show you? What are you going to determine by the results of this

blood test?" I was constant, on them, on them, on them. I mean, I would find the doctor, hunt down *the doctor, grab him, and say, "In the child's chart it says _____. ... Explain that to me." And he's like, "Well, that's the nurse's writing." And I would say, "I don't care whose writing it is. You're the doctor, you tell me why!" I wasn't afraid to do that. I wasn't one of the people who wouldn't look at the chart because that's a "private" thing. I don't care. If it's there, I'm the mother, I'm gonna read it, you know? So I was on them constantly, and I wanted them to know that I was there, and I wanted them to know that I wanted to know and I wasn't going to take no for an answer. I think they gave me, I don't mean to say "preferential treatment," but maybe people thought of me as someone to contend with and to be slightly leery of and "If we don't do everything right, we're going to hear about it." And I'm not a nasty person, but I had to do what I had to do for the sake of the kids.*
—Pam

This mom was very assertive, and her style may be different from yours. You can advocate effectively using a variety of styles, as long as you are constructive. Being constructively assertive involves
- Not attacking the doctors and nurses personally
- Sticking to "I" statements
- Assuming that the medical staff has your baby's best interests at heart
- Working toward collaboration, not conflict

For instance, to begin a dialogue instead of a war, try this approach: Instead of saying, "You make me so mad. How could you do that?" try saying, "I am so angry about my baby's setback. Please, can you tell me what happened?"

Remember, as your baby's advocate, it is your goal to be informed, vigilant, and protective so that your baby receives care that you understand, approve of, and agree with. You are *supposed* to ask: "What are the side effects and risks of this test or treatment?" "Will this hurt—can you give my baby something for pain?" or "When can my baby medically tolerate kangaroo care?" Assume that you have a right to know and you have a right to object or disagree with care plans when they are experimental, risky, or their outcome is uncertain. When, in your opinion, something is not clearly in the best interests of your child, you can propose another path.

We were a pain, but we felt that was our right, our kids' right. I think they knew that we weren't going to go away, that they had to deal with us—and that if we weren't satisfied with what was going on, we would seriously question it and we'd call a meeting to figure out a solution or to have them make us understand exactly why they were doing it. They understood that. —Betsy

Being There for Medical Procedures

As your baby's advocate, you might also feel strongly about being present for certain medical procedures. Hospitals and even members of the health care team vary on how comfortable they are with the presence of parents at these times. But it is your right to be with your baby, as long as you can conduct yourself responsibly, cooperatively, and quietly, and you do not interfere with the medical treatments being carried out, the staff's ability to do its job well, or a sterile environment (which is why you can't be present during surgery).

On the other hand, it can be very difficult for most parents to be present for certain procedures. Your deep empathy with your baby can cause you great pain, or your general queasiness can get in the way of your being able to handle yourself properly. So remember, you don't *have* to be at your baby's bedside during certain procedures if you feel squeamish or too distressed. It is better—for yourself and for your baby—to leave than to force yourself to stay when you're having trouble tolerating the situation. After all, if you're having difficulty holding yourself together, you have little or no spare energy to help your little one cope. Instead, from a safe and calming distance, you can send your positive thoughts toward your baby and then comfort your little one when the procedure is over.

Watching Over Multiple Preemies

If you have twins, triplets, or more in the NICU, you may feel an even larger obligation to stay informed and advocate for your babies. This can be very challenging because all of your babies will rarely be experiencing the same thing at the same time. You may have many conditions, complications, and treatments to learn about in order to stay on top of things.

Being able to keep things straight can pay off, though, because one peril of having multiples is that sometimes, although rarely, multiple babies get mixed up. For instance, Pam's baby girl, Riley, got abdominal X rays, but her baby boy, Banning, was the one with necrotizing enterocolitis (or NEC, a bowel disorder). Banning's theophyline medication levels were checked, but Riley was the one who was receiving the drug for apnea. So Riley was exposed unnecessarily to radiation, and Banning received an unnecessary blood draw. Pam talks about taking charge:

> *At that point I said, "Nobody does anything to either one of these children without prior consent, no ifs, no ands, no buts. If it's an emergency and if it's life-threatening, then sustain life and then call me. But nothing is to be done." And I hated to be such a jerk about it, but I had to be. These babies couldn't speak for themselves, so they needed somebody to do it, and I thought that was my job, you know? —Pam*

Don't assume that the medical staff will resent your efforts, or that you'll be interfering. They know you're not trying to take over their job. By being involved, you are just doing your job as a parent. Plus, participating in your babies' care will build your confidence. As their discharge approaches, you may feel less intimidated by the prospect of taking over all of their care.

Dealing with Regrets

If you are looking back on your time in the NICU, you may be wondering if you should have or could have been a "better" advocate. You may have wondered about this even while your baby was still in the NICU. Or perhaps you felt comfortable with your degree of advocacy at the time but, in retrospect, now believe that you should have been more active or vocal. You may wonder how you could have behaved so compliantly or felt so disconnected from your baby's medical care. There may be other things that bother you now, things that you ignored or were oblivious to at the time. How could you have been so "out of it"?

On the other hand, you may think you were too overbearing, too aggressive, too detail oriented, or too angry. You may regret not having had more tranquil relationships with the nursing staff or the neonatologists. You may wish you could have been more constructive. In either case, you may wonder why you behaved differently in this situation than you usually do in other aspects in your life.

Looking back, many parents wish that they could have been more constructively assertive during their preemie's NICU stay. But most parents need time and experience in the NICU to build up their strength and courage to be assertive and to acquire skill at being constructive. Some parents just need to survive this experience and get out; only in hindsight can they see that they might have been lacking. Other parents are too stressed to have the energy to communicate judiciously. Whatever your style or timetable, remember that you were who you were. Also remember that it is much easier to be an effective advocate when you are working with professionals who understand and respect your advocacy. Although second-guessing yourself is a normal part of parenting in the NICU, give yourself credit for doing your best at the time under the circumstances.

Could your observations or assertive demands have made a difference for your child? It is likely that your baby's outcome (in the highly skilled hands and under the attentive care of your NICU's medical staff) would have been the same, even if you had behaved differently. And after homecoming, as you deal with pediatricians, therapists, and perhaps repeat hospitalizations, you may develop a more assertive approach. The process of learning about caregiving, becoming skilled at it, and growing as a parent to your child is ongoing.

Points to Remember

- When your baby is whisked away to the NICU, it is normal to feel lost, left behind, and out of the loop.
- Give yourself time to get used to the NICU. Early on, it is natural to be intimidated by the technology, equipment, and terminology, not to mention the busy, knowledgeable medical staff. Very soon, you will learn your way around the NICU and come to trust the nurses and doctors who are caring for your precious baby.
- State-of-the-art, family-centered neonatal intensive care provides each baby with individually tailored, developmentally supportive care. It involves parents and encourages them to get close to their babies. Medical technology is important for preemies, but so is nurturing and the parents' touch.
- As a parent, you should be supported, too. You may be frustrated sometimes by a lack of sensitivity or responsiveness to your needs. Try to remember that your medical team is also trying to learn how to balance and integrate medical and emotional issues. Be your own advocate and

make your needs known.

- As a parent, it is your job to ask questions, learn, make mistakes, have intense feelings, be informed, and advocate for your baby. Tell the doctors and nurses what you need to do your job well. An important part of their job is to support parents and share information.
- Your needs for information can fluctuate, depending on your emotional condition. When you're overwhelmed, you may unknowingly shield yourself from the grim realities while you get your bearings.
- To keep the lines of communication open with your baby's medical team, approach them in the spirit of collaboration, telling them what kinds of information and support you need.
- Remember that *you* are your baby's parent and, when informed, your baby's best advocate.

CHAPTER EIGHT

Becoming a Parent in the NICU

Becoming a parent to a baby in the NICU is very different from parenting a healthy newborn in the privacy of your own home. You may find it difficult to act and feel like a parent when so much separates you from your newborn. It takes time and practice to feel competent at meeting even the simplest of your tiny baby's needs.

I wanted to touch him, to stroke his face and skin, but that felt unsafe. He seemed so fragile. I felt distanced because of the tubes and wires. I was afraid of pulling something out. I felt I had to wait for instructions from the nurse. That wasn't what I was expecting when I first met my baby. —Laurie

I felt very detached, though I tried desperately to be involved. I pumped milk for him from day one, saw him every day, touched him, then later held him, read stories, sang, spoke, but there was still that detachment because we had to leave him every night and go home to a babyless house. It was odd. There were flowers, balloons, and cards from friends and family, but no baby. It was a very empty feeling. —Sherilyn

Even for seasoned parents, becoming a parent to a preemie is a formidable task, presenting many challenges. Your little one arrived before you were ready, doesn't look or act like a newborn should, and is medically fragile. Plus, you are facing the task of developing a sense of yourself as a parent to a baby who is separated from you. If you've never been a parent before, this situation can make it doubly hard to believe that you are a mother or a father—and that you are important to your baby even when health care professionals are taking care of him or her.

I had no idea what I expected to feel or what kind of parent I thought I would be, but I do know that dealing with this threw everything completely out of whack. It was really hard for me to feel like a real parent to Nicholas for the first few weeks. After all, I was not his primary caregiver, and that felt just plain wrong to me. —Sterling

There's so little you can do. I remember them coming in soon after he was born, and I asked them, "What can I do? Does he need my kidney? He can have it. Anything that he needs, he can have." And there wasn't anything I could do, except give him breast milk. So that's what I did. And be there for him. I did those things with everything I had. —Marcia

I wanted to hold him and mother him in my own home and on my own terms. —Claire

When your baby is hospitalized right after birth, you face many hurdles that keep you from feeling like a "real" or a "normal" parent. You may struggle with any or all of these feelings:

- Uncertainty as to when you will feel like a parent to this baby
- Emotional turmoil, marked by both positive and negative feelings about your baby
- The desire for privacy with your baby
- Concern about your own medical problems
- Fears for your baby
- Worries about getting past the medical barriers in the NICU
- Feeling displaced by your baby's medical caregivers
- Lack of confidence in your ability to take care of your baby, in both caregiving skills and parenting abilities
- Uncertainty about parenting from a distance

- Concern about whether your baby is benefiting from your presence

At first, many of these hurdles may seem insurmountable, but as you adjust to parenting in the NICU, you will discover that you can get past them to forge a relationship with your baby. In time, your confidence will increase, and you will get your bearings. This chapter explores each of these hurdles and offers suggestions for overcoming them.

Wanting to Feel Like a Parent

Suddenly I was no longer pregnant, and yet I was far from being a mother. Where did this all fit into that glowing dream of motherhood? Where did I fit into it? What could I do for my baby but look at his tiny body, covered in wires and tubes, and tell him over and over that I was sorry?

Our boy did remarkably well, yet day in and day out I watched over this child, hovering, always frightened, always waiting for something to go wrong, always wondering what the next day would bring, always just two steps in front of exhaustion, hoping that today would be the day that I would feel like a mother. Waiting to be able to do more for my son, waiting to feel like I was worth something more in this baby's life than just a jar or two of breast milk, waiting to feel something other than desperation.

At night I'd dream that I was pregnant and wake up full of hope— and then remember that I wasn't. I'd lie in bed at night and wonder if my baby was peaceful, if he was calm, was he agitated, did he need his mummy, and instead of peeping in his bassinet, I'd have to phone a nurse and ask. I wasn't a mother. —Leanne

To most parents, newborn babies elicit thoughts of soft blankets, sweet-smelling skin, spit up, diapers, cooing and giggles, and lack of sleep. My newborn memories include hours watching my tiny son paralyzed by drugs, aware but unable to respond, to avoid the expenditure of calories he could ill afford to waste kicking his legs or waving his arms. I remember learning about pulse ox, and brain bleeds, and perforated bowels. My newborn memories include medical discussions of how to wean my morphine-addicted infant once the painkiller was no longer required. While other new parents learned to change diapers, we learned to change the adhesive bag covering his ileostomy. —Susan

When you have a baby in intensive care, you can feel both intensely like a parent and, at the same time, entirely unlike one. Although you know intellectually that your baby has been born, emotionally, you haven't caught up. Separation from your infant doesn't help. Are you really a new parent? You may resist the idea outright.

My heart broke at how tiny she was, yet she still didn't seem real to me. I was concerned that the nurses would think I was unfeeling, but I just didn't know how to react or feel about this baby. All I knew was that one moment I was pregnant and looking forward to my final trimester. And the next moment found me in a NICU, staring at a creature that did not look, act, or sound like a baby. I feared she would die. I feared we would bring home, if ever, a handicapped child. —Renee

It seemed so surreal. Nothing was happening the way it was supposed to. At first, I couldn't believe that I was pregnant. Then right around the time I started believing I was pregnant, I had her. So then I had problems believing I was a mother. The way you think about being a mother is, "I'm a mother. I'm sitting here. I've got my baby." But of course, for me, it never happened like that because she was in the hospital for so long. So I didn't feel like a mother right away. I came in when she'd been in the NICU for two or three days, and the nurse says to her, "Oh look, Mommy's here!" And I'm like, "Whoa! Stop that. I'm not a mother." And they're like, "Yeah, you are." And I'm like, "Well, yes, I am, but don't call me that because I'm not quite ready to accept that yet." —Brooke

No matter that you delivered your baby, your mind is still pregnant. It took me a long time to adjust to that, to not feel pregnant, to see a pregnant woman on the street and not think, "That's what I am." Because your mind is scheduled for a nine-month pregnancy. You want to be pregnant. And you don't want to face the preemie thing. —Gallice

For a while, Katie wasn't our baby. She was the NICU's baby. We were in this odd state of limbo. —Mark

Feeling remote and powerless can be disorienting, even disturbing.

Especially early on, you may feel out of sync with what you know other parents do with their newborns. You want so much to do all those nurturing, cuddly things that are supposed to be good for babies, but your baby cannot tolerate the kind of caregiving you want to offer. When you are unable to feed, dress, or even hold your little one, you may feel a confusing mixture of disconnect and longing. While intense longing is painful, it reassures you that you have parenting urges. Feelings of disconnect may make you wonder if there is something wrong with your parenting ability.

I was very sick and was kept about a week in the hospital to recuperate. I remember that I did not feel "connected" to the baby and was disappointed that I not only didn't learn to recognize his cry right away (never did, really) but, embarrassingly, could not even recognize him visually. ... I worried that someone was going to realize that I couldn't recognize my own baby. —Shaina

I think the worst part, afterward, was trying to make myself believe that I did give birth to a baby, he didn't die, and I could take care of this child when he came home. —Ami

You may have other concerns about your ability to parent. You may feel discouraged about your ability to meet your baby's needs because they are so far beyond routine newborn parenting. You may feel hesitant and clumsy, unqualified to even touch or hold your tiny baby. You want to get close, but you don't want to do anything wrong. You may struggle with painful feelings such as fear, guilt, inadequacy, wanting to keep your distance, and wondering if your very presence could be harmful.

Strange, but I can't remember [holding him for the first time] very clearly. I was still so afraid I was going to lose him. I do remember that I was afraid that I would give him germs. Seven weeks with PROM [premature rupture of the membranes] had made me very frightened of germs. —Inkan

I didn't get to hold her for eight days after surgery, and then when I could, I didn't want to do it. I was afraid to do it. They said, "Do you want to hold her?" and I said, "No." I was scared that I would hold her and she'd have another setback and it would be twelve days before I could hold her again. Or weeks—and I'd never get to hold her and she'd die. I'd do something wrong: knock the ventilator by mistake, or kill her. —Beth

The thing I remember most was the fact that I couldn't get close to him. I felt as if I had hurt him so badly and that I could never make it up to him. I also remember feeling helpless and extremely useless. —Jenny

It took me quite a few hours before I'd go back in to see Sean. I was scared, I guess. I didn't know what to do with him. I felt guilty, too. I just knew I had to have done something to cause this to happen. It had to be my fault because I'm his mommy and my job was to protect him from everything. And if I couldn't even protect him before he was born, how was I going to protect him now? —Ami

You may also feel powerless to protect your little one from invasive or painful medical procedures. These treatments are necessary, but they seem so rough. During the intense crises, you may feel inadequate, believing that you have failed as a protector, the most basic of parenting jobs.

Nicholas was just taken downstairs, but it might as well have been in another world for all the access I was allowed at first. They kept telling us that we would be able to go right down and see him … but then they wouldn't let us. The longer they made us wait, the more frantic I got—thinking that something really horrible was happening to him and I couldn't be there. —Sterling

At the age of three weeks, Seleste coded for the first time. … Within a minute or two, they started doing CPR—and I've never seen anything so brutal in all my life. … There were two things on my mind: One, "I've got to stay under control so they don't kick me out of here. I want to be here," and two, "Stop, stop, you're torturing her!!!" It just looked so inhumane. —Suzanne

The biggest thing I felt was inadequacy. Every time one of his alarms beeped, I felt as if I had done something wrong. I was petrified that I was holding him the wrong way or that he would stop breathing on me. Once, I was holding him while he struggled to come back from an apnea. I was devastated because I couldn't help him and felt as if it was my fault that it had happened. It was a stressful situation, different each day. —Claire

You may also keenly miss the chance to be constantly present and involved in your little one's everyday life, experiencing both the ordinary and the special. Not being there for all of your baby's "firsts" can feel as if the nurses are stealing such milestones as the first bath or diaper change. However insignificant particular milestones may seem to others, they can be immensely important to parents of preemies. Whatever activities and opportunities you hold central to the parenting role are those you'll miss the most.

That's the rub of it all. They may be crappy milestones, but they're all we've got. And I wasn't even there. And it makes you feel like you're not even the mother—like you're just a visitor. It just really hurt me so badly, you know, because I wanted to get pictures. She was in some big girl bassinet now, and I wasn't there to make sure everything was okay. And I'm supposed to be her mom. —Beth

You may also harbor many feelings that don't seem appropriate for a mother or father: sadness, anxiety, fear, failure. You may curse or resent the obstacles that separate you from your baby, even as you acknowledge that they are necessary for your baby's survival. There may be many heart-wrenching times for you. And yet, this emotional turmoil is normal and a natural part of wanting to feel like a parent.

Each evening I'd blow my child a kiss through his plastic walls and walk away, every nerve ending screaming that this was wrong, every fiber of my being wanting to hold that child close and never let go, and yet night after night I left. How could I do this one more day? —Leanne

The first time I really held Ricky was when he was almost a week old. I felt as if I was holding him away from me, so I wouldn't hurt him anymore. I thought that this was all my fault, and I couldn't bear to hurt him any more. He felt heavy, not like a burden but like a weight around my heart, pulling and pulling me toward him. I wanted to hold him forever. I looked up and saw that I was not the only one crying. The nurses who took care of Ricky knew my pain; they had seen it before. I just held him and looked into his eyes and begged him to forgive me for failing him so miserably. He didn't open his eyes, but he did yawn and wriggle. I held him that way for about five minutes, and then the nurse told me I had to put him back. I was so happy that I had finally gotten to hold him, but I was hurt deeply at having to leave him there. I went home and laughed and cried and fell into an exhausted heap at my husband's feet. —Jenny

Embracing Your Intense Emotions

Intense and bewildering feelings are part of the process of becoming a parent. Emotional turmoil is natural and universal during the last trimester of pregnancy and the weeks after delivery, even for the parents of term babies. This turmoil is considered adaptive because it mobilizes the mother's and father's emotional energy toward adjusting to parenting and forming a relationship with their baby.

Of course, the challenges of adjusting to parenting a preemie and forming a relationship with your little one can seem formidable as your last trimester of pregnancy is cut short and the weeks or months after delivery are marked by separation from your baby. But your turmoil can be adaptive, too. This emotional roller coaster, although uncomfortable and overwhelming, is not only natural but also mobilizes your emotional investment in your baby.

Still, as the shock and numbness wear off, many parents of preemies are concerned about the intensity of their emotional turmoil. You may wonder if there is something wrong with you. Try to remember that the intensity of your feelings reflects your investment in this baby and in experiencing a rewarding parenthood. The stress and calamities you're enduring add to the painful mix of your emotions, naturally making your turmoil more intense.

I didn't have a sense of joy regarding Emma for most of her ICN stay. Just sadness and fear and guilt and more sadness. —Diane

I expected Katie to do the roller coaster thing, but my emotions were even more out of whack. I wanted to hold her and love her. I wanted to be that strong parent—and found myself in tears a lot of the time. —Angel

Health care providers or the NICU staff may attribute your tears to postpartum depression alone, making you feel that they are dismissing your feelings, discounting the traumatic nature of this experience, trying to "normalize it," and implying that if you received treatment for postpartum depression, you wouldn't be struggling. By misreading your reactions and misunderstanding how hard this experience really is for you, they can inadvertently discourage you from getting extra support. Here is how one mother felt:

> They kept saying, "Oh, you have postpartum depression. You have it really bad." I was furious. Yes, I was crying every single day. Somebody couldn't say something that I didn't cry, whether it was just something with the girls— anything, I was bawling. But I didn't think that it was to the point that I needed to go to therapy. The Christmas thing, it really bothered me when they told me I could just go spend it with my family. These babies were my family. They didn't know why I was crying, and they were going to send for the psychiatrist from the hospital to talk to me. But postpartum depression wasn't the problem! —Julia

Of course, some parents are more emotionally distraught than others. Your situation, your personality, your history, your baby's condition and prognosis—all these factors can affect how much turmoil you feel. Whatever the direction and intensity of your emotions, they are yours. It's important to accept your partner's degree of turmoil as well, because it's unique to him or her.

If you are concerned about your degree of emotional turmoil (or your partner's) and you feel comfortable doing so, ask your baby's nurses or doctors if your reactions seem in line with what they've observed in other parents of preemies. If they show concern or if you continue to feel uneasy, don't hesitate to talk with a mental health care provider. Your hospital's social worker should be able to refer you to a counselor who works specifically with parents of preemies. A good counselor can help you untangle your emotions and reactions so that you can figure out more adaptive ways of dealing with your difficult circumstances. Your baby's primary nurse, an experienced parent of a preemie, or an empathic friend may be able to give you needed boosts as well. Keeping a journal about your feelings can provide a release and help you develop insight into this special situation. Remember, you're not the one who is flawed. It's the *situation* that is so abnormal. Most parents need some help adjusting.

Claiming Your Parental Identity

What helped me feel like a mom was just living it—accepting it—because it was something I had to do day by day by day. Also, seeing her react to me. And talking about her really helped make her a lot more real. All my coworkers would ask me, "How's she doing?" and they didn't understand half of what I was saying, but they still asked. —Brooke

Maybe when I was in that mixed-feelings state of not wanting to cope with that whole situation, maybe at that point—I've sort of forgotten about it because it's embarrassing—but we didn't know if he was ever going to be a normal baby. He was not there; we did not want to admit it. But people were so reassuring. I think that gave us right away all the optimism we needed, and it transferred to him, and then we felt pretty good about him. ... I found him so cute. I realize that he was not the most beautiful baby for other people, of course, but for me, he was the cutest baby in the world. —Gallice

The birth certificate lady asked, "What did you have?" "A boy." "What's your son's name?" I said, "Oh, my son." I hadn't said "my son"—those words—[before]. I hadn't thought of him as my son. I loved saying those words after she said them. —Nettie

It's difficult to sort out your complicated feelings while at the same time trying to feel like a parent to your hospitalized infant. The suggestions that follow can help you get past feelings of hesitation and ambivalence, as well as help you see that even your painful emotions are an integral part of your devotion to your baby.

- *Forgive yourself and your baby for not being the way that you had imagined.* Let yourself get to know *this* baby, rather than waiting until he or she seems more like the baby you had envisioned.
- *Remind yourself that shock and numbness follow trauma.* Feeling detached isn't a sign that you don't or cannot care about your baby. It is merely an expected aftereffect of trauma. As the situation stabilizes, so will you.
- *Accept that you may have mixed feelings about your baby or about going to the NICU.* It is normal to feel frustrated by limited access to your baby. It is also normal to feel reluctant about spending time with your baby,

especially at first. It is natural to need to warm up to your baby.

- *Give yourself time to acclimate emotionally to the NICU.* The confusing and dismaying sights and sounds of the NICU can add to your feelings of detachment from your baby. The more you stay and the more you learn, the more familiar this place will become—and the more able you'll be to focus on and warm up to your baby. As your baby becomes a part of your everyday existence, you'll feel more and more like a parent.

- *Remind yourself that your painful emotions reflect your heartfelt connection to your baby.* If you didn't have a connection to this child, you wouldn't be so emotional.

- *If this is your first baby, recognize that part of what you feel has to do with never having been a parent before.* All new parents feel incompetent, overwhelmed, and anxious at times. Having a premature baby magnifies the intensity of these feelings, of course, but they are a natural part of being an inexperienced parent.

- *If you have older children, recognize that this baby may challenge your self-image as an experienced parent.* It's difficult to go from feeling confident about our abilities to feeling unsure. Remember that parenting a preemie is *different.* It's natural to feel like a novice as you learn how to meet this baby's needs.

- *Take the time and energy to face your anger, sadness, and disappointment about the circumstances of your baby's delivery and hospitalization.* If you don't deal with these negative feelings, you may displace them onto your baby. Working through these feelings can make it easier to see your baby in a positive light.

- *Let yourself cry when you feel like it.* You may find yourself moved to tears while you pump or while you hold your baby skin to skin. Tears of joy and sadness can mix together, and floods of emotion are natural. Your tears won't harm your baby. Shedding them can help you manage your grief.

- *If you feel anxious about being around your baby, talk about your feelings with someone you trust.* If you are worried that your presence might harm your baby, keep in mind that your worries are based on your intense wish to protect and nurture your infant—even if you conclude that doing so requires you to keep your distance. Inkan confesses: "I was very afraid about giving him any infection. It felt more secure to stay away from touching him." This sentiment is profoundly parental.

- *Talk about your emerging parental identity with a trusted friend or with other parents of preemies.* Seek out reassurance and support for doing the things you want to do with your baby in the NICU. There are many good books that support parents' desires and needs to be close to their babies. (See Appendix C, "Books for Parents of Preemies.")
- *Refer to your little one as "my baby."* Even if it feels awkward at first, practice using the phrase in your mind and on your tongue.
- *Refer to yourself as your baby's "mother" or "father."* Although you may not yet feel competent in the role of mother or father, you *are* your baby's parent. Even when you still have much to learn, you have a unique relationship and connection with your daughter or son.
- *Trust that your baby knows who you are and that you are someone special to him or her.* Follow your intuition about this connection. You don't need concrete evidence. Just sense and feel the connection—and build on it.
- *Keep in mind that you can create your own "firsts"*—the first bath you give, the first diaper you change. You or your partner will also be the first to breast-feed, the first to give kangaroo care, and the first to take your baby home. No one else can do those parenting tasks.
- *Decorate your baby's temporary home.* Ask the medical staff where you can place family photos, small toys, and special name tags or signs. Bring a baby blanket from home to drape over the incubator. Bring preemie clothes for your baby to wear. Doing these things can help remind you that this baby is an individual and an important member of your family. (For more ideas on this subject, see "Making the Most of Your Absences" later in this chapter.)

It is also very important to understand that it is natural to approach your baby tentatively at first, staying for short periods and touching with just fingertips. Subdued interactions are appropriate and not necessarily a sign of detachment. After all, parents of a term newborn imitate their baby's behavior in an instinctive attempt to avoid overwhelming their infant. Parents of preemies have this same instinctive reaction. When your tiny baby is inactive and unresponsive, it is only natural for you to tune into and respect those signals. Keeping some distance can show your connection and empathy with your little one.

They were on warming tables in the NICU. There were tubes and wires everywhere. I was afraid to touch them, but I asked the nurse if I could, and she said it was okay. I stroked their feet. It seemed like the only safe place to touch them. —Lorraine

Finally, it may also help you to view your baby's hospitalization as the third trimester. While this is not the third trimester you'd envisioned, try seeing this time as the continued gestation of your baby and the continued incubation of yourself as a parent. Your baby needs to grow and develop, and you have much growing, developing, and learning of your own to do. Viewing the NICU days as an unwelcome intrusion into your pregnancy, rather than as a thwarted newborn period, can sometimes help. When your baby is ready for discharge, you can still savor a newborn period at home.

Finding Privacy

Forging a connection with your baby is an intimate, heartfelt activity. But there are many eyes and ears in the NICU. You may feel exposed and self-conscious trying to make this connection while surrounded by medical staff and other parents of preemies. You may find yourself listening to or watching other parents out of curiosity or a desire to learn—and realize that they may be doing the same thing.

I was taken to see my girls on the third day of their life. It was not a pleasant experience. The nursery was crowded and noisy. My husband was constantly trying to explain what all the machines were doing for them. At that point, I really wasn't interested in listening. I just wanted to pick both of the girls up and go to a quiet place and hold them. —Kimberly

At first, when the NICU is unfamiliar, you may be especially sensitive to the lack of privacy. Screens are available in some units—ask for one if you think it would help you feel more comfortable. As you become used to the NICU, you may develop territorial feelings about "your" space. You may be able to tune others out, or after a while, you may not care anymore. As your baby's condition improves, you may be able to take him or her to a more private space in the unit when you're there. If the lack of privacy bothers you, ask your nurses to help you find the privacy you need.

The best of times were at the end of the NICU stay, when we could go to a
private room and nurse lying on a bed, all alone. I used to sing soft lullabies to
him and dim the light. In the NICU there were so many other people all the
time, and it was hard to relax in the same way. —*Inkan*

Dealing with Your Own Medical Hurdles

When I first saw Selina, I was still having a hard time getting out of the
anesthetic. It never really occurred to me that she was my baby. I guess I
denied that she was mine and that she even yet existed. After all, babies aren't
born at that gestation (yeah, right). I had very severe complications after her
birth and was in ICU for a long time myself. I guess that the first time I
actually did get to see her without my mind being hazed out by drugs was
when she was three weeks old. Even then I felt terrified and still denied that
she could possibly be mine. My idea of babies was that they were big, seven to
eight pounds, and healthy—not two pounds and struggling to live. ... All I can
remember seeing is that she looked like a toad that I had killed and that had
been sitting in the sun for too long. The tubes and monitors were surprisingly
comforting to me. I was shocked to see her. *I had never seen anything like that*
in my life. —*Jodi*

You may have your own set of medical hurdles that keep you from being with
your baby. If you have feelings of detachment from your baby during your
recuperation, it is important to remember that those feelings come in part
from your physical condition. They do not indicate some inherent inability to
love and nurture this child.

Give yourself the time you need for your own physical healing. If you
are quite ill, you may need weeks of recuperation before you can turn your
attention toward your baby. And when you can finally be with your newborn,
give yourself the time you need to adjust to your baby and the NICU.

The first day, I was so sick that I did not want to see her. I can hardly believe
that now!! The second day I wanted to see her, but I knew that I would be

*way too weak to hold her. By Saturday, after everyone I had talked to had
asked if I had seen her yet, I was ready—and very upset—crying hysteri-
cally—because I had not seen my baby yet.* —Stacy

If you feel strongly about wanting to be with your baby in spite of your
special needs for physical healing, you may hesitate to follow your feelings.
You may give in to the orders of your own health care providers to stay away
from the NICU, even if that means going against your own better judgment.
Trust your intuition about how to balance your physical needs with your emotional needs as a new mother. For some mothers, the emotional benefits of
being with their baby seem to facilitate physical healing. Do what you feel is
right *for you.*

*One of the hardest things was leaving him. I was there most of the time
during the day, but I was still in the hospital, post–C-section, and the nurses
just kept saying to me, "You have to take care of yourself. You are post-op
yourself. You've got to take care of yourself. Get out of here. We are kicking
you out of here. For three hours we don't want to see your face." Then I'd go
to leave him, and he would start crying. It was so hard to leave him because at
that point it was clear to me that he knew.* —Micki

*I was taking longer to heal, and I had some complications afterward. The
nursing staff would tell me, "You know, maybe you should stay home, take a
day and just rest, do some things for yourself, go have your hair done, or
whatever." And what I really wanted to hear was somebody saying, "Good for
you. What you're doing is so important." That's really what I wanted to hear
because there was no way I was staying home. There was no way. I wasn't
going to have my hair done. And rest? I had to get up every three hours to
pump anyway. I wasn't getting any rest. I might as well be at the hospital.
There's no way anybody was going to talk me out of being there.*

*Do whatever you need to do. Don't let anybody talk you out of it. I
went every day. It took me longer to heal, but I healed. It was more important
that I was there with him.* —Marcia

Facing Your Fears

Deep down I felt completely out of control. I would lie awake at night in a panic imagining her living with awful handicaps. How would we be able to take care of her? What if she was a "vegetable"? What if she lived for three or four months and then died? It was an awful time. ... I wanted to be sure that if Shayna were to die, I would have no regrets about how everything was handled. So I planned for the worst. I made my sister-in-law pick out a family plot and talk to the funeral director about different options. (I couldn't bring myself to go there; my husband wanted nothing to do with this.) I know this must sound terribly morbid, but it gave me a sense of control. I needed to be ready for anything. —Karen

Becoming a parent in the NICU includes learning to deal with your fears. It can be very disturbing to see your baby covered with all kinds of tubes and wires, surrounded by humming, blinking, and sometimes beeping machinery. Your imagination can run wild.

My babies did not look like babies. They were so small. I knew I was supposed to feel an overwhelming love for these children, but all I could feel was fear. I was scared to get any more emotionally involved because I knew he chances of their survival were very slim. I was scared to touch them. —Kimberly

The thing I was most afraid of was that she would die. The very close runner up to that was that she would be severely disabled. I was picturing basically a vegetable. They are there, they're breathing, but they're gone. —Brooke

Especially early on, your anxieties may mount each time you see your baby: Has my baby's condition changed? How can I risk getting close to a baby who looks so sick? What can I possibly offer as a parent? What if this baby dies? In the dark recesses of your mind, you know that not every NICU baby goes home. You may try to ignore your more overwhelming fears, but you pay a price; you may have heightened concerns about other issues or unusually strong reactions to certain events.

Throughout this time we worried quietly to ourselves, never voicing our concerns. I am usually very expressive about my emotions, but I was too afraid to say anything, certain that my biggest fears would come true if I gave them a voice. I also was in denial that anything was really wrong. Still, I would dread going to the hospital in fear that there would be bad news and that I would have to face it alone. Sometimes there was. Other times I would have my husband call ahead to get a report before I went to the hospital. —Laura

I tried not to let myself think that they are going to die, but each moment was so scary—like, "What does that machine mean?" In the beginning, I had to wonder, "When that beeps, is my baby dead?" —Stephie

I didn't read any books for a good four months, and I listened to the radio because I didn't want to be in the middle of a good book or listening to one of my tapes that I really like when I got the phone call that she had died. ... I didn't want to taint it. So I did crossword puzzles because I figured, "I hate crossword puzzles. If she dies, it's okay because I [already] hate crossword puzzles." —Brooke

I don't know how I managed the fears. I certainly didn't acknowledge them at the time. When Sarah was born, I didn't allow myself to really consider her death. I knew it was a possibility but never once spoke of it aloud. I approached any physical or mental impairment the same way. It was never spoken of. ... What was I most afraid of? Going down to the unit and not finding the baby where she was supposed to be. —Cindy

On the second or third day, after I was getting around pretty good on my own, I waddled over to visit her in her original incubator parking spot. I knew she was doing well, had been fine the night before, but when I walked in, she was gone! That cold fear feeling you get when you have a close call with disaster came over me. I can't really describe it other than "chilling"! On the outside I appeared calm, but my insides were mush. ... I asked someone, and that's when they told me about moving her to the transitional nursery. Whew! —Linda

No matter how your baby is doing in the NICU, it is normal to have fears about what's going on, what's next, and what the future might bring. It

Becoming a Parent in the NICU

can be scary to admit those fears, but doing so will not make them materialize. Only by facing your fears squarely can you overcome them. Instead of your fears being another emotional barrier between you and your baby, they become something you deal with and put aside, allowing you stay mobilized and involved with your baby. Instead of being paralyzed by what *might* happen, you become engaged with what *is* happening

Voicing your fears also enables you to seek relevant information and to ask for reassurance from the doctors and nurses. They may not always be able to give you the comfort or guarantees that you need. But information can help you cope by countering your imaginings, which can be much more scary than the reality. For example, perhaps another infant born at the same gestation as yours is battling grave complications, and you may conclude that this is par for the course. Instead of entertaining these grim possibilities unnecessarily, ask your primary nurse about the implications for *your* baby. You may find that because your baby had a relatively straightforward delivery, she or he is not at the same risk for those complications. The nurse can shed light on your baby's unique profile and assure you that every baby follows a unique hospital course.

Fears about disabilities or death are especially frightening. Still, facing these fears brings them into the light where you can deal with them. Ask your questions, gather information, and remind yourself to focus on what is happening *now*, and what your health care teammates *do* know, rather than what might happen or what is unknown. And remember that if either of these fears becomes a reality, you *can* cope, adjust, and find meaning. (For more on discovering disabilities, see Chapter 18; for more on coping with the death of a baby, see Chapter 11.)

Balancing Fear and Anger

Sometimes when parents disregard their fears, the balance of fear and anger becomes upset, and anger dominates. You may be seething at your baby's doctors, nurses, your partner, or others close to you. You may be furious with yourself, your body, the breast pump, the ventilator, medical technology, fate, God. To your dismay, you may find yourself even feeling angry with or disappointed in your tiny baby. (See Chapter 9, on bonding, for reassurance that these feelings are normal.)

Just as fear is a normal expression of parental anxiety, so are feelings of anger. But if some of your anger is merely covering your fears, this anger can unnecessarily seep into your relationships or interfere with other parts of your life. Misplaced anger can also exacerbate feelings of detachment from your baby. Your goal is to feel angry at what is frustrating or enraging and to feel afraid of what is scary.

To restore the balance between fear and anger, it is important that you acknowledge the fears and disappointments that lie beneath the rage. Do you fear that your tiny baby may fade instead of progressing? Do you fear you're not up to the challenge of parenting this child? Are you afraid that your child will have delays or disabilities? Are you afraid your baby may die? It is frightening to face an uncertain future and not know what will be asked of you. It hurts to think that your child may suffer. It's devastating if you see your fondest hopes being crushed.

Coping with your anger includes getting in touch with your deep feelings of grief and hurt—hurt that this had to happen to your precious child and family. Working through your despair frees you to get close to and love your child for who he or she is. Whatever the prognosis, over time, you *can* move beyond your anger and other disconcerting feelings about your baby. (For more on this subject, see "Getting to the Bottom of Your Grief" in Chapter 3 and "Perspectives on Parenting Your Preemie" in Chapter 15.)

Negotiating the Medical Barriers in the NICU

He was taken down the hall to the NICU, but I felt as if he were a million miles away. I had been carrying him around for seven months, and I could not get used to the idea that I had to look at him in an open warmer with tubes in him. We couldn't hold him because he was on an oxygen hood, so all I could do was lay my hand on him and cry uncontrollably. —Jenny

I wanted so badly to pick him up. To hold him close to me. To rock him and sing to him and feed him. But all I could do was reach in and touch his tiny hand. I couldn't even stroke him. Any more stimulation than just a touch would be too much for his little system to handle just yet. I was crushed. This was not how it was supposed to be. I should have had my boy in my arms— not in this bed. I went back to my room and cried—again. —Ami

• • •

I can remember that right after the surgery I could not touch her. At all. Period. If I touched her, she had a tachycardia. She would [set off] her alarms. And the nurse said, "I have to tell you not to touch her because you're disturbing her and stopping her from healing." And I just sat and cried and cried. It kills you. ... Going through that was the worst thing that's ever happened to me in my life. The absolute worst. —Beth

Particularly when your baby is in critical condition, there are many medical obstacles between you and your little one. It's hard to get past the tubes, wires, machines, and the plastic walls of the incubator. Sometimes, your baby may be too sick or overwhelmed or tired to be held without compromising his or her vital signs. Even when your baby is stable, you might feel intimidated by how much you don't know about your baby's medical status and care.

Getting to know your infant when obstacles stand between you is difficult. Medical conditions and immaturity can prevent your baby from responding to you. You may have trouble discovering her or his personality and preferences because of all the medical treatments and equipment. You cannot even see your baby's face for the tubes and tape and eye masks.

I had a tendency ... I never looked at her, I was always watching the monitors. And then one day this one nurse came in and said, "All right, we're going to fix this," and she took a blanket and just threw it over the monitor. And I was [gasp], and the nurse said, "If it alarms, we'll know it, but you can't sit there and just keep staring at the monitor." Because every time her heart rate would go 160, 140, 150, I was panicking. So [covering the monitors] helped a lot. —Suzanne

Hindered by the barriers of medical technology, you can feel terribly disconnected and helpless. As a parent, you want more than anything to be able to *do* something, to get involved, to *nurture* your little one, yet you do not want to interfere with your baby's care or hurt your fragile infant. You know that these technological obstacles are necessary for your baby's survival, and yet they are so *in the way.*

Tony held her first, and then it was my turn. My surprise and shock was with the way they have to do it all, because of the ventilator and everything. And I said, "I don't have her," and they said, "Yes, you do," and I said, "No, I don't have her," and they said, "Yes, you do." It was just that concept of not realizing how extremely light she was. I mean, I felt as if I were holding a blanket. —Suzanne

Especially early on, you may feel keenly that your newborn is inaccessible to you. You may believe that you have no place in this tiny one's life when you can see how urgent his or her medical needs are. In the days and weeks following delivery, your ability to get past the medical barriers depends on what you can tolerate, absorb, and accomplish. But as your distress lightens and as you adjust to the NICU, your abilities and confidence will grow.

At first, I was scared to touch T. J. He was so fragile. Also, I was overwhelmed by all of the machines and the information that I had been given. I didn't feel as if I was really his mother because I had so little control over what was happening to him. Gradually, I became more confident. —Claire

I wished I'd taken more control right away. By the first week's end, I was just going in and picking her up, but those first few days, I'd wait to be offered, as if she belonged to these strangers and not me. I would touch her through her little incubator, apologizing still. —Linda

There were all those damn machines and people and procedures and tests. I never really felt like Sarah was in my control until she was moved from the critical area. Once she was in a regular bed like a full-term baby, swaddled for all she was worth, I began to feel more like a parent. That's when I started becoming less frightened and more protective—because I could protect her. I knew (or thought I did) what she needed to feel secure and loved. —Cindy

It is natural for you to hang back at first. As your baby's condition improves, some of the barriers will disappear, and you'll be more confident about negotiating the remaining ones—and the gap between you and your baby will become narrower. In the meantime, when you can't have your baby in your arms, let your voice, your touch, your presence hold your little one. When you can't be at the bedside, let your heartfelt thoughts forge a bond.

• • •

I just sat there beside him, talking to him. We tried massaging him, but he couldn't take the stimulation until much later in his hospital stay. So we settled for just hanging out. —Sterling

I discovered that they all loved to be read to. I would sit there and read to them, go from station to station. So I knew I could do something to make them happy. So even when I couldn't hold them, I could still care for them. —Julie

Tips for Overcoming Barriers

It's quite challenging to negotiate your way around the medical barriers the NICU imposes. Here are some suggestions that can encourage you to overcome the hurdles:

- *Give yourself time to orient and regain your trust in yourself.* The early days and weeks of your child's life may be frightening and uncomfortable, but in time, you will find your voice and your sense of competence. As the NICU becomes less foreign, you will begin to feel less hesitant about joining in your baby's care.

- *Recognize that your feelings of inadequacy arise from your devotion to your tiny baby.* Your devotion is apparent in your desire to nurture your baby in your own way, as well as in your recognition that your baby needs medical support and specialized handling. Your feelings of limitation or inadequacy reflect your baby's medical condition, not your competence as a parent.

- *See your frustration as a sign of connection.* When you feel frustrated with the barriers between you and your baby, are impatient with the medical situation, or feel envious that other parents are able to be with their babies, consider these feelings signs of your growing courage and involvement with your newborn.

- *Focus on your baby, not the medical equipment.* Ignore the "stuff," and see the little person behind it all. If you tend to watch the monitors, try watching your baby instead. To gauge your baby's condition and progress, even your health care teammates rely largely on their observations rather than on monitors and measures.

- *Ask your health care teammates to show you their "tricks of the trade."* You might ask them to show you, for example, how they handle your baby without disturbing the wires and tubes. Ask them what kinds of handling your

Parenting Your Premature Baby and Child

baby can benefit from and how to get your baby out of the incubator and into your arms. Model their behavior, and soon you'll build confidence about working around the lines and equipment.

- *Try any avenue you can to relate to your baby.* You may find yourself doing "strange" things in an effort to feel close to or get to know your baby, such as taking joy in hearing your baby's cry. Remind yourself that you are facing unique challenges in parenting and in forming a relationship with your little one. Unique challenges often call for unique behavior.

The first time Josh got off the ventilator, we kind of tortured him, as only a parent of a preemie could do, but we wanted to hear his voice. He liked the pacifier by then, and we kept pulling it out just so we could hear him cry—because it was so magical to hear any kind of voice. We would put it back in and pull it out just so we could hear him complain. It was so amazing to us to hear that. Some of the stuff we did, it just wasn't normal. But it was all we knew. —Stephie

Eventually, as your confidence and competence grow, you will begin to feel more like a parent in spite of the medical barriers. In the meantime, remind yourself that you are doing the best you can in a difficult situation. Rest assured that, over time, your best will become even better.

Feeling Displaced by Your Baby's Health Care Providers

It seemed so wrong to give birth to this baby and then leave him for someone else to take care of. I was supposed to do it. I'm his mommy. Not these nurses. Not the doctors. Me. So it should be me taking care of him. It wasn't fair. That's all I could think. It just wasn't fair. —Ami

When they're in the hospital, it's not your baby; it's their baby. You have to ask to do everything. Or you feel like you have to ask to do everything. Even though you probably don't, you feel like you do. —Beth

It was not me [taking care of my babies], it was the doctors and the nurses. And I hated that, and I was resentful of the fact that they were the ones who were taking care of our children instead of me. But I'm not a doctor, and the doctors and nurses were giving the babies the life-sustaining whatever they had to have, but they weren't nurturing them the way a parent would. I mean, the nurses were very wonderful. I would see the nurses in there holding babies just because they wanted to. But you're a nurse, you're not me. You know?

At home is where I actually feel like their mother. In the NICU, I was their supplier of food and that was about it. I bathed them, I changed their diapers, and I did what I could do. I held them, I rocked them while I was there. But it's like babysitting. You give them back. They couldn't come home. —Pam

When your baby is in the NICU, you may feel displaced by the health professionals who are taking care of your baby. Feeling like your baby isn't quite *yours* builds yet another barrier between you and your little one. You may feel that the nurses and doctors are your baby's primary caregivers because their jobs seem so much more critical than yours does. After all, they are *saving a life.* All you can do is hold a tiny hand and whisper endearments.

Feelings of displacement can give rise to envy and frustration, especially when you see how adept the nurses are at holding and taking care of your baby. You want more than anything to know what they know, and to know it *now* so that you can contribute to your baby's care with confidence. Yet although you appreciate their ability and expertise, you may also resent it. Knowing that you alone can't meet your baby's needs feeds your feelings of frustration, helplessness, and parental incompetence.

When I had to return to work, the long hours away were torture. I counted every minute until I could bolt to my car, wolf down the portable food I kept there, and race across town to the hospital. I ran breathless up the stairs, sprinted to the NICU, and looked eagerly for a task I could participate in to remind me that I was a mommy. I will forever carry the rage, the wounding, I felt when I faced nurses who backed me down, forced me to the sidelines, and asserted their authority at the cost of my parenting. —Susan

I always had to ask permission to touch her or hold her. Much later on, she was almost off the vent, and I was more comfortable picking her up while she was on the ventilator. I did it by myself without asking, and I thought that was a really big deal. It seemed like I was always asking permission. I wasn't encouraged a whole lot to do things for her. —Suzanne

After a few days, I became possessive. I wanted to change his diaper, take his temperature, feed him. One day, I was running a little late, and I had called to say I was going to be in at this time and I want to do everything, and his nurse said, "Okay." Well, she went on break, and the nurse who took over went ahead and fed him. I was so upset because I felt like they were doing my job. They get to do all the medical things that I can't do, and so the few things I get to do, I want to do them to feel like I'm a part of this baby. ... And I remember I was really down in the dumps that day because I didn't get to do my job. —Vickie

While I was thrilled that Josie was doing so well and was at a good hospital, I couldn't help but feel that her nurses were far more competent than I was. They were so confident holding her and changing her diaper. I was a nervous wreck just picking her up. It took me twice as long to change her diaper, and I actually dreaded bathing her, even though the nurses highly recommended it. I wondered why she would need a bath when she wasn't out playing in a sandbox or making mud pies, but I felt too intimidated by these skilled nurses to question them. —Rebekah

You may feel frustrated, thinking that if only they'd step aside, you could really be with your baby, yet at the same time, you may dread being given that chance because you feel so inadequate and unsure of how to handle your infant. You don't want to fail your little one. This fear of failure can make you back off even more, and being so removed can make you feel like even more of a failure. This can turn into a vicious cycle that deepens your feelings of detachment.

Probably one of the rougher aspects was saying, "No, I'm the mother, I'm supposed to be the one to do this. You're not supposed to be doing this. This is supposed to be my job." But I was so scared of her. I didn't want to touch her because I was afraid that, like, her arm would fall off, which of course is a completely irrational fear but one that was very real in my mind at that point in time. It was like a double-edged sword. On the one hand, I was really happy that other people were doing [the caretaking] because I didn't feel quite ready to, and, on the other hand, it was, "Wait a minute here!" —Brooke

I remember one time when my husband was pushing me to change her diaper, and he was saying, "C'mon, Michelle, they have to watch you do it. They need to know you can do this." And I was like, "Why? They do it all the time. Let them do it. I'm too afraid to touch her. She's too tiny." I felt like, "You know more about it, you just do it." —Michelle

One of the things that got frustrating was that some nurses would let me go in and change a diaper or hand me [one of] the babies and walk away, and other nurses wouldn't let me touch them. Or they would say things like, "Your baby is so overstimulated today," or "Your baby doesn't like to be touched." Excuse me? I know my baby. You never even had my baby before today. But I couldn't defy them and put my hand in there and touch. Since [these babies] were my first, I didn't really know. If that happened today, I'd say, "Sorry, I'm touching my baby. Go get the doctor if you want to kick me out of here. If my baby starts desatting, I'll take my hand away." But back then, it was, "Okay, this nurse says no," so I didn't do it. There's a sense of powerlessness. —Stephie

My lack of knowledge made me feel completely powerless. I visited her in the NICU but did not know what to say or do. I felt useless and conspicuous standing beside her bed. To make matters worse, days later I still felt no connection to her. —Renee

Even as your baby's condition improves, your feelings of helplessness and detachment may persist. You may find it hard to believe that there is much that you can do, and decide that it's better to leave your tiny baby in the care of the people who "really" know how to do things for him or her. You may wonder if your baby even knows who you are.

Building Confidence in Your Ability to Take Care of Your Baby

The antidote to feeling displaced is getting more involved in the care of your baby. Becoming more involved takes time. In the beginning, when your baby needs such intensive care, it is normal to hesitate. You need encouragement from your health care teammates and opportunities to practice caregiving skills so that you can feel comfortable taking care of your baby. Here are a few pointers that may help:

- *Remind yourself that one of your responsibilities as a caring parent is entrusting your little one to the skilled care of others when that is necessary.* You are parenting your baby around the clock with your thoughts and, when you can be there, simply by your presence.

- *Accept your own grief.* Knowing that you need medical staff to teach you how to care for your baby and to supervise you as you learn can be disheartening. It's okay to feel sad, angry, and disappointed that your baby requires professional monitoring, intervention, and instructions—that what was supposed to be so simple and natural is instead so complicated and unnatural.

- *Go easy on yourself when you feel awkward or unsure.* Nobody expects you to be comfortable with your tiny baby right away. When you're feeling incompetent, remind yourself that nobody is more protective of or cares more about your baby than you do. If you had the power to make everything better, you'd do it.

- *Break the fear cycle.* If you are afraid to fail, to make mistakes, or to show your inexperience, your fear may keep you from relating to your baby. A way to break this cycle is to confront your fears, which will empower you to tap your courage, take the risk, and step up to the plate. Try telling your baby's best nurses that you're unsure of yourself. With encouragement and support from your health care teammates, time, and practice, your confidence *will* grow.

- *Spend blocks of time caring for your baby.* If you live far from the NICU, ask the hospital if there are accommodations for parents who wish to stay overnight. Spending large blocks of time learning and practicing caregiving skills can really help you build confidence.

- *Be persistent in your requests to be involved.* If you ask for a more active parenting role but are refused, continue to bring the subject up with your baby's doctors and nurses. Encourage them to review the research for themselves. Give them a copy of the "Growth of Developmentally Supportive Care" section in Chapter 7, or share other resources with them.

- *Practice speaking your mind as you begin to feel more sure of yourself.* If you have a question or an opinion, voice it to a staff member with whom you feel some connection. Over time, you will develop the confidence to speak directly with others on the medical team.
- *Ask for the information you need.* Remind your medical teammates that you want to be knowledgeable about your baby's medical conditions and needs because eventually you will be taking your baby home.
- *Consider your health care teammates to be your allies.* Remind yourself that you all share the same goal—the best care for your baby—even when it seem as if your teammates are keeping you from your baby or taking away your choices. If you are afraid that voicing your concerns or preferences will compromise your infant's care, talk about your fears with a staff member you feel you can trust, with the charge nurse, or with the head neonatologist. If your concerns mount and medical decisions must be made, do not hesitate to seek a second opinion from another doctor, hospital, or medical practice. You have the right to do this.
- *Recognize that the responses of individual staff can affect your degree of involvement.* The actions and attitudes of individual nurses can affect your ability to join in your baby's care. Some will welcome your presence and involvement and will teach you in a way that nurtures your parenting spirit. Others will feel uncomfortable handing over caregiving tasks. Embrace the welcoming messages and ignore the negative messages.
- *Recognize your essential role as nurturer.* If you feel that the nurses don't nurture your infant as you would, consider it proof that you are central to your baby's care. You, the devoted parent, are the one most able to provide the nurturing your baby needs and to make sure that he or she feels loved. You are the one responsible for this aspect of your baby's care. As such, you are an irreplaceable part of your infant's NICU health care team.
- *Remind yourself that you are your baby's emotional support.* As you learn to tune in to your baby emotionally, you'll increasingly be able to read your baby's cues. You'll learn what soothes him or her and be able to identify

when there is a problem. As you note that, "Hey, I was right," you'll begin to trust your instincts and intuitions about your baby. So, try whatever seems right to you to soothe your little one. Ask the niggling questions or request an assessment of your baby's condition if you are worried. Give yourself permission to do the kind of parenting you want to do.

- *Recognize what constitutes parenting.* Your thoughts, your questions, and your attempts to do practical things for your baby all count as "parenting." You also have special qualities that no neonatologist or nurse has: an intense love for your baby and a special familiarity that your baby finds calming. You also have a vision of a future together.

One long night, a midnight shift nurse told me that I was perfectly capable of performing some of the tasks involved in caring for my son. She recognized my motherhood—and stunned me, honored me, by helping me do the same. —Susan

When I finally got to hold Sean for the first time, he was three weeks old. I finally held that tiny child, and cried at how beautiful he was and how much of a precious miracle he was. I realized then that this little boy needed me as much as he needed the doctors and nurses that were caring for him. —Ami

As he grew, I could hold him to my breast, and even though he wasn't supposed to be able to nurse, he could rest and be comfortable there. —Inkan

Parenting from a Distance

Perhaps the biggest barrier to parenting a preemie in the NICU is physical distance. Even if your home is around the corner from the hospital, your baby is not there. You cannot see and touch your baby whenever you want.

Parenting your baby from a distance can seem an insurmountable challenge at times. Even if your preemie is your only child and you are able to spend a lot of time in the NICU, there is still a sense of distance between you and your baby. Most parents have other obligations and limitations that make it impossible for them to be with their baby as much as they'd like. If you have other children to care for, your heart and your time are pulled in opposite directions. You may feel as if you are never in the right place. Whether you ache to have your baby with you or feel detached and wish you didn't, you are grappling with the painful feelings of separation that come with having a baby in the NICU.

I hated being a mother during the times the girls were in the hospital. I was a new mother, and yet I had no baby to show off. It was strange. Even after Ashley came home right before Christmas, it wasn't the same. I still had one other baby at the hospital and was still cheated out of being able to bring my twins home together from the hospital. —Rosa

Carving out the time, energy, and (especially if your baby is far from home) even the money to be with your little one as often as you'd like can be challenging. Many parents struggle to fit a caregiving schedule into complicated lives. If you live close to the hospital, you may feel even more pressure to spend lots of time there, neglecting your other responsibilities. Not being there as much as you think you should be may cause you to feel guilty for being unavailable to your baby.

And if you live far from the hospital, you may have mixed feelings: at times wishing you lived closer so that you could go more easily and, at other times, feeling relieved that the miles give you an "excuse" for taking a break.

Whether you live nearby or far away, it is natural to feel selfish for needing a break, wanting more time for other responsibilities, and resenting the constant trips to the NICU. When you think that your baby is struggling just to live and breathe and grow, you may feel embarrassed for complaining about your own problems.

Most parents, whatever their circumstances, must work to find a balance. That balance may change over time and as your baby's condition changes. And then after homecoming, there's a whole new balancing act to manage!

Of course, one disadvantage to living far from the hospital is that your options aren't very flexible. Parents who live close by can stop in just because they want to. But if you live farther away, spending time with your baby takes more effort and planning. Even an hour's commute each way can be time consuming and draining when done regularly. When you live some distance from the hospital, you may feel scared and especially unsettled that your baby is so far away from you.

Making the Most of Your Presence

How can you make the most of your time spent in the NICU? Figure out what you need from each stay. Is it meeting with the doctors face to face? Talking with your baby's nurses? Watching your baby, even as she or he sleeps? Holding him or her? Taking photographs? Fussing over the toys and homey touches in your baby's incubator? Learning caregiving tasks, such as bathing, changing, and feeding?

As you read all the ideas in this book, you may feel that you must concentrate lots of parenting into very small segments. But don't expect each precious stay to be perfectly satisfying. Each time will be what it is—a typical slice of your newborn's day. Expect variety in what happens, as well as in how you feel. You can also adopt Janet's perspective: "There was no 'most meaningful' way. Every minute we got to spend with her was meaningful."

Many parents—even the ones who go to the NICU daily—don't feel like much of a parent until their baby comes home. You may find yourself feeling restless and dissatisfied even if you are able to spend all day, every day at the hospital. No matter how much time you spend in the NICU with your baby, it's still less than what you would wish for.

Many NICUs try to accommodate the needs of parents who live far from the hospital by sending them postcards, photographs, or e-mail. These tools can forge connections over the miles. As computer technology becomes more affordable and widespread, faraway parents can connect over the Internet to see digital photographs or even videos of their baby and to communicate online with hospital staff (video-conferencing).

Also remember that physical distance need not equal emotional distance. If you are concerned about the "bonding" time you are missing, remind yourself that you can pick up where you left off each time you go to the NICU and when your baby comes home. If you are concerned that your baby won't know you, be assured that your baby recognizes there is something special about you. Watch how different your baby's reactions are to you than to the nurses.

If you are concerned that you aren't getting the practice you need to learn how to take care of your baby after homecoming, ask your hospital about "rooming-in" with your baby before discharge. A preemie who is stable can sometimes be moved to a private room adjoining the nursery. Some NICUs have facilities for this and encourage parents to use them. Living with your baby around the clock for a couple of days and nights at the hospital gives you the chance to practice caregiving with the reassuring presence and advice of your baby's nurses. During this time you are the primary caregiver, the one in charge, and the nurses are your trusted consultants.

Making the Most of Your Absences

Making the most of your absences means discarding the idea that when you and your baby are apart, you are disconnected. When you can't be with your baby, you can still maintain contact in ways that have meaning for you. If the hospital has a toll-free number, call often. Try to telephone at a scheduled time when your favorite primary nurse can speak with you at length to give you a full report. When you spend time at the hospital, leave behind something containing your picture, your smell, or the sound of your voice (such as a recording of you talking, reading, or singing to your baby). Just knowing it is there can help you feel close. Similarly, take something home with you that has your baby's picture, smell, or voice. If it helps to write to your baby, talk about your baby, or just think about your baby, do it.

> *I always made sure that Dominique had a little something—a charm—to help kept her safe while I was away.* —Rosa

> *Having two other kids at home and trying to finish up some of my work, I was not the most present. Some parents stay night and day. I wanted to be there a lot, especially when he was awake, but if he was sleeping, it was okay for me to leave him asleep—since that's what he had to do a lot. We gave him some animals and a blanket to feel at home. I was there mentally even if I wasn't there physically. He was in my thoughts constantly.* —Gallice

Making the most of your absences also means taking care of yourself when you're not in the NICU: keeping your home life running as smoothly as possible, maintaining healthy habits, and doing things that nurture you and give you respite. By tending to yourself and your other business when you're away from your baby's bedside, you can really attend to your little one when you *are* there. You can be more nurturing and soothing when you're not feeling that the rest of your life is pure chaos. Leaving your baby is one of the most difficult parts of parenting in the NICU. But your absences are inevitable, even necessary. By using your absences to take care of yourself, they benefit both you and your baby.

For a little while, our son was very fragile. We could go there and hang out, but we couldn't even open the incubator, so we didn't go as much or for as long. How were we helping our child? We were doing normal activities, seeing friends, getting support, sleep, food, time together, downtime. We were healing ourselves, too! —Maren

Baby Diaries

Baby "diaries" are notes written by the NICU nurses "from" the baby to the parents. This idea, which originated at Simpson Maternity Hospital in Edinburgh, Scotland, grew out of the messages and notes the nurses would leave for their replacements coming on shift. The nurses began sharing these "diary" entries with the babies' parents, who were delighted and comforted by these little notes "from" their babies. Here is an example, the first note Susanne and her husband received, followed by this mother's recollections of how the note affected her:

Good morning, Mummy and Daddy, I just woke up from a lovely long sleep, and I have been a very good boy. My special breathing machine is making breathing a bit easier for me: small boys like me need some help. I have a cozy wee house a bit like a greenhouse but more comfortable. I have some lovely blue stripey socks on, and I think I look very handsome. There are lots of funnily dressed people here to keep an eye on me, and I have worked out how to make them come and visit me by making my bells ring!!! Hope you had a long sleep, Mummy, and that you can come and see me today if you feel better. Daddy said you will have to get rid of your drips [IVs]. I need mine for a wee while longer till I grow a bit bigger. Phew, I must stop now because I am tired with all this typing. It is hard work when your fingers are only small. Bye Bye. Love, Connor XXXXX

Well, you can imagine I was both delighted and overwhelmed with emotion. It was very powerful and comforting, and after having never seen this baby they all told me I had, all of a sudden I really felt as if I did have a baby after all. It also prepared me for how Connor would look to an extent in a lighthearted way. Over the next few months when they had a minute or two, the nurses would add to Connor's "diary," and when we would arrive, a little note was taped to the end of his incubator. And even though we knew it was done by the nurses, we would laugh and say, "If he could talk, these are the things he would say." Good days and bad, when he put weight on or when he had to be reintubated, he sent us a lighthearted note, which gave us a relationship with him and made things easier. It helped us immensely. I can never stress to anyone enough how much this meant to us. —Susanne

Even if your NICU doesn't provide baby notes, you can write them yourself if the idea appeals to you. Share the notes with your partner as a way of conveying information about your baby and your solitary treks to the NICU. Writing notes from a lighthearted point of view can help to ease the trauma of your baby's hospitalization and help you see your baby as a person, a member of your family. (For more on baby diaries, see Appendix A, "A Note to Caregivers.")

Recognizing the Importance of Your Presence

As you begin to feel more like a parent, you'll learn to recognize the importance of your presence in the NICU and your participation in your baby's care. At first, your attempts to hold your baby's hand or cup your baby's head can seem so small next to the life-sustaining medical intervention he or she is receiving. But, in fact, many experts believe it can make a significant difference in promoting weight gain, in how soon your baby gets off the ventilator and how well she or he continues to breathe without it, and in reducing the length of hospitalization. Your baby benefits greatly from your nurturing. As you get to know your baby, you will observe how she or he is soothed by your comforting presence.

He would calm down if I stroked his head in the incubator. My husband noticed that his vital signs would change when I spoke near his incubator or when I would stroke him. I never noticed that because I didn't look at the monitors much, but they were somehow comforting to my husband. —Laurie

I always felt that he knew me, even from the beginning. I spent every day by his bed talking to him and making sure he knew that we loved him. He always

Parenting Your Premature Baby and Child

was very calm when I was with him—very rarely did he have any bad times when I was by his bedside. If he was upset, I could open the porthole and put my finger in his palm, and he would settle down. —Kelly

A nursing student was holding my son, and he was crying inconsolably. I took him from her, and he stopped crying instantly. My presence helped them thrive. They loved being touched and held and cuddled. —Erica

Even when her eyes were still fused shut, Emma would acknowledge our visits. Her little eyebrows would raise up and down. —Diane

I was pretty sure he knew me after a few days. I know he could recognize me by smelling me. He wouldn't do it every time, but I got the feeling of him turning toward me or moving when I got there, or when he was sleeping, he would start to do little imperceptible movements, when he was perfectly quiet before, but he could feel that I was there. And against me, he was just breathing, not getting agitated but just breathing quietly against me, and I'm sure he knew it was me. —Gallice

When you start to see that you are not simply another set of hands to your baby, you are beginning to embrace your parenting role. Realizing that you're special and important to your infant can be very comforting. Of course, with this realization comes the belief that you should be even more available to your baby. Discovering the powerful effect your presence has on your baby makes being away that much harder.

Despite the importance of your presence to your little one, though, your baby does not need you at the bedside constantly. Your preemie can benefit from long stretches of uninterrupted sleep. Your baby also needs you to be healthy and resilient, so taking time to rest, run errands, or have lunch with a friend is time well spent. Put aside your guilt. You do not need to remain hospitalized with your baby.

Finally, keep in mind that staying informed, advocating, and making the most of your presence (and absence) are all ways of staying meaningfully connected to your child. Recognizing the importance of your presence doesn't refer only to your presence at your baby's bedside but also to your ongoing presence in your baby's life.

• • •

It's painful to be separated from your baby when he or she needs you, but be reassured that the time you spend with your baby really matters, and the benefits don't disappear when you leave. Your nurturing presence builds your baby's capacity to endure your absences. Have faith in your baby's ability to manage when you're away.

Spreading Yourself among Multiple Babies

If you have more than one baby in the NICU, it may seem that there is not enough of you to go around. You may feel torn between babies, wondering which one needs you more.

When they were first born, Evan was so much smaller and so much sicker that we were just really concentrating on him. If we had to sit by somebody's bedside, we'd sit by Evan's bedside. I would go and look at Josh and make sure he was okay, and I would talk to him, but we concentrated on Evan. And then a couple of days later, they did the brain ultrasounds, and we found out that Josh had a grade III brain bleed. And that's when the thought of having twins that are so sick just really got to me. How can I do this? How can I sit by two babies who need me so much? [tears] Josh really needs me, he's got this brain bleed, and Evan is so little and so sick. How can I do it? I just didn't know how. —Stephie

I was so wrapped up in Jacob, I wasn't thinking that I had other children. I still had Claire and Emily to worry about. I realized that I had better start paying attention to all of them. It wasn't just Jacob who was critically ill, that any one of them could have had problems. I guess I was feeling like a pretty lousy mother. ... I wish I could have cloned myself and stuck one of me next to each of them. I felt pretty inadequate—like I didn't have enough of me, I didn't have enough to give. —Julie

When you are the parent of multiples, you cannot give any one of your infants your undivided attention. This may make you feel especially neglectful. It is important to remember that you are putting your energy and resources where you think they are needed the most. You can't do any better than that. Trust yourself to give each infant what he or she needs on any given day—or even hour by hour. Also remember that it isn't so much the amount of time but the quality of your focus that's important. For instance, Pam discovered that when her twin babies were each in a different section of the hospital, she could focus really well on whichever child she was with. She felt that both babies benefited from her being able to devote her full attention and energy to them one at a time. For her, spending half her time really being with each one was better than spending all that time ricocheting between the two.

Also give yourself permission to share the job of nurturing your babies with your partner. If one day you feel especially drawn to one of your babies, spend more time with that one and encourage your partner to focus on the other(s). Have confidence that your babies will do just fine even if your attention is split at times.

Also let yourself appreciate and rely on the attention your babies' nurses give them. The nurses are there to help you care for your little ones. Finally, remember to give yourself credit for being your babies' round-the-clock advocate. One mother talks about doing what she could and trusting that her triplets would get the rest of what they needed from the NICU staff:

> *When you have three babies in the NICU and you're going from one to another to another, dealing with what each one of them has, you just have to know that they're in the best place that they can possibly be and that they're going to be taken care of. And that there's nothing you can do to make them better but advocate for them.* —Betsy

Gaining Confidence

Over the course of your baby's hospitalization, as you see your preemie respond to your voice, your touch, and your scent, you'll feel more confident in yourself as a critical partner in your baby's healing. Your tentative touch will gradually develop into a more confident, protective hold. Your hesitant requests will become more assertive and your convictions more firm. Only your preemie's own growth will rival your development as an involved parent.

> *There are so many things I learned about myself, walking in there. I'm a very confident person anyway, but to realize that there's a certain amount of confidence you need to be able to go in there and do what the nurses do. You know, they're flipping these babies around, and they're not afraid of this stuff.*

As the days go by, you start learning, okay, I can have the confidence to hold this baby, to know what cord is for what, and when to be alarmed and when not to. —Vickie

We set up vigil at his bedside and reminded the occasional hurried medical student to wash his hands between beds, asked janitors to avoid clanging trash cans near his bedside, argued with doctors about placing infected babies adjacent with single nursing care when beds got scarce. —Susan

As you get more involved in your baby's care, you may also notice an emotional shift. You may begin to let go of some of your sadness and guilt. You develop ways of relating to your preemie that go beyond grief and shock about the premature birth. You slowly begin to feel more like yourself. Most significantly, in bits and spurts you have moments of feeling "parental." You feel bolstered by the simplest things—being referred to as your baby's mother or father, being asked for permission to perform a medical test or procedure, or even noticing a family resemblance. As you start to use the words "mother" or "father" to refer to yourself, you begin to feel more like a parent. The more you feel like a parent, the more you can behave like one.

As you start to see yourself as a parent, you also begin to recognize that your baby doesn't depend entirely on technology and skilled care. Your baby also depends on you. Gradually, you gain assurance that your eyes can see what your baby needs and that your touch can soothe and comfort. You begin to feel more in sync with your baby. As that rhythm develops, you realize that you are connected and important to your baby. This realization is both reassuring and a bit anxiety provoking. After all, your last big job as a parent was to complete a pregnancy. Remind yourself that no matter why your pregnancy ended early, your ability to parent this child remains intact.

During his first week, he was so critically ill that he did not respond to anyone. When he was more stable, he began to respond to my voice, by trying to open his eyes. At around the same age, he began to show high sats and fewer bradycardia episodes when one of my breast pads was laid next to him, within sniffing range. Once I was able to hold him, he began gaining weight at a more accelerated rate than when I was not allowed to hold him. The first time I held him for an hour, he gained seventy grams that night. —Jayna

• • •

In fact, as you become accustomed to the monitor bleeps and more comfortable with the tubes and wires (or as they disappear), you may find that the simple, basic things that you had hoped to do with your newborn are things that you now can do. Holding, cooing, singing, soothing, reading to your baby, even just sitting nearby—all of these activities, when done with care, can foster increased intimacy and connection between you and your little one. As your baby grows, you'll be able to do more things, such as feeding, bathing, dressing, and more interacting. The more you are able to meet your baby's needs, the more connected and confident you'll feel.

As Nicholas grew and I got more comfortable with him, we got to know one another. I guess we all end up adapting to the NICU environment in our own time. But pretty soon, I was doing almost everything for him—so, in a sense at least, maybe he saw me as one of his primary caregivers and hopefully the one that wasn't causing him any pain. —Sterling

If you have twins, triplets, or more, remember that becoming a self-assured parent of multiple newborns challenges all parents. Give yourself the time and space to become a parent to each child individually and to become adept at meeting their inevitably various needs.

No matter where your baby sleeps, you are still the parent. No matter how much skilled care your infant needs, you are ultimately the one in charge of your little one's welfare. Above all, remember that your identity as a parent and your confidence in yourself will grow over time. Even if you begin to parent this child from a distance or with some ambivalence, a shaky start doesn't doom your parenting forever. As circumstances change and as you grow and develop into a successful parent, you'll look back and wish you had been able to imagine this comforting future.

Managing Your Regrets

Some parents fault themselves for not being the "perfect," sacrificing mother or father during their baby's hospitalization. You may regret not spending more hours in the nursery, or you may feel burdened by your constant vigil, believing that all the hours you do spend are still not enough. Keeping round-the-clock watch at your baby's bedside can sometimes be an attempt to compensate for feelings of guilt, inadequacy, numbness, and failure. You may be wrestling with the pain of feeling distant from your baby and unlike a parent. You may feel down on yourself, whether you're in the NICU all the time or hardly at all.

If constant attendance in the NICU is wearing you down, remember that although being with your baby because you *want to* can be good for both of you, being with your baby because you feel as if you *should* or you *must* to quell your anxiety or grief is not necessarily beneficial. It might do you more good to take some time and energy to work through your feelings of obligation, worry, and grief by journaling, going to counseling, or talking with a supportive friend. This emotional "clearing" can keep you from emotional and physical exhaustion. Setting aside ten or fifteen minutes a day or an hour a week to write, think, or talk can enhance your ability to be "present" for your little one. Also try viewing all that you are doing for your baby as if in hindsight. Doing so might help you give yourself the credit (and the breaks) you deserve for the magnitude of everything you *are* accomplishing.

> *I drove myself into the ground trying to watch over Vincent while he was in the NICU, and it left me very fragile. —Anne*

> *If I had to do this again, I wouldn't beat myself up so much. I'd take a day off when I needed it without feeling guilty. In the months my kiddos were in the NICU, I was there all day every day but one. I was so exhausted that day that I broke down in tears at the thought of [finally] driving in at 9:30 at night to see my babies. I look back now and can't believe I pushed myself so hard and didn't totally fall apart mentally and physically. —Julie*

If your regrets center on feeling distant from your little one, about not "being there" emotionally or physically for your baby, your guilt may grow after homecoming, as your relationship and connection with your baby deepen. Looking back, you may wonder why you avoided the NICU or felt so removed from your little one. But instead of faulting yourself, recognize that it's hard to feel like a parent when all your interactions with your baby take place in a NICU filled with equipment and trained caregivers. Be compassionate with yourself. Remember how flooded with feelings and fears you were. Recall your baby's condition and all the medical obstacles in your way. Even in the most family-centered NICU, at times you probably felt out of place and unable to nurture your baby in the way you wanted to.

I can think of all sorts of things I wish had been different, but mostly I realize that none of them were possible because I couldn't figure out a way to [deal with] my own anxiety, fear, frustration, anger, sadness, and on some levels, resentment. ... I believe the bottom line is that I wish I could have felt more a part of the whole situation, rather than like a spectator at a horrific accident. —Sheila

The very nature of parenting in the NICU can give rise to feelings of inadequacy. If you have regrets, it is important that you grieve for them and forgive yourself for being unable to do more. Recognize that most of the limitations you had to work within—such as your baby's medical status, your physical and emotional conditions, having more than one baby in the NICU, your other family obligations, the distance between your home and the hospital, the NICU policies—are largely out of your control. Instead, commend yourself for the ways in which you are trying to work within or overcome these limitations. It's also important to remember that there's no such thing as a perfect parent. Reaching for being the best that you can be every day is a worthy goal, but on the days you feel as if you're falling short, reassure yourself that it's okay to be "good enough."

Especially after homecoming, it is natural to look back and agonize over what you wish you would have done or felt differently. But with hindsight, as you hold your little one close, you may also wonder how you could ever have doubted your devotion to and ability to parent this child. Things that bothered you then can seem inconsequential. With time and experience, it is normal to have regrets and recognize mistakes, but it can also be easier to give yourself the benefit of the doubt, to accept that you did your best under the most difficult circumstances.

Points to Remember

- Becoming a parent to a baby in the NICU is different from becoming a parent to a term baby who is home with you. It can take time to adjust to this unfamiliar situation.

- You are likely to be flooded with confusing and overwhelming feelings as you try to feel your way into the job of parenting your tiny baby. Acknowledge your feelings and accept the role they play in mobilizing your development as a parent.
- When your tiny baby is inactive and unresponsive, it is only natural for you to hold back. In fact, your distance can be a sign of your connection and empathy to your child, rather than of detachment.
- Recognize that many parents need a certain amount of privacy to forge a close connection to their infant. As you adjust to the NICU, you'll be able to carve out the quiet, private moments you need.
- No matter how your baby is doing in the NICU, it is normal to have fears about what's next and what the future will bring. Voicing those fears can be scary, but doing so will not make them happen. By facing your fears, you can decrease their power to disturb you and keep them from intruding on your relationship with your baby.
- When in the NICU, it can be easy to feel inadequate as a parent. Try to remember that no matter how much technical care your baby needs, your presence is extremely important to your baby's healing and to your own adjustment.
- Trust any intuitive sense you have that your baby knows who you are and that you are someone special to him or her. Sense your connection—and build on it.
- Your caregiving schedule will depend on many factors in your life. If you can't go to the NICU as often as you'd like, try to find other ways to feel close to your baby.
- Parenting multiples in the NICU challenges your view of yourself as a "good enough" parent. It's normal to worry that there isn't enough of you to go around. Remind yourself that your babies don't need all of you all the time. They can thrive on small bits of your focused attention.
- Parenting a premature baby demands that you build confidence in the face of some unusual obstacles. Gaining experience with your baby, getting support, and giving yourself time and space to adjust will all help you become the confident parent you had imagined being before your preemie was born.

CHAPTER NINE

Developing a Relationship with Your Baby in the NICU

Many parents of preemies in the NICU worry about how to relate to their baby and develop those special feelings of love, devotion, and competence. Central to forging a meaningful, two-way relationship with your baby are bonding, feeding, and becoming attuned. These are all nurturing ways of giving care that a baby responds to. But with this tiny newborn, your attempts to nurture can feel compromised because of your baby's prematurity and the NICU setup, which create barriers to the natural growth of your relationship. At first, it's hard to trust in your ability to connect with your baby and provide meaningful and nurturing care. And your preemie can be very hard to feed, relate to, or feel at ease with.

It is important to remember that the process of becoming acquainted with and adjusting to the needs of *any* newborn can be stressful. With a premature baby, relationship development is both complex and delicate. This chapter provides information, tips, and support for connecting with your preemie in ways that you'll both find rewarding.

Enjoying Your Baby

You may hear from your family and your baby's health care providers, "Just enjoy your baby." But if your baby is struggling or in critical condition, this suggestion may confuse or infuriate you. You may wonder, "How can I enjoy my little one when I'm feeling so anxious, numb, and detached? Where do I find those moments of joy with this fragile infant in this public setting? Enjoying your baby means learning to pay attention to those little moments when he grips your finger or she turns to your voice. It means appreciating each moment you can touch him and every time you can be with her. It means being genuine and heartfelt with your baby. Even in the midst of your worries, your anger, and your regrets, you can stop and smell the tiny roses.

Bonding

Many parents of preemies are concerned that their infant's early birth and hospitalization will interfere with their ability to establish a parental bond. When access to your baby is limited, you worry that you'll feel emotionally distant from your tiny newborn. Amid a NICU experience clouded with grief and fear, you may wonder about your ability to form a meaningful connection with your little one.

I wish I could say here that I soon bonded with my daughter. I'm not at all sure I ever did while in the NICU. It was weeks before I felt she was mine. Perhaps my heart was afraid to get too close to an infant who could die at any moment. I was becoming increasingly depressed, for perhaps the first time in my life. I was concerned about my lack of emotional closeness to the baby. I felt that I should feel more for this baby, that I should love her more than I did. My feelings of failure over her birth were multiplied by my guilt over not feeling loving toward her. —Renee

A nurse brought me pictures of her, and I studied them very closely. Was this really my baby? She looked so strange and unfamiliar. Why don't I immediately feel close to her? Shouldn't I immediately feel close? We didn't have that initial bonding that so many books advocate. Does that mean we'll forever feel distant from each other? —Rebekah

How Premature Birth Affects Bonding

I remember devouring the sight of his face—trying to see the person inside. I remember his hands flailing and having a sense that he was afraid. I wanted to soothe him but wasn't sure what I could do. ... I remember that he seemed to weigh nothing. I kept trying to orient his weight to know how to hold him. He was so bundled that it all felt awkward and unreal. I couldn't get any sense of connection because I couldn't feel him at all. I felt like I held an empty blanket. —Laurie

Bonding refers to the connection that parents feel toward their baby. (The connection your baby feels toward you is called attachment, which is discussed in Chapter 13.) Bonding is associated with activities such as carefully preparing a cozy nursery for your baby and snuggling with your newborn immediately after birth. But when your baby is born too soon, you face a nursery lined with bleeping monitors and the inability to hold your baby for days or perhaps weeks after delivery.

It is natural for you to grieve deeply over the loss of these expected firsts, but in the long run, these activities are not critical to becoming emotionally invested in your infant. More significant are the characteristics of bonding that hold true for parents of full-term and preterm infants alike: bonding is a process that occurs over time, the process has peak moments, and it is flexible and resilient. As you learn more about the process of bonding, you may be reassured by how close to the mark you can be with your tiny baby. Still, most parents of preemies worry about bonding during crisis, so let's look at that issue first.

Bonding during Crisis

The first real look I had was a day after the C-section, when I was able to sit in the chair beside the incubator. His eyes were closed, and I felt like I wasn't really sure this was my baby ... and I looked for signs of problems more than looking at him, I suppose. —Inkan

He really didn't respond to anything. This really was hard. You always hear how a newborn knows his mother's voice, and I wondered if he had had enough time in the womb to know mine. Would we have the bond mothers and babies have? Does he know I'm his mommy? —Cynthia

My son was so inactive that it was hard to believe he was even alive sometimes. —Terri

When a baby is born prematurely, many mothers and fathers worry about the typical "bonding" experiences they are missing. Where are those moments of meeting your newborn with extended skin-to-skin closeness and eye contact? Where are those intense feelings of pride, love, and devotion? Instead, the moment of birth may be followed by a quick glimpse of an alien creature surrounded by people in gloves and gowns. Later, after your baby is installed in the NICU, your fragile emotional state influences how you relate to your tiny infant. You may stare in disbelief at a scrawny, feeble being who is neurologically immature and unresponsive to you. At a time when you want to feel completely connected and in tune with your infant, you may instead feel shocked, detached, and terrified to even touch him or her.

The first time I held her, I didn't really feel much. It sounds bad to say that. I was happy, but at the same time I was just really numb. I don't remember feeling, "Yes, I feel this wonderful outpouring of emotion," because it wasn't really like that. I was just there, and she was just there, and there wasn't really any connection. —Beth

Bonding was by no means an immediate occurrence for me. For a long time I looked at those babies and thought, "They're cute, but are they really mine?" I wondered if I would ever "bond" with them. I knew I should love them, bond with them, be a mother to them, but I didn't feel anything! I felt numb. I didn't cry—and I feel I should have. Why didn't I? It wasn't until a month after they were born that I cried. —Sara

It's really weird, but I kind of felt bonded to her and detached at the same time. It was like I was bonded to her but I didn't want to be because I didn't know how she would turn out. I didn't want to get too attached if she was just going to die on me. I didn't let myself feel like a mom until I didn't have to worry so much about losing her. —Brooke

• • •

Although feelings of detachment can make it seem as if you don't feel anything for your baby, your detachment is, in fact, just a temporary phase of coping with the trauma of premature delivery and hospitalization. It's normal to need time to recover emotionally before you can reach out and to feel emotionally reticent when your baby is so unfamiliar, unresponsive, and his or her medical condition is critical. It's normal to feel distant when you can't hold your baby.

But as you become able to get closer physically and as you gain experience taking care of your baby, the process of bonding proceeds naturally. It may take a while, but as your baby's condition improves, you'll begin to feel more emotionally calm and open. You'll feel a surge of devotion when your baby finally squeezes your hand, and you'll feel more actively nurturing when you can hold your baby in your arms. As you do more caregiving, your love and investment in your little one will naturally grow. It may take days or weeks for these reactions to surface, but you *will* experience them.

> *I didn't see my son for a week after he was born. Those days were horrible. I went into a deep depression. When I finally got to see my son, he was off the oxygen and breathing on his own, and I got to hold him the first time I saw him. That was when it was all worth it—it didn't seem real until then.* —Cyd

> *I was afraid to really let myself believe that he was real and was mine. But when he was a little more stable and I had a little more say as to how he was cared for, then I began to look at him as my baby. But it really wasn't until I had some semblance of control over the situation that I could allow myself to feel that.* —Sterling

> *For me, that bond wasn't really there [in the NICU]. Yeah, she's my baby, but until we really got her home, it wasn't as significant. As she got healthier and bigger, it was definitely easier. The bond was there. But in the first month and a half or so, it was hard.* —Sandi

As your emotions rise, keep in mind that bonding involves more than just positive feelings such as love and joy. There is also a dark side to feeling invested in your baby. You may worry about the terrible things that might happen. It will hurt you to see your baby struggle. You may struggle as well.

• • •
277
Developing a Relationship with Your Baby in the NICU

You may feel rejected when your baby can't tolerate handling. It can be tiresome and depressing to pump breast milk when you'd rather just put your baby to the breast. It can be frustrating to seek out and absorb information about your infant's medical care. The setbacks are devastating, and you may be filled with feelings of anger and dread. Particularly if your baby continues to be medically or developmentally challenging, your feelings will remain mixed. Most parents experience a wide variety of positive and negative feelings about their premature babies.

> *It's different. It has to be so different. Especially with the firstborn [who was full-term], I was just amazed when I came home and this child was lying in a bed next to my bed, and I'm thinking, "This is mine now, and no one's going to come and take it away. This human being, this beautiful creature I was given as a gift." With Erin [the preemie], there was so much in your head, going around, there just wasn't any peace—from "Is she going to have problems when she's older" to "Are the oxygen sats levels at 100 all day?" There was no time for me to think about the beautiful things. It was just more of the awful things. I kept thinking of all the things that had to be done. ... And you get to the NICU for the day, and they explain what's going on—and just trying to remember all the medical stuff. There just wasn't that much time to lean over and look in the incubator. The love was the same, but the worry was higher. —Charlie*

You may be concerned that having any negative feelings about your baby signals a lack of devotion to your preemie. But feelings of stress, avoidance, regret, guilt, anger, and being overwhelmed by the demands are all part of "normal" parenting, even for parents of term babies. Of course, you'll probably experience all these feelings much more acutely than parents of term infants do, but this only makes your journey more intense, not "wrong."

Your connection to your baby will reflect all the joy that comes with parenting *and* all the agony that comes with crisis. Recognize your fears for your preemie and your desire to shield your infant from harm as evidence of your deep emotional investment in this child. Worrying about your ability to bond shows your desire to continue investing in your baby. Unfortunately, others may not always accept your mixed emotions. Medical staff, relatives, and friends may try to simplify your reactions with comments such as: "You love them, don't you?" or "Why can't you just be happy—your baby will be fine!" You may sense that these people would rather not acknowledge the range of intense and complex emotions you feel about your baby. This lack of recognition of your emotions can make you feel as if they are not legitimate or as if there is something wrong with you. In response, you may try to bury your contradictory feelings.

But refusing to acknowledge negative feelings makes it impossible to work past them. And when you suppress your negative emotions, you tend to suppress your positive emotions as well, becoming generally numb. That's why facing the negative can be key to building a positive connection with your premature infant. So, if you're feeling distant from or angry with your baby, remember that these feelings are natural. Rather than trying to follow a script that doesn't fit you, turn toward your baby and all of your own heartfelt reactions. Facing *all* your feelings lets you behave more naturally and spontaneously with your baby and strengthens your growing connection to your little one.

Remember, though, that at times numbness is a really effective coping mechanism. It's a way to avoid feeling overwhelmed, a way to suppress negative feelings such as frustration and anger—feelings that you imagine might cause others to label you a "bad" parent. Then as time passes and you recover your balance, give yourself permission to own and express your negative feelings about your baby, so that you can also tap into the positive feelings that enable you to enjoy your little one.

If you are so flooded with depression, anger, and/or fear that you consistently avoid your baby and the NICU, seek help from a qualified counselor who has experience with parents of preemies. You don't have to feel incapacitated. Even if you simply have some nagging concerns about your parental feelings, you deserve to get help and support. Ask your health care providers, local hospital, support group, or other parents of preemies for referrals. And stay in touch with your grief over your baby's early birth. When you can feel your painful emotions, you can also feel the joyful ones. Parenting a baby is such a precious time—and it passes quickly. You and your baby deserve to experience all its complexity and richness.

Characteristics of Bonding

Bonding Is a Process Contrary to myth, bonding does not happen within seconds after birth, when parents first lay eyes on their baby. Instead, bonding is a powerful and complicated *process* of falling in love with one's baby over time.

When parents think about bonding, they often imagine instantaneous rapture upon their baby's delivery. Although this emotional spike may happen for some, it doesn't happen for everybody. For many parents, falling in love with their baby is a slow burn, not an explosion. And even for parents who do experience "love at first sight," bonding remains an ongoing process of emotionally investing in their baby.

In fact, for many parents, the bonding process starts even before conception, when they imagine holding their future baby in their arms. It is ongoing throughout pregnancy, and then continues after delivery. When a baby is born early, the pregnancy and contact right after birth are cut short, but the bonding process isn't cut short. It just continues on. Whether a baby is born at term or before, parents continue to bond *after* their baby arrives, when their responsive, interactive relationship begins.

> *I loved Alex before he was born. I felt very connected with him, when I carried him inside. ... When he was born, he was wisked out of the room, and I had to ask if he was a boy and was alive. But I felt so close to him it was like we shared memories. When I entered the NICU for the first time, it was like I saw it from his perspective and from my own. —Allison*

Your baby's hospitalization complicates the development of your feelings of parenthood and connection. Feeling distant isn't evidence of failure, but a natural reaction to separation from your baby. As you carve out a comfortable space for yourself as a parent in the NICU, you will feel more at ease with your baby. Your bond will continue to deepen as you feel more knowledgeable, more in sync, and more in charge.

You may worry about the impact of missing out on the early opportunities for closeness that other parents have, such as being able to hold your slippery little newborn against your body or spending that first hour together in peace. But since bonding is a process that occurs over time, those early experiences won't make or break your bond. You may feel bereft, and you will grieve for these experiences. But missing them needn't stand in the way of the bonding process.

I felt terribly lonely and cheated when T. J. was whisked away to the NICU. I wanted desperately to hold him and to marvel with my husband at the little miracle we had created. I felt I had been robbed of the initial closeness to my child. I just wish I could have held him right after I had him. However, now, I feel as if we bonded just as well afterward. —Claire

Over time, you'll experience many opportunities to be close to and feel your growing bond with your premature baby. Although not the ones you had anticipated, these opportunities can be just as precious, extraordinary, and meaningful—even though you may have to wait for them. For example, as your baby stabilizes and matures, you'll appreciate eye contact or the turn toward your voice that much more. Touching your preemie or holding your little one can be such a tender and endearing experience, one that is special every time. Homecoming may mark another turning point, when you really begin to feel the intense bond you've been wishing for. (For more on bonding at home, see Chapter 13.)

I bonded with him the first time I put cream on his leg—because that was all we could do. Every day, he was like a little white ball of cream because that was all we could do. —Nettie

For me, the realization that he was mine was when the nurse wrapped him up and handed him to me and I was able to hold him. I was looking at him, and I couldn't believe how a baby could be so small. I mean, I know they're that small when they're inside of your stomach, but how could this baby be so small and be alive. ... And he just looked at me, and he probably couldn't see past his eyelashes, just staring right at me, and I just remember crying and thinking, "This is my baby. How wonderful. How wonderful." —Vickie

Bonding Has Peak Moments Bonding between parent and child has many peak moments that occur over time: when a couple receives a positive pregnancy test result, when they see the baby's image on an ultrasound screen, when they feel the baby move for the first time, when they see and hold their baby after birth, when they watch their baby sleeping peacefully. The father experiences his own special peak called engrossment—gazing in wonder at his newborn after birth, as if the rest of the world no longer matters. In general,

Developing a Relationship with Your Baby in the NICU

peak moments are when parents feel a heightened level of commitment and devotion. Spending these sweet times with their baby and remembering those moments reinforces the parents' bond with their little one.

You've already been through the peaks of pregnancy test results and perhaps ultrasounds and feeling the baby quicken. But once your baby is delivered, it's hard to imagine when you'll be able to experience another peak moment. You may feel surrounded by valleys instead. But although the peaks may be brief, bittersweet, or few and far between, you *will* experience significant bonding moments. And you'll find them when and where you least expect them.

They came up with a picture, a Polaroid picture—oh, that's him. ... It didn't seem real to me up to that point. But when I could hold him, I can't even describe it. ... I was just trying to hold him as close as I could—I guess ... trying to put him back. You're not ready yet. It was a big moment.
—Marcia

I held my son the night he was born. I had to beg them to let me hold him. When they put James in my arms, I started to cry. But it was the most wonderful feeling in the world, holding my son. I could only hold him for a few minutes, and I didn't want to let go. When I held him, I felt that everything would be all right. —Jennifer

Fabian didn't need to be intubated on the spot. He was breathing and he cried, and so I even got the chance, which I never even imagined could be possible, but they put him on my breast for a few seconds. ... It makes me cry. ... That was one of the most beautiful gifts on earth, to be able to have him on me. It was really good. Because at that point, you're so scared you don't know what's going to come out of you. And I could see, of course, he was really tiny, but still he was a baby and doing well and to just have him on me, that was really wonderful. —Gallice

The baby I held first was Jacob, but that's only because the nurse bent the rules. He was twenty-eight days old, and they were getting him ready for the first of his surgeries ... and one of the nurses said, "Why don't you hold him while I get the bed ready? ... What if I pull up a rocking chair and you can sit down and hold him?" ... I'll never forget. It was at that point and time I knew everything was going to be okay.—Julie

Some parents are too dazed or scared to appreciate the peak bonding moments when they occur. It can be difficult to feel warm and fuzzy when your baby is in peril. Nevertheless, in spite of your worries and hesitation, when you feel so thankful that your baby is alive, when you hold or feed your little one for the first time, when you start making discharge plans, or simply when you savor thoughts of how precious this new life is, you are experiencing a peak moment. Sometimes the feeling may seem closer to terror than to love, but it is still a peak moment.

I remember that I started to cry before we even entered the room the babies were in. It felt as though my heart was attempting to get out of my chest, and I was shaking. —Michele

About a couple of weeks after my son's birth, a nurse practitioner called me with some results of a brain scan and described a small bleed to me over the phone. We had been told he hadn't had any bleeds they could find, so this was quite a shock. ... I spoke to the neonatologist that night, and he explained the brain scans. The news wasn't nearly as bad as I had thought, and the bleed was so minor they didn't even classify it as a Grade I, but I was hysterical. This was the first time it really hit me that this is a real baby—and he was mine to protect and raise. —Andrea

The first time I really felt close to my son was when Sean was three weeks old, the day I finally got to hold him. It was only for ten or fifteen minutes, but I got to hold him. I sat in the NICU rocking chair, looking down at my tiny infant son. The realization suddenly hit me for the first time that, rather than wasting all this time and energy feeling sorry for myself, I should be giving him love and encouragement. At that moment, as I looked at this miniature baby bundled in his blankies, cuddled up in my arms with all his wires and tubes and such, I was suddenly hit with an overwhelming feeling of love and pride for this little boy. He had fought so hard, come so far already. He amazed me. He was my miracle. ... I was going to take care of this baby the best that I could. I would give him everything I had. This little boy was

•••
283
Developing a Relationship with Your Baby in the NICU

going to live. It didn't matter anymore what I had to do to make that happen.
—Ami

I didn't get to see my son for five days after his birth because I was very sick also. I had expected to see a big, bubbling baby, and instead there was this little tiny thing lying there, and I was afraid to touch him. He had all these tubes and pipes coming from everywhere. The nurse was very friendly and helpful, and she finally got me to touch his hand—and it was the most electrifying experience. I've been holding that hand for three years now. —Jonette

Bonding Is Flexible The bonding process is flexible—flexible enough to overcome obstacles such as anxiety, illness, the NICU, and separation. For example, you needn't go through a term pregnancy, much less see your newborn upon delivery, to fall in love with her or him. Just ask any adoptive parent. Snuggling, feeding, and cooing immediately after birth are not mandatory for bonding to occur. Even if you haven't yet been able to nest or nuzzle, you are bonding with your baby simply by wanting what's best for him or her. Whether you're able to look past your baby's medical fragility and necessary treatments or you agonize over them, your reaction is a measure of your intense devotion—and your bond.

I looked at them, and it was the standard, classic, overwhelming feeling of total and complete love for these babies. ... From the moment I found out I was pregnant with them, I was in love with these babies. And then, looking at them, I could see beyond the wires and these monitors, these little teeny tiny humans that were my children, that will someday run and play and have a good time. I wasn't focused on the situation. I could see beyond that and see these tiny babies with their teeny tiny hands, and I saw a term baby in there. I loved these little babies, regardless of how different they looked. —Pam

No way could I look past their prematurity. It was like a knife in my heart. My fondest wish on bed rest was that they would be boring [need few interventions] to neonatologists. As it turned out, they weren't boring. I was tortured by their fragility because it meant that they needed things that I couldn't give them. ... I desperately wanted to be able to give them everything they needed, and everything I had.—Rikki

• • •

You may have additional concerns if your postpartum recovery is prolonged or coupled with your own medical crisis. If you are unable to leave your bed for days, you may feel detached from your baby because of your physical condition or emotional shock. This is normal, and your bond with your little one will prevail during your recovery. Or you may feel intense longing and agony over not being able to be close to your baby. This longing, even when it's accompanied by fear, is an expression of your growing bond to your little one. Whatever your reaction, rest assured that if you cannot be at your baby's bedside, your baby will not become more attached to the nurses than to you or not know who you are. Your baby will still find you familiar and continue to prefer your touch, smell, and voice, even over the course of a long separation.

When your separation is prolonged, your partner (or close friend or family member) plays a critical role by spending time with your baby in the NICU. By listening to your partner's reports and emotional investment, you can continue to feel connected as well. Your partner's presence at your baby's bedside can also be immensely comforting. Although you may long to be there, you can rest and recuperate knowing that your baby is being watched over.

Remember also that you and your partner may show devotion to your infant in different ways. One parent may learn every medical term and pore over the chart; the other may want time spent with the baby to be jargon-free. One parent may spend hours over the incubator, while the other may work overtime to pay the mounting bills. One may search medical libraries, and the other may want only to count toes and sing silly songs. All of this is bonding.

> *When she was first born, I was already thinking that whatever it took to keep this child alive, if I had to go into debt and live in a shoe box, I would live in a shoe box to keep this girl with us for the rest of our lives. ... I would make sure this girl would be happy.* —Charlie

Bonding Is Resilient If you had a very high-risk pregnancy, you may have tried not to become invested in your baby. If your baby was unlikely to survive, you may have refused to see your little one at first. Even if you find yourself "falling in love" right away, you may fight the feeling, hesitant to invest emotionally in an infant who looks too frail to survive.

It was like the whole thing was a dream. It didn't feel like I was looking at my child. [I was] afraid that if I got attached to him, I would only end up getting hurt, because I didn't see how such a little person so sick would ever survive. —Susan

She was extremely tiny—transparent skin, I could visualize her every vein. She was beautiful. Such a sweet, innocent, frail little baby. My baby. And I fell deeply in love with her from the moment I laid my eyes on her even though I tried so hard not to love her because I was so afraid of losing her. —Jillian

Reluctance to get close to this baby is a normal and natural reaction, a way of trying to protect yourself from grief. It may take you a while to adjust to the reality that this baby has arrived—and is possibly here to stay. Even if you try to stay detached, your love remains, just waiting for an opportunity to bloom.

I watched as she was wrapped in warm sheets and handed to me. I think that was when I realized she was a real baby. I could hold her and kiss her just like a full-term baby. It was a moment in my life that I will never forget. Until this point, I was unconsciously holding myself back from loving this child. That ended when I held her. She was so small and innocent, I could not help but feel an overwhelming surge of love for her. —Kimberly

The first time I saw Liam was beautiful. Here was this little baby I was so scared to get attached to but couldn't help it. Here was the baby I kept thinking I was miscarrying. Here he was. And once I saw that face, I immediately started crying. I had tried so hard not to love him when I was pregnant for fear of getting hurt ... but it turns out that I did love him all along. I kissed his head and took in his smell. I will never forget those first few minutes. —Kimi

It may also help to recognize that holding back won't prevent you from bonding. Your feelings of devotion, like Kimi's, will grow in spite of your attempts to protect yourself. And if this baby dies, you would be devastated, no matter how much you try to harden your heart. If you avoid spending time in the NICU and then your baby dies, you will always wonder what small but

• • •

powerful knowledge of your child you might have gained had you spent the time you could have with your newborn. And if your baby does have long-term challenges, you will grieve over them and for your child whether you are in the NICU for fifteen minutes or fifteen hours a day. So you might as well reap the benefits of involvement. Dare to get close to your baby. Dare to feel like a parent. Parental bonding is a wonderfully powerful, resilient, and flexible process. You *can* bond during the most anxiety-filled pregnancy and infancy. You *can* feel the full depth and joy of parental love during the months after your preemie is born. The road can be challenging, but the rewards are immeasurable.

In some ways, we are even more bonded. We know what it's like to almost lose them—to be faced with that. Maybe we're even more appreciative of just having them. —Debbie

To make a long story short, I overcame my fears of my child and of the NICU. I could not love my daughter any more than I do now. The special circumstances of her birth just required some adjustments in my thinking! —Kimberly

Kangaroo Care

Kangaroo care is the practice of holding your diapered baby on your bare chest (between your breasts if you're a mom), blanket draped over the baby's back. Both you and your preemie can benefit greatly from this skin-to-skin contact. After the trauma of an early delivery and the physical obstacles that are so often placed between you and your baby in the NICU, the sensation of having nothing between you acts as a balm to heal the wounds of your separation. Holding your baby close can transport you to a different world.

This dear nurse asked if I wanted to hold him. She got him out, and we were able to kangaroo for almost an hour. It was the first time I had cried since the whole emergency began. It was so wonderful. He spent only a little time looking at me or awake, but it didn't matter. —Trish

Of course we were excited about the prospect [of kangaroo care]. The doctors finally relented and allowed us to hold Sarah after she weighed enough. Sarah handled kangarooing so well the doctors were amazed. And I felt alive finally—at least for those few, short minutes each day. —Cindy

When I was allowed to hold Alycia, I kangarooed her and loved every minute of it. The warmth of her skin against mine was a feeling that I cannot describe! I felt like a mom for the very first time! And each time I held my babies, I felt a bond that no one will ever be able to take away. The hardest days were the ones on which I wasn't able to hold them. —Michele

I remember the feeling of pure joy. I don't think I had ever been that happy before. I could see the relaxation in Glen's face. I could tell it was so much more comfortable for him than lying in the warmer. —Sharon

As appealing as the idea of kangaroo care is for many parents, you might be a bit reluctant to hold your tiny baby, especially at first. The fragile look of a preterm infant puts some parents off, and your normal fears of hurting your baby may stand in the way of your enthusiasm to hold her or him. If you feel guilty about the early delivery or your baby's condition, the opportunity to hold your baby so close to your body might feel both exciting and frightening—after all, you may not yet have banished the feeling that you and your body are agents of harm. Rest assured that your scent, your touch, and the rhythms of your speech and breathing are familiar to your baby. Your little one needs you, and you need your little baby.

Frankly, I was terrified of picking her up—she was so tiny and weak. I was actually somewhat relieved that the doctors didn't want me to hold her at first. In just two days, though, the nurses told my husband and me about kangaroo care. I held her frail body against my bare skin and slowly started to feel like, yes, this was my child. —Rebekah

The first time I held Zane, our smallest triplet, it was by kangaroo care. He weighed just over three pounds at birth. I was so surprised and comforted when I held him and found that he felt just like a baby. He looked so tiny and fragile that I think I assumed he would be like china, but he was soft and warm and cuddly. ... We calmed and comforted each other. I could feel myself relax as I held Zane, and I could see from his monitors that he was relaxing, too. —Jill

Kangarooing seems so natural that, with permission and encouragement, most mothers and fathers seize the opportunity eagerly. After a gentle initiation, even the most hesitant parents can become ardent kangarooers.

They put her on me kangaroo style. She felt like a wet dishcloth. That's what went through my mind. They placed her on me, us both unclothed, right between my breasts. I have never felt more content in my life. —Timmesa

The Benefits of Kangarooing

The physical and emotional benefits of kangaroo care are many. Research indicates that it only takes a few minutes of kangarooing per day to see results in babies and their parents.

Infants:
- Maintain their body warmth more easily
- Achieve more stable heart and breathing rates
- Spend more time in the deep sleep and quiet alert states (explained later in this chapter, under "Becoming Attuned to Your Baby"), and less time crying
- Gain weight more quickly
- Are more successful with breast-feeding

Parents:
- Grow more confident about their ability to parent
- Are more eager and able to take their baby home
- Feel closer, more "bonded," to their baby
- (Mothers) tend to have more success with breast-feeding and a better milk supply

For parents, the emotional benefits of kangaroo care are important. When you can enjoy closeness with your baby, you may feel more positive about your baby's premature arrival and NICU experience. When you feel you are doing something significant and nurturing for your baby, it can boost your morale. Most parents believe that their baby reaps emotional benefits as well. If you have multiple babies, you can also try kangarooing them together on your chest.

Thaddeus cuddled right down when I would hold him against my heart. I had the feeling that that was familiar to him. He was quite peaceful that way right from the start, and that told me he felt safe there. —Laurie

While he was in the hospital, I felt he needed to be held—[he] couldn't just be in the incubator all day, only held when the nurses needed to feed him. He needed that interaction. That was pretty much why we were there. —Richard

The Emotions of Kangarooing

Kangaroo care, especially the first time, is an intense emotional experience for many parents. It's a potent catalyst for releasing pent-up emotions.

Instead of watching your baby through plastic, you can finally snuggle up, smell that sweet baby smell, and touch soft skin. Knowing that your preemie is responding well to kangaroo care can also strengthen your recognition that you can finally do something meaningful to help your baby recover and grow. Nurses and doctors, for all their skill, do not do kangaroo care with the babies in the NICU. Only parents hold their baby with such intimacy.

The kangaroo care, that for sure helps so much. You've got your baby on your skin, and he's yours and you feel him and he's living and he's breathing, he's warm and he's a real human being. ... Everything else in the world disappears. There's nothing else but your child. You feel him and he's just ... you forget all about the whole situation, the fears, that you're scared for his life. You forget everything, and he's just on you. It was just so relaxing. At the same time, you remember that that's still where he's supposed to be, so he should be there. It's the best thing to have in the world. You forget all about time. You'll never forget that feeling, it's so special. —Gallice

If you feel like crying during kangaroo care, your tears may have many sources. As you feel your tiny baby curled up on your chest, calm and content in your protective embrace, you can rejoice at your closeness, and at the same time grieve for your cruel separation. Kangaroo care can also build your hopes: you may start to feel confident that your baby will survive and that you can have a close relationship with this child. As you hold your baby, you may feel more certain that you can monitor your little one's health and safety. If you've been feeling displaced or inadequate, the way your baby sinks into your bare chest can make you feel valuable and capable. If you are struggling with guilt, you may sense that this child forgives you for all that you imagine to be your fault. You may even begin to forgive yourself.

Your tears will not hurt your baby, who can be in a deep sleep and undisturbed by your crying. If you'd rather not cry in the NICU, you might try to visualize kangarooing your infant and having a good cry before you go in.

Some nursing staff may be uncomfortable with your tears and try to take your baby away. One mom bitterly recalled, "A nurse ripped my baby away from me when I cried. Told me it was bad for the baby." But as long as your infant is resting comfortably, there's no evidence that your tears are bad for him or her. You can be assertive even through your tears: make it clear that as long as your baby is content and comfy, you're going to continue kangarooing.

When your kangaroo session is over, your baby may protest being removed from you. This won't undo the benefits of kangaroo care. Your baby was able to have a valuable rest. Research also shows that right after kangaroo care, babies sleep better. For that reason, you might consider kangarooing in the evening, so that the benefits to your baby continue into the night. You want to encourage your baby to sleep well at night, partly because of the NICU routine (in units that practice developmentally supportive care, night-time may provide more opportunity for uninterrupted sleep) and partly to encourage a day-night cycle that matches your family's.

Arranging to Kangaroo Your Baby

If your hospital's NICU is hesitant about kangaroo care and you feel up to it, you can be an agent for change. Many books and articles touting the incredible benefits of skin-to-skin contact have been written in recent years. (Check Appendix C, under the section "Books for Parents of Preemies.") Consider sharing these publications with medical staff.

In some NICUs, preemies are kangarooed only when they are medically stable and in good condition, but research is now identifying the benefits of kangaroo care for younger and sicker babies as well. Some hospitals use kangaroo care from birth onward. This makes sense because babies may need kangaroo care the most when they are struggling, which is usually when the doctors and nurses want to surround them with machines instead of their parents' arms and skin. It can be logistically possible to kangaroo a wired, intubated, hooked-up baby, machines and parents working together. This kind of kangaroo care has been tried with great success in many NICUs.

If you feel strongly about wanting to try kangaroo care to help your tiny baby improve or become stable, talk to your baby's doctors and nurses. Encourage them to review the research for themselves.

If your baby is very sick and the doctors tell you there's not much more they can do, *you can do kangaroo care*. If they believe your baby is dying, there is absolutely nothing to lose. Kangaroo care probably won't save your baby's life, but it will give you a chance to be intimately nurturing at this important time, and it will provide memories you will cherish always.

If you are never allowed to kangaroo your baby or if you must wait for weeks and weeks to do so, know that you can still form a strong bond with your baby. Kangaroo care is simply one of many ways in which parents and their babies can be close.

If you and your baby are home now and the idea of kangaroo care still appeals to you, the two of you can still enjoy the many benefits of skin-to-skin contact. Kangarooing at home can help heal your disappointment over not having a "normal" birth, one where your naked baby is placed on your bare skin. It offers a chance to reclaim the intimate holding and snuggling that you missed in the early minutes and hours of your baby's life. Your baby's health and growth can profit from kangarooing at home, helping your baby fall asleep more easily; calming both of you after a fretful period; and even reducing, interrupting, or preventing crying spells or fussiness. A sick baby may recover faster if he or she spends time sleeping on you, even when you are both fully clothed. Consider holding and lying down with your baby to be the best way to invest your time. Enjoy the respite for yourself, too. You will cherish these sweet times and the treasured memories they make.

Infant Massage

The greatest happiness we had together when he was a baby was when I massaged him. I tended to get lost in the beauty of his little body, and our interaction seemed much more instinctive and comforting to us both. —Anne

Whether or not your NICU encourages kangaroo care, you and your baby can benefit from the touch of infant massage. Your touch can calm your baby and promote healing and weight gain. The first step is simply to contain your baby by cupping your hand around his or her head, chest, or by holding your baby's arms and legs in a flexed position. Cupping can be very soothing to a preemie. As you become accustomed to massaging your baby, experiment with different kinds of touch and pay attention to what your baby seems to enjoy. Most babies prefer small amounts of firm, gentle stroking. Avoid anything that seems to irritate, startle, or overwhelm your baby. You can also try using nonirritating natural oils or a gentle unscented lotion that your baby's doctor recommends. Your NICU may have a nurse or therapist who can teach you more about infant massage, or you can find information in books or consult with a massage therapist. (Look in Appendix C under "Parenting Style and Caregiving.")

Okay, so you can't hold the baby—the baby's in the incubator. And I'm asking the nurse, "Can I touch the baby, can I put cream on the baby?" It's that skin touch that gives you that connection. There's not much to touch, but just being able to make a connection skin to skin, that was so important. And I know it's important to the babies. It's got to be. Because being in an incubator or a warmer is not the same as being in a mom. ... It was a few days before we could hold Peter, and I knew that I just had to have my hands in there to just touch him—to touch his toes if that was the only thing I could get to, or a hand. That's what I did. —Vickie

Cobedding for Multiples

If you have twins, triplets, or more babies in separate beds, you may be sensitive to the fact that they cannot snuggle together. Besides missing your womb, they might be missing each other.

In many hospitals, babies from a multiple gestation are placed together in the same bed in a practice called cobedding. There are reports of putting twins together when one twin is struggling to stabilize, sleep, stay calm, or eat and gain weight. Within minutes, the struggling twin stabilizes, calms, and starts to improve.

Multiple siblings can benefit from cobedding because they are comforted by the familiar touch and boundaries the others provide. As their sleep-wake cycles become synchronized, they cuddle with, suck on, and provide mutual

Developing a Relationship with Your Baby in the NICU

warmth for each other, and they support each other's ability to stay calm and adapt to life outside the womb. Just as kangaroo care mimics the comfort of the womb, cobedding mimics cohabiting with one's womb mates.

Parents of cobedding multiples take comfort in the thought that their babies are together in the NICU. They perceive the NICU to be a gentler place when their babies are snuggling with each other. Perhaps most important, when the babies are bedded together, the parents can practice and gain confidence in taking care of them at the same time, instead of alternating between or among stations. Finally, parents report that their babies' synchronized sleep-wake cycles make it easier to take care of them in the NICU and especially after discharge. Overall, cobedding of multiples can reduce stress in the parents *and* their infants and raise the parents' confidence in their caregiving abilities. When parents believe a reasonable practice to be good and nurturing for their babies, they're usually right: it generally *is* good and nurturing for their babies—and for the parents too.

In the final weeks before my twins came home, my son was doing fabulously. But before we could take him home, he had to have some surgery. They did four surgeries at once, which included bowel resection (from NEC), hernia repair, circumcision, and ROP Stage III laser surgery. Well, after this surgery he was a "mess." He stopped eating and took about five giant leaps backward. My once fairly docile son would not stop screaming. It was like all the pain he had suffered bubbled to the surface. No one or no amount of fentanyl could calm him. One day one of the nurses decided to sneak my daughter into his incubator to see if maybe that would help. Well, lo and behold, the minute she was laid near him, he took one look at her, reached for her hand and held it, and fell quietly asleep—and a calmness had returned. It was one of the most miraculous things I had ever experienced. The entire nursery was silenced by the beauty of this. I get teary just remembering. That night he started eating again, and his fentanyl was discontinued.

After they connected like this, I insisted that I wanted to start kangarooing them together—so they let me when the docs weren't around. I had always felt that my kids had been cheated out of the "twin bonding" by being born prematurely, so I think cobedding and cokangarooing is an absolutely wonderful idea. —Becky

• • •

294

If your multiple babies have had the opportunity to cobed, you may be familiar with the advantages. If you would like your infants to try cobedding, your health care teammates may be open to the idea, particularly if your babies are breathing room air, stable, and without infection. If the staff express concern over confusing the babies, suggest color-coding everything, including lines, monitors, charts, supplies, medications, and wrist and ankle bands. As some of the parents in this book can testify, twins can get mixed up even when they *aren't* in the same bed. It can sometimes be easier to keep them straight when they *are* together.

Cobedding can also be a workable option after discharge. Whether or not your babies had the opportunity to share a bed in the hospital, you can try cobedding them at home.

Feeding Issues

Even under ideal circumstances, the feeding—and growth—of newborn babies occupies a substantial portion of new parents' time and energy. When a baby is in the NICU, parental concerns about these issues become amplified because parents are quick to understand how important physical growth is, both as a marker of improvement and as a criterion for discharge home.

Before you had your preemie, you probably spent some time thinking about how you wanted to feed your child. For most parents of term babies, the choice boils down to formula in a bottle or milk from the breast. Parents of preemies have to look at things a bit differently:

- *Method of feeding:* Bottle only, bottle and breast, breast only, or for babies who are unable to suck or swallow, a feeding tube. Depending on the situation, your child might move through all of these possibilities.
- *Substance that is fed:* Breast milk only, breast milk and formula, breast milk and fortifier, formula only.

You'll make some of these feeding choices while your baby is in the NICU; others will come up later. Some of these options will work well for you and your baby, and others will spur you to explore alternatives. Even if you're told that a certain method or substance is a surefire cure or the way to help your baby grow, if your intuition tells you otherwise, speak up. Not all babies respond the same, and your observations are valid.

In addition, because you lose so much control when your baby is born early, feeding decisions can take on enhanced meaning. Your decisions are important—and your infant's success at feeding and growing can be emotionally charged as well. Because of the emotion surrounding this issue, it can be helpful to sort out how you feel about the situation and your options.

Formula Feeding

Although breast milk is best for most babies, not every mother of a preemie can or chooses to provide it. In some cases—such as when the mother has a disease that can be transferred to her baby in her milk or when she must be on medication (or is taking street drugs) that shouldn't be passed on to her baby—it is not recommended that the mother provide breast milk. A mother who is critically ill following delivery may not have an adequate milk supply or may be in no condition to express her milk. The ordeal of having a critically ill baby and the emotional trauma it entails can also affect some mothers' milk supply. Some mothers may not choose to breast-feed because of cultural factors. Others may find the idea of spending time pumping, rather than being at their critically ill baby's bedside, unbearable. Occasionally, a mother's hormones don't orchestrate milk production or release.

Although there is agreement that breast milk is medically and nutritionally superior to formula, most newborns can do just fine on formula. But for a premature baby, breast milk has what might be termed "medicinal" qualities. Your baby's health care providers may encourage you to furnish what you can.

Staying with Your Decision to Feed Formula If you had planned all along to feed your baby formula, you may have had many reasons associated with your lifestyle, your own health concerns, your culture, or your employment. Despite your baby's early birth, these reasons may still be applicable and important to you. You may not want to give up certain aspects of formula feeding, or you may hold on to your decision to formula-feed as a way to maintain some semblance of control over the situation. If you interpret caregivers' encouragement to provide breast milk as pressure, you may deeply resent these efforts to "make you change your mind." It could seem like another challenge to your autonomy as a parent and exacerbate any guilt or failure you are already feeling.

It is very important for you to recognize that your baby's health care providers are obligated to educate you about the medical facts and benefits of breast-feeding for your preemie. They are not out to get you, trying to force you to breast-feed, or implying that you are obligated to provide breast milk in order to make up for your baby's early birth, appealing to feelings of guilt or inadequacy in the process. If you feel pressured, guilty, or inadequate, recognize that you are already feeling these sentiments, and this decision is merely bringing them to the surface. It can help you to write about or talk about these feelings with a supportive listener. If you conclude, after consideration, that formula feeding is definitely best for you, say so clearly. Your health care teammates should support you in your decision. Although they may encourage you to breast-feed, they also recognize that it's acceptable for mothers to decide not to do so.

Changing Your Mind and Deciding to Breast-Feed If you had planned to formula-feed, you may decide that breast-feeding is a better alternative after you hear what your baby's health care providers have to say. You may make this decision gladly, yet feel embarrassed and unsure about breast-feeding because you are unfamiliar with the mechanics. Even mothers who had planned all along to breast-feed can feel embarrassed or unsure at first. Most mothers have to learn the skill of breast-feeding. It's normal to feel awkward in the beginning. The lactation support you receive should help you feel more confident and certain as time passes.

> *I didn't plan to breast-feed, but the doctor kind of pushed me into it, saying it was the best thing I could do for him. Once I understood the fact that breast-feeding would be the best thing for my baby, I had no problem doing it. It made me feel more like a mom to him, that I was the only one providing food for him. —Christine*

If you are resisting changing your mind about your feeding decision, but a part of you is wondering "what if?" you may find it helpful to ask yourself these questions to sort out your feelings:

- *Are you resisting because you don't like surprises or sudden change?* Try taking a flexible approach. Consider supplying *some* breast milk. You can attempt a trial of providing colostrum and breast milk to see how you feel about the process. Your breasts will produce these in any event, and your baby will benefit from whatever you can provide. If you give it a try and it doesn't work for you, you can always stop.
- *Are you resisting because you're not sure what your partner, friends, or relatives will*

think? Remember, *you* are your baby's mother—and only you can decide whether this is right for you and for your baby. If those close to you object, enlist the support of your baby's doctors and nurses, or contact a lactation consultant or a support group such as La Leche League to help you counter their objections. If providing breast milk is meaningful and healing for you and good for your baby, others have no valid basis for undermining your choice. You can insist that they respect your decision and your feelings.

- *Are you resisting because you want to feel that you are still in control?* Remember that this decision is yours. You need to choose what's right for you and your baby. Just as you shouldn't choose breast-feeding against your better judgment only because you don't want to disappoint the "authorities," don't choose formula feeding just because you feel compelled to go *against* the authorities. Reacting against the advice you're getting instead of making a thoughtful choice may keep you from doing what's best for you and your baby. If you decide to do the opposite of what the "authorities" are recommending simply to spite them, you are still letting them control you.

Switching Back from Breast Milk to Formula If you decide to try breast-feeding despite your original decision to formula-feed, you are to be commended for your courage and willingness to try. Still, you may come upon barriers that even the staunchest breast-feeder would find insurmountable. Maybe you feel that the time it takes to pump is time you need to spend with your newborn. Maybe the addition of pumping to your tasks at this time is just too much. Perhaps you work and work to express milk and find it painful—or you cannot establish a supply. You may lack the support you need to continue. Perhaps you are told that your baby cannot tolerate your milk or that he or she will be unable to use it until some far-off future time—and you feel it's futile to keep trying when your baby can't digest your milk anyway.

If you determine that continuing to try to produce milk and/or breast-feed your preemie is simply not feasible, you may worry about disappointing the medical staff or others, or going against their recommendations. Your decision to switch back to formula may add to your burden of guilt and frustration, particularly if you had warmed to the idea of breast-feeding. Remind yourself that you have made the decision to return to formula just as carefully as you made your earlier decision to try to supply breast milk.

Breast-Feeding (and Pumping)

Breast-feeding your premature baby may have been the obvious choice for you all along, or you may have decided on it after pondering the options. If you feared you'd be unable to breast-feed because your baby was born preterm, you were probably relieved to find out that you still could. However, you probably won't be able to put your baby to the breast at first. Instead, you'll need to provide breast milk by pumping it and then taking it to the NICU, where a tube will be used to deliver it to your baby's stomach. Eventually, as your baby matures and gains strength, you should be able to try to nurse.

Still, you may hesitate. If you feel betrayed by your body, you may second-guess your decision to breast-feed, finding it hard to believe that your body could produce anything useful for your little one. Anger or grief about your baby's preterm delivery and hospitalization might color your feelings about pumping breast milk. If you had imagined putting your baby to the breast in the delivery room, you might feel overwhelmed by the distance you feel from your little one and discouraged when you are confronted with a cold electric pump instead of a warm, hungry baby. Pumping is not what you'd planned.

I was pumping breast milk for Alison to get. I hated it. My milk production was not the greatest. I thought of pumping as very unnatural. It emotionally tore me apart. I mentioned the poor milk production to some of the nurses, and they didn't really say anything except get lots of rest and drink lots of fluids. They also mentioned something about relaxing. Yeah, right—when you want your baby home with you, you're still not recovered from the complications, it hurts to sit and hurts worse to get up. —Stacy

I felt resentment. Of course I wanted Emma to have breast milk—it's what's best—but I didn't think the lactation staff were too understanding of what an ordeal expressing breast milk would be. They certainly seemed far too chipper about the whole thing. —Diane

I really had a hard time making myself do it because I just felt so much like a science experiment anyway, with the bad pregnancy and then the pumping was just so mechanical. —Terri

Developing a Relationship with Your Baby in the NICU

I felt revulsion at having my milk being drawn from my body by a plastic cup attached to a machine, only to watch a nurse feed it to my son a milliliter at a time through a tube, while my breasts ached to feel his lips and my heart broke because he couldn't. —Leanne

Despite facing the pump, for many mothers providing breast milk helps to soothe the anguish of being unable to prevent the early delivery. Mothers of premature babies often note that their expressed milk is the one thing that only *they* can provide for their baby. Providing breast milk and then working to learn to breast-feed is one way to try to make things normal again. Knowing that your baby gets so many health benefits from your milk can boost your confidence in your ability to nurture and nourish your tiny newborn. Breast milk can also seem like an antidote to the medical technology that surrounds your baby. Though you may have mixed feelings about providing breast milk—you resent the pump, the schedule, the hassle, the mechanical nature of it all—the rewards can be well worth the price.

Despite the fact that I hated being trapped by that horrible machine six times a day for half an hour each session, I knew that keeping it up would only benefit my baby. He would grow stronger because of it. —Christine

When they were trying to feed him, that was a big thing where I felt I was off on the sidelines. I wanted to nurse him. At first, he was too small to nurse, so they had to tube-feed him. Then I couldn't be with him around the clock to nurse him, so he had to learn to take a bottle. I pumped for six months. That's all that I could do. I'm sorry I missed out on breast-feeding, but what's important is that he got the breast milk. I feel good that I did that for him. —Marcia

Having to pump my breast milk was difficult and easy at the same time—difficult because it made me sad that it wasn't the baby eating normally, and easy because I knew the importance of the nutrition I could provide for her. —Cindy

If you decide to try providing breast milk, give yourself credit for being flexible, brave, and willing to attempt something new. Even if you switch to formula later, you and your baby will benefit from any breast milk you supply.

Meeting the Challenges of Breast-Feeding in the NICU

I breast-fed my older [term] son with no problems. I know what it takes—and believe me, trying to breast-feed a baby who isn't there is pretty difficult. Add to that the fact that your two daughters are still in the hospital and you don't know when or if they will be coming home soon. Now that's a task. —Rosa

The NICU is not the place to get a great start, but ... like everything else about the preemie experience, you don't have a lot of choices, do you? Preemies have weaker, sometimes less coordinated sucks; they tire easily; they distract easily (which I thought was more difficult than the tiring); and it's so hard with tension, hormones, and milk-engorged breasts. —Sheila

I really wanted to breast-feed her right away. I did keep up the pumping and did eventually get to breast-feed, but they convinced me that bottles were better to start. I really feel bad to this day for letting them take charge because I know now that this is not so. Still, who was I to know? They were the professionals. —Linda

Unfortunately, while your preemie is hospitalized, you may not always receive effective guidance and support in your attempts to breast-feed. Sometimes, despite the health care team's encouraging you to supply breast milk, your baby is given formula. Or the staff's decision to bottle-feed your breast milk to your baby may make you feel that they are more interested in your breast milk than in helping you master breast-feeding. Your desire to breast-feed or the pace that you had imagined for feeding your baby might not match the staff's routines. When you're trying to assert some control as a parent, it can be frustrating to have to negotiate all of this with your baby's medical team. And sometimes, you and your baby simply will not be able to breast-feed. This can be a tremendous blow if you had had your heart set on breast-feeding exclusively. (For more on this subject, see "Supplementation and Bottle-Feeding" later in this chapter.)

The next day I was desperate to pump some more milk for my son, but the nurse on duty wouldn't help me. She said okay and then never showed up, so I kept calling her to help. Finally she told me that she was waiting for the lactation specialist to come in at 10:00 A.M. I was mad and shot her a dirty look. I don't think she realized how important it was to me to get some more milk to my son. I am still mad about it four months later. I was also mad at the NICU people who fed my son formula because they didn't have any of my milk. Didn't they realize that I had plenty of it but that I just couldn't get it to them? Why didn't they come get my milk—I was only a few corridors away? If my milk is so much better than formula, then why???? The more I think about it, the madder I get!! —Ruby

Trying to breast-feed her turned out to be quite traumatic for both of us. She would latch on but, after thirty seconds or so, would become exhausted and fall asleep. The nurses would weigh her before and after our breast-feeding sessions, and more often than not, she would have lost weight. I was very disheartened. I reasoned that breast-feeding her would be an opportunity to make up for our lost bonding experience, but it only proved to be very distressing for both of us. I tried to get her to breast-feed for six weeks once she was home, but I finally had to give up. At that point she was "hooked" on the bottle, and I couldn't get her to change her mind. I do wish the NICU nurses had told me that once she took the bottle it might be hard for her to switch to the breast. —Rebekah

Even if you end up succeeding in breast-feeding, the process can be quite trying and drawn out. Because preemies often take a long time to learn to coordinate sucking, swallowing, and breathing, breast-feeding can require a lot of patience. Your baby may take two steps forward and then one step back. Do keep in mind that most term babies don't learn to nurse until they are around forty weeks' gestation. Try to give your preemie credit for accomplishing as much as he or she does. Comfort yourself by imagining a future in which you and your baby have mastered nursing. Envision it. Allow yourself to hope for it. Then do what you can to try to make it happen.

I was absolutely determined to breast-feed my preemie (not knowing at the time how difficult such a thing is!). I arranged special permission with the NICU staff to be able to breast-feed him every time he was bottle-fed, supposedly to try to keep him used to both. He didn't have any trouble latching on to me, though. Well, sometimes he did seem to have trouble, as if he was frustrated and didn't want to latch on. And I'd get all discouraged and depressed. And, of course, the staff didn't really care about making sure I breast-fed the same number of times as he bottle-fed—it was all up to me to push for it to happen. But I kept trying (stubborn mom that I am!). Lots of ups and downs, but we were exclusively breast-feeding by a few days after his due date. Patient stubbornness goes a long way, I think! —Sandy

Here are some suggestions for tackling the challenge of breast-feeding in the NICU (some of these apply to establishing breast-feeding after homecoming as well):

- *Discuss feeding options with your baby's nursing and medical staff.* If you very much want to breast-feed, discuss ways to increase your breast-feeding practice without compromising your baby's progress.
- *Seek out support for and information about breast-feeding preemies.* Talk to other breast-feeding mothers of preemies. If you are not satisfied with the lactation support provided by the NICU, don't hesitate to look for another lactation consultant: a nurse, midwife, or doula (a woman who gives emotional encouragement and physical assistance to a new mother) can also be a good source of support. There is plenty of information available in print and on the Internet. See the resources in Appendix C for some suggestions. (Chapter 6 also contains lots of information on the advantages, the mechanics, establishing and enhancing your milk supply, and overcoming physical challenges to breast-feeding.)
- *Recognize that you and your baby form a unique breast-feeding partnership.* Whether her baby is term or a preemie, every mother has to do a certain amount of figuring out what works best. For instance, if your baby has trouble latching on to your nipple, you might try using your pump's suction to draw out your nipple before putting your baby to your breast. If your baby is overwhelmed by your milk spurting out at the beginning of the feeding, you might pump just enough milk to decrease the pressure or volume so that your baby can keep up with the flow without swallowing so much air or choking. Look for answers that work for both of you. Problems don't indicate failure—they only indicate a need for solutions.
- *Know that some babies are easily distracted or overwhelmed by external stimuli.* Ask if you can feed your baby in a quiet, darkened room. Experiment with different methods of holding your little one, such as wrapping or

unwrapping him or her in a blanket.

- *Incorporate kangaroo care into your efforts to breast-feed.* Research indicates that skin-to-skin contact inspires the instinct to suckle. You might try starting your breast-feeding sessions by placing your baby against your bare chest to rest, relax, and soak up your warmth and nurturing. (Check out the section on kangaroo care earlier in this chapter.) If your baby starts rooting around on your skin, follow this cue and guide her or him to your nipple. Enjoying and relaxing with your little one is a priority, whatever feeding method you use.

- *Be flexible.* You may want your baby to receive only breast milk, but allow yourself to consider supplementing with formula if it's necessary. You may want to exclusively nurse your baby, but let yourself consider bottle-feeding if that seems to be a solution. If you have one baby, make decisions uniquely for that baby—no matter what your sister or cousin or nurse chose to do with her child and no matter what you did with your earlier babies. If you have multiples, the same principle applies: make choices that are unique for each child—a good general practice for raising multiples. (For more on feeding multiple babies, see the section later in this chapter.) Being flexible doesn't mean that you've given in. It means that you recognize that the situation is not what you'd anticipated. Adjusting your plans to fit the situation is a wise decision.

- *Allow yourself to mourn your losses.* Give yourself permission to experience your feelings—sadness, frustration, disappointment—about the options your baby's premature birth has ruled out.

- *See the feeding relationship itself as meaningful for you and your baby.* Free yourself from society's definition of successful breast-feeding. For you and your baby, successful breast-feeding may mean that your baby takes a bottle filled with your pumped breast milk. Or it may mean putting your baby to your breast for a bit and then providing a full formula feeding afterward. Don't think in either-or terms. Experiment and adjust. Use the combination of breast milk and formula, bottle-feeding and breast-feeding that works for you and your baby.

- *Recognize that you supply many valuable things to your baby—not just breast milk.* The amount of breast milk you supply and the outcome of your attempts to breast-feed say nothing about your desire to nurture your baby or about your competence as a parent.

- *Persist through the ups and downs of your milk supply.* When you are pumping into that clear bottle, you are well aware of variations in your milk supply. If your supply seems to be decreasing, you may simply need to get more rest, drink more water, or pump more frequently to maintain or build up your supply. (See Chapter 6 for more information on this.) If your baby takes a turn for the worse, your milk production may diminish overnight, and you may feel too depressed to try to maintain your supply. If your breasts seem unproductive in spite of pumping, you may be tempted to give up—but try to keep pumping. This is a critical time for you to receive the support you need to keep your breasts primed. As your baby improves, your supply may build up naturally in response, and you can continue to reap the rewards of breast-feeding.

I'm so thankful to the lactation nurses at the hospital because, when Fabian got so sick, my milk production completely stopped. When I was pumping, I think I got two drops out, and they would tell me, every day, to continue pumping. I hated it at the time. It was horrible, but I did stick to it. I had to write how much I pumped on each side, a drop here, a drop there; a quarter of an ounce here, a quarter of an ounce there when things got better. For three weeks, I hardly had anything coming out. But when he got better, suddenly my milk came back in, and I got home, breast-feeding him completely. It was amazing. To see that he was going to survive and make it, and not being scared for his life, that's when the milk started to get better. And I'm so thankful for the support. Without them, I would have never been able to keep it going. —Gallice

Waiting and Stockpiling It can be days or weeks before your premature baby is given anything to eat by mouth—even by tube—and your breast milk may accumulate in the freezer. You may have mixed feelings about seeing your frozen milk stacked there: it can be a visual representation of what has not yet happened—your baby isn't able to take the milk that was made just for him or her. You may not be able to imagine a time when that milk will be useful. It may be difficult to imagine your baby ever being able to consume that much milk. In addition, your baby was supposed to take that nourishment directly from your breast. Seeing those ounces accumulate, you might think about all the milk that you wish had already been in your baby's tummy.

Expressing milk at home just reminded me that I didn't have my daughter home with me. It was horrible. —*Diane*

But that stock of breast milk in the freezer can also represents a bountiful harvest. You may feel proud of your production and glad that only you can provide this treasure. You would never, ever want to see it run out.

It was like a feast of plenty, tangible evidence that I had enough milk for my babies. I would have preferred that they could have gotten it from me directly, but at least they were going to get it at some point. —*Rikki*

Intake and Weight Gain A common source of parental impatience associated with breast-feeding is wanting your baby to master this skill and consume vast quantities so that she or he can go home sooner. If you begin to worry that breast-feeding may be holding back your baby's weight gain, remember that neither bottles nor formula can guarantee that your baby will be able to come home a single day sooner. Give your milk and breast-feeding the benefit of the doubt. Who knows? Maybe your milk will help your baby fight off an infection or get healthier sooner. Maybe your breast-feeding will help your baby gain weight faster and thus go home earlier.

Intake is another source of impatience or anxiety. Because you're in a medical setting, your baby may be weighed before and after feedings to determine exactly how much he or she consumed. The attention intake receives may cause you to worry that your baby is not getting enough breast milk. It is easy to resent the fact that something so natural has to be so closely scrutinized. But as your baby grows healthier and bigger, and especially when you take your little one home, you can let go of these intake anxieties and learn to trust your baby to regulate his or her own consumption. As your baby thrives, you will see that the two of you work as a marvelous milk-producing and milk-consuming team.

Supplementation and Bottle-Feeding Particularly if your baby was born very early, supplementation with preemie formula or human milk fortifier may help him or her grow. You may resent the implication of supplementation: that your breast milk alone is inadequate to meet the needs of your preemie. Or you may resent the attitudes of those who second-guess your decision to supplement, especially when it may be a painful decision on your part.

Similarly, your baby may receive your pumped breast milk in a bottle. You may be relieved that your baby is being nourished by your milk, even if it comes from a bottle, or you may be concerned that your little one will get used to the bottle and resent the intrusion of your efforts to breast-feed. While some babies do learn to prefer the bottle, research is starting to show that when the mother isn't present to put the baby to the breast, babies who are bottle-fed may actually do *better* at breast-feeding than babies who continue to be tube-fed. Apparently when babies can practice sucking skills with a bottle, this practice may transfer to better suckling at the breast. Some professionals believe that it is better yet to feed preemies with a cup or a spoon; this can offer practice eating by mouth but avoid nipple confusion.

Your decisions about supplementation or bottle-feeding may be influenced by research, medical staff, or by your desire that your baby eat a measurable amount, grow quickly, and come home. But even though some decisions can be medically beneficial to your baby, they might overshadow your maternal preferences and intuition.

By the time the doctor was ready to stop supplements, I was not able to satisfy Stephen. This is still my biggest single regret. I knew nursing was best for my baby, I knew he was big enough and strong enough to nurse, he was my fourth child so I knew to trust my instincts, and yet I still followed the doctor instead of my heart—and as a result lost out on nursing my baby. —Tracy

Once she had developed the suck-swallow-breathe reflex at around thirty-three to thirty-four weeks adjusted age, I got enormous pressure from the nurses to give her a bottle. But I wanted to nurse her as long as I could—practice sessions, really, because she was too small to complete a feeding—before the bottle was introduced. This was a major source of tension between the nurses and myself. Many thought it was cruel to deny Charlotte the pleasure of a bottle for this period of time. ... But eventually we had to introduce bottles because she couldn't go home being gavaged, and I think the number of bottles she has had has interfered with her ability to breast-feed. —Kate

It can be quite frustrating—and even demoralizing—if you are working hard to breast-feed but your baby begins to resist nursing, finding it easier and faster to take a bottle, or if your supply falters. If the medical staff doesn't support you in your desire to breast-feed, you may feel that your attempts to do what you believe is best for your baby are being undermined. Ideally, your baby can breast-feed when you are present and bottle-feed only when you aren't there, or as a supplement *after* breast-feeding.

Some babies take to breast-feeding only as they grow older or healthier. Some babies take to breast-feeding only in the quiet of home. (See Chapter 14 for more information on breast-feeding at home.)

Providing Breast Milk without Breast-Feeding If your baby cannot manage to breast-feed, resolutely prefers the bottle, or still relies on tube-feeding, you'll need to decide whether to continue to pump to maintain your milk supply so that your baby can benefit from receiving at least some breast milk. You must also decide how important or feasible it is for you and your baby that the tube or bottle contain breast milk only. You can pump part time and feed formula part time. You may decide to keep pumping while your baby is tiny and move to formula later. Or you may find a pumping routine that works for you and continue to feed your baby breast milk exclusively or in part. Even in your disappointment over not being able to put your baby to the breast, pumping can reinforce your involvement in your baby's feeding and give you the boost of knowing that you are supplying your baby with vital nutrients. If your baby doesn't take to nursing, this is not a rejection of you, a reflection on your mothering ability, or your fault. Some babies just have naturally strong preferences or the tendency to resist change, and when they get used to the bottle, they don't want to drink from anything else.

If you were really looking forward to nursing, you will need to grieve the loss of this special way of relating to your baby. Just keep in mind that you *can* have a close and rewarding relationship with your baby without breast-feeding. You can experience the satisfaction of providing breast milk. You can mimic the intimacy of breast-feeding by cuddling your baby against your warm skin; holding (instead of propping) the bottle or tube; silently letting your baby observe your face or feel your skin; and remaining soothing, comforting, and responsive to your baby during feedings. It may not be the same, but it can still be very rewarding for you and your baby. However you feed your baby in the NICU, you are nurturing your little one.

I had always planned on breast-feeding my baby, but he definitely changed all of that. I pumped the whole time he was in the hospital (three and a half months). It was the only thing I could do for him, and it made me feel like a mom even when I felt completely helpless. But when it came time to start breast-feeding, he couldn't take in my nipple. It didn't take long for me to give up. I thought he'd had enough struggling to survive. I didn't want him to stress out over feeding. —Sharon

If You Must Stop Providing Breast Milk Even with the best intentions, efforts, technique, and support, for a variety of reasons, some mothers find that they can no longer feed their baby at the breast or pump milk. And some babies cannot tolerate breast milk. Although breast milk is easier to digest than formula, some preemies' digestive systems are so compromised that even their mother's milk is too much for them to handle. Some babies just need time for their systems to mature or heal, but other babies will have long-term problems adjusting to breast milk. A mother can find it unbearably difficult to continue to work so very hard to produce milk when she's not sure that her baby will ever be able to be nourished by it.

If you must stop providing breast milk for any reason, this can be yet another deeply felt loss. You may try for weeks or even months before finally letting go of your hope to provide breast milk for your preemie. But when the costs of pumping become greater than the rewards, it is quite reasonable to turn your energies toward the many other ways you can nurture your baby. Know your limits and respect them.

Breast-feeding was definitely something I wanted to do, but it was never something that was going to be an issue with me. If I couldn't do it, I couldn't do it, and that was the end of it. And I had gotten to a point with Charlie, after pumping and pumping and trying to get milk for about a week, that I said: "You know what? I have got way more on my head to deal with. I can't cope with this. This frustration is an emotion that I refuse to deal with. So bottle-feed him!" —Jaimee

It breaks my heart that I was not able to [continue pumping]. I felt very unfulfilled and like even more of a failure than I already did for what had happened. ... I am tired of feeling inadequate because I chose to bottle-feed my baby. Yes, breast may be best—but I wish that they would make it known that it is not best in all situations. —Stacy

If you had your heart set on providing breast milk, you may feel a deep sense of failure, anger, disappointment, or loss that it didn't work out.

I pumped breast milk for three months for Casey. I felt that he needed breast milk more since he was premature, and I thought it was the only thing I could still do for him. He stopped digesting breast milk when he was three months old and had to be switched to formula. I cried that day—yet another failure to take care of my baby. —Kelly

It is important for you to acknowledge these painful feelings so that you can find pleasure in other ways of feeding your baby. Talk about your feelings with someone who can listen supportively or write in your journal, perhaps as if you're writing to your baby. Do whatever helps you make peace with the situation. You can achieve feelings of closeness during feeding times, however you nourish your baby, and you can always put your baby to your breast for comfort, without having to produce breast milk. Sometimes, stopping *is* the best thing to do. Look at it this way: You didn't fail, you *finished*.

I'm a mother. I want the very best of everything for my daughter. I love her. I would do anything for her. If I had my choice, she would still be breast-feeding. But you know what? I didn't have a choice. My daughter wasn't able to tolerate even a milliliter of breast milk. She was orally defensive, and I had completely dried up well before she came home, despite the fact that I had a really good breast pump. —Brooke

It's really a toss-up whether more mother tears are shed each day over an incubator in the NICU or over a breast pump. ... All mothers would benefit from being empowered to take control of feeding their child and doing it in a way that's perfect for the two of them, period. —Sheila

Feeding Multiple Babies

When you have multiple babies born preterm, your may need to reconsider your earlier plans. If you had planned to formula-feed, you may look to a breast-feeding relationship to ease the separation from your babies or to provide a nutritional boost. If you had believed that you could successfully breast-feed multiples, you might waver when confronted with the need to pump enough milk for several babies for several months.

Multiples present the challenge of doing what is best for two (or more) little ones. It is common for parents to make different choices for different babies. If one baby is more critically ill than the other(s), the mother may pump milk for one infant (or feed from the frozen supply) while giving the others formula. Similarly, if a mother has been pumping throughout her babies' hospital stay and finds that one baby learns to nurse but another does not, she must decide how to proceed. Does she breast-feed one and pump for the other? Does one get formula? Does she pump for both? Does she stop pumping entirely? Trying to coordinate pumping, breast-feeding, and bottle-feeding can be overwhelming for parents of a single premature baby. If you are a parent of multiples, feeding can be the most complex and time-consuming task you face—especially if your babies are slow eaters!

It is also normal for you to have mixed emotions about all of the complicated options and decisions you make. For example, you might have otherwise been content to supplement with formula but now feel enormous guilt doing so for a small, ill, premature twin. Or you may grieve if one baby cannot take breast milk while the other(s) thrives on it. Take your time figuring out what works for you and your babies. When you can, keep your options open. Also expect circumstances to change and your babies to be different. It is the rare set of multiples whose needs and preferences remain identical and unchanging. If one baby prefers the bottle, consider pumping for that baby while you put the other(s) to the breast. If you feel you can't possibly provide breast milk for all your babies all the time, give yourself permission to supplement with formula and reassure yourself of the benefits of whatever amount of breast milk you can provide. If one baby does better on breast milk and another does better on formula, meet their unique needs. Don't worry about treating your babies exactly alike. Each one will benefit from being fed however and whatever he or she thrives on.

Becoming Attuned to Your Baby

As your baby grows and matures, you'll be able to do more than just hold and feed your little one. As your infant's awareness and responsiveness increase, you'll be able to interact more. With practice, you'll become more and more attuned to your baby and learn how to encourage his or her interest in the surroundings—and in having a relationship with you. Becoming attuned to your baby is a cornerstone of nurturing your baby.

Every newborn has a unique temperament, as well as particular sensitivities and thresholds for stimulation. Because preemies' nervous systems are so immature, they generally have more extreme sensitivities and thresholds than do term newborns. For example, some preemies have strong aversions for certain sights, sounds, or touch. One preemie may have trouble handling noise and also have difficulty noticing soft voices, leaving a very narrow range of sound that is "just right." Lack of responsiveness or escape from overstimulation are two reasons preemies spend a fair amount of time in a state of drowsiness or sleep. Preemies who have trouble regulating themselves may disintegrate into fussiness when under- or overstimulated because they cannot calm themselves when they're unable to attend to or tune out stimulation.

Fortunately, parents can figure out their baby's sensitivities and thresholds by learning to interpret their infant's behaviors. With practice, you can use your baby's many cues to "read" her or him—to recognize what kinds of stimulation she prefers or his readiness to nap, eat, or play. You can also discover what bothers your baby, what keeps him soothed, and what restores her to calm. The following sections explain how to decipher your baby's behaviors and reactions so that you can confidently respond to your little one's preferences and needs.

Reading Infant Behavioral States

Much of your response to your baby's cues will be instinctive: when your baby cries, you'll want to do calming things. When your baby is sleeping quietly, you'll feel compelled to leave her alone. When your baby is bright-eyed, you'll feel like getting his attention. But sometimes your baby's cues will be more subtle than a silent snooze or a lusty yowl. In fact, a baby's level of sleepiness, alertness, and fussiness can be categorized into one of six states of awareness called behavioral states. Familiarity with the signs of these states—and how these states affect your baby's behavior and responsiveness to you—can help you respond more effectively to your preemie's needs.

- *Deep sleep.* Your baby is fast asleep, breathing regularly, eyes closed and motionless, with no bodily movements except the occasional involuntary twitch. In this state your baby is difficult to awaken, will not respond to your voice or touch, and cannot effectively eat from breast or bottle.

- *Light sleep.* This sleep state is associated with dreaming. Breathing is irregular; eyes are closed but moving beneath the lids; and your little one may move, suck, or fuss although still asleep. Your baby can be awakened enough to feed but probably not enough to play.
- *Drowsy.* Your baby is in the transition zone between wakefulness and sleep. The eyes may open and shut, the arms may move voluntarily, and breathing may become more rapid and shallow. Babies who have been awake are ready for a nap when they become drowsy; those who have been asleep may be ready to wake up and enter the quiet alert state.
- *Quiet alert.* Your baby has a bright, wide-awake look and can focus and attend to the surroundings. Because your baby is so focused, he or she may not move much or make much noise. This is the best state for playing with your baby because your little one is calm and attentive.
- *Active alert.* Your baby is awake and slightly agitated. Breathing is irregular. Your baby may move and startle more easily in response to sights, sounds, and touch, and may be fussy. Your little one cannot tolerate much more stimulation without dissolving into crying or drowsiness. Try lowering your voice, stilling your touch, or averting your gaze (or all three, depending on your baby's sensitivities and thresholds) to see if he or she can return to the quiet alert state or take a needed nap.
- *Crying.* Your baby is awake and agitated. Breathing is irregular, shallow, and rapid. Your infant can no longer tolerate or attend to playful interaction or feeding or cope with any stimulus that isn't calming.

Being able to recognize your baby's state lets you know when to encourage sleep, coax a feeding, or take advantage of readiness for play.

Reading Other Physical Cues

There are other observable physical signs—called physiologic cues—that suggest how your baby is perceiving and coping with the surroundings. For instance, look at your baby's color, breathing (respirations), movements, and eyes. The description that precedes the dash in the list below indicates that your baby is calm; the one that follows the dash indicates stress:

- Is your baby's skin tone healthy, even, glowing, pinkish undertones— or pale, mottled, gray, or bluish?
- Are your baby's respirations stable—or uneven?
- Are your infant's limb movements smooth—or jerky?

- Are your baby's eyes bright—or are they glassy, squinting, frozen, or looking away?
- Is your baby leaning into your touch and settling into your hold—or startling easily, arching his or her back, or squirming?
- Are your baby's muscles toned—or limp or rigid?

When your baby is alert and calm, he or she is able to attend to and tolerate the stimulation or interaction that is occurring—and is open to its continuation. When your baby begins to show signs of stress, she or he is telling you that whatever is happening is too much or too unpleasant—and that it's time for a change, a break, or a nap.

Engaging Your Baby

To effectively engage your baby, you need to support your child's growing ability to stay calm and attentive during interaction. Some preemies can regulate themselves, sucking on their own hands, looking away, or falling asleep when they need a break or some soothing. These efforts can help them stay relaxed and, if they aren't too tired, stay interested in their surroundings. Unfortunately, their repertoire of regulating actions is quite limited. Tiny babies can't cover their ears when it's too noisy, walk away when they're tired of visiting with somebody, or find something else to do when they're bored or overwhelmed. They haven't yet figured out how to "change the channel." And so, all newborns rely heavily on the responsiveness and protectiveness of their caregivers.

Extremely premature babies don't interact much with or show much interest in the world for a few weeks or even months after birth. The same is true of very sick babies, who need all their energy to get healthy. But as the intensity of your baby's care drops and as your baby grows and matures, she will be able to become more interested in the world around her. As your baby approaches his due date or discharge, he will be able to tolerate more stimulation and interaction from you.

You can try all of these strategies to bolster your baby's growing ability to engage with you:
- Follow your baby's lead.
- Honor your baby's attempts to moderate stimulation.
- Protect your baby from overwhelming or unpleasant stimuli.
- Provide the kinds of touch, sounds (voice), and other stimulation that

soothe your baby and sustain his or her interest.

You probably know these strategies instinctively, but when confronted with a tiny preemie in the chaos of the NICU, you may be afraid to trust your instincts and your intuitions. The next time you are with your baby, notice how easy it is to do these things and how "right" you feel doing them. Don't second-guess your intuitive abilities. Instead, follow your baby's lead—and your heart.

Follow Your Baby's Lead Eager to attract and hold their baby's attention, many parents become more active and engaging. This approach can overwhelm premature babies, though, and cause them to disengage their attention. Instead, it's important to tone it down and imitate your baby's actions and level of interest. When your baby averts her gaze to rest, you can rest, too. When she is ready to reengage, she'll look at you, and you can respond by smiling and looking back. This intimate dance shows your baby that you are responsive to her pace. By imitating her and following her lead, you encourage her attentiveness.

Honor Your Baby's Attempts to Moderate Stimulation Touching or making eye contact with your baby can be very rewarding, but it's important to remain responsive to your baby's ability to notice and handle your advances. As you get to know your baby's signals of distress, you can adjust your interaction. If your baby arches his back, change your touch or stop completely. If he averts his gaze, let him go and wait until he is ready to come back for more— which may not be until after a good nap. If he tries to reengage, try changing your interaction. In a similar vein, let him sleep when he is tired and feed when he is hungry.

When your preemie gets overwhelmed, she may recover if you back off—or she may quickly pass the point of no return. Recognize that your baby's inability to recover is not an indication of your parenting abilities, but a measure of your baby's fatigue, young age, unique temperament, and immature ability to stay calm (to self-regulate).

As you learn more about your baby, you'll become more sensitive and skilled at reading cues. As you become more experienced and as your baby becomes more mature, the two of you will be better able regulate the amount of stimulation and to extend fun playtimes.

Protect Your Baby from Overwhelming or Unpleasant Stimuli If you notice that your baby is particularly sensitive to light, sound, or touch, you can take steps to protect him or her. Ask that the overhead lights be dimmed, request that the monitors be turned down, and do what you can to figure out what kinds of touch your baby finds soothing. Put a sign in your little one's incubator to remind your health care teammates to take these sensitivities into consideration as they work around her or him. Ask that your baby be given eyeshades and earmuffs for sleep. Unfortunately, in the NICU, as in life, you cannot always protect your baby from unpleasant or overwhelming stimuli. To compensate, you can be there to soothe and nurture.

Provide the Kinds of Touch, Sounds, and Other Stimuli That Soothe and Sustain Your Baby's Interest Individual babies respond differently to sights, sounds, touch, taste, smell, and movement. Like all parents, you need to figure out through trial and error what your baby finds tolerable and interesting. Read your baby's physiologic cues to figure out what's calming and what's stressful. You and your infant, working together, can figure out what keeps him interested but not overwhelmed.

For example, how does your baby react to a noisy environment? Does your baby drift off to sleep, stay awake but unfazed, remain alert and interested, or startle easily and become fussy? Discover the kind of voice your baby turns to by experimenting first with a high pitch and then a low pitch; then try a soothing voice and finally, an animated one. Figure out which things (including you) your baby likes to suck on. Provide sights that your baby prefers to look at: does he or she respond best to your face when you smile gently and silently, or when your smile is lively and you're talkative? Figure out the kinds of touch that your baby leans into. Some babies like to be swaddled (wrapped in a blanket or other covering); others like to hang loose. Some babies like to be held firmly; others just want to be cupped with the hands.

By providing the kinds of stimulation and interaction that interest and soothe your baby, you are helping your baby stay calm and attentive to the surrounding world. That the world (including *you*) is intriguing, fun, and safe is a significant lesson for your baby to learn. Your emerging ability to provide a calming attitude, a soothing touch, and an interesting distraction is a skill that you will use effectively throughout your child's life.

The nurses said that she was more calm when we were there, from very early on. In the first few days, we could cup our hands around her feet, or lay our hands on top of her to give her boundaries, and she responded well to this. It was so important, because this was the first direct thing we could do to help. —*Mary*

My son opened his eyes a little and watched us, but mostly he slept. He rarely cried when we held him but watched us very closely when he was awake. We talked to him very quietly when he was awake, and he seemed to respond very well to our voices by having really good readings on his sats and no apneas or bradycardias. —*Andrea*

There will be plenty of times, especially early on, when your baby won't engage with you. Instead of feeling rejected, remember that your baby's ability to fall asleep or to turn away from you is a sign of his or her ability to control the amount of stimulation being taken in, in an attempt to avoid becoming overwhelmed. This reaction is much like they way you behave at your favorite museum: even though you're fascinated, after a while you need to take a break from the exhibits. When your baby tries to find a balance between paying attention to what's interesting and becoming overwhelmed, this is evidence of growing adaptation to the outside world. (For more support and information on this topic, see "Tuning In to Sensitivities and Thresholds" in Chapter 16.)

As you become more responsive to your baby, your baby can become more responsive to you. Your infant's growing attentiveness and your emerging ability to engage and sustain that attention are reassuring signs that you are building a rewarding relationship.

If you have more than one baby in the NICU, you may struggle to get to know and connect with each one separately. Getting to know your multiples would be a challenge even if they were not premature and in the NICU. It takes time to discover each baby's preferences and sensitivities. It takes energy to engage each baby and to decipher each unique set of cues. It takes practice to become responsive and to build a rapport that suits each baby's special style. Give yourself the time you need to get to know each of your precious babies.

Points to Remember

- The bonding process is flexible. You will develop a connection to your baby that is resilient and that changes over time. Your bond can thrive in spite of your baby's premature arrival and this period of hospitalization.
- Kangaroo care is an important way of feeling close to—and providing respite for—your baby. Other beneficial forms of touch for preemies in the NICU are massage and, for multiples, cobedding.
- Decisions about how to feed your baby are central to your parenting identity. Seek out the information and support you need, and give yourself permission to make flexible decisions for you and your baby.
- When your preemie is very young, unstable, or unhealthy, you may feel frustrated by his or her lack of attentiveness to you. Rest assured that your baby will be able to show interest in you and the surroundings as he or she heals and matures.
- As you get to know your baby, you will learn how to read your baby's behaviors, respond to cues, and accommodate unique sensitivities and thresholds. These skills will enable you to follow your baby's lead and to become adept at engaging your baby's attention without overwhelming him or her. This success will help you feel that you are building a rewarding relationship with your baby.
- Bonding with, engaging, and making decisions about feeding twins, triplets, or more involves assessing each baby separately and responding to each one's unique needs.

CHAPTER TEN

The Roller-Coaster NICU Experience

At the beginning of your baby's NICU stay, you may feel as if you are holding your breath. "How will my baby survive being born so early?" you may wonder. It may be weeks before you can exhale.

> *I thought, "He's actually alive. Now what?" I had tried desperately to prepare myself for my son's simultaneous birth/death. But he was alive, and I was incredibly shocked and horribly scared. I felt terrible for not having the faith in my son's strength to live but was incredibly fearful of the impending outcome/pain he would endure.* —Andrea

> *I stare down at the gauze over his eyes and the IVs in his scalp, and I remember how people have asked me if I think I'm being tested. No, I don't. A test is something you go through only to see if you can go through the real thing.* —Jeff

The experience of having a premature infant in the NICU has often been compared to a roller-coaster ride. As your baby navigates the ups and downs of even a typical preemie medical course, your emotional journey will correspond, and it can be arduous. All of the unpredictable twists and turns leave you wondering what is waiting around the next corner. What new setback, what new apparatus, what new treatment, what new complication, what new struggle lies in wait? The uncertainties can rattle you to the core.

As you become more familiar with the medical and nursing interventions and as your baby improves and becomes more predictable, you may feel more hopeful and assured about what's next. Or the opposite may happen: as your baby improves, your emotions may catch up with you, making you feel worse just when you think you should be feeling better. Whatever your experience, you may not be able to shake that feeling of being on an emotional roller coaster for quite a while, even after your baby needs less intensive care.

[When she was moved to a bassinet], they lost her preemie pacifier. It must have fallen on the floor and they threw it away, and it was the only one. They didn't have any more. And then I was going to have to drive all the way to stupid [a distant town] because that's the only store that carried preemie pacifiers. And I was just furious and angry and upset. Just so many emotions all at once. I couldn't even begin to cope with them. And my milk started to dry up. Well, of course, I hadn't had a lot of rest, and it was finally starting to take its toll. She was getting better, and I was falling apart. —Beth

Whether your baby has a relatively smooth NICU stay or a very rocky one, you do a lot of waiting. How you feel about that waiting is related to the uncertainties you face, the setbacks that occur, and the balance between your hopes and fears for your tiny baby. This chapter offers some suggestions for surviving the waiting. It also looks at other aspects of this roller-coaster ride, among them the comparisons you may make between your baby and other preemies in the NICU, making life-and-death decisions, and the extended stay.

Waiting

Buddy was out of surgery in a few hours. Those were hard hours. Very frightening. Minutes seemed like days. —Ed

During an NICU stay, so much time is spent just waiting: waiting for the doctor to come, waiting for a test result, waiting to confer about a decision, waiting to see what will happen next. You'll find yourself waiting for your baby to breathe on his own, to open her eyes, to eat, to grow, to recover. You'll wait for the chance to hold your baby close. And then you'll wait for your baby to come home with you.

Each little milestone was so important. Things most people take for granted, we couldn't. Things you don't even think you'll ever need to consider—like sucking. We had to teach her. Remembering to breathe. There was nothing we could leave to chance. We were in the NICU forever. At least it seemed like it. Babies came and went. Even seasons changed. But our little family held on. —Cindy

As your baby's hospitalization drags on, you may feel intense impatience. Even when your baby's NICU course is relatively short, straightforward, and without crisis, the waiting is traumatic in and of itself. Why should you have to wait for the joys of parenting that are supposed to occur right after birth? Why does your family, your baby, have to wait for the rewards that other families get without much effort or forethought? Your greatest source of frustration and distress may be what your baby has to endure. You may wish that you could take your baby's place—to spare your little one the pain and to spare yourself the watching ... and waiting.

The nurses called her a "feeder and grower"—all she needed to do before she could come home was gain weight. Still, my husband and I worried about her constantly. Is she gaining weight adequately? Doesn't that tube they're feeding her with bother her? Will she need the bili lights? Why is there blood in her stool? Do the lights bother her eyes? We asked lots of questions about her condition and visited her as often as possible. —Rebekah

Whether your baby is doing poorly or relatively well, waiting is agonizing. Waiting can make you feel helpless. There is nothing you can do to make time go faster. Indeed, you may feel separated from the rest of the world, in this foreign space where time seems to stand still. You are powerless to make things happen any faster than they will: you can't, for example, make those test results come back more quickly. To top it off, when something finally does happen, it isn't always what you were waiting and hoping for.

I cried a lot. The worst for me was the waiting. Every single day we didn't know if he was dying on the inside. Or waiting for test results. I would walk around just hyper, literally shaking and trying to think of things to do to pass the time. Numerous times, we were told, "If this doesn't get better in two days, we'll do more tests." So there's another couple of days of waiting. ... I did a lot of pacing because I couldn't get the worries off my mind. And the worst part of it was that I did a lot of it by myself. —Stephie

We got to walk with the surgeon and the anesthesiologist to the elevators, and at that point you kiss your baby good-bye and you don't know what's going to happen from there. ... Okay, now we sit and wait. ... [Tears] It was probably the longest hour of my life, waiting. ... The lady from pastoral care came down, and the nurses tried to talk to us, but you really don't want to talk to anybody—at least we didn't. They were trying to be comforting and reassuring, but I didn't listen—basically, I didn't want to be bothered. I didn't want to have anybody try to comfort me. I just wanted to be by myself. —Pam

Waiting takes on a whole new aspect when you are told that your baby's condition must be dealt with *immediately*. To most of us, *immediately* means "right now," so when things don't happen right away, the wait can seem interminable. Then if another doctor examines your child and decides that the condition isn't critical, you may not know what to think. Should you relax, or get yet another opinion? Whom should you believe? When you've been put on high alert, it's hard to lower the volume on your questions, worries, and impatience.

We followed the ambulance to the Children's Hospital, and when we got there, we waited around forever. So we're just waiting and waiting, and they didn't even have the eye doctors come look at him. And here I'd been told if he didn't have this surgery, he was going to be blind—and nobody was looking at him because they had other stuff they were doing. I just sat there. And then the head eye doctor and about ten other doctors all looked at Josh and said, "I have no idea why your hospital sent him over here—his eyes are fine. This child doesn't need surgery and probably isn't ever going to need it. We're sending him back tonight."

So then you start questioning things, like every decision that had been made up until then—and who do you believe about the eyes? This is not something you want to mess with. But he was sent to the Children's Hospital because they were the experts, which I kind of did intuitively believe.

But then after that [back at our "home" hospital], it was horrible because, almost every other day, they kept telling me he was going to need the laser surgery. For days they were checking him, and then they were checking

Evan too, even though he didn't have the same problem. And they kept telling me, "He's going to need surgery still, any day." And I kept telling them, "No, he's not. They told me at Children's he's not." And then they thought I was being this really rude parent and not believing them, like I was in denial or something. It was awful. All those days of not knowing—does he need surgery or doesn't he? And questioning everything they were doing. Not knowing who to believe. —Stephie

Dealing with differing medical opinions is a particularly trying part of the NICU roller-coaster ride. It is common for different doctors to have not only different ideas about your child's condition, but different approaches to diagnosis and treatment. Some tend to "wait and see"; others do every test available to them. One doctor may be very aggressive about intervening; another might suggest trying the least invasive treatment first—and then going from there. Of course, you may be more in tune with one approach than the other. If you're lucky, you'll have a doctor whose philosophies match your own. In any case, if you have questions or concerns about how a doctor is planning your baby's care, you can seek another opinion. You may want to contact either your baby's primary doctor or the specialist you trust for consistency and guidance. And if you're given contradictory opinions, you have to put your parental intuition to work—and trust what your gut and heart are telling you.

Waiting with Uncertainty

The doctors said they just didn't know, but that she was growing and that was good, but they needed to get her off the ventilator. They tried every ventilator they had. Julie would get off a little, and then she'd have a setback. And if one thing would get better, then another thing would get worse. And this went on and on. —Tim

Especially when your baby is in critical condition, having to "wait and see" is painful. The uncertainties can seem vast and unrelenting. You may feel frustrated that the doctors and nurses cannot tell you when things will improve. In fact, the doctors may not even be able to guarantee that your baby will survive. You may have few promises on which to pin your hopes.

Being in the NICU is difficult, whatever your situation. Even if your baby is doing well, you may feel on edge, mistrusting that trend until it is well established and resisting getting your hopes up only to have them painfully dashed. Gallice remembers, "For three weeks we didn't want to believe how well he was doing."

James was a feeder and grower. There was nothing medically wrong with him that time wouldn't and hasn't cured. That did not mean that I didn't spend the whole of every night with one ear listening for the phone, my body aching at its emptiness. And when the phone did ring, the fact that my child was doing so well didn't stop my heart rate quickening and didn't change the feeling of dread as I answered that call. It did not mean that my heart didn't break when I had to leave my baby every day he was in the hospital growing. —Leanne

Along with not knowing how your baby's medical course will play out, there are so many other uncertainties to cope with. If a treatment is not foolproof or if your baby seems to be struggling too much, the doctors won't be able to tell you *for sure* how effective that remedy will be for your baby. You'll need to wait and see. If your baby is too unstable or sick to tolerate being held, the doctors won't be able to tell you *for sure* when you'll be able to do more hands-on care and snuggling. You'll need to wait and see. In the beginning, your baby's caregivers won't be able to set a *firm* date when your baby will be able to come home. They may tell you to expect to take your baby home around the original due date, but they won't be able to promise it—and they won't be able to tell you what you and your baby will have to go through in the meantime. You'll need to wait and see. And nobody can guarantee that your baby will emerge from the NICU unscathed.

Scary. Incredibly scary. Like a living nightmare, one in which you don't know where the dark tunnels are going to lead. You just go with what comes and try to make the best of it. When we didn't think we could handle it, we sought somebody to talk to about what we were going through. —Andrea

Perhaps at some point, your baby's care providers will be uncertain which treatment option is the best one for your baby. When feasible, they will set up a series of trials to see which approach your baby responds to. If a choice must be made, they should turn that decision over to you. With their counsel, it will be your job to examine the possibilities and bring your values and intuition to bear. Making medical decisions for your baby in the face of uncertainty can be painfully difficult and nerve-racking.

If you normally have difficulty tolerating ambiguity and uncertainty, waiting in the dark will be especially hard for you. If you prefer to make rational choices, forming medical decisions intuitively can be unsettling. If you aren't very comfortable with suspense, or if you prefer to have all your ducks in a row and all your loose ends tied up neatly, your baby's NICU hospitalization and medical course can feel torturous.

Living with uncertainty proves emotionally and physically draining for most parents of preemies. It's difficult to endure the wait when you can't count on a bright future at the end. If your baby's very survival is in question, it's hard to know whether to welcome this child or to start saying good-bye. The tension and the conflicting emotions that arise from ambiguity can be paralyzing. If your baby is close to death, you may find yourself wishing for a speedy conclusion because the suspense and tension are so overpowering that they are threatening your sanity. You're not the only parent of a preemie to have these feelings. Your wish that the ordeal would come to an end is a powerful testament to how difficult this situation is. It is important for you to recognize that there is nothing wrong with your feelings. It's the situation that is so wrong.

When she was three days old, I remember sitting there, just bawling my eyes out ... saying, "If she's going to die, I want her to do it now. I don't want her to wait a couple of weeks." I felt horrible saying that, but on the other hand, it felt better for me to let that out. And it was true. If she was just going to die anyway, I wanted her to die before I had a chance to really fall in love with her. ... That was part of it, and another part was that the sooner it happened, the sooner I could pick my life up and move on, instead of agonizing over the next couple of months, "When is she going to die?" —Brooke

Here are some approaches that can help you cope with all the uncertainty of your baby's situation:

- *Know that uncertainties are most plentiful and loom largest early on and during crisis.* As each situation resolves, many uncertainties resolve as well.

Some disappear entirely, some merely shrink, but each resolution generally reduces the scope and number of uncertainties. You may not always like the outcome—and if your child has special needs, there will always be some degree of uncertainty about the future. But as your baby gets closer to discharge, you'll have more certainty to pin your hopes on.

- *Take it one day at a time.* Try to live in the present and not worry about the future. Of course, it is normal to worry to some extent about the possibilities that may unfold, but you can vow to spend less energy pondering events or situations that have not yet occurred, remembering that they may very well never happen. (For more about this, see "Waiting with Your Baby" later in this chapter.)

- *Believe in your own assessment of the situation.* Trust your evaluations of the information you are being given and your appraisal of the doctors' opinions. Recognize the validity of what you observe and know about your baby. Also rely on your parental intuition.

- *Care for yourself.* Get as much sleep as you can; eat nutritious, wholesome foods; and exercise so that you can better withstand the stress associated with uncertainty. See Chapter 6 for more on this important coping tool.

- *Take breaks and use relaxation techniques.* Take frequent minibreaks, particularly when you're feeling especially tense. Consciously relax your muscles, releasing the tension in your shoulders, your jaw, and your forehead. Get into the habit of being mindful of your breathing and practice deep breathing.

- *Seek out support.* Connect with the people in your life who can help and support you. Avoid spending time with people who drain you.

- *Focus on the stable aspects of your life.* Continuing (or creating) a weekly routine of pleasurable activities gives you something that you can rely on and look forward to. Routine can be especially comforting in the midst of uncertainty.

- *Realize that anxiety about an uncertain future is normal.* If your child's future remains uncertain at and after discharge, you can still imagine a rosy future with your baby as you become more comfortable with the questions that remain unanswered. Even if the outcome is full of challenges, you will learn to cope in time, with support.

- *Hold on to life philosophies or spiritual beliefs that help you make sense of this experience.* These beliefs can also reinforce your resilience in the face of uncertainty. The following suggestions are descriptions of some perspectives that parents have found helpful. Read through them and see if any resonate for you.

▲ Control what you can and let go of what you can't. Life is a mystery that unfolds, not a problem to be overpowered.

▲ Take comfort in religious perspectives about why bad things happen. Look for personal and spiritual meaning in the midst of this situation.

▲ Work toward spiritual acceptance, toward recognizing that you are witnessing a part of nature's cycle of health and illness, birth, and even death. Seek harmony with nature, rather than fighting against it.

▲ Believe that your baby chose this life to learn the lessons that are necessary for enlightenment or the soul's progress. In kind, you chose your life for its lessons and enlightenment as well.

▲ Adopt a "wondering" attitude about the future. Instead of specifying your wishes for an outcome, hold onto the idea that everything will unfold as it should and that there are higher spiritual reasons for this child to be on this particular journey.

▲ Rely on prayer, with the awareness that prayers may be answered in ways we can't always understand.

▲ Believe in miracles, remembering that sometimes a miracle isn't what we think it should be. Miracles can be found where we least expect them.

Waiting with Unpredictability

He started off pretty well, and I really thought he was going to do very well. Every time he would come off [the ventilator], I would get all excited because it was a step forward. Then he would go back on, and I would be crushed that he was so fragile. He looked so big compared to most of the babies in the NICU, so I expected he would be progressing more quickly. —Tracy

We didn't think there was going to be another problem. I guess we didn't read far enough ahead in the book. So we felt that we were in the clear, and Jacob just needed to grow and get stronger and Claire and Emily just needed to grow and get stronger. We were at that stage—and all of a sudden, we have somebody sitting there saying, "In the next two weeks, we'll figure out if your son is going to be blind." It was extremely hard to take. It was almost like the final blow. —Julie

The unpredictable nature of your baby's medical course can be the most strenuous and terrifying part of this roller-coaster ride. With each unforeseen crisis, there is a renewed feeling of helplessness and lack of control. Every setback, every new downturn, strikes fresh fear into your heart. Even things that you thought wouldn't bother you are terrifying when they actually happen.

All these weeks with my friend [who's preemie was diagnosed with ROP], I was thinking, "What's the big deal? It's only the eyes [not life or death]!" Then they tell me that if Josh doesn't have laser surgery that afternoon, he's going to be blind. And all of a sudden, it's "Oh, my God, it's the eyes!" The eyes became everything. I was hysterical. After all these babies have been through, they deserve perfection. They don't deserve blindness. They don't deserve anything bad, you know? —Stephie

If your baby remains in critical condition for a while, waiting can become oddly comforting. As you get used to the current set of medical issues, their familiarity and stability let you relax somewhat. But typically, just as you master one set of medical issues, it's on to new, unfamiliar challenges.

It would be such a relief if your baby's medical course could be displayed on a graph that showed a straight, upward-slanting line representing your baby's steady growth and improving health. And it would be especially comforting if you could see that graph *in advance.* Unfortunately, many preemies experience plateaus and setbacks while in the NICU, and this unpredictable sequence of gains and losses can frazzle even the calmest of parents. Parents of babies who experience many setbacks feel especially on edge because they know how fragile their baby's progress is.

Every day was a milestone for Zachary, but at the same time, there was always some new threat coming up. —Marcia

We'd get over one thing, and then there'd be another one. Whenever there was a lull, so to speak, we're like, "All right, what's happening now? Something is building up." And there were times we'd be, "All right, this is going too good. There has to be a setback somewhere." —Brooke

One time the NICU called, all excited, to tell me that Josh was off the ventilator—and by the time I got there, he was back on it, so I didn't even get to see him without it. —Stephie

Your premature baby may have an initial honeymoon period, including some growth and improvement, followed by a setback. Setbacks such as losing a few grams or having slightly increased oxygen needs can be relatively minor from the medical staff's perspective. But to you, these setbacks feel *major*. Setbacks such as pulmonary hemorrhage or infection, which are generally major from a medical perspective, feel tremendously grim to a parent.

Whether minor or major, your baby's complications may frighten you, disappoint you, or fill you with grief. Every new difficulty can remind you of the losses you've already endured, and each one starkly emphasizes how *unfair* this situation is. If your baby faces serious medical setbacks, devastation and fear can overwhelm you. Each time your preemie has a setback, the future again becomes unpredictable—and you must wait with that unpredictability.

During Stuart's surgery, we waited forever, when a social worker told us that all was going beautifully. On her heels, though, arrived the surgeon, who told us that Stuart had crashed as they prepared to close. This tiny, terribly scarred boy was not expected to survive the next twenty-four hours. Yet he did—slowly, painstakingly, with many setbacks and battles. He was to be moved several times from conventional vent to the "oscillator" to the jet ventilator. He needed the same surgery yet another time. ... Yet come home he did. —Susan

You were probably told when your baby was born that you should expect many ups and downs—that these setbacks and improvements are "a preemie thing." This knowledge comforts some parents, once they adapt to this new definition of "normal." Reminding yourself that your infant is doing typical things for a preemie may help you to calm down. It can be a revelation to find out that a particular setback doesn't rule out a good outcome.

For others, though, every setback feels like yet another violation—an inability to hold on to the progress that has been made. It can seem so unfair that you and your baby must go through this.

Here are some actions you can take that may help you to get through this unpredictable cycle of progress and setbacks:

- *Record the dates and details of your baby's progress and setbacks*—weights, feedings, conditions, illnesses, treatments, procedures, caregivers' assessments, being held, kangaroo care sessions, being put to the breast or bottle, reactions to you—whatever facts, observations, and experiences you feel are significant. Doing so can help give some order to the chaos. It can also clarify your memories of what you and your baby have gone through and help you to see how far your baby has come—ups, downs, and all. Many parents treasure this record as a testament to their endurance and to their baby's triumph. If your baby should die, this journal can be a treasured keepsake that affirms your baby's life.

- *Ask for the explanations and information you need when your baby has complications or setbacks.* Being told "It's just a preemie thing" may reassure some parents, but if that explanation doesn't comfort you, ask for more details.

- *Seek out parents of NICU graduates who had issues similar to your baby's.* You can find these parents through your unit social worker or your hospital's parent-to-parent support organization (if the hospital has one). If there are no local avenues, try the Internet—Preemie-L has a parent mentoring program. (See the "Internet" section in the Appendix C.) Hearing about another infant's ups and downs—and especially seeing that the family came out the other side—can be very reassuring. It's also nice to talk with someone who understands how difficult this experience is.

- *Give yourself time to adjust to the situation.* Even if you've been told that your baby's setbacks are insignificant ("normal preemie things"), it is natural to feel discouraged or distressed over them. Trying to distance yourself from your baby's ups and downs (even the small ones) is not realistic, especially in the first days and weeks of your baby's NICU stay. However, as the days pass, you'll be less thrown by small variations in weight, feeding amounts, or oxygen needs, but you must come to this frame of mind in your own time. As you adjust, you'll learn to ignore the hourly or daily ups and downs and to focus on your baby's overall progress over several days or weeks.

- *Accept that you may not get used to your baby's ups and downs.* Even though the NICU roller-coaster ride is "normal," every downturn can be frightening, and you may protest the ride with every fiber of your being. It's natural to be buoyed by good news and crushed by bad. That's especially true when the downs aren't so minor.
- *Be kind to yourself.* If you feel like crying, go ahead. If a "small" setback triggers a large reaction, go with the flow. You have so much to grieve. Cry and scream and rail against the unfairness of it all whenever you need to.
- *If nursing or social work staff suggest that you shouldn't cry or be sad near your baby, remind them that what you need most is to be near your baby.* Your tears will *not* harm your preemie. If you feel the need to cry by the incubator, you have every right to do so. If the staff feel uncomfortable with this, show them Appendix A, "A Note to Caregivers." If they insist that you cry in private, you can insist that they provide you and your baby with a private place.
- *If you need to scream at the top of your lungs, pound things, throw objects, or run as fast as you can, find a safe place to do these things.* If you need to disappear to a private area go ahead. If someone follows you and you want to be alone, say so. When you feel more composed, return. Let them know you're okay and thank them for giving you the space to protest the agony of all this.
- *If your baby is making great progress and you want to celebrate, do so in ways that reinforce your joy and hope.* Commemorate your baby's gains with a trinket, a picture, or a note in your journal. Remember to take pictures of the "firsts." Even if you fear that your baby will be intubated again, pictures of your little one's face without a ventilator tube are still to be cherished.

Waiting with Your Baby

Sometimes, waiting with uncertainty and unpredictability can take the place of being with your baby. This is understandable. Until you have some answers, you may dwell obsessively on what the future might bring. You may focus on your worries, or you may believe that your life will begin again when you and your baby leave the NICU. Unfortunately, waiting in this way makes it impossible to stay emotionally in the moment with your little one. Instead of parenting in the present, you're focused on the future.

There is another way to wait—and that is waiting *with* your baby. Of course, concern about the future is part of being a responsible parent. But waiting with your baby means focusing mainly on the present. While you wait, you watch and see everything that is happening with your infant. You keep vigil. This is not a passive process. Here are some suggestions for waiting with your infant:

- Worry only about what's happening *today*.
- Learn about your baby's *current* medical conditions and treatments.
- See your baby as an individual and a member of your family.
- Notice your baby's preferences and personality.
- Learn what you can do *now* to comfort and care for your baby.

Waiting with your baby makes waiting rich and meaningful. When you look back at this time, you will know that you were very much a part of your baby's life during this ordeal. By waiting with your baby, you are laying the stones on your shared path through life.

Balancing Hopes and Fears

When Lauren, my daughter, was born, I guess I never even thought babies survived at that low of a weight, so boy, did I have a lot to learn. But, in the beginning, I was scared of everything ... The neonatologist told us that she might have learning problems due to prematurity. It scared us, but he did use the word "might"—not "will." —Shirley

When your baby is in the NICU, fear may dominate your emotions, but clinging to your hopes can improve your ability to cope. Hoping for the best and fearing for the worst are on opposite sides of the fence. Most of the time, the most effective approach is to straddle this fence between hopes and fears. Striking a balance isn't easy, but it can help you prepare for whatever may happen—and help you wait *with* your baby.

Though it may seem that your hopes for the future are going up in smoke, remembering your dreams and wishes for your baby and your family helps you hold on with optimism. This can help you cope with much of the uncertainty and unpredictability that is natural during a baby's NICU stay. Being surrounded by hopeful health care teammates can also help keep you afloat in a sea of fears and ambiguity.

When we visited Neil the first time—me wheeled there on a gurney, an hour after his birth—the first thing the nurse attending him did was congratulate me. I didn't see much to be congratulated on. My body had just committed the ultimate betrayal and kicked out my baby far, far too soon. Yet congratulations are so much better than an "I'm sorry"—and being congratulated made me start thinking that maybe there was something to be happy about, that maybe things weren't quite as bad as they seemed. —Tara

Although it's important to hold on to your hopes, shutting out reality won't help you cope with this situation. Avoiding your fears can be paralyzing. Acknowledging your fears, on the other hand, can give you the power to face the difficulties. (For more on this subject, see "Facing Your Fears" in Chapter 8.) This mixture of hope and fear makes parenting any child a powerful job.

The one thing with Banning that I fixated on—and I knew I had to stop— I was fixating on his weight. And he got down to a point where he was one pound ten ounces from three pounds six ounces—and it was like, I can't ask anymore *because, every time, he's losing weight, he's losing weight, he's losing weight. I've got to focus on something* positive. *So I would write things in his journal, the things that I could see that he was doing, the progression, his milestones, no matter how small they were. If he had taken an extra ounce of milk that day, it was so exciting. So I wrote a lot. —Pam*

When the going is rough, the balance may shift too much toward fear, and it can overshadow your hopes. You may worry about hoping for too much or hoping too intensely—afraid to "jinx" your baby. You may hesitate to express or even think about your hopes for your little one—so that whatever happens might be easier to bear. In the face of monumental uncertainties, wishes can seem impossible, and fear can dominate hope, but dwelling on your fears can keep you from focusing on your baby.

If you look deep inside yourself, you'll find those hopes and dreams you had during the pregnancy. They don't just disappear when you deliver prematurely. They are still a part of you. Allow your buried dreams to slowly emerge into the light.

In addition to these buried dreams, as your baby's hospital course progresses (especially if it is difficult), new hopes and wishes will evolve. At first you may continue to hold on to elaborate dreams for the future, but when you realize that these are unrealistic or distant, you may gradually revise them to more achievable goals. You may begin to feel satisfied with small increments of progress as your baby attains one small goal at a time. For example, at first you may say to yourself, "I just want my baby to breathe on his own." Then if this process is taking a different path than you'd hoped for, you might say, "I just want my baby to have good sats on the vent." Shirley put it this way: "I just wanted her to be healthy. ... I would worry about the developmental stuff later."

As your baby improves, you may gather the courage to reclaim some modified form of your original wishes. You may hope for larger things, such as feeding your baby yourself or taking your baby home, healthy and free. As your baby's medical path becomes clearer, it's easier to allow yourself to hope, even if that means rethinking the future. Although you will still grieve for what you've lost, you can also rejoice in the adjusted dreams that are coming true.

At any time, you can also build hope by finding special meaning in the things that happen around you or your baby. Perhaps your favorite nurse postpones a vacation, and you take this as a sign that the universe is working in your favor. Perhaps you find comfort in a gentle snowfall, a mother bird's nesting in your eaves, or a shooting star. Others may dismiss these things as superstition or happenstance, while you, caught up in the mystery of birth, may find yourself more open to the wonders that surround you.

The point when I realized things would "probably" be okay was when I came to the NICU to find my son, who was very heavily sedated, lying on his side with his hand cupped over his nose and mouth—an unusual position impossible for him to get to on his own—and the nurses said they hadn't positioned him like that. This was the same position my grandmother (who had passed away when I was in junior high) always slept in. I felt at that moment that she was there with him, watching over him, and that things would be alright.
—Ami

I started to look for omens. It obviously goes to show my state of mind at the time, but if I didn't see kangaroos on the drive to the hospital (we have lots of bush and lots of 'roos), I'd think it was some sort of bad sign. My mum also had a plant that she was obsessive over. When I had Ngioka, the plant was "sick." She was convinced that she had to keep the plant alive and then

Ngioka would survive. Another mum had a thing about parking spaces (which were at a premium at our hospital). If she drove into the car park and got one, it was going to be a good day. —Jo

You can also build hope by reassuring yourself with positive thoughts. Be aware of the things you tell yourself. Instead of obsessing about how awful the situation is, try to remind yourself that "This too shall pass" and that "In life, the one constant is change." Even when hope is hard to find or when it appears so frail that you're afraid to lean on it, try to hold on to your faith that things will get better. Take to heart the positive signs you observe and your intuition that things will turn out for the best. Try to replace negative thoughts with positive ones. Remember that many preemies do just fine and yours can too.

Some parents find it easier to focus on optimistic thoughts after their baby has gotten past a certain point: perhaps birth, or after he or she has made it off the ventilator, or when their baby proves the doctors' negative predictions wrong. If, deep down, you believe that in the end everything will be okay, trust and focus on that feeling.

Every hour there was a different emotion with each of the children, but we always tried to stay positive and we always thought that they were strong, and they were as relatively healthy as they could be at that point, and that they were just going to get through it—that it would be a long haul, but that they would get through it. —Betsy

My fears and my worries were all before he was born. After he was born, I never remember thinking one time, "He's not going to be okay." I really was convinced that he was [going to be] fine; nobody led me to believe any differently. I didn't think that he would have any neurological problems. I just really thought that everything was okay. —Jaimee

Up to that point in time, I was just kind of living with the idea that she was going to die. The doctor said, "She's going to die," so that's going to happen, right? Then [when they told us she wouldn't make it through the night], all of a sudden, I had this weird sort of certainty, where I knew she was going to make it. And she was going to go, "Ha ha, fooled you!" —Brooke

•••
335
The Roller-Coaster NICU Experience

Although your optimistic thoughts may not change your child's outcome, they may very well affect your child's quality of life. Instead of holding back your emotional connection with your baby, you can invest in him or her with optimism. In the face of uncertainty, positive thoughts are free— it's the negative ones that can cost you dearly.

You may always have concerns about your child. Especially when your little one is out of immediate danger and the NICU stay has become routine, it is natural to turn your sights toward the bigger picture and the future. But instead of imagining future catastrophe, put that "worry" energy into picturing an optimal future—not a perfect or even a typical future, but one that is the best it can be. Visualize that whatever challenges lie ahead, you will have the strength, the courage, and the wisdom to cope and to seek the paths that will bring your family the most happiness and satisfaction. And whatever happens, assume that your child will be blessed by destiny.

When Your Health Care Teammates Dash Your Hopes

Naturally, you hope that all will be well for your little one. But when you're struggling to hold onto hope, hearing medical staff or others tell you not to expect too much can be terribly frustrating. Explain to these individuals that your high hopes are simply your parental wishes for your baby, not unrealistic expectations. Besides, it is normal for you to want your baby not to need medical intervention to survive and thrive.

Cling to hope and optimism wherever you find it. If one doctor is giving you doomsday predictions, but another is upbeat, rely on the optimistic opinion. Don't ever be afraid to hope.

Of course, choosing which predictions and opinions to hang on to can be challenging. Pronouncements from your health care teammates can strongly affect your emotional state. Reassurances from medical staff are comforting, but their pessimism is devastating. Sometimes you want to hear their honest assessments; sometimes, you don't. The safest setting in which to hear these assessments is during an extended conversation, when you can ask questions and get the support you need. The worst time is in passing, at your baby's bedside.

> *One well-meaning doctor gave us an update on our son's condition after a tough week of complications. As he finished, he said, "You know, he might*

actually make it," as though it were a slim possibility. "Not making it" had never crossed my mind. My faith, hope, and certainty that he would survive were the only things getting me out of bed every morning. That seemingly positive comment devastated me. I cried for over an hour. —Laura

Some of your teammates may not understand the pain they cause by urging you to have "realistic" expectations. They may not recognize that you need some hope (and even denial) to cope. Sometimes it's easier to be brave when you don't know about all the painful possibilities and harsh prognoses! Or they may inappropriately share their own feelings of hopelessness or anxiety with you. In your state of vulnerability, you may find it very difficult to ignore these comments from well-meaning but misguided medical caregivers. You might have to remind them that you need their help to find a balance between hope and fear, especially if your baby's medical course or prognosis is uncertain.

It is the special caregiver who can offer hope without making promises. Susan explains her reactions to the very different comments of two health care teammates:

The chasm between the acts of kindness and the acts of cruelty was deep. Three days after the death of our firstborn, his twin underwent life-threatening surgery. For days I asked questions of every professional who came near us, questions designed to elicit hope. No one could offer any. Everyone was understandably guarded and careful. One quiet afternoon, as I sat watching, waiting, asking nothing of anyone, one brave doctor knelt down next to me, put his arm on my shoulder, and said, "It's okay to hope, you know. Some of them do make it." On another, quite later afternoon, just after we had emerged from a second, unexpected bout of NEC, I sat next to my baby's bedside, tears seeping down my cheeks, feeling incredible relief. Remarkably, he had turned another corner. Inexplicably, a nurse felt it necessary to advise me: "Don't relax now. You will be dealing with this for years. Even if he does recover from this, you will spend years rushing in and out of the hospital dealing with strictures and other medical complications. It will never be over." —Susan

Acquiring realistic expectations for your preemie is a drawn-out process. Don't let others' remarks discourage you from having hopes and wishes.

When Hope Shines More Brightly

If your baby starts out his or her NICU stay in critical condition, you may have days or even weeks of high anxiety. As your baby's condition improves, it can be difficult to change gears. Moving from the twists in the roller-coaster ride that are fraught with peril to those that are relatively minor is a significant transition. It can be a challenge to start thinking of your baby as a "grower and feeder" instead of as a medical case that must be watched closely.

As your baby's discharge date approaches, you may still find it hard to believe that your hopes are coming true. Learn to trust that your baby is on the road home and work on letting your fears recede. Doing so will free you to put your energy toward getting better acquainted with your baby and his or her caregiving needs. When your hopes burn brighter than your fears, relax and enjoy the feeling.

> *As my son became more stable, I tried hard to keep up and make the transition to being a mom of a stable baby instead of a critical preemie. ... It was a more disjointed process for me than what my husband experienced, but the three of us did come out the other side feeling extremely close to one another.*
> —*Maureen*

As you and your baby head toward home, if your baby's future development remains unknown, your hopes are tempered by uncertainty. Because infants are so resilient and unpredictable, your baby may do relatively well. This is a hope to hang onto. And if your fears about delays or disability are eventually confirmed, hope still endures, even as you grieve and adjust. (For more on living with uncertainty, see Chapter 17; for more on coping with delays and disabilities, see Chapter 18.)

When Hope Changes Direction

If your worst fears should become reality and your baby is dying, you can still have hopes for your little one. Your hopes take a new direction when your baby's journey seems to be turning away from home. You may hope for the chance to hold and caress your little one free of the tubes and lines. You may want your baby to spend his or her last minutes or hours peacefully in your arms. You may plan to hold your baby skin to skin or to your breast. These desires to protect and be close to your precious baby are an extension of your earliest hopes, when you thought the path led toward home.

When hope changes direction, your heartfelt dreams and worst nightmares all loom large. Rest assured that this intense combination of opposing images is both natural and necessary. The passion of your hopes and your fears reflects your profound relationship with your baby. (For more on grieving and coping with a baby's death, see Chapter 11.)

Multiple Realities–
Multiple Roller Coasters

When you have more than one baby in the NICU, you have more than one set of worries and wishes for feeding, growth, health, and development. You have multiple medical courses to keep track of and manage. You have more than one baby to advocate for.

To add to this burden, your babies will probably have different patterns of progress and setbacks. You may find it nearly impossible to catch your breath between the dips of these simultaneously running roller coasters. Parenting multiples in the NICU can be a gargantuan and dizzying task.

They couldn't bring him back easily, because of pulmonary hemorrhaging, but he finally seemed to stabilize again. We had just seen our first trauma using emergency procedures. And we were pretty scared about that. In my mind, I remember thinking [Daniel's survival] was a very iffy thing. I didn't know what his outcome was going to be, and when the phone rang at 3:30 in the morning, I thought they were announcing that Daniel had died. I was sure. But no, they weren't calling to say Daniel had died, they were calling to say that Shayna had begun pulmonary hemorrhaging. So it was frightening and it was ugly. I remember Debbie hanging up and screaming and crying, "I can't take this, I can't take this!" It was pretty horrible, about as awful as it gets. —Mitch

If your preemies' hospital course is filled with serious complications, there is always *something* that has just happened, that is threatening to happen, or that one or more of your babies are only now recovering from. Anxiety is your constant companion. You might feel as if you have not been able to relax since before these little ones were born.

I would go back and forth because when one would be sick, then the other would be okay. And then it was not only, "How can I do this, be there for two babies?" but you could never enjoy yourself because if one baby was doing okay, the other baby was inevitably really sick and about to die. So for months, there was never a day when you could even, like, just let your shoulders down and collapse and be okay. They were so sick, and there were so many things that were going to kill them. —Stephie

Most parents of multiple preemies have to cope with numerous, and often alternating, ups and downs. If you're extremely lucky, your preemies will follow similar medical courses, but you'll still have to keep pace with each of them separately. And in spite of their differences, you may still anxiously compare your babies with each other. How much weight is each one gaining? How much supplemental oxygen does each need? Any apneas or bradycardias? You want your babies to thrive individually but also together, as a unit. And you hope that the healthiest of them is a harbinger of how the others will fare.

With multiples, you may also have a special set of worries about the future. You want each baby to be okay, but you may also worry about how their outcomes may differ. If one of your babies is disabled or developmentally delayed, not only will you mourn for that child, but you may also fear the loss of that mystical bond between siblings who are twins, triplets, or more. If one has significantly more limitations than the other(s), you might worry that he or she will be left out. And if parenting healthy multiples is a challenge, you may wonder how you will possibly manage to care for a medically fragile or disabled child in the mix. If one or more of your babies die, you will grieve for the one(s) you miss and the lost chance to raise these children together, even as you celebrate the life of your survivor(s). (Turn to Chapter 11 for support around this grief.)

Here are some strategies that can help you deal with the multiple rollercoaster rides of having more than one baby in the NICU:

- *Keep a small notebook for each baby.* Use these notebooks to jot down each infant's daily events, milestones, and medical issues as they occur. Separate notebooks can help you to keep the stories straight, and you'll worry less about missing or forgetting something in the midst of the chaos. If you want, each notebook can also become a journal—a place for you to write about your feelings and thoughts for each child and situation. You'll be glad to have these records to bolster your memories and help you make sense of the journey.

- *Assume that your babies will have unique medical courses.* Just because one of your babies has a certain frightening complication doesn't mean your other baby(ies) will develop it.

- *Be prepared for the ups and downs.* Remember that one baby's ride may get bumpy just as another's smooths out. Knowing that this seesaw effect is common can make it a bit less distressing.

- *Rest assured that you will be able to catch your breath down the road.* Take one day at a time and remember that this too shall pass.

- *Focus on progress over the longer term, not on daily differences.* Your babies may have medical courses that are very different day by day, but in hindsight their overall picture may look quite similar. Avoid focusing on the daily differences. Look, instead, at their weekly progress. Even when the overall picture is different in the short run, your babies may have very similar (and excellent) outcomes down the road.

- *Grieve both the obvious and the subtle losses associated with having multiple babies.* If your identical twins are struggling with different issues, own the feelings you may have about them not sharing identical outcomes. If your triplets are not allowed to cobed, acknowledge the feelings you may have about the fact that they cannot snuggle together the way they did inside you. These acknowledgments will help you cope and move on.

Making Comparisons in the NICU

Seeing other kids in the NICU posed problems, since we weren't supposed to compare. Some other kids weren't doing as well as our girls. It was tragic. It was very depressing and made us recognize how limited any parent's control is. On the other hand, I remember that triplets were born and released after just a few days. I remember Rikki thought it was unfair and that she had let the girls down by not holding them in longer. —Dwight

Even in the NICU I felt inadequate, especially around more "experienced" NICU parents. It was the only place I felt somewhat normal, but even then ... I just felt like a freak. —Diana

• • •

All these other preemies were so sick, and I had one of the only ones that was doing really well. I felt embarrassed that mine was doing so well, and I felt so bad for them. I was so happy, but because of them I felt ashamed that I was so happy. —Gallice

In the NICU, you are surrounded by babies and their parents, but you may hesitate to make contact with them. Early on, you're so focused on your baby, you may not be very aware of the others. But when your baby stabilizes, you may look around and compare your situation to these others. You may wonder

- Do these other parents understand what I'm going through—because every situation is different?
- Is it normal for me to feel competitive about whose baby goes home first with the least medical equipment? Do these other parents feel the same competitiveness toward my baby and me?
- If I talk to parents whose babies are doing better than mine, will I envy or resent them? If I talk to parents whose babies are doing less well than mine, will it be too depressing? Will I incur their envy or resentment?
- If I talk to parents who are focused on their fears, will I be able to hold on to my hopes? If I'm overwhelmed by my fears, can I tolerate parents who talk only about their hopes?

Talking with other parents of preemies can benefit you enormously, despite any uncomfortable undercurrents of emotion. These conversations let you establish your "credentials" as parents who understand each other's emotional ordeals. As you share information about your children, you can form bonds. In fact, when you are a newcomer to the NICU, you may feel an odd sense of comfort when you see new preemies like your own arrive. New admissions mean that you aren't the only novice struggling to acclimate to the NICU and grappling with harsh realities. But as time passes and you grow more accustomed to this place, it may hurt you to see new parents arrive. Your heart goes out to them as you remember what a struggle those early days were. The longer your time in the NICU, the less you'll care about the situational differences, competition, envy, resentment, and whether the talk focuses on hopes or fears. What will matter most is the common ground of parenting a precious baby in the NICU.

It was hard, going in there every day and passing by the babies that were smaller than him. ... But by the same token, we were sharing the same heartbreak of not being able to take a baby home with us, going through the experience of being on that unit, and the grief and agony and joy of going through the hurdles. —Vickie

Finding out how other babies are doing can give you some perspective about your child. You can feel fortunate for the complications your baby has avoided. When you learn how babies older than yours are faring, you can begin to imagine what might lie ahead and prepare yourself for the possibilities. The flip side is that when you look at babies who aren't doing well, you may feel terrified about your baby's future.

Making comparisons is inevitable and natural. It can help to remember, though, that every baby's course is unique. Another baby's roller coaster isn't necessarily a gauge of how your baby will fare. Even though another baby's progress is faster than your baby's, your little one's outcome may be just as good. Comparisons become more pointed when other preemies die, or when other preemies go home.

When Other Preemies Die

The hardest part of NICU life was seeing some of the babies die. You sympathized and mourned for them, feared for your own child, and were secretly thankful it was not you. —Laura

Whether or not your unit encourages contact between parents, it is likely that you will get to know some other families whose babies are in the NICU. Even if you do not know each other's names, you will recognize one another. If a baby is not doing well, the parents and the medical staff will often reflect this reality—the unit may seem more grim, more fearful. And as you sit by your baby's incubator, you are faced with stark evidence of what could have happened—or might still happen—to your baby.

I think one of the saddest experiences was, the second day after Andrew was born ... I went with another NICU mom to go see our babies, and I just remember looking at her baby, thinking, "I feel so lucky. How did I get this, a baby who had a better chance than her baby?" Then I went back to another room, and I wasn't there ten minutes and the nurse came and told me that that mom's baby had just died. ... I think that was the first time that I realized the seriousness of having a premature baby. I didn't realize that if there's one thing a preemie will do, it will keep you guessing. A baby may be looking good right now and in ten minutes be coding. ... I think that was the first time I actually cried after Andrew was born, realizing what we might be in for. —Vickie

When another preemie dies, you may grieve right along with that baby's parents. Knowing how painful it is to have a critically ill baby, you identify closely with those parents. You recognize the depth of their bereavement. You can hardly bear to imagine being in their place. If you have already experienced the death of a baby, either before this delivery or among your multiple preemies, you may feel overwhelmed by grief upon this other infant's death. You aren't just identifying with those parents; you've been there. And you can only hope you won't find yourself there again.

Whatever the extent of your childbearing losses, when someone else's baby dies in the NICU, the grief you share with that family is compounded by the grief you carry for your own.

Our closest friend in the NICU lost her son after six months, two weeks before our son was discharged. How do you express your feelings of such deep loss? How do you comfort someone who has lost something you still have? How could we possibly understand what she was going through? How do you look at a beautiful little baby in a doll-sized coffin? How do you put him in the cold, dark ground in the pouring rain? All she kept saying was that he was getting wet. ... After his death, we hit our breaking point. We needed to get out of there. We pushed, and two weeks later we took our son home. —Laura

I'm so upset [about Nathan, my son's young classmate]. ... Nathan's father was one of the pallbearers, and he watched as they lowered Nathan into the ground. He was so brave to do that. But then, that's what being a parent is all about, I guess. Always watching over your baby and making sure that [he's] safe, whether it be warm and comfortable in an incubator, while riding a bike, or ensuring that his coffin is set down softly and gently. —Leanne

If your baby is in critical condition, a death in the NICU may prompt an eerie feeling that your child could be the next to die. This response is natural, but remind yourself that one child's condition has no impact on another's. Also keep in mind that most NICU babies survive—neonatal intensive care works most of the time. If you've been afraid to bring up the possibility of your baby dying, another baby's death can give you an opening to discuss your fears with your health care teammates. Ask how your baby's situation differs from the other child's, so you can get some reassurance.

When Other Preemies Go Home

Whether you spend days, weeks, or months in the NICU with your baby, you are bound to see other infants who are getting ready to go home. Discharges can give you some hope for the future—babies really *do* leave this place. But these discharges may bring up a variety of painful feelings as well. You may

- *Feel intense sadness, envy, even anger.* You want to take your baby home with you, not just watch others take their babies home!
- *Feel impatient, as if you and your baby will never get out of here.* Watching babies come and go is so hard—especially if your baby has had a long stay and the babies going home were admitted to the NICU after your baby.
- *Wonder whether your baby's discharge will be similar.* Will your baby be that healthy or look that robust?
- *Feel competitive.* If a baby with continuing medical needs is discharged, you may wonder why your baby can't go home as well.
- *Feel fearful.* If a baby with clear medical or developmental needs is discharged, you may worry whether you could care for your baby at home with needs like those.

Talk to your health care teammates about any of these feelings. If you wonder whether your baby's discharge may be complicated or delayed, ask. Comparing your baby with other NICU graduates and looking ahead is normal. Ask your teammates for information about your baby's unique prognosis.

What to Remember about Comparisons

The impulse to compare your baby with others in the NICU may make you feel uncomfortable. It can help to keep these things in mind:

- *It is normal to compare yourself and your baby with others in the NICU.* Comparisons are part of getting acquainted with the landscape and forming relationships. As you get to know other parents of preemies, you'll feel surrounded and comforted by this community.
- *Making competitive comparisons may signal the need to work through your loss(es).* When you find yourself comparing your baby competitively with other NICU babies, recognize that you may need to identify and work through a particular loss. This might be, for example, having a baby who still needs oxygen while surrounding babies are on room air.
- *Each preemie is different.* Comparing your baby to others can provide perspective, but will not necessarily give you an accurate view of what is in store for your child.
- *Maintain some separation from others' heartbreak.* If you are especially sensitive to and empathic with others' heartbreaking situations, calm yourself with this mantra: "It's not me. It's not my baby. Right now, we're doing okay. It's not us."
- *Celebrate your child's accomplishments, even if other babies have not reached that stage.* Other parents may envy you and your baby, but you also give them hope for the future.
- *Your experience is valid!* No matter how early your baby's birth or how complicated or straightforward the hospital course, your experience of loss, trauma, and disorientation is valid.

When we were in the NICU, we saw so many come and go while we waited to see if our survivor would survive. I couldn't identify with people [who were] there so briefly, dealing with a temporary, resolvable problem concerning their baby(ies). I couldn't understand how someone could fall apart while dealing with premature infants (especially multiples) who were comparatively healthy, who would all go home soon. Truth be told, I felt a sort of contempt, not to mention raging envy, at their reactions to the less daunting challenges that they faced.

And then I saw people lose their only child, both their twins, all of their triplets. I saw tragic, beaten parents leave that godforsaken NICU with no one, with nothing to show for their suffering. And I realized that I was to them what the others were to me. I realized that suffering comes in degrees, yes, but whatever degree is thrust upon you seems unbearable because it is the worst you have known. I realized that any parent dreaming of a healthy pregnancy, a normal delivery, a beautiful child—the parent that each of us is at the beginning—any parent who ends up in a NICU, for whatever reason, for whatever period, has something to grieve. And our grief expands to fill whatever void it marks in our lives. —Susan

Making Life-and-Death Decisions in the NICU

On the NICU roller coaster, many parents are faced with the need to make difficult medical decisions about their preemies. Of course, you make these decisions in collaboration with your health care teammates, who provide information, statistics, and their opinions. You bring your values, preferences, point of view, priorities, and hunches to the process. You also bring your heartfelt hopes and fears for your baby's future, and your parental devotion to do what is in your baby's best interest.

Some decisions are a matter of course. When there is more than one treatment option, though, and it's not clear which one is the way to go, you may be consulted as to which intervention you think is best for your child. If a treatment is experimental or of questionable effectiveness for your baby, you must decide whether to consent to its implementation. Other decisions are much more grave, a matter of life and death: do you want the medical staff to intervene aggressively or do you wish to let nature take its course?

All of these decisions can be unnerving, but our focus here is the challenge of coming to terms with life-and-death decisions. If your baby dies, please also read Chapter 11 for additional support related to decision making, as well as grieving and coping.

Parental Decision Making in the "Gray Zone"

Parents usually face life-and-death decisions with their baby because the baby's prognosis is uncertain. This is often the case with babies who are born just at viability or within a few weeks after that date or have developed life-threatening complications before or after birth.

It is not clear in this climate of uncertainty, or gray zone, whether medical technology will help or harm. The doctors can't know how a specific baby will respond to intervention. When the "right" choice is unclear, parents and doctors must collaborate on decisions about medical treatment. If your baby's prognosis is uncertain, health care providers must involve you in treatment decisions because it is you who is ultimately responsible for the care and well-being of your child. You must live with the consequences of treatment decisions. When it is not clear what is in your baby's best interests, the decision is largely subjective, and it rightly rests with you, for it is your values, your intuition, your heart, and your judgment that matter the most.

Making life-and-death decisions for your baby is an immense parental responsibility. It involves weighing the risks and benefits, assessing the severity of your baby's problems, poring over the options, and changing your mind a dozen times, or choosing to rely on the doctors' recommendations. And when you've made the decision, you'll have to wait for and face the outcome, whatever it might be.

If you have to decide how aggressively to treat the most devastating complications of your infant's condition, you may feel the most protective of your baby and the most connected to him or her. What a crushing time to feel the full weight of parenthood.

> *At one point, when he was about two days old, they told us they didn't think he'd survive through the night. They asked me, if he stopped breathing completely, did I want him to be resuscitated. Before he was born, I automatically said that yes, I wanted him to be saved. But after he was born, I tried to think about him and the pain he must be in and how it might be better for him if I just let him go. But I finally decided I couldn't do it. We had to sign papers saying that they could try to save him. I felt terrible, like I was causing my baby all of this pain. But I couldn't let him go. It was something I really agonized over. —Jennifer*

If you decide to try aggressive medical intervention, you are betting that the benefits will outweigh the risks or harm. If you decide to decline medical intervention, your instincts as a parent are leading you to protect your baby from invasive and painful procedures. Whatever you decide, you believe it is the most compassionate choice in your baby's situation. You make your decision with the best of intentions and with the deepest love.

If, during your baby's NICU experience, you were unable or not permitted to make important, life-and-death decisions for your baby and you disagree with the decisions that were made, you have your own special grief to bear. It is especially important that you come to terms with your exclusion. There are several approaches you might take:

- *Write a letter to the doctors and the hospital.* Start out by venting all your anger, your objections, and proposed solutions. Then slowly and carefully edit out the venom, leaving just the constructive parts. Focus on conveying information, rather than on "shoulds." For instance, instead of writing, "You should have done X," try, "It would have helped us if X had happened." Consider sending your revised letter, especially to the hospital ethics committee. Keep the "uncut" version for yourself.
- *Talk about the situation to anyone who will listen.* Telling your story can help you work out your anger and resentment.
- *Write in a journal about your regrets and your feelings.* Get down your deepest fears and your ugliest thoughts. You are not a terrible parent for having them. You are simply reacting to a terrible situation.
- *Write a letter to your child, expressing your sorrows, regrets, and guilt.* Then write what you imagine your child's response would be. Write from the heart.
- *See a qualified therapist to help you work through your feelings.* You may be tempted to see a lawyer, but they are generally not qualified to help you get what you really need to be able to move on with your life.

Dealing with the Uncertainties

The doctor couldn't tell us when the outcome would be hopeless, and that's the problem. There are no hard-and-fast rules, like, "Okay, we've done twenty shunt revisions; now it's hopeless." I'd say to the doctor, "You can't just keep doing these surgeries." And he'd say, "Well, sometimes we'll just do shunt revision after shunt revision, and then you won't see them for ten years." So that's kind of what we were hanging in there for. —Suzanne

When you're faced with life-and-death decisions, you view the ambiguities and uncertainties of intensive care in a different light. You have to make crucial decisions with limited information. It's impossible for the doctors to tell you exactly what will happen with your child if you choose aggressive intervention. Even if the doctors say that your child will be significantly impaired, often they can't tell you exactly how, or how much. Some children outgrow problems, but it is hard to tell when. Other serious problems, such as cerebral palsy or severe developmental delays, often cannot be firmly diagnosed until the first or second year of life. Decisions involving the following simply add to the uncertainties you face:

- Complicated or obscure diagnoses, such as certain birth defects, brain abnormalities, or severe feeding disorders
- Conflicting opinions about a treatment's benefits, risks, and outcomes for your baby
- Experimental treatments
- Applying research statistics on treatment outcomes to *your* child
- Lack of consensus about what constitutes futile intervention

To make this most important decision, you have to rely on incomplete information, the doctors' best guesses, your values regarding life and death, your bias toward medical technology or nature, your spiritual beliefs, and your gut instincts. Ultimately, you have to *sense* what is in your baby's best interests and go with your heart.

Although uncertainties can add immeasurably to your distress, being involved in the decision-making process gives you some measure of control over what happens to you and your baby. After all, if nobody knows for sure the right way to go, you might as well be the one to choose—because you and your child are the ones who will travel that path.

When Seleste was approximately three weeks old, the neonatologists sat my husband and me down and we began the discussion on whether or not to discontinue life support due to the poor prognosis she had with the level of brain and lung damage she had endured. We put off the decision for a while, until she had two codes with full resuscitation needed. ... We just could not stop life support because to us that would be giving up. But we decided that a compromise that felt good to us was to put a "Do Not Resuscitate" on her so that if she crashed again, they would let her go. We were kind of saying, "We'll let God decide, or let her decide." —Suzanne

I made it clear to the doctor that I was calling the shots, not him. He had an obligation to do everything to save Casey. I knew that he would survive if I didn't give up, and I wasn't about to let a doctor tell me what my future was going to be. I knew that if Casey died after they had done everything they could, then I could live with that. I could not live with the idea of giving up! The outcome of that decision was certain. —Kelly

I was told I needed to think about what I wanted to do if there were complications. If he coded, what did I want to happen? The doctor said, "We can work on a kid for forty-five minutes, but at that point there can be so much damage, especially with a child his age, that what you save may not be worth saving—for him, for you." So I said, "I want him to have quality of life." —Micki

Wrestling with Guilt and Second Thoughts

Somehow, we were reconciled to his death yet couldn't bear to allow it to occur without extending him every possible chance. We consented to surgery, something I'll always regret, but only in hindsight. Soon, we were holding our tiny son as he died in our arms. ... If only I had known what I know now. —Susan

No matter what decision you make, you will probably wrestle with guilt and second thoughts. If you decide to take a chance with medical intervention and your baby's outcome is superb, you may feel guilty if you considered, even briefly, withholding or withdrawing aggressive intervention. Remember that, given the information and statistics at hand, your hesitancy was sensible. You were struggling to make the best possible choice for your baby.

Before we were told they would induce labor, we were asked if we wanted them to intervene. I didn't say anything before my husband answered with a definite "yes." I was going to say "no." I had a terrible time getting over the question, "What if I had said no?" I wouldn't have a wonderful child. I still torture myself with that on occasion. —Andrea

As Geoffrey was born, not breathing, looking so pitiful, I wondered if we should have done a DNR and just let Geoffrey pass. For he was obviously not comfortable and looked so little and frail. The guilt I felt was with the question "Were being selfish and putting a baby through all of that so we could have a baby, and me a son in particular?" –Shaw

• • •

351

The Roller-Coaster NICU Experience

If your baby lives, but at a price, you may say that if you were to face a similar situation in the future, you might very well not choose aggressive medical intervention because of the odds and what your surviving child has had to endure. If so, you are not the only parent who has emerged from the NICU and said, "Never again."

> *I honestly don't know what I would do if I went into preterm labor again. I might not run to the hospital. I hope I never need to find out. Sometimes, I think you need to let nature take its course. Alex suffered a lot with all his surgeries. I can't imagine life without him, even though it would be a lot easier.*
> *—Mo*

Indeed, some parents of preemies say, in hindsight, that the right decision would have been to let their child die as a newborn, rather than put him or her through a painful life. As Suzanne points out, even though there were moments of joy, she believes the suffering was too high a price to pay.

> *If I faced this decision again, I don't think it would be as hard to decide. I wouldn't blink an eye about stopping life support, or not beginning it on any baby who had little or no chance for survival, or when survival would probably mean enduring a life of continued suffering. I'd be sad and I'd grieve, but I'm not willing to take those odds. I'm not willing to have my child take those odds. —Suzanne*

If your child is severely disabled or suffers chronic illness or pain, you'll naturally have doubts about whether you made the best choice. This is an integral part of your ongoing grief over what might have been and your continuing adjustment to raising a child with special needs. (For more on this subject, see Chapter 18.) And no matter what you decide, if your child dies, second thoughts are a natural part of your mourning. (For more, see Chapter 11.)

Some parents (and many health care providers as well) worry that their decisions are tainted because they are made under duress. But life-and-death decisions cannot be totally rational. They involve a huge and crucial emotional component. Your emotional duress plays an important role in your judgment. It enables you to make this decision with your heart and gut, as well as with your mind. Your decision is grounded in your caring, protectiveness, and deep emotional investment in your baby.

Other parents find themselves wishing that someone else could make the decision—someone who knows more, who can think more clearly, who can foresee the future. But there is no such person. Because decisions such as this deal heavily in matters of the heart, parents are the most appropriate decision makers for their babies. It is a heavy responsibility to bear, but your decision is the best one there is.

Decide now. And you do. I did. In a split second. With a lifetime to revisit that moment, reconsider that decision, a lifetime left to deal with the consequences of that choice. We went for broke. We did everything we could to give our sons the chance to cling to the life we had thrust upon them. One died anyway, after ventilation, chest tubes, surgery, after lying on a board in artificial light under a piece of Saran wrap. One lived, after more ventilation, more chest tubes, more surgery, more time on the board under Saran wrap. Four years later, I don't yet know the scope of what we did—don't yet know the price. —Susan

Imagining the "what-ifs" is a normal part of coming to terms with your decisions. Having doubts is a natural reaction to making such difficult, painful decisions. As you deal with your feelings, particularly your anger and guilt, and as you come to terms with your baby's difficult life and/or death, you will eventually notice a subtle shift in your attitude toward your decision. You will come to accept reality—it happened, you made a decision, you can live with it—instead of fighting it. Lingering what-ifs become reflective daydreams rather than attempts to change reality. The what-ifs may become gentler and broader: "If only he hadn't been born so prematurely" rather than "If only I had made different choices." In time, you will be able to let go of what might have been and accept what is.

If you can't seem to stop wrestling with your doubts over the decisions you made, remember that you were not deciding your child's outcome. What you decided was which medical route you believed was in your child's best interests. The ultimate result was not within your control. If you had had that kind of power, you would have chosen for your child *not to have the ailments* that required this hard decision.

Also remember that you feel bad because you made *difficult* decisions, not bad decisions. An alternate decision wouldn't necessarily make you feel any differently. You are the only one who can let yourself off the hook. Try to understand that, in fact, you've done nothing that needs forgiving. Instead of being upset about the decisions you made, be upset that you were put in that predicament.

Also appreciate that wrestling with second thoughts gives you the opportunity to evaluate, solidify, and embrace the beliefs, principles, and intuitions that guided your decisions. Even if you are struggling mightily with guilt or doubts, you can make peace with the decisions you made. Over time, as you mull over everything that happened, you will come to accept that your decisions were right for your baby and your family *in that particular situation, at that time, with the information at hand.* You will recognize that your choices were based—rightly—on what you could see, hear, and know at that time, not on what you couldn't. As you adjust to your baby's death or your baby's life, you will reconcile with your guilt, your doubts, and your second thoughts. In the meantime, be gentle with yourself and give yourself credit for facing an impossible situation with courage, faith, and love.

> *My child is a scarred survivor of a battle that I waged. He was drafted, unable to choose his own course. And my child is my joy. He is the frame of reference for anything that has meaning to me. It makes no sense. I can't explain how the two can coexist. But I can look—I have to look—at the scars, at the outcome, in the harsh light of life. Looking at the path he has traveled through fuzzy mommy glasses denies the magnitude of who he is. I can't look at the joy and deny the toll. So I can't declare that it was all worth the pain, worth the cost. I can only love and love and love. I can only shield and aide and strengthen. I can only be a balm and be a bridge—ever reaching toward the child who is, after all, my own broken heart. —Susan*

Decisions about Long-Term Care

Some parents face agonizing decisions about long-term care when their baby continues to require significant and ongoing caregiving, intervention, or equipment beyond the NICU. When a baby's condition has been stabilized and is no longer critical, he or she can move to a rehabilitation hospital or a long-term care facility. When an institution is the best place for a child to receive appropriate care, parents can still be very much involved. If parents decide that neither home nor an institution is the answer, they can relinquish their child to a foster or an adoptive family who can manage even complicated medical needs or severe disabilities. This can happen straight from the NICU or down the road.

God didn't do this. This is not God's plan, nor is it his will. It just happened. What I have decided is that God wants to help me through this by guiding me in making decisions. This may mean that eventually Alex goes into foster care. ... Sometimes God does give you more than you can handle. —Mo

If you face decisions about how to meet your baby's significant and ongoing special needs, just as with life-and-death decisions, you can rely on your devotion to your baby's best interests; your careful consideration of all the available options and information; and what your mind, heart, and gut tell you. Know that your decision is based on love, not rejection. Acknowledge your limitations honestly, and remember that thoughtful, realistic decisions are responsible and healthy. There is no right or wrong choice, but simply what you believe is best for your baby, you, and your family. Also keep in mind that most decisions are not written in stone. As needs and situations change, you may be able to reevaluate. Finally, accept that difficult decisions entail painful feelings. Whatever you decide, you will have losses to grieve, cope with, and recover from. (For more on the emotional aspects of parenting a child with special needs, see Chapter 18.)

The Extended NICU Stay

For many preemies, the prediction that they will remain in the hospital until their due date is an accurate one. Parents can prepare to have their baby home with them at about the time they had originally expected. Being able to see the "light at the end of the tunnel" makes it easier to believe you will prevail—and to see the NICU stay as just temporary. But when complications prolong the NICU stay and your baby's discharge date remains uncertain, it's like running a never-ending marathon. You may begin to feel as if the hospital NICU is your baby's only home, and your second one. The separation from your baby and the disruption to your life can become more difficult to tolerate.

If your baby's hospital stay is much longer than expected, your hopes may have been raised numerous times, only to be dashed by many sudden deteriorations or crises. You may find it hard to trust the news that your baby's condition has improved. It becomes harder to balance your hopes and your fears. You may not dare to imagine your baby's discharge. You may also know that a long stay in the NICU does not always end with a triumphant homecoming. Some preemies are not discharged home, but to a long-term care facility. Others spend many months in the hospital only to die. You may wonder if this will happen to your little one.

As the hospital stay lengthens, you may find that you start to feel distant from your baby. This is a natural way to protect yourself from the blows of repeated disappointments or extended uncertainties. Although you cannot completely avoid the hurt, distancing can sometimes help you to survive this endurance test.

Pacing yourself through a not-just-temporary NICU stay is challenging. You may agonize about the amount of time you are spending at the hospital, especially if the demands of older children, distance from the hospital, or other stresses pull at you. Usually, at least one parent returns to work, but sometimes, both must. Single parents generally have more urgency about returning to work than do those with two incomes. In addition, you may struggle with how to allocate any leave time—how much to spend at the hospital with your struggling preemie and how much to save for a much-anticipated but delayed homecoming.

As you search for a balance, guilt is natural. You wish that you could do everything for your child—but real life intrudes. Despite doing the very best you can to balance everything over the many months your baby is in the hospital, it is common to feel that every aspect of your life is suffering.

Although balancing work, home life, and caregiving at the hospital is very tiring, establishing a routine can give you some welcome predictability. Over time, as the hospital becomes more familiar, you'll find it easier to fit your caregiving into a routine that works for you. Routine will help you experience some sense of normalcy.

As you recover and are eventually able to look back on your baby's NICU stay, you will do so with wonder. You'll realize that when life is most challenging, you do what you have to do. It wasn't an easy time, but you prevailed, and even grew. You may have some regrets, but you'll be able to look back at the bigger picture with pride. You did the impossible—and you did it well.

$\bullet\bullet\bullet$

Points to Remember

- Most preemies follow a medical course that is a roller-coaster ride of ups and downs, triumphs and setbacks. Parents of preemies experience the same bumpy, unpredictable ride.

- Waiting, especially in the face of uncertainties and unpredictability, can be frustrating and unnerving. As you settle in, you can learn to wait *with* your baby and to find richness and meaning during this time.

- Establishing a routine that balances work, home life, and hospital caregiving can make it easier to cope with this roller-coaster ride. The ability to look forward to scheduled respites can rejuvenate you and give you the fortitude to keep going.

- Maintaining your balance between hopes and fears isn't easy, but working at it can help prepare you for whatever may happen—and it can help you wait *with* your baby.

- Each time your preemie faces a setback, you must wait, hope, and fear all over again. As your baby's medical course goes up and down, so do your emotions. It is normal to be buoyed by good news and crushed by bad. Cry when you need to and dare to celebrate when you can.

- Comparing your baby with others in the NICU is an inevitable part of establishing a much-needed connection with the parents of other preemies. Neither you nor your baby is a contestant in the NICU. Each family's experience, however easy or hard, is its own, to grieve and celebrate. Be comrades instead of competitors. Also remember that each baby is an individual—and that your baby will not follow in the exact footsteps of any other.

- Having two or more babies in the NICU at once is exhausting. As one baby's ride smoothes out, another's may take a plunge—and it may seem impossible to catch your breath. Keeping individual journals for each baby and accepting the caregiving help of others can help.

- If you face or have made life-and-death decisions for your baby, know that your love and devotion guide those decisions. Wrestling with guilt or doubts is a normal part of coming to terms with your baby's life and/or death. If you feel bad, it's not because you made a bad decision. It's because having to make such a decision, and the decision's consequences, can be very painful. In time you will be able to make peace with your

• • •

decision, to let go of what might have been and accept what is.

- If your baby has an extended NICU stay, your feelings of helplessness, anger, and impatience can mount. It can be particularly important to establish a routine that injects balance and respite into your life.
- Despite the difficulty of riding the NICU roller coaster, when you look back at this time, you'll see that you prevailed and even grew. You may have some regrets, but you'll recognize that you did the impossible, and you did it well.

CHAPTER ELEVEN

When a Baby Dies

I always viewed our son's prematurity in this way (a view not shared by all): If my son is blind, I will see for him and teach him how to interact in his world. If he is deaf, I will hear for him and teach him how to function in his world. If he can't walk, I will carry him, for the rest of my life if need be. But I'm frightened of the vent and the bowel problems because I can't breathe for him and I can't eat for him. In the end, that which I couldn't compensate for took him from us. —Ed

For parents whose baby spends days, weeks, or months in the NICU, death is a frightening prospect. When you are in the unit, you can't help but notice that this outcome is a possibility for premature infants. You may not let yourself think about death, but you may still feel haunted by it. When a baby dies, how do the parents survive this most terrible loss? How would you?

This chapter is written especially for parents whose beloved baby dies. It provides support for grieving, affirming the baby, approaching the challenging tasks of coping and adjusting, and making peace with any difficult end-of-life medical decisions that might have been made. If the unthinkable should happen to you, please also consult Resources (Appendix C) for additional sources of information and emotional support.

If your baby is struggling in the NICU, or even if your little one is doing well, you may feel drawn to read this chapter. Please do so—at least skim the sections that seem to speak to you. Gaining information and insight won't build a shield against the possibility of painful grief, but it is a step toward empowerment. Knowing that you could survive the death of a precious child—as the parents who recount their experiences in this chapter have done—can provide some reassurance. In particular, some sections in "Affirming Your Baby" ("Being with Your Baby" and "Keepsakes") contain ideas for nurturing your baby and for collecting memories and mementos that will bring you comfort now *and* down the road—whatever happens.

Grieving a Baby's Death

As you now know, when your baby is born too soon, you grieve for your prematurely ended pregnancy and your hospitalized infant. Over time, though, your expectations adjust to fit this new reality, and you go on. But if your baby dies, you face the immense grief of obliterated expectations. Death magnifies all your feelings of guilt, failure, and longing. Your emptiness seems endless. When your baby dies, you require a lot of time and emotional work to eventually be able to "go on."

I had never experienced losing a child, and I wouldn't wish it on a person I hated. To plan a funeral, to find a cemetery plot, to do all that—stuff I'd never done before. To do that was just unbelievable. —Charlie

I feel very old right now. Until this happened, I'd always been happy-go-lucky, kind of immature—and all of a sudden I feel so old. I look in the mirror and I look old. I feel tired all the time. It's probably taken some years off my life. It's just a lot of stress. —Tim

Grief can be intense and overwhelming. It's natural to feel lost and afraid. The following sections can help you navigate this painful journey by providing some perspective on:
- How the grieving process helps you *gradually* adjust to your baby's death
- The complexity of grief and the wide range of emotions it entails
- The importance of having realistic expectations for yourself and grief

- Coping with and working through your emotions
- Ways of affirming your baby or babies
- Making peace with difficult decisions about medical treatments

An Overview of the Grieving Process

Your grief at the death of your baby arises out of your deep attachment to and heartfelt investment in parenting this child. This section explains how the grieving process generally unfolds, and it touches on the emotions shared by many bereaved parents. It's important to keep in mind that real grief is not this neat or this simple. What *is* true of the grieving process is that it lets you *gradually* come to terms with your baby's death.

In the early hours and days following a death, pervasive numbness and shock are common reactions. As your mind tries to grasp the horrible reality of your baby's death, it also tries to protect you from the full blow of this information. Especially if your baby's death was unanticipated, the fact may not truly register for several days. You may appear to be unaffected by this tragedy or to be taking it in stride, largely because its full weight hasn't hit you yet.

Throughout the weeks following your baby's death, you may continue to feel occasional periods of numbness, when your baby's death seems unreal or you seem unaffected by it. But the pervasive numbness is usually limited to the hours and days immediately following your baby's death.

As the reality of your baby's death sinks in, you can no longer avoid it. Naturally, you protest—and feelings of anger arise. You may feel angry with the doctors, the nurses, your partner, the world. If you are religious, you may feel angry with God and question your faith. You may feel angry at nature, at other pregnant women, at new parents, and at anyone who doesn't understand your sorrow. You may even feel angry at your baby. All this is so unfair.

Guilt can cause you to feel angry with yourself as well. If your baby had birth defects along with prematurity, both parents may wonder about their genetic contributions. Mothers in particular tend to assume a fair amount of guilt—after all, you carried this baby in your body. Concerns may arise over the effects of any bad habits or false steps you made during or even before your pregnancy.

Anger and guilt can arise from believing that you should be in charge of your destiny: You make plans; you follow them. You have goals; you attain them. Then tragedy strikes. You feel cheated, angry, and betrayed by medical technology, Mother Nature, fate, or God. You may feel that you failed to control your destiny or wonder if your baby's death is your fault.

Gradually, as you work through your anger and guilt, you come to the realization that you are vulnerable—that terrible things happen to the best of people, even you. Out of a clear blue sky, lightning can strike and change your life forever. You recognize that you don't have total control over your life and what happens to you and your loved ones. This can be a frightening realization.

As you look behind your anger, you begin to recognize deeper feelings: sadness and despair. Getting to the bottom of your grief can be excruciatingly painful, but it is the only path to adjusting to your baby's death. Grieving is what enables you to eventually find peace and healing.

Realistic Expectations for Your Grief

Your day-to-day, minute-by-minute experience of grief will be more fluid and more complex than the pattern described above—and quite bewildering at times. Although many parents share common reactions, your personal journey is unique. Predicting how you will feel one hour, day, week, or month after your baby's death is impossible. There are no timetables.

Expect to find your own irregular path of ups and downs that will slowly smooth out over a period of several years. This may seem like an interminable length of time, but as the months pass, the ups do become more frequent and longer lasting, and the downs become gentler and more fleeting.

In addition to sadness, anger, guilt, and vulnerability, you can also expect to experience a wide range of other powerful and agonizing feelings that will emerge over time. These feelings will include yearning, preoccupation, anxiety, irritability, failure, hopelessness, distractibility, regret, and despair. You'll probably also experience physical symptoms, such as aching arms, tight chest, poor appetite, insomnia, and fatigue. You may feel like "a mess," but these are all normal facets of grief.

> *My garage used to always be spotless and organized. You can go out there, and it's a metaphor for our life right now. It's just a mess. Everything is just kind of helter-skelter. Things are thrown wherever. —Tim*

> *I walk through my life looking and acting normal, but I'm not. I feel like I should wear a badge announcing that I am not okay, that it isn't okay that*

my son died, that I still remember him, I still hurt for him, that there will always be a not-okay spot in my heart and my life. —Susan

When your baby dies, there may be moments when you doubt that you can survive this ordeal. Indeed, a few months down the road, it is quite normal to feel worse, rather than better. Your pain may run so deep that you may doubt that you will ever emerge from this abyss called grief. Healing seems impossible when mere survival is in question.

It's normal to feel that you don't have the will to go on. **If you find yourself making plans to commit suicide, however, seek help. Suicidal plans are a hallmark of serious depression. This qualifies as A MEDICAL EMERGENCY—you require prompt medical treatment. Do not allow crippling grief to kill you.**

When Travis died, I felt like killing myself. I had no reason to live with him being gone. I just didn't want to live, and yet I could hear Travis saying, "Take care of my brothers." I could just hear him saying that, deep down inside. "You've got to take care of the two that are here." That was something that gave me strength. —Charlie

Grieving is hard work and takes a lot of energy. Your feelings are valid and natural, however and whenever you experience them. You're entitled to all your feelings—and you are not the only bereaved parent to have them. It is also natural to seek professional help. If you think you would benefit from counseling, get it. You are worth it.

Anniversary Reactions As you grieve, you can expect to have "anniversary reactions." At first, you may feel most unsettled or sad at certain times of the day or week. As time passes, you may notice that you feel especially blue at certain times of the month or year. Your body and heart automatically "remember" important dates and times, and "remind" you with feelings of grief. When you're having an especially hard time that seems to come out of nowhere, take a look at the clock or calendar. Acknowledging these anniversaries can help. Take advantage of these opportunities to release your feelings and let your grief flow.

A week ago, I woke up crying in the morning and I couldn't stop crying. I couldn't stop. I was just inconsolably tearful all day. A few friends called and we spoke, and I told them Yoni would have been two months old that day. I knew that in my head but it did not register, it absolutely did not register— until late afternoon, when I was driving down the street and all of a sudden it hit me, oh my God, he would have been two months old today, and I lost it. I was crying so hard that I had to pull over to the side of the road. I wasn't able to drive. And then I went out to the cemetery and went to his grave, next to my mom, and then I went to the separate children's section and I thought of all the other babies who had died too. And then I just cried and cried, that gut-wrenching cry. Since then, it's been a little easier for me—not easy, but a little easier. —Micki

Anticipatory Grief Particularly if your child's illness was lengthy, you may have done a fair amount of anticipatory grieving. By the time death came, your dominant feeling may have been relief. As Suzanne recalls: "You can never prepare yourself emotionally, but I'd say I did 80 percent of my grieving before she died, throughout her life and toward the end. And in the end there was such a relief, not only for her to be out of pain, but for me. I'm not the mother of a handicapped child anymore."

This honest assessment may seem shocking to outsiders, but it is a testament to how draining the whole experience of parenting a critically ill child can be for parents. You may have worked diligently to behave selflessly toward your child, but along with your grief, it is normal and natural to feel relief that this ordeal is over—not only for your child but also for yourself. If you experience any guilt about these feelings, remember that your wish wasn't to be free of your child—your wish was for your child to be free of pain and suffering, and for yourself to be free of this ordeal. And you knew that death was your child's only escape. As that reality sank in, you turned away from hope for survival and toward hope for an easy passage.

Although anticipatory grieving serves as a "gradual good-bye" before death, it does not erase the need to grieve after your child dies. Even when relief plays a part in your response to your baby's death, it will be accompanied by many profound and agonizingly painful emotions.

Multiple Realities and Grief

Such a hubbub around Megan, and not around Elizabeth, who I still couldn't believe had died. I had my time with Elizabeth. But I didn't get to spend as much time as I would have liked because I wanted to get to Megan. I was so afraid I might not be able to get to her before she died. So I sacrificed the only time I had with Elizabeth so I could see Megan. —Timmesa

If your babies were twins, triplets, or more and one or some of them died, you have especially distressing "multiple realities" to deal with. You may wrestle with many of these issues as you grieve:

- You grieve not only for the baby(ies) who have died but also for the lost chance to raise twins, triplets, quads, quints, or more.
- You are immensely grateful that one or some of your babies are alive, but the contrast between those you miss and those who remain seems particularly cruel. You may have felt torn between wanting to spend time with a baby who was dying or had died and being there for the baby(ies) who still lived. This tug-of-war adds to your grief.
- If one or more of your babies died earlier in the pregnancy, you will need to grieve for those babies even as you care for and worry about the surviving baby(ies) in the NICU.
- Just as you need to grieve for the baby(ies) who died, you also need to delight in the baby(ies) who lived. Others can have a hard time grasping this. They may shy away from your grief, as they also downplay your desire to rejoice. A baby shower, in particular, can be a way to celebrate all your babies, yet most people won't understand this.
- You may be reluctant to admit how difficult the ups and downs of the NICU roller coaster are to bear with your surviving baby(ies). After all, you may think, ups and downs are far easier to cope with than death. You may believe that you should just be grateful to be on that roller coaster at all. Instead, give yourself permission to experience your feelings, whatever they are. Expect to be distressed by even small setbacks. Each is a reminder of how very vulnerable your surviving preemie(s) are.
- You may feel jealous of other parents of multiples in the NICU, even if their babies are really struggling. This feeling may be difficult to talk

about. You may think others couldn't possibly understand why you would wish for what they might see as simply more suffering for a baby. Of course, you're not wishing for more suffering. You're wishing for your baby who died.

- You may feel angry or simply dumbfounded when others suggest that you are "lucky" not to have to endure the ups and downs of multiple babies in the NICU. You want to explain to them that you'd give anything to ride more NICU roller coasters simultaneously.

- Your need to devote much of your emotional energy toward being with and raising your surviving baby(ies) will complicate your grief for the one or more who did not make it. On the one hand, you may be so grateful that you still have one or more babies to take care of. On the other hand, you may feel that you have no opportunity to grieve for the baby(ies) who died. And others may not give you the extra support you need. Rosa explains: "No one has asked how I've been dealing with my baby's death. Because I still have one baby, they do not ask me any questions about Dominique."

- After homecoming, you may believe you don't deserve to complain or ask for relief from caregiving duties. Admitting that you need or want help may intensify your feelings of guilt and inadequacy. After all, you were "supposed" to have even more infants to care for. But asking for help with fewer babies doesn't mean that you didn't deserve or couldn't manage *all* of your babies. Taking care of even one baby is hard work, emotionally and practically. Needing assistance is normal, and accepting it is the responsible thing to do.

- Raising surviving baby(ies) can bring both joy and pain. The survivor(s) are a precious delight, but you may also feel twinges of sadness as the little one(s) constantly remind you that you should be seeing double, triple, or more.

Your challenge is to find a healthy balance between parenting and grieving. You may be swept into the future with the baby or babies who live, even as you want to linger in the past with the baby or babies you miss. As a parent of multiples, expect your timetable for healing to be longer. But rest assured that, as time passes, especially beyond the NICU, you'll be able to find more opportunities to remember and to say good-bye. Give yourself permission to grieve in the face of parenting and also to parent in the face of grief.

. . .

Having Ashley does help me to keep going but also to never forget Dominique through her. —Rosa

It both helped and hindered me that I had a critically ill child in the NICU when Spencer died. It helped because I had something to focus on, to fight for, someone depending on me to be there for him. It hindered because I couldn't grieve without distraction, couldn't surrender to my sorrow. We had been through so much, were going through so much, we were just trying to hold on. We didn't plan a funeral for Spencer; I couldn't bear to leave Stuart's bedside. And, I think, we were waiting, fearing, dreading the possibility that there might be another funeral to plan. We didn't have baby showers. We didn't send out birth announcements. We just held on. It was like hanging from a window ledge by the tips of our fingers. We couldn't seem to do anything but try to get through this moment, and then the next and the next. One at a time. —Susan

Coping with Grief

Grieving is a distressing process that entails facing your painful emotions and moving through them. Here are five key components to coping with your grief:

- Accept your need to grieve.
- Identify the feelings you are experiencing.
- Embrace your need to dwell on your baby.
- Pursue those things that help you cope.
- Have faith that eventually you will feel better.

Accepting Your Need to Grieve Because grief is so distressing to endure, many people believe that grieving is something bad, something to be avoided or gotten over as quickly as possible. But grieving isn't a problem to be solved—it is a process that unfolds naturally, one in which you yearn, rant, and cry over what you have lost. As you release your feelings, you also let go of what might have been and adjust to what is.

Certainly, there will be times when you conceal your grief. A flood of tears may not be appropriate or comfortable at certain times, in certain places, or with certain people. But you can save your grieving for later, rather than burying it forever. It is your grief that will take you to the other side. As you grieve, you are also healing.

Identifying the Feelings You Are Experiencing Identifying the individual feelings that make up your grief will make your grief seem more manageable, instead of simply a confused mass of pain. Here are some of the common feelings parents report.

- *Shock and numbness.* Early on, you don't feel much of anything, largely because your baby's death and all its ramifications have not yet sunk in. As Charlie puts it, "It's such a nightmare, you're not even using your brain."
- *Denial.* You harbor unspoken fantasies that this can't be real, that your baby is still alive somewhere, that you can somehow recover your baby, or that you will soon awaken from this nightmare.
- *Yearning and preoccupation.* You ache to hold your baby in your arms. You are consumed by thoughts about your baby. Your world revolves around your baby's short life and death, and you probably have trouble concentrating on anything else.
- *Failure.* You feel as if you have done a poor job as a parent, a spouse, a man, or a woman.
- *Responsibility.* As the parent, you feel that your baby's welfare was ultimately your responsibility and that you should have been able to do something to protect your little one.
- *Guilt.* You feel anger toward yourself, that you must have done something terribly wrong to bring this on, or that you deserve this sorrow because of past or present failings.
- *Anger.* You are mad, frustrated, impatient, irritable—because your baby's death is so very unfair and infuriating. You ask, "Why did this have to happen to me and to my baby?" Feelings of helplessness—knowing that there was nothing you could do to prevent your baby's death—also breed anger.
- *Isolation.* You may feel abandoned by friends or relatives who don't understand or who make themselves scarce. Some people are impatient with grief and will urge you to "move on" long before you are ready or able to. (Ignore them.)
- *Sadness and despair.* You feel devastated, distraught, empty, hopeless, and hurt.
- *Vulnerability.* You realize that you are unable to always avoid tragedy. Vulnerability can be a scary, unsettling feeling, but it allows you to stop trying to control everything about your life and lets you adjust to what has happened.

When you can identify your feelings, you have taken the first step to dealing with them. It's not necessary to analyze them or to justify them, but simply to name them.

Embracing Your Need to Dwell on Your Baby Immediately after your baby's death, you may think constantly about your little one and be filled with longing and yearning. You may still feel the sensation of your baby kicking inside you, or you may wake up at night and wonder for a second why your belly is so small. You may think you hear your baby crying or have vivid dreams about your baby. You may want to return to the hospital to search for your infant, feeling that you should be able to recover this baby, if only you could figure out how. You may cuddle, dress, and sleep with a baby doll. If you're the mother and still lactating, your milky breasts will remind you that you *should* have a baby. The longing may seem too much to bear.

Consumed by grief, you may feel scattered and distracted. You may question how everyone and everything can keep going after your world has come to a screeching halt. Everything else can seem pointless and trivial.

> *I don't have focus. My mind wanders. ... You just feel like you're going through the motions. I've kind of lost a lot of enthusiasm. I used to be a little wild, enthusiastic and goofy, a big sports fan. I watch sports now, and I'm not involved at all, just kind of watching. I used to be excited. I've just lost a lot of enthusiasm since this. —Tim*

Your distractibility, longings, and preoccupations are signs that your mind (and body) is fighting the reality of your baby's death. You still have powerful biological and psychological urges to nurture and protect your baby. Especially as a mother, the powerful biochemical postpartum changes in your body put you into parental overdrive. Your preoccupation can lead to hallucinations and mothering behaviors that make you question your sanity. But you are not insane. You are bereft of the very thing that would give meaning to those natural feelings and behaviors: a baby.

As time goes on, your obsessions and urges will fade. For now, accept yourself for where you are. If it helps you to dress and sleep with a baby doll, write letters to your baby, or talk to your baby's ashes, do it. Your parenting urges are evidence of your biological parenting instinct, as well as the depth of your parental love. There was a baby, and you will always be that baby's parent.

I feel his presence much of the time and feel very strongly that he is involved in our lives. Yoni will always remain a part of our family. —Micki

An important part of grieving is dwelling on your baby. Do those things that help you feel close to your baby. They will help you experience a more gradual, gentle good-bye.

Pursuing Those Things That Help You Cope Along with accepting grief, identifying your feelings, and dwelling on your baby, many other actions and resources can help you grieve, and thereby heal.

- *Set aside time for yourself and your grief.* Caress your keepsakes. Visit the cemetery. Do those things that help you feel close to your baby and your grief. Let your emotions flow.
- *Respect your own needs.* As you grieve, be gentle with yourself. Recognize that you deserve to get what you need. Figure out what you can do to get through this.
- *Talk about your baby.* Telling your story many times to friends, relatives, or anyone who will listen supportively can be very therapeutic.
- *Write about your baby.* Keep a journal of your memories, your thoughts, your feelings. Unloading your feelings onto paper can relieve you of your burden and create a special keepsake. Talking and writing about your baby are ways to affirm your little one. (See "Affirming Your Baby" later in this chapter.)
- *Write or talk to your baby.* Addressing your baby directly can help you feel close to him or her.
- *Attend a support group.* Meeting and talking with other parents who truly understand what you're going through can be extremely helpful.
- *See a therapist.* An experienced counselor can acknowledge and validate your feelings and help you to process all that has happened.
- *Accept others' gestures of support.* Let others help you, however clumsy their attempts to do so may be. Tell people what you need. True friends will appreciate your candor.
- *Write letters.* Address these letters to those you need to communicate with: the rude neighbor, the kindly stranger, the doctors, the hospital, God, Mother Nature, fate. Don't send these letters; the writing is for you. Particularly if you have regrets, write a letter to your baby. If you wish, imagine or write your baby's reply.

• • •

- *Read books and articles.* Literature about coping with grief, personal accounts of loss, or books and articles on medical, emotional, or spiritual issues can be valuable sources of support. Be open to advice that seems helpful; discard advice that isn't right for you. Keep in mind that some of the suggestions or ideas that don't fit your current situation might work for you later on.
- *Do something creative and/or athletic.* Activities that draw on your creativity or those that get you moving physically encourage the expression of emotions or release of tension. They also remind you that you can accomplish something constructive.
- *Find comfort in religion or other beliefs.* Lean on the aspects of your spiritual beliefs or religious faith that give you comfort.
- *Ask for guidance or reassurance from other parents who've been there.*
- *Find respite in those things you can enjoy.* Taking breaks from your grief when you feel like doing so renews your energy for coping, adjusting, and healing—as well as managing other areas of your life.
- *Make a conscious decision to survive.* You can decide to get through your grief without letting it destroy your life. After a while, you can choose whether to move forward with what you've gained or to remain stuck with what you've lost. Many parents mention that they eventually reached a point where they just decided to stop wishing it hadn't happened and started learning to live with it. When you are ready, you can do that too.
- *Remember that your grief is normal—and that you are not alone.*

Having Faith That Eventually You Will Feel Better Instead of imagining grief as a bottomless pit, imagine it as a tunnel. When you are in the middle of it, you may not see any light. But as you work through your deepest feelings, you *will* come out the other side. Here's another way to think about grief: you will need to shed a certain number of tears or feel a certain number of pangs before you can come to terms with your baby's death. Every time you cry, every time your heart aches, those particular tears or pangs are behind you and you've moved along in your healing. No tear is wasted.

In spite of the unpredictable ups and downs of this painful journey, you can expect your grief to slowly soften over time. Eventually you will discover that you can remember your baby without falling apart. Your sadness and longing for your little one won't disappear entirely, but they will mellow considerably. You can also acquire a sense of peace. You'll never forget, your life will never be the same, and you'll always bear scars, but your broken heart will heal.

Affirming Your Baby

I was someplace and someone asked me, "Do you have any children?" And I said, "I have one son, but unfortunately he died." And then someone else who knows me said, "Wouldn't it have been easier to say you don't have any children?" And I said, "That's not true. I have one son, but unfortunately he died." —Micki

When your baby dies, affirming your baby's spirit and existence can help you grieve and heal. Affirming your baby can include
- Remembering your pregnancy, labor, and delivery
- Seeing and holding your baby after birth
- Naming your baby
- Collecting keepsakes, such as photos, videos, charting notes, incubator signs, ink or plaster handprints and footprints, locks of hair, infant clothing, and anything your baby used or found comforting
- Performing religious rituals that pertain to birth and death
- Having a funeral or a memorial service
- Knowing where your baby's body is buried or where the ashes are
  All of these actions, memories, and keepsakes acknowledge that your baby was important to you. Your memories of your baby's existence and appearance can help you understand whom you are grieving for. Seeing and holding your baby can make her or him more tangible. Keepsakes let you say your good-byes more gradually. Rituals help others recognize the depth of your loss. In short, affirming your baby can make your grief more manageable.
  At first, you may be distressed, unsure, or uncomfortable at the thought of being with your dying baby, seeing and touching your baby after death, or taking photographs or a lock of hair. With support and encouragement, most parents are able to overcome their reservations and realize how much they need and want to do these things.

Being with Your Baby

Initially the nurses were saying, "He knows who you are." And I said, "Oh, come on. I believe that when a baby is eight or nine months old, it knows who its mother is, but I don't think when babies are this premature they know." And they kept saying, "Yes, he does." So by the second day, when I was saying I just don't believe it, they said, "Come in and don't say a word. Look at the monitors. Then touch him and watch what happens." His respirations got more stable, his heart rate got more stable, and he always responded. I put my finger into his hand and he rolled his fingers around my finger, so I said, "Reflexes." The nurse said, "You want me to do it?" So the nurse did it, and there was nothing. So I put my finger near his toes, and he rolled his toes around my finger. When the nurse did it, nothing. So I said, "Yoni, I guess you know who I am." —Micki

With my son Gavin, I am glad I was able to hold him while he left this life just to be able to let him know that I was there for him. ... I remember holding him, when they took off the vent, and he looked at me as I started to cry. His look was almost as if to let me know that he was gonna be okay. It's a look that will be burnt into my memory forever. —Jamie

As you grieve, you can reflect on memories of being with your baby. During your pregnancy, your baby was cradled inside you or your partner. You can remember the kicks and stirrings of a little life. If you were able to touch your baby after delivery, you can try to remember how he or she looked and felt. Your experiences of holding your baby, however brief, can be exquisite memories for you. You may have been able to hold your baby against your bare chest, providing kangaroo care even as he or she was dying. This can be a deeply meaningful way to "be there" for your baby and to forge powerful memories. If you were able to hold your baby as he or she died, you can call on memories of nurturing your baby through that passage. If you delivered more than one baby, you may have had the chance to see and hold all your babies together, validating the experience of "my twins" or "my triplets" or more. Although these cherished memories may never seem like enough, you will carry them in your heart forever.

It was pretty clear to me he was dying. I asked the doctor whether or not she thought there was any hope. She said, "In my professional opinion, no." So I said, "Then take him out of the incubator, I want to hold him." And it was the first time I held him. He couldn't maintain his own body temperature yet, he wasn't strong enough to be taken out ... [tears] And I held him for maybe an hour, and I rocked him and I told him how much I loved him, and he died in my arms. —Micki

Some people may wonder whether seeing and holding your baby will make your grief more painful—whether it will cause you to become "too attached." You can remind them that you have already held the baby in your womb and felt a bond long before your baby's death. Others may wonder if it's wise for you to get to know your baby, only to have to say farewell. Still others may believe that it will only distress you to hold your dying baby or to see your infant who is so very tiny and fragile. But, of course, being with your baby makes parting easier to cope with—and having memories of those last days, hours, or minutes is such a comfort.

We have felt that if Buddy had passed on earlier, it would have been more difficult. There were still some things we needed to do to say good-bye. Laurel was able to give Buddy a bath for the first (and only) time, and we were able to hold him a great deal. We read to him, sang to him, prayed with and over him, and did all these things that we had wanted to do with him. ... Laurel read The Velveteen Rabbit. *(She now refers to [Buddy] as more "real" because of the extended time we had to bond and care for him.) I read some important religious material to him. I gave him a blessing (something I can do in my faith). We took pictures. We sang to him.*

We told him stories and made promises. I still owe him a day of kite flying, bubble blowing, and a baseball game. ... I held him, and we spoke to him and stroked him, and I did get to rock him to sleep with no medical staff looking on. We lived two hours away from the hospital, and this was the first time we spent days with him. It helped us say good-bye. —Ed

They called at 5:00 A.M. and said that he was going down quickly. So I rushed over there and I got to hold him like any baby. It was so neat. He was just so beautiful and so perfect. It was weird too. He was dying but you don't

really see it. Then they took him away, and then they took the respirator stuff off, and he died right away pretty much, so I got to hold him some more.
—Charlie

The placenta was in terrible shape. It just kept pulling away, so had he stayed inside of me any longer, he could very easily have been a stillbirth—which for me would have been much worse. Some people have said, "Wouldn't that have been easier, *because you wouldn't have gotten to know him?" And I said, "No, it would've been* worse*—because I wouldn't have gotten to know him." —Micki*

If you are able and encouraged to do so, spending time with your baby's body after death can be remarkably comforting. Seeing your baby's face can reassure you about the peacefulness of death. Touching and kissing your baby's skin and holding the body close can give you a chance to express loving good-byes. Holding on to your baby's body for a while may give you a gentler, more gradual physical separation. Even if you feel squeamish about parchment skin, funny shapes and colors, or escaping body fluids, observing those things helps you experience the body's lifelessness and the fact that your child's spirit is no longer in that body.

They were wonderful. They let me stay with him after he died—for about seven hours. They said to me, "Whenever you're ready." And I said, "I'll never be ready, so you'd better tell me when I need to [give him up]." —Micki

All I wanted to do was go down to the funeral home and spend all day with her, and so I did, and it was pretty nice. I spent like six or seven hours there, and I did a lot of touching and a lot of kissing, a lot of stroking. ... And it really helped me settle the physicalness of it, that it wasn't her anymore.
—Suzanne

Even if you had many opportunities to see and hold your baby, it is still normal to have regrets, such as not having had more time, not having taken enough pictures, not examining every inch of your baby's body, or not doing nurturing things such as cuddling, kissing, or dressing your baby's body. If you gave birth to more than one baby, you might not have been encouraged to hold them simultaneously or to photograph them together. At the time, many of these things might not have occurred to you, or you may have felt uncertain about what behavior was appropriate. Although doing so is painful, it is necessary to grieve for these missed opportunities. You can cope with your feelings more easily if you pinpoint these moments and talk or write about your regrets. If you believe that your baby's spirit is still present, it may help you to write or talk to that essence.

If you have regrets, it may also help to know that you are not alone. Most parents express regret that they were unable to spend more time with their baby or to do certain things with him or her. Even parents who feel that they spent a lot of time with their baby will always wish they could have had *more time*—a lifetime—with that child.

> *I think if Sue had been there too, I think it would've been easier for her—and for me. She never got to see Travis alive, so it was hard for her to accept that he had passed away. It was very hard for her. ... Still to this day, six years later, she is upset about the whole situation: What happened? How did he die? What did he die of? Was he peeing?—you know, all of that. Whereas I saw him and held him and saw him pass away. I [was] able to say, "Okay, I'll see you when I die." I talked to him while I held him, and I told him I'd see him, whereas Sue never got a chance to do that. There was never a good-bye.*
>
> *If I could do it over again, I'd say, "Let's keep him alive a couple of hours, get my wife down here, or bring the baby there, whatever you gotta do," just so she could have held him. —Charlie*

> *My biggest regret is that I never once held my son Spencer when his little body was free of medical equipment. In their haste to let us hold him as he died, they handed him to us with the IV connections and other tubes disconnected but still attached. He was wrapped tightly in a blanket, and though we showered his tiny head and face with tears and kisses, I never stroked his slender fingers, never explored the arms, legs, knees, and elbows that had tumbled and danced in my womb.*
>
> *I handed his body back to the nurse never realizing that I should have stayed with him, unwrapped and untaped him, that I should have been the person to send him from this earth bathed in a mother's love. I never dressed or undressed him. I didn't even pick out the only gown that he ever wore. I don't*

even know where it came from.

I think that the nurses were trying to protect us. He had just been through major surgery, and he didn't look well. His color was gray-blue, his eyes were old and sunken, his body horribly bruised and scarred. But he was my baby, my firstborn, and somehow, though I ached for his wounds, I still saw him as lovely, beautifully formed, my sweet, precious baby.

I had no previous experience with death. I certainly had not been willing to consider, to plan for, to gather information and make choices about what I would do if my own child died. I spent every moment of his life focused on his survival. As he was dying, I simply was. I couldn't question, act, plan. I was just there. I was there with him.

I blame myself for many things, but not for not knowing what my options were when my son died. I was his mommy, and my entire being yearned for his life. I don't blame the medical staff. I think they tried their best to be sensitive in a situation that wasn't their own, wasn't personal. They did what they could without knowing what it is like to live through the death of your own child.

I just regret that I didn't kiss and stroke, breathe my heart and bury my face into his little body. —Susan

Bringing a Dying Baby Home Sadly, not every baby goes home to live. Some babies go home to die. Although some people may be horrified at the thought, taking a baby home to die can be a very healing thing for parents to do. If you are facing this situation, you may see taking your baby home as a chance to create some very special memories, weave your baby into your family life, and nurture your baby in ways you simply can't in a hospital. Especially if time is short, do whatever holds meaning for you. Take plenty of photos or videos, kangaroo your little one, invite people over. Soak up your baby's presence, and do whatever nurturing you can, such as bathing, dressing, or nursing. Even if you can bring your baby home for only a few hours, this is an opportunity to be cherished.

If your baby's dying process is lengthy, you may have a keen sense of death lurking in the shadows. This may sound morbid, but to those who are intimately involved in the process, it can seem quite natural. With a dying child, you focus on how precious every moment is. Preparing for death means appreciating life to the fullest. Knowing that your baby is dying structures your memories of this time and brings new meaning to everyday occurrences.

Parenting a dying baby means ardently embracing as well as gradually letting go. You may experience a mixture of relief and tenacity, both looking forward to your baby's release and dreading the end. Over a period of time, you will need to carve out some space for yourself, to step back, refuel, and reengage. This is the natural pattern of any relationship. You may have twinges of guilt when you step away from your baby, but these healthy separations arise from the fact that you are separate individuals with your own destinies. You may want to be there when your baby dies, but know that you cannot control the timing. Not every child dies when the parents are there. Death will come on your baby's own terms. Rest assured that, forever and always, you will hold this baby in your heart.

Keepsakes

> *Finding ways to symbolize the place Spencer will always hold in our hearts and our lives has been an important expression of our love and grief. As one example, my husband had three stacking rings made for me, one for each of my children. Each has a name, birth date, and birthstone. Spencer's is on the bottom, closest to my heart, and I wear them always.* —Susan

There are many kinds of baby keepsakes you might collect, depending on what is meaningful and comforting to you. Create a special container in which to keep them—a baby book, a photo album, a box, a drawer, a wooden chest. Make sure that they are easily accessible so that you can go through them whenever you wish.

You might gather and preserve any of these items:

- *Pregnancy mementos.* Ultrasound pictures, medical records, special maternity outfits, and photographs taken during the pregnancy
- *Birth mementos.* Birth certificate, birth announcement, a newspaper or magazine published on that date, or cards received from family and friends
- *Keepsakes collected at the hospital.* Photographs of your baby after birth, a lock of hair, handprints and footprints, or a blanket your baby was wrapped in. If you declined the opportunity to take photos, hospital staff may have taken and saved photographs for you. Be sure to ask for

them if you later decide you want them.

- *Things you acquired for the baby's incubator or homecoming.* Infant clothing, toys, cards, gifts, a tiny diaper, a blood pressure cuff, a pacifier, a knit cap, a bedside journal or photographs
- *An unlaundered blanket or outfit* that holds your baby's scent
- *The contents of the nursery you had set up at home.* If you had the chance to prepare a nursery, don't rush to put things away until you feel ready. If your baby spent some time at home, set aside those things your baby used that hold special significance to you.
- *Gifts others purchased or made for your baby.* If you didn't have the time or opportunity for a baby shower, but you know that certain close friends or relatives had already purchased or started making gifts for your baby, tell them how much you would treasure having these mementos of your baby's short life. They may be uncertain about what to do with their gifts and glad to know that they would mean so much to you.
- *Mementos that symbolize your baby and/or your love for your baby.* Plants, flowers, jewelry, dolls, ornaments, stuffed animals, figurines, artwork— anything that speaks to your heart and reminds you of your baby falls into this category
- *Your own beautiful creations.* You can memorialize your baby by creating something beautiful. Knitting, sewing, building, planting, weaving, drawing, composing, painting, engraving, sculpting, writing, and designing are just some of the talents you can use to create something to remember your baby by. You can write about your baby's short life. You can compose a poem or a letter to your baby, spelling out your wishes and dreams, regrets, and grief. You can have a portrait made of your baby. If you don't have a photograph, an artist may be able to render a likeness from your memories and a composite of family baby pictures.

If you had a multiple pregnancy and more than one of your babies died, gathering mementos for each baby can help you acknowledge their individuality, as well as their specialness as twins, triplets, or more. Particularly if you are raising a surviving baby or babies, it may be very important to you to acknowledge the survivor's membership in a set of multiples. If you don't have photographs of all your babies together, having a portrait done that includes them all is one way to acknowledge their special relationship.

By helping you hold on to your memories, the objects you collect and create let you feel close to your baby. Photographs in particular can affirm your baby's existence. You may want to share photos with the friends and relatives who never got to see this child. As Charlie says, "When Travis died, my sister-in-law said, 'It's just a miscarriage.' Then she saw pictures of me holding him, and it blew her away." Or you may prefer to tell them about your baby. Micki points out, "I haven't had a wallet-sized picture made yet, and part of it is because I would rather that people hear stories about him as a feisty little vibrant kid than see a picture of him and not be able to see past the tubes." Better yet is being able to talk to people who were able to see your baby and can share some memories with you.

While he was in the hospital, I used to tell everyone, "Come on over. I want you to meet him." Because I wanted people to get a sense of this feisty kid, of Yoni, as being who he was, and not imagine, "Okay, what's missing, what's wrong, what part of his anatomy isn't there? What's a one-pound baby?" He's a perfect little teeny weeny, weeny one-pound baby. So I had a lot of people come over, and that's been very helpful to me because at least there were other people who saw him for who he was, and he's not just a story. —Micki

Rituals

I sang to my son, right before he passed away, "Now I lay me down to sleep, I pray the Lord my soul to keep." And now before I go to bed every night, I say that, to keep him knowing that I'm here and I'll see him some day. This way, when I die, he'll know where to find me. —Charlie

Rituals are ways to memorialize your baby's life and express your devotion. Common ones include naming, baptism, burial, funeral and memorial services, sitting shivah, and recognizing significant days such as due dates and birth dates. Some religious or cultural traditions have prescribed rules and rituals around death. These can be comforting and reduce some of the decision-making pressures.

Even if your religious or cultural traditions do not provide rituals that you find comforting, you are free to come up with your own or to adapt existing rituals to fit your needs. Rituals can be ceremonial or subtle, public or private, elaborate or simple. They can take place immediately after your baby's death or down the road, when you feel ready and able. Rituals can also be ongoing, such as the verse Charlie repeats each night; lighting a candle on special days; planting and tending a tree; working on a handmade memento; wearing a special adornment; or commemorating your baby with a plaque, gravestone, or memorial fund. Rituals can be painfully sad, but they can also give comfort as they provide a framework for acknowledging your memories and your feelings. Find the rituals that feel right for you.

We have no family in the area, and though they wanted to come when Spencer died, strangely we didn't want anyone there. Jack and I formed a cocoon around Stuart [our surviving son in the NICU], we enveloped one another and supported each other's grief. It was a private and personal time. We went together and arranged for his cremation. —Susan

Naming Giving your baby a name is a way to acknowledge his or her existence and individuality. A name is something personal and lasting. Your baby deserves to be named. You may choose the name you had in mind all along, or you may select a special name after you discover this baby has died or is dying. Whether the name is formal or an endearing nickname, given at birth or long after, it provides a way of referring to this child and including him or her as a member of your family.

My therapist says my baby's name is "Yoni-I-wish-that-he-still-could-have-been-inside-me-growing-bigger-and-stronger-every-day." That's his name. —Micki

Burial or Cremation When your baby dies, you may find it difficult to choose between burial and cremation. Neither is a comforting thought. You might feel pressured into making this important decision—one that you will have to live with forever—before you are ready. The sense of urgency can be very distressing, and making any decision in a state of shock is very difficult. You may also be outraged at the whole concept. You don't want ashes or a casket—you want a baby!

Whether you bury your baby's body, scatter the ashes, or keep the ashes in your home, it should prove comforting to know where your little one's remains are. Their location can give you a place to go when you want to feel close to your baby or to release some grief. If you have regrets about any of your decisions, express your sorrow about them and figure out how to create a place that memorializes your baby. Plant a tree, mount a plaque, erect a bench or statue, or simply dedicate a favorite spot where you can remember and acknowledge that precious life.

Services Funerals and memorial services are ways to gather loved ones around you at a time of great sorrow. They are also another way of honoring your baby and of saying good-bye. A funeral is a chance for others to pay their respects. A memorial service can be held when you feel ready or decide it's something you want to do. These farewell rituals can help you work through your grief. You can arrange for a formal service and invite many people, or you can keep the gathering small and informal. You can even have your own private service. Do whatever feels comfortable and comforting to you.

Remember, your decisions regarding rituals are based on your circumstances, mind-set, needs, and available options at the time. It is never too late to memorialize your baby in ways that are meaningful to you.

Healing

Healing accompanies grieving. Some people call healing the "resolution" of grief: but your grief doesn't completely disappear, you move on to a place where it doesn't hurt so much. When you begin to feel that you are adapting, adjusting, and integrating your baby's life and death into the landscape of your life, you are beginning to heal.

The healing process involves
- Coming to terms with and accepting what happened
- Making a conscious decision not just to exist, but to reinvest in life
- Discovering that your bond with your child doesn't terminate, it just changes
- Emerging with a stronger self and establishing a new "normal"
- Feeling more comfortable letting go of what might have been
- Integrating this experience into your life
- Moving on and taking your memories with you
- Finding treasure in adversity
- Always keeping a place in your heart for this child

The simple passage of time forms a vital component of healing. Early on, few parents can consider integration, finding meaning, or moving on. At first, all you can see is that your baby's death is entirely unacceptable. You fight this reality with every ounce of your being.

But eventually, as you work through your grief, you will emerge from the depths and take stock. You can accept that it happened and that you must endure. In trying to make sense of your life again, you begin to look for meaning or try to extract something positive from this ordeal. Some parents find meaning in philosophies or religious beliefs about life and death. Others take comfort in what they learned from their baby or how they grew through this experience. Many parents speak about changing their priorities and per-spectives or discovering personal strengths. Others undertake new pursuits that have become meaningful to them because of their baby's life and death. Although finding treasure in adversity can be a struggle, doing so can help you integrate this experience into your life and find peace. It can also help you honor your child's memory.

I'm just trying to get through this year. It's been the worst year of my life. But in a lot of ways, it's made me appreciate other things. The way I look at Julie's life is that maybe we didn't appreciate everything we had in our lives. It made me appreciate my family, my friends, the community I live in, the kindness of strangers more. —*Tim*

I see "healing" as a process of acceptance and integration of the deceased person's spirit into the lives of the living. It's very hard work—but also ulti-mately soothing and enriching. For instance, Yoni taught me a lot about what is important. I get stressed about much less now—and have concluded that if it's not a matter of life or death, it's not ultimately that important. —*Micki*

Tons of good things can come out of tragedy and did for me, but it still doesn't make it right. It doesn't make it worthwhile. But it did happen, so what are you going to do with it? I like to think about the changes that we are making in the NICU, especially with developmentally supportive care, and if I can give one speech and it turns one doctor or nurse around and that makes a dif-ference in the comfort or developmental outcome of one child, then it will honor Seleste's memory. —*Suzanne*

Discovering meaning or positive aspects to this experience is something others cannot do for you—and should not try to do. It is up to you to find your own way on this journey. If others' insights or pronouncements about "blessings in disguise" feel intrusive, you can gently inform them that you appreciate their attempts to help, but that this is something you must determine for yourself, in your own time. When you are ready, you will discover meaning or special significance. From this will come serenity.

Thoughts on losing a child

The first time I held my son in my arms, he was dying. Nine days old, two pounds heavy, big brother to his younger, smaller twin by all of one minute, and dying. His face was drawn and gray. Those lovely, long fingers I'd so admired were wrapped tightly in the blanket that covered stray bits of medical equipment not yet untaped from his impossibly small body. Sometimes it was me, sometimes it was his father who held this tiny soul in his enormous arms as we wept, whispered, and prayed him into another world.

It is three years later. I work. I call people. I meet deadlines. I'm up early. I go to bed late. Life, as they say, has gone on. I'm even raising two boys. Nineteen months apart, yet in some ways disturbingly like twins. But not. I am finally a mommy. But I am a mommy connected to another world, a murky place I cannot see or know. I am connected to a baby I had, but do not have. I am the living mother of a dead child. ...

A customer calls. A nice man. A man who likes, I believe, working with me and my company. He is upset. Marketplace conditions have slowed our ability to fill his orders. His work is backlogged. Our business relationship has become tenuous. I drive to his office. We work together, devise a plan to improve our response time. We are creative. We are innovative. We are friends again. We discuss houses, weather, vacations. Driving back to the office, I wonder: what might those fingers—those lovely, long fingers—what might they have done?

I am a better person for having lost a son. I treasure my children. I marvel at them. I willingly surrender to their needs. They are the magic in my life. I am more empathetic to those who suffer. I am more grounded. Less afraid. I know, sadly, unwillingly, of what I am made. I know what I can endure.

And yet I am not better. I have lost a connectedness, the ability to relate to those who have no frame of reference for my grief. Less afraid, I am more frightened. I know what can happen. I check, I watch, I hover, I pray, not again. Please never again. I am needy, looking for assurances that aren't there. That never were there.

Before my son died, I sat with him one day, stroking, I think, some small patch of skin not pierced or taped. I can't recall if he had his Saran wrap blanket on, but I remember his eyes. The gray-blue eyes of a very old soul sought mine and, finding them, held fast. It wasn't a baby gaze—open, full of wonder. His look was weary, patient, willing. His look held a question.

I wanted this child. I needed this child. I had done all in my power, more than should have been in my power, to bring him into the world. And he had worked harder than few ever will to remain in this world. I met his gaze. "It's okay," I told him. "It's okay. Rest. You've fought enough. It's okay to rest." And, of course, he died—the next day.

And I lived. I live. I continue living. I look for ways to connect to him, to here. Mostly I wonder. I am, for the most part, silent. People don't want to hear about your dead baby, don't want to know about dead babies, don't want even you to think about your own dead baby. So I listen to the echoes, I finger the edges of a shape, of a place that isn't there. I am going on, knowing that there is no getting over. —Susan

Making Peace with Difficult Decisions

As we explained in Chapter 10, if your baby's prognosis is poor or uncertain, it is your right and responsibility to be involved in decisions about whether to pursue aggressive medical intervention or to let nature take its course. These decisions are some of the most difficult you'll ever make.

Truthfully, the decision-making process was harder for me than when my daughter actually died. I think it is because you feel so responsible, and that no matter how good or bad the outcome is, you are the cause. That is an awesome responsibility. —Suzanne

I was making decisions, and I didn't know what decisions to make. I'd never made any before, I had no one to call, and I knew no one, friends or family, who'd ever made decisions [like this] before. It was all a bad nightmare. On the way home, I just couldn't drive because my eyes were so full of tears. I almost had to pull over because I couldn't see the road at all, the whole way home. Very, very, very painful. —Charlie

Decision Points

If your baby dies after you collaborate with your doctors in deciding to induce labor, it may help you to remember that this decision was based on the information at hand and right for your circumstances. Your infant had a better chance of surviving outside the womb than inside. But it's now clear that it was only a chance, not a guarantee. Most important, your decision was based on your love for your baby and your desire to be his or her parent.

In the NICU, if your baby's prognosis is uncertain or leaning toward grim or if your child takes a severe turn for the worse, you are faced with decisions about withholding or withdrawing aggressive medical intervention. You are confronted by the reality that although modern medicine offers benefits, there are risks and failures as well. If your baby's future is unclear, you and your partner have the right to be fully informed, to weigh the evidence, and to make these critical decisions about which path to take. Being the parents, guided by your values, intuitions, and devotion, you are uniquely qualified to discern and honor your baby's best interests.

If it is clear to the doctors that your baby will not survive, then there really isn't a choice to be made between comfort care and aggressive intervention. Comfort care, which includes warmth, holding, and pain control, is the only reasonable option and ultimately in your baby's best interests. Although this news is staggering, if your health care teammates can gently inform you that your baby is dying and that medical technology cannot save your baby's life, they spare you the unnecessary burden of refusing intervention and help you see that this fate is unavoidable. They can also focus on supporting you during this heart-wrenching time. Instead of discussing medical regimens and statistics, they can help you turn away from intervention and toward your baby. With comfort care, you must face a painful reality, but you also have the chance to nurture your dying baby and make the most of the time that remains.

The doctor said, "I want you to know that we'll take your advice on a code." And I guess the morning that he died, they could have called a code. His heart rate was dropping, his sats were dropping, and I knew there was reason to worry. But to me, the only major decision I had to make was whether to leave him in the protection of the incubator as he died or whether to hold him. And there was no question. I held him. —Micki

We decided to remove support to speed along the inevitable and to make him very comfortable. For the first time in his life, we held him with no tubes or wires, and he gently fell asleep. ... Edward Allan ... III—"Buddy" to his friends—slipped quietly and peacefully to the other side while being held in my arms. —Ed

The Illusion of Control

Whatever decisions you made, remember that you did not choose whether your child would live or die. You simply chose the next step on the journey. Having options only gives you the *illusion* that you are controlling fate. Aggressive medical intervention may offer you a chance, but life may still prove elusive. Turning away from aggressive medical intervention simply means conceding the inevitable. If death is in the cards, it will happen with or without medical intervention. If you are still wondering whether you or your baby's medical staff overlooked some option or opportunity, know that no matter what you might have discovered or done, your child's life or death was not in your hands.

Our priest talked to us, and he said, "She can't die of failure of the brain stem, she's got to die of stopping breathing. The more you do for her—the more oxygen, suctioning—that's just going to prolong things. And withholding, that's not euthanasia." —Suzanne

If you decided to turn away from aggressive medical intervention, you may wrestle with feelings of responsibility for your child's death. But your child did not die because of your decision. Your child died because there was no effective medical treatment for his or her catastrophic problems. Death happens because there are no better options—and that's what you based your decision on. Your child died because he or she could not live.

Regrets about Intervening

When Seleste was born, they might have said something to the effect of "Do you want us to try and save her?" And geez, well, yes, I guess so! I had no clue about how hard it would be to save her, or what it would take and what the consequences of that would be. —Suzanne

If you decided to intervene and your child died despite those attempts, you may wonder if your decision was futile. But at the time, refusing intervention may not have seemed like a feasible option. Perhaps you needed to give your baby a shot at life, however long a shot that was. Maybe you wanted to make sure that all the available options were explored. Intervention is also a way to buy time until your baby's fate becomes clearer. All of these intentions were noble and loving. Your decision wasn't futile. It just didn't achieve the desired outcome.

If you eventually turned away from intervention after giving it a trial, you may regret putting your baby through that trauma. But it was reasonable to give intervention a try, to check out possible options for saving your child's life. You had to witness your child's deterioration firsthand to know for certain that intervention wasn't working. Don't blame yourself for pursuing the trial. It gave you the evidence you needed to, in good conscience, let nature take its course. It takes time and experience for many parents to recognize that comfort care is the right choice for their baby.

Reviewing your child's medical course can make you question some of your decisions. But it's important to remember that you did not have the benefit of *hindsight* when you made your decisions.

You won't always be filled with regret as you look back on the decisions you made during your child's short life. As time goes on, hindsight will teach you that your decisions were based on what you believed to be your child's best interests at the time. Every decision was evidence of your loving devotion to your baby.

Second Thoughts about Refusing Intervention

If you decided to turn away from medical intervention, doubts and second thoughts will be a normal part of your grief over your baby's death. You miss your baby so very much. It is natural to wonder: "If we had tried something more, would my baby have responded better than expected? Would she or he be alive, happy, and with me today?"

Although painful, doubts and second thoughts about your decisions are a normal part of coming to terms with your baby's death. Over time, you will find your own answers to those doubts. Eventually you'll be able to let go of "what might have been" had you taken a different path. You'll protest less and accept more.

Some second thoughts may arise from the uncertainties that surrounded your baby's condition and long-term outcome. Your decision to refuse intervention may have come down, in the end, to a gut feeling or intuition. Indeed, if you felt in your heart that your child would not beat the odds, you would have been remiss in forcing medical intervention on your child. You may have struggled with your intuition, but you were wise to let it guide you. Suzanne explains: "I always had this feeling in my heart that she wasn't going to live. But there was this other part of me that was afraid it was a self-fulfilling prophecy. On the other hand, I was always right about knowing when she was in shunt failure. I didn't *want* to be right, but I was always right. And I didn't want to be right about the fact that I felt she wouldn't live."

There was something very, very special about him. He had such a zest for life. I said to him, "You just keep fighting. I may regret these words when you're a toddler and an adolescent, but you just keep fighting." He was just an incredibly feisty fighter. On the last day, when I knew how sick he was, I didn't need them to tell me, you know? It was intuitive. I always wondered if I'd have the mother's intuition. I had the mother's intuition. I was standing at his bedside and I said, "When it gets to be too hard and you can't fight any more, it's okay to let go"—because I had to give him that permission. Did he understand it? Most probably no. But if he got anything that made it easier for him to make that transition, I had to do that. I had to let him go. Because I certainly didn't want him to suffer. I think those last few hours that he was in the incubator, he was suffering. And then I held him, and he just calmed right down, like he knew. —Micki

For me, it was so important to look into my child's eyes, to see into her soul, and then I knew I was making the best decision for her. —Suzanne

•••

389

When a Baby Dies

Rest assured that *your* best judgment was the best one of all. You were in the best position to sense your child's odds. No one was closer to your baby in blood, body, and spirit than you. For a different baby, you might have made different decisions. Trust in your assessment of what was best for this child.

Julie was stable but deteriorating little by little. I stayed that night and slept a couple of hours, and when I got up the next morning she was okay, hadn't gotten worse. ... The nurse started doing all the things she needed to do after the doctors came on their rounds. I told her, "I'll go out and go for a walk and get some fresh air and then I'll come back, so you can do what you have to do." Because I'm not big on the blood and everything, so I didn't want to be around when they were cleaning wounds.

It was a real nice day, and it seemed like I'd been at that hospital all winter, which, you know, I had. And I knew the nurse had a lot of things to do, so I thought I'd walk around a little more. I knew how close I was to the lake, so I walked around and looked at some houses and went out and sat by Lake Michigan at the end of this dead-end street, and I'd never done that before. Then I walked back, and when I came back in, the head nurse saw me and said, "Where have you been? We've been looking for you and looking for you. Go in there right away!" So I went in and they were working on Julie very feverishly, and they explained to me that she had coded while I'd been out for my walk. They said I needed to call my wife, Janet, and tell her to come in.

Janet had asked me the night before how Julie was doing, and I said that she seemed to be deteriorating. And Janet said, "I just don't know how much more she can take," and that was my feeling at that point too, how many bullets can you dodge? I mean, every time she seemed to make a little bit of progress, something else would happen.

So they took me in the "family room" and one doctor said, "Look, if you want me to operate again, I'll operate again ... " and you could tell that he would operate, but he found it very distasteful. The other doctor took the other side and said, "You know, if you don't operate, she's going to die and I want you to understand that." I said, "Well, I think I know what I want to do, but I'll wait until my wife gets here."

Then Janet came and the doctors gave their sides and Janet was asking them all these medical questions, and we didn't seem to be getting anywhere as far as coming to any conclusion about what should be done. One of Julie's primary nurses was sitting there, and finally I said to her, "What is your take on it? What do you think?" And she said, "I think you guys need to think about what's best for Julie." And we knew this nurse was a real fighter and she never would have said something like that if she thought there was any hope.

So they left us alone, and right away I said, "I don't believe there's any hope." I felt Julie had been through enough, and so did Janet, and I just didn't feel it was fair to make a decision to put someone that little through so much pain. She had fought for so long. To this day, it's interesting to me that this all happened when I happened to go on this long walk that I'd never done before. I mean, I'd never been more than two blocks from that hospital for four months—when Janet was in the hospital, or when Julie was in the NICU. Never. I was always near a phone or calling and saying, "This is where I am." That was the first time nobody knew where I was. And I said, "I just think it's time [to let go]." And Janet said the same thing. —Tim

Finally, know that your child didn't feel abandoned by you. Depending on your spiritual leanings, your child now either knows nothing or knows all. And if the latter is the case, your little one knows how grim the prospects were and how much he or she was wanted, loved, and cherished.

Gaining Perspective on the Decision to Let Go

If your baby's prognosis was uncertain or looked grim, you may have alternately willed your baby to live and secretly wished for your baby to die. If you feel any guilt about hoping that your baby's death would be quick, remember that your wish arose from a knowledge that *some fates are worse than death*. Sometimes, death *is* the only escape from suffering. Unfortunately, many parents assume that wishing for their child's death must mean that they are bad, selfish, rejecting parents. They question their motives and focus on what they have to gain.

Try to remember the bottom line: you didn't want your little one to suffer so much. Remind yourself how much pain your baby seemed to be experiencing or how difficult it was watching your child languish. Your worries and heartache, your agony over your child's condition, were terrible burdens. Of course you wanted the ordeal to end—for yourself but also for your baby. If you felt numb and detached or tried to shield yourself from loving this child, you may look back at your motives with greater suspicion. But even if you were afraid to let yourself feel attached to your baby, your wishes for the suffering to end arose from your intense devotion to nurturing and protecting your little one. Remember as well that your goal was not for your child to die. It was that your child be set free from pain—and you knew that risky or life-prolonging medical interventions were not the way to go. You wanted both to hold on to your child and to spare your child from suffering. There was just no way to do both.

> *McKenzie Anne, twin number two, had a difficult and short life. She never stabilized completely. About five days after her birth, she was receiving ten times as much medication as my other daughter. They were pushing the limits on everything. Finally, the neonatologists explained that they had done everything they knew how to do, but they were going to keep trying new combinations of drugs to help her. My husband and I prayed over this matter. While we wanted McKenzie Anne to live, we were concerned about the quality of life she would have. It seemed terribly selfish to keep her alive just for our sakes. We met with the doctors several times. Finally, after many hours of tears and prayers, we decided we wanted all additional medication stopped. We had the respirator turned off. They kept only enough medication going to keep her from feeling pain. It was an agonizing decision to make, but even more difficult to carry out. I held her as she took her last breath. As difficult as the entire process was, I know in my heart that we made the right decision for McKenzie Anne. —Kimberly*

Deciding to turn away from aggressive medical intervention can be the ultimate act of parental devotion. The urge to hold on to your child at all costs can be so strong, yet your sense of what is "best" for your child prevails. Letting go takes a lot of courage and love. Even after you make the conscious decision to refuse aggressive medical intervention, your embrace remains. You will always hold this child close to your heart.

> *I remember thinking, "I can handle this. You know, she just lies in her bed, we can G-tube–feed her, she's got oxygen, she's not in pain. I could do this forever. It's okay." And even before that crossed my mind, I thought, "No, it's not okay, it's not okay for her. It's no life for her.*
>
> *When she died, oh, her face changed dramatically, from this tortured,*

slack, no-tone [look] to just so peaceful. And I literally really think I could see her spirit lifting, and I was like, "Go for it. Go, baby." … All I could think was that she was out of her pain, out of her suffering. —Suzanne

You may feel a sense of having played an intense, indispensable role in your child's life. Choosing between nature and medical technology is surely one of the most passionate parenting experiences. This decision made your relationship with this child extraordinarily profound and poignant, concentrated and heartfelt. These are treasures that you can claim.

One of the highest versions of love is letting somebody go and die. … I can't help but feel that Seleste was a really mature soul, [one] that maybe needed to go through this experience or whatever, but I always felt that she was older than me from the time she was little bitty. There was such a sense of tranquility, sweetness, and niceness about her all the time. How could she have come in and been a wiser soul in that short a period of her life? I don't know if there is such a thing as reincarnation. I'll find out later. But I think some people confuse the fact that because I say that, yes, in hindsight I should have stopped life support at birth, that I don't give value to who Seleste was and what a wonderful person she was. But I do and I think that would still exist, and maybe we might not have known it, but it would be there whether she lived five minutes or three and a half years. —Suzanne

If you believe that we choose our destinies, remind yourself that your child chose you as his or her parent, knowing that although life would be short, he or she would experience what it is to be truly loved.

Being with your dying baby, from a dad who's been there …

Almost three years ago in July we watched helplessly as our former twenty-four-weeker, "Buddy," went from condition to condition that ultimately led to his death after 140 days in the hospital. Let me share how we handled it.

First, we asked the doctors a lot of questions. We just needed to know that we had thought of possible remedies and had good reasons why they wouldn't work. I needed to know that there was a good reason for letting go. Perhaps it was just a way of expressing how helpless I felt.

Second, we asked the doctor what it was going to be like when he died. We asked about physical reactions—what would he look like when he went, would he gasp for air, would he convulse, etc. The doctors told us that they would remove all the connections but not the "stuff" that was in him (i.e., the intubation tube in his mouth, the IVs), but everything on him (temp monitor, etc.) would go. We made sure that the alarms were turned off. We were assured that Buddy would get one big shot of morphine before they removed everything. [The doctor] indicated that it was likely that Buddy would just fall asleep and not wake up. He also said that Buddy might turn a bluish green color and that was normal. He also told us that Buddy might "gasp" for breath or kind of convulse. These were normal instinctual-level reactions but were not indications that he was trying to breathe and just couldn't. He was too far gone for any of that to work. Buddy didn't gasp or anything, but I think not knowing and having it occur would have bothered me forever.

Third, we discussed with the doctor how we wanted things to go. He explained we could let [Buddy] die in his bed, we could go to the parent conference room, we could have lots of people around, we could have very few people around. We could even leave the unit and let them take care of it and inform us after he died. We chose to hold Buddy in the conference room. It had a couch, privacy, and some soft lights. We also chose it so that other parents wouldn't be disturbed by seeing a baby die.

Fourth, we discussed between ourselves who would hold Buddy last. We decided that I would do that. Laurel held Buddy while they removed the connections and then handed him to me. We walked to the room, and I remember saying repeatedly how much we loved him and would miss him. We also reminisced about the days before, doing all the things we wanted to say we'd done.

Fifth, had we known, we would have brought something to clothe him in for transport to the morgue. The unit had some clothes, and we used a really cute boy's jumper.

Finally, I believe if you have to let your child go that it is the absolute hardest thing you will ever do in your life. It's okay to cry. It's okay to hurt. It's okay to feel empty and lost and betrayed by the universe. It's okay to be angry. It's okay to be tired, and it's okay to want to hide. I will tell you it gets easier over time. One day you will be happy again, you will find joy in things, you will laugh again, and not betray the memory of your child. —Ed

Points to Remember

- Grieving is a complex, unpredictable process that enables you to gradually say good-bye, to let go of what might have been, and to come to terms with the death of your precious baby.
- By facing and expressing your painful feelings, you loosen their grip over your life. Set aside the time and find ways to work through your feelings.
- Have realistic expectations for your grief and pursue those things that help you cope with painful emotions.
- Grief entails many ups and downs. Over time, you'll feel better for longer periods.
- Find ways to affirm your baby's life and importance. Collect keepsakes and dwell on your memories.
- Grieving lets you heal. You'll always remember this experience, but painful emotions fade into bittersweet as you hold on to pleasant memories of your little one.
- If you feel mired in your pain and suffering, counseling can help you move to a more comfortable place with your grief. Writing about your feelings and memories in a journal can be therapeutic, and connecting with another bereaved parent can be a lifeline.
- If you faced difficult decisions, it is normal to have feelings of responsibility and doubts. These are a normal part of your grief. Feeling bad does not mean that you made a bad decision, but that it was a painful decision to make. Also remember that making decisions only gives us the illusion that we have control over death. Death happens, not because of the decisions we make, but because medical intervention cannot always avert death.
- If your baby is dying, ask the doctors what that process will be like so that you can be better prepared for what you will witness. Spend whatever time you can with your baby, before and after death, and do those things that have meaning for you. Although this is an excruciatingly painful time, it can also be rich and profound as you help your baby turn toward the path you cannot yet follow.

CHAPTER TWELVE

Discarge and Homecoming

Discharge and homecoming. *These two words are loaded with meaning for the parents of preemies. Day after day, perhaps week after week, with a lump in your throat, you try not to notice other new parents being escorted out the hospital door, taking their babies home while yours remains in the NICU. You eagerly anticipate the day that the word* discharge *will be directed at you and your baby. You may believe that your life will finally be back on course when you can celebrate your little one's homecoming.*

> *The night before Ryan was discharged, I was sitting there with him and Elizabeth [Ryan's twin], who had already been discharged and saying good-bye to all the nurses—we all cried tears of joy! I remembered early on seeing the nurses parade around with a baby ready to go home and thinking, "Will that ever be us?" When it finally was us, it was incredible! —Sara*

In the beginning, discharge and homecoming are faraway dreams that can seem elusive and even impossible. You may wonder if your tiny baby can *ever* grow big enough and strong enough to leave the NICU. Then as time passes and you witness your baby's growing size, strength, and resilience, you may feel a mixture of hesitancy and impatience. If your baby has had many setbacks, you may hesitate to get your hopes up in order to guard against possible disappointment. Even when discharge is around the corner, you may be afraid to let yourself really count on it, lest you somehow jinx it. The thought of taking your baby out of the relative safety of a hospital setting and into the dangers of the real world may worry you. It is common to feel increasingly impatient and filled with suspense. Will your baby be coming home this week or next? If a discharge date has been set, you may feel overwhelmed with anticipation about getting your little one home.

Suddenly, when the day of discharge came close, I felt confused because I longed for it so much, and still I wasn't prepared. I felt that taking him home could be dangerous, considering germs, and I didn't trust my ability to take care of him. I was very happy that we could pack our things and go home, but I [knew I] would desperately miss the contact with the nurses. After the doctor told us we were going to get to take Sarah home the next day, I walked around in a fog. I was thrilled, excited, scared, and generally nuts. —Cindy

Approaching discharge is like returning to the wild part of the NICU roller-coaster ride. Opposing emotions tug at you: you may feel grateful and hopeful, but also anxious and unprepared. Even though your baby's graduation from the NICU is exciting, in some ways, you may dread it.

Looking back, I think that despite our protests that we wanted them home as soon as possible, we got very dependent on the order and expertise represented by the NICU setup. We were confident and skilled at being proponents for our children but not ready for a primary caregiving role. I also think we got used to the lifestyle—as inconvenient as it was—of having our schedule of visiting them and leaving our parental responsibilities at the door of the NICU. What made it even scarier was that we surprised ourselves by hearing out loud how vociferous our objections were in reaction to the news that they'd be coming home. —Dwight

For us, since we had two other kids at home, we were not that anxious to have him home as soon as possible. For me, the longer he could stay in the hospital with good care in a pretty safe environment—of course, hospitals can be a source of infection and all sorts of bad things, but I saw it as a safer place than our house full of germs. —Gallice

Until your baby's caregivers begin to discuss discharge dates, you might not realize how nervous and vulnerable you feel. You may not even recognize your hesitancy until your baby is finally turned over to you. Still, in the push and pull between wanting your baby to stay in the NICU and wanting your baby to come home, home wins.

When it finally came close to time to take Sean home, I became really nervous. On the one hand, I wanted my baby home more than anything. It seemed like it had been forever since I had given birth to him. On the other hand, I was scared. What if something happened? What if he stopped breathing and I panicked and forgot what to do? What if? What if? What if? (I'm a worrier by nature, anyway, so I was just awful at that time.) But I finally decided I could do it. I figured God wouldn't give me this beautiful, strong-willed boy, let him grow, and then when I got attached and brought him home, take him away from me. So home we went. —Ami

It was not until we unhooked her from the monitors that I realized how scary this would be. Thus far, she had been supervised around the clock. Her vital signs were monitored at every moment. Suddenly, it did seem too soon! I was afraid that she would stop breathing at home and we would not know. But more than that, I wanted her at home with us. I could not wait to lay her in a real crib! As I carried her out of the hospital, it began to feel right. —Renee

In many ways, the feelings associated with the discharge and homecoming of a preterm baby are similar to those felt by parents of term babies with no complications. But in addition to the typical anxieties and adjustments of taking on the care of a newborn, you must learn about your baby's very real medical needs and potential developmental concerns. You may also have mixed thoughts and emotions about bringing home *this* baby—not the full-term baby you had imagined during your pregnancy. Although being home at last with your baby can be a joy and a relief, there is also a sense of disorientation and feelings of grief. This chapter addresses all these feelings and offers strategies for coping with them, as well as tips for gaining the confidence you need to take over the care of your little one.

Transferring Back to Your Local Hospital

If your baby was delivered or taken to a regional center and you live far away, a wrinkle in discharge is the issue of transferring your baby back to your local hospital. If transfer back to your local hospital was a goal, the move may feel like a triumph. If you did not want your baby transferred but the move was made for insurance reasons, you may feel angry and scared. It can help to remember that the reduced level of care at your local hospital is most likely appropriate for your baby. If you are worried about the transfer, state your concerns, ask questions, and protest vigorously if you are not convinced that a transfer is in your baby's best interests.

If your baby was admitted to (or delivered at) a distant hospital so that he or she could receive a higher level of care, you may have felt both distressed at the distance and grateful for the top-notch care that your baby was able to receive. Later, if your baby is transferred to your local hospital, you may be both grateful to have your baby closer to home and distressed at the changes in care. The physical transfer back can also be a nerve-racking experience.

The actual transfer was scary. [Both babies were] loaded into the same incubator with tons of equipment and one NICU nurse. We followed them down to the ambulance bay and watched as they were loaded into an ambulance for a fifty-mile ride, mostly on big-city toll roads. I almost panicked as the ambulance pulled away. They had never been outside the NICU before, let alone careening down a toll road at sixty-five miles per hour. —Julie

After your baby enters the new nursery, you must adjust to changes in care and protocol. For instance, you may have become quite accustomed to the degree of technology in the bigger NICU, and it may worry you that the local unit doesn't have all those bells and whistles. It's important to remember that your baby now requires a different level of care. Much of the technology you came to see as comforting is no longer necessary.

You may also miss the doctors and nurses you had come to know and trust. Will this new crew give your baby the same careful treatment? You can expect your baby's new doctors and nurses to be just as careful as the staff at the first NICU, even though they may appear less concerned about your now-thriving infant. Remember, your baby no longer needs such intensive care— that's why transfer to your local hospital was recommended. As long as your baby is doing well, consider a more relaxed environment to be a good sign.

Parental anxiety is normal after the transfer. But just as you needed time to get acquainted with the landscape and the medical staff in the first NICU, you'll naturally need time to get to know this new landscape and staff. If you want the team at the first hospital to communicate with the team at the new hospital about your baby's care plan, kangaroo care, or your level of involvement with your baby, speak up. Health care professionals are generally eager to share their expertise and willing to do what benefits the babies in their care.

As you adjust to your baby's changed needs and get to know the new doctors and nurses, you'll soon become comfortable in this new setting. You'll certainly appreciate the shortened travel distance, the ease with which you can spend time with your baby, and the extra time for tending to other priorities.

Getting used to the new NICU was very hard. Our local hospital is only a Level II NICU, and they just weren't used to dealing with babies who had my trio's history. I felt better knowing that the neonatologist at our local hospital had studied under our neonatologist at their birth hospital, but it seemed I knew so much more than the nurses. The first day was a frustrating round of evaluations from neonatologists, respiratory therapists, anyone even remotely responsible for Clare and Emily's care. I felt they were being used as guinea pigs because the staff in the local hospital rarely had the opportunity to care for micropreemies. The gals were exhausted and cranky for days. Things were more lax than at the large hospital. Since Clare was only on a tiny amount of oxygen, they didn't take it as seriously as they should have. Luckily, I was holding her when she had an apnea episode. (They were doing periodic weans at the time.) Scared the heck out of everyone. After that, there was a respiratory therapist sitting bedside during any wean. But "lax" also worked in our favor. Aunts and uncles as well as grandparents were finally able to visit the gals. Clare and Emily were showered with attention and someone holding them practically every hour of the day. It made me feel better knowing they had so many visitors because I was still occupied with Jacob, who was still at the birth hospital an hour away from home. —Julie

The Transition to Discharge: Practicing Care

In many hospitals, preparation for discharge involves several steps. As your baby stabilizes, the nurses may invite you to participate more in your infant's basic care. You may have extensive practice diapering, bathing, and feeding your little one—but all under the supervision of the nurses. Many hospitals have what they call a stepdown or transitional unit for babies whose primary needs are to master feeding and to continue to grow. Babies in stepdown are often cared for less by nurses and more by parents. A stepdown unit is a calm, encouraging environment in which you can become more familiar and comfortable with your baby and her or his particular needs.

As your baby's hospitalization continues, you may ask to take your baby into a nursing room or a parent room so that you can parent in private, without the hovering and watchful eyes of staff. Some hospitals may encourage "nesting," where you can spend a day and a night or two in the hospital with your baby. This can feel like a "test" of your abilities, but it's really a chance for you to gain confidence as your baby's sole caregiver while you have the security of your health care teammates nearby for consultation.

> *The doctor said we could take him home if we stayed overnight in the hospital. Yeah!!! We got everything ready, and I was so excited I forgot to wash my hands when I got him. The nurse wheeled him in with his crib into the little room. She instructed us finally on how to care for him. I felt a little scared when she said that even a cold could put his life in danger, but I hardly listened because I was just in bliss holding him.*
>
> *That night I did kangaroo care all night long. We didn't even use the lame crib they wheeled in for him. I was so excited. I changed his diaper every three hours and fed him whenever he wanted it! I was feeding him on demand and I was proud of it, although the nurse seemed to be surprised. I was most afraid of them thinking I was unable to care for him, though. But I didn't need the nurses' help at all the whole night! After that I was very confident that I could take care of him myself and I could hold him all I wanted and cuddle with him all day and all night. —Ruby*

The day before he left the NICU, we had all kinds of training to complete, and that night I had to stay with him alone in a room to prove that I could do it. I was so nervous that I would do something wrong and they wouldn't let us take him home that I barely slept a wink. When we walked out of the NICU, I couldn't believe they were actually letting us take him with us, and I shed a few tears. —Mindy

Not all hospitals are alike: some hospitals encourage transitional steps like these, whereas others either are not physically set up for such experiences or are not philosophically inclined to provide them. If you do not have the chance to experience these transitional steps or if your opportunities to practice caregiving are limited, you may feel especially anxious about bringing your baby home. After all, you may wonder, if you're not considered competent enough to take your baby from the nursery to a private room or to decide when he or she is hungry, how could you possibly be able to care for your baby outside the hospital?

I was completely unready for coming home with her—not even close to emotionally ready for coming home with this child. I suppose you are never emotionally ready to come home with a child, but I wasn't even close. I didn't feel like I could handle her. You feel like everyone must be able to see how incompetent you think you are. You feel like you have a big neon sign over your head flashing "Incompetent mom, incompetent mom. I don't know what I'm doing. Take this child away from me!" —Beth

When she got to the point where it was obvious she was okay and coming home, I was afraid of new motherhood. I mean, it took two shifts of nurses to care for her around the clock. How could I do it alone? —Kelli

Especially if your baby has experienced medical complications, the thought of discharge home may be frightening. How can you be sure that your baby will not have another downturn while in your care? If your baby requires ongoing monitoring or treatment, how will you continue that kind of care at home? Even if your baby had a fairly easy course or is going to be discharged with a completely clean bill of health, you may feel a bit apprehensive about being solely responsible for your infant's well-being. After your baby has

• • •

403

been surrounded by medical professionals and technology, it can be hard to imagine that everything will be okay under your watchful eye alone.

As we drew close to the discharge date, not so much with Shayna's but surely with Daniel's, I knew he was going to have an apnea attack and turn blue on me one night and I would have to do infant CPR. It felt comparable, I think, to standing at the edge of a platform about to do your first high dive, your first bungee jump, your first skydive. I was trying to psych myself up: "Okay, you can do this. Pay attention." They made us go to an infant CPR class. It was required, and I took it very seriously. I needed to know this because I felt that Daniel was going to need to be resuscitated once or twice by me. So did I feel like a parent? Not really. I felt like I was going to have to be the doctor, not the parent. —Mitch

Gaining Confidence in Your Caregiving Abilities

The last night, I roomed in with him in an isolation room, and what bliss it was to have him all to myself! Of course, the nurses were still coming in to check his vitals, but he was mine! The next day, amid much fanfare and videocameras, we took Stephen home. It felt so good to walk into my house with him in my arms. I sat on the couch and just held him and held him for hours. Finally I could make the decisions on when or how to feed him or bathe him or dress him! —Tracy

Most parents build some measure of confidence about taking their baby home. It helps to have support and reassurance from health care teammates who have confidence in your parenting abilities, lots of hands-on experience taking care of your baby, and a baby who has shed all the monitors and complications and is responsive to you. All of these things build confidence.

I got to room in with her in a private room the night before she came home. That was really special. They wanted to make sure I was comfortable with her home apnea monitor. We spent the night just cuddling. I thought how lucky I was that I already really knew my baby, whereas moms who have a two- or three-day-old baby are rooming-in with a stranger. We had ten weeks under our belts and knew each other well. That was nice. —Kelli

Some parents feel confident in spite of reluctant medical staff who don't encourage them to take on much of their infant's care. In the face of such professional doubters, your confidence may be borne of defiance and impatience. You may be more than ready and pushing unequivocally for discharge.

The doctor explained his concern that it was too soon, that she needed to become more adept at bottling. He told us how hard they had all worked to ensure her survival and how they hesitated to send her home too early. I told him, simply and forcefully, that I had also worked very hard for the same things and that it was time for me to become her mother. I explained that I had risked my very life to bear her—and that we felt she would thrive at home. Our family physician was contacted and he agreed to assume responsibility for her release from the hospital—and we took her home! —Renee

But most parents feel a mixture of confidence and apprehension. Even if your child's caretakers are assuring you that your baby is ready for discharge, you still may wonder if *you* are ready. You may believe your anxiety signals a basic incompetence. You might fear *you* will be the undoing of your baby once you go home. It can feel jarring to have close monitoring and support one day, and none at all the next.

This natural fear reflects the wound you suffered when you could not protect your infant from a premature birth. With your sense of vulnerability heightened, you may feel apprehensive about your baby's discharge because you can't wholeheartedly believe the common platitude that "everything will be all right." Your attitudes about parenting are not so casual anymore, and your confidence is shaken. But going home is exactly what you need to do, because it will give you more time and experience caring for your baby, which in turn will rebuild your faith in yourself as a strong and capable parent. (See Chapter 8 for more on how to bolster your sense of competence as the parent of a baby in the NICU, Chapter 14 on "Coping with Feelings of Vulnerability," and Chapter 15 on becoming the kind of parent you want to be.)

Coping with Imminent Discharge
Here are some things that you can do during your baby's last days in the hospital (and beyond) that can help soothe your apprehension about parenting your preemie effectively at home:

- As your baby grows and improves, let yourself imagine what it would feel like to leave the hospital with your own little bundle in your arms. Visualize being a calm and nurturing presence for your baby at home. Specifically envision holding and feeding your baby, and make a list of all the soothing techniques you can try during fussy times. Visualizing success increases your likelihood of attaining it.
- Start to assert your position as a parent (if you haven't already). State your preferences about how your baby is dressed; participate in feeding, changing, and bathing; and take part in decisions about his or her care.
- Even if you have returned to work or live far away, try to spend as much time as you can with your baby in the days before discharge. Ask a primary nurse to be available, if necessary, while you take over your infant's care. Even if your hospital does not offer a formal "transition" procedure for the shift from hospital to home, try to provide one for yourself.
- If you are breast-feeding, see if you can stay overnight in the hospital to establish around-the-clock feeding for your baby before discharge.
- Even if you are not breast-feeding, ask if your hospital has a "care by parent" unit where you and your partner can stay with your baby for one or more nights before homecoming. Think about doing this a few days before discharge so that you will have time to accomplish all of your other preparations and will have one final night's sleep before the big day.
- Request that any necessary training (CPR, monitor, other specialized instruction) take place several days before discharge. Trying to learn these critical-care tasks at the last minute is likely to make you feel anxious and unprepared, making it more difficult to retain the information. When you train in advance, you have time to absorb the lessons and the chance to come back to the unit with your questions or concerns.
- When you find out that discharge is imminent, you may be tempted to spend *less* time in the hospital. You are likely to be preoccupied with setting up the baby's room; stocking up on diapers, wipes, clothes, and any necessary medical supplies; perhaps even arranging for some child care. You may try to clean house, run all your errands, and tie up all your loose ends, much like any parent whose due date is fast

approaching. (If you have multiples and are bringing them home at different times, you are preparing to be stretched even further, with two or more babies in different locations.) Although these "nesting" activities may seem pressing, be sure to spend enough time nesting at the hospital with your baby, taking on more caregiving responsibilities. Your homecoming will benefit much more from a greater acquaintance and practice with your baby than from a clean house and a stocked nursery. Remember, too, that cleaning, preparing, and shopping are practical things that eager friends and relatives can do for you. Do only those home-nesting tasks that are most meaningful for you.

- You may be especially anxious about your baby's homecoming if the attitudes and expectations of your child's medical team have not encouraged confidence in your ability to parent your tiny baby. But remember that hospital policy and unit attitudes are totally separate from how ready you and your baby are to be home together. Recognize that larger systems are at play here. Even if your unit discourages you from becoming more autonomous in your baby's care, this approach has to do with policy. It has nothing to do with how ready the staff believe you are to take over or how capable you actually are. Some units simply keep parents at arm's length from their infants until discharge.

- Whatever your situation, if you think you would benefit from more hands-on experience with your baby, ask your primary nurses about it. You might tell them that you feel unsure about your abilities and would like to practice certain things while they watch you and give you feedback or suggestions. You might tell them that you need to experience being the primary caregiver for extended periods in the NICU, while you are still able to rely on their presence and consultation. Most nurses take pride in their abilities to teach and coach parents and would be glad to have such an eager pupil.

- If you have questions about your baby's care, medical needs, future risk factors, or follow-up, ask them. Ask the questions a second time if you are not sure about the answers. Get instructions or information in writing if that helps. Don't be afraid to go back to the neonatologists and nurses to clarify anything that you don't understand.

- Remember, you can always call the NICU to ask questions or for reassurance once you and your baby are home.

•••

Discharge with Medical Equipment ... or Without

Some preemies are discharged from the NICU without monitors and without clear ongoing medical or developmental needs. Other preemies go home with monitors for detecting breathing or heart rate irregularities. Still other preemies are discharged with medical devices—for example, supplemental oxygen by cannula, a colostomy or an ileostomy, a gastrostomy tube or button, or a tracheostomy and a home ventilator. Leaving the hospital without any equipment—or with it—prompts a variety of feelings in parents. Naturally, your reaction to how your child is discharged reflects your attitudes toward your child's medical needs.

Monitors

Having a monitor come home with their baby means different things to different parents. If you have seen the medical and technical support in the NICU as nothing short of miraculous, you may feel extremely anxious if your baby is being sent home without monitors. You've become accustomed to an alarm telling you if your baby has had a spell of apnea or bradycardia. You're used to knowing your little one's exact oxygen saturation levels. You've depended on technology to tell you that your baby is okay, and you may not trust that you can monitor your baby's condition by observation alone.

Although monitors can be comforting in the NICU, your baby may no longer need them. If your health care teammates believe that your preemie is no longer at risk for life-threatening complications that require constant monitoring, it might take a while for you to feel reassured that your baby will be safe. In fact, it's possible that you may disagree with your teammates' assessment and feel strongly that your baby is still at risk. It's okay to fight for monitoring equipment at home—even if you use it only for a few days to help with the transition. It's a legitimate request.

Before she came home, she passed the "sleep" test, and we were not required to bring her home on a monitor. Nevertheless, for our own peace of mind, we did anyway. It only lasted for a few days. I could see that she was fine, so by the end of the first week we returned the machine. Basically we just got tired of the wires and carting the thing around. —Diana

In contrast, if the neonatologists want to send your baby home with a monitor, you might wonder if the hospital is discharging your baby too soon, in too fragile a state. Although you may be so eager to have your infant home that you don't mind the technical gear, it may give you pause. If you don't feel comfortable with your baby's discharge, talk to your baby's doctors about your concerns, and you may postpone homecoming until you *and* your baby are more ready.

They almost let us take him home without a suck. I wanted this baby home more than anything, but I was very uncomfortable with that. I was [gavage feeding] in the hospital, so I knew how to do it, but I was not going to take it on at home. I knew that Charlie had apnea, and I knew that we were going to have to come home with him attached to an apnea monitor. I was not, on top of that, willing to do the feeding part. Just having the monitor was really scary. —Jaimee

Similarly, later on, when your pediatrician decides that it is time to discontinue the monitor, you may feel intensely anxious. You have come to depend on this equipment for peace of mind. Talk to your doctor about weaning your baby *and* yourself from the need for monitoring or equipment. Ask the doctor to explain specifically what he or she looks for so that you can learn to make the same astute observations. Also, as in the NICU, practice focusing on your child rather than the monitor. Finally, if you believe that your baby's doctor is tuned in to your little one, trust this professional assessment of your preemie's growing resilience. Ask for the reasons the doctor feels confident now and allow yourself to feel confident too.

Another factor to keep in mind is that different hospitals have different guidelines about which babies should be sent home with a monitor. Don't compare your preemie's discharge plan with another preemie's. Not only is every preemie different, but every neonatologist makes this judgment call differently. Also keep in mind that monitors do not offer some sort of magical protection. They don't *prevent* problems, they merely point to them, sometimes with a hypersensitivity that is less than helpful. Talk to your health care teammates about the pros and cons of having a home monitor for *your* baby.

Medical Devices and Equipment

Sometimes preemies who still need significant medical intervention are truly ready to come home. The decision to discharge a medically dependent premature baby is multifaceted. Getting this infant out of the NICU reduces the risk for infection, and babies tend to thrive at home, where parents can have more intimate contact with and control over their baby's care. For some parents, finally being able to take their baby home supersedes their feelings about the medical technology that comes along with their little one. Especially if your baby's survival was uncertain, coming home with medical equipment may seem peripheral in the big scheme of things.

If you are faced with the choice between your preemie remaining hospitalized for many more weeks or taking him or her home with medical equipment, you may feel grateful that your baby has come this far and thrilled at the opportunity to bring your baby home. Bringing the hospital home with you might even seem appealing after months of bringing yourself to the hospital. In fact, that equipment can offer a safety net, as it did to Lara, who brought home oxygen tanks.

It's funny, but Gracie probably could have been off the oxygen a good month or so before we took her off it. Our pulmonologist, a wonderful, intuitive sweetheart of a guy, knew that I had to be weaned as much as Grace. He had told me that we would do a sleep study once she came off, but we never did because it was abundantly clear she was ready once we decided to do it. —Lara

Other parents feel betrayed when their infant needs equipment at home. Especially if you were told that your preemie would eventually recover without complications, coming home with medical equipment feels like a disappointment, tarnishing the joy you expected to feel. After all, you probably assumed that graduation from the NICU meant that your baby would simultaneously graduate from requiring ongoing medical care. Not only did you want your baby discharged from the NICU, you also wanted your baby discharged from the need for monitoring and medical devices. You wanted this whole experience to be *over*.

I was absolutely devastated at the idea of bringing the twins home on oxygen. I had really believed that by the time they were ready to go home, they'd be

• • •

ready, *and I could leave the hospital behind. I wanted to go home, but not like that, not with the hospital following me. It took away some of the thrill of discharge. It was like a heavy cloud over us.* —Rikki

If bringing home a medically dependent baby violates your hopes, this adds a layer of grief to discharge. Medical intervention can be a double-edged sword, providing a sense of safety for your baby but intruding on your family and home. You may also believe that your baby's ongoing medical needs are strong evidence that your baby is too fragile to be discharged into your care.

The most emotional and worried that I got was in reaction to the idea that we would be bringing the girls home while they were still on oxygen. It seemed very risky and seemed to require too much from us. We may have secretly believed that we were supposed to be handed children that required no special medical assistance, that the kids would stay in the NICU as long as they were "abnormal" or "catching up," and that we would get them to take home only when they were all done needing any special help. The fear that they were not ready for life outside the NICU and that we would fail them (or that the act of being released would fail them) was palpable. —Dwight

If you are bringing your infant home on medical equipment, there is an emotional struggle with how to make sense of your baby's condition and ongoing recovery. Your adjustment often depends on how you feel about the medical equipment itself. The equipment reassures you of your baby's continued growth and survival; you know that you can feed your baby a measured amount through a tube or have access to oxygen and turn it up when needed. But it can also signify to you that your baby could become a chronically ill child, one who will never be like other children. The sight of a feeding tube or nasal cannula may remind you of a sick relative and bring back a flood of grief and fear. The thought of bringing your preemie home with a gastrostomy tube or button may paralyze you with anxiety. Or you may alternate between assurance and fear.

Parents hope that with their baby's homecoming they will join the ranks of "regular" parents—but a preemie's ongoing medical needs make this impossible.

• • •

I wanted to leave like other parents with their new babies. I was devastated that I'd have oxygen tanks in my house and that my babies wouldn't be like other babies. I felt like a failure. I was embarrassed. I had been assured that they'd be off oxygen by the time they came home, so I also felt angry and betrayed. What made it even worse was that [the NICU staff] didn't get it that I was devastated. Like I was just supposed to be glad that my babies were coming home. —Rikki

If you are grieving your child's discharge with medical equipment, you might get little sympathy or even be afraid to mention your mixed feelings to anybody. You may fear appearing ungrateful for your child's medical progress and homecoming. You may worry that others will misunderstand your feelings, criticize you for having such "high expectations" for your baby, or consider you selfish or rejecting.

But your mixed feelings are normal. Having a baby come home with special needs is not what you'd wished for. This situation violates your expectations and your hopes for a completely "victorious" homecoming.

When we brought Carter and Zane home to join Sara, Carter was on oxygen and monitors. I was very resentful—I couldn't carry Carter like I could the others. I hated [the equipment] and I know Carter hated being connected to [it]. But [it was] his lifeline, and I had to come to accept that. It was very difficult. —Jill

Coping with Your Baby's Ongoing Medical Needs
To cope with the idea of bringing home monitors or medical equipment as well as a precious baby, try the following suggestions:
- Give yourself permission to feel however you feel. Feeling glad that your preemie has survived to go home is normal, but so is feeling upset that your little one is encumbered with all this equipment. It is natural to wish that your baby didn't need all this stuff—and normal to wish that you didn't have to become an expert at disabling alarms or setting up a feeding pump. Isn't having an infant supposed to be less technical than this?
- If you feel extremely uncomfortable with the idea of taking your baby home with monitors or medical equipment because that suggests to

you that he or she is too fragile and not ready for discharge, say so! Insist on speaking with your baby's doctors about this. Share your concerns and listen to their explanations. Do not let them placate you with "trust me" statements. Ask specific questions about your reservations. You have every right to understand their reasoning and the basis for their medical decisions. You have a right to protect and care for your child as best you can.

- Give yourself permission to change your attitude about the medical equipment over time. After all, the technology is there to assist you in meeting your baby's complex needs. These devices represent your baby's will to live. You may be angry and protest at first, but as you gain confidence and get into a rhythm, you'll find that you can adapt.

- You, your baby, and your family will benefit if you can enlist and accept others' help. A good home health care agency can provide immeasurable assistance and support. If one is available in your area, see if your insurance will cover these visits. Often, public health nurses and occupational, respiratory, and physical therapists will come to your home. See about getting a case manager to coordinate your baby's care. Your hospital social worker and your pediatrician should be able to guide you to resources.

- For friends and relatives eager to assist, make lists of all the chores and errands that need to be done and learn to delegate. It is so important that you get the ongoing emotional, logistic, and financial support you need to care for your medically dependent baby.

- As you mourn having a "tethered" baby, you will adjust to having medical equipment at home. And as you get to know your baby better, you'll be able to look at your baby and see your child, rather than the tubing and devices. When your child is weaned from this equipment, you will still have those victorious feelings you long for.

- In contrast, if you equate medical devices with life and safety, you may need to be emotionally weaned from them at the same time your child is physically weaned. If you are reluctant to let go of technological support, ask your pediatrician to provide you with the extra time and reassurance you need.

Finding a Pediatrician

One of the main tasks in preparing for your baby's discharge is to decide who will follow your baby's medical care beyond the NICU. Selecting a medical caregiver can be comforting because it ensures that you won't be adrift and isolated from medical support after discharge. Some families already have a pediatrician or a general practitioner or chose one before the preterm delivery. In many NICUs, these practitioners have minimal contact with the baby during the hospital stay, becoming involved only upon discharge.

If you had a chance to interview some pediatricians before you knew that you would have a preemie, the questions you asked then may only partially cover your concerns now. Now that you have a preemie, your ideas about medical care are bound to have changed. Your requirements have risen because of your baby's special beginning and ongoing needs. You may have a clear sense of what you need in a relationship with a pediatrician. You certainly want to find someone who is knowledgeable, thorough, responsive, available, and reassuring without being dismissive. Part of your role as the parent of a preemie involves clarifying both your baby's needs and your own needs—and seeking a physician who will respect and honor them. Especially if you considered yourself a member of the NICU health care team, you will want a pediatrician who considers you to be a teammate as well.

I remember thinking, when he came home and got sick, "I don't know how to deal with this. They did." There was a real sense of fear. I remember calling my pediatrician and apologizing. And he said, "You are the one mom in my practice who gets to be a hysterical mom. Don't ever try to do it yourself. Call me. We'll get past this stage, and things will settle down." —Kathy

If you are choosing a new pediatrician or want to discuss your baby's unique needs with one who you had tentatively chosen, here are some issues to consider:

- Is this doctor in independent practice or part of a group? How is on-call and vacation coverage arranged? How do you reach the doctor in an emergency?
- Does this doctor see your vigilance as a healthy adaptation to having a fragile newborn or a sign of pathological anxiety? Will this physician

honor your job as parent and partner in your baby's care?

- What is this doctor's approach to collaborating with other physicians and specialists? Does this fit with your ideas and your baby's needs?
- Who will coordinate your baby's medical care if she or he must see multiple specialists?
- What is the doctor's stance on breast-feeding? How much support and encouragement can you expect if you are committed to breast-feeding but are struggling?
- Is this doctor specifically experienced with premature infants?
- What is this physician's attitude toward developmental follow-up?
- Do you get the impression that your questions or concerns will be taken seriously and not brushed off?
- What sort of support do you feel you need as the parent of a preemie? Does this doctor appear to be interested and able to provide this type of support?
- What does your intuition tell you about how well you and this doctor can work together? Do your styles of relating mesh well? Does this physician seem warm and open to you?

Deciding on a pediatrician can be challenging for any new parent. It's okay to make a choice and then switch after a few months if the fit is not good. Trial runs are part of finding a caregiver who will collaborate with you as your child grows. When you have additional concerns, whether they are medical, developmental, or emotional, honor those needs. Look for a pediatrician who values your input and boosts your confidence in yourself as a parent. There are many pediatricians who work very well with premature babies and families, and you shouldn't have to settle for less. Don't be afraid to ask for what you want and continue looking if you have not yet found it. You and your baby deserve to get the extra care, reassurance, and support you need.

> *I do remember calling, saying, "His oximeter reading is __. His heart rate is __." I asked the doctor months later, "What do you think about a parent like me, giving you all of these numbers?" He [told me], "You're just like the parent who calls in and says, 'He's breathing real fast. His heart is racing.' It's the same thing. You're just giving me the numbers. Don't worry. You're not an abnormal mom." —Kathy*

• • •

It's important to find a pediatrician who knows about preemies. They say it doesn't matter because once they're home they've left the hospital and left all those things behind. But it's important. If it's important to you that your friends understand, it's 100 times more important that your pediatrician understands. —Marcia

Finding Caregivers You Can Trust

After your baby comes home, you may enlist at least the occasional help of other caregivers. You may use these individuals for simple assistance with having a new baby at home, for day care, for occasional babysitting, or for help with an infant who has complicated or special needs.

Attitudes toward Sharing Care

Although there are obvious advantages to employing additional caregivers, you may resist the idea with a passion that surprises you. There may be several reasons.

- After the highly skilled care your baby received from the NICU nurses, it might be hard to imagine ever leaving your tiny infant in the hands of anyone less than thoroughly trained. Even if you never leave the premises, you may feel anxious when someone else is "on duty." If you worry about inadvertently harming your preemie, you may be extremely wary about bringing in additional caretakers.

- After relinquishing your infant's care and control to others in the hospital, you may want nothing more than to take total charge of your little one. Even if home nursing support is available, you may be reluctant to take advantage of the opportunity. You may even hesitate to rely on close friends or family.

- You may be struggling to regain autonomy after having had it so rudely taken from you. There is a certain sense of triumph in being able to manage so much without outside assistance. If you feel anxious before your baby's discharge, taking total control of your home and your baby's care can be a way to accelerate feeling competent. You may reason that if you don't accept help, you will just *have* to figure it out on your own.

- After your prolonged separation, you may vow never to let your baby out of your sight. If you had planned to have help at home during parental leave from work, you may wonder if you'll now resent the intrusion. If during the pregnancy, you had assumed you'd return to work full time and put your baby in group day care, you may be revising your plans. You may even decide that returning to work in the near future is no longer an option.
- You may recall fearing that you'd never get the chance to care for this child. In your mind asking for help now might mean that you don't deserve to be this child's parent. If you still harbor feelings of responsibility or guilt for your baby's preterm birth, you may think that by doing everything yourself, you are paying back the immense debt you owe your child for the premature delivery and the NICU. You may believe that asking for help indicates weakness, failure, or lack of devotion, and you want to be strong, successful, and devoted.

I didn't want to hire anybody after so many strangers had taken care of [my babies] in the hospital. I was adamant about doing as much of it myself as I could. —Stephie

I was tired of help. I was tired of someone else taking care of them, tired of someone else making the decisions and not me. So when they got home, I didn't want any help—which, I suppose, was a mistake. But that was how I felt at the time. —Debbie

Other parents fall at the opposite end of the spectrum. They step away from their baby and willingly abdicate a great deal of responsibility to other caregivers. If this describes you, perhaps taking over the care of your preemie is daunting and you assume that you will not be able to meet your baby's needs. You may cling to feelings of failure and guilt around the premature birth, compromising your ability to face the challenges at hand.

If you have difficulty caring for your baby at all, you may be rightly worried about your feelings of detachment. You need more emotional support than you are getting. Consider seeking out counseling to help you with your experiences and emotions around the birth and the NICU. Try writing in a journal about your experiences—your feelings, your worst fears, and your greatest hopes. Also consider the role that postpartum depression may be playing in your feelings (see Chapter 6). You deserve to experience all the joys and challenges of raising your preemie instead of being confined to the sidelines. Explore those parts of Chapters 8, 9, and 13–16 that address bonding, responsive parenting, and emotional adjustment issues.

Somewhere between the two extremes of total immersion and detachment are the parents who want to be intimately involved in their baby's care but who also know they'll want help. They include, among other situations, parents with older children, those who need to return to work soon, and those who need practical help caring for a high-need baby or for multiple preemies. Whatever your situation, it's a good idea to consider getting some assistance soon after homecoming because the adjustments involved in bringing home a new baby can be exhausting. You may be able to rely on relatives or close friends for the short term. But if your situation requires a long-term commitment, you most likely will need to hire someone.

Finding someone with whom you feel comfortable is not always easy, especially if your infant has special needs or if you have multiples. Caretakers you interview might minimize your baby's special needs or may be overwhelmed and shy away. Be persistent. Ask your pediatrician, the hospital social worker, discharge planner, or the nurses for referrals, as well as parents of preemies, parents of multiples, or any other parents you know. When you find the right caregiver, you'll know it. You'll see warmth and confidence and recognize that you feel safe about this person helping you care for your preemie.

Making Room for Other Caregivers

If, after homecoming, you find that you could really use more relief than you expected, it's never too late to ask for help. As your needs and your baby's needs change, there may be more room for other caregivers. But it is a rare parent who brings a premature baby home and immediately feels confident about asking for and receiving help from others. The decisions you make at first about your baby's postdischarge care are not hard and fast. Experience, practice, and time will give you more information and insight, and you can alter your choices for a better balance.

It's important to remember that asking for help when you need it is a sign of strength, success, and devotion. It's also a sign of health, courage, and wisdom. You deserve emotional and practical support. Having a new preemie at home is hard work. Getting help does not mean you deserve your baby any less.

My parents came and stayed for a few days, and they knew I hadn't slept in four days. In the middle of the night, my dad came in and took the bassinet and said, "Don't worry." And of course I'm thinking, well, how sensitive is their hearing? And what are they going to do, and what if somebody has something going on in the middle of the night? But that night I slept. I was dead to the world. —Mitch

In contrast, if you arranged for caregivers to help out once you brought your baby home, you may find that you've handed off too much control for your baby's well-being. After a stint in the NICU, where you become accustomed to feeling like the "second string," it can feel natural to re-create this scenario at home. It's never too late to assert your authority as a parent and your intimate relationship with your infant. If you and your partner disagree about how best to manage your baby's care after homecoming, you will need to work out your differences. One of you may never want a stranger to care for your baby again—while the other yearns for a bit of a break from infant care. Remember that each of you is entitled to your view of the situation. Sit down and talk about each of your visions. Brainstorm about ways to compromise if you disagree.

The bottom line is that every parent has needs that are unique. Don't compare your child care situation with that of other parents. If people are gently suggesting or even scolding you to spend more time or less time with your baby, remind yourself that they aren't you, and they certainly don't know your baby as well as you do. Assume that you are the best judge of what feels right and works for you and your baby. Also assume that what works will change over time and with circumstances. Making adjustments is a natural part of raising children. You can figure it out and do what you need to do.

Discharge with Multiple Babies

I was filled with mixed emotions when my babies came home! First of all, Karlianne came home two days before Alycia. I actually felt a little guilty for being so excited about Karlianne coming home. —Michele

• • •

Bringing multiple babies home from the NICU involves extra challenges: staggered discharges, simultaneous arrivals, multiple needs. Nothing is simple.

If your babies are discharged at the same time, it might feel rather like a circus! Learning about their individual needs, practicing caregiving, setting up at home, arranging for any necessary medical equipment—all of this is a big job! If a part of you is dreading the onslaught, this is only natural. It is especially important for you to enlist some type of home assistance, whether it be from family, friends, community outreach, or employed help.

Many times, multiples do not come home together. You may feel alternately relieved and distressed at the thought of your babies coming home one at a time. Although you don't want to leave anyone behind, staggered homecomings can ease your anxiety about discharge, allowing you to get the hang of each baby individually. On the other hand, you are bound to feel pulled in ways that would have seemed impossible before one baby came home. Jill recalls: "I was so torn. I was thrilled Sara was coming home, but I felt guilty that Zane and Carter were still in the hospital."

When they were better, they were next to each other in the NICU for a long while. And then Riley got to come home. And then it was like—tugging on my heartstrings here again—Banning was saying, "My sister leaves, and I'm here all by myself." You know? And then I'm thinking, "Oh, he's going to think we abandoned him and that I love her better because she got to come home first." But from the time he was born, I was real honest with him. When I would hold him and talk to him, I would tell him everything. I don't know if he knows or understands [tears], but I told him everything. —Pam

If your babies are discharged one at a time, try to adapt to their homecoming step by step. You may worry about having one baby at home first because you're afraid that you'll become more attached to this baby (or maybe to the baby in the hospital, to compensate for the separation). Or perhaps you'll become accustomed to caring for one at a time and resent the additional load when they're all home. You also might feel that having only one baby at home means that you are still in limbo—unable to really enjoy homecoming until they are all there. Still you may appreciate the chance to gradually adjust to being at home with multiple preemies. Pam, who just acknowledged the difficulties of bringing home one baby at a time, here talks about the advantages. Then Betsy reflects on how appreciating the nurses' devotion helped her let go of her guilt when her triplets were discharged separately, a month apart.

Having a previous child, I know what it's like to take care of babies. I know they need a lot of attention. I was happy because [the twins] could come home one at a time and I wasn't overwhelmed with both of them. And I could get to know Riley [at home] for those weeks because I knew her but she wasn't like she was mine. And when Banning came home, it was the same thing. ... So I was happy they got to come home one at a time just so we could do the bonding and getting to know each other. —Pam

Dylan's nurse was almost like his mother. I knew that she was constantly there taking care of him, giving him baths, brushing his hair, just doing the things that he needed her to do. He had that nurturing, and everybody would ask me, "Doesn't that make you feel weird?" No, I'm so happy that I can walk away and know that she's there and that he's being taken care of. They each had a special nurse, they each had somebody who I knew would be there for them. I could walk away and know they were okay. —Betsy

In the case of your babies' staggered arrivals home, joy at the homecoming of one baby does not negate the attachment and longing you feel toward the other(s).

Homecoming, at Last

I will never, ever forget the moment when we brought Anton to the car. I walked along the corridor leaving the NICU, carrying Anton in my arms. He was dressed in the smallest available winter overall, and he was so small, it almost felt like there was no baby in all those clothes. When we went through the door and got outside, I suddenly looked at the outside world with new eyes. The air was so cold to breathe. ... I felt the security from the NICU was over, and now Anton had to face reality, even though we would do our best to keep him away from the greatest dangers as long as possible. —Inkan

Actually having a baby home was so incredibly joyous! All I wanted to do was hold her and look at her and just plain enjoy being a mommy for the first time since I had given birth to her. Finally, there was no one telling me what to do and when to do it with her. I could hold her whenever I wanted, for as long as I wanted! —Sara

After weeks or months of intensive care, picking up your preemie at the hospital, settling her or him into the infant car seat, driving home, and walking in the door can be an almost unreal experience. It's also one of those events you'll never forget, a delicious and memorable occasion.

Bringing him into our home was like taking the deepest, most cleansing breath of fresh air you ever could. My whole head cleared and my body tingled. We settled in, and the three of us cuddled all together for the very first time. It was bliss. —Laura

We didn't tell anyone he was home for a whole day so that we could have him all to ourselves. We would fight over who got to hold him. —Ruby

Of course, like most other parts of this journey, homecoming can be emotionally overwhelming. You may readily admit to feeling excited, but not so readily admit to feeling grief, anxiety, and unease. Terri puts it this way, "It was satisfying but also very strange." Once the initial rush of excitement has passed, many parents of preemies describe an array of mixed feelings.

We said our good-byes to the rest of the nurses and made our way home—a family at last! We got home and put both babies in their cribs, and I cried for hours! Relief, fear, pity—"why me?" —Sara

It was very emotional. [That day] I cried the whole way to the hospital. I cried the whole way home. I think it was a little bit of everything. I was bringing him home, which was so emotional. A lot of it was a relief to me— like, it was over, it was done, he was out of the hospital, he wasn't hooked up to anything except this apnea monitor. And there was definitely a piece of it that was a little scary. You know, this is still kind of a young baby, and I kept thinking to myself, he's still not supposed to be here. This is still really early.

But most of it was relief—I was so glad that he was coming home. ... It was very emotional, and actually very nice. —Jaimee

I really had some funny feelings that day [of baby's discharge]. They lasted about twenty-four hours. By the next day or a couple of days later, most of those feelings had passed and he was part of the family. —Richard

Being so tired really dulled the emotional experience. More than a joyous occasion, we were relieved to not have to make the drive to see her anymore. The first thing we did when she came home was eat lunch and take long naps! —Mary

You probably consider your baby's discharge an end point of sorts. Exiting the hospital doors with your baby in your arms feels like a victory or a grand finale. But as soon as you drive off, the awareness that homecoming is a new and overwhelming beginning may quickly replace that feeling of conclusion.

The Emotional Fallout

Most parents of preemies experience some degree of emotional fallout after homecoming. The remainder of this chapter examines feeling unsettled, dropping your emotional guard, and being patient with any surge of grief. Chapter 13 looks at more emotional aspects of your adjustment to being home with your preemie.

Feeling Unsettled

Now that you're home with your baby, you might expect to feel only joy and celebration, yet you may also feel unsettled.

It was nice—and it was scary—having her home. It was the hardest thing I've ever done in my life—even harder than having her in the NICU, because you're on your own. I got home with her, and the first thing I wanted to do was go back. I was thinking, "This isn't right. I don't want to be here. I want to be back there. It's safe in there." —Beth

Feeling unsettled has many sources. Now that your baby is home, the uncertainties that you all faced at birth have lessened, but it's unlikely that they have entirely disappeared. Your baby may still have medical needs that remind you of his or her tenuous beginning, and questions about developmental outcomes prod you to watch your baby vigilantly. You may feel pressure to provide "perfect" care, to minimize your baby's exposure to germs and to maximize your baby's progress. Or you may struggle to avoid being overprotective and hypervigilant, vowing not to let your baby's prematurity affect your parenting. In any case, you're probably not the carefree parent you long to be. Being home can be quite intimidating.

When you bring your preemie home from the hospital, it's also normal to feel somewhat disoriented. Having your baby with you can even feel odd. As much as you longed for this time, everything suddenly feels so different. This is only natural. After all, you've left behind trusted caregivers and your baby's first nursery. And it's all up to you now. The anticipatory anxiety you felt before discharge has followed you home. As Mary says, "We were relieved and happy to bring her home, but I was somewhat anxious that our round-the-clock source of information wasn't as accessible."

> *Something I didn't expect was a feeling of emptiness when we got home. We had spent the last ten weeks with a whole family of people taking care of this baby. There were all the doctors and nurses, and we were just two of the people "helping out." And all of a sudden it's, "Here's your baby. Take him home, and you're not coming back unless there's a problem." —Richard*

> *We plopped her down on the floor in her car seat and stared at her and said, "Now what?" —Sandi*

Finally, you are all too aware of how long you have been waiting and how much you have been looking forward to being home with your baby. You may have high expectations for how wonderful it will feel. You want to celebrate and be a normal family, in a situation that is not quite normal.

> *The boys were so excited. They were running around their room and holding him and picking him up, and it's crazy now when I look at it, but you know, we wanted it to be a happy event, and not start saying, "Now be careful. Don't touch, don't, don't," don't." We were not comfortable at all about letting that*

happen, but we wanted them to feel comfortable about this homecoming, not to fill it with negatives and don'ts. The baby should not be a big don't. —Gallice

When we brought Sara home, I didn't feel completely like a parent because Carter and Zane were still in the NICU. Once we were all home, I thought I had to make it up to them—try to hold them for all the days I couldn't hold them. My actions were out of love but also out of guilt that I couldn't be a mother to them like I wanted to when they were in the NICU. —Jill

I shudder to think what this must mean, but one of the first things I wanted to do when I brought her home was to take photographs: posed pictures in frilly dresses with pink backgrounds. It was a disgusting obsession and very unlike me. I think I wanted to pretend her preemie experience had not happened. —Renee

At a time when you had imagined putting your baby's traumatic birth and NICU stay behind you, you might be surprised to discover that the roller coaster part of this emotional journey isn't over yet. You want to find emotional equilibrium. But settling in at home with your baby is a process that takes time and has its own set of emotional challenges.

In fact, after your baby is home, you may begin to grieve fully for what you and your baby have lost.

Dropping Your Emotional Guard

Especially if you cruised through the NICU stay without too much turmoil, you may be shocked to suddenly feel despondent. But many parents feel safe enough to experience their deep sorrow only *after* the initial danger has passed. Fathers, especially, may finally feel that they can afford to face their emotions without undermining their ability to support their partner. Jaimee talks about how her husband finally allowed himself to cry the day they brought Charlie home:

[Seeing my husband cry] was really, really hard, but I knew it was because he was so happy that [the baby] was home. I felt like he knew that now I knew that this baby was mine and was safe and I had nothing to worry about—and so it was the same sense of relief. But for a very short second, I got upset

because I thought, "Oh, my God, he's afraid." Since then, we've talked about it, and he said, "That's the whole reason why I could never do it before. Because you would never understand that it was me just being able to have feelings too, and you would think that I was worried." —Jaimee

Because of the sense of relief that homecoming brings, you can let your emotional guard down. It is normal for all the regrets, trials, and memories of your baby's hospitalization and separation from you to come rushing to the foreground. You may sort through your experiences, examining them, re-experiencing them, and trying to make sense of and find meaning in them. These are all-important parts of grief work. Particularly if you had multiple preemies and one or more died, homecoming can bring your grief to the forefront.

I attended a national business meeting the October after their birth and Spencer's death. (I brought Stuart and a grandmother to watch him while I was in meetings.) I remember the grief I was feeling. I didn't realize it at the time, but I was steeped in grief. I should never have tried to carry on so normally, attending meetings and attending to business as if I were normal and everything were all right. I couldn't focus, couldn't concentrate, and couldn't care about the things being presented to me. I sat in meeting after meeting chronicling in my head all that I had been through, trying to give it some order, some sense, some meaning. At one point, I even took an unused deposit slip from my checkbook and wrote down each thing in the order that it had occurred. I carried that slip of paper around and stared at it during the meetings, trying to comprehend it all, remembering. —Susan

Even if you feel that you did a fair amount of grieving while your baby was in the NICU, when you're finally in the comfort of your own home, cradling your precious infant in your arms, more feelings will probably come tumbling out. As you settle in and relax little by little, you'll have the energy and time to deal with more of your feelings about what you've been through, as well as what you're still going through.

If you buried some of your feelings while your baby was in the NICU, you can expect to start feeling them—and perhaps even to be flooded by them—when you bring your baby home. You may be wracked with anxiety over your baby's condition, even though the doctor tells you your little one is doing fine. When you are feeling frustrated or inadequate as a parent, you may be filled with intense guilt, sadness, and regret, and then wonder what's the matter with you. Remember that the source of your intense feeling is what you've been through over the past weeks or months. Take the time to look back. In the safety of settling in at home, you may finally be able to acknowledge that your baby's premature birth and hospitalization was a traumatic crisis. Take advantage of this opportunity to deal with your feelings when they come up.

If your baby has ongoing special needs or if you have multiple babies who demand vast amounts of your emotional resources, you may still try to bury some of your feelings. Especially if one or more of your babies died and you are raising one or more survivors, you have so many emotions to deal with.

Whatever the difficulties of your situation, you may want to focus solely on the joy. When joy meets despair, though, you really have to face them both. Carving out time to deal with your distressing emotions can benefit you and your baby tremendously. By facing your pain, you can truly tap into the joy. Acknowledging all your feelings and getting the support you need will free you to have a loving, close relationship with your baby. It's never too late to work through painful feelings and unburden yourself.

Homecoming has been a huge relief. ... Most of what I feel is very happy, but there is an undercurrent of pain from this experience. It's just below the surface, and I know I need to find ways of working through it so it won't always color parenthood. I felt it recently when I took Charlotte to the lab at the community hospital to check her anemia. I stood by her on the table while the lab tech prepared to draw her blood, and when the lab tech began rubbing the alcohol wipe on Charlotte's foot, Charlotte howled loudly. The lab tech was so shocked and kept saying, "I haven't even stuck you yet!" I knew that the smell of alcohol—so present in her memories of hospitalization—made her afraid. It saddened me to think of how Charlotte spent the beginning of her life in such an environment, and I'll never really know how it has affected her. —Kate

Having Patience with Your Grief

As you settle in after homecoming, you may finally start to feel like a *real* parent, but you may also feel frustrated by how distant "normal" still is. You want to have the "regular" homecoming that you imagined during your months of pregnancy. You want your baby to have a "regular" infancy. You want to be a "regular" parent. You might wish that you could forget the whole high-risk hospital stay and your baby's NICU experience.

It's important to remember that your recovery from the trauma of preterm birth can span the NICU stay, homecoming, infancy, and even early childhood and beyond. You will benefit from staying in touch with your feelings and finding constructive ways to express them. Just because your baby is home doesn't mean that prematurity is behind you. Many parents notice that painful feelings rise to the surface just when life starts to feel more stable or relaxed—because they are in a place where they can afford to deal with those feelings. Give yourself permission to feel your emotions—painful or joyful or mixed—whenever they appear.

> *I was walking with the stroller outside. It was March, and the sun was shining, and I could smell spring in the air. I tried really hard to feel like any mother walking with her baby, and I think I looked like one, but I was crying all the time, remembering my terrible fear only a couple of weeks before. I was so happy that I was walking there, in this sunny moment, with a little healthy son. This was so much better than I had ever dared to hope for. It was probably much more intense than the moment a "normal" mother gets her baby on her chest right after delivery. This was my moment, and it was two months after delivery. But it was a moment that only a mother of a premature baby would understand. —Inkan*

Bringing home a preterm baby is momentous. It is a triumph for all of you. Things did not go as planned, but you prevailed. You traveled through a difficult phase of this journey and made it home together. No matter how much you long for normalcy and to forget the past, give yourself opportunities to reflect on how far you have come with your little one. Looking toward the future does not mean discarding the past.

Points to Remember

- Discharge preparation is a process that can help you gain confidence. Just as your baby must go through several steps to be considered ready to leave the NICU, you also have developmental steps to take as a parent before you can feel ready and able to take over your baby's care completely.

- Your NICU should encourage you to practice caregiving, even to room in before leaving the hospital, so that you feel confident about being in charge of your baby's care. Ask for repeated opportunities to do this if you think more practice would help you.

- If your baby will be discharged with monitors and/or medical equipment, you may have strong feelings about the situation. If you believe that your baby is still too fragile to come home, talk to your health care teammates about this. Similarly, if you want certain equipment to come home with you for reassurance, ask about this as well.

- Before you leave the NICU, you'll want to find a pediatrician to collaborate with. Doing so will reassure you about your baby's continued care. Arrange for other caregivers (family, friends, professionals) to assist you after homecoming to help your adjustment.

- Your baby's discharge is a truly momentous occasion. In the midst of celebrating, it is also normal to feel worried or sad when your baby leaves the NICU, especially if your experience with your child's medical team has been positive.

- Being home with your baby may feel different than you expected. Just when life starts to feel more stable or relaxed, painful feelings may rise to the surface because you are in a good place to deal with those feelings. Give yourself permission to feel your emotions—painful or joyful or mixed—whenever they come up. Let your feelings flow.

CHAPTER THIRTEEN

Settling in at Home

After they bring their baby home, many parents of preemies go through a honeymoon period. They are filled with enthusiasm and are delighted with their twenty-four-hour access to their beloved little one. Then reality and exhaustion set in—and the honeymoon fades. The challenges of caring for a preemie build up, and it sinks in that twenty-four-hour access to your baby means being on duty twenty-four hours a day. In the hospital, you had a team of caregivers who were assigned to shifts. At home with your baby, you alone are covering all the caregiving and all the shifts. While this new arrangement has its advantages, it can also feel formidable.

For the first few weeks, we walked around the house like elated zombies, and wished someone could have dropped by to pick up an afternoon shift so we could get some sleep. —Sherilyn

Unfortunately, during this exhaustion phase, you may feel that when you need support the most, you're getting it the least. Your baby's first follow-up visit comes and goes; any support the NICU offered is a distant memory; and you're still isolated from all your germy friends and relatives. You may also feel oddly disappointed or let down—after all those weeks of fantasizing

•••

about being home with your baby, all you're doing is feeding, soothing, changing diapers, and if you're lucky, sleeping.

The truth is, caring for any newborn is a full-time job. And having your preemie at home can be especially taxing because a small, neurologically immature baby is likely to require a great deal of soothing and feeding. Especially if you have multiple babies or your preemie is still very young or medically fragile, you may be overwhelmed. As much as you have endlessly longed for the chance to care for your child, actually *doing it* endlessly can be exhausting. In fact, sleep deprivation alone is a huge problem among parents of preemies.

> *We'd be lying in bed, the closet light would be on, and Daniel would make noise in the bassinet. I would get up and lean over and open my eyes wide to get used to the light and stare at his face and determine what color he was—so that was the kind of sleep I was getting. —Mitch*

If you are really, *really* lucky, your baby will sleep a lot, eat well, soothe readily, and generally fit into your life and your home. But for the vast majority of preemies and their parents, adjusting to home is much more complicated.

> *I was terrified. My babies were so tiny—both under five pounds. I had no idea it would be so much work. —Erica*

Adjusting to being a round-the-clock caregiver takes time. Figuring out ways to juggle your child's unique needs, getting to know your little one on your own terms, and learning to listen to your own instincts take effort and support. This chapter explores the variety of adjustments that you face as you settle in with your preemie at home.

Your Reorientation

Liberation—and Anxiety

After homecoming, it is natural to feel a sense of liberation from the rules and restrictions of the NICU. Now *you* are in charge, finally free to make your own decisions. You don't have to ask to pick up your baby; you don't have someone looming nearby, telling you that it's time to put your little one back in bed. You decide everything. But unexpectedly, you may find that you are second-guessing yourself. Being away from the "protection" of the NICU can make you feel nervous.

It is normal to have some anxiety about your new role. In the NICU, knowing that your little one was in able hands offered some comfort and satisfaction. After homecoming, yours are the able hands that your preemie needs. Your eyes will assess his or her health, and your judgment will prevail. But how will you know that what you are doing is right for your child? What if you are not protective enough and something terrible happens? How will you even *know* if something awful is happening?

You may also worry about your ability to meet your baby's simplest needs: medications, feedings, sleep schedules. After being closely supervised in the nursery, you now realize that you have not only the *freedom* to decide what to do with your baby but also all the *responsibility*. This realization is both exciting and frightening.

Responsibility—and Fears of Inadequacy

When you were in the NICU and your baby was surrounded by technology and medical professionals, you may have struggled with feeling incompetent as a parent. Now that your baby's care is in *your* hands, the reality of this responsibility is daunting. It can stir up tremendous fears: what will happen if you actually *are* incompetent?

As new feelings of inadequacy arise, you realize how accustomed you had become to the NICU standards of care. Comparing your fumbling home care to the nurses' polished hospital care may make you feel awkward. It is also natural to miss the familiar and predictable NICU routine and practices. You may even try to re-create the reassurance they gave you by looking for a scale to weigh your baby's diaper, taking temperatures, and checking heart and respiration rates.

If your baby comes home with the need for ongoing monitoring, then keeping track of input, output, apnea alarms, and oxygen levels is important, just as it was in the NICU. Remember, though, that when your baby is discharged home, she or he most likely doesn't need the same *degree* of intense monitoring as in the NICU or stepdown nursery. Ask both your baby's neonatologist and your pediatrician for their views of your baby's ongoing needs. If you feel that they are either minimizing or exaggerating your infant's need for monitoring and follow-up, discuss your feelings with them. You may also need more information, reassurance, and experience to quell your anxieties.

As a parent, you need to find a balance between scientific monitoring and careful observation of your baby. Some parents are more comfortable relying on technology, scales, thermometers, and stethoscopes; others are more comfortable relying on their own observations and intuitions about their baby's condition and progress. After a stint in the NICU, it takes most parents a bit of time to adjust to being on their own and trusting their own judgment.

Of course, you're not entirely on your own. Your baby has a new health care team, and you can work with your pediatrician and other specialists to figure out what you need to do to make sure your baby is doing okay. (For more on dealing with your own vulnerability, see "Coping with Feelings of Vulnerability" in Chapter 14.) You may also find it helpful to rely on certain people to whom you can turn for feedback and with whom you can discuss your observations, opinions, and important decisions. Lean on people you trust as you develop your own instincts as a parent to this baby. And remember, this little one is your *baby*, not your *patient*.

Anger—and Reclamation

Even though you can be grateful to your NICU health care teammates for your baby's well-being, you may also have renewed feelings of anger about temporarily abdicating much of your role to them. Now that you are no longer under the thumb of the NICU staff, you may feel that you can afford to be angry about the ways in which you weren't able or allowed to parent your baby.

Any anger you feel reflects your growing connection to your baby and your appreciation and reclamation of your rightful position as your baby's parent. Now that you can gradually integrate your whole range of feelings, preferences, desires, and beliefs into your parenting style, you will feel more like yourself again. As you become more adept at figuring out what your baby needs and what kind of parent you want to be, you'll feel more confident in your parenting skills. However, don't reject in anger everything you learned in the NICU, even if you had a hard time there. Hold on to the good advice and tips you received and toss only what doesn't work for you and your baby.

Reclamation—and Confidence

As you reclaim your parental role, you join the ranks of other parents who have their new babies home with them. Just like them, you struggle to figure out what your baby needs and work toward meeting those needs. Yet you and your baby are not like those other families because the road you took to get to this point was different. Upon homecoming, you may have the advantage of knowing your baby for a while longer than the parents of a term infant, but your baby's needs may be more complicated and your struggles may be bigger. Your support networks are most likely inexperienced with preemies, instead of ready and able to guide you.

As you sort through their opinions and advice, you may feel isolated and at odds with the world around you. When you don't see your experiences reflected in parenting magazines and well-meant advice, you may feel somehow less acknowledged and validated as a parent. When you feel "set apart" you receive little confirmation that you're doing the right thing, and your confidence can be undermined.

The transition from parenting in the NICU to parenting at home can be exciting but also exhausting, confusing, and challenging. Consider the following ideas and tips:

- Try to remember that despite the traumas of early delivery and hospitalization, your parenthood has expanded over the weeks and months since your baby's birth. You may not have really felt like a parent until you brought your baby home, but recognize that you were a real parent all along, even though your role has now grown.
- Preoccupation with your baby is an integral part of your ability to be a nurturing and protective parent. Your concern for your baby's well-being is what energizes you to instinctively meet his or her needs.
- When concern turns to anxiety, it can deplete your caregiving and parenting energies. That's why it's so important to get support from others for your emerging parenting instincts. When you begin to feel overwhelmed, having the backing, encouragement, and cooperation of your partner, your pediatrician, and your relatives and friends should help you feel energized instead of paralyzed. Their support reassures you and gives you the ammunition you need to overcome your worries. Create a circle of close friends and advisors who can support you and your efforts.

- Try to let yourself enjoy the process of figuring out how to best care for your preemie. Look again at the ideas you had about parenting before the preterm delivery and see if those goals still feel good to you. If they do, figure out ways to make them work. Doing so may mean being flexible, but that is a way of honoring your baby's unique needs. If you had hoped to breast-feed, sleep with your baby, or carry your baby in a sling, these goals may still be possible—or they may need to be modified. For example, babies on oxygen or monitors are tougher to carry in a sling, but they benefit just as much from the close body contact. Maybe you had never considered sleeping with or "wearing" your baby, but after experiencing (or reading about) the joys of kangaroo care, you might like to try that approach. Give yourself time to experiment and figure things out for yourself.
- Naturally, friends and relatives may be eager to offer the strategies they used with their healthy term babies. Their ideas may or may not be appropriate or effective. Thank them for thinking of you, then take the advice that fits and discard what doesn't.
- While you and your baby are settling in together at home, you already have a lot of experience and coaching under your belt that most new parents don't get. Your lack of confidence may have very little to do with your abilities, being more a reflection of the trying transition from hospital to home and your adjustment to being the one in charge. Settling in can be a tumultuous process, but you will adapt and prevail. Find value in the path that you traveled to get home with your baby.
- Continue to advocate for your baby. Hear your internal voice and trust yourself. You know your baby better than anyone else does. Others are entitled to their opinions, but you are blessed with your knowledge.

Your Baby's Reorientation

Until now, the NICU has been the only home your baby has known outside of the womb. Because your preemie's neurological system is probably still immature at homecoming, her or his adjustment to the feel and routine of your household is often more complicated and uneven than you expect. If you had anticipated a baby who would be easy to schedule or who would sleep well, you could instead have a baby who is unpredictable and restless. Even babies who had established firm feeding routines and slept most of the time while in the NICU may become erratic and wakeful at home. This change in your baby can be a natural part of maturation and reaching "term," as well as an adjustment to the different sights, sounds, and smells of home. Plus, if your NICU followed a "reverse" schedule (where babies are bathed and weighed at night and the night shift is quite active), your baby may have days and nights reversed.

To ease your baby's adjustment to home, you can try to simulate the familiar NICU. If your baby's NICU had active nights, you might try keeping the lights brighter and the sounds louder at night, dimming them slowly over a week or more. If your baby still sleeps better with constant background noise, you might try playing a CD of soothing ocean waves or womb sounds at low volume throughout the night. Try keeping the daytime softer, quieter, and calmer at first, so your baby can be awake without being overstimulated. Over time, your baby will adjust and mature, and you'll figure out ways to entice her or him to sleep better at night and be awake and more calm during the day. Trust yourself to evaluate what your baby needs to settle in.

Reorientation with Multiples

Shayna came home first. She was cute—she was this little doll. She was always swaddled in her blanket. We'd get up, give her a bottle. She was not that hard. Then Daniel was discharged, and that was an entirely different story. He was uncomfortable, and he screamed and screamed and screamed. It was tough. And once there were two of them at home, within thirty-six hours we were wiped. There was an unbearable amount of sleep deprivation, and not just for a bad couple of days, but when it continues for a week, it's hard to function. It was really hard in the beginning. —Mitch

Homecoming with three tiny babies can only be chaotic. Both Clare and Emily came home on apnea monitors and medication for apnea. Jacob came home [later] with no equipment but with lots of medical care needs and extreme feeding issues. Between weight checks, follow-up visits, and Jacob's specialists, we were packing up babies and equipment to visit some doctor at least twice a week. Moving three babies from place to place is hard enough but then to lug equipment! It made for some interesting times. Caring for my tiny babies

437
Settling in at Home

became a full-time obsession. But it was, and still is, a labor of love. When their care would start to overwhelm me, I'd think of how extremely lucky I was to have all three of them home with me. —Julie

If you're bringing home multiple babies, being overwhelmed with their care can be a mixed blessing. After all, there were no guarantees that you would ever see this day. Still, having tiny, often irritable, perhaps medically needy babies at home compounds the normal exhaustion that comes with having multiples. Plus, in addition to trying to keep track of who was fed when and how much, you may also be juggling numerous medications, dosages, schedules, and pieces of equipment. It can also be hard to keep track of which baby is which. And if (when) there are mix-ups, you'll be making embarrassing calls to the NICU. You won't be the first parent to do this, nor the last.

Even after coming home, you may discover losses you had not expected. For example, you might have looked forward to bedding your babies together, but if you brought them home with oxygen or monitors, the tubing and wires might keep getting crossed; you may end up separating your little ones to make things safer and easier. Additionally, feeding may not be the idyllic scene you'd pictured.

Here are some tips for coping with multiples in the early days at home:

- If you don't like the idea of having someone around during the day, consider getting help at night. An eight-hour period when you can get a good night's sleep will vastly improve your ability to cope. This is a common recommendation even for parents of multiples who are born at term. If you don't have enough volunteers for the night shift, consider hiring someone. (Ask your pediatrician or other families of multiples for recommendations.) Even if you must stretch to afford it, strategic use of nighttime help is an investment in your mental and physical health and in your relationship with your babies.
- Accept offers of help. You may have a fair number of friends and even acquaintances that you trust and who are eager to pitch in, especially during the early months when they know you're making the transition from hospital to home.
- If your babies are discharged on different dates, enjoy the opportunity to focus on them separately. Remember, the quality of your attention can be just as important as the quantity.

• • •

- If your babies continue to need monitoring, medication, or medical devices, color-code everything (including the babies) to make it easier to move them around, give doses, and carry out other caregiving tasks.

Finally, it's important to allow yourself to grieve for your disappointments, even the subtle ones. If you'd idealized the experience of having twins or more, you may need to revisit and adjust your expectations.

Enjoying Your Baby

As for my parenting the boys when they came home, I was elated. I didn't care if I had to have bottles in my hands twenty-four hours a day, which it seemed like I did. I needed to make up for lost time and to finally feel like these babies were mine. —Stephie

One of the first adjustments that parents notice after they are home with their preemie is that they can spend as much time holding, snuggling, feeding, and playing as they (and their baby) desire. Without the watchful eyes of the NICU staff, you probably feel freer to pick up your baby "just because"—and to play, sing, or talk. If your NICU's setup was very open and exposed, having your little one home may feel delightfully cozy. At first, you may even hold your baby most of your waking hours! The luxury of having that opportunity and the privacy of home can be intoxicating.

I didn't feel like he really knew who I was until after he was home. It was the way he would look at me when I picked him up and the way he would snuggle into me. —Sharon

As you learn to enjoy your baby, it is natural to bask in being together. Unfortunately, others may discourage you from doting on your baby. You may even wonder if you are "spoiling" your little one. Rest assured that babies benefit from being held. If your baby seems to enjoy being held and wants more, that doesn't mean you should do it less! In some cultures, babies are held next to their mothers' bodies nearly constantly for the first year.

If you take joy in holding your baby close, celebrate it. Surround yourself with people who understand this and who rejoice with you. Your desire to hold your baby comes from a positive instinct to nurture, and it is good for both babies and parents.

> *I just wanted them near me all the time. I was very idealistic. I was never going to leave these babies. I was never going anywhere without them—lots of "nevers." It was actually a very long time before we left them with anyone. ... We just had the intense need to be with them and heal. Just the thought of being able to hold my baby whenever I wanted to—I said: "I'm never going to put them down. Once I get to hold them, I'm going to hold them forever." And then like after two days, "Okay, we can lay them down here a little bit now." But we were very much like that. Once they were home with us, we were glued together. —Stephie*

> *Because Daniel was small, any time there was an opportunity to try to feed him, we would. He would always wake up between 11:00 P.M. and 1:00 A.M., and I would always get him—and you know what? I didn't mind getting him. The fact was, when he started getting bigger, I loved getting him. I'd bring him down, I'd turn on the light over the kitchen sink, and I'd give him a bottle. I used to hold him real high on me, and I'd just put my cheek on his while I gave him his bottle, and I just thought he was the sweetest thing in the world to give a bottle to. So I didn't mind getting up. —Mitch*

If you'd like to hold your baby more, but he or she doesn't tolerate it well, there are several things you might try. First, find out what positions and holds your baby likes. Some babies prefer to be held upright on the parent's shoulder, and others like to be curled up against the parent's chest (like they're in a sling). Still others like to be cradled on their back in the parent's arms or lap, and some like to be held like a football, tummy down, pelvis supported by the parent's hand and head supported by that arm's elbow. Some babies like to be held still; others like to be carried around; still others like to be rocked back and forth or up and down. Some babies like to be swaddled. Others like their arms and/or legs to be unconfined.

Next, figure out when your baby likes—and doesn't like—to be held. During feedings? When asleep? When fussy? When awake and alert? When there's a lot going on? When things are calm?

Then honor your baby's preferences, remembering that over time they will change and may become more flexible. Remind yourself that all babies have preferences associated with being held, whether they are born early or late and whether they have expert or novice parents. Your baby is a uniquely wired individual. It's your job to help your little one learn that the world is a responsive place where she or he can fit in comfortably.

Mixed Feelings about Your Baby

It is perfectly normal to feel a mixture of joy and sadness as you settle in with your preemie. Your joy comes from relief, hope, and love. Your sadness is for what you have lost and for what you fear you may still lose. You may miss the support and camaraderie you got in the NICU. Of course, you miss the respite NICU care provided.

> *I felt a deep sense of loss leaving the NICU. It had been my home for more than three months. Just by the act of taking Jacob out those doors, I no longer belonged. When Jacob was just a couple of weeks old, we returned to the hospital for a day of doctors' appointments. The NICU allowed me to use the refrigerator on the floor to store Jacob's bottles. When I walked in to get them, I felt like an intruder, a total stranger—when just two weeks before, I had belonged there. When so much of your emotions are wrapped up in one experience, it's unsettling to be set free. —Julie*

There is also the possibility that, given the stress you may be under as you adjust to your new role, you are experiencing postpartum depression. (See Chapter 6 for more information on depression.) If you continue to feel distant and disconnected from your baby after homecoming, you might benefit from setting aside some time and energy to work through some of the emotional pain of the last few months. Remember, if you want to feel the joy, you also have to deal with your distress. You may find it particularly helpful to work on forgiving yourself for any perceived inadequacies, past or present.

Forgiveness can happen when you know you can be responsible for taking care of your baby without carrying the blame for his or her premature birth. Taking responsibility makes you feel strong, competent, and empowered; blaming yourself makes you feel weak, incompetent, and undermined. Taking responsibility helps you move forward in a positive direction; blaming yourself keeps you stuck on your transgressions. By recognizing your valuable contributions and seeing yourself as a devoted parent, you are taking responsibility; the emotional benefits will spill over into your relationship with your baby. (For more ideas and support, review "Moving through Guilt" in Chapter 3. Also be sure to read "The Emotional Fallout" in Chapter 12.)

Know that the care you can give this baby is special, *if you let yourself give it.* You probably also require some extra nurturing yourself, which will in turn better enable you to nurture your baby. Get the help you need and deserve. You—and your baby—are worth it.

Your Dynamic Bond with Your Baby

Because of your baby's unusual beginning, you may continue to have concerns about your relationship with this child. You may worry that any difficulties between you are permanent results of the detrimental effects of prematurity. But your relationship with your baby will naturally ebb and flow, and your bond is resilient. As you settle in at home, you become better acquainted and have more opportunities to express your devotion. The quality of your relationship may improve slowly over time, or you may experience a dramatic "moment of truth" where you realize the strength of your bond.

My next baby has made me realize how severely my relationship with my [preemie] son was affected. It took a very long time to get over what I had done emotionally to protect myself from loss. I can't really describe the kind of barrier that seemed to be between us in his infancy, but I didn't have anything like the feelings for him that I have for my daughter. I felt I had to "work" at developing those feelings. ... I now have tons of "evidence" that he was a very emotionally healthy infant. Our attachment relationship at thirteen months was fine. Other than being still slightly "overprotected," I don't think he has suffered any long-term emotional ill effects. (We're actually pretty close now!) —Shaina

An event after Molly's homecoming highlighted and strengthened my feelings for her. Six weeks after she came home, I found myself crouched in a parking lot with my daughter while a tornado passed over. I held her tiny body beneath me while hail pelted us and the wind threatened to snatch her from my arms. It was a terrifying experience! But I discovered, incredibly, for the first time, that I wanted my girl to live. I fought for her life in that parking lot, and things were not the same after that. —Renee

It is normal for the parent-child relationship to grow and adjust over time—a lifetime. As a baby develops his or her own distinct personality and becomes a separate individual, the relationship expands to accommodate the child's "otherness." As the baby grows and leaves the breast, then leaves the lap, then leaves for school, and then leaves home, the bond doesn't lessen or disintegrate—it simply stretches and becomes more complex. The nature of the connection also becomes richer as the child grows and develops. It includes more and more of what the child brings to the relationship, and it makes room for all the relationships that the child forms with others. If the child remains dependent into adulthood, the bond doesn't stretch quite so much, but the relationship does accommodate change as the child grows and the parents alter their caregiving.

Occasionally the relationship breaks down a little—when the child receives less attention because the parents are undergoing heightened daily stresses or if the child is going through a challenging stage that produces a lot of conflict. And certainly, when your baby was taken to the NICU, and perhaps for the duration of your baby's hospital stay, you felt varying degrees of disconnect. But any breakdown is usually temporary. The parents search for solutions in books, by talking to other parents, or by consulting a family therapist to help them get back on track. When things seem darkest, trying to find answers and getting help are signs that the parental bond is strong. Even if you make the heartbreaking choice to place your child in another's care, you express your devotion by giving your child what you believe is best.

Remember that all relationships ebb and flow. For parents and preemies, early hospitalization is an unavoidable obstacle. There are other times, developmentally, when parents and children are naturally more distant. There will be moments when you will be particularly unhappy with one another. But your bond will persist through the rough patches because it arises out of your underlying devotion to each other. Your bond is what will motivate you to get whatever extra help and support you need to parent this child. (For more on bonding, see Chapter 9.)

Your Baby's Attachment to You

Of course, your relationship with your little one is a two-way street. *Bonding* refers to the connection that parents feel to their baby; *attachment* refers to the connection that the baby develops to the parents. Just as you may worry about your ability to bond with your baby in the NICU, you may also worry about your baby's ability to develop an attachment to you. How can your baby learn to trust and depend on you when so many others were providing care in those early weeks or months?

Just as bonding is a process that occurs over time and with experience, so is attachment. Attachment emerges over the first year, as the infant experiences consistent nurturing from devoted caregivers and as his or her knowledge of the surrounding world becomes more sophisticated.

In the early months, although your infant may be especially soothed by *your* presence, he can accept soothing from anyone who appropriately meets his needs. Through this he learns that the world is a safe, nurturing place. By the second half of the first year (corrected age), your baby figures out that you still exist even when you're not there, and she begins to protest when you go away. This protest of your absence is commonly referred to as "separation anxiety," and it persists throughout childhood to some degree. As your child learns that she can especially rely on *you* to meet her needs, she will naturally form a strong preference for you and will protest if others get too close. (This is commonly referred to as "stranger anxiety.") You can see the evolutionary advantages of these anxieties and protests: it's more likely that you will survive infancy if you can compel your favored caregivers to keep you close by.

So, by around age one, your baby will show evidence of a secure attachment to you (and to other consistent caregivers) by

- Depending on your comforting presence
- Preferring you over less-familiar people
- Being soothed by you when upset

Your baby's attachment to you forms because of your bond with him or her—your ability and willingness to be there for your child. But your bond alone isn't all that's needed for attachment. Your infant must also bring certain abilities to the table. For instance, your little one must be able to

- Stay calm, your presence and overtures can make a positive impression
- Be interested in her or his surroundings in order to learn about the world, including you
- Respond in positive ways to your face, touch, and voice in order to keep you involved

The nurturing you provide—emotional responsiveness and empathy, communication, touching, holding, feeding, and soothing—are all ways in which you help your baby be calm, interested, and responsive. They are also the ways you express your devotion and emotional connection to your baby. When your actions are met with a calm, interested, responsive baby, it's easy to stay devoted and connected. Even in the NICU, you were able to freely offer this kind of nurturing. Despite the barriers there, your presence and your growing bond provided a foundation for your little one to become attached to you. After homecoming, you can really get into a rhythm of cuddling, interacting, and enjoying time together.

Unfortunately, some babies do not invite or tolerate much interaction. If your baby seems unusually placid, undemanding, or withdrawn; if your baby is often fussy, inconsolable, avoids eye contact, and doesn't like to be held; or if you feel generally unneeded, ignored, or rejected by your baby, have your infant evaluated by as many specialists as it takes to get to the root of the problem. A thorough evaluation will take into account how you respond to and interact with your baby, but many factors should be considered. They include problems with the brain, eyes, ears, digestion, metabolism, central nervous system, circulatory system, organ systems—any conditions that might make your baby withdrawn or miserable. Try to determine what is getting in the way of your baby's attachment to you so that you can reach for a more rewarding relationship.

Also keep in mind that some natural differences are to be expected and are not serious impediments to your child's forming an attachment to you. For example, you and your baby may have very different temperaments. If you are more active or outgoing and your baby tends to be more placid, you may worry that your child is too quiet when, really, he or she is fine—simply different from you. Or this child may be different from a sibling. If your older child loves to cuddle, but your preemie squirms and would rather be on the go than on your lap, you may worry about this when, really, your baby is just more active and independent than your older child. Also consider all the aspects of attachment. Maybe your squirmy one isn't a cuddler, but if she or he shows a definite preference for you and is soothed by you when upset, chances are that your relationship is solid.

If you are concerned about your baby's attachment to you and want an evaluation, do what is necessary to get one. You'll receive either reassurance or the help and support you need.

· · ·

Getting in Tune with Your Growing Baby

I started to enjoy him more and to get in lots of kisses and cuddles. Before then, I'd always been affectionate only up to the point where his muscle tone increased, and then I'd quickly stop. But he always had that "More! More!" look in his eyes. And I definitely had the "More! More!" feeling in my heart.
—*Anne*

As your preemie approaches his or her due date, you may notice major changes in alertness, activity level, and fussiness. Depending on when you bring your baby home, you may observe a few more weeks of "preterm" development and then see a shift as your baby reaches term and beyond.

Often, a change in your baby's routine, needs, preferences, or behaviors means a growth spurt. Fussiness, clinging, sleep disruptions, prolonged or more frequent feedings, or general discontent can signal that your baby is gathering steam to make a jump in physical, intellectual, emotional, or social maturation. Your baby may even regress slightly before advancing—taking one step back, then two steps forward. If you are breast-feeding, you could find yourself nursing for seemingly endless chunks of time (perhaps most of several evenings in a row) when your little one is stepping up your production to fuel physical growth. For some babies, teething is a stressful time. Fussiness can also occur when babies know what they want to accomplish, but need more practice before they can achieve it.

It may help to remember that most babies find comfort in predictable routines, such as when lunch is followed by cleanup, a story, and a nap. But infants vary in how well they respond to timed schedules. Some babies are such regular eaters and sleepers that they do best with regularly scheduled mealtimes, naptimes, and bedtimes. Others do best when parents play it by ear, because their eating and sleeping needs and times can vary daily. If your baby seems to respond best to schedules, try to meet those needs. If your baby's schedule is naturally variable, on the other hand, you can still impose set mealtimes and bedtimes, as long as you stay flexible. Allow for variations in appetite and provide makeup snacks. Expect some wakefulness and the need for unplanned catnaps.

If you have multiple babies, even as you are working to be responsive to their individual schedules, your little ones can cope with the introduction of some structure into their lives. In fact, with multiples, *you* might require some scheduling and structure to meet your own needs for downtime. You can gently nudge your babies into a reasonable routine (after the first few months at home) without being rigid or insensitive. Finding a balance between your babies' needs and your own is an ongoing parenting job.

Your baby's needs and behaviors are bound to change countless times over the weeks and months to come. With each growth spurt, you may first worry that something is wrong—is your baby getting sick? If you determine that your baby's behavior is not about illness, you can probably chalk it up to a developmental leap. Still, you may feel frustrated or discouraged when your "bag of tricks" doesn't soothe or entertain your baby as it used to. And at times like this, you may especially miss the ideas and encouragement you used to get from the NICU nurses.

Just remember that when your baby is making a developmental leap, you are required to do the same and expand your abilities as well. Indeed, the only constant in parenting is that you must continually decipher your growing child's emerging needs and discover new solutions and approaches. Also remember that you can turn to your support network of trusted friends, family, professionals, and other parents for ideas and encouragement. You don't have to figure it out all by yourself.

Here are some general tips for tuning in to your baby's needs:

- If you were able to practice tuning in and responding to your preterm baby's cues in the NICU, those efforts provide a strong foundation for getting in sync with your baby after discharge. You became sensitive to the levels of stimulation, activity, and holding that your little one needed in the first days or weeks. You can continue to use and refine your skills and intuitions at home.

- When your baby grows and changes, expect some struggle as you both adjust. After all, you must typically cope with extra fussiness and regression, plus figure out how to respond to your baby's new needs. It is important to remember that your struggles aren't a sign of your inadequacy but a sign of your baby's growth.

- At times, even as you try to follow your baby's lead, you may be frustrated because he or she can't use words to tell you what is causing this discomfort or unhappiness. There is a certain amount of trial and error involved in figuring out (or stumbling upon) what your infant needs.

With practice and as you get to know your baby, you'll become a more effective parent-detective.

- Turn to your trusted friends and advisors, but also tune in to your own intuitions while you keep pace with your baby's ever-changing needs.

Over the first few months, your anxiety, exhaustion, and confusion will lessen as you master your tuning-in skills and figure out what works. As your baby becomes more responsive, those little smiles will make all your struggles worthwhile and do wonders for your morale. The following sections offer specific suggestions you can add to your "bag of tricks."

Responding to Your Baby's Cues

Being home with your preemie, you'll discover that you spend most of your baby's waking hours attending to her needs. When your baby fusses or cries, your job is to figure out what she needs—and then to meet the need, soothing and quieting her. Your baby tells you what's wrong by her behavior. You can learn to read her cues and respond appropriately.

Your responsiveness is important because it builds your baby's trust in you as a nurturing caregiver. It also encourages her to stay calm and become interested in her surroundings, as well as responsive to you. This growing trust, calmness, and interest are important early developmental milestones for your baby. And having a trusting, calm, and interested baby gives you pleasure and confidence. Being able to calm your crying baby is not a mission impossible but a skill you acquire.

As you continuously observe your baby's preferences, sensitivities, and temperament, you'll learn how to soothe him and what keeps him happy and calm. You'll figure out that your baby loves certain noises, sights, touches, and positions, and gets fussy with certain other kinds of stimulation. You'll recognize how he signals his need to be fed, held, played with, and entertained. You'll master how to soothe him to sleep when he's tired. You'll find out whether your baby prefers to suck on a fist, a pacifier, or you.

Being responsive to your baby's cues does *not* mean that you must respond correctly and instantaneously every time. Sometimes you'll need a period of trial and error, and sometimes your baby will have to wait a minute or so. The key is to aim to minimize your little one's frustration. Natural and inevitable small delays won't interfere with your baby's learning that the world is safe and that you can be trusted. Of course, babies vary as to what they consider "minimal" frustration.

If your baby is easygoing, she may tolerate the wait while you figure out what she needs or when you put her off for a few minutes while you tend to something else. But if your baby is high spirited and sensitive, she will usually need your prompt intervention. For instance, if your baby becomes highly distressed very quickly, you'll discover that the faster you can respond to a need, the more effective your response will be in calming her. Otherwise, your baby will reach the point of physiological hyperarousal, or "meltdown." Then, even when you finally meet the original need, your baby will be past the point of no return and will require more effort to soothe. Learn your baby's threshold for frustration and respond accordingly.

Using a Basic-Needs List

Especially if your baby is extrasensitive, you might find it helpful to keep a list (mental or on paper) of basic needs and appropriate responses that you can quickly review. If one response doesn't soothe within five to ten seconds, try another one. Before you know it, you'll have hit the mark before your baby reaches the point of no return. A "basic-needs" list with responses might include the following:

- *Baby is hungry:* feed. (Always consider this option, no matter when your baby last ate.)
- *Baby wants to suck:* provide pacifier, breast, finger, etc.
- *Baby has a wet or full diaper:* change it.
- *Baby is bored:* provide sights and sounds that are interesting but not overwhelming to your baby, including your face and voice, music, and toys.
- *Baby wants to be held in a certain position:* try cradling in your arms, the football hold, or holding upright on your shoulder.
- *Baby wants to move:* try walking around, swaying, rocking, or putting your baby in a swing, rocking cradle, or vibrating chair.
- *Baby wants to be swaddled:* try loosely or firmly wrapping your baby in a light blanket. (If your baby hates to be undressed for a bath, try cleaning your baby in sections, wrapping all but the part that is being washed and working your way around the body.)
- *Baby wants to be soothed with skin-to-skin touch:* try gently massaging your baby, taking a warm bath with your little one, or kangaroo care.
- *Baby is chilled or too warm:* add or remove a layer.

- *Baby is in pain:* determine cause (e.g., scratchy seam, prickly tag, uncomfortable position, light/sunshine too bright, tummy ache, illness) and relieve if possible; if no cause is apparent, try holding, moving, warm bath (even take your little one into the tub with you), massage, kangaroo care, swaddling, or sucking as soothers. If your baby has colic, food intolerance is a likely suspect. If you are breast-feeding, exclude common allergens and gassy foods from your diet. (See suggestions in the "Breast Care for Breast-Feeding Mothers" section of Chapter 6.) If you're using formula, talk to your pediatrician about trying hypoallergenic, predigested protein, or soy-milk brands, or avoid "iron-fortified" kinds and see if your baby improves.
- *Baby is tired:* soothe baby to sleep. For some babies, this means being left alone in a quiet, dark room; for others, it means being held in comfy arms and sucking or nursing; for others, it means going into the swing, on a walk (in a sling or stroller), or for a drive—or listening to a humming dryer or a CD of nature sounds. (Ignore the "experts" who warn against letting your baby fall asleep in your presence. However your baby falls asleep easily is the *right* way for him or her!)
- *Baby is sick:* you may be able to tell by your baby's temperature, listlessness, or unsoothable discomfort that something isn't "right." Also, if none of the other situations fit or strategies work, your baby could be ill. Call your pediatrician and describe your baby's symptoms and behaviors, and your concerns.

Keep in mind that your baby's needs—and effective solutions and soothers—will change over time and with the situation. Most of all, your baby will benefit from *your* staying calm. Frantically rocking a baby never did anyone any good. Remember, also, that this is not a contest: you won't be penalized if your baby turns out to be inconsolable. Backup assistance also helps—because an inconsolable baby can test the mettle of the calmest parent. Let others help you help your baby.

Encouraging Attachment in the Face of Discomfort

Whether your baby is robust or fragile, it is inevitable that your little one will need treatments that are unpleasant or painful. Whether you are suctioning a stuffy nose, taking your infant to therapy sessions, or preparing your child for surgery, you cringe at the thought of making your child undergo any more discomfort. How can you be a nurturing advocate and also an agent of intervention? One mom put it this way, "It seems odd: I put saline in his nose and suction it, making him scream bloodcurdling screams, then I pick him up and comfort him." How can your child not see you as one of the "bad guys"?

Yet, your child still turns to you for comfort, showing a healthy attachment. This is because she or he can feel the caring in your caregiving, and you respond to her or his distress with empathy. Your benevolent intentions and your attempts to comfort are what count.

Indeed, many parents notice that their premature babies grow into remarkably empathic children, and parents wonder if it is because of the suffering their little ones have endured. But that's not it—it's because of the empathy and comfort they received from loving parents.

Finally, keep in mind that as children age, they scream less and cooperate more—their growing abilities to understand help them cope. But babies scream in protest, to express their discomfort, and to inform you that this had better not last long. To help you cope, try to see those screams as positive evidence that your baby is standing up for him- or herself, protesting (instead of passively accepting) pain, and communicating need.

Like most parents, especially those whose children have special needs, you'll be inspired by how your growing child copes with challenges and adversity. Your child's coping skills may be even better than your own!

I'm always amazed at how much Jacob has gone through and still goes through and what a wonderfully loving and calm little man he is. He has every right to be angry and spiteful, but he isn't. Both Hal and I share (take turns) with the truly nasty medical interventions (like blood draws for med levels). Right now, Hal is taking Jacob to physical therapy because I got burned out. But Jacob still adores both of us equally. As Jacob gets older, it's easier for him to understand why painful things are happening to him. It's harder on us (and him) when he realizes an operation is coming up and anticipates pain, but at least he understands why it has to happen. (Heck, I'm already obsessing over their next set of vaccinations.) —Julie

As Conor got close to going home, I had to learn to put in his nasogastric tube. This was the first hard thing I had to do to him. Then it just progressed. ... Just feeding this kid was torture to him. Not to mention fifteen doses of med-

ication for a kid who had major oral aversions, regular nebs, zillions of doctor's appointments and blood draws, and more. ... It soon got to the point where I was the only one Conor trusted to do things to him. I am always sure to hold him tightly, rub his feet or back, and sing softly in his ear to calm him for anything that bothers him.

Conor is the most forgiving child I've ever met. No matter how hysterical he would get during a procedure, he would always go over and hug the doctor or nurse and say "It's okay," as if to make them feel better. When his sister hurts him and I discipline her, he always runs to her defense. He is the sweetest thing ever. ... When he sees others suffer, he is so incredibly compassionate. He amazes me. —Laura

During the first year, Ali got a number of very resistant bacteria in her urinary tract and had to take a few medicines that she hated so intensely that each day was marked in four-hour battles, followed by hours of tears and sadness. I used to hate that I was forced to do this to her. I still can't quite describe the depths of my angst and despair. I was tormenting her, and it didn't seem to really help. I so worried about permanently damaging my relationship with this particular child, who has always been so intense and stubborn, yet fragile and reluctant to show affection.

I let her nurse well past her third birthday, something I never intended to have happen, yet a bond and emotional release for both of us prevented me from taking any action that wasn't totally lead by her. I took a god-awful amount of criticism about her lengthy nursing. I even wondered myself (quietly and privately) if perhaps I'd lost my always-tentative grip on sanity ... but for me, this was my way to prevent permanent damage to my maternal relationship with my daughter.

I know for us this turned out to be a real salvation. At age six, she still talks about when she nursed. From the language she uses and the times she recalls it, I know it's fundamental in the way she thinks of me. I'm glad, because I'd hate to think of "Mom" being conjured up by the thought of vile antibiotics being forced down [my child's] throat.

I go on each day believing that my children will take all of the experiences of their childhood into consideration when deciding how they feel about their mother ... and that as long as I continue to lead with my heart, in the end it will be all good. —Sheila

• • •
452

Juggling the Needs of Multiples

Your twins, triplets, or more won't get the vast amounts of undivided attention you could give to a single baby. That's not necessarily a bad thing. Just as there are certain benefits to being raised as an only child, there are certain benefits to being raised with siblings—especially siblings of the same age. They get to experience the magic of the "multiple bond." And as your little ones grow, instead of relying solely on you for interaction, they will also have each other.

When there truly isn't enough of you to go around, you can ask for and rely on other caregivers to help you. In fact, babies can benefit from having more than one or two consistent caregivers. Instead of focusing on the potential drawbacks to your babies of being a twin, a triplet, or more, focus on the special benefits.

Don't spend time worrying about treating your babies alike. It's far more important to treat them as individuals and provide them with what they each require. If you are worried that one baby might feel rejected when you spend more time with the other baby, rest assured that your infants are not keeping track. If your babies feel that they are valued and responded to as unique beings, they won't feel deprived and notice who gets what or how much. The bottom line is that each child is getting a "good enough" amount of just what she or he needs.

As you settle in at home, you may discover challenges you had not expected. For instance, it is normal to notice both your babies' similarities and their differences. In fact, you should *expect* differences between your babies. All infants have distinct preferences, personalities, and developmental paths. Some differences may be striking and others subtle. As a parent of multiple preemies, you face a special challenge. Your sensitivity to your babies' developmental and medical risks complicates your comparisons between babies. If some developmental or temperamental differences concern you, ask yourself whether you are interpreting normal variations between children as problematic—especially if you are hypervigilant about development or if you want your multiples to be similar to one another. If one or more of your babies are having marked difficulty, you might feel anxious, angry, or sad that your children are not progressing together. Try to focus on each baby as an individual and appreciate each baby's strengths. If there are weaknesses that need to be addressed, your positive focus on and appreciation of each child will help

* * *

you guide your little ones without undermining them.

Also be aware that each child will have traits and go through phases that you will enjoy, as well as traits and phases that will be more challenging to tolerate. That you may prefer some traits more than others is only human nature. However, some parents find themselves clearly preferring, attending to, or identifying with one baby more than the other(s), and that is a concern.

If you do favor one baby more than another, it is important to admit your feelings so that you can work free of them. Take a close look at your assessment of the less-favored baby, identifying positive points and downplaying negative ones. Get to know the whole little person inside the fragile body or behind the funny quirks. Also take a look at your vision of the "ideal" baby. You may need to let go of unrealistic expectations—and the disappointment associated with them. Expect each of your babies to have his or her own strengths, weaknesses, and idiosyncrasies. If your favoritism persists despite your best efforts to compensate, seek professional counseling.

Family members who play favorites can be a problem as well. In response, you may feel fiercely protective of the "rejected" one or you may identify with either the "chosen" one or the "rejected" one. Mixing up who you are and who the baby is not only hinders that child's sense of self but also puts a wedge between you and your other baby(ies). Counseling can help you sort out this situation.

Finally, if one or more of your babies died, you may have mixed feelings as you watch the others grow up. Grateful to have them, you will also be reminded of and miss the baby(ies) you won't get to raise. Watching your multiples get to know one another, you may imagine the sibling relationships they will miss and the losses they must also endure. Bearing this grief while raising surviving multiples can be overwhelming. (See Chapter 11 for support in dealing with the death of one or more infants.) Find people who understand. Turn to them when you need to talk or just to be with someone who will let you feel your grief as well as your joy.

Points to Remember

- Settling in with your preemie can be a time filled with joy—as well as anxiety and exhaustion.
- It is normal to need a period of reorientation when you come home with your preemie, even if this baby is not your first. Parenting a premature baby is different, and you are a different parent after having a preemie.
- Recognize that your baby may have a period of reorientation, too. Find ways to ease this transition from NICU to home for both of you.
- Being attuned to your baby's ever-changing needs can be challenging. With time and practice, you can develop the skills you need to be responsive and soothing to your little one.
- Settling in at home with multiples is challenging under any circumstances. Attending to the various needs of each baby, as well as your own needs, is quite a balancing act. Getting to know each baby as an individual takes time. As you settle in and get the hang of it, though, you will learn their preferences for feeding, sleeping, soothing, and activity, and find you have more energy to devote to each child.

CHAPTER FOURTEEN

Meeting Caregiving Challenges at Home

As you settle in, get reoriented, and get in tune with your baby, you will experience the joy of having your little one home, at last. However, just as you will experience the rewards, there may also be some caregiving challenges to meet, challenges that you may or may not have expected. This chapter explores the feelings of vulnerability that most parents of preemies encounter, as well as support and practical suggestions around managing feeding issues and the ongoing medical interventions that some premature babies require.

Coping with Feelings of Vulnerability

Vulnerability and Preemie Parenthood

For most parents of preemies, some sense of vulnerability lingers after homecoming. Many parents find themselves vigilantly watching for any signs of trouble, ever ready to intervene and fearing that the saga of prematurity will never end.

> *Hypervigilance—I'm not sure it ever completely goes away. I think I have developed an awe for my children, that they can overcome anything, but a fear that they may still have a lot to overcome. As soon as one of them wheezes, I*

am taken right back to the panic of the ICU. I think I will always be afraid that I might lose them still. Every parent must feel that to some degree, but I know I probably check occasionally [to see] if they are still breathing.
—Stephie

Feeling vulnerable is a natural reaction to what you've been through. The more fragile your baby was at birth and the more precarious the hospital course, the more likely you will be to continue to see your child as vulnerable—regardless of the current outcome. You may pay close attention to your baby's breathing, sleeping, and eating. You may watch anxiously for developmental milestones and work overtime to shield your little one from infection.

Like most preemie parents, we were quite obsessed with her "numbers"—how much she ate and how much she weighed! I kept charts of everything! It was also weeks before I was comfortable while she slept. I had to check on her constantly, to be sure she was breathing. She visited the doctor weekly for a while, to be certain she was gaining sufficient weight. We also took her to a developmental clinic on a regular basis. —Renee

*I will admit that I tend to be on the neurotic side of things ... but this whole experience with Nicholas has just about pushed me over the edge. I am constantly jumpy with him. If he doesn't eat well one day, I watch him like a hawk and have everyone up in arms in case there's something wrong with him. Whenever we go out to the store, I clutch him to me as if I'm afraid someone might breathe on him, which in all truthfulness, is exactly what I'm afraid of.
—Sterling*

I do remember being very paranoid about her health. A small child once tried to touch her fingers, and I almost screamed at him. I was always thinking, "Get away from my baby!!!" This was tough because we had our own toddler at home. But we always had her wash her hands before "playing" with her sister. It really bothered me when visitors would not understand. I guess you have to have been there yourself. One friend came over with her two-year-old daughter, who wanted to "touch" the baby. I asked her please not to. My friend's response was, "Oh, she is very good with babies." I wanted to scream at her, "This is not the issue, you idiot!!!" Germs are very scary to preemie moms. —Linda

Acknowledging the Risks When you express concern about the risks of infection for your baby, others may suggest that you are being "overprotective." However, your vigilance is justified: parents of preemies have some very serious issues to worry about. When some of your friends and family tell you to relax and treat your baby "normally," they are really just expressing their wish that your baby were a regular, hardy kid. But wishing does not make it so. It is your job to be mindful of the real risks and to take precautions that will make a difference for your baby. It is also your job to be mindful of your baby's growing resilience and strengths, and to avoid impeding your child with your needless or unfounded worry. (For more on this, see "Vulnerable Child Syndrome" in Chapter 17.)

Separating Real from Imagined Threats Distinguishing between reasonable fear and unreasonable worry can sometimes be difficult. You may sense that you overreact sometimes. You may know that your sense of vulnerability has been heightened by trauma. But your baby *did* spend time in intensive care and *does* need special handling. *How* special is something you must determine with input from trusted advisors (pediatrician, friends, family). It is perfectly appropriate to protect your infant from real risk. Doing so is not being "overprotective"—it is being careful. (For more on protecting medically fragile preemies, see the next section in this chapter.)

No matter what you do, though, your control over your baby's health is limited. This can make you feel intensely vulnerable.

> *I was very scared that Alison would get sick if she came into contact with someone who was sick. Since she was so little, this could have been deadly. It bothered me that everyone insisted on holding her (which we said no to many, many times) and getting in her face. —Stacy*

If reasonable protective measures don't calm you, and you feel constantly anxious about your baby's health or development, your struggle may be less about the actual risks to your baby and more about your own feelings of defenselessness. Here are some suggestions for feeling less intensely raw and powerless once your baby is home. (For more ideas and support, see "Getting to the Bottom of Your Grief" in Chapter 3, as well as "Protective Parenting" in Chapter 15 and "Managing Heightened Vigilance" in Chapter 17.)

- Acknowledge your feelings without trying to justify them. You have been through a grueling ordeal. You don't have to defend your feelings.
- Try to define what you fear most. Doing so can help you sort out what is generalized anxiety and what is specific and potentially preventable danger.
- Gather information about what you fear. The more you know, the less you'll be haunted by unknowns. Then you'll have more energy to attend to real risks and implement realistic protective strategies.
- Ask your baby's health care providers what they consider to be the real dangers to your baby and question them about your worries. Figure out sensible precautions that will reassure but not consume you.
- Remind yourself that needless worrying and wondering can consume enormous amounts of time and effort—all of which can be much better spent either enjoying your baby or nurturing yourself.
- Wondering "what if?" can be a normal aspect of mastering the ordeal you and your baby have been through. Some anxiety is constructive if it motivates you to do your best to protect and nurture your baby. But if you feel obsessed with the "what-ifs," you deserve to get relief. Find a mental health professional who can help you sort through these painful thoughts and feelings. If your distress persists, your therapist may discuss the potential benefits of using medication along with therapy.
- Separate imagination from reality. Are your anxieties based on imaginary scenarios about what *might* happen or are they based on what you have observed and what is actually happening? Calm the worries that lurk only in your imagination and pay attention to those worries and intuitions that are related to things that are really happening. For example, are you anxious because you know it's flu season and you can *imagine* the shoppers in your aisle sneezing near your baby while you're in the grocery store? Or are you anxious because you've spotted someone who is sneezing, and your intuition tells you that this person is highly contagious? Spend your energy being vigilant about what *is* happening around you, and take the steps you need to safeguard your baby. Remember that your concern is what makes you an attentive parent, as long as that concern doesn't overpower your perceptions or your common sense.
- Ask your baby's health care providers for an honest assessment of your

baby's resilience, strength, and ability to overcome germs or other challenges. If you're the only one who feels your baby is fragile, ask yourself whether this is because others are clueless about the actual risks or because your baby is perhaps more robust than you realize. Let yourself entertain the possibility that your baby is not in jeopardy. When you look at your growing baby, do you still see that tiny, frail infant in the hospital? Let yourself see that strength. As your baby becomes robust, allow yourself to trust that progress.

- Don't be afraid to get skilled help and respite. Even a few visits from a home nurse can be immeasurably reassuring.
- Let your love come through along with your worries. Try not to let worry take the place of loving.
- Remember that your child is on his or her own journey. You are not the one who has the power to change the ultimate course. Let go of your urge to have all the control, and you won't feel so powerless.
- Remember that your baby is a survivor in the strongest sense of the word! In the absence of evidence to the contrary, trust that if your little one could survive as a tiny infant in the NICU, she or he has already survived the toughest tests.
- Give yourself the benefit of the doubt—that over time, and as your baby demonstrates health and growth, you'll relax more.

She was so tiny that when she cried you could barely hear her. That changed as she gained weight, and I think that was a defining moment for me—being able to actually hear her let out a rebel yell! —Janet

We made it through these first few months without any major sicknesses, and I am almost ready to let her catch something. I am not nearly as neurotic as I was those first few weeks. —Linda

Now I feel better because he's growing and he's getting tougher, and now I've seen him get sick a couple of times this winter with a bad cold or a stomach virus and it hasn't affected him too badly. Like he reacted as a regular child. He's grown enough to cope with all sorts of germs, and he's ready to go out into the world. —Gallice

Riley had an apnea monitor at home for nine months. Even after she passed her home apnea test, I was scared to death to give it up. I didn't call the monitor people to collect it because it was reassuring, peace of mind, that if she stopped breathing, the monitor would go off. So that first night after she passed that test, she goes to bed, and I left the leads on because she still had that monitor and we were still gonna use it until I was comfortable with her not using it. ... In the middle of the night, I hear beep beep beep beep, and I look at her, and she's got the leads in her hand, all three of them, and she's just holding them. And I think, all right, she's telling me something. She knows that she doesn't need these any longer. She must know that she's okay, and I've got to—as much as it's against everything I believe in—I've got to trust her natural instinct in this. So I did. And I don't know if she ever stopped breathing in the night. That night I was up a thousand times, looking, listening. But it was a sign when she took those leads off. —Pam

The Medically Fragile Baby

If your baby continues to struggle with significant medical issues, your feelings of vulnerability are based on these ongoing needs. Your baby's health may not inspire much confidence. Still, many of the suggestions in the previous section can help you face your feelings about your child's situation and find ways to cope. Even if your baby is truly vulnerable, you can manage your anxiety by keeping perspective and holding on to reality. Doing so will help you be a more effective advocate in getting your baby the care he or she needs, rather than spending precious energy on unnecessary worry or precautions.

Isolation as a Protective Strategy—and Its Effects If your baby is at risk for developing complications from ordinary cold or flu germs, your neonatologists and pediatrician may advise you to protect your baby. After all, there are very real dangers out there, and you may worry about your ability to keep your baby safe from disease, especially if you have older children at home. You must take precautions to protect your little one from anything that could cause serious illness, possible complications, and rehospitalization. Your sense of vulnerability and responsibility can be intense.

My biggest fear was that Sean would contract RSV [respiratory syncytial virus], be readmitted to the hospital, and die. The fear that bothered me most was that my husband would bring something from work. Living with that fear was tough. —Maxine

If your baby comes home in the summer, you may be able to enjoy a few relatively "germ-free" months. Because viruses can spread more easily when people are confined indoors, summer is a time to taste freedom and reconnect as you share your baby with friends, family, and neighbors. If you're coming out of a long winter of isolation, you may take a deep breath of relief, having less fear of infection and the chance to reduce your degree of watchfulness. But when winter approaches, the doctors may remind you that it's time to "hibernate" while germs proliferate in enclosed, crowded public spaces. What a discouragement when you may have just started to feel "normal"!

You may have difficulty complying with quarantine, because although isolation is good for your baby, it's probably not good for you emotionally or socially. First, there's the loneliness you may have to cope with as you strive to protect your baby. You may have relationships with other parents and families whose company you value and enjoy, but when the weather turns and play-dates have to move indoors, you must decline. If your baby comes home from the NICU during cold and flu season, you may feel as if you've proceeded from one confined space straight to another. You can't even invite your neighbor over because she has a young child with an always-dripping nose. During the year-end holidays, when you're accustomed to celebrating with others, you may feel even more frustrated and lonely. You may resent your own need to avoid public places so that you don't bring home nasty germs. You know that doing so is in your baby's best interest, but it's still aggravating.

What will be most difficult to give up is his playgroup. He will miss the kids, and I'll miss the contact with moms who have a similar parenting philosophy. That will be the biggest hardship. —Maxine

Many parents confront another battle—dealing with people who disrespect their precautions. Instead of offering understanding and compassion, some people may accuse you of being paranoid, excessively restrictive, or obsessed with germs. Others may resist your precautions head-on instead of simply complying. People may "forget" to tell you about their sore throat or

• • •

463

Meeting Caregiving Challenges at Home

claim that they have allergies, adding to your fear that your baby will be unknowingly—and unnecessarily—exposed to germs. It is normal to feel angry and resentful that you must justify your legitimate need to protect your baby.

I felt like the world was full of ignorant people—when they treated us like we were overdoing it. —Clark

I couldn't believe [it] when my nurse friend told us our pediatrician was way too excessive—it was time to treat him like a normal baby. Then she told us the hospital had made us paranoid. —Kerry

My friends thought I should be back at work with my son in a day care and getting on with my life when he was still so small and vulnerable and subject to RSV [respiratory syncytial virus]. We even opted out of family celebrations at Christmas because we didn't feel like our son could handle the stimulus and the exposure to various illnesses, particularly RSV. I felt like everyone thought I was being overcautious. —Terri

You may struggle with how to discourage visits by family or friends who do not comprehend the risk your baby faces. Although it can be scary to discuss the possibilities, you may get more cooperation and support from friends and family if you point out to them that your baby could die if infected. Tina told people point blank, "They are preemies, and RSV [respiratory syncytial virus] can kill a preemie."

No matter how diplomatic you are, some misguided people will even be offended. Some will feel that you are rejecting *them* instead of just their germs. Others will feel insulted that you think they even *have* germs or that their germs could really hurt your baby. Remind them that germs don't care that their carrier "means well." No matter how much they love your baby, their germs can still be very dangerous. If they still take offense, remember, that's their problem, not yours. In the choice between protecting your baby and protecting the feelings of others, your priority is clearly protecting your baby. If others can't appreciate, understand, or share that priority, then you may very well need to avoid them along with their germs. You might find it preferable to be quarantined in your house with your baby than to deal with these problem individuals. (For more on dealing with others, see Chapter 20.)

Tips for Coping with Isolation You have very real needs for support, companionship, and respite from baby care. There are creative ways to meet those needs. Here are some suggestions for coping with isolation:

- Develop a supportive network of friends and caregivers who can acknowledge that following the doctor's recommendations and protecting your baby is vital. The people who understand and respect your judgement about isolating your baby will be the ones who will go out of their way to help you continue to feel connected with the outside world.
- Remind yourself that isolating your baby from germs is a small price to pay to avoid serious illness, hospitalization, or even death. You know that any of these possibilities are far more stressful, draining, isolating, and tragic than vigilant hand washing and quarantine. Remembering these facts can help you keep your priorities straight.
- Give yourself permission to be upset that you must treat your baby with extra vigilance. Allow yourself to feel frustrated with this situation and sad that your social life with your new baby is different than you had anticipated.
- Decide on rules for who can visit and under what circumstances. Some people may act like spoiled children and test your rules, but if you stand firm, they'll get the message that the rules apply to them, too.
- Allow yourself to enjoy visits from people whom you deem "safe."
- If you have a reliable, healthy sitter or family members to depend on, ask them to come in once or twice a week. Use this time to enjoy their company or to leave the house for an hour or two.
- Use the phone *a lot* to keep in contact with supportive friends. Set up a regular phone date for the times you and each friend are most available. Dates will give you something to count on and look forward to.
- Take your baby to the window to show to friends.
- Join an online support group (for parents of preemies, mothers, or breast-feeding, for example) or become active in an online chat room.
- Recognize that this period of isolation is a relatively short part of your life. It will end soon enough.
- Instead of dwelling on the disadvantages of isolation, focus on the potential advantages. You can, for example:
  - ▲ Spend endless hours enjoying your precious baby
  - ▲ Form a stronger, closer bond with your little one
  - ▲ "Make up" for the lost time when your baby was hospitalized

- ▲ Develop your parenting style without criticism from others
- ▲ Build confidence in your parenting skills
- ▲ Celebrate with a small "coming-out" party once isolation is lifted

It can be hard to imagine, but as your child becomes less vulnerable over time, you will begin to feel less vulnerable as well.

We kept Josh and Evan in for a long time, except for doctors' appointments. We were in doctors' offices so frequently that I finally decided, if Josh and Evan could be in a doctor's office, they could be at a person's house or in a mall. —Stephie

I think this is the hardest thing for me, balancing a respectful caution for the risks with a healthy desire to treat Gabe like any child. I suppose I will err on both sides from time to time—but hopefully, never to the risk of his health and safety. —Maren

The remainder of this chapter examines the challenges some parents of preemies face in dealing with medical conditions that linger after the NICU, including feeding challenges, respiratory complications, and rehospitalization.

Feeding Issues

After homecoming, feeding issues may become less intense, or they may remain as problematic as they were in the NICU. If you are breast-feeding (or trying to), review Chapter 6 for tips on the physical aspects. Also, whether you're trying to breast-feed or not, reread the "Feeding Issues" section of Chapter 9: much of that information and support may continue to be useful to you after you bring your baby home. You may also want to look ahead to "Growth Charts, Developmental Timetables, and Trusting Your Child's Path" in Chapter 16. If your baby relies on tube-feedings, turn to "Coping with Feeding Complications" later in this chapter.

Breast-Feeding

Some preemies are able to complete the transition from partial to full breast-feeding. Others' nutritional needs will be met by some combination of breast milk and formula, bottle-feeding and breast-feeding. If you have your heart set on total breast-feeding, your baby's transition to that goal may continue after homecoming. (For helpful tips on this, refer back to the bullet points in "Meeting the Challenges of Breast-Feeding in the NICU" in Chapter 9. Also refer to other books listed in "Books for Parents of Preemies" and "Breast-Feeding" listed in the Appendix C: Resources.) If your baby completes the transition, it can bring about a sense of accomplishment—and normalcy. As Sheila points out, "For mothers who came through the alienating world of the NICU, nothing could be more important than putting that relationship [with the baby] back together the way it *could* have been if a thousand tiny turns had happened differently."

If putting your baby to the breast is important to you but your baby continues to struggle with it, you may feel a deep sense of disappointment. Even if you are dedicated to long-term pumping and your baby thrives on bottles of your breast milk, you grieve for the *nursing*.

> *Breast-feeding has become a very sore subject! I have just come to the conclusion that Charlotte is not going to be able to nurse. I had been planning all along to breast-feed—even with her early birth—and I have been pumping religiously eight times a day since then! (I'm still pumping.) I'm not one to give up, but it doesn't seem possible anymore, and I need to let go of this struggle. And, this is yet another loss I've had to face—first losing the last trimester of my pregnancy and now, the experience of nursing. It's really hard for me. —Kate*

> *I had the hardest time adjusting to the reality that she wouldn't be able to nurse and that I would have to pump for a long time. I have coped pretty well because it was easy for me to do whatever was best for her health. There have been times, though, that the grief returns now and then. I talk to other women about it—my husband is wonderful but it is hard for him to understand why this is sad for me. —Mary*

Of all the topics covered in this book, breast-feeding is one of the most passionate for mothers, perhaps because it can feel so central to a nurturing mother-infant relationship. This book encourages breast-feeding. However, when the transition to full breast-feeding doesn't work out for moms, we also encourage *flexibility*.

In coming to terms with the situation, it helps to stop idealizing breast milk or total breast-feeding. Breast milk may be the superior food, but formula is also excellent nutrition for many preemies. Total breast-feeding is convenient, but bottle-feeding—even tube-feeding—is quite manageable too. And breast-feeding is just one of many ways you can connect with your little one. You can be a wonderful, nurturing mother and have a close, loving relationship with your baby without total breast-feeding.

It can also help to adjust your definition of "breast-feeding" to fit your special circumstances. Think of it this way: if you are pumping, you are breast-feeding. If you are just pumping part-time, you are breast-feeding. If your baby suckles at your breast but gets most or all of her or his food from a bottle, you are breast-feeding. Breast-feeding is what works for you, your breasts, and your baby.

It is also helpful to broaden your views of what it means to feed and nurture your baby. If you are struggling to breast-feed, keep the bigger picture in mind: forging a warm, intimate, loving relationship with your baby. If feeding is becoming a source of pain, take the pressure off yourself and your baby. You can take a break for a time and simply pump and bottle-feed breast milk. Hold on to the hope that as your baby matures, he or she may eventually take to the breast. However you feed your baby, focus on the cuddling, the visual and vocal interactions, and your enjoyment of and relaxation with your little one.

Even if your baby doesn't get enough to eat from breast-feeding alone, you can feed from the bottle and offer your breasts as the effective pacifiers they can be, even if you quit pumping and feed your baby formula. You can do this even if your baby doesn't suckle, but simply calms to the skin-to-skin contact with the soft warmth of your breasts.

I did nurse Gabe but also used a bottle to supplement calories. I've had to work hard to get over some of my own self-imposed guilt over not being able to nurse alone, and that he weaned himself so early in favor of the bottle. The last thing we need is other people thinking their "breast-only" soapbox is appropriate for everyone. —Maren

We need to stop repeating the notion that you must choose between putting your child to your breast or giving him or her a bottle. ... There is no [either-or]

• • •

choice, except our continuing decision to see it as such. You need to feed your child, and you need to nuture your child, and you should be encouraged to use absolutely everything at your disposal to do it. Whether your child does nothing more than "comfort-suck" at your breast and receives all his or her food from a bottle is not anyone's business but yours and that child in your arms. You shouldn't be told, "Well, if you're not going to use your breasts as sole nutrition, then there's no point." —Sheila

Finally, let go of the belief that if you had just tried hard enough, done the "right" things, or figured out the way to make it work, you and your baby would have been able to rely on breast-feeding. Perhaps you *were* able to exclusively breast-feed and would have been a smashing success at it—except that your baby didn't hold up her or his side of the bargain. Forgive your little one for not wanting or being able to take you up on your loving offer and give yourself credit for being responsive to your baby.

I always thought I was the one who would decide if Bronwen would breast-feed or not. Wrong! Bronwen decided. I can't make her do things. I can only give her the choice. When I realized who was in control of the breast-feeding, I was able to relax, and I felt a whole lot better. Then when I decided to stop trying, I didn't feel quite so bad about it. Bronwen was telling me she couldn't do it. Eventually, I listened. —Nola

It finally became very clear that clinging to breast-feeding was more for me than for him, that I needed to give up that dream and concentrate solely on my son and his health. I still mourn the fact that we didn't have a breast-feeding relationship, but I look at my son and am so grateful for his existence that I can't focus on how he's fed. —Tara

Giving Up the Pump

I cannot emphasize enough how emotionally painful it was for me to give up the idea of breast-feeding. My mother-in-law was very distressed about my decision and suggested I just keep pumping. But I had learned to hate the sight of that pump, and I felt resentful that she was making such a painful decision even more painful for me. Thankfully, my husband and my own mother supported my decision. However, I still hear those voices of well-meaning friends saying, "Well, didn't you try this?" or "Didn't you try that?" The truth is I had tried so many different things and worked so hard at it that my poor baby started tensing up whenever I came near her. That's when I knew that I had to give up. —Rebekah

If your baby isn't nursing and you decide, for whatever reason, to stop pumping, this can be a tremendous loss to grieve. You may feel a mixture of relief, regret, and mostly sorrow. If you also have feelings of failure, do remember that as you implement the feeding method that works best, your baby senses your care and love.

I was even more set on breast-feeding my son due to the premature birth. This was very important to me, since I felt I was doing what I could to help him survive. I expressed for six months and felt very positive. But he developed colic after coming home, and it turned out to be in response to my breast milk. That was when we had to go to formula. I felt bad because it was another rejection toward my capabilities of being a good mother, but my husband and the doctors were very assertive about the fact that it was not my fault. —Andrea

I had always planned on breast-feeding my babies. But with Nicholas, as small as he was and in need of supplementation for as long as he was, it was just too hard for him to nurse. ... When I brought Nicholas home, pumping was almost impossible. The stress of having him home and trying to breast-feed while still trying to find time to pump was just too much. Eventually my milk supply dropped too low to even feed him for a day. I didn't really let myself get too bogged down in how disappointed I was that I couldn't nurse my baby, until he was home for five weeks and still not nursing. Making that decision to finally stop the pumping and let my milk dry up still makes me cry. (And if I had known that formula feeding was going to be this disgusting—he spits it up all over the place—and expensive, I would have kept pumping for the rest of the year.) But I just convinced myself that it was in Nicholas's best interest not to push him. I had enough milk frozen while he was hospitalized to last until he was almost five months. That's a lot longer than most term babies get to breast-feed, so I just tell myself that I did the best I could for him, gave him all I could, and he's better off for it. —Sterling

Many mothers who decide to stop pumping hear from well-meaning family and friends, advising them on the benefits of breast milk and the rewards of persistence. When you're grieving and regretful, it can be difficult to handle the comments and criticisms of others second-guessing your approach to feeding. Their statements just feed into the frustration and power-lessness that you may already be feeling about the situation. Maren plans her responses, "just to avoid getting into a defensive position." Here are some examples:

I could simply say: "I don't think you understand the barriers for a preemie to be able to breast-feed. Do you have any idea how difficult it is for a premature infant to learn how to suck, swallow, and breathe all at the same time?" Or: "You know, I don't really care how my child is being fed, by breast, by bottle, by tube, as long as she is getting enough nutrition to grow and her brain to develop." With people who are in my life for good, I take the teacher position and say: "Neurologically, eating by mouth is a very difficult thing to learn when your nervous system is very immature. Most preemies need to start feeding by mouth while [they are] still in the NICU, in order to go home, oftentimes weeks before their actual due date, still [weighing] only a few pounds, with wires and monitors and IVs [attached]. Breast-feeding in the NICU is a victory, not the norm. The mother's flow can reduce due to fatigue, stress, pumping. [Preterm] babies can't suck hard enough to get enough nutri-tion from the breast. Bottle-feeding is often required because a child has to have more than twenty calories per ounce due to lung disease or other complica-tions." Sometimes a photo of the child in the NICU is enough for them to realize they are in over their heads. [It's] worth a thousand words.

Or, the shock response: "We're lucky she/he is eating by mouth at all. We could be feeding him/her with tubes down the throat or permanently implanted in the stomach." Or, for those stubborn and insensitive people who don't ever get a clue, lay it on the line: "Since you have a healthy, full-term child, I know it is difficult for you to understand how trivial the bottle-versus-breast argument is to me at this point. I am simply grateful for my child's just being alive." —Maren

If you're struggling with feelings of failure and regret over your decision to stop pumping, you might try letting go of any "shoulds" you are carrying around. For example, "I should have tried harder to breast-feed" or "I should have been able to provide more breast milk." First, recognize that these "shoulds" are beliefs that you adopt, and they become something you repeatedly tell yourself. But these "shoulds" are only beliefs, not truths. Still, they have the power to stimulate feelings of inadequacy, anxiety, and sadness around the ways you are feeding your baby. To stop the "shoulds," catch them as they are going through your mind. Imagine what it would be like to step away from them, away from regret, and toward acceptance—of yourself, your baby, and the situation. What would it feel like to think, "I am feeding my baby the way he needs me to feed him"? Take your time and sit with this. How does it feel? What else do you notice? As you come to accept the reality of the situation, the blame and regret will fade. (For more support on giving up pumping, see "If You Must Stop Providing Breast Milk" in Chapter 9.)

Your Baby's Weight Gain

While your baby is in the hospital, the medical staff supervises his or her eating and weight gain. If your baby has difficulty tolerating feedings, the nurses will identify the problem and take steps to remedy it. Once your baby comes home, however, attention to these details rests largely on your shoulders.

Your baby's ability to eat can generate a great deal of worry. You want to be sure that your child is progressing, both in how much he or she is eating and gaining and, later, in how well he or she is managing solid foods. You should know that breast-fed babies gain weight at a slower, but not inferior, rate in comparison to formula-fed babies, and that many growth charts are based on formula feeding. Be sure you know to whom your doctor is comparing your baby. Ideally it will be to others of similar gestational age at birth, similar hospital course, and similar feeding method.

Weight gain is loaded with meaning for parents of preemies. You will most likely consider weight gain a salient measure of your baby's health, growth, and robustness—and thus of your competence as a parent. Many preemies tend to be smaller and thinner than their full term peers, and it is natural for you to want your infant to grow out of the "preemie look" and become a typical chubby baby. You want your tiny baby to "fill out" in order to eradicate this reminder of her or his early birth and your pain.

If your little one remains in the lower percentiles, try to examine your feelings about your baby's weight. You want to ensure that your approach to the weight gain issue is clearly about your child's needs, not about your own anxieties and grief. Here are some suggestions:

- Face your feelings so that you can respond with emotional awareness instead of just reacting.
- Give yourself permission to trust your child's individual growth curve.
- Let go of standards that don't fit.
- Focus more on your child's health and improving feeding abilities than on the amount of weight gained.
- Focus more on providing your child with nutritious foods than on the amount of food he or she eats.
- Look at the week as a whole if you must measure intake for each meal.
- Ask your pediatrician or a nutritionist for information about nutritional requirements. Many toddlers and young children need amazingly small amounts of food because they aren't growing as much as they were as infants. Also remember that appetites vary widely among children; what one child requires can be far too much for another child.
- Avoid power struggles (which usually backfire). Allow feeding to be your child's domain. Give your little one a chance to explore and enjoy food.

Most important, don't let concerns about weight gain rob you of your ability to enjoy your child and to have a warm, easy relationship, especially around feeding times. And when you can't help but worry, get professional support.

Consultations with an occupational therapist and a nutritionist were very *helpful for this! Now, we obsess less, and she has started to gain weight again!* —Mary

About slow (halting) weight gain—it is so hard to be constantly reminded of it. I know how it can be like this black cloud hanging over you and your child, sort of shutting out the rest of the world and the rest of the joys of motherhood.

It made me so sad and mad at the same time, worrying all the time about Gabe's size, trying to feed him when he just didn't care. I felt like I had been robbed of the simple joy of being a mom. It interrupted my days and nights. And there was a time when I was hardly aware of him as a whole child with a whole life of bright lights and laughter and joy.

• • •

Please try to let it be sometimes—not that you will stop searching for answers or doing everything you can, but just in your thoughts and in your heart, try to let it go for periods of time. Just tell yourself that, in the long run, if your child is going to be a very small person for the rest of his life, you and he can live with that and still be grateful for everything else.

It is not easy to do sometimes, or to maintain that attitude, but your worry and anxiety will only exhaust you and cut you off from your joys and will not make him grow. ... It seems so simplistic as I write it, but when I was able to do this, to put all my worry in a different place outside my heart and head, and just have fun being Gabriel's mommy, it was like the world was twice as bright and Gabriel was just fine and beautiful just as he was. No matter what was coming down the road, I was so in love and so grateful for being given the gift of being his mommy. —Maren

If your concerns about weight gain are tied to any other physiological symptoms, such as aversion to eating or drinking, continual fussiness, vomiting, listlessness, or anything else that makes you suspect undiagnosed problems, consult with your baby's health care team. (For more information and support on these issues, see "Coping with Feeding Complications" later in this chapter, as well as "Grappling with Oral Feeding Difficulties" in Chapter 16.

Managing the Needs of a Medically Fragile or Technology-Dependent Baby

I want to give her a normal babyhood—without all the tubes and wires and various other contraptions that we have hanging around here. And I hate, hate, hate the fact that I can't. —Brooke

I was very worried about being unable to provide adequate care for a baby with medical needs. I didn't feel qualified to be home with him at first. —Terri

If your baby comes home with medical needs and equipment, you may have mixed feelings. You may be grateful that technology makes it possible for your baby to come home, and overall, managing the caregiving may feel easier than managing the hospitalization and separation from your little one. Still, at times you may feel intimidated by some aspects of the caregiving, your home can feel like an extension of the NICU, and you can feel more like a physical or respiratory therapist than a parent. Two of the most common medical issues that follow preemies home from the hospital are eating and breathing. These common medical complications are discussed here, and there is more on feeding issues in the "Grappling with Oral Feeding Difficulties" section of Chapter 16. For information on other developmental and disability concerns, turn to Chapters 15–18.

Coping with Chronic Respiratory Complications

"I wish I could breathe for you" is many parents' closely held wish for newly born preemies struggling to breathe. When you recovered from the initial shock that your newborn had respiratory complications, you were probably grateful for the technology and hopeful that it would work further miracles. In fact, the array of oxygen delivery devices surrounding your baby could have given the illusion that everything was completely under control.

It is natural to assume that after some time on respiratory support your infant will be weaned, with no sign of ever having been in distress. But sometimes it's not that easy: the medical team must try one strategy after another to get your baby off the ventilator or oxygen. If weaning fails and you have to bring home all this equipment, what once seemed like a miracle can now seem burdensome.

If your baby comes home with a nasal cannula and oxygen tanks or a tracheostomy tube and a ventilator, you probably have some strong feelings about what it means for your baby to continue to need respiratory support. At first, the prospect of dealing with chronic respiratory complications can feel jarring, uncomfortable, and unwelcome. Fears that your baby will never be able to breathe independently are common. It is possible that you wrestle with your desire to get your baby off oxygen because *you* want a sense of normalcy, downplaying what your baby really needs. Or, you may continue to wish that you could breathe for your little one.

There was so much anxiety for me. Getting them off the cannula was like my life goal. To me, having my babies on oxygen meant there was something wrong. That's what sick babies need, and that didn't fit in with my view of my babies. Plus, you couldn't just pick up a baby and leave the room. You couldn't just put a baby in a sling and walk around. And I couldn't see that this was transitional. It had been such a long time, between bed rest and their hospitalization, so I felt like it would never end. I'd been chained down for fifteen weeks, and I was still chained down. —Rikki

Even if you became quite competent administering respiratory treatments and medications in the NICU, it is normal to feel terrified when you have to do it all on your own at home, especially at first. During your baby's NICU stay, you were confident that your health care teammates were supervising your baby's care. After discharge, you are the one who must decipher the signs of respiratory distress. This is an awesome responsibility and a frightening role shift. It can cause you to jump at every sniffle and panic at each cough out of concern that your baby will develop a horrible respiratory illness.

In addition to being overwhelming at times, respiratory complications are a constant reminder of the premature birth. The sight of your baby and all this breathing equipment may occasionally transport you back to the beginning, a beginning filled with distressing images and conflicting emotions. Your baby's bronchopulmonary dysplasia (BPD), asthma, or complications from respiratory syncytial virus (RSV) can exacerbate your frustration with the questions from others or your own anxiety. For months and even years after homecoming, you may continue to legitimately fear rehospitalization and to feel very alone in your struggle.

Feeling intense resentment and grief over the diagnosis and ongoing treatment of your baby's respiratory condition is normal—and it does abate over time. Give yourself permission to experience the whole range of feelings you have about this issue, so that you can separate what *you* need from what *your baby* needs. Facing your emotions and working through them will enable you to come to terms with your baby's respiratory condition and reduce the level of anxiety you feel about your baby's special needs.

I was very anxious for Gabe to come off oxygen because I felt it was a sign that Gabe was okay and also [a chance] to have some normal life. It was pretty much all about my experience, my needs, not Gabe's. That is not easy to admit, but it's true, and I simply didn't make sure I knew what we were dealing with when we took him off, with the pediatrician's blessing (but as we know, that doesn't always mean much). Nor did we follow up well enough. I don't think I truly grasped, or wanted to accept, that he could still be vulnerable, that he could be using too many calories for breathing/oxygen exchange and not for brain growth, weight gain, and development. I wanted so badly to believe that he was healing, that he was over his vulnerability, I ignored the cautions. I feel lucky that Gabe has done so well because I think it is clear to me now, two years later, that Gabe's growth did drop off directly after we took him off oxygen and has been at a slower pace than is really the best. —Maren

When you feel anxious to be rid of the oxygen or the nebulizer, face your feelings about your child's dependence on respiratory treatment so that you can make decisions based on your child's needs. As you work through painful feelings over time, you will notice that your baby's complications become less important in your view of him or her: your baby's lungs will take a back burner to other things in the parent-child relationship. Monitoring a baby with ongoing respiratory issues becomes a natural part of daily care. Instead of considering the oxygen, cannula, or nebulizer the enemy, you can learn to see them as aids to healing your baby's lungs and promoting growth. Your increasing ability to cope emotionally will be a gift to your child, one that encourages him or her to cope with any adversity as well.

Coping with Feeding Complications

When we think of feeding a baby, most of us see images of an infant cradled in a parent's arms, eagerly sucking on a bottle or nursing at the breast, then falling contentedly asleep with a full tummy. What could be easier or more natural? Unfortunately, some preemies encounter problems that make oral feeding a struggle or even an impossibility. If your baby resists eating or vomits often, feeding becomes an anxious time that can consume many hours a day. (For more, see "Grappling with Oral Feeding Difficulties" in Chapter 16.)

When a baby (or child) is unable to take in sufficient nutrition by mouth, she or he must be fed by tube. This section focuses on tube-feeding, including the often emotional decision of placing a gastrostomy tube.

Coming Home from the NICU with a Feeding Tube

When we were told that the tube would be put in, we struggled with the idea that our little boy wouldn't be able to eat "normally." My feelings were ones of overwhelming sadness. We were never asked for our opinion regarding the tube placement. We were told it was necessary, and that was that.

    When I first saw the tiny tube protruding from my baby's tummy, I cried. No child should have to eat like that. My dreams of a "perfect" child were dashed. Of course, that sounds very selfish. I hated the tube at first. It symbolized to me the struggles that my son would go through to be "normal."—Marsha

If your baby is unable to tolerate any oral feedings, placement of nasogastric tube (NG-tube) or a gastrostomy tube (G-tube) is a necessary intervention, and even when you know that it's best for your baby, you may grieve. If your baby is exclusively tube-fed, you miss out on those early milestones: when your baby learns to hold the bottle, to drink from a cup, or to eat solid foods. You may feel terribly sad that she or he hasn't had the chance to taste and to enjoy eating. You may worry about the future and wonder if your child will ever eat by mouth.

    Along with your sadness and fears, you may feel angry. If your baby is still using an NG-tube, you probably detest the inevitable replacements. If your little one has a G-tube, especially before a button is installed, you may resent the extra care it requires. Tube-feeding can feel more like performing a medical procedure than providing nourishment. But, of course, it's both. And it's normal to have mixed feelings about it.

    It's not the way I had pictured feeding my son. I have looked at other mothers feeding their children from a bottle with no apparent problems and have envied them. I wish I could tell them how fortunate they are that their children can eat without the necessity of a feeding tube. I think it is more difficult for me than for my son. He doesn't know any other way to deal with eating. Hopefully he won't remember any of this. But I know that I always will. I will look back with sadness that I missed out on "normal" feeding experiences. At the same time, I will be thankful that my son was able to grow and gain weight and be healthy. ... The tube was in his best interest and that it was only temporary. After many tears and much soul-searching, I found the inner peace to know that for my son, the G-tube is "normal." —Marsha

Before your preemie was born, you were likely unfamiliar with feeding by tube. It can take some getting used to. But as you become an expert, you can figure out ways to make it a cuddly and relaxing time. Also remember that tube-feeding doesn't affect all the other wonderful ways of connecting with your little one, including singing, playing, bathing, and skin-to-skin contact. Seeing tube-feeding as only one part of your nurturing can help it feel more "normal" to you.

It became very normal to tube-feed our little baby once his digestive system was able to handle pumped breast milk. It was so normal it became a treat even for relatives and friends to visit during the time he was fed so they could hold him and the little syringe of milk as it dripped down the tube. We just wanted to be a part of his daily life so badly that it didn't matter if we were feeding him through a tube or a bottle. —Katrina

Making the Gastrostomy Tube Decision After homecoming, when a baby (or child) is continually unable or averse to taking in food by mouth, parents are faced with deciding whether to consent to surgical insertion of a gastrostomy tube. A G-tube can be gentler for the baby than continual replacement of the NG-tube, and it can help a baby gain weight when oral feedings are too much of a struggle. As a parent, you may be presented with this decision in the NICU or after homecoming. Some parents see a G-tube as a welcome option. They accept it eagerly as a step toward getting their baby discharged sooner or as a way for their child to receive a measurable amount of nutrition with a minimum amount of fuss.

They had to continually put NG-tubes down, which was very difficult and upset Caleb. He would also pull the tube out frequently. When the surgeon operated to reconnect Caleb's intestines, we specifically requested that a G-tube be placed to spare him the ongoing trauma of an NG-tube. It was a good move on our part because it has taken Caleb almost a full year to be able to recover and attempt full oral feedings again.

I suppose it was hard at first, but now I am grateful for the tube. To us, a feeding tube is neither a failure nor some kind of major handicap. True, I wish Caleb fed like a normal child, but Caleb does few things like a "normal" child, and the tube is convenient, easy to care for, and doesn't seem to bother him in the least (and believe me, he would let me know!). —Eva

But many parents resist the G-tube. This may be true for you if a feeding tube represents frailty, abnormality, invasive medical treatment, and dependence on technology—all those things you want to leave behind at NICU discharge. You may not want your child to endure yet another surgery, more anesthesia, more pain, more hospitalization. If this is your baby's first surgery, it can be frightening to contemplate. You (and your friends and relatives) may also associate the feeding-tube decision with end-of-life issues. Relying on a G-tube can seem like a setback, and such a mechanical way to nourish your child. You grieve for your child's inability to drink or eat with ease. Most of all perhaps, you yearn for feeding to be a relaxing, soothing time, instead of a chore. Unfortunately, your hesitancy or your desire to avoid G-tube placement could mean that you and your child struggle mightily over feeding issues for many months or years.

> *We went through years of fighting the battle. Fighting to get Taylor to eat. Fighting with therapists as to what to do to get him to eat. Fighting with my husband, fighting with family, but mostly fighting with my own conscience. ...*
> *I fought placing a tube for over four years. I convinced myself that I was saving Taylor from more pain and from a surgery and hospital stay. I played all the guilt issues out in my mind. Not being able to feed your own child really cuts to the quick of how we view ourselves as parents. I convinced myself that I was being a better parent by doing all that I could to prevent having a G-tube placed. I could not have been more wrong! —Tammy*

Once parents recognize that a G-tube is what their child truly requires, they are surprised at how easy it is to decide to get one placed and what an improvement it makes in their daily lives and their relationship with their child. You discover that instead of signifying failure, G-tube insertion can offer relief. Instead of being a setback, it is a jump forward. It's not an end-of-life issue, but an option that can help your child thrive. It is more natural and less invasive than force-feeding. And although you may need to face the grief that insertion of the tube raises, you spare your child the suffering that eating by mouth can impose.

> *If I had it to do all over again, I would have placed the G-tube as soon as it was suggested to me. The years of pain and fear he has had to endure from all*

the years of throwing up, feeling so out of control, and fighting every bite is far worse than the pain from the surgery of placing a tube. The emotional scars he will forever carry from his food battles will stay with him forever and are far deeper than any physical scar from a G-tube. ... If I would have given in and had a tube placed, we could have avoided so much heartache. He could have just gotten strong—and put his concentration into all the wonderful exploring and learning that babies are supposed to concentrate on. I can't help but wonder how much faster and easier his battle to "catch up" would have been if he would have been stronger and weighed more. I know that his toddler years would have been much, much happier if it weren't for the constant eating battles. And he most certainly would have a much better attitude about food now. —Tammy

We spent his first nine months at home trying to get Chris to bottle-feed. We measured every milliliter and how long it took for him to take it. We added rice cereal and other supplements. It seems like we fed him constantly and he never grew very well. The doctor pushed us a number of times for a G-tube with a fundoplication, but we really were afraid to do it. We didn't want Chris's anatomy messed with.

    Finally we saw a pediatric gastroenterologist about the reflux when Chris was nine months old, and she assured us his reflux was resolved enough to place a G-tube without doing a fundoplication. The first two weeks he had the G-tube he grew two inches and gained two pounds! He never gained at that rate again and never got past the tenth percentile, but at least he looked a bit chubbier. I was happy to tube-feed him. It was a relief from the worry. After a while, you come up with a system and routine that works for you, and it becomes easy to feed your child no matter where you are. It nevered bothered me to tube-feed Chris in public. —Amy

    Feeding Jacob has always been frustrating. He had a poor suck/swallow/breathe, was slow to eat, and would frequently give us back all we had struggled to get into him. By the time we coaxed in the right amount of formula, revisited it, then coaxed it in again, it was time for the next feeding. Funny, when I type this, I remember all the frustrations, but I still could not bring myself to give in to a G-tube.

    We fought for six and a half years to avoid placing a G-tube. Jacob

•••

481

teetered on the edge of dehydration/malnutrition due to poor oral motor coordination and oral defensiveness. Feeding Jacob became our main passion. When, at age six and a half years, Jacob dropped to twenty-three pounds, we faced the inevitable. Finally, I knew it was the only option. Jacob was so sick by the time we agreed to have a G-tube placed. I looked at him one day and knew he was going to die if I didn't come to terms with my fears of that tube. The hardest part was trying to keep from feeling like we had lost, and that all we had done for six and a half years to avoid that tube was for nothing. It was one of the lowest times in my life with Jacob.

Even after tube placement, knowing it was the only option, I still questioned our decision. It's such an unnatural way to nourish your child. But as Jacob began to thrive and grow both physically and cognitively, I came to terms with Jacob's way of taking in foods and was able to separate feeding from loving. Nourish the body does not mean nourish the soul. Luckily, I had someone in our community to mentor me, someone who had gone through the same experience and could help me come to terms with our decision. Now I can say I love that G-tube.

I look back on my six-and-a-half-year avoidance of the G-tube and shake my head. It seems so foolish now to have given that G-tube almost monster characteristics. It's just another small part of what makes Jacob whole. —Julie

Even though a G-tube can be a blessing, some babies' digestive issues are so complicated that it can take a while before the health care team presents a G-tube as a viable option. If your doctor downplays the severity of your baby's problems, you may be the one who pushes for surgical intervention. You can see the G-tube as a positive move rather than a defeat.

It has to be remembered that when a child is in a desperate situation that requires a feeding tube of any sort, that the act of eating/digesting, and so on, can be as calorie-intensive as a thirty-minute aerobic workout. A feeding tube can provide effortless calories that can be used for growing and, eventually, getting back on the oral feeding track. It takes stress out of your lives and gives you back a bit of freedom. —Joanne

The most important thing you can do for your child right now is give him every possible means to get strong and healthy and happy. *If he gets strong, the rest of his development will be easier. If he is constantly working so hard just to eat and gain weight, the rest of his development will suffer and take a backseat.*

Getting a tube is not *a failure. It is simply a tool to help your child gain strength, and for your family to keep some sort of sanity. — Tammy*

If you've been concerned for a while about your baby's fussiness, reluctance to eat, vomiting, or failure to gain weight but your doctor is reticent to discuss these problems, you may feel frustrated and unheard. Consider this a *serious situation* even if your pediatrician dismisses it. Consult with pediatric gastroenterologists, ask for feedback from all members of your baby's health care team, talk to other parents of preemies with feeding problems, do research, and trust your intuition. As the head of your child's health care team, this is your prerogative. If your teammates undermine your efforts, you have every right to be persistent—and angry.

We were not told that Chris might have long-term feeding problems, even though he was showing classic signs already in the NICU—trouble with nippling, suck-swallow-breathe problems, oral-tactile defensiveness, and fighting the feedings. Finally, he was diagnosed with severe reflux. I cried when they told me. He had been in constant pain from the undiagnosed reflux. After the reflux was diagnosed, Chris was placed on a forty-five-degree-angle sleeping wedge, kept upright most of the day, and given medications. Within a couple of weeks, he was a completely different baby—happy and no more constant crying. We were very angry to find out how long he had had to suffer, and we know this suffering was the biggest contributing factor to his feeding problems. —Amy

Alex's problem wasn't getting it down but keeping it down. The reflux was horrible. I was an experienced mom (Alex was my seventh child); my others spit but never had the projectile vomit that Alex displayed with each meal. They also gained weight well despite the spitting up. Alex didn't. I was patted on the head and told not to worry.

Well, a twelve-month-old kid who weighed eleven pounds worried me

• • •

483

nonetheless. It was also mentioned that the projectile vomiting was "normal" for severely brain-damaged kids. That might well be, but it didn't mean it was a good thing or should be allowed to go on. It was finally the insistence of his early intervention physical therapist that forced the doctors to sit up and take notice. She refused to do PT on him, saying he was burning muscle since there was no fat to use for calories, and PT could have serious health consequences. It took six months of testing before they decided on a G-tube and fundoplication. No one discussed the possibility of the surgeries till then, and then suddenly it was, "Hurry up and decide—your baby is in trouble!" (duh!!!)
—*Joanne*

Addressing Other Feeding Issues G-tube placement isn't the only component to resolving to your child's feeding problems. There's still the question of what kind of nutrition he or she will tolerate best, and what quantity at what frequency should be delivered. If your child has other throat, stomach, or intestinal problems, those will need to be addressed separately. Just when you think you may have the answer—a G-tube—more detective work may be in order.

In the beginning, the G-tube resulted in as many problems as nursing/bottle-feeding had. We were instructed to bolus feed him four times a day, but he could not tolerate bolus feedings at all. He retched and gagged so badly and even on occasion vomited. The doctors refused to take the issue seriously and said this eighteen-month-old kid who weighed seventeen pounds was gagging on purpose because he liked to. Oh, please!!!! We were even required to see a developmental psychiatrist to make sure the mother-child relationship was normal.

Thanks to the Internet I found out about psuedo-obstruction, as well as a GI doctor who was familiar with it. Delayed gastric emptying was indeed a major issue in the feeding. He did much better with very slow overnight feedings than with bolus feedings. He even began to eat orally again.

When we had so much trouble with the gagging at the start, it was a real low point. I felt there was no way, oral or mechanical, that I could feed my child. Once I learned how his digestive system worked and the feedings went much easier and I could see him thriving and growing and gaining developmentally in front of my eyes, the G-tube was no longer an emotional issue but a victory over doctors' predictions of a severely brain-damaged child.

•••
484

(He's entering regular first grade this fall with adaptive tech supports to deal with his cerebral palsy.)

If it came down to Alex's needing the G-tube again, I wouldn't hesitate for a second. It again is important to understand how your child's digestive system is working, though, and to do what the child is comfortable with rather than a set idea of the therapist. —Joanne

Besides digestive or anatomical problems, some babies have coordination difficulties or oral aversions that can interfere with learning to eat by mouth. This developmental piece of the puzzle needs to be addressed with therapies attuned to the child's particular challenges, which may persist for many years. For example, many babies and children with oral aversions have trouble coordinating the use of their tongue, which is critical for moving food around the mouth and swallowing without gagging. A speech pathologist who specializes in motor-speech disorders can offer real solutions.

Most parents report that the G-tube is temporary. With appropriate therapy and calm encouragement, their baby learns to eat. If your child's dependence on the G-tube continues, though, this is not a reflection of failure on your part or a matter of willpower or waiting for your child to "snap out of it." Tube-feeding addresses a real need, and your child will grow out of that need when the conditions are right. (For more on this subject, turn to "Grappling with Oral Feeding Difficulties" in Chapter 16.)

Rehospitalization

When you walk out of the NICU with your baby in your arms, you may hope fervently that you will never darken that door again—except for triumphant visits with a healthy, growing child. But no matter how much your baby weighs at discharge or how healthy she or he seems, you may worry about your preemie's ongoing health and growth. You know that preemies are vulnerable to serious illness. Your awareness and concern motivate you to do your best to keep your baby healthy and growing, and to avoid rehospitalization.

In spite of the best precautions, some preemies have setbacks, get sick, or require surgery for which they need rehospitalization. Some preemies reenter the hospital unexpectedly; others, such as those returning for follow-up surgery, go back according to plan. Whether the rehospitalization is expected or not—and even when surgery is necessary for your baby's growth and well-being—your first reaction is often fear. You may worry about your baby's safety, comfort, and survival. Being back in the hospital, even years later, can rekindle old memories and anxieties, particularly around the separation and your connection with your little one.

No matter how minor the surgery, how frequent, or how "experienced" I become, I still become manic days before Jacob goes under. What gets me most is when we take a healthy, happy Jacob in and get a sick, sad, and sore Jacob in return. —Julie

When she was extubated several days later, she would not smile or maintain eye contact. ... I asked the nurse about these new developments, and she said it was not uncommon for [re]hospitalized infants to react in such a manner. This news broke my heart. I dedicated myself to gaining my daughter's trust. It was a long time before she would look at us and longer still before she began to smile again. —Renee

Not far behind the fear may be feelings of guilt over real or imagined lapses on your part. You may rack your brain figuring out how your baby got sick or what caused the setback, wondering what you did and what you could have done differently. If you disregarded the doctor's advice or ignored your own instincts, you may be agonizing over your actions. "What if?" and "If only ... " thoughts may consume you. Dealing with these feelings while trying to attend to your baby can be overwhelming.

Finally, as you gaze down at your preemie lying in yet another hospital bed, you are reminded that there are limits to how much you can control. No matter what boundaries you set around your home and your little one, you are not all-powerful. Just as with the premature birth and NICU course, bringing your baby home to grow up holds uncertainties. Your baby's rehospitalization confirms your vulnerability.

For me, the NICU is not the pinnacle of the preemie experience that it is for others. For us, it is followed up by many other hospital stays and complications. The NICU was difficult ... but returning to the hospital for a long-term stay after I thought we'd left that behind us was even more devastating. —Eva

• • •

Coping with Rehospitalization

When your baby is rehospitalized, it is normal to experience many of the same feelings of fear, vulnerability, guilt, anger, and sorrow that you felt in the NICU. You may resent this intrusion on your relationship with your baby and on your family life after homecoming. You may have flashbacks or feel as if you're overreacting because of what you went through earlier with your baby. You may see the medical interventions as more cruelly invasive because of your heightened emotional sensitivity. As Susan says, "I would rather have blood extracted from my veins via hacking with a screwdriver than to let a skilled phlebotomist draw blood from my son."

But even though there are many emotional similarities between the NICU and hospitalizations that follow, in many other ways, they are different. You must now orient to the pediatric floor or to pediatric intensive care. On many such units, parents are expected to perform their baby's basic caregiving and to room-in. If you are breast-feeding, the health care team should encourage you to nurse your baby whenever possible. Although the ways in which the pediatric team incorporates you will vary (just as it does among different NICUs), it is more likely that your input will be taken seriously and sought out. And now that you've spent some time at home with your baby, you may feel more assured in your parenting role.

After weeks or months in the NICU and some time at home, you are not the same parent that you were when your preemie was first born and hospitalized. Although your confidence may be shaken if your baby is very ill, you are likely more sure of yourself and have an easier time voicing your preferences for your child. Feeling more like a parent and being more certain and assertive about your role can help you deal with new challenges. Your struggles to develop your identity as a parent in the NICU will bear fruit during repeat hospitalization.

Dylan has so much love and support from so many people, just everybody. Surgery is going to hurt a lot and it's going to be really difficult for him, but he's going to know that we'll be there for him and he'll be loved and supported. That's the only thing I can give him, the only thing that we can say that we have some control over.

And just staying on the positive side of it, I know it's going to be hard for him, but I also know it's going to be so much better for him. Another thing about being positive is that you can't say, "Oh, my God, I don't want him to have to go through this." Of course, I do wish that he didn't have to go through it, but he does, and there's nothing we can do about that. It's just something that we have to get him through, and get him through in a positive way so that it's something that we can all handle.—Betsy

Here are some tips for coping with a rehospitalization:

- Speak up, advocate for your baby, and remember that you remain a critical part of your baby's medical team.
- See yourself as a seasoned veteran. Recall lessons learned from your time in the NICU and use your acquired skills to manage during this time.
- Find ways to stay close to and involved with your baby. Do kangaroo care, or at least touch and hold your baby whenever possible. Doing so can hasten recovery.
- If you are breast-feeding, make sure that you can keep nursing and/or pumping. Call on the hospital's lactation consultant if you need assistance.
- Learn as much as you can about your baby's setback, illness, or surgery. The more information you have, the more empowered you can feel. Information can also quell anxiety.
- Face your feelings as they arise. Remind yourself that they are natural and normal.
- Take care of yourself as best you can. Ask for help from others and accept it when it is offered.

If you are feeling to blame for your baby's hospitalization, be compassionate with yourself. You have faced the most difficult juggling act a parent can deal with and have struggled to balance the needs of your preemie with those of others in your family (including yourself!). You did not have a crystal ball. It's so hard to know whether you could have done anything to avoid this rehospitalization. Give yourself credit for doing the best you could do at the time and for learning through experience.

Her second hospitalization served to remind us that she was a premature baby. We became extracautious about germs and her contact with other people. We observed her more closely and paid greater attention to her health. —Renee

Do what you need to do to get through this stressful period. When you return home you will have a chance to reestablish your routine and settle in again with your precious child.

Points to Remember

- Regardless of your baby's condition at discharge, you are likely to continue to feel vulnerable. These feelings come from legitimate worry and a deep fear of further loss.
- Become informed about your baby's risks and distinguish between real and imaginary threats. Figure out ways of taking sensible precautions that will reassure but not consume you.
- If your baby must be kept isolated to avoid infection, you can develop a supportive network of friends to help you continue to feel connected with the outside world.
- If you continue to struggle with breast-feeding, it may help to redefine your expectations of what "breast-feeding" means for you and your baby. Try to let go of the "shoulds" that give you feelings of regret and failure.
- Don't let concerns about your baby's weight gain rob you of your ability to have a warm, easy relationship, especially around feeding times. Make the priority filling your child with love, not just food.
- If your baby comes home with ongoing medical complications, you may feel deeply disappointed—but your expectations of "normal" will adjust over time.
- Instead of considering medical equipment to be the enemy, you can learn to see it as an aid to helping your child develop and grow stronger. Your growing ability to cope will be a gift to your child, one that encourages him or her to cope as well.
- If your preemie is rehospitalized, you may feel devastated. Use the skills you acquired in the NICU and rely on your developing confidence as your baby's parent. You will prevail.

• • •

CHAPTER FIFTEEN

Becoming the Kind of Parent You Want to Be

The birth of a premature baby gives most parents a heightened appreciation for how precious their children are. Preemies remind us how susceptible we all are to life's misfortunes. Your child's special beginning may inspire you to become a special kind of parent—and the best parent you can be.

> *I think I am a much better parent than I might have been had this experience not happened. I mean, I think I would have been a good parent regardless. But having been through the experience of being so close to losing my son, I learned very quickly how much this new little life meant to me, and that I needed to do everything in my power (sacrifice whatever I needed to) to protect him and make sure he has every opportunity possible for a chance at a good recovery and good life. I don't take him for granted, and never have. I realize the tremendous responsibility I have to him. ... This is what made me a better parent. —Andrea*

Along with feeling energized at the prospect of parenting your preemie, you may also approach parenting in a whole new way. You don't—you can't—take parenthood for granted, nor can you simply copy the kind of parenting you see all around you or the kind you received as a child. You become more conscious of your role and strive for your own emotional health so that you can be responsive to your child's needs. In general, your ideas about parenting may become more flexible and open.

I would have to say that I am much less judgmental since I had a preemie. I had planned to be rather strict, but I am much more tolerant. I used to despise parents who had children who had temper tantrums or wouldn't behave in a public place. I knew that when I had kids, they would be model citizens. Now, if I see a tantrum in public, I am more inclined to wonder if the child has a problem, rather than the parent! ... Now I know better. —Mo

In many Western cultures, parents receive a fair amount of social pressure to conform to certain ideals. In some camps, being in tune with your baby is considered "spoiling" rather than responsiveness; allowing your little one to be dependent and clingy is considered "permissive" rather than nurturing; being flexible and negotiating with a child are considered "giving in" rather than being adaptive and generous. Because of these attitudes, some of your relatives or friends may be skeptical of your attempts to be sensitive to your little one. You may be scolded for being protective and warned against ruining your youngsters with attention and affection. But you can decide for yourself what style of parenting suits you and your children. If that means going against the grain of those around you, so be it!

My daughter's neonatologist gave me her release orders and told me the following: "Now, Rhonda (very condescendingly), don't make the mistake that most preemie parents make. Do not spoil this child."

As tears welled up in my eyes, I replied, "This child missed three months in my womb and didn't get to lie in my arms for two weeks after she was born and spent the last two months in a brightly lit, noisy room where she was separated from me twelve hours per day. I think it would be okay to 'spoil' her and her brother. They deserve it."

Let me just say that my children turn one next weekend, and I smother them with kisses every chance I get and take excellent care of them and they are very happy, well-adjusted children. ... Let's take each case on an individual basis rather than making sweeping judgments about how we should/should not treat our children. —Rhonda

It amazes me when people who have not had a preemie, or a critically ill newborn, or another major health problem concurrent with the birth of a child can straight-faced criticize another parent for how they are raising/handling their child. It is ridiculous for a person to think they could know what is "best" for such a baby and [his or her] parents.

Even three years later, I am still shocked into a sort of numbed silence, which grows into anger and resentment, when people make comments or express criticism or "suggestions" on how I "should" or "should not" be raising/handling Gabe. I know that Gabe still has preemie-related behaviors and health issues, and maybe they don't realize these are still issues. ... Too many people just think that preemies are simply tiny versions of newborns who will simply catch up in size and be typically developing children. They just don't know or believe the real difficulties that a prematurely born child can face and how parenting these children doesn't fit any of the baby book "wisdom" tossed around at play groups. —Maren

If you're lucky, you have supportive friends and relatives who respect your instincts and choices about how to best nurture your baby. In any case, seek out those who support you as you develop your parenting preferences and patterns with your preemie.

This chapter looks at your continuing development as a parent to your preemie. It offers encouragement to support you in becoming the kind of parent you want to be.

Following Your Nurturing Instincts

After you and your baby are separated at birth, you may at times be both bewildered and impressed by the intensity of your desire to be close to and nurturing toward your baby. Particularly after homecoming, when you can finally stay close to your baby, you may be reluctant to deny that part of yourself that is consumed by your infant.

Revisiting Parenting Approaches

In the past decade or so, innovative pediatricians, psychologists, child psychiatrists, anthropologists, and parent educators such as Stanley Greenspan, John Kennell and Marshall and Phyllis Klaus, Eda LeShan, Meredith Small, and

William Sears have written parenting books that question many of the old rules about how to raise babies and children well. (See "Parenting Books" in the Appendix C: Resources for a full list of recommended books and authors.) They point out the disadvantages of "one-size-fits-all" parenting, rigid parent-set schedules and rules, ignoring a baby's cries, discouraging dependency, punishing emotional outbursts, and viewing misbehavior as purposeful manipulation. They highlight the advantages of

- Trusting an infant's cues (babies know what they like and need)
- Respecting a child's temperament (every child is unique)
- Meeting dependency needs (a need doesn't go away until it's filled)
- Having realistic expectations (babies aren't bad, they're just *young*)
- Teaching children to identify problems and create and implement effective solutions (kids become more responsible with guidance rather than commands)
- Consciously adopting a set of consistent, clear, basic values and being a role model for how to live by them
- Making room for feelings and teaching children to verbalize their emotions (rather than acting out)
- Recognizing that children do well if they *can* (and if they can't, we need to figure out why, so we can help guide them toward real solutions)

All facets of a child's development are tied to receiving nurturing and responsive caregiving. Attentiveness, affection, flexibility, empathy, negotiation, and firm, gentle guidance are now viewed as effective, emotionally intelligent parenting skills. These skills are so effective because they teach children to

- Trust others and themselves
- Value their own uniqueness
- Become independent and interdependent
- Internalize rules, values, and goals
- Adopt emotionally healthy responses
- Respect their true needs

All of these attributes help a child grow into a happy, well-adjusted adult.

Now endorsed by the experts, this nurturing and responsive parenting style is nothing new. These ideas are an integral part of ancient mothering wisdom that has a long, rich, cross-cultural history: some of the best parenting ideas can be observed in gentle tribal cultures around the world whose ways of living have not changed much over the past few centuries.

•••

Traditional Mothering for Modern Times

In recent years, parents in developed nations have begun to consider the fact that human babies have thrived for thousands of years under "primitive" conditions. Remember, diapers, bottles, strollers, cribs, and master bedrooms are modern inventions and still not accessible to most of the world's families. Until the last century, babies were held most of the time, were fed on demand, slept with the mother, and breast-fed for many years (the current worldwide average is more than four years). Babies also grew up surrounded by the attentive care of family and friends living in small communal groups.

Then along came the Industrial Revolution and with it, factories, assembly lines, commutes away from home, standardized time zones, multibedroom houses, widespread economic prosperity, and the scientific method. Around the same time parenting came under the scrutiny of "experts" who saw "modern progress" all around and decided that what was good for society would be good for babies. So babies began to be raised using an assembly-line approach—put on schedules, kept in their own rooms, fed scientific formulas, carried around in strollers, and generally held at arm's length and treated alike so that they would grow up to be self-reliant, productive, conforming citizens. Emotions and individual differences were considered signs of weakness and not to be tolerated in parent or child.

When Dr. Spock entered the scene in the late 1940s, the tide slowly began to turn away from the idea that children can and should be molded to conform to some ideal. We began to view children as unique individuals from birth, individuals who need emotional sensitivity and nurturing plus firm and gentle guidance from their caregivers. Then in the 1970s, researchers and experts began rethinking the bias against the primitive or the foreign. Since the 1970s, researchers have been finding sound biological, psychological, and developmental evidence for embracing much of what mothers have always known. Many traditional ways are gaining respect and acceptance in the modern world because they are relaxed, efficient, make good sense, and most of all, feel satisfying.

These traditional ways rely on the valid assumption that babies respond to their own internal cues and can indicate what they need in order to grow and develop. Even newborns give clear signals about what they like and dislike. Parents can observe their baby's cues and respond accordingly.

Traditional ways also give weight to the idea that each baby's genetic,

···

inborn makeup and biological heritage greatly influences his or her development and behavior. The idea that biology is largely responsible for development and behavior is gaining more credibility with new advances in genetic and brain research. We already take for granted, for example, that genetics or biological conditions will determine when a child's teeth come in or the thickness, color, and length of her or his hair. We would never scold a child whose baby teeth fell out later than those of his or her peers, and we don't try to coax a bald baby to hurry up and grow some hair. Now we are starting to realize that many aspects of development, behavior, and temperament are ruled by biology.

Of course, a baby's temperament and behavior can be exacerbated by environmental influences, but characteristics such as sensitivity, shyness, disposition, and activity level are largely inborn and consistent throughout childhood. We are beginning to appreciate why giving an active, risk-taking child a "time-out" doesn't persuade that child to adopt a more passive, cautious approach to life. Scolding or ignoring a child with a sensitive or introverted nature doesn't compel the child to "snap out of it" and adopt a more carefree or extroverted personality. Instead, we are learning to work with—instead of against—a child's nature. (For more on this subject, see "Nurturing Your Child's Nature" in Chapter 16.)

Likewise, there are biological roots to how a child perceives, interprets, and reacts to situations and surroundings. For instance, we are beginning to appreciate the biological origins of learning disabilities, emotional imbalances, and sensory integration dysfunction, abandoning the belief that we can simply reward or encourage such a child to "learn" or "behave." When a child's behavior or development appears off track, uncovering and addressing the child's biological, brain-based strengths and weaknesses allows us to design effective treatments. Real progress can occur when we tailor environmental influences (including therapies, medication, nutrition, stimulation levels, verbal play, education, expectations, and parenting style) to fit the child's biologically determined needs and capacities. (For more on this subject, see "The Brain-Behavior Connection" in Chapter 16.)

The many facets of a child's behavior and development—including physical, emotional, social, linguistic, artistic, intellectual, spiritual—are influenced by environment *and* biology, nurture *and* nature. And a child will do best when environmental conditions (such as opportunities, situations, surroundings, interpersonal relationships, nutrition, therapeutic support) are a good match for the biological components of his or her temperament, physiology, abilities, and limitations. The best interventions simply improve the match between what's going on inside and outside the child, changing the surroundings, relationships, nutrition, medication, education, and activities so that the child's unique nature and development are supported.

While this may sound complicated, it is actually quite simple and intuitive; for eons, many caregivers around the world have been instinctively tailoring their responses to children in nurturing, sensitive ways. Unfortunately, our increasingly complicated modern human societies downplay intuition. Our instinctive wisdom is often muffled by the fast pace, barrage of information, and technology in our busy lives. Modern societies also isolate families, limiting their support. It truly does take a community to raise a child. Modern parents who wonder why they are losing their grip trying to raise their children in relative isolation can look to the past. Throughout history, nuclear families typically lived with extended family in small, closely knit communities. Children had intimate and longstanding relationships with other adults and kids. Getting together was spontaneous and easy, a matter of course in regular daily cooperative living—not meticulously scheduled between commitments and errands.

Nowadays, full-time parenthood is *spectacularly* challenging. In our society, families are typically cordoned off in single-family homes, and most primary caregivers' needs for support, companionship, and relief from child care go unmet. If you are chronically depleted, you're likely to resent the burden of child care, and it is much more difficult to listen to or act on your intuitions about the kind of care that is best for your child. Searching for solutions in isolation deprives you of the collaboration, wisdom, and perspective of others who can be sounding boards or who've been there before you.

It is important that you find ways to meet your legitimate needs for community. When you feel ready and able, find ways to spend time with other parents and kids with whom you feel comfortable. If you're so inclined, look to the Internet for supportive groups of parents of preemies, such as Preemie-L (see Appendix C: Resources). In general, find ways to ensure that your various needs are met, so that you will be better able to meet your child's needs.

Tips for Nurturing Parenting

Honor your nurturing instincts toward your baby. Keep these thoughts in mind as you work to establish your own nurturing style of parenting:

- Take advantage of your eagerness to be close to your baby and to be a responsive parent.
- Listen to your nurturing urges and listen to your baby. Follow your baby's lead, build on your little one's abilities and interests, and do what feels most nurturing to you and your baby.
- Tune in to and respect your own temperament, strengths, and weaknesses. Learn to appreciate and work with your nature, not against it. Your insights into and acceptance of your own constitution will help you gather insight into and acceptance of your child's.
- Resist the pressure others may place on you to get away from your baby. For instance, if you don't feel like going out on weekly dates or overnights alone with your partner, you don't have to. Having a strong marriage is clearly important to your family, but a strong marriage can survive the naturally intense focus on a baby during infancy.
- Don't worry about being "manipulated" by your baby or young child. Assume your child is communicating a genuine need. After all, manipulation requires a fair amount of planning, emotional control, and calculation—concepts and abilities that are beyond babies and young children.
- It is always appropriate to be emotionally generous. Meet your little one's crabby moods with calm and a gentle smile or acknowledgement. Remember that your ability to stay calm can be more powerful than your child's unpleasant outbursts.
- Babies and young children do not engage in infantile behavior to control or trouble their parents. Nor do they cling, nurse, cry, explore, or chew on things out of bad habit. They do these things out of internal drives and needs. Little children aren't bad, they're just young.
- Letting go is an important part of parenting, but it should be a gradual, child-driven process. A child's competence and independence arise from having dependable and responsive caregivers during infancy and childhood, as well as getting the uniquely tailored support he or she needs.
- Remember that your goal as a parent is less about pushing your children toward independence and more about leading them toward it.

· · ·

Rather than focusing solely on independence, also encourage interdependence: the ability to form and rely on close, mutually satisfying relationships with you and others, balanced with developing autonomy. It's healthy for your child to need you, to want to be with you. Your child's attachment to you is how she or he learns about emotional closeness and connection. Your child should learn that it's okay to need and ask for help and comfort. By your example, he or she will internalize the importance of assisting and supporting others.

- Although books and friends offering support and advice can be invaluable, remember that you are the ultimate expert on what feels good for you and your baby.

- Relax, dote on your little one, and enjoy yourself and your baby. Especially during the first few months after homecoming when meeting your baby's needs will consume most of your time, try to have realistic expectations for yourself. Nurturing yourself and your infant are your top priorities. Everything else can wait or be delegated.

Protective Parenting

I'm not saying I love my children more than a mother of a full-term baby does. I'm just saying it's probable that I appreciate them more, and I think that any child who has missed as much time in the womb as mine have, and [who has] spent as much time with main lines in their heads and collapsed lungs, etc., deserves *special attention. Of course, I won't be smothering my children with kisses when they are older. But for now, all of us need this.* —Rhonda

Because of the trauma you've been through with your preemie, vigilance and protective feelings may remain prominent, even as your baby grows. Others may warn you against being "overprotective" and thereby hindering your child's development, but you can be protective in ways that promote your child's progress without being overprotective. Preemies have unique needs, and your sensitivity and attempts to meet those needs are important.

I know I was hypersensitive to her needs during the first year. She was easily overstimulated, and we were always making excuses to avoid social gatherings or to leave early. —Diana

• • •

499

As Alex is mildly autistic and learning disabled, he doesn't relate to others like most kids do. Although it is often not obvious by his actions, he is aware—but his way of responding has a different feel, appearance, and quality. This was especially hard for both my husband and myself because we are very expressive parents. Yet in many ways we are closer to him than parents of "normal" children. In some ways we are like his "interface" with the world, to use a computer term. I believe that when professional researchers notice this behavior in parents of children with ADHD [Attention Deficit Hyperactivity Disorder], for example, they think that the parents are overly controlling. They don't understand that as parents we are helping our child interpret and interact with the environment. It's almost a symbiotic relationship. Of course, part of the job is to guide your children toward independence. But it doesn't come naturally, as with our other children. —Allison

There is a difference between being *over*protective and *appropriately* protective. Protecting your tiny baby from infection in the early months at home is not being overprotective; it is an appropriate response to real risk. Staying tuned in to your infant's sensitivity to overstimulation is not overprotective, but appropriately supportive. Gradually, as your baby becomes more resilient and tolerant, she or he will outgrow the need for your vigilant protection. However, if your child continues to be vulnerable to serious illness or if each foray out into large, loud groups leads to a meltdown, it is appropriate to continue your vigilance long past infancy. In any case, appropriate protection means responding to your child's vulnerabilities and needs at each developmental stage. Overprotection happens when your actions are based on your *own* vulnerability. Overprotection has more to do with your anxiety than with your child's needs.

I don't have any other experience to compare it to, but I do know that all my family and friends say that I am an extremely protective parent. I constantly need to know what Ty is doing, where he is, and so forth. I almost have panic attacks if he isn't where he is suppose to be or doesn't answer me when I call him. I am terrified of him dying. Nightmares are a regular occurrence in my lifetime. So I guess it has affected me in a negative way. —Dawn

Overprotectiveness can also become a vicious cycle. In general, your child's behavior and beliefs will reflect your hypervigilance. If you are overbearing, your child will either rebel, in which case he will be short on cooperation, or fall in line, when he will come to believe that he needs rescuing and that the world is full of danger. To avoid rebellion or overdependence in your child, don't rush to his or her rescue, showing your anxiety, or anticipate or respond instantly to your little one's every request. First ask yourself, "Is it safe for me to step back in this particular instance?" Then try letting your child fumble with a toy or struggle with a task. Let your little one figure out some things for herself. Remain calm and encourage your child to explore and experiment. Let him make mistakes and learn to cope with frustration and disappointment. If you are trying to compensate for your child's difficult beginning by being overly protective or by being the "perfect" parent, remember that the goal is to empower your child, not to render him or her helpless.

If your protectiveness arises more out of *your* needs than your child's, seek counseling. You deserve to get the help you need to deal with the anxiety, guilt, or grief that remains present in your life. You deserve to experience the joys of parenting, and your child deserves a parent who recognizes his or her needs for freedom as well as protection.

> *In my opinion, if you baby them and coddle them and keep them in a little glass ball, they're gonna be different from every other child—and I don't want them to be different. I want them to be normal. I want them to be perceived as normal. I want them to perceive themselves as normal. ... I have a friend who had a baby at Children's for a very long time and he was critical for a very long time, and the way she treats him now, she doesn't let that child do anything. She does everything for him. And he's just going to be a lost, sad little boy, and I don't want my kids to be like that.* —Pam

Guidelines for Protective Parenting

More than anything, protective parenting refers to safeguarding your child's individuality and self-worth. Protective parenting can apply to all children, not just preemies, and includes these skills:

- Responding to your child's needs
- Using effective discipline
- Helping your child deal with a wide range of emotions

- Respecting your child as an individual
- Being your child's advocate
- Letting your child follow his or her own path while providing protective boundaries that expand over the years

As a protective parent, you may strive to master all these skills. It is also imperative that you expect yourself to be imperfect.

Protective parenting does *not* mean sheltering your child from life's inevitable pains and complications—although the idea of doing so can be tempting. When your child encounters limits, mistakes, negative feelings, and obstacles, she or he is experiencing valuable life lessons. Give your kid the tools he or she needs to grow and cope with adversity. Strive to find a balance between holding on and letting go.

- Encourage your child to do what she is capable of doing. If you do for her what she can do for herself, you rob her of practice, feelings of achievement, ownership, and a sense of control.
- Help your child learn to negotiate and to deal with limits and rules. If he offers major or ongoing resistance or if a rule seems unenforceable, either drop it from your priorities or see if you can make it more realistic for his current abilities and interests.
- Let your child learn from her mistakes and face the natural consequences of her behavior. Resist the urge to lecture. The less you say, the more she can listen to her own voice, which will help her internalize the lesson.
- Support your child through his negative emotions. Negative emotions are a normal part of a child's life, not a sign of parents' personal failure. Instead of trying to fix or erase negative emotions, acknowledge and validate them, just as you want others to do for you. Help your child move through his feelings, not away from them. Your empathy and understanding will help calm and comfort, diffusing rather than escalating his feelings.
- Help your child face obstacles and cope with hardship. Life is supposed to be messy and complicated, even difficult and painful at times. Teach your child that there's nothing wrong with experiencing a hard time. Don't try to confine your child to the shallow, smooth waters. You won't always be able to prevent your children from being unhappy or hurt, but you can always offer a listening ear.

• • •

Protectiveness and Your Child's Vulnerability

All that I know about myself is that I am an excellent mother and I plan to stay that way. If I'm overprotective, I have a right to be. I'm the one who sat beside my son day in and day out, not really sure that I would get to bring him home at the end of everything. Even up to two and a half months, we didn't know if he would live. If I am overprotective, then it is not because of something new (cerebral palsy diagnosis), but more likely something old (months in the hospital). —Lissa

When your child has ongoing medical vulnerabilities or complications, disabilities, or developmental issues, whether they be major or minor, his or her need for your protection in certain areas may be ongoing or more extensive than it would be for a child without any special needs. Your vigilance will help you be on the lookout for problems as well as appropriate interventions. You will be conscientious about being a bridge between your child and the outside world, translating your child's signals and responding to his needs as you learn to decipher them. When your child is young, you will shield him from being overwhelmed. As he grows, he will take on parts of that job himself, and you can support him in doing this.

Although your protectiveness may be appropriate most of the time, sometimes you may catch yourself being hypervigilant or more cautious than necessary. Your feelings and perceptions can guide you, but they can also get in the way if they impede your ability to stay accurately tuned in to your child's actual medical and developmental needs. Here are four common, often interrelated emotional sources of being overly protective:

- *Wanting a feeling of control.* You may be wrestling with the loss of control over your life and your child's life. When you can't "fix" what's wrong, hypervigilance provides an illusion of control.
- *Trying to manage your anxiety.* Struggling with anxiety about your child's condition or development, you may have difficulty setting limits or encouraging your child to struggle, stretch, and grow. Instead, you may feel compelled to pounce and rescue whenever your child meets a challenge, and you may tend to focus unduly on the problems rather than on your child's strengths.
- *Assuaging your feelings of regret, fear, and sadness.* Intense feelings of regret

about the past, fears for the future, and sadness for your child's struggles can lead you to try to "undo" the damage done by becoming overprotective. In particular, residual feelings of guilt can drive you to try to "make it up" to your child by being overly permissive or vigilant.

- *Misperceiving your child's vulnerability.* When your vigilance is in response to your child's *actual* vulnerability, it mobilizes you to be accurately responsive to your child's needs. But if your vigilance is more a reaction to your own anxieties, it can disconnect you from your child's actual medical or developmental situation, and your protectiveness becomes *over*protectiveness. (For more on this issue, see "Vulnerable Child Syndrome" in Chapter 17.)

If your child has lasting complications, it is important to be aware of your grief so that it doesn't impair your ability to meet your child's needs.

Your little one has so much to learn, and with a combination of your guiding involvement, your appropriate expectations, your focus on his or her strengths, and your stepping back to give your child room to explore and experiment, you are his or her main teacher. Don't abdicate this role or let your worries or your sadness and pity get in the way of effective parenting. Working through your painful feelings better enables you to practice a parenting style that is less about reflecting your pain and more about doing what is good for your child.

It may also help to remember all that your child has already survived. In spite of lasting complications, as they get older, many of these children can tolerate a little frustration, deprivation, or disappointment when they come up against a limit they don't like or a hurdle they can't surmount. They can learn from making mistakes, tolerate cleaning up after themselves, and figure out how to pick themselves up after a fall. Depending on the particular issues that your child faces, you can learn about and gradually come to terms with his or her weaknesses so that you can support him or her through times of frustration, allowing your little one to build what strengths he or she can build even within a more limited framework.

As you become more conscious of when your grief shuts you down and when it mobilizes you to be an effective parent to this child, you can gain confidence in your parenting skills and you can set appropriate limits without anxiety or fear. You'll fine-tune the balance between protecting and letting go. You can also become a guiding light to your child. Remind yourself that even when your child's problems seem huge, you, the parent, are bigger still. You can be the wiser, stronger, calmer one, and as you learn about your child's unique needs and vulnerabilities, you can use this strength to support your child's growth and development.

Instead of focusing so much on what you want your child to become, you can focus on becoming that kind of person yourself. Also remember that your feelings of guilt, anxiety, or sorrow do not mean you are a bad parent. Painful feelings simply indicate that you have had a difficult row to hoe. Dealing with your feelings makes it less likely that you will taint your child's experiences with your own fears or beliefs about yourself. It may also help to remind yourself that your calm presence and your faith in your child's capabilities can boost his or her coping abilities and confidence. It is better for both of you that you focus on your child's strengths, even as you are aware of the weaknesses, and that you reach for growth.

Your appropriate protectiveness can help you reclaim your parenting role. Your intuitive, empathic connection to your child is valuable. As Bess says about her protective urges, "This is me defending the rights I had taken away for so long. This is me allowing myself to be the lioness. This is me finally trusting myself to be a mother."

Your Personal Growth as a Parent

As you grow into your identity as a parent to your premature baby, you adjust and learn how to become a different kind of parent to a different kind of child. This section focuses on your development and ways to approach challenges, nurture yourself, and get the support you need to become the parent you want to be.

Adapting to the Long-Term Process of Parenting a Preemie

In her book *Nobody's Perfect*, clinical psychologist Nancy B. Miller identifies four overlapping processes of adaptation to parenting a child with any kind of special needs: survival, searching, settling in, and separating. To some extent, all parents of preemies experience these processes because all premature newborns have special needs that present parenting challenges. If your child continues to have special needs as he or she grows, this process of adaptation will be ongoing. Whatever your situation, this explanation from Miller may help you to make sense of your many reactions to parenting your preemie in the NICU and beyond.

Surviving is what you do to get through the day when you are overwhelmed by the situation. You may feel numb or you may be overcome with raw emotion and intense grief. Naturally, right after your baby is born, it's all you can do to put one foot in front of the other. You just do what you have to do and let go of the rest.

You may plunge back into survival mode again when your baby needs surgery, when a serious setback occurs, or when you receive a grim prognosis—perhaps even when your baby first comes home.

Searching is what you do to find answers. Looking for information on what happened, what's going on now, and what will happen in the future is termed **outer searching.** In the beginning, you want to know about diagnoses, treatments, and prognoses; later on, you want to know about discharge plans and services. Further down the road, you'll want to inquire about testing and schooling. **Inner searching** is when you ask, "Why me? Why my baby?" Your search for answers and understanding begins immediately and, on some level, lasts a long time.

Settling in is what you do when survival mode wanes, when outer searching becomes less time consuming, and the treatments or services your child requires are in place. Settling in is also a time of slowing down and not feeling so frantic. You can see your journey as a process—and grasp that time is on your side. You may decide to reorder some priorities or attempt to find a better balance. You have identified resources and developed a support network to rely on. You know some shortcuts to solutions, and you feel more competent and confident.

You may feel a sense of settling in while your baby is still in the NICU and then again at home—or you may need a few years before you get there. With each new crisis you may dive back into survival and searching, and later come around again to settling in.

Separating is a gradual process that begins at birth. It refers to "letting go," a process all parents must go through with their growing children. Because your preemie is so vulnerable at first, you may not be able to imagine ever being able to see your little one leave your arms, much less the nest. But as your baby grows and begins to explore and have experiences with other caregivers, you learn to trust that she or he can do things alone, without your careful watch. You guide your child toward independence and self-sufficiency. If your child has special needs, this process can be slow. As you find therapies, schools, and community placement that are good fits for your child, he or she will take steps toward independence, and your relationship with him or her will broaden.

Over the months and years as your baby grows, you will recognize these processes of adaptation in yourself and your child. And over time, you become more adept at coping with challenges, finding meaning in your emotional experiences, and discovering healing solutions.

Nurturing Yourself

Being a good parent does not mean being a martyr. Some parental sacrifices are inevitable and important, but total selflessness will wear you down and reduce your patience, flexibility, warmth, and self-respect. Your children will benefit from your efforts to maintain a balance between your needs and their needs. Your needs for sleep, relaxation, and order are just as important as their needs for attention, nurturing, and spontaneity. The best way to ensure your ability to meet your children's needs is by getting many of your own needs met too.

Finding a balance can be challenging. Depending on the child, the right balance may be meeting many of his or her needs to just one of your own and occasionally making sacrifices or depleting your own reserves to guide your child through a rough spot. For some preemies, the first *years* seem like an interminable rough spot. But try to get your needs met most of the time: it's the only way you'll have the energy and creativity you need to face the challenges you must deal with every day. Like many preemie parents, you may struggle with this balance, but remember that recharging yourself always translates into better parenting.

> *I am a shell of my former self. Before Conor, I had a very busy, involved life. I had an amazing job, an amazing social life, and a great lifestyle. Conor has completely consumed the last three years of my life. I've lost all contact with old friends and activities. I can't even begin a conversation that does not completely revolve around preemie issues. Well, Conor's just turned three and is healthier than ever. We've just bought our first house. Things have finally started to go right. ... I'm making an early New Year's resolution to get on with "my" life*

• • •
507
Becoming the Kind of Parent You Want to Be

and to stop living Conor's. Besides, pretty soon it's going to be Conor's story to tell—not mine—and I've got to learn to respect that! —Laura

I really felt like a loon for most of Lars's first year, and Mat's confidence and support kept me going. ... Trying to meet all of our needs was a challenge— just meeting Lars's needs was a struggle, and there is no way to meet your baby's needs if your own are too neglected. But it often felt selfish to both of us to take time for ourselves, both individually and as a couple. We all did better, though, when the adults' basic needs were cared for as well as the baby's. —Kris

Getting the Support You Need

Along with nurturing yourself, also accept help and nurturing from others. It can be quite draining to try to get by on four hours of sleep or to pace the floor with a fussy baby. Accepting help from others is an effective way to balance your needs with your baby's needs: outside assistance provides the respite you need from constant caregiving. You might get a massage, walk or talk regularly with a friend, or let someone cook for you. Your partner, trusted friends, or close relatives are the first people you can turn to for support. (See Chapters 19 and 20 for more on these relationships.) And remember, when others nurture you, they are gladly contributing to your ability to nurture your baby.

If you are isolated with a preemie who is essentially quarantined, it is especially important for you to find ways to get support from others. When a primary caregiver is alone for most of the day with small children, she or he is in fact *very much* alone. Meeting your children's constant needs can consume all of your energy—and you may feel your aloneness most keenly when your emotional and physical energy stores are not replenished. Especially if you have multiple preemies, it is important to take breaks from constant caregiving to refuel yourself.

Getting the outside support you need is also paramount when your child is sick or fussy or if your little one is generally "high need"—for example, hypersensitive, easily overwhelmed, highly active, technology dependent, disabled, or developmentally delayed. The more special needs your child has, the more intense and draining your life will be. If you experience these intense sorts of demands from more than one of your children, you are likely to be particularly overwhelmed and depleted. If you find your child

especially difficult to live with, your anger, sadness, frustration, and desperation can be so intense that you may at times feel you are losing your sanity.
You may fantasize about giving your child up for adoption or consider placement in an institutional setting. **If life ever becomes that unbearable,
you and your family need more support of help than you're getting.**

Such thoughts and feelings are painful. Although you may feel ashamed
of your reactions, be honest about them. Let them help you determine
whether your situation is becoming intolerable so that you can seek solutions.
Then, do *whatever* you must to get the assistance you need: insist on evaluations
by the most qualified specialists, get social services involved, or go to the emergency room at your local hospital. You deserve to get the resources you
require. If other attempts have not helped, recognize that placing your child
in an institutional setting or a special foster home might be in your family's—
and your child's—best interests. Remind yourself to look at the whole
situation; remember to be kind to yourself.

Dealing with Parenting Anger

> *There were many terrible times at home, particularly during the first year. I felt
> guilty that I'd been unable to carry this child to term, and I was angry at her
> for putting us through the ordeal. I recognize these feelings of anger as
> "wrong" and "bad," but sometimes I still feel them. I know it wasn't her
> fault, but since we have never figured out why it happened to my body, I
> continue to want to put the blame somewhere. I always wished there had
> been some obvious medical reason (an infection, high blood pressure, something
> else) to explain it all. —Diana*

You may wish you could be the perfectly calm parent, with never a harsh
word, ugly feeling, or impatient moment. But any intense and loving relationship has conflict, and it's impossible to always react gently. It may help to
remember that this child is not perfect, and it's okay that you aren't either.

When you are angry, remember that anger is a normal parenting
emotion. Many factors can underlie parental anger. Children need a lot of
nurturing, attention, supervision, and repetitive caregiving tasks. Children are
time-consuming, messy, noisy, test the rules, and try your patience. When your
child's conditions, behaviors, or disabilities are challenging to deal with, you

may feel that your life is overwhelmingly complicated or out of control. You may feel inadequate as a person and incompetent as a parent. When the challenges are chronic, you can love your child but acknowledge that this existence can at times be just *too* hard. Your anger is a natural response to this stress.

Instead of trying to banish your anger, pay attention to it. When situational stress is a factor, your anger can help you acknowledge your limits and motivate you to get the support you need. If physiological stress is contributing to your irritability, your anger can remind you to reach for biochemical balance through adequate sleep, nutritious food, frequent exercise, sufficient leisure time, or medication to treat imbalance.

Trigger Thoughts "Trigger thoughts" can also contribute to your tension. These thoughts are prompted either by a deep anxiety or depression or by the general difficulty of your situation. Trigger thoughts include

- Assuming your child is misbehaving deliberately: "He should be able to control himself." "She's just doing this to push my buttons." "He's just trying to get his way."
- Catastrophizing—magnifying the situation in your mind or jumping to extreme conclusions: "I can't take one more minute of this." "She's *always* so rude." "He's *never* going to outgrow this phase." "If he can't do this, he'll never have any friends."
- Assigning negative labels: seeing your child as selfish, demanding, irresponsible, wild, spoiled, clumsy, manipulative.

Not only do these general, unrealistic assessments of your child or the situation add to your tension, but they also contribute to your overall sense of inadequacy, lack of control, and helplessness. When the tension becomes intolerable, you explode. As an example, let's say you're rushed, trying to pick up a few things at the grocery store before going home. Your child pulls over a display of cereal boxes. Already stressed from your attempt to get home as quickly as possible, a trigger thought like one of these sets you off: "She did this just to defy me." Or "Everybody is staring at me because I can't control my own kid." Or "Now we'll be even later getting home and starting dinner, and our evening routine will be ruined." Who wouldn't explode when prompted by trigger thoughts like these?

To diffuse this kind of anger, first of all make sure you aren't chronically stressed or running on empty. Nurture yourself, get support, and build rest, relaxation, and simplicity into your life. Then, become aware of making faulty assumptions or having overgeneralized, catastrophic thoughts. Try to identify those situations that prompt you to have these overreactions so you can be on the lookout. Next, when you catch yourself having trigger thoughts, dispute them. Talk back to them with more realistic expectations for your child and with more realistic perceptions of the situation:

- If you catch yourself making negative assumptions about your child's intent, remember that brain and behavior are connected. Your child wants to function smoothly, make good decisions, and behave appropriately. But temporary stress (being tired, hungry, or overwhelmed) or chronic stress (a chemical imbalance such as anxiety, trouble integrating sensory experiences, or trouble dealing with frustration or situations that demand flexibility) will compromise your child's ability to conform to even realistic expectations. Assume that your child wants to behave well but simply *can't*. Also keep in mind that misbehavior can arise from an unmet need. Your child's behavior isn't intended to push your buttons so much as it is meant to communicate a need—for example, for stimulation, your attention, more choices, a nutritious snack, a good nap, or something else that's lacking.
- If you catch yourself magnifying the situation, remind yourself that you *can* stay calm and handle this incident. It's only temporary. Things can still turn out okay for your child. This behavior is not indicative of a disastrous path toward antisocial, out-of-control maladjustment or certain failure.
- If you catch yourself assigning negative labels, remind yourself to see your child, instead, as
  - ▲ Acting her age (rather than immature)
  - ▲ Energetic (rather than annoying)
  - ▲ Enthusiastic (rather than loud)
  - ▲ Assertive, holds high standards (rather than demanding)
  - ▲ Persistent (rather than stubborn)
  - ▲ Passionate (rather than moody)
  - ▲ Discriminating (rather than picky)
  - ▲ Unique (rather than strange)
  - ▲ Overtired or hungry (rather than crabby)
  - ▲ Overwhelmed or sensitive (rather than emotionally unstable)
  - ▲ Struggling to learn from mistakes (rather than incompetent)

• • •

▲   Distractible or disorganized (rather than careless)

▲   Just trying to get what she or he *needs* (rather than selfish or demanding)

No one wants a loud, stubborn, moody, picky, demanding child. But who could resist an enthusiastic, assertive, persistent, passionate child who has discriminating tastes and holds high standards? (For more on temperamental qualities, see "Nurturing Your Child's Nature" in Chapter 16.)

Talking back to your trigger thoughts helps you feel less downtrodden. Your child will benefit from your ability to empathize and to accurately size up the situation. After all, if you can assess the real cause of your child's behavior, appraise the actual extent of the problem, and replace negative labels with neutral descriptions, you'll be able to see your world more objectively. The cognitive technique of talking back to triggers can powerfully reduce your stress and reshape your thinking.

If these distressing thoughts are merely the tip of the iceberg, though, simply reframing them may seem superficial or meaningless to you. Instead, try to identify the underlying sources of your frustration and these triggers so that you can deal with the root causes. What is it about your child's behavior that is especially enraging or embarrassing? Why is this behavior so irritating—and not other behaviors? Does this behavior relate to attitudes from the past or aspects of your history? Take a close look at the ways in which your trigger thoughts reflect larger struggles in your life. If you have a history of anxiety or depression, these sorts of thoughts may be all too familiar to you—not just a result of being a stressed parent. Anger can also be a way of lashing out against inner feelings of shame.

If your frustration or sadness in dealing with your preemie seems like an extension of other battles you have waged, consider giving yourself the gift of some time with a skilled therapist. Characteristic patterns of thinking and looking at the world don't just disappear. If you have spent years viewing yourself or others through a particular lens, it is not surprising that you might extend this view to your relationship with your preemie. Counseling can help you understand how these thoughts develop and why they feel so irrevocable and powerful. It can also support your efforts to adopt gentler views and reactions.

When the root cause of your frustration and your trigger is really that your child is testing your rules and standards (because that's what kids do), express your irritation in ways that will motivate your child to genuinely care about where you draw the line. You can also negotiate what's negotiable. And remember that children are also susceptible to stress and trigger thoughts. Help them lead simpler lives and teach them to talk back to their triggers, too.

Also remember that when you are responsive, supportive, and guiding, you draw your child into your embrace. In contrast, being insensitive, combative, or controlling creates separation and distance between you and your child. These negative attitudes create friction and resistance, because they *force* cooperation. You can consciously strive to be the kind of parent who *encourages* cooperation.

Finally, be honest about your faults. You won't always be kind and patient. You won't always know the right thing to do. Admit your mistakes and apologize. Seek outside help often. Your children will respect your honesty and decency, and you'll make a fine role model.

Perspectives on Parenting Your Preemie

Questioning What's "Normal"

In her book *Expecting Adam*, Martha Beck likens adding a son with Down syndrome to the family to going to the pet store to get a puppy, the same kind that all her friends had, but instead coming home with a kitten. For a while, she tried to teach that kitten to bark and fetch and wag its tail. But then she realized that kittens are special, too—and she finally stopped trying to turn her kitten into a dog. She learned to accept that she was raising a kitten and to appreciate her growing cat.

Preemie parents with differently abled children may be able to relate to Beck's metaphor. Their children are not easily pigeonholed. They may do some tail wagging and try occasionally to bark, but they may also purr or swim or chirp. Nobody knows quite how best to raise these unique beings. The only thing that is really clear is that you definitely do not have a dog—and this precious creature won't respond favorably to being treated like one. But chances are, if you follow your offspring's lead, you can figure out how to take care of this unique being, teaching, meeting needs, and cherishing your child for who he or she is naturally.

Ask yourself: "What is my definition of 'normal'? Must my child fit into what others consider standard?" Alternately, you may find it helpful to think of your child as a normal or even gifted kid, who just happens to have a dis-

•••

ability. You can also focus on your child's continuing progress rather than on how his or her development compares with the norms.

If your child is not in sync with the "norm," it is especially important for you to become a different kind of parent to this different kind of child. Focus on being a parent who sees beyond your child's eccentricities, appreciates the spirited being you've been given to raise, and recognizes your child's wonderful gifts.

> *He looked back at me with steady eyes, and I knew what I had known—what I should have remembered—all that time: that his flesh of my flesh had a soul I could barely comprehend, that he was sorry for the pain I felt as I tried to turn him into a "normal" child, and that he loved me despite my many disabilities.* —Martha Beck, from Expecting Adam

Thinking about the Future

> *I worry daily when I see her reactions to being overstimulated—meltdowns that just aren't "normal"—but I have to really hold back the judgment whether it's a preemie issue or just a personality issue. I'm still trying to iron all that out, and listening and learning.* —Donna

Your child's early birth and medical course may mean that he or she exhibits different patterns of behavior from other children or lags behind in certain areas of physical, emotional, social, or intellectual development. Like all other children, your child will have his or her own unique constellation of strengths and weaknesses, gifts and challenges, easy adjustment and difficult struggles. But it can be difficult to know what the future holds if your child's strengths are accompanied by worrisome weaknesses.

Others may tell you to stop worrying about the future. But as a parent, it's hard not to. Still, most parents have the luxury of imagining routine or even rosy futures for their children: for them, looking ahead is not painful or anxiety provoking. Rest assured that your concerns about the future are a legitimate aspect of raising your child, whatever your situation.

> *Ian is nearly caught up; we will see what time will tell. Alex is severely mentally impaired but making strides. He isn't making the leaps and bounds we*

hope for, but steady, slow progress. And some progress is better than none. He will most likely always live with us, and we will have to make special plans for him after our death. If we die young, he will probably go into foster care since the family doesn't want to deal with him. That's depressing for us. —Mo

Also keep in mind that your worries will not necessarily become reality. Some worries may seem like premonitions; others grow from baseless fears. Hindsight might be the only way to distinguish the two. In a few years, when you look back, you may very well see that things haven't turned out as badly as you feared—and that one of the hardest parts of the experience was those pesky worries. You wish you could have a crystal ball, so that you could know which worries to heed and which to dismiss. Try to give the future the benefit of the doubt. Hope for the best. Know that whatever happens, you can find solutions, meaning, and peace.

I am very excited because we have an educational plan in place for Stuart next year. He has made tremendous gains the last few months. It is really wonderful. His teacher has come full circle from recommending he return to [preschool] for a third year to recommending that he enter regular kindergarten. We have had two meetings with the school and are awestruck by the support available to him and their total enthusiasm for his inclusion. I feel so grateful, both for his gains and for the support the school will offer. I have heard so many horror stories from other parents regarding the schools, so the uniqueness of all of this seems enormous to me. We have researched many other options, not feeling great about any, so this is a huge *weight lifted.* —Susan

Pondering Disability

When you observe your child, certain behaviors or reactions or delays may bother you. You may wonder if they signal deeper, catastrophic problems. Even if your child's impairments are mild, your reaction is not necessarily mild. The verification of any disability or delay can be emotionally devastating and overwhelming. You are certainly grateful that the situation is not worse, but mostly you're sad that it's not better. You grieve that your child has to suffer or struggle at all. Perhaps you fear what these disabilities will mean to you, your child, and your family. Parents of preemies, whatever the situation, share many common worries:

- What if our child doesn't outgrow the need for medical intervention (feeding tube, oxygen, medication, therapies)?
- How will this child fit into our family?
- Will our financial situation worsen?
- What if we are unable to meet this child's complex needs?
- Will our relatives and friends abandon us?
- Are my child's problems a sign of my personal failure?
- Am I selfish or unworthy if I don't embrace the possibility of raising a disabled or medically fragile child?
- Who will take care of this child if something happens to us?
- Is institutionalization in this child's future?

Some parents are reluctant to admit that they are worried about delays or disabilities, especially mild or temporary ones. They may feel ashamed that anything less than perfect is a disappointment, that any kind of struggle is devastating. In contrast, for other parents anything better than the worst is a triumph. What's your baseline? How does reality compare with your readjusted expectations?

As you entertain future possibilities, you may find that you have certain biases—that you believe you could cope better with certain kinds of delays or disabilities than with others. Would it be easier for you to tolerate physical disabilities or mental disabilities?

> *I have to admit, while I had no problems accepting that our child was destined to have some neuromotor abnormalities (she has low tone), I was most frightened that she might not develop intellectually as well as I hoped for my child. I kept telling myself that I would love her no matter what she might grow up to be, and that the most important thing was that she would grow up to be happy. However, I know how important intelligence is in this society. I wanted my daughter to be smart.*
> —Christoph

Your biases may be affected by whether your child is a boy or a girl. The qualities you view as essential to being male or female may affect your wishes for your child. It can be especially difficult for a father when his son is affected. How will you raise a son unlike you, a son who is different? Will you still be able to teach him what it means to be a man? How do you define being "a man"?

Facing your feelings and pinpointing your fears helps you deal with them. Gather more information. Ask your health care providers if your baby's prognosis is as dire as your projections. Read books written by parents who've been there. Identify organizations and parent groups that offer support. Find out whether institutional placement is as grim as you imagine it to be.

It may also help to explore "the worst." What, in your mind, is the worst thing that could happen if your child is mildly, moderately, or severely disabled? What if your child has overwhelming medical needs or remains medically vulnerable? What are some of the other "worst" scenarios that could happen? How might you cope with them? Remind yourself that if any of your worries come true, you *can* learn to live with them.

Also have faith that you can transform yourself into the kind of parent who can accept his or her child, no matter what. For many parents, coming to grips with developmental disabilities involves letting go of the wished-for "normal" child and accepting the unique and special person that their child actually is. Although your sorrow runs deep, your joy can reach the loftiest heights. With delays and disabilities comes a greater appreciation for what is healthy, fun, and unique about your child. With this perspective, you can achieve a sense of peace.

There is great reward and cause to celebrate in our special little people's lives. I didn't always see this and came from the same despair and uncertainty that any parent starts with. Jacob will never be "normal"; he'll never be just like his sisters. He'll never be just like anyone but himself. He doesn't walk below us but alongside of us on a different plane. Jacob will always be just that: Jacob—and that makes him perfect! —Julie

For some parents, the therapeutic move is to admit that imperfection is okay—that it's acceptable for themselves and for their children to have flaws. Imperfection is both a reasonable and a healthy state. Being imperfect is just fine.

I am realizing, late for my (newly) forty years, that living means accepting imperfection—no, embracing imperfection. I have always been driven toward perfection. Member of everything, summa cum laude, president of the corporation, trying to protect myself, I think, through my achievements. Surely children would be the culmination, the validation of it all.

We had friends over last night, friends locked in what seems a victorless battle. Both desperately want children—she, only through adoption; he, only biologically. They have constructed a "perfect" life, save for this one problem. Discussing adoption, he said, "How do we know we won't end up with some 'crack baby.'" I said, "Even biologically, ours isn't perfect." Because she loves my children, my friend cried, "He is perfect!" and I said, "He is not. And he is fine."

And he is not. And he is fine. And my marriage, my family, my dreams are not perfect, are far from what I aspired to, are sometimes so hard and draining that I long for a release from their imperfection. But finally, they are my life, my living, my me. And I can no more separate from them than I can be perfect, or find perfection in any aspect of living what is this strange and lonely journey toward connectedness from undeniable isolation. —Susan

Valuing Complexity

Different people in a child's life will inevitably have different perspectives on that child, especially if he or she is "unusual." "Typical" kids are much easier to decipher. They are the round pegs that fit easily into round holes. Many people (and school systems!) like kids they can put easily into round holes. Unique, different children have many complexities and facets. They don't fit into the standard round holes. And they can be so easily misread.

For instance, if a child is very shy and quiet, some people will see a child who is dull; others will see a child who thinks deeply. There is a story about a little kid who sat in the school sandbox at recess, day after day, fingering the sand and looking off into the distance. Different adults made different assumptions. Some thought he was shy; others thought he was antisocial. Still others thought he was intellectually impaired. Finally, a wise adult thought to ask him what he was doing. He replied, "I'm trying to figure out how mountains turn to sand and which mountains this sand came from."

With complex children, people may try to simplify where there is no simplicity, and they may make faulty assumptions based on their own prejudices or viewpoints. So many people don't make that extra effort to engage the child, get to know him or her as an individual, or learn to appreciate the child's myriad strengths and challenges.

Every child deserves a comfortable hole that fits, perhaps one designed especially for him or her. Some kids are square pegs who simply need square holes. Other children are triangles or trapezoids; still others are ovals. And some are stars.

Choosing Your Perspective

Some people embrace the philosophy that how you choose to perceive and react to the people and situations you encounter is more powerful in determining your life path than the people and situations themselves. Even when you feel that the situation is beyond your control, you still can decide how to view and respond to what goes on around you. You can consciously choose to

- See the humor in a situation
- See the positives
- Not take offense
- Not take unmerited criticism personally or to heart
- Assume that others' intentions are benign
- See the vulnerability, fear, and hurt that others carry and forgive them for their transgressions

Although you can't necessarily shrug off your child's challenges, delays, disabilities, or medical complications by simply looking at the situation with a positive attitude, you can certainly diminish the minor, everyday inconveniences of life. For instance, when someone makes a clueless comment about your baby's prematurity, you can assume that they are either oblivious or making a legitimate attempt to comfort you, and aren't trying to insult you personally. If someone's children are acting up and bothering your child and the parents aren't intervening, you can assume that the parents are simply overwhelmed, and if you want, you can handle the situation yourself. If you are in for a long wait at the doctor's office, you can see it as a chance to have some downtime, and assume that the timing will work out in the end.

Albert Einstein once said, "The single most important decision any of us will ever make is whether or not to believe the universe is friendly."

Points to Remember

- After an early delivery and separation from your baby, you may feel a strong desire to be close to and nurture your little one. Be inspired to become a special kind of parent to your special child.
- Give yourself permission to respond to your nurturing instincts. Ignore those who discourage you from doting on your little one. Resist their suggestions that your infant is "manipulating" you, that "all babies require the same thing," or that your attunement and responsiveness to your baby's needs are wasted or misguided. Draw on traditional parenting wisdom.
- Consciously adopt the values, perspectives, and parenting goals that are most satisfying and meaningful to you. Be the kind of person that you want your children to be.
- Remember to simply enjoy your baby. You can find ways to hold, interact and be close that both you and your baby will enjoy.
- Honor your protective urges, but also examine them as your child develops and his or her needs change. Appropriate protectiveness is a respectful response to your preemie's medical and developmental needs. "Overprotectiveness" is a response only to your anxiety.
- Remember that protective parenting attempts to shield a child from challenges or pain, and that's where life's valuable lessons lie. Protective parents balance holding on and letting go. They empower their child to grow and learn and become a well-functioning person.
- Respect your own development as a parent. Learn to nurture yourself, get the support you need, and manage parental feelings of anger.
- Staying tuned in to your child means respecting the unique developmental path that he or she takes. This path may not be the one you envisioned, but it is just fine.
- Explore your fears and hopes for the future. Find a new definition of "normal."
- Consciously adopt positive perspectives and make positive assumptions. Decide that the universe is friendly.

CHAPTER SIXTEEN

Supporting Your Child's Development

One of the most challenging aspects of raising a preemie is that there is no timetable for your unique child's physical, emotional, social, intellectual, and linguistic development. There is no way to know for sure what is within your child's range of "normal," whether your child is falling needlessly behind, or how far your child can go.

As a parent, one of your main jobs is to guide and enhance your child's development. As the parent of a preemie, you may be eager for additional information about how to support your child's development because

- You may not find information geared to your situation in regular baby books
- You are committed to avoiding any "wrong" moves
- You are eager to get your baby "back on track"
- You know that your baby (like the vast majority of preemies) has extra needs during early infancy
- You may have worries about your preemie's developmental progress
- You may be hesitant to trust your intuition
- You may wonder whether you and those close to you are up to the challenge of guiding this child

This chapter offers practical ways to think about your child's development and suggestions for fine-tuning your caregiving to help you support your preemie's progress, build your confidence, and enhance your relationship with your child. Some of these suggestions may work for you and your child; others won't. As the parent, it is your responsibility to know your youngster, consult your intuition, consider various parenting approaches, experiment, and then select what fits for you and your child and toss out what doesn't. The bulk of this chapter explores some of the important ways you can support your child's development from infancy through childhood. The final section discusses evaluations and labels.

Like many parents, you may also struggle with managing heightened vigilance and living with uncertainty and ambiguity with regard to your child's development. These emotional aspects of supporting your child's development are the focus of the next chapter.

Six Basic Skills for Supporting Your Preemie's Development

I had a wonderful pediatrician who was very good at letting me know what I should do differently from [what I would do for] a normal full-term baby. There was so much [that was] different. —Rosa

There are many general ways to support your child's development: Give freely of your attention and affection, talk and read to your child, provide imaginative toys, offer your child opportunities to explore, provide nutritious foods, set reasonable limits, discipline gently and firmly, cultivate a supportive network, and more. Underlying these parenting skills are six basic concepts that can guide you as you attempt to meet your growing baby's unique needs:

- Take into account the connection between brain and behavior
- Tune in to your child's sensitivities and sensory thresholds for stimulation
- Empathize with your child's feelings, perceptions, and abilities
- Follow your child's lead
- Encourage your child to reach beyond his or her current abilities
- Enjoy your child and your relationship

Though some of these concepts may sound complicated, they are really fairly easy and intuitive, and you will naturally start practicing these basic skills as soon as your baby is born. These concepts are also intertwined, and your skills build on each other. For example:

- Recognizing the brain-behavior connection motivates you to ...
- Tune in to sensitivities and thresholds, which requires you to ...
- Empathize with your child, which entails ...
- Following your child's lead, which enhances your capability to...
- Encourage your child to reach beyond current abilities, which rests on
- Enjoying your child and your relationship, which includes ...
- Recognizing the brain-behavior connection ...

Your abilities to tune in, empathize, follow, encourage, and enjoy also promote your baby's ability to tune in to you, follow your lead sometimes, respond to your empathy and encouragement, and enjoy your relationship. This reciprocity or synchronous dance between the two of you is key to promoting your baby's development.

As you get to know your baby and engage in this synchronous dance, you can see how your responsiveness, empathy, lead-following, encouragement, and enjoyment can help your infant reach his or her first significant milestone: to stay calm while maintaining interest in his or her surroundings. This critical developmental step forms the starting point from which your baby is able to engage in meaningful relationships and communication with others, as well as continue her or his physical, intellectual, and emotional development.

Not only do these six basic concepts reflect a general attitude and approach to parenting, but they also can

- Strengthen your confidence and skills as a nurturing parent
- Give you appropriate and hopeful expectations for your child
- Help you guide and encourage your child to reach his or her full potential
- Enhance your ability to enjoy your child and your parenthood

The bulk of this chapter explores these six basic concepts and discusses how you can incorporate them into your parenting. To learn more about these six basic concepts, turn to the books listed in "Supporting Your Preemie's Development" in Appendix C.

The Brain-Behavior Connection

All of us have known children who were picky eaters and children who would eat anything that was put before them. We've known kids who napped until they were five years old and kids who gave up naps before their second birthday. We've known children who are cautious and kids who are bold. We've known children who love to sit and draw and others who run circles around us. What do all of these children have in common? Their behaviors reflect how their brains function.

As medical science continues to unravel the mysteries of the brain, the idea that humans have "free will"—control over their behavior if they choose to exercise it—is being modified. We now know that brain chemistry and functioning play a significant role in everything from emotional characteristics (such as depression, anxiety, and autism) to behavioral characteristics (such as hyperactivity, compulsivity, eating disorders, and drug abuse) to learning issues (such as dyslexia, attention deficit disorder, and giftedness) to personality characteristics (such as shyness, optimism, and adaptability).

Despite its biological nature, the brain doesn't operate in a biological vacuum: everything a child is or does is *not* neurologically preprogrammed or genetically determined—but neither is a child a blank slate for the parents, society, or surroundings to write on. Environmental influences (such as family functioning, the quality of the parent-child relationship, neighborhood, school, climate, nutrition, culture, social network, and everyday experiences) and biology (such as genes, physiological chemistry, and neurological functioning) are intertwined and often inseparable in affecting behavior and all areas of development. For instance, brain chemistry and functioning are affected by environmental influences, ranging from caffeine intake to the quality of interactions with others. In turn, the specific effects of interactions with others and caffeine intake depend on one's biological tendencies, strengths, and weaknesses.

Interactions with others are particularly powerful influences. Now that scientists can observe brain function and structure by measuring electrical brain waves and using sophisticated medical scanning equipment, there is clear evidence that human interaction, especially interaction with caregivers, can shape brain development. Accurately attuned responses (for example, soothing, containing, structuring, and guiding) can actually have a positive effect on the physical development of your baby's brain and can even help to modulate (but not cure) certain glitches in your child's neurology.

Similarly, the sights and sounds and feel of your baby's surroundings also have a tremendous effect on his or her brain development. These effects are tremendous because the newborn's brain is still a work in progress, a wiring system that is a virtual tangle of neurological connections that need refining. Connections are strengthened or weakened according to the sights, sounds, smells, tastes, and touch that an infant experiences. Unfortunately, in order to develop optimally, the immature brain of a premature baby requires the muted experiences of the womb, not the high intensity of a busy NICU.

If a preemie is bombarded with glare, clamor, and abrupt handling instead of the darkness, muted sound, and soft envelope of the womb, then the brain's refining process can be quite different, affecting to some extent how the infant's brain is wired, and ultimately, how he or she learns, organizes, reacts to, and makes sense of experiences.

That's why developmentally supportive care is so important in the NICU—and at home. The ideal environment imitates what your baby would have been exposed to in the womb (muted and gentle experiences) or what your baby would normally experience at birth (held to the mother's breast, cradled in the father's arms, family closeness). Conditions that fulfill your preemie's needs give your baby the best chance for healthy brain development. If your infant experienced less-than-ideal conditions, by accommodating your child's needs now you can still make a positive contribution to his or her brain development. Especially during infancy and even in childhood, the brain has "plasticity," meaning that it continues to refine its connections according to the experiences to which it's exposed. The more we learn about the brain, the better we are able to understand how to affect neurology and how to discover and design treatments that really work. Besides addressing the surroundings and interactions with others, treatments can involve other environmental influences that have important effects, depending on the biology of the individual's brain. Treatment may include

- Medications that regulate the brain's chemistry
- A diet free of toxins (toxins can include usually benign substances such as dairy products, wheat gluten, yeast, mold, alcohol, or other elements that have toxic effects on some people's systems because of genetic and/or environmental sensitivities)
- A diet that supplies missing nutrients or other requirements

- Surgery to remedy physical malformations or malfunctioning
- Practicing new ways of thinking and interacting that enrich brain function
- Exposure to natural sunlight (which has been shown to affect mood)
- Basic physical maintenance, such as adequate sleep and rest, regular exercise, and keeping blood sugar levels even (all of which can enhance mood and functioning)

In short, our brains benefit from the intake of nutritious foods, and if necessary, supplements and medications, as well as from engaging in a variety of healthy activities and interactions with others. Even if a child's brain has certain permanent limitations, aiming for maximum brain health is aiming for maximum developmental and behavioral health.

If a child is misbehaving or having trouble, it's important to look to the brain for pieces that can help solve the puzzle. For example, if a child can't stay organized, content, and focused at morning preschool, the brain's needs may dictate the solution. Here is a list of possible underlying problems and their associated solutions for this hypothetical scenario:

- If the child is uncooperative because her blood sugar is low, she doesn't need a time-out, she needs a nutritious snack or meal.
- If the child is tired because he really needs a morning nap (circadian rhythms, or natural sleep/wake cycles, can be hard to change), he may do better in an afternoon preschool program.
- If the child is bored, she may need a more stimulating or individualized program to fit her needs.
- If the child has trouble integrating sensory input, he will likely benefit from occupational therapy to give him the types and intensities of sensory stimulation he needs.
- If the child has trouble processing the teacher's verbal instructions, she will benefit from language therapy as well as nonverbal instructions.
- If the child is fearful, the teacher's interactions with him may be cool or abrupt, and either orienting the teacher to his needs or switching to a different teacher may be the solution.
- If the child is anxious, depressed, or stressed, she may benefit from attention to her emotional needs and identification of whatever is over-whelming her, as well as encouragement and guidance in verbalizing feelings and using self-soothing techniques.

- If the anxiety or depression is intractable, he may benefit from antianxiety or antidepression drugs or nutritional measures to improve brain chemistry.

There are many possible scenarios. Your job is to be a parent-detective. When you can identify the real problem, you can find a real solution that takes into account the brain-behavior connection.

I think we've both known for quite a while that "there's something just not quite right" with Curtis. He's bright and articulate but wants to be in the same room with us nearly all the time. He talks constantly. He can't follow multistep instructions. But the first few times (over several years) that I mentioned to Jeff that he might be ADD (because I knew that it's common in preemies), Jeff wasn't willing to admit that there was a "problem." He always said, "I knew he was perfect when he was born, I loved him before he was born, he'll be fine." Finally, this fall I had a major breakthrough in getting him to consider there might be a problem. It's partly because my nephew (full-term, now in third grade) underwent a full battery of educational and psychological testing last year and was finally diagnosed with mild ADD and dyslexia. Jeff saw how much better he did in school with the correct diagnosis and help. ... We know Curtis is very bright and want him to have every tool he needs to succeed.

Right now we're in a "wait and see" stage as we adjust his dose of [ADD medication] to see if it will work for him (the doctor was reluctant to try stimulants because of anxiety). It's frustrating dealing with side effects but rewarding seeing an occasional glimmer of the child he can be with his impulsive behavior moderated. He gets along better with his sister and with other kids. Today he admitted that a box of 100 crayons I accused his sister of spilling in the car wasn't her mess but his and helped to clean it up! Six weeks ago he'd have sworn on his life that he had nothing to do with it even if I'd seen him spill it! —Melissa

Tuning In to Sensitivities and Thresholds

Every baby and child has unique preferences for stimulation, but preemies tend to have more exaggerated sensitivities, including higher or lower thresholds for stimulation, inflexible preferences, and stronger reactions than term infants. That's why your baby's behaviors may seem like troublesome barriers to building a relationship. Especially as your confidence grows and you feel more enthusiastic about interacting with your baby, you may feel frustrated when your overtures are rebuffed. It's hard to play with a preemie who falls asleep or falls apart every time you try to make contact. (For a helpful review of infant behavioral states, reading and responding to cues, and engaging your baby, turn to the sections "Becoming Attuned to Your Baby" in Chapter 9 and "Getting in Tune with Your Growing Baby" in Chapter 13.

It is important for you to remember that your baby's sensitivities and thresholds for stimulation are biologically based. They are not a measure of your competence as a parent. How your baby takes in, processes, and responds to sounds (including language), sights, touch, taste, smell, movement, emotions, and interaction is determined by the particular ways his or her body and brain operate. By learning to recognize your baby's unique constellation of tendencies and preferences, you can help your little one tune in to and ultimately interact with the world. To support your child's growth and development, you can tailor your interactions so that they play to your child's strengths and minimize the demands on his or her weaknesses. As you enhance your baby's strengths, you help your little one acquire tools for developing those weaker areas.

Expanding Your Baby's Sensory Abilities Some premature babies cannot tolerate more than one bit of stimulation at a time. For instance, your infant may not be able to tolerate both visual and auditory stimulation, being held and talked to at the same time, or being fed when there is a lot of activity, noise, or light. These limited tolerances are not a reflection of your baby's feelings for you; he or she simply finds it too exciting and overwhelming to use more than one sense at a time. Keep in mind that your baby's brain needs time to mature. Before you know it, she or he will be able to take a lot more in stride.

In the meantime, there are things you can do to help your baby tolerate using and integrating multiple senses. First, ask yourself, "What senses is my baby using right now, and what is she or he sensing?" Then, try to figure out what your child enjoys and what irritates him or her. Use the information you gather to help your baby build on strengths and shore up weaknesses.

For instance, here is a list of observations you might make about your baby's strengths and weaknesses:

- Your baby is unresponsive to low voices and you discover that she

attends to higher-pitched voices
- Your baby brightens more to singing than talking
- Your baby is overwhelmed by your sustained efforts to maintain eye contact, and you discover that when you are quiet and let your baby set the pace, he looks away when he needs a break but easily comes back to you in his own time
- Your baby is uncomfortable with light stroking, but enjoys firm massage or soothes when you hold onto a hand or foot or when you cup her head and body in your motionless hands
- Your baby takes little interest in the world, but becomes alert when you move him in rhythmic ways or talk to him in an animated manner

As you discover your baby's sensory preferences, you can strengthen your child's ability to tolerate and attend to certain kinds of stimulation, one at a time. Perhaps your little one enjoys being held. In that case, as you hold her quietly, gradually try different positions or motions, and widen the variety of holds she can tolerate. Perhaps she enjoys singing. As you sing to her in her infant seat, you can also try talking in a sing-songy voice, thereby extending her ability to attend to language and sound.

Then, try combining the types of stimulation your child finds pleasant and soothing. Try singing softly to her while you're holding her and see how she does. The next step is to pair something your baby finds soothing or interesting with something that is more challenging: for example, you can encourage your baby to tolerate eye contact (the challenge) when you hold her in her favorite position or sing to her (soothing things). After some time, your infant may eventually grow to tolerate eye contact without the soothing props. Swaddling, sucking, holding your baby upright over your shoulder, or skin-to-skin contact, such as kangaroo care, are among other props that can help your baby extend and integrate his or her senses.

For many preemies, a big challenge is eating, because it can involve eye contact, holding, touching, talking, rocking, and sucking. Reduce the number of stimulating components by looking away from your baby often, feeding him in dim light, swaddling him, or keeping the rocker still. If your baby can't tolerate a lot of handling before feeding, just pick her up and feed her, leaving the diaper changing and interacting for after she's had her fill.

Many babies also find it challenging to make the transition between waking and sleeping states. If your baby fusses when ready to sleep or wake up, you can provide containment and soothing that will help him or her fall asleep, stay asleep, or awaken calmly. Try soothers such as swaddling, holding, motion, background music, and sucking. These are helpful supports for your infant.

Capturing and Holding Your Baby's Interest Figuring out how to engage and maintain your baby's interest without overstimulation can take some detective work and real effort on your part. Experiment with different strategies and ask your baby's NICU nurses, developmental specialists, therapists, or other parents for pointers. By learning what your baby can handle and being sensitive to his or her cues, you are teaching your infant that the world is a fun and interesting place that responds to individual needs. As you get to know your baby better, and as your baby becomes more resilient and robust, tuning in to those unique sensitivities and thresholds will become easier. In turn, as your baby develops and learns that the world is fun and interesting, her or his ability to stay engaged improves, and she or he becomes increasingly motivated to attend to the surroundings, including you.

Tuning in to your child's sensitivities and thresholds is something you'll want to continue throughout your youngster's childhood. This skill feeds your ability to assess your child's strengths and weaknesses, capabilities, and growth, and it will help you to support and encourage your child's continued development.

Empathizing with Your Child

At birth, a baby's limbic system—the primitive, reactive part of the central nervous system—controls his behavior. Your baby's response to feeling an emotion is simply to react. Helping your maturing child to identify his emotions with words enables the child to express feelings constructively and respectfully *and* builds connections from the reactive brain to the thinking brain. The more your child can practice this, the more connections will be formed, and the easier it will be for him to stop behaving impulsively. Instead of simply reacting, your child can identify the emotion, think of an appropriate response, and behave accordingly. Identifying emotions is the hallmark of emotional intelligence. Emotionally smart kids are cooperative, motivated, and able to get along with others.

Teaching Your Child about Emotions So, how do you help your child identify her emotions? Use your empathy—your ability to see and appreciate your child's perspective—to provide emotional coaching. Teaching your child about her emotions also builds your relationship with her, which can further enhance all areas of your child's health and development.

Having empathy with your child does not mean always giving in to his demands or giving him emotional free reign. Having empathy means listening, trying to understand, helping your child label his emotions, setting clear limits, and teaching your child how to express emotions respectfully and constructively. Such parenting behaviors will convince your child that he can trust you and turn to you for guidance—and they ultimately help your child develop self-control.

Another aspect of being an empathic parent is recognizing the role of temperament in your child's behavior. We call this nurturing your child's nature.

Nurturing Your Child's Nature A child's personality, or temperament, used to be considered largely a product of the environment, something parents could mold, by force if necessary. If parents did a good job, conventional wisdom had it, they could produce children who were passive, happy, easygoing conformists. Needless to say, many parents "failed." In the 1970s, however, Drs. Stella Chess and Alexander Thomas unveiled research showing that on nine qualities of temperament, children remained consistent from infancy (two months of age) through childhood, implying that these qualities are inherent to a child's nature. Babies with sunny dispositions, for example, tended to be sunny ten-year-olds, whereas babies who were more serious tended to be serious ten-year-olds. Chess and Thomas's nine qualities of temperament are

- General mood (happy vs. serious)
- Sensitivity (easily startled or upset vs. nonplussed)
- Intensity (whimpers vs. screams when upset; chuckles vs. shrieks with delight)
- Persistence (moves on easily vs. doesn't give up)
- Activity level (active vs. passive)
- Regularity (naps and eats at the same time vs. naps and eats at different times every day)
- Adaptability (resists vs. embraces changes in plans or situations)
- Distractibility (easily distracted vs. intensely focused)
- Approach/withdrawal (bold vs. cautious)

Most children fall between the extremes in each category, but some children tend to fall at one extreme or the other. Children may behave at the extremes temporarily because they are stressed—tired, hungry, bored, sick, or dealing with major life changes. Allergies and food sensitivities or other physical problems that make a child feel generally uncomfortable can also push a child's temperament toward the challenging ends of the spectrum. If your child's usual behaviors fall at the extremes in many of the categories, you will find support and ideas for helping her or him in the books mentioned in Appendix C: Resources at the back of this book.

The concept of inherent temperament has tremendous implications for parenting. You can more effectively deal with challenges when you see them as inborn or biological. Rather than forcing your child to exhibit personality traits that are not a part of her nature, you can work with your child according to her temperament. For example, instead of forcing the cautious child to be bold, you can work with him when caution gets in the way of progress. The rest of the time, you can be grateful that your child tends to "think before he leaps."

It can also help to recognize your own temperament. If your child's temperament doesn't match yours very well, you can experience a good deal of conflict if you don't make room for your child's own tendencies and preferences. Or, if you and your child share certain temperament qualities that you criticize in yourself, you will likely devalue those qualities in your child. It is important to be aware and accepting of the temperament differences and similarities between you and your child, so that you can learn to appreciate and work *with* them. Indeed, knowing and accepting your child often entails knowing and accepting yourself.

If you find certain aspects of your child's temperament challenging, one of the most helpful and sanity-restoring things you can do is to appreciate the strengths each quality can carry. For example, children who persistently whine for what they want also tend to work persistently on a problem until it's solved or on a project until it's finished. A child who is sensitive to sock seams may also notice other little things, like dewdrops. The distractible child can be easily steered away from electrical outlets if given something else to do; the child who is not easily distractible is committed and focused.

We admire all of these traits in successful adults. It helps to keep in mind how useful these characteristics will be when your child reaches adulthood. Your job as a parent is to understand and guide your child's tendencies into positive pursuits and appropriate channels.

· · ·

Naturally, parents like to take credit for their children's developmental accomplishments and positive personality traits. Unfortunately, when you do this, you also have to shoulder a lot of the blame for your children's faults and difficulties. In the long run, it's easier to acknowledge that your children's temperament qualities, sensitivities and thresholds, strengths and weaknesses, and inborn developmental timetables play a huge role in their growth and development. And a more realistic view of parenting is to give your child most of the credit (and responsibility) for most of his or her growth and development. Give yourself credit for providing a facilitating environment, encouraging and appreciating your child's strengths, and learning how to understand, cope with, work with—and yes, even appreciate—your child's challenges. By helping your child get in tune with his or her qualities of temperament, you also teach your child to deal with situations in ways that work with, instead of against, his or her disposition. Your child may be unique in so many ways, some that are wonderful and integral to his or her spirit and others that call for your assistance and guidance. Your youngster will always benefit from your unconditional support; as you embrace your child's essence, it will become more familiar and manageable.

Following Your Child's Lead

Following your child's lead means recognizing that your child's developmental timetable will be as unique as he or she is. Following your child's lead also means trusting that his or her development will unfold naturally.

All parents have to learn to provide the right conditions to support their children's development. And for most parents, following a child's lead is fairly clear-cut because standard expectations, common approaches, and popular parenting techniques fit well enough.

Raising some children can take more ingenuity and effort. Their parents may turn to books that write about the "spirited" child or the child who "drives you crazy." Following a child's lead when she or he is spirited can be a struggle, but by trial and error and with conscious effort, parents can figure out how to respond to their unique child.

A third group of children dwell "outside the box." For these families, there is often a huge mismatch between what the parents expect and know how to provide and what the child requires to thrive. Even the books on "spirited" children don't offer the right kind of advice or insight, and well-meaning friends and even professionals may be as stumped as you are. If you have this type of child, you will need to do more than your share of research, experimentation, adjustment, and learning by trial and error. Naturally, your parenting experience will be extra bumpy because few have traveled the road before you. Following your child's lead will require improvisation, intuition, and a lot of trust.

For example, if your child craves certain kinds of movement, activity, and sensory experiences, don't expect him to "snap out of it" or to respond to reward or punishment. This will only lead to failure and disappointment. Instead, understand that your child is trying to nourish his brain with the kinds of stimulation it needs to stay alert and organized. Follow your child's lead and guide your little one toward safe alternatives. If your child wants to jump on the bed, put an old box spring on the floor or get a mini-trampoline. If your child loves strong smells, provide flowers, herbs, or extracts to sniff. If your child doesn't like the feel of certain fabrics, buy cotton knits with gentle elastic and remove the tags.

Also provide your child with a sensory diet that includes alerting, organizing, or calming activities that fit your child's needs. Oversensitive children benefit from calming activities such as sucking on a pacifier or Popsicle, swinging, rocking, massage, and warm baths. Undersensitive children benefit from alerting activities such as bouncing, jumping, taking showers, and eating crunchy foods. Some children are a combination of under- and oversensitive, and they require a combination of calming and alerting activities. Also keep in mind that certain activities help organize and coordinate a child's physical movements, such as hanging by the hands on a bar, pushing or pulling heavy loads, getting into an upside-down position, and eating chewy foods. You can also offer play experiences that engage multiple senses, such as cooking or baking (and then eating) food; dressing up in exotic feathery, silky, or furry costume clothing; or playing with toys in water, sand, rice, flour, popcorn, or mud.

Making Adjustments Kids will usually show problematic behaviors when their needs are not being met. As a child, you knew when conditions were all wrong for you, and your behavior reflected your discomfort. Sometimes you were listened to, and sometimes you weren't. Of course, following your child's lead doesn't mean listening and yielding to proclamations that ice cream is the only edible food and that regular bedtime should be past midnight. There is a difference between wants and needs. Rather, following your child's lead means listening, observing her or his behavior, and assuming that if your child is obviously struggling, acting out, misbehaving, or generally being difficult to live with, some important needs are going unmet. Figure out the conditions that will meet those needs and you'll produce a happier, thriving child.

Here are some things your child may need when you see him struggling:
- Nourishing snacks throughout the day
- More sleep, including naps or adjusting bedtime
- More attention from busy parents
- An emptier calendar or slower paced schedule
- More help with troubles at school or with peers
- More guidance and limits at home
- More autonomy, responsibilities, or choices
- Reassurance about fears and anxieties, coaching on how to talk back to anxiety, or permission to be more dependent than the parent might expect
- Challenges, things to do that he or she finds interesting, or opportunities to be more independent
- Fewer demands placed on sensory weaknesses, such as protection from overwhelming touch, sounds, and social situations.
- Support for special physiological needs, such as a special diet to address digestive sensitivities, eyeglasses to correct vision, therapy to help coordinate eating and swallowing, or medications or other measures to address biochemical imbalances in the body or brain
- Different parenting or teaching approaches that support special emotional, cognitive, social, or physical needs. For instance, a child who is distracted and uncooperative because she cannot follow verbal directions will need extra assistance in understanding what to do before she can attend and cooperate. A child who is distracted and uncooperative because he is devastated by criticism or scolding will need gentle discipline and more encouragement.

If your child is experiencing problems, you can also try parenting "against type." For example, if your child is aggressive and angry, instead of lashing out and escalating the aggression and anger on your side, be the calm presence that is firm about rules such as "no hitting." If your baby is fussy, be the calm presence that soothes with empathy and warm baths. If your baby isn't interested in interacting, try to woo your little one instead of leaving him or her alone.

Without help, your child may develop a habitually withdrawn or oppositional stance toward others. Recognize that this approach is simply your child's best effort to get what she or he needs. Your child is not acting out or withdrawing in order to drive you crazy. Assume that, if she or he could, your child would much rather be happy, physically and emotionally healthy, getting along with others, growing, or learning a new skill. Your job is to figure out what remedy your child needs to grow and be healthy. To determine which conditions and approaches work best, try a variety—and observe what's most effective. If something isn't working, that doesn't mean you need to do it longer or harder, it means you need to try something different.

> *My daughter, Mackenzie, suffers from anxiety issues. There is an article I read about a year ago that was very enlightening, on multiple areas of hidden disability. It discussed common behaviors they had found in extremely low–birthweight school-age children. [The behaviors] included high activity, needs urging to respond, distrusts own ability, anxious, gives up easily, seeks to terminate, prefers only easy tasks, needs constant praise and encouragement. I read it and was floored at how many of the behaviors Mackenzie had—I thought it was something I was doing wrong! Well, since then we have done some alternative therapies to help her (and me). Homeopathy has been wonderful! She is seen by a classical homeopath (which is different than buying a homeopathic remedy at the store), and I see significant improvements. Her grades have excelled! Not because it's made her any smarter, but her anxiety is low and self-esteem is up. ... [Homeopathy] just makes one balanced. Balance is taken from our children immediately at birth.—Dianne*

Each child holds the desire to blossom and flourish. If you follow your child's lead, you can provide the right conditions for your child to thrive.

> *One of the responsibilities I feel most keenly right now is the desire to protect and celebrate the differences that are Stuart's gifts, yet to maximize his ability to live effectively in the "normal" world. I have read everything I can get my hands on about the different approaches to working with children who have similar challenges. Some of the behavior modification programs that show*

success, while effective in teaching interactive and self-care skills, seem to do it by stamping out the things that make these children so special. I look at my tender little boy who has been through so much and realize I want to nurture him into this life, not push, prod, and demand compliance. However, we do use some behavior-mod techniques with him in specific areas, particularly eating. But our underlying approach is to let Stuart lead the way. We have to support him, to enable and enhance his growth, to challenge him, but most of all, we have to let him lead the way. —Susan

Following your child's lead means accepting that your child must form his or her own image. When your child is having trouble, do your best to gently guide your little one in positive directions that complement his or her self-determination. Indeed, following your child's lead helps you become the kind of guide your child can follow.

Growth Charts, Developmental Timetables, and Trusting Your Child's Path

Anytime I get a written report about them, it makes me angry when they put an age to anything. I get really mad that they don't have standardized tests for preemies. It's unfair to compare them to "normal" kids, and just adjusting for age doesn't quite cut it for kids who are born this little and this early. I wish there were people who could say, "This is normal for a five-year-old who was born at twenty-three weeks." I would just like to know how they are doing. I know they are doing phenomenally, but their speech is still very delayed, and they're going for occupational therapy and are going to go for physical therapy, but I'd like to know, compared to kids born this early, is this normal? It's very frustrating being a pioneer, and there isn't anything I can read about development. And anything that is written, there are so many variables that affect developmental outcome. It's frustrating. —Stephie

Naturally, following your child's lead is tempered by whether your child fits in with what is normally expected at a given age. Growth charts and developmental timetables are often used to evaluate whether a child is on track and whether interventions are indicated.

Unfortunately, most preemies don't follow the standard growth charts and developmental timetables, which can make parents tremendously anxious. Even when age is adjusted or "corrected" to reflect how old a preemie would be if he or she had been born at term, growth and development can take years to "catch up."

Indeed, for some preemies, "catching up" is not a goal that makes sense, because it perpetually labels them as "behind." Especially if your preemie doesn't comply with the standards, drop the urge to compare, and consider your child to be on his or her very own growth chart and developmental timetable. Look for progress, not conformity.

We were told Stuart would "catch up" by one year. Then two. Now at three years, three months, his prognosis is as uncertain as it has always been. He struggles with many delays yet triumphs with many accomplishments. As potential "diagnoses" are proffered and retracted, we try with varying degrees of success to focus on the individual and his sweet, unique personality. —Susan

With regard to physical growth, your pediatrician should be able to supply you with growth charts calibrated for preemies. (You can also find these charts in Tracy and Maroney's book, *Your Premature Baby and Child;* see Appendix C: Resources for more information.) Still, instead of focusing predominately on age and charts, concentrate on

- Providing a nutritious, well-balanced diet
- Encouraging your child to enjoy eating
- Cultivating a warm and nurturing relationship with your little one
- Trusting that your child will grow, even if it's not according to a standard growth chart
- If your child needs additional calories, it is particularly important that you focus on building your child's enjoyment of eating. Consult your pediatrician or other specialist to help you come up with a plan.

Similarly, regarding development, concentrate your energies on

- Providing fun and interesting surroundings and activities
- Cultivating a warm and nurturing relationship with your little one
- Trusting that your child will learn what he or she learns when he or she is ready

Note that both lists include "cultivating a warm and nurturing relationship with your little one" and "trusting your child." Cultivating your relationship is perhaps the most important factor in your child's growth and development. It is also fun and deeply rewarding for both of you. Trusting, on the other hand, can be challenging, especially when you have anxieties about growth or delays. You may fear that if you follow your baby's lead on eating or learning, he or she may never reach maximum potential. If this is one of your fears, remember that it is far more important that your child slowly build strong foundations based on early milestones rather than being pushed before she or he is eager to move on. For example, your child must

- Be proficient at suck-swallow-breathe coordination before he can learn to breast-feed or drink from a bottle
- Be competent at tongue coordination before she can learn to eat solid foods
- Be comfortable with making eye contact before he can experience intimacy
- Understand how to communicate with gestures before she can use words meaningfully
- Be skilled at standing up before he can walk
- Learn her letters before she can read

It doesn't matter when or how fast your child acquires those latter skills as much as it matters that your child builds a strong foundation of the former skills on which his or her abilities can grow. When your child is older, how well she or he can do these things will be far more important than how old your child was when he or she first learned to do them. Don't fall into the trap of rushing your child ahead. Doing so can make for weak foundations and shaky starts, undermining skill development.

His little cousin was very early with everything she did, so the comparison was even more warped. Everybody compares. That is normal. We always had to remind ourselves and others that the development range is large and there are so many variations. As he was and is making continuous progress, that's just fine.
—Sarah

It is frustrating to see kids the same age (sometimes I forget to correct her age) or younger doing so much more than she is doing. I know that she will eventually do [these things] and that all kids develop at a different rate. My comment to parents "complaining" about their child becoming mobile at an early age (or bragging about doing anything at an early age) is that the only thing that Alison has done early is come early. That normally gets a chuckle and the conversation moves on. It is just reassuring to see her healthy and gaining weight. She is gradually doing more and more things—on her *time schedule. —Stacy*

Of course, some medical complications or disabilities make growth and development more of a struggle. If your child is not progressing and nothing seems to help, you may long to uncover and overcome whatever is interfering with your little one's growth and development. If the "experts" are not providing answers that work for you and your child, you have nothing to lose by striking out on your own. March to the beat of your child's drummer. Trust that you and your child can form a powerful alliance to figure out what your child needs. Respect your child's uniqueness and work with (not against) your child to help him or her reach for health and growth. Your child's development is his or her own journey. You can be a companion, a guide, and an assistant navigator, but let your child do the driving.

I know that my son is an incredibly bright, incredibly sensitive little soul with so much potential. I am learning that his potential will unfold in his own time frames, according to his own motivations, and that my job is to provide every avenue to enhance that process. —Susan

Grappling with Oral Feeding Difficulties

I have a white-knuckle grip on the conviction that Lars will grow out of his feeding problems (with lots of help), and grow, and overcome his speech delays (we are introducing sign but so far he shows no interest ...). I realize that in so many ways we are very lucky, but the feeding issues are unrelenting and overwhelming. Will we all be "fine" when his feeding issues resolve? I hope so, but I feel so far removed from "normal" that I couldn't make you, me, or anyone else any promises. And today is a good day. —Kris

Feeding is a significant and challenging issue for many parents and preemies. It can be particularly important to follow your child's lead in this area, especially if your child has such feeding difficulties as oral defensiveness, lack of appetite, or physical complications such as reflux or those necessitating tube-feeding. Because feeding is such an emotionally laden area for parents, you may struggle greatly along with your child.

It was a struggle to feed him, and he was labeled Failure to Thrive. Of course I took that "failure" label to heart. What kind of mom was I that I can't even nourish my child? —Julie

A child who will not/cannot eat normally is a recrimination of our parenting ability. For more than five years, my child's every meal, every nutritional substance, has been a struggle, a total focus on surviving. There is no sharing of M&Ms, never the chance to leave a hungry child to a good meal, never the ability to relax, to enjoy, to be normal. Every family outing is focused on carrying enough PediaSure, every meal centered around prompting each and every bite after self-feeding was finally coaxed from a reluctant four-year-old.

I think my biggest weakness as a parent to Stuart's younger brother is my total indulgence to dessert, to treats, to the sheer pleasure of eating. My inability to share the joy of eating with Stuart leads to my overindulgence with Justin. I feel guilty for what Stuart can't do (eat normally); guilty for what Justin doesn't do (eat healthily). —Susan

You may also have questions about whether your baby is becoming "too" dependent on his method of feeding (e.g., the bottle, the tube, your spoon-feeding) or whether the barrier to progress is physical or psychological. You want to balance your child's developmental needs with nutritional ones.

When it comes to feeding, nutritional, physical, psychological, and developmental issues are intertwined. Your child's inability to suck from a bottle, tolerate solid foods, or self-feed can be directly related to developmental lags as well as digestive or physiological problems such as reflux. Oral aversions can have a basis in memory of negative experiences along with coordination problems with chewing and swallowing that lead to gagging and choking. Finding a physician or other specialist who can give you the diagnoses and treatments your child needs can be hard, but it is important to trust your intuition and persist until you get the help you need.

A topic that I feel is minimized by the medical profession is the tendency for preemies to be troubled with varying degrees of feeding problems. I resent the fact that I took my preemie home without that knowledge—and struggled for nearly a year before getting help. And now, nine months later, we're still trying to undo the damage of silent reflux. —Angela

If your child eats, but eating is a struggle, try to step back. Pressure to eat often leads to power struggles, which can undermine your relationship with your child and your child's progress. Trust that your child knows what his or her body can handle—even if it's to be fed mainly by gastrostomy tube. If you swear your child would starve if you didn't tube-feed, you may very well be correct. When your child requires or is dependent on tube-feedings, his or her appetite or oral consumption of food doesn't increase with a decrease in feedings. This evidence doesn't mean you should break that dependency. It means you should *honor* it by providing the means your child depends on to get the nutrition she or he requires for optimal growth.

Jacob now gets most of his nutrition through a G-tube. We fought to avoid this for six and a half years. I was so creative with getting calories into him, and he had worked through a good deal of his oral defensiveness issues. He was eating table foods!!! This past spring, Jacob had a series of seizures that left him without the desire/ability to eat. He dropped a scary amount of weight, and we finally agreed that the tube was needed. Since having his tube, he's been gaining a steady amount of weight and has also begun to grow cognitively at a faster rate. Feed the body, feed the brain. —Julie

Many parents are heartened by how the G-tube results in marked growth and developmental strides. Joan says, "As he grew developmentally, I felt the G-tube was the neatest thing since sliced bread." But even though nutritional problems can be solved by tube-feeding, problems with oral feeding may remain, and they can be frustrating and tenacious. If your child has medical clearance to eat but resists swallowing or even putting food in his or her mouth, you may second-guess your consent to the feeding tube. You may wonder if you should have kept trying to get your child to eat more. If the feeding tube was placed during infancy, you may wonder whether you should have given your child's natural eating "instincts" more time to kick in before agreeing to the tube. You may also crave the normalcy of being able to feed your child from the family table.

I tube-fed Chris for three and a half years, and the length of time was very frustrating (we were told it would be for a maximum of six months). The greatest source of frustration was that Chris stopped eating anything (except for a few Cheerios) by mouth within a month of being tube-fed. We tried feeding therapy, sensory integration therapy, bribery, etc., to get him to eat, and he'd just chew it up and spit it out. It was so hard to see other kids chow down on food and my child be so difficult—even though I knew it was his oral tactile defensiveness.

I was angry a lot, especially after trying to prepare something nice for the family and Chris wouldn't eat it. I don't think we ever got into a power struggle over it because I knew I had no control over his eating, but there were times the smell of vanilla PediaSure was enough to drive me insane. —Amy

As with so many issues, it is very important that you stay in touch with your feelings of grief over the issue of feeding, so that you are not compelled to override your child's real needs. Also consider that the aspects of your child's condition that necessitated the feeding tube have prevented your child from connecting with his or her natural eating instincts. In other words, it may not be the feeding tube itself that creates the oral aversions, but your child's *brain development* and *physiological conditions* that keep him or her from developing the coordination to eat and the association between eating and satisfaction. Knowing this can help you be more patient with your child's progress, as Julie can now attest:

Jacob gave up oral eating right after getting his tube (almost two years ago). He's now back to eating orally three or four times a day and is working on regaining his cup drinking skills. It just takes time ... more time if hunger is no longer a major motivator and if the child associates eating with pain or unpleasant sensations. —Julie

If you've ruled out esophageal, stomach, and intestinal problems and your child still can't shake oral aversions to eating, this can be a sign of *significant* coordination or sensory difficulties. Your child should be evaluated by a speech pathologist or another professional who has experience helping preemies learn how to suck, chew, and swallow. If you are seeing a professional who advises you to force-feed your child or who insists that the problem is merely a power struggle or that it stems from you alone, you are not getting the assistance or support you need. Parents who have been down this road can tell you that those approaches don't help, that they produce guilt and discomfort. There *are* professionals who can identify the root of your child's problem and help you encourage and teach your child without force. (Check out Appendix C: Resources at the back of this book; also see "Feeding Issues" in Chapter 14 for more information and support.) Also ask other parents for practical suggestions.

> *Even though Taylor's feeding problems had a physical basis, the trauma of the years of fighting, puking, force-feeding, and on and on [recommended by therapists!] caused an "eating disorder." After a gag episode, he would refuse all foods and liquids for days. We were told to force-feed him. He is telling me right now (as he reads this over my shoulder) that [he refused to eat] because he was afraid that he would puke. ... Today, he is physically capable of eating any type of food [after finally seeing a speech pathologist who specializes in motor speech disorders]. But believe me, it is a daily struggle. He still carries a huge phobia about eating. —Tammy*

If in spite of topflight evaluations, treatments, and therapies, your child does not seem to be making progress, assume that there are developmental or physiological keys that have not yet been uncovered. Stay in touch with the professional community and the community of parents who have children with feeding problems. Along with providing camaraderie and support, parents form valuable networks that share information on the latest research, therapies, and practical suggestions that have worked for them.

Of course, your ultimate goal is that your child eventually learn to eat *and* enjoy food. Whatever your child's situation, focus on making mealtimes enjoyable. One way to do that is to provide a variety of nutritious foods, and then let your child determine choice and quantity. And if your little one wants to taste something and spit it out, recognize that that is progress. To find the patience you need, focus on the fact that continuing reliance on the feeding tube is just a part of the process.

> *We have several structured "mealtimes" a day during which we introduce solids on a spoon before giving him his tube-feeding. No luck in getting him to*

swallow anything or show any interest so far, but it's still early in the game. The tube is so easy and he is gaining, so I can't really complain. —Eva

Immediately after tube placement, Jacob gave up on oral eating for a while. The pressure was off him, and all that unpleasantness of eating food with his mouth was gone. Slowly, Jacob began to want to eat orally, to beg for food in his mouth. Because of the tube, we could make eating fun, not a necessity to maintaining life. Today, almost two years after tube placement, Jacob is eating about half his calories orally. He is learning to feed himself and even uses a spoon on his own. Eating is a game because nutrition goes in through the button in his belly. Fun goes in through his mouth. He's almost caught up in size to his sisters and is making great gains cognitively and physically. We've had the healthiest winter ever. He hasn't had to choke down those nasty bitter seizure meds in almost a year. I can keep him hydrated in hot weather. Loving that tube. —Julie

Also make meals a special time for the family to gather together. You may be concerned about how to integrate your child into mealtimes when he or she cannot or will not eat. Include your child at the table, providing items to occupy his or her attention (and hands) during mealtimes. Encourage your child to join in the conversation. Make mealtimes more about togetherness than eating, even if it's just the two of you. Also consider inviting friends and other loved ones for special meals or extended visits, to reinforce the fact that meals are about socializing and fun.

Chris was finally "cured" at age three and a half by a two-week visit from an out-of-state friend and her three kids, who all had very healthy appetites. Chris wanted to be like them, and they encouraged him to eat what they did. Within a few weeks, Chris was eating totally by mouth. I would have invited them a lot sooner if I'd known that would work!! —Amy

Of course, no approach is surefire. Success depends on numerous factors, such as timing, your child's developmental stage, implementation, and applicability to underlying problems. In the meantime, keeping friends and relatives informed of your goals may help discourage them from offering simplistic, inappropriate, or undermining suggestions. (For more on dealing with others, see Chapter 20.) In fact, a G-tube may quiet some people's comments, as it visibly documents your child's feeding problems. Still, you may encounter the occasional ill-informed person who believes that "if you just removed that tube, your child would have no choice but to eat"—as if your little one was choosing to starve just to be conniving and manipulative!

> *People tend to disregard our concerns as overreacting to normal toddler behavior. They compare his daily projectile vomiting to a bout with the flu or normal infant spit-up. They act as if we haven't tried every trick in the book to get him to eat. Here are some examples of common comments I receive:*
> * *"Have you tried ice cream? Bananas? Noodles? Chocolate?" (Of course we have; I've thrown away enough food to feed a Third World Nation!!!!)*
> * *"Maybe he'll eat for me." (In other words, I'm not doing it right, or he doesn't like me.)*
> * *"You have to be firm with him."(I'm too lenient, and this is a behavior problem?)*
> *—Laura*

Following your child's lead in certain areas of development isn't always easy, especially if your child's behavior presents tough challenges or if you have your own anxieties about a particular area. Following your child's lead means trusting that your child will follow the developmental path that's right for him or her, having realistic expectations, implementing unique solutions that fit your unique child, providing the conditions under which your child thrives, and working *with* your child.

Encouraging Your Child to Stretch beyond Current Abilities

> *First we thought maybe our kids would need a wheelchair. Then, when they learned to walk, we crossed that item off the list. Then, we worried about talking. Ian finally learned to talk, but we are still working on Alex. Now, I am considering pre-kindergarten for one of my boys. It's not that we aren't thankful for the miracles along the way. The issue is that we want the best for our children. So we keep researching and pushing, hoping to help them go farther. We know it's a miracle that they walk and talk and do as well as they do, but I think it's simply human nature to want to keep on pushing. Even if*

they were "normal" kids, we'd do the same. We all want our kids challenged. Some just have different challenges. —Mo

For every parent, encouraging a child's development also requires finding that delicate balance between trusting the child's developmental pace and encouraging the child to stretch and reach beyond current abilities. Respecting your child's needs, abilities, limitations, and temperament as you encourage him or her to stretch is an important part of being a responsive parent. As you work to find that balance, consider these ideas:

- Encouraging stretch means staying mindful of what is just beyond your child's ability and what is too far beyond it. If development is like a ladder, you want to encourage your child to reach for the next rung, not the rungs that are out of reach. It's okay to ask a child to stretch; it's too much to ask a child to leap.

- When your child's needs, abilities, or temperament differ from the norm, figuring out what is a reach and what is a leap can be challenging. Knowing how much to expect when your child's developmental potential is unknown is a huge question. Follow your intuition and your child's lead. (For more ideas and support around this, see the previous section "Following Your Child's Lead.")

- Cultivate the art of balance—by following your child's lead even as you encourage stretching. All children, including children with limitations, benefit from appropriately high expectations that encourage them to stretch and grow. It's okay to take a firm, loving line and expect your child to toe it. If your expectations turn out to be unrealistic, you can redraw the line.

- When you're on an unrealistic track, you'll know it by lack of progress, absence of resolution, or the bad feelings that arise. If you are pushing too hard to get your child to accomplish something, you'll feel the tension, the uncomfortable balance of power, the gnawing in your gut. You'll observe your child withdrawing or acting out. Listen to your intuitions, and lay off or try something else for a while.

- Trust your child's intuitions about what fits; what works; what feels right, good, and comfortable. For instance, if your child continually resists doing certain activities or being with certain people, assume that there is a good reason for the discomfort, such as your child senses a lack of fit or nurturing. Likewise, when your child eagerly (or with minimal protest) takes part in activities or goes to other caregivers, know that he or she is feeling comfortable—or at least comfortable enough to manage the stretch.

- Follow your child's interests and inclinations. Encourage your little one to stretch and expand on existing abilities by joining her in pretend play, in which your child can follow her interests, but you can playfully challenge her, draw her out, and compel her to expand on her repertoire of abilities and emotions. For instance, when your child asks for juice, extend the interaction by playfully asking what kind, what cup, how about this kind—whatever keeps your child engaged and purposefully communicating with you. Your child will be more receptive to your teaching if you follow her interests and inclinations while stabilizing and broadening the abilities she's practicing.

- Take your child's temperament into consideration. If he is naturally shy, value his introversion and make sure he gets the "alone" time he needs, but also give him opportunities to socialize, even though he might not ask for them. If your child is naturally active, provide plenty of opportunity for running around, but also encourage occasional quiet time, starting with short periods.

- If your child is inflexible, easily frustrated, and has frequent meltdowns, recognize that she may need more practice being flexible and tolerating frustration. The meltdowns can indicate that she's in over her head. She needs to work on this in baby steps. For now, lessen your demands that your child be flexible—which often means that *you* will need to be more flexible (just think what a good role model you're being!)—and make situations less frustrating while you help your child remain calm and consider the options. In that way you encourage and support your child's growing ability to be flexible and to tolerate frustration. **For a child who struggles unduly with frustration, medication or dietary measures may be crucial in getting her brain chemistry in order.**

- Observe what makes your child feel pride of accomplishment and what makes him dissolve into frustration or helplessness. Guide your child gently, with patience, and support—as well as your confidence that he *can* do this. Your job as a parent is to pull your child *through* these

• • •

548

feelings, not out of them. And you can capitalize on your child's strengths as you encourage him to work on weaknesses.

- Finally, accept that, in general, your child will follow the developmental path he or she is meant to follow. While you can guide and support, you and your child also benefit from this attitude of acceptance.

Expecting Too Much As the parent of a preemie, you may be susceptible to pushing your child too hard if you harbor guilt about the preterm delivery or the NICU course or try to compensate for your imagined shortcomings. Vigorous prodding can be detrimental to your child and his or her development—and it certainly does not address or even ease your guilt. You may be struggling with this issue if

- Others tell you that your expectations are too high
- Your relationship with your child is marked by conflict or distance
- Feelings of guilt, incompetence, or grief nag or haunt you
- You anxiously fill your child's schedule with lessons, playdates, sports, therapies, or other activities that take your child away from you or home for most of your child's waking hours (beyond school or day care).

If you recognize yourself in any of those descriptions, try to step back and examine your tendency to push. Face your painful feelings and seek support or counseling. By attending to your emotional needs, you'll be in a better position to effectively encourage your child's development. (For more support in this area, reread Chapters 2 and 3, and look under "Guilt" in Chapter 18.) If your child is in day care or school, it can be even more important that he or she have down time, hanging out with you. This kind of relaxation and connection with you can actually fuel your child's development and improve her behavior and emotional well-being. Doing everyday activities with you can be just what your child needs.

Expecting Too Little Some parents push too hard; others don't push enough. They may consider their child too fragile, or they may want to protect their child (and themselves) from the disappointment and frustration that can accompany stretching toward new abilities.

It is important to remember that out of struggle comes real growth. If everything is made easy for a child, she misses out on the special feelings of accomplishment, competence, and confidence that result from overcoming hurdles. Like butterflies, children need to experience some struggle on their way out of the cocoon or their wings won't develop properly. Cultivate

Supporting Your Child's Development

accurate expectations by allowing enough room for you and your child to take some risks. Don't make the certainty of success a prerequisite for trying.

Enjoying Your Child

As you work to be the parent you want to be, remember that it's more important to try to enjoy your child than to do everything "exactly right." Your natural desire to contribute to your child's progress may lead you to focus on what you can *do*, but it is even more important to relax and delight in your child. Give yourself permission regularly to let go of your worries about growth, development, and the future, and simply *be* with your child. Pay attention to who your child *is* and not merely what he or she *does*.

Even as you fine-tune your parenting skills, concentrate on parenting *from the heart* rather than on parenting perfectly. Your connection, affection, respect, alliance, and devotion are paramount and irreplaceable to your child's growth and development. As the parent, you can provide that unique responsiveness, compassion, encouragement, confidence, admiration, and joy about who your child is. The warmth of your relationship will also determine how effectively you can motivate your child to live up to your reasonable expectations. Holding these attitudes is central to enjoying your child.

If your preemie has ongoing special needs, it can be quite difficult to "just enjoy" if you feel unable to relax, let go of your worries, or to hold on to positive attitudes. You may feel trapped in the job of constantly putting out fires, with very little downtime or reward. You may find yourself often acting like a physical therapist or speech therapist or a nurse to your child. Your anxiety about what your child is accomplishing can be a trap: you may become so involved in monitoring and shaping your child that you miss some of the simple pleasures of enjoying and living with your precious little one.

> *Looking back, it seems that all I did was live from milestone to milestone. I was so excited when each milestone was reached, but never allowed myself to enjoy the times in between. That is one of my biggest regrets and one that I would caution other parents about. —Sue*

> *I wish I had relaxed and enjoyed Alex more. If I had known how things were going to turn out, I might have worried less. I could have focused my energies more on the most important issues. —Allison*

I mean, I was so in love with her, but I was so detached. ... I wrote down how many milliliters she took, I gave a report to the home nurses, and they gave [reports] to me. I even started dressing like the nurses. ... I remember once, my sister picked Seleste up and bounced her up in the air, and she said, "You are such a cute baby." And I was taken aback ... it was the first time I'd ever seen her as a baby. —Suzanne

I just got sick of correcting his posture all the time and watching him to see what he was doing wrong. I took the "therapist" role seriously, but I didn't enjoy it. ... Our relationship now is much more affectionate than it was in the early days. I don't hover around him when he's playing. The habit of looking at him in a critical way is gone. I just see this gorgeous little boy and think, "Yum!" And he's always in the mood for a cuddle. I think of our first year together as a kind of emotional anorexia. I feel we'll be making up lost ground for a long time. —Anne

As you practice becoming responsive to your child's unique needs, you'll get better at balancing your concerns with simply enjoying your little one. Whatever your child's outcome, enjoying him includes giving him room to grow into himself; providing a home and family environment that feels nurturing; and looking for the right schools, friends, and therapists with whom your child thrives. You learn to focus more on her happiness and less on her "progress" or "success." Above all, you trust that love is the best medicine, and there is always room for hope.

I rejoice in everything she does. Somewhere along the way I have learned to love her for who she is and not for what she was "supposed" to be. And I think, well, if she never progresses beyond this point, that's okay because I really love this stage of her development. —Kathie

Part of a parent's role is to be the single source of unconditional love and acceptance. No other person on the planet actually has that engraved into their job description. Yes, we are supposed to teach and challenge and promote and encourage ... but at the end of the day, if we don't do any of that ... there are plenty of others who are designated hitters ... but in the acceptance department, if we aren't there ... the deck is empty. —Sheila

•••
551
Supporting Your Child's Development

Evaluations and Labels

This is very typical for preemies, that they need help all along the way.
It does not end when you walk out of that unit. It just doesn't. —*Vickie*

Developmental evaluations may be a regular part of your child's NICU follow-up care, or you may seek out testing because you have concerns about your child. Evaluations can provide reassurance if your child is doing well, affirmation if your child is struggling, and a reason (which you may have suspected all along) for his or her lags in development, idiosyncrasies of movement or language, or challenging temperamental qualities. Evaluations also give you information that can help you provide what your child truly needs, as well as giving you peace of mind.

> *When Khalila didn't gain weight, having the support and respect of our pediatrician—who referred us out of system for a consultation—was so helpful. Having the support and information from the occupational therapist who consulted with us regarding [Khalila's] eating was priceless. I felt much more at peace after that, and haven't felt as worried since then.* —*Mary*

If you voice any concerns to your pediatrician and he or she agrees, you have the start of a cohesive treatment team. If your child's doctor resists further investigation or seems to dismiss your observations and your child, you are likely to feel both frustrated and alone. If your family or friends are not attuned to what you see happening with your preemie, they may even oppose your suggestion of testing or visits with specialists. You may feel undermined and misunderstood. (For more on dealing with others, see Chapter 20.)

If, instead, you are confident that your child is doing well but others are expressing concern, you may feel frightened and angry. You may wonder why they expect so much from this child who has been through so much. You may feel that *whatever* he or she achieves is miraculous and that others are putting your child under a microscope and second-guessing your assessment.

If your view of your child is quite different from the results of a professional evaluation, try to determine whether the professional evaluation has merit or whether it is full of holes. How does it compare with *your* evaluation? Does it shed light on some of what you see (or don't see) in your child?

Evaluating Professional Evaluations

Frankly, I was terrified about what I might hear. I'd left the NICU naively believing that now we just waited for Stuart to catch up. In the years that followed, discovering the subtle and pervasive effects of his prematurity left me feeling as if I were tiptoeing through a minefield, and waiting for the results of this evaluation was like waiting for the next explosion. I quite literally wasn't sure I could face it. So it was critical to choose a professional I felt would be qualified not only to make the assessment, but also to be compassionate and constructive in communicating his findings with us. —Susan

The quality of evaluations—and evaluators—can vary widely. As your baby's parent and advocate, it's important to be aware of factors that increase the likelihood of receiving an accurate evaluation—or a misleading one.

The Accurate Evaluation A meaningful and accurate evaluation involves a number of different measures, assessment tools, and sessions. Activities can include

- Looking for patterns in your child's behaviors
- Observing how your child spontaneously interacts with caregivers
- Noting how your child spontaneously plays with toys he or she finds interesting
- Consulting with caregivers, teachers, and others involved with your child to assess their experiences, observations, and evaluations
- Exploring how your child takes in, processes, and responds to stimulation
- Noting your child's specific strengths and weaknesses
- Formulating a treatment plan
  Other aspects of an accurate and constructive evaluation include:
- Along with a clear and meaningful diagnosis, a topflight evaluator will also provide parents with affirmations. Most reassuring is when a specialist can say to a parent, "Your observations are in line with mine and consistent with this diagnosis. There is nothing you could have done to cause your child's condition or behaviors. This is nobody's fault." When a professional gives you these messages as you are first hearing a diagnosis, your predominant feeling may be relief. You may think: "I'm not crazy, I'm not making things up. Not only is there a *name* for this, but it's *not* my fault. And my child isn't the only one who has it." Another

affirmation is when an evaluator makes treatment referrals in a way that respects you as a parent, bolstering your ability to act on new information and meet your child's identified needs.

- Competent evaluators predict a child's future only with great caution and with sensitivity for the parents' feelings. They generally provide a range of possibilities. If the evaluation results must dash certain expectations, the evaluator offers new expectations to take their place.
- A thorough evaluation includes the opportunity to discuss findings, ask questions, and raise any doubts. If the evaluation turns out to be accurate and surprising in ways that are painful to you, the evaluator should be responsive to your reactions and your requests for more information. They may use unfamiliar terms; ask for clarification about words or labels that concern you. Also note that evaluators sometimes use terms for the sake of "the system"—to ensure, for instance, that health insurance will cover the recommended treatments.
- A good evaluation is holistic—that is, it looks at the whole child and the big picture. Some assessments may focus on what is delayed, disabled, or "wrong," but an accurate and effective evaluation also assesses and acknowledges a child's strengths and overall adjustment. This type of information can be immensely reassuring to parents. A good evaluator recognizes that there is a person inside the little body that is being examined and tested, and she or he also acknowledges a family's strengths and coping abilities. Even in the face of devastating deficits, these affirmations can strengthen your hope and your confidence.
- Along these lines, another mark of a good evaluator is when he or she sees your child as a precious human being. Whether your pediatrician takes the time to cradle your baby, a therapist connects emotionally with your child, or a specialist gives your kid a warm hug, you may be struck by their kindness and caring sensitivity. Knowing that someone else values your child can warm your heart and calm your fears.

It's been almost five years since we walked into his office after he had completed a comprehensive evaluation of my then three-year-old son. I was nauseous, nervous, shaking, feeling as if he were about to pronounce the totality of Stuart's lifetime potential. Fortunately, we'd chosen well ... a wonderful neuropsychologist who did a ten-visit, multiple-location, multiple-

approach evaluation of Stuart. He wasn't focused on labeling as much as he was on assessing in order to review [Stuart's] program and make treatment/ therapy recommendations, many of them for my husband and me to utilize. I felt confident that he really understood Stuart's strengths and challenges. He was very gifted at not taking away my hope for my son, and I left his office feeling strangely peaceful about things ... as if I might just make it after all, knowing that my child had gifts and challenges, and that no one could define or limit his future at this tender age. —Susan

The Misleading Evaluation

The first time the boys were tested, they needed to shake a rattle. The rattle they were given was way too big and heavy for their hand, so they couldn't even hold it. Of course, the therapist said they couldn't do it. I don't know why they can't have scaled-down tests, to fit these babies. —Stephie

Just because [the evaluator] didn't see her perform the milestone, it didn't mean she couldn't do it. I believe this is key. It is when parents' comments are not considered—or worse, that they take the child away from the parent—that you are not going to get a "true" picture of the child's abilities. —Shirley

Unfortunately, some evaluations do not present an accurate portrayal of a child's abilities, strengths, and weaknesses. For example, some specialists evaluate a child by spending a limited time administering tests that aren't much fun or interesting. Then, when the child doesn't cooperate, smile, interact, sustain interest, and so on, they may proclaim the child has pervasive delays and autistic tendencies. At the other extreme, a variety of specialists each evaluate only one small piece of the child and, without seeing the big picture, assess the child's performance as "good enough." With a stack of "good-enough" assessments, how is a parent to question the results?

No one ever told me that they suspected that Alex was multiply impaired until he was almost three and transitioning out of [an early intervention program]. I was told he was doing well. The pediatrician said he was doing well because he was physically healthy; the ophthalmologist thought he was doing well because his vision was correctable. All the professionals looked at their little piece. Then we had the multidisciplinary evaluation, and I almost fainted when the psychologist casually said something about dealing with mental retardation to this degree. Then they handed me a pamphlet about a stipend from the state for severely mentally impaired children. I had thought he was still just "delayed." They thought that I knew that there were serious problems. ... When we have commented on Alex's lack of progress, we have been constantly told that our neurologist is not known for making mistakes. Yet, two years later, we have seen virtually no progress. I'd rather hear the truth even if it stinks. —Mo

In general, seek another opinion if

- You believe that your child's evaluation resulted in a diagnosis based on information collected under conditions that were stressful or unnatural for your child
- You believe that your child was not assessed in a way that accurately displayed his or her strengths, weaknesses, and behavior patterns
- Your child is viewed as a bunch of separate parts instead of as a whole, where all areas of development are considered together along with their interplay
- The evaluation does not point to specific plans or referrals for treatment that can be tailored to your child's unique strengths and weaknesses
- The evaluation is based solely on how your child interacts with the professional during one session of standardized testing
- The evaluation doesn't take into account your observations
- A diagnosis places your child with other children with whom he or she might have just one aspect in common
- A prognosis is offered by an evaluator who did not pose a wide variety of appropriate, interesting tasks in familiar settings
- A prognosis is based solely on images of your child's brain

Also keep in mind that even "experts" can undermine, misinform, or mislead parents. If an evaluation, diagnosis, or treatment plan—or a professional's advice or any piece of it—doesn't feel right to you, question it. Ask for clarification, elaboration, and specific examples that illustrate the professional's assessment. If your specialist can't answer your questions or tolerate your doubts about the assessment, find another professional to help you. Worst of all, if an evaluation offers no hope, definitely question it.

I had a very painful meeting with Stuart's teacher this week. She really forced me to look hard at her assessment of him. She wanted me to realize that Stuart is significantly impaired in almost every major area. Those words just do not describe the little boy I live with and love every single day. And though he does have significant challenges, he also has areas in which he truly excels: music, math, letters, and spelling. He is very bright, very sensitive, very emotionally responsive. I don't know who I am arguing with. I just feel stripped of my hope for him. —Susan

Remember that you know better than anyone what is going on with your child. You may not have all the terminology or ideas for treatment, but you know when something is amiss—or not. You are in the best position to differentiate between a problem that must be dealt with to help your child grow and adjust, and simply a different path that your child is taking to get where he or she is going. Even if you are coming to the realization that your child may never "catch up" or keep pace with his or her peers, you can still have hopes for your child's future. Having hopes is not the same as being out of touch with reality. Your hopes adjust to fit reality and give you faith in your child's journey. When teachers or other professionals minimize or ignore your knowledge and intuition about your child, examine their views with an open mind. Don't, however, let their opinions make you doubt what you know or second-guess what your heart, gut, and intuition are telling you.

Somebody said to me at a Twins Club meeting: "Trust your instincts. If you think that something is wrong with one of your kids and the doctor says, 'Oh, they're fine, they're fine,' get a second opinion, get a third opinion, get a fourth opinion." It's not just going in until you find someone who'll agree with what you're saying, but just to make sure. Because so many times, you know when something isn't right, and the doctor is just, "Oh, it's okay." If you think something's not right, call another doctor and keep calling another doctor until you get the response that you want, [the one] that can give you a valid explanation. —Julia

If you are having trouble getting others, especially professionals, to see the situation from your perspective, videotape or audiotape the things about your child that you want them to see. If an evaluation doesn't give the examiner the opportunity to observe the crux of the matter, tell the professional that his or her observations are not complete. For many children, one evaluation or one session can't reveal everything. Find evaluators who understand that some of the most valuable information about a child comes from the parents' observations, as well as those of teachers and other caretakers. Also obtain the opinions of trusted specialists who already know your child. Ask them for their insights and use them as sounding boards for your questions about completed evaluations.

If you feel that your child needs help for something, unless you say, "I'm seeing something; I want help," a doctor is not going to seek that out for you. What we've learned is that if you see something and think your child needs help, you go for it. If you don't get it [from that professional], you go to the next one. If you don't get it there, you keep going until you get help, whether it's medical, emotional, physical, whatever it is for your child. I think that's one of the strongest things I've learned, that just because a doctor is a doctor doesn't mean you have to totally believe or trust. But it's a good thing to find someone you can believe and trust in, too. —Vickie

Once the dreaded words "autistic spectrum disorders" were spoken [by a school-system therapist], I threw myself mind, soul, and body into becoming a walking expert on the topic. I read everything, buried myself in the Internet and the proliferation of information available there. I felt so intensely the responsibility to make sure that Stuart was getting the right, the best treatment, and based on all of my past medical experiences, I felt no one could adequately make those decisions but me. And the treatment options available were astounding. Everywhere were stories of miraculous cures based on one type of intervention or another, and nearly every one hinged on doing lots and doing it early. I needed a team of twelve to twenty people to work intensely with Stuart twelve to eighteen hours a day! I had to hurry! We were losing ground! I had to pick a course of action, but which one would save my little boy (they all disagreed with one another). I drove his two pediatricians crazy with calls, faxes, e-mails, consultations. They are wonderful, patient women who gave us lots of time and support. They finally called a joint meeting during which they suggested gently among many other things that maybe I should see a therapist to deal with my anxiety about the whole thing. That really got my attention,

558
Parenting Your Premature Baby and Child

and together with their comments and opinions about the need to let Stuart be a little boy and the fact that there are no miracle cures, not to mention the fact that neither one of them even considered him to be autistic, *I was able to put the brakes on, regroup, and breathe again.* —Susan

Adjusting Your Own Evaluation If you disagree with your child's outside evaluation even though it meets the criteria of an accurate and constructive evaluation (see the previous two sections), this should raise a red flag about your perceptions. Another red flag is when you disagree with an assessment with which other professionals, friends, and relatives are in general accord. A third red flag is when you dismiss the news, but a piece of it keeps resonating for you, or you can't shake some of the insights it offers. If you recognize any one of these red flags, you need to consider the possibility that you might need to adjust your own evaluation of your child. To do this, look inward for answers.

If you are resisting a diagnosis, you may find yourself turning away from matters that need attention because you cannot bear another loss or another shift in how you view your child. Perhaps you feel okay about how your child is doing, and you don't feel like you need to call it something and then get treatment for it. Or you may believe that there is nothing to be concerned about and that others are making a big deal over little issues.

Even as developmental issues make themselves clear, you may push away or gloss over evidence that your child is affected by prematurity. Instead, you may strive to put the preterm birth and NICU stay behind you, acting as if this child's prematurity never happened, or at least doesn't matter.

If you were told that your baby was doing fine at follow-up, you may have taken the news as a guarantee. You don't want to have to change gears and let go of that good news.

Even now, I think they are too small to be expected to do developmentally [age] appropriate activities. ... I guess I still haven't fully adapted to the perceptions of others about my kids. I think they are doing beautifully, but on any developmental test they are way behind. It hurts every time I get a written report about them, and I am terribly nervous every time they get tested. —Stephie

Of course, resisting a less-than-positive evaluation at first is normal. But if you are still resistant after some time has passed, it may benefit you to face any anger, disappointment, guilt, or sorrow the evaluation brings up. If you can face your feelings, you will be able to face the news.

Also, you may very well have intense feelings about the preterm birth that haven't found expression yet, and an evaluation may bring on a flood of feelings that you're trying to hold back. Such a deluge can be overwhelming. Give yourself permission to fall apart. You *will* be able to put yourself together again. When you deal with your feelings, you empower yourself to deal with current reality.

If you are resisting news that your child is "normal," you may still see prematurity reflected in much of what your child does or doesn't do. You may identify strongly with the experience of delivering early and raising a premature baby and be struggling to see beyond the fragile, helpless newborn who is now your growing child. You may be mistakenly looking for preemie-related complications as a way to make sense of your child's unique but essentially normal developmental path.

Know that your child can be "normal" and *also* a preemie. The original trauma of your baby's birth and hospitalization may be the source of your continuing overreactions to the typical, common problems of childhood. These problems don't indicate that something is wrong with your baby. How prematurity affects a child's development varies greatly. It is not always possible to determine why a child is developing along a certain path.

> *I had an insight that seems so obvious now. ... We (my husband and I) over-react all the time. I don't mean taking [Lars] in to the doctor every time he gets a sniffle—that's not overreacting—but emotionally. We spent the night at Mat's folks' house this week, and Lars slept very poorly—up for three hours, or at least needing attention so we couldn't sleep. Instead of thinking, "Oh, he had a bad night in a strange environment, no biggie," our response was, "What a disaster! We're never doing that again!" It made me realize that our emotional response to every little thing is way out of whack. ... I'm tired of emotional hangovers all the time. I hope recognizing the pattern is the first step in breaking free of it. —Kris*

Try to separate your anxiety about your child's progress from your observations of your child. Rely on others' assessments to help you uncloud your vision and see your child more objectively. Identify your fears and determine which of your worries have a basis in reality and which arise from your fertile imagination. Let go of the latter and get the support you need to deal with the former. Doing that can diminish your anxiety.

If you are wrestling with feelings of guilt, you may be convinced that your child will have problems as a cosmic payback or punishment for your contributions to the premature birth. Try to see this for what it is—your unresolved guilt talking. (For more on working through guilt, review Chapter 3. For more on separating your pain from your parenting, see "Protective Parenting" in Chapter 15.)

Finding Specialists You Can Collaborate With If your child is having difficulties, dealing with professionals who discount your concerns can be discouraging. You may resent the fact that you must be the one to do the research and try to solve the mysteries. But after all, you are the leader of your child's health care team. It is your right and your obligation to be the one to ask the questions, examine the options, and choose the treatments that you believe best fit your child's needs.

Sometimes a multifaceted approach is necessary, but sometimes answers can be found by a specialist who addresses one critical underlying piece. Specialists who insist that their one little piece is the linchpin are more likely to be correct if they are

- Looking at the situation from many angles
- Seeing your child's strengths as well as the constellation of problems
- Able to talk about the big picture

In general, trust your own assessment of proposed or ongoing treatments. Value the therapists, specialists, or teachers with whom any of the following is true:

- Your child is growing or thriving under this individual's care
- The caregiver's ideas are consistently on track and backed with explanations and clarification that makes sense to you
- The caregiver's instincts seem to be in line with yours, and he or she seems interested, available, connected, and willing and able to really tune in to you and to your child
- You feel that you can look to the caregiver for support, hope, inspiration, collaboration, or active attempts to find answers
- The caregiver is willing to talk about painful topics and to stay with you

as you process the information and review your perspective.

It can certainly be a relief when you find someone who sees what you see, who can assess the situation in ways that make sense to you, and who attends to all of your questions, ideas, and concerns. Remember, though, that you are not looking for someone to just concur with your observations; you want someone to help you explain, expand the framework, and intervene. Your trust is based on the specialist's ability to be empathic and present with you through the process, and allow you to feel that your viewpoint is respected even when he or she has a perspective or assessment that differs from yours. You're also not looking for someone who can just give you all the answers, but someone with whom you feel like a partner in your child's care. When you sit down together to compare notes, your child's specialist hears what you have to say and responds to it—either by explaining it from a different perspective or by integrating it into his or her framework and treatment approach.

If you're taking a multifaceted approach and enlisting the aid of multiple specialists, when even just one of them collaborates well with you, you're more likely to discover the real underlying problems, whether mild or severe, and find solutions that address them. You can also be a more effective advocate for your child when you have the support of at least one professional you are working with. This key professional can help you facilitate collaboration among all of your child's specialists.

The best specialists are also not bound by charts and timetables or restricted to hard science and research. They have a natural instinct, an ability to see your child as a unique individual who requires a unique approach. And they understand that a child's whole being cannot be summed up through the lens of one specialty. Find specialists who are interested in your child as a whole and who recognize the complexity of your child's problems, even if they only feel "qualified" to evaluate their small piece of the puzzle.

A real blessing during all this was our pulmonologist. Unlike most of [that specialist's] babies, Alex stayed on as a patient as he grew. This provided some real continuity, and it was so nice to work with someone we didn't have to prove ourselves to. He could talk to us about Alex's problems while pointing out how far he had come. He always made us feel like we were doing a good job, despite the overwhelming task we faced. It was wonderful to have his support. —Allison

•••

The best specialists also see your child in the context of your family, community, and school or child care, and they consider your need for support and guidance with regard to parenting this child. Whether they provide that guidance or refer you to a family counselor, you may feel relieved and comforted by their acknowledgement that it is normal and natural for parents to sometimes respond in ways that are less than helpful to a challenging or troubled child. And when you know they value you and your relationship with your child, it is easier to trust their advice on how you can more effectively respond to your youngster. Their suggestions "feel" right because they strengthen your connection with your child.

Understanding Labels

If your child is encountering challenges, you will want to identify the problem—to find a "label" for it. But having a label with which to identify your child's difficulties is a mixed bag. Though it is often a relief, a label can also be a terrible blow because the term can bring up frightening images, assumptions, and associations. Having a label forces you to come to terms with what's wrong. The other side of the coin is that a label also enables you to seek more information. It can be comforting to know that there is a definitive diagnosis—and that other kids have this problem, too.

Generally, when a child has physical disabilities or a chronic medical condition, caregivers assign labels so that a care protocol can be established. For instance, if your child is diagnosed with gastroesophageal reflux, retinopathy of prematurity (ROP), bronchopulmonary dysplasia (BPD), or cerebral palsy (CP), the label can be helpful in guiding treatment.

Still, these kinds of labels are incomplete descriptions of your child. And labels for developmental disabilities or delays are even more incomplete: the brain is involved and there is so much we don't understand about its inner workings and development. Different specialists may propose contradictory explanations and treatments. So labels aren't always helpful in defining treatment, although they can provide clues or some guidance.

Labels can also be misleading. Some labels focus on symptoms observed during testing, which may or may not be indicative of a child's true condition or abilities. Some labels just scratch the surface, describing what is observable but ignoring a child's underlying problems. For instance, if a child is labeled "unresponsive," is it because he or she is overwhelmed by auditory stimulation, cannot process language, or cannot respond verbally? An accurate label should reflect something meaningful about a child's experience as well as how he or she relates and responds to other people and to different sorts of tasks.

Yet even when labels may not be especially illuminating or helpful, many parents seek them, and many professionals try to assign them. Especially if your child has "invisible" disabilities, you may want a label so that you can tell people what's going on, succinctly and with professional backing.

> *So many people will come up to Brayden and talk directly to him, which I do not mind at all, but they expect him to respond, and he doesn't respond in any way, so then they look at me, waiting for an explanation. Brayden's issues are so complex that I simply do not have the energy or time to explain it to every stranger who doesn't get a "hi" from him.* —Jayna

> *I was relieved when Jacob got his chair because then there was an outward sign to others that there was a lot going on with him. It also helps that I can give a simple explanation of cerebral palsy, which at least the general public has a clue about. I usually tell them Jacob has a hard time responding but understands everything they say to him and loves to be talked to.* —Julie

> *There are differences when those disabilities are visible versus invisible. One of the things we [Julie and I] talked about was how relieved we were (in a weird way, I grant) when our kids got their orthotics, or in Jacob's case, his wheelchair. ... now the "don't-have-a-clue" folks could see that our child was disabled and not ask quite as many dumb questions. ... When Stephen had his walker and later his orthotics, I was glad that I could stop having to explain that he was disabled and not a brat.* —Tracy

Over time, as you observe your child's development and learn about his or her challenges and capabilities, you will discover that your child is so much more than any label could capture.

After all, if your child is labeled as having a medical condition, such as ROP or BPD, that label describes only one tiny facet of who he or she is. We say, "She *has* reflux" not "She *is* reflux." The labels for developmental disabilities, on the other hand, more often describe the whole person, however

...
564
Parenting Your Premature Baby and Child

inaccurate that may be. Unfairly, we often say, "He is autistic," or "She is delayed," or even, "She is disabled"—as if that's *all* he or she is. Such over-simplifications dismiss the wonderful complexity and uniqueness of our children. It is far more appropriate to say, "This is my child, who has a wide range of attributes and also happens to have this disability."

In any case, when it comes to their development, most preemies defy labels. Many are significantly delayed in some areas and appropriate or advanced in other areas. One child may have trouble with motor skills but be able to think circles around peers. Another child may have exquisite speech but have poor social skills. Still another child may be smart and athletic but highly inflexible and intolerant of frustration.

Unfortunately, the developmental delays and disabilities that show up in preemies have not been extensively studied. Assessing preemie outcomes is complicated because evaluations must encompass medical, emotional, social, verbal, physical, behavioral, and intellectual aspects of development. And there is no well-defined disease or syndrome whose symptoms are predictably uniform from individual to individual. Instead, each preemie has a unique prenatal and NICU course and a unique constellation of complications that gives rise to a unique constellation of abilities.

The lack of research and information is frustrating for parents and pro-fessionals alike. The scarcity of knowledgeable doctors, therapists, and educators can be very discouraging for parents who are trying their best to identify their preemie's difficulties, pinpoint the sources, and find solutions.

"Preemie Syndrome"

Because so many preemies carry a baffling mixture of strengths and deficits, and have disabilities that are not clearly predicted, defined, or treated, some parents use the descriptive term "preemie syndrome". For them, this broad, informal label describes their children who were born prematurely and who have unique behavioral and developmental profiles that defy conventional labels.

> *My son, Alec, is now nineteen years old and a freshman in college. His school years, particularly primary, were very difficult times for him and, consequently, for me. There was so much that I didn't understand about him and his behavior, things that I couldn't quite put my finger on but knew were not quite*

• • •

565

Supporting Your Child's Development

right. Doctors and relatives would dismiss my concerns as being overreactive. I'd see the knowing glances exchanged between my two older sisters whenever I'd mention a behavior or problem as, perhaps, being a result of his early birth.

Alec's issues in school were mostly social. Academically he did fine. In fact, in any subject related to Language Arts—reading, spelling, grammar, etc.—he was gifted. Math has always been a problem with him and continues to be his worst subject. With peers, however, it was a struggle. Alec has always been a contradiction when it comes to children his own age. He was both more immature than they and more mature. ... His passions have tended to be more mature than children his own age. He has always loved movies and could quote from them, tell anyone who would listen details of scenes, dialog, stars' names, the director, and much more than anyone would want to know. This started at an early age and hasn't gone away. He is like that in regard to music as well. This obsessiveness often leads to very one-sided conversations with him doing all the talking while the listener gives subtle signs of being ready to move on that he takes no notice of.

I spent years trying to find ways to help him. I've been to several therapists to talk about my concerns about him socially. I even got him in to speak to two of them. Their recommendations and insights were of no use. The fact that he was quite premature was never a factor. In fact, it would be dismissed. No one seemed to know anything about preemies and the issues that follow them. When pressed on the subject, one said that it seemed like an area of study that really should be researched. Another suggested Ritalin as I'd mentioned that he had difficulty paying attention. We declined to put him on it and I honestly can't imagine that it would have helped him.

Now, at nineteen, he is still somewhat a loner but seems to be well-liked by most of his peers. I think as they've matured they have become a bit more tolerant and also may recognize the gifts that his obsessiveness has given him. He is, in a way, quite amazing in his depth of knowledge in the particular areas he is most interested in, i.e., music, movies, acting, etc. My hopes and prayers are that this will lead him to a career where his obsessions and single-mindedness will work to his advantage. —Madeleine

Perhaps with better research, such a condition [as "preemie syndrome"] can be adequately described at some point, but I expect we will continue to find prematurity causes a vulnerability or increased risk, rather than directly causing any particular set of symptoms. ... That said, I am entirely sympathetic to the need for a label or diagnosis. Whether the "cause" is "prematurity," or "brain damage subsequent to the vulnerability inherent in prematurity," most children born extremely prematurely have some additional challenges that would not have been present if they had been born at term. Many of these children seem especially responsive to interventions—interventions they are less likely to receive without some way to acknowledge a "condition."

My child has "clumsy hands" and terrible visual-perceptual integration. He is at the top of all his honors classes in a demanding high school. The only accommodation he needs at this point is a keyboard. I am keenly aware that he would not be functioning at this level had we not recognized his visual-perceptual issues very early and made sure it did not hinder his academic progress. He still has no official diagnosis ... and will not be eligible for accommodations on the SAT because he would not meet anybody's definition of "disabled." Not being able to color in tiny circles quickly with a pencil is not [considered] a disability. Can anybody think the results of such a test would reflect his ability to function in college? Did I say that I am very sympathetic?! —Shaina

If your preemie's condition or development defies conventional diagnoses and treatments, it can be reassuring to know that you and your child are not alone. But remember, even if you adopt the term "preemie syndrome," far more important than any label is identifying your child's strengths and weaknesses. When you do this, you can help your child use his or her strengths to work on or compensate for those weaknesses. Any irremediable weaknesses your child exhibits may not form an obvious pattern, but you will eventually stop trying to make sense of them and learn simply to embrace them. You will reassess the value of "normal," modify your expectations, and go with the flow.

"Special needs"?? I haven't come to terms with that yet. Each time that phrase is used in reference to my son, it hits me like a blast of cold wind. What does that mean? What will it mean for my son, for whom there are still so many unknowns? Do those words have some sort of power over his future, his potential? "Special-needs kids" are some other kids with some other problems, kids I've felt vaguely sorry for, not real people that I know and love. My son is this gentle little creature, a person with talent and rare gifts. How can he be a

special-needs kid? What does that mean?

   I guess where I am right now is trying to understand the labels, take what is useful or helpful, and reject the rest. —Susan

Points to Remember

- As the parent of a preemie, you may need additional information and assistance to support your child's development effectively.
- Recognize the brain-behavior connection; tune in to your child's sensitivities and thresholds; empathize with your child's feelings, perceptions, and abilities; follow your child's lead; encourage him or her to reach just beyond current abilities; and most of all, *enjoy your child as the extraordinary individual he or she is.*
- Seek out books, articles, professionals, and peers who share your goals and can validate your perceptions.
- Discover the kinds of stimulation your baby enjoys and the senses he or she enjoys using. Pair what your little one likes with diminished or modified versions of what she or he doesn't like. Your recognition and support of your child's sensitivities will help your little one use his other senses, build tolerance levels, and enjoy interacting with you.
- Raising a preemie means confronting "normative" growth charts and timetables. Give your child space to develop at his or her own pace and in his or her own way.
- Let your youngster take the necessary time to build the strong foundations that will support further development. Don't try to rush your child or encourage shortcuts: doing so risks undermining the solidity of your child's future growth. Instead of focusing on *when* your child learns a skill, focus on *how well* she or he learns it.
- If your child has special developmental needs or medical challenges, recognize that you may need to modify how you relate to your preemie to best help him or her grow. Share your insights with others so that they can support your efforts to be a responsive parent.
- Following your child's lead means having trust that your child's developmental path is right for him or her, having realistic expectations, implementing unique solutions that fit your unique child, providing the

conditions that your child thrives under, and working *with* your child.

- Stay tuned in to who your child is *now*. Enjoy the present and revel in his or her joy in mastering even small things.
- Be active in any developmental evaluation process with your preemie. Be sure that evaluators collect a wide range of information and that your experience and perceptions are not discounted.
- If your child is evaluated, accept the assessments that seem useful, appropriate, and in line with what your intuitions tell you. If you are receiving assessments that appear to be well done and with which others agree but you cannot accept them, you may need more time and support to come to terms with the results.
- Consider the ways in which labels can help or hurt you and your preemie. When applied accurately, labels can both validate and guide. When assigned without sufficient care, however, they merely describe one element of behavior without considering the whole child. Always look at the whole child.
- Trust your instincts and find others who can support you.

Parenting Your Premature Baby and Child

CHAPTER SEVENTEEN

Watching Your Child Grow

Devoting attention to your child's well-being and having hopes for your child's future are natural parts of parenting. Your attention to health and development arises out of your efforts to guide and support your child's growth and maturation. Your aspirations, hopes, and dreams for your child are similar to those of the many parents who have come before you—wishes for happiness as well as healthy growth and development that will lead your child to build an independent and satisfying life of his or her own someday.

But when your baby is born early and requires medical intervention to survive and grow, you may go beyond mere attentiveness to your child's growth and development—you may watch vigilantly. Knowing the risks for health complications, developmental delays, behavioral issues, and disabilities that preemies carry, you may wonder if your baby will be among those who have special needs. Uncertainty and fear can cloud your hopes and joyful anticipation for your child.

I was very worried about developmental delays, even if small. It seems like an eternity waiting for your baby to catch up and worrying that he won't. —Terri

Throughout the whole time, we were scared that complications might arise. We examined the flow sheets, looked at the labs; I even listened to our daughter's heart when I thought nobody was looking. When our baby was discharged, I dragged her to a neurodevelopmental specialist to examine her, and I continued to do neurodevelopmental examinations myself until she was two years old. When she looked cross-eyed at me once, she was seen by a top-notch pediatric ophthalmologist the next day. Our anxiety level was very high. —Christoph

Vigilance coupled with continuing uncertainty about health and development is a nerve-racking part of parenting a preemie. You must wait and see as your child grows and develops. It can be difficult to know what constitutes a problem or even what is "normal" for a child born prematurely.

He's fine now—we're a little overprotective—but we're always wondering if something about him is due to his prematurity. He's always had sleep problems, and we're always wondering, "Is this because he's a preemie?" He's so tiny, a tiny little boy—is that because of his prematurity? Is that something he's going to outgrow, or is it genetics, because I'm pretty tiny myself? Or potty training. He's not doing well with that. Is that because of his prematurity? They're not major things like his eyes or his lungs, just normal developmental things. But we're always looking back and wondering. [Prematurity is] always there even though we're past it. It's always there lurking as a possible reason for the things that he does, and we don't have answers for those things. It could be. —Marcia

Naturally, parents vary as to how vigilant they are. Your degree of vigilance is a reflection of how you perceive your child's vulnerability and can be related to the uncertainty of your baby's prognosis. Parents also vary as to the *focus* of their vigilance. You may focus on the here and now and deal with things as they crop up; you may be vigilant about one aspect of your child's health or development and not others; or you may delve into every aspect in order to feel a sense of mastery.

Because most parents of preemies find that they are more vigilant than they might otherwise be, this chapter explores this experience, as well as living with the uncertainties that may arise around a child's health or developmental prognosis.

"Catching Up"

One of the things I sort of liked about Sean's being born so early was the fact that I got to keep him a "baby" for a little longer than most moms do. After a while, though, I started to get impatient, waiting for the first smile, first laugh, first everything. A lot of his stuff has been "on time" by his corrected age. But I still get a little impatient and have to remind myself that he's only five and a half months developed, not nine months (or whatever the case was at various points). That has been hard for me to keep in mind. Now, for example, I keep waiting for him to walk. I keep thinking, "He's nearly fourteen months old now. He should be taking a couple of steps at least." Then I have to stop and remember that actually he's only ten and a half months. Then I realize that he's really not too behind. It's just keeping it in mind that's hard. —Ami

Because your baby was born early, you might have been told to expect your preemie to lag behind, physically and developmentally, until about the age of two. Knowing this can be comforting at first, but if your little one had extensive complications or was born extremely early, this expectation could be unreasonable. Instead, you may need to "correct," not only for prematurity, but also for weeks and months of critical illness in the NICU or after homecoming. And at some point, you may stop correcting and just accept that your child is where he or she is.

I think that they do a great disservice to us when they tell us that micropreemies will be caught up by age two. If you have a twenty-five-weeker who was in the unit for three months, how do you expect them to be caught up by age two? That's still eighteen months adjusted. And there is a huge difference between an eighteen-month-old and a two-year-old. I always said that I didn't expect my boys to catch up until they were six and entering kindergarten. Now, it seems that Ian may not be caught up by then and that Alex will never catch up. I am so glad that I didn't expect them to catch up by two. I would have been devastated. I think that Ian won't really "catch up" but that the delays will become insignificant. Is a ten-year-old's speech pattern all that different from a twelve-year-old's? The vocabulary may be better, but by then all kids are speaking in sentences, can carry on a conversation, and so on. If Ian's learning curve keeps going the way it has, his speech may always be eighteen months to two years behind, but it soon won't matter. —Mo

I never expect them to do things at the same time as other kids, and I think it's unfair that early preemies are expected to "catch up" and not be adjusted after age two. What a joke. All it does is set parents and kids up for failure. Someone should come up with norms for when preemies do things and make it okay to be on that schedule. —Stephie

Still, wishing for your child to "catch up" is a normal reaction, and it has many facets. It reflects your natural desire for your baby to grow and reap the benefits of sound physical, intellectual, social, and emotional development. You want your child to be able to weather common childhood illnesses and have physical strength and stamina. You hope your child will be curious, make discoveries, and enjoy learning. You want your child to be able to communicate needs, adapt to change, and be well adjusted. Perhaps most of all, you want your child to be able to join in and keep up with other children. Because of your baby's tough beginning, you may worry that he or she will never catch up to peers born at term; will act, look, or feel different; and will be made fun of or preyed upon. Waiting and watching to see how your child will fare with peers can be agonizing.

Glimmers of hope may flood you with happiness. Progress also bolsters your faith in your child's unique developmental path.

Because of having a preemie, I spent many agonizing and wrenching hours, weeks, months—almost two years, actually—wondering if my darling son would ever be one of the kids, or would always be on the outside, unable to participate. And my own isolation of having a preemie—because no one in my family or circle of friends, my support network, could understand what I was going through—made me fear my son would also be forever isolated. So the first time I watched him sit in the circle at day care during story time just like all the other kids, I sobbed. And the first time I see him playing a team sport, I think it will be the same—just wrenching at my heart in my incredible need to know that he won't be on the outside, that he'll feel a part of this world. —Maren

Stuart is blossoming. I am always terribly concerned about his challenges and making sure that we are helping him appropriately, but even that concern is being tempered by his progress of late. Potty training really helped, because I was really worried that it never would happen, and that reality is daunting to consider. But I think my biggest source of hope and happiness right now is remembering his last two birthdays. When he turned three, he truly had no clue. I had no sense that he knew what the day was, he was totally uninterested in presents (totally uninterested). Last year, when he turned four, he was a little more cognizant, but still largely unaware and uninterested. This year he truly gets it. He is counting down the days. He can't wait for his party, talks about getting presents, and even asks each morning if he can have his presents today rather than on his birthday. That change in and of itself gives me so much hope that other things that aren't clicking for him may come together sometime in the future. As my more patient husband often says, he does things in his own time frame. So the part of me that has been afraid to hope is daring to hope a little more each day. —Susan

The community of other preemie parents provides another source of hope. Many preemies have similar idiosyncrasies that defy conventional labeling. They share similar milestones—such as getting off the home monitors, oxygen, and medications—milestones that are not necessarily appreciated by "regular" parents. Sharing observations and information with other parents of preemies may provide the comfort of knowing that your child is following a course that is common to other preemies.

I also felt a little secluded because some milestones—like getting off theophylline or not having to use the apnea monitor anymore—those were things that no one else could understand. And it could be the biggest news in the world to you, but when you told a family member outside the household, they didn't see the importance because it wasn't "normal" and they just wanted to know if he was sitting up yet! —Terri

Finding this Internet list and finding out that Chris's medical, developmental, and psychological problems are common to preemies was a huge relief. It gave me access to a huge amount of anecdotal information that years of research about his specific problems (taken out of the context of prematurity) couldn't give me. Yes, information about a specific diagnosis is very important. But it never answers the questions of "why?" and "what about the future?" Because doctors can't seem to put two and two together and get "prematurity," they send us parents off on wild-goose chases or tell us they don't see a problem, when all we need is another preemie parent to tell us, "Oh, my child does that, too!" and the mystery is solved. —Amy

Watching Development Closely

It is common for parents of preemies to worry secretly about bizarre effects from prematurity: "Will she grow teeth?" "Will he ever have hair?" But these worries usually mask more terrifying concerns: "Will she walk, talk, relate to me, and make friends with other kids?" "What cognitive, behavioral, or motor disabilities may be waiting to unfold?"

After I stopped worrying about whether he would just live, I started worrying about how "normal" he would be. —Teresa

We had so many immediate worries about them [as infants], but then began thinking about what they're going to be like as three- and five- and ten- and thirty-year-olds and what their quality of life will be, given their beginning. —Debbie

Even if you're told that your baby is "doing well," it's natural to wonder about the effects that premature birth and medical complications may have on your child's future development. If your preemie had a long and complicated medical course, you already may be discussing this with your baby's health care professionals. If you were involved in making difficult treatment decisions, you are no stranger to considerations of quality of life and long-term outcome.

Whether your preemie's NICU course was complicated or smooth, you may be highly sensitive to irregularities you observe in your child's behavior or development. Especially if you sense that something isn't quite right about your child's development or if your baby hasn't caught up by the age you were told to expect, you'll have suspicions. But many health care providers prefer to give babies more time to grow before they assign firm diagnoses. They are hesitant to make pronouncements because infant development is very resilient, and they don't want to burden parents with a diagnosis that doesn't hold up over time. Still, it's hard for parents to wait. That's why it can be so helpful for health care providers to acknowledge the basis for parents' concerns and support them through the waiting.

If you later get confirmation that your toddler, preschooler, or school-age child has delays, special needs, or disabilities, this can be quite unnerving. If you had inklings or concerns all along that were dismissed, you may feel quite aggravated that your judgment was not affirmed earlier. If health care providers or follow-up clinic personnel assured you that your baby was right on track, you may now feel misled, even if you suspected there were problems. You may feel particularly devastated by less-than-positive findings if your baby's NICU course was relatively smooth, because after believing that you had dodged a bullet, you now feel ambushed. When delays, special needs, or disabilities are identified later, you might regret your naivete or the months or years of early intervention that were missed. (For more on this, see "Guilt" in Chapter 18.)

Because her NICU stay had been so relatively easy, with so few complications, it made it even harder to accept that she has permanent brain damage. We went to an NICU reunion when she was about a year old and saw children who had been much sicker in the hospital, and born much younger, who were "fine." I was jealous. I am jealous. —Diana

When she finally hit three years old, that is when I began to notice how far behind she was in comparison to her peers, so I arranged for another developmental checkup. After the results of that checkup, that's when I finally broke down and cried because now I knew our future was uncertain. She tested okay in some areas, but in other areas she had up to an eighteen-month delay, and I wondered, "How could we have let things slip so far behind?" —Kathie

Gabe's low tone/low strength in his upper body wasn't identified until he was fifteen months old. He was in a developmental follow-up clinic every three months his first year, but due to how well he was developing, he didn't qualify for Early Intervention. I took that as a promise that he was fine. Instead, I missed out on learning about what he really needed as a tiny infant to develop his upper body strength and tone. —Maren

*If I had left the hospital with information about sensory integration dysfunc-
tion and its relationship to prematurity in a packet to refer to, I maybe could
have recognized this problem earlier and had Skyler in therapy. We need to
leave the NICU with information on behaviors to look for as possible problems
that we may encounter, and what steps we need to take when and if our child
shows any of these certain behaviors. —Ashley*

Other parents experience the opposite: the doctors give a grim prognosis about their baby's development based on observed brain damage that
appears to suggest future disabilities. Receiving this kind of news can be
devastating, and you may plan for the worst. But some babies' brains do an
incredible job of healing or compensating, and although they experience
some challenges, these children defy all predictions. (For more on this, see
"The Elusive Brain" later in this chapter.)

*We found out a couple of months into Caleb's second hospitalization that he had
also suffered severe brain damage. ... The doctors were not optimistic, especially
the neurologist, who told us, "I hope he will develop the ability to recognize you
in some capacity." We were in tears for days and nearly went insane.*

*We had a rough winter, but we managed to avoid any further hospital-
ization ... and Caleb is just a dream. Despite what everyone has said, Caleb
has improved magnificently. He is figuring out how to sit independently and
roll (and is very proud of himself!). He can make all kinds of sounds. He
grabs toys, shakes them, and lunges toward things he wants. These seem like
subtle things, but overall they have changed him so much. He is so interactive
and happy (as long as he gets his way). This from a baby they told us would
not do much of anything, as in be blind, not walk, be retarded, and so on.
They painted a grim picture. But now everyone is so optimistic! I hesitate to
write about it for fear I will "jinx" him. —Eva*

Because predictions can be unreliable, no matter where your child falls
on the developmental spectrum, you'll probably hold your breath for a
while—watching, waiting, and hoping. If you are anxious about your child's
future, you might hesitate to hope that your child will do much better than
expected. Even if your child is doing fairly well, you may obsess about
problems that could be lurking in your little one's brain or body. You may be

hypervigilant about feeding amounts or slow growth. You may look constantly for signs that your child will one day outgrow preemie-related difficulties and be indistinguishable from peers born at term. If you finally feel confident that your child's development is progressing normally, you may feel both relieved and triumphant.

> *If they're around other babies, it depends on how old the baby is or what the other baby is doing. If the baby is younger and doing more, then I feel bad, like "Are they going to catch up? They should be doing that. Why aren't they? What's wrong?" If they are doing more, then I say, "Oh, look at what they're doing," and I feel proud that they're doing well. —Julia*

> *Last year I cried during his school conference when the teacher told us that he was the finest example of early intervention at work that she had ever seen and that if she didn't know his background she would never have guessed he was a preemie. —Mindy*

> *Follow-ups have continued to be enjoyable and educational. They have provided us with tools to help Sarah catch up to her full-term peers. And catch up she has. At eighteen months she was determined to be age-appropriate. Hip, hip, hooray! —Cindy*

If your child has no clear residual affects from his or her premature birth, you may be ambivalent about how closely to watch for difficulties. Should you continue to be on the lookout for problems? Should you tell anyone that your child is a preemie? Would the school's knowing benefit your child? If your child has no special needs, deciding whether to share this information may be difficult. You may wonder how long you need to hold on to the circumstances of your child's birth.

Waiting for the Other Shoe to Drop

After weathering the ups and downs of an NICU stay and the irregular path of preemie development, you may feel on guard for the next challenge your child will surely face. Many parents of preemies experience this ongoing vigilance: they wait for the other shoe to drop and worry about discovering another consequence of prematurity.

But really, when does it stop? I wonder what will happen when he starts big school next year. What he will face when he gets to primary school and starts to encounter peer group pressure. And what of other possible problems? Could they manifest themselves at a later stage? I feel so far removed from "normal" that I don't quite know what it once must have felt like. —Jo

Even if your preemie's hospital course is rather uneventful and your baby quickly gets on track developmentally, you may continue to be ever vigilant, watching for problems that might crop up. Grateful for your baby's safety and growth, you're still affected by your baby's precarious start.

I am doing very well, and so is Charlotte. She is developing in leaps and bounds and does not seem like a preemie. Many others have said the same. Of course, I don't forget how it all began, and I think about her two-pound body with much humility. She is a charming, fun and robust little girl. ... But I am always mindful of how precious this little being is, and at times I have to deal with my baggage of thinking that at some point the "other shoe" has to drop. The choice to continue to stay at home with her is, I think, influenced by my experiences and wanting to stay in close touch with her development since she was premature. —Kate

Particularly if your child was a micropreemie or had serious medical complications, it's hard to believe that he or she could come through this experience unscathed. Even if your child is doing well, you may continue to brace yourself for a hidden developmental or behavioral glitch to show itself as late as school age or beyond. But it doesn't really matter what your baby's gestational age or NICU course was; it's the *trauma* you experienced around your child's early birth and hospitalization that escalates your anxiety, compels you to look for problems regardless of whether they actually exist, and results in your hair-trigger reaction to even the most subtle irregularity.

The repercussions of their prematurity we will never know. Thank God they are overall normal, healthy, wonderful children. But I guess there's a little something in the back of my mind that wonders what damage has been done to them because they were so early. There's just no way that they could come out of that experience without scars. But what those scars are, we don't know. I wonder about the effect of missing those three months of pregnancy. That's a long time, a lot happens in those three months. Emotionally, did that hospital experience scar them in some way? I just wonder, sometimes. —Debbie

I really missed out on a lot by being so totally consumed with the proper physical and emotional development of my twin preemies. I didn't even realize what was happening until Nicholas, the first to stand up all by himself, was standing there—and instead of celebrating that my little man was standing for the first time, I was down on hands and knees making sure his feet were flat on the ground and that his posture was good. At that point I realized how much I had missed of my babies' infancy, enjoying all the milestones to that point and just really enjoying them as infants rather than as babies who might not be developing properly due to their prematurity. From that point on I decided to celebrate every teensy little thing they did and not obsess so much over the little things they didn't do or didn't do properly. —Barb

Some parents outgrow this vigilance gradually or suddenly when their child reaches a particular milestone. They believe that they have "made it" and that this is a sign that everything will be okay.

After Sarah came home and we began reaching for those milestones, I found myself nervous because she couldn't lift her head easily. For me, that was the big milestone. I thought if she could only lift and hold her head up, she could do anything. Once she reached that, I let go of my worry and nervousness about her development. In my heart I have known she would reach and exceed any expectation anyone set for her. —Cindy

After this turning point, these parents stop waiting for the other shoe to drop, and they relax. This relief can be bittersweet for parents who are raising a surviving child from a multiple birth. For them, joy may mingle with grief.

Today we attended the memorial service that is held every year at the cemetery where Leah, Naomi's twin, is buried. After the service we brought flowers to Leah's grave. As we were walking away, Naomi turned and said, "Dye-dye, a-uh" (Bye-bye, Leah). She said it again, and Jim heard it too, so I know I was not imagining it. Of course, I sank to my knees and sobbed. How do you

express joy for her learning to say something so wonderful and then feel
crushing pain that she needs to say it under these circumstances? —Shoshana

For other families, their baby's severe prematurity and/or difficult
hospital course puts long-standing question marks around the future. If your
baby continues to have medical problems and/or developmental delays, your
vigilance may remain dramatically heightened. You may feel that fate is still
actively toying with you. You know there are twists and turns yet to come on
this roller coaster of life.

I often fear that he will die. That we aren't being aggressive enough with
his treatments and diagnoses and some unknown factor will sneak up and
snatch him from us. I never voice these concerns. People would think I was
overreacting. —Laura

I feel traumatized. I can't believe how anxious I get about Vincent. I really
feel like I could go mad with worry. I've been having fantasies about getting a
job and leaving the house each day (with some magic person taking over my
responsibility for worrying about Vincent), or us moving to some remote place
in Tasmania (where Vincent isn't vulnerable), or just leaving, or taking up
narcotics, etc., etc. Only fantasies, but alluring just the same. —Anne

Whether your preemie was born recently or a while ago, your vigilance
can be a lingering legacy of the trauma of an early delivery, the NICU stay,
and possibly raising a medically fragile child at home. Even years later, your
body may retain this alarm function—always on alert for danger, ready to step
in before a crisis. It's no wonder that you may fantasize about escaping to a
less stressful, more idyllic existence.

Your chronically heightened awareness makes you notice very subtle
signs, which can be an advantage when something is amiss. If your child has
feeding difficulties, you might be able to hear reflux from the next room. If
your little one has motor delays, you might pick up on subtle changes in
muscle tone long before the pediatrician notices them. Unfortunately, your
chronically heightened awareness can make you worry about tendencies that
really pose no problem. Your vigilance can even make it more difficult for you
to take normal variations of development in stride. You may also be on the

lookout for any emotional difficulties your child might show, worried that his or her reactions are atypical and connected to that stay in the NICU. It can be hard to know whether your child's behavior has more to do with experience or with inborn temperament. (See "Bonding" in Chapter 9 and "Enjoying Your Baby" plus "Encouraging Attachment in the Face of Discomfort" in Chapter 13 and "Nurturing Your Child's Nature" in Chapter 16 for reassurance concerning your child's emotional resilience.)

You may also be more vigilant in an effort to compensate for feelings of failure or powerlessness. Although you couldn't prevent the preterm delivery, you may believe that if you just work hard enough, you can prevent the effects of prematurity on your child's development. You may want to "make it up" to your child by exerting more control now than you could when your baby was first born. Maybe, you think, your vigilance will pay off this time, and your feelings of failure and helplessness will dissipate.

I think one of the hardest parts of raising a preemie has been the constant need on my part to prove what a good parent I am, and what a good outcome my child has had. It's as if I need to prove this over and over, since I failed in the one thing everyone else seems to do so easily—bear children. —Sue

Vulnerable Child Syndrome

Of course, it is normal and natural for you to see your preemie as vulnerable when he or she is struggling in the NICU. But like many parents, you may still see vulnerability where vulnerability no longer exists, even after you bring your baby home. You may feel haunted by your time in the NICU, still harboring visions of your tiny baby surrounded by medical technology, experiencing complications with breathing, heart function, infection, digestion, feeding, brain bleeds, or eyesight. If your baby experienced repeated setbacks or canceled discharges, these events can undermine your confidence in your infant's ability to thrive. If your baby was monitored until the moment of discharge, that too can reinforce your perception of your infant's continuing vulnerability.

Depending on the baby and the outcome (and the parents too), most parents of preemies have a touch of what some professionals call "vulnerable child syndrome." This is a pattern of attitudes and behaviors including seeing unfounded vulnerability in the child and lacking confidence in the child's ability to overcome challenges and develop optimally. As a result, the parents are hypervigilant and overprotective to an extent that interferes with their child's development. Their perceptions of their child's vulnerability become a self-fulfilling prophecy. Symptoms and signs of "vulnerable child syndrome" that result for the child include prolonged separation anxiety, infantile behaviors, discipline problems, psychosomatic complaints, and school underachievement. Of course, some of these problems can have temperamental, neurological, medical, or physiological sources. But these problems can also arise if you repeatedly treat your youngster as though he or she can't be healthy, handle challenges, or abide by limits on behavior. Your child internalizes these lowered expectations, your anxiety around taking risks and reaching beyond what is comfortable, and adopts the stance of "I can't." Even when your child's vulnerability is imaginary, the handicap is real.

If you see yourself or your child in some of these descriptions, this is *not* an issue for you to feel guilty about. This is an issue for you to be aware of and demand support around. According to neonatologist Dr. Peter Gorski, one of the pioneers of developmentally supportive care for babies *and* parents, vulnerable child syndrome is not about the parents failing the child, it's often about the NICU and follow-up health care systems failing the parents. If you don't receive emotionally sensitive and developmentally supportive care in the NICU, or if you feel abandoned by the medical system after homecoming, you may lack confidence in both yourself and your baby. You may displace your grief, anxiety, guilt, or feelings of vulnerability onto your baby, treating him or her with unwarranted vigilance and overprotection.

As your baby outgrows his or her vulnerability, it is important for you to move beyond it as well. But it is difficult to do this alone. You may benefit from the encouragement of trusted advisors to help you adjust your perception of your preemie, so you can learn to see your child as he or she really is, *not* as your child *was* or as you fear he or she *could* be. Request feedback from the people who know you and your child best—perhaps your child's neonatologist, primary nurse, pediatrician, therapists, or teachers. You may also rely on your closest, most empathic friends and relatives or other parents of preemies. Ask them about their perceptions of your child's level of vulnerability and whether your vigilance corresponds or is over the top. Recall your youngster's earlier vulnerability and ask them to help you observe the current realities. It can be quite eye opening to hear others' assessments of your child's strength, health, and capability. Of course, your judgement and intuition are paramount, but don't allow these valuable parental assets to be clouded by anxiety, guilt, pity, distressing memories, outdated beliefs, or imaginary perceptions of vulnerability. *Don't let your grief and anxiety become your child's biggest hurdle.*

If you're staying aware of your child's *real* vulnerabilities and you are being protective *and* coaching him to stretch beyond his abilities, others may see you as being hypervigilant when you are actually providing the extra support your child needs to thrive. If you can be clear about where your anxieties end and where your child's developmental needs begin, you'll find it easier to respond to their judgements. Here are some steps that may help you see your preemie's situation clearly and provide appropriate support.

- Identify and work through your painful emotions so that you can reach for emotional balance and see your little one with fresh eyes and an open mind
- Focus on your child's resilience and victories, entertain the possibility that his or her struggles are normal developmental phases, and remember that there is benefit to a reasonable amount of struggle
- Be aware of your child's weaknesses and rely on his or her strengths to promote development
- Acknowledge the real risks and ignore the unreasonable worry
- Know that your positive attitude and confidence in your child will build his or her positive attitude and confidence

She tries to do her best and is determined do well in school regardless of her potential. She is doing very well, and I feel very proud to be her mother. A lot of hard work but it is worth it. I do work with Tanya every day. ... I teach Tanja to believe in herself that she can do everything. Maybe it will take her a little longer than other kids but she will get there if she believes in herself. —Milka

Managing Heightened Vigilance

The fears, of course, are intense. Even when the doctors told me before delivery that my baby would probably be "fine," I couldn't help but think, "But she won't be her very best," or that there must be something "wrong" with her. Even today, I keep waiting for it to surface. I can't believe that we got off so good. —Linda

I was a lot less concerned about her physical development than I was her emotional development. I so wanted to "undo" all the emotional damage I believe resulted from her weeks in the hospital. —Renee

I am frustrated [that I'm not listened to]. I don't want people to think that I'm one of those hysterical first-time moms, but of course I worry about baby James a lot. —Marina

Hypervigilant? Yes, I was. No apologies for it either. I do not mean to sound insensitive or trite, but a parent of a premature baby doesn't have the luxury of regular worries, like "What color should we paint the baby's room?" or "Will she cry all night?" —Cindy

Our first NICU follow-up appointment was at three months adjusted age, and I was apprehensive about them being "evaluated" and so afraid that they would find something wrong. I had a knot in my stomach and was feeling I was responsible for their development so if something was wrong, it was my fault. —Sara

Vigilance around your child's development can be a full-time occupation for parents of preemies. Although this attention to detail has its place, it can also be exhausting and intrusive. To keep your vigilance from getting in the way of your child's health or development or interfering with your relationship with your little one, try the following tips:

- Make an effort to see your child as a "whole" instead of focusing on specific parts. For example, see how your child's social, emotional, physical, and intellectual strengths come together to create your son or daughter. Focus on how happy and well adjusted your child is, rather than on a specific weakness.
- Enjoy your baby's or child's accomplishments. Don't accompany each triumph with a "Yes, but ... " For example: "Yes, he's crawling, but will he ever walk?" "Yes, she's starting to speak more clearly, but what about her stuttering?" If you have multiple babies, you may fear that one child will progress faster than the other(s), leaving his or her sibling(s) behind. Try not to let your response be "Yes, but what about my other baby(ies)?"

- When your little one is enjoying new skills and feeling triumphant for accomplishing something she or he has worked hard at, stay in the moment. Try to immerse yourself in the present joy of your child's accomplishment, reflecting back your child's triumph without immediately tacking on a moment of worry. Even if your appreciation is bittersweet, you and your child have every right to enjoy each small sign of progress. There is plenty of time to focus on your concerns.

- If something about your child's development or health is bothering you, get the information you require. Trust your intuition. Also trust information that rings true and comes from sources you have confidence in.

- When connections between your child's premature birth and his or her development are unclear, don't concern yourself with trying to prove or disprove them. If making connections helps you make sense of your child's path, then go ahead and rest on them; if not, release yourself from the task of drawing connections.

- Recognize that anxiety can compel you to look for problems where none exist. Try to determine whether you are harboring fears that are blown out of proportion or that have nothing to do with your child's *actual* development—but are related to your feelings of loss about the premature birth. Facing your grief about your baby's early arrival and hospitalization may quell some of your anxiety about your child's outcome and reduce your heightened awareness.

- If you carry any guilt, face those feelings. Letting go of self-blame may make you less likely to perceive unfounded vulnerability in your child. Instead of holding onto guilt, work toward accepting your child's premature birth as an indispensable part of his or her—and your—unique life journey, a part that was beyond your choosing or control.

- Remind yourself that your degree of vigilance is not a measure of your devotion to your child, nor will it control the uncontrollable. You can be relaxed *and* committed to your child's best interests. Reassure yourself that if a delay or disability is showing up in subtle ways, it's okay to wait and see, to bide your time. Trust that if something alarming were going on, you would recognize it and act on it immediately.

- Remind yourself that your child's development is not a marker of your parenting. Your child's development will unfold in certain ways, and you are not ultimately responsible for your child's outcome, nor do you have control over his or her journey. Also, appointments with the pediatrician and NICU follow-up visits are not intended to evaluate *you*, they are for your preemie. You are not the one being tested.

- Remind yourself that young children can be emotionally resilient when they have at least one devoted caregiver who shows empathy, interest, and acceptance. Also try to admire the adaptive coping skills you observe in your child. With your continued support, your little one can overcome any emotional trauma.

Feeling vigilant about your preemie's development is a normal aftermath of a preterm birth. Over time, though, you must find some balance between maintaining control and letting go. (For more support and ideas, refer to "Getting to the Bottom of Your Grief" Chapter 3, "Balancing Hopes and Fears" in Chapter 10, "Coping with Feelings of Vulnerability" in Chapter 14, and "Protective Parenting" in Chapter 15.) Vigilance is a very important parenting job, but as a parent it is also your job to focus on *who* your child is, not just on what your child can—or can't—accomplish.

Living with Uncertainty and Ambiguity

Josh had no oxygen for numerous minutes. I remember asking, "What does that mean?" and the doctor said, "Well, it could mean brain damage, but we don't know if it takes repeated incidents to produce brain damage, and it's not usually the kind of thing that shows up right away. It could be years later." You don't know how to react because they don't even know what's going to happen. —Stephie

All families live with uncertainties. No one knows for sure how kids will turn out. Most parents can assume that their children will survive and turn out fine—and most probably will. But as the parent of a preemie, you may feel that you can't assume too much. To add to the confusion, you and your partner may hold different projections for your child.

For the past year since my son has been home, he has become our life. My husband plays the role of the optimist. His strong religious belief tells him that God will make sure everything is okay. I am more of a pessimist. I know [our son] will have problems and I don't have the faith my husband does to believe that we can get off without them. —Raquel

I've been worried about one of my daughters, who seems to be starting to stutter. One evening last week, he was home with the kids and I called from work to check in. I asked, "How's her speech?" He said, "Fine, but I could panic if you'd like." ... I'm the worrier. He's more inclined to say that they're fine. I'm more inclined to have a heart attack. —Rikki

With any child born prematurely, delays or disabilities may or may not crop up. As a parent, there is a sense of uncertainty that you must learn to live with. Even if your child receives a diagnosis of a chronic medical problem, a disabling condition, an emotional or behavioral problem, or a developmental delay, there are still many uncertainties and unknowns, including the extent, effects, treatments, and prognoses. Additionally, diagnoses are sometimes reevaluated, leaving you doubly uncertain as to what the future holds. Only time will provide the answer.

It may feel as if the NICU roller-coaster ride is continuing. Your child may finally turn some corner in development and then be set back for months by some physical ailment. Or your child may be growing ever healthier when an unexpected complication suddenly appears. These dips can be agonizing, but they sometimes help to clarify the big picture. They may lead to improved solutions that help your child's health and development.

Along came his first seizure to burst my bubble. I was angry! I felt cheated! I felt insecure. As with anything Jacob has led us through, we learned we could handle the seizures. Sure, he's had some doozies that have scared the pants off of us and landed him in the hospital, but most are very controlled. We have learned to sense when one is coming. We've learned to avert most with tests and medication changes. And there's the silver lining. We've hit on a combination of drugs that seems to have lifted Jacob's fog. —Julie

Dealing with relentless uncertainty can make you feel confused, immobilized, fearful, out of control, anxious, or depressed. Uncertainty can be physically and emotionally exhausting.

•••

589

From time to time things still go wrong with Vincent. Recently he had a "neu-rological aberration" that might have been a seizure while he slept. He has had three of these in his life, and they almost drive me insane. Apart from the fear, my focus narrows so completely that it seems like there's no room for anyone in my heart but him. ... At times like this I can barely think. ... In my experience, it's hard to be wise, mature, and tolerant when your child or baby is sick and you're desperately worried. —Anne

It is impossible to describe the pain you feel when you look at the child you created. The child you want everything and more for, the child that you would sacrifice anything for—and you see him struggle to connect with the world around him, to comprehend the choice of yes or no, to answer a question in a direct fashion. And you do not know what the future holds for this child. You hope for the best, dread the worst. Every accomplishment causes hope to sprout anew. Every delay pierces your soul. The fear for this sweet child's future is indescribable. ... Sometimes it seems too much to face. Yet of course, your child faces it all daily, so face it you must. —Susan

First, not knowing is the hardest. It was so much easier to accept Alex as mentally impaired when we were told he was mentally impaired. It was as if we just said, "Okay, he's mentally impaired and we need to deal with it." Then the neurologist says he's not mentally impaired and he'll approach normalcy. So now we keep looking for this normalcy, and it's not here. It was easier when we thought he was mentally impaired. I still think he is, but I hesitate to "accept" it because now it seems as if I do not believe in him. —Mo

When answers are elusive, it's impossible to experience emotional closure. Your exhaustion and emotional pain reflect your sense of loss, but in the face of lingering uncertainties, you may find it difficult to grieve because you can't be sure exactly what you've lost. This confusion can freeze your grieving process. You may even chastise yourself for not holding on to high hopes or for being less than grateful. Your child is such a gift to you and so beautiful in his or her own way. How can you mourn? But unless you grieve, you cannot accept and move on. And as always, your mixed feelings are normal.

I will spend a lifetime living with the outcome, waiting each day to see, to know the cost, to find the answers to the questions that no one, not one single one of the endless parade of doctors and therapists now woven into the fabric of our lives, can answer. He is, as my husband says, who he is. And he will be who he will be. I am totally captivated with him, by him. I am terrified for him. —Susan

I don't think I've quite accepted Alex's situation yet. As I said before, it was easier when we were told he was mentally impaired. But then to be told he's not and to have an MRI with no brain damage ... and still no real improvement. I thought last night that I wished God would answer our prayers and heal him. Then I thought that maybe the answer was no. For a brief minute I felt relieved. Maybe I could quit asking for a cure and move on to acceptance. But it's just so hard when there is a glimmer of hope. I wish the MRI had shown brain damage. Then I would have an answer and could move on. The not knowing is killing me. —Mo

The Elusive Brain

For some preemies, a vast uncertainty is the condition of the brain. Early in your journey, you may focus all your attention on this area. Technology lets us peer inside the brain, but it's important to recognize that test results may not indicate much about a child's development, much less what the future holds for that child.

Babies' and children's brains can develop and change remarkably. When parts of the brain are damaged, other parts may take over and compensate. Or they may not. Each child's response to brain injury—the specific damage and how the brain compensates—is unique and often unpredictable. Unless the entire cortex is devastated, predicting developmental progress or outcome can be very difficult.

Furthermore, interpreting the result of brain scans is a tricky matter. Plenty of parents have discovered that a terrible-looking brain scan can belong to a kid who is doing pretty well, and a great-looking scan can belong to a kid who is doing quite poorly. Brain scans cannot tell you how your child will ultimately grow and develop. At best, the results might provide some explanations and names for what you and your medical team have already observed.

Finally, there are many uncertainties and unknowns regarding the effects of your baby's prematurity on his or her brain development. Gestational age at birth can contribute significantly to outcome, as the more immature the brain, the more shaping it receives from caregiving and the baby's surroundings after delivery. But there are so many other influences as well. Before birth, a brain's potential is influenced by the roll of the genetic dice or by the course of the pregnancy or delivery. Some babies' brains are compromised from conception or during prenatal development. After birth, the more serious and numerous the medical complications and required interventions, the greater the possibility that the developing brain is significantly affected. But no one can tell you exactly which postnatal influences will lead to which specific outcomes for your individual baby.

Still, in general, there is increasing evidence that the preemie's brain development can be affected by the weeks or months spent in the stressful environment of the NICU. Even in the most developmentally supportive nursery, many preemies must occasionally endure the unavoidable bright lights, loud sounds, invasive medical procedures, and separation from parents. Researchers are just beginning to examine how chronic stress or trauma affects the structural and functional development of the immature brain, including the mapping of neuropathways, the release and uptake of neurotransmitters, and the regulation and integration of brain function. When the developing brain repeatedly responds to stress, it is compelled to form pathways and chemical reactions that are different than they would have been under a less stressful beginning.

You can only guess at the relative contributions of genetics, the pregnancy, the prematurity, the NICU stay, or the continuing medical complications and treatments on your baby's developing brain, and the ultimate effect on his or her health, behavior, temperament, or overall progress. But you might focus on the NICU's potential effects on your child's outcome, especially if it stands out for you as being terribly stressful for your preemie. You may wonder about how detrimental the NICU's policies and caregiving approaches may have been for your baby's developing brain. You may wonder whether some of your child's physical or psychological reactions or challenges result from experiencing stress and trauma in the NICU or beyond.

I think there is some level at which our son's body remembers what happened in the NICU. I don't know what the term would be, but it seems like some positions are encoded—in a way that ties in physical and emotional. I don't think it is a conscious memory—rather, a very deep, physical memory. For our son, it was apparent. Whenever he was laid on his back, he became immobile. Handy for changing but unnatural. He eventually wriggled around on the changing table like crazy, but this reflex remained for years. If he was knocked or fell down on his back, he would get a very stunned look on his face and freeze. It was spooky. It has gotten better over time, but we are talking years and years. —Allison

When you learn that brain development can be compromised by the effects of prematurity and hospitalization, you may feel overwhelmed with worry. However, learning what you can about brain development and its influences can help you make sense of your child's uniqueness or help you find keys to meeting special needs. (For more on this, see "Perspectives on Parenting Your Preemie" in Chapter 15, Chapters 16 and 18, and "Supporting Your Preemie's Development" in the "Parenting Books" section of the Appendix C: Resources.)

It is also important for you to remember that your baby's brain continues to develop and be shaped by experience *for years after* hospitalization. Your relationship with your preemie is especially important, because responsive and encouraging interactions help your child reach his or her potential. As time passes and you see how your child behaves and develops, you may become less curious about what his or her brain looks like, less intent on the connections to prematurity and hospitalization, and more able to simply take in the reality of who your child is.

Coping with Uncertainties

If your baby's prognosis is uncertain, it can help to first face the fact that some expectations have changed. Then, identify those losses that are clear or obvious, so that you can grieve them. Doing so can reduce the burden of dealing with the remaining uncertainties.

You don't need a specific diagnosis or treatment plan before you can acknowledge that your child's health or development isn't what you thought it would be. You can grieve for the loss of a "typical" child. If your baby requires special precautions and caregiving, or if you are swamped with doctor and therapy appointments, you can grieve for the loss of a simple, blissful infancy. If you are watching closely for delays, illness, or disabilities and feel responsible for keeping your baby "on track," you can grieve for your lost ability to trust that your baby will thrive and develop well at his or her own pace with little effort on your part. You can grieve over the lost peace of mind about your baby's health, temperament, and development.

Also hope for the best while staying grounded in the present, facing the disappointing and fearsome realities as they arise. Your optimism gives you reason to go on. Your realism allows you to follow the path that fits best for now, even though you don't know exactly where that path is going. Your focus on the present lets you stay focused on your child.

- As your child grows, it can be helpful for you and members of your family to share your perceptions. Your views of reality and uncertainty will naturally differ. Sharing helps you understand and appreciate each other's perspectives and assessments of the joys and challenges you each face. Sharing may also help you to notice characteristics of your preemie that you had missed.

- Reach out to others outside the family. Outsiders can provide emotional or logistical support, but they can especially help enhance your grip on reality by reflecting your situation and struggles in their reactions and perceptions. Involvement with outsiders can also help you become more flexible in how you view and approach problems.

- Consider modifying your ideas of what it means to be a successful parent and to form a loving family. Observe and listen to others who appear to be successfully managing situations similar to yours.

- When you have trouble dealing with the uncertainties and unknowns, remember that it's not because there is something wrong with you, but because there is something wrong with the situation. Uncertainty and ambiguity are difficult for everyone to cope with.

- Manage uncertainties by making positive changes. Internal changes might include figuring out a more constructive way to view your situation or problems, or requesting medical records to fill in the gaps of your memories or knowledge. External changes might involve getting a second opinion from another doctor or replacing a therapist who scares your toddler. Constructive adjustments like these help you adapt and feel more settled, rather than immobilized by the uncertainties.

- Seek out spiritual or religious philosophies that help you accept ambiguity and uncertainty. (See "Spirituality and Religion" and "Getting to the Bottom of Your Grief" in Chapter 3 and also Chapter 23 for ideas.)

Even if your child's outcome remains uncertain, you can eventually get to a place where you can settle on what you generally expect for and from your child. Over time, you can adjust your expectations according to the unfolding of your child's development. If tangible difficulties emerge, you face yet another layer of loss associated with your child's preterm birth. You recognize that the 100-yard dash of preterm delivery and the NICU stay has become a marathon. Although having some certainty might make your life *easier*, it won't necessarily make it *easy*.

When Caleb was born prematurely, I of course grieved for that perfect pregnancy and all the attending pleasures ... holding him after birth, breast-feeding him, the joyful homecoming ... but when he went home after two months in the NICU, I was hopeful I could leave that experience behind. I of course worried on a daily basis that his prematurity could have long-term effects on him, but I now realize that nagging worry was nothing compared to the certainty *I now have that his prematurity will have long-term effects on his health/development. To live with that knowledge is painful.* —Eva

The following chapter addresses discovering delays and disabilities in your preemie, including more about testing, evaluation, intervention, grieving, and coping. Even if this information does not apply to your situation (yet or ever), you may feel curious about what that path can look like for parents and their children.

• • •

Points to Remember

- It is normal to wonder how your child's prematurity and medical complications will affect his or her long-term development, health, and behavior.
- You may have many mixed thoughts and feelings, hopes and fears about your preemie's future.
- No matter where your child ultimately ends up on the developmental spectrum, you'll probably hold your breath for a while—watching, waiting, and hoping. Your vigilance is important and can help you tune in to your child's needs and feel more in control—but it's important to find a balance between being on high alert and being relaxed about your child's development.
- As your baby outgrows his or her vulnerability, it is important for you to move beyond it as well. You may benefit from the special encouragement of trusted friends, family, and professionals to help you adjust your perception of your preemie and see your child with fresh eyes.
- No matter what worries lie ahead for you, try to immerse yourself in the joy of accomplishment with your child. Try to enjoy each small sign of progress and to celebrate.
- Although uncertainties are hard to live with, hoping for the best while staying grounded in the present and facing disappointing realities as they arise can help you deal with not knowing what the future holds for your child.

CHAPTER EIGHTEEN

Discovering Disabilities

For most preemies, development is naturally delayed in the early months. It is difficult at first to determine what, if any, delays will show themselves to be long-term disabilities. Many preemies will gradually make up for lost time. For others, questions about development intensify as "corrected" time begins to run out.

> *We hung on the words we'd heard from* so many *people, doctors and nurses included, that "preemies always catch up by the time they're two, if not sooner." So we waited. ... By the time she was nearing her first birthday, we already suspected that there were problems. She could barely roll over, couldn't sit, couldn't really hold things in her hands. I always kept giving her time "allowances" in my head. I'd use her adjusted age, and then double the premature time, and take off for the time in the hospital too, but eventually there was no denying her developmental delays. We started physical therapy and occupational therapy when she was thirteen months old, but her official "cerebral palsy" diagnosis wasn't made until a few weeks before her second birthday. —Diana*

If you are unaware of the various developmental complications that premature babies can experience, you may be caught completely by surprise by your little one's lack of progress.

I clung to the statistics provided to me regarding the outcomes. They showed survival rates of 90-plus percent. Surely after all that I had been through, that was the overwhelmingly likely outcome. It is so ironic and painful to me now that all I understood at the time was "survival" versus death. I had no concept of the many variations in between. I would learn. ... —Susan

They never spoke to us about how even babies who look good can still have some developmental and sensory integration problems and things like that—all the things to expect from a preemie. ... Now I know that all preemies do not do that well. And how can they tell you, even if your baby is breathing well at birth, that he's not going to experience other types of problems? Nobody ever mentioned anything about developmental problems. —Gallice

I had to know that "serious handicaps" was much more likely than death, yet I never, ever, imagined a child with even a mild handicap. Never. Not even after I brought home a healthy but hypotonic infant and had difficulty eliciting reflexes. Not when I acknowledged unusual state regulation. Not while worrying about apparent seizure activity, lethargy, and low tone. I continued, however, to obsessively check his breathing in the night. In fact, I continued to check to make sure he was breathing up until he was almost eight years old— when I brought home a new baby to worry over. (I'm still checking her breathing!)

I have to really think about this now and what it means for parents in follow-up clinic. How many people are hearing—but not hearing—that possibility? How many of those parents who swear no one ever told them their baby was at risk for mental retardation, cerebral palsy, or other developmental problems have simply not been able to imagine those possibilities? —Shaina

Even if your little one is showing clear signs of disabilities, it may take a long time for you to consider the possibility, much less let yourself see the very real manifestations in your child. You may find yourself turning away from issues that need attention because you didn't expect this and can't believe it. You may find excuses for your child's atypical behaviors because you don't want to face the possibility that your child won't simply outgrow these quirks. If you don't have a firm diagnosis or prognosis, or if others are downplaying your concerns, it's especially easy to deny the existence of a disability.

At first I would pooh-pooh the therapists when they would show a concern. To me, they were just having unrealistic expectations. I was giving him too much leeway, making too many excuses for his shortcomings instead of aggressively pursuing the milestones. He was so perfect and so amazing in my eyes. I got lulled by all the doctors who were also blinded by his spectacular advances [that were] "beating the odds" not to see the obvious delays.

Family and friends added to that lull. Every time I would raise a concern, they would dismiss it and tell me I was overreacting. I just didn't want to be labeled an alarmist. —Laura

I never really expected him to have delays because I had other preemies and they did great. Wow, what a big shocker, when he is now turning a year old and still not rolling by himself. So I guess I was very unprepared in that area. I mean, I knew that it could happen that way, but I guess I just didn't really expect it to happen. —Angie

I remember the first time someone mentioned bringing them in for some sort of early intervention. I was irate. "My babies are fine. What are you talking about?! My babies made it through this. They're okay." The thought that they might be delayed took a long time to sink in because, to me, it seemed normal that they should be delayed. It didn't seem like a bad thing—they had reason to be delayed. It didn't seem like something they should have to get help for. They were in therapy before they were a year old, but for a month there, it really was a struggle to admit, or to even allow myself to think in those terms—that a child can be okay and still have things that they need, that they could use help with some things. I still struggle when I learn new things about them. —Stephie

Getting a Diagnosis

When you're ready to take a close look at your child's development, the search for answers can be grueling. Visits with specialists, testing, and interpretation all take time and great effort. Sometimes, it takes a while to clearly define a disability or sort through a series of diagnoses. With each piece of the puzzle that is found, you must survive, search, and settle in all over again. (For more about this process, see "Your Personal Growth as a Parent" in Chapter 15.) If the news gets progressively worse, you may feel as if you are on a downward spiral.

We realized after a couple of months that we had no contact with him. Everything you read in the books was actually Fabian—no contact with his environment, no eye-to-eye contact; he was in his own world. It took a while before my pediatrician would realize that. I was telling him, and he was still thinking that it was a prematurity thing, just a delay. And then we thought it was purely visual. Since he had been doing so well, we thought maybe it's not a developmental thing, so we started hoping it was purely visual and putting all our hopes there. And I remember telling people, "Well, if they tell me that Fabian will need glasses, it would be the most wonderful news you could give me." So we did all these tests for the eyes, and that's when we learned that the eyes were actually functioning, but the brain was not processing the image, so it was a cortical type of impairment. It was a while before we could put our finger on that. And then a month later he developed infantile spasms, and so that was the answer to all that was happening. With him, we kept going from worst to worst to worst, and we kept saying with each time, "Well, now we've had the worst. It can't get worse." And each time, it would be worse. —Gallice

A diagnosis of disability marks a turning point in the developmental lives of both you and your preemie. It's difficult to deny the existence of a problem (or cluster of problems) that has a name. Some of the uncertainty recedes as problems become better defined. The future may look a bit clearer, even if it also looks more distressing.

Identifying a disability means making emotional adjustments. A diagnosis means letting go of the hope that your child will simply outgrow these challenges. Now that you face a future with a child who has special needs, you must consider what this new reality will be like.

I had a very hard time accepting that after the babies survived they would ever have [special] needs. My thinking was very black and white, live or die—if they live, they'll be okay. There was no middle ground. Once I learned the babies had low muscle tone and needed therapy, it was very sad and hard to take. I got them (and still do) all the therapy they needed, but it is still hard to adapt to sometimes. —Stephie

When I was pregnant with Stephen, I can remember thinking, "I can handle just about anything as long as my child can communicate with me." Then when he had his intraventricular hemorrhage, I was told that this would most likely affect his motor controls, if anything. Again, I thought, "Oh, good. I can handle that." Well, here I sit with a little guy who is going to need lots of help *learning to communicate. And I can't help but be a bit ticked off at the man upstairs for having chosen the one area that will be hardest for me to adjust to. —Tracy*

Over time you adjust your dreams to your reality. Maybe you start off wishing for Yale and end up hoping for entry to an LD (Learning Disabilities) college. This adjustment period is hard, very hard. —Allison

Facing a diagnosis of disability can be a shock and a sorrow. But it can also be a relief, especially if it has taken a long time to pinpoint your child's condition. If you've suspected that something was not quite right, a diagnosis can ironically be a boost to your confidence, a confirmation of your astute observations and judgment. It puts a name to your findings and the concerns you have voiced. Having accurate names for the challenges your child faces also empowers you. With a diagnosis, you can search for specific information and learn. You can also make more informed choices for your child and arrange for the necessary interventions.

For me it is important that I know what I am dealing with. ... I think it would help me feel less like I am struggling against an unknown. This would be an enormous relief. With his health issues, I have always known what I was dealing with and therefore could approach it with information. With his neurological situation and "delays," I don't really have a place to look for information since I don't have a name to look under. —Tracy

Unfortunately, not every condition can be clearly diagnosed. If your child's challenges or developmental delays remain unidentified, and particularly if health care providers are unable to prescribe productive treatment or therapies, you may continue to feel on edge about your child's future.

Somehow parents need to be warned that they may never get a concrete answer to their questions about "Why is my child behind?" And since Alex looks "normal," people have different expectations of him. Sometimes we wish he [looked abnormal] because then there would be a visual cue that something is wrong. —Mo

Furthermore, some diagnoses are so vague that their causes, treatment, and prognosis aren't known. Other diagnoses are so narrow that they don't begin to describe the complexity of your child's issues. Or your child may receive a range of diagnoses, each treatable individually, but hard to treat in combination. (For more about evaluations and labels, see Chapter 16; for help in dealing with uncertainties, see "Living with Uncertainty and Ambiguity" in Chapter 17.)

Facing Reality, Facing Feelings

With or without a firm diagnosis, health and developmental issues make themselves clear as your baby grows. As you gather more experience and observe your little one over a longer period, reality—and the attendant feelings—will replace denial. This can be a distressing revelation. Seeing your little one unable to keep up may make you feel both helpless and frustrated that you can't make it better. As your child learns that he or she is different, you may worry about your little one's frustration, pain, and isolation. As your child gets older and the disparity between age and abilities grows ever larger, your devastation may intensify. Facing reality and facing feelings go hand in hand.

I knew there was something wrong. I just didn't want to accept it. Since she's still little, I can still do everything with her. I can still carry her here and there. But I think when she's older and weighs more, when we can do fewer things—that's when it's finally going to start crushing me. —Charlie

As I've started including Conor in more activities with the mainstream population and as he gets older, I do see his "disability" becoming more apparent. It was very eye opening for us to have him in soccer with other kids his age and to truly see the disparity in his skills overall. In our little vacuum we call home and school, Conor is making huge advancements—for him. But when he's out in the "real" world, I see how far he really has to go. —Laura

I don't look at the charts anymore, so I really don't know what she is supposed to be doing. Of course, I use her peers as a good barometer. And when her friends are up on the fort and she's down on the ground because she doesn't have the strength to climb up, I feel sorry for her. She is unaware of all this, but someday she may realize that she can't do all those things, and I do worry how this may affect her. Nobody wants to be different from everyone else. —Kathie

Other parents can't tell the differences, but I see the sensory and language delays affect how they relate socially. They are just more immature. I don't mind, but sometimes it's a little sad that the other kids are making friends and they aren't. —Stephie

Stuart has been doing so well and making such progress, but last night he participated in a "graduation ceremony" from a pre-K safety program through the schools. The distinctions between his premature self at five and the normally developing kids were stark. My husband said, "He breaks my heart." —Susan

As you face reality, you will also face many painful emotions of grief. But recognizing that there are problems will make it possible for you to search for solutions. Although draining at times, the turmoil of grief can energize you toward getting the intervention that your child needs and the support that you and your family deserve.

By facing reality and your feelings, you can also come to terms with your child's special needs. If you can acknowledge the extent of your child's challenges, you'll be able to let go of romanticized hopes and acquire realistic expectations. You can reorganize life around what *is*, instead of remaining stuck in what might have been.

You may see this same dynamic in others around you—relatives, friends, your child's pediatrician. When they acknowledge the extent of your child's challenges, they too are able to deal more effectively and realistically with the situation. If they can face their own hurt and sorrow, they will be able to support you as you work through your own. Surround yourself with those who can face reality and deal with a wide range of feelings. They are the people who can walk with you down this rocky path.

•••
603
Discovering Disabilities

Oddly enough, it was the respiratory specialists who helped me be more at peace with the idea that he will likely have long-term delays and possible mental disabilities. They were the first who would actually look me in the eye and tell me that Stephen might be mildly retarded. All the others have talked around it. It was hearing it straight out that allowed me to begin to assimilate it and learn to adjust my life to it. The most frustrating thing of all the delays has been that "delay" implies a lag that will be made up. I kept waiting for Stephen to "catch up." Now that it has been put into terms implying a permanent situation, I can deal with it as part of life and not wait for an ending that won't come. —Tracy

If others minimize your concerns about your child, you may wonder if you're mistaken or if you should simply be grateful for what your child *can* do. Try to remember that those who minimize your worries are trying to shield you—and themselves—from the grief that comes with having a child with delays or disabilities. But you are entitled to face reality—and your feelings about it—as it unfolds over time.

For families who must live with glaring question marks, not knowing encourages denial. You needn't wait for final answers to get on with life. What is important is the current reality. Live in the present. Deal with each day as it comes. Stay in tune with your child.

Grieving This New Realization

I was going through grief for the second time in my daughter's life. The first was during the crisis of her early days, when I realized how sick she was. The second period was when I realized that my daughter wasn't going to look like those "super-preemies" who came toddling or running up to the NICU door to greet their former caregivers. —Karen

I always dreamed we'd be perfect, happy parents. I always thought we'd give them all the time and things they needed. I never dreamed those things would be doctors and medicines. … When my son was born, I prayed every day to God for my son to be healthy, happy, loved, intelligent, kind, and successful— in that order. Of these six things, I can only be sure he'll get one of them. All six is not too much to ask. He certainly deserves it. —Laura

As you confront the reality of your child's disabilities and special needs, you face more grief: your child's losses, as well as your own. Although you've been healing from your disappointments around the premature birth and hospitalization of your little one, you may feel as if you're returning to square one. And now that your little one faces a less-than-excellent outcome, you'll need to rework some of your grief over the avalanche of events that brought you to this point.

This has been a weird time for me. I am realizing that what is making it so difficult is accepting that Stuart isn't going to "get better," for lack of a more accurate term. I am experiencing the death of a dream at the same time of year that I experienced so many other tragedies four years ago. ... I am grieving anew the fact that I now know that it will never be over. That it isn't a matter of reaching this milestone or that. That our lives—most of all, my son's life—will continually be gauged by where we end up considering from whence we came. And I am tired. —Susan

Since you began this journey, you, your child, and your family have benefited immensely from your willingness to face your feelings and come to terms with reality. Still, you may worry that the grief you are feeling now is unfounded or that you are overreacting to these latest developments. After all, your child's outcome could be a lot worse. That's true—but it could also be *a lot better.* As always, you are entitled to the entire range of your feelings, especially in light of these new developments.

It really broke my heart to see him next to that [term] baby. I guess I was kind of in denial as to how small and how far behind he really is until tonight. When she left, I sat and held Chris and just cried, but then felt guilty because I know there are little ones who are having a harder time than he is, and maybe I shouldn't be so upset. No one has ever said that Chris will never do this stuff. They just tell me he is very far behind—so maybe I have no right to these feelings. I should just be grateful that I have him, regardless of what he does and doesn't do, or how big or little he is. —Angie

"If only. ... Please, I will trade her sight if only she can hear ... Oh, she can't hear? Then let her walk. Oh, she can't walk? Let her be happy ... " I

was so thankful to read this when I did. I remember sitting and sobbing as I read it, so happy to have someone give voice to my feelings. We convince ourselves that something isn't a big deal when, in another framework, it would be a big deal. It's good that we work this way, or all of our lives we would live in despair, but it goes back to the point that it is all relative. —Julie

Coping with Your Feelings

Ever-Present Grief

I cannot even think about the future. I live one day at a time. I love him and enjoy him. AND he limits my life and lifestyle and career. I am one of the parents who goes in and out of chronic grieving patterns. ... I find I am always looking for a way to be at peace about Vic, his disabilities, and how he does or doesn't fit in ... and peace about my role as lifelong caregiver. —Chris

Many parents of children with special needs remark that their grief never ceases. New losses can keep cropping up as your child grows. Uncertainties complicate your adjustment: you can't know exactly what you've lost or how to modify your expectations. Just when you think you've mastered a certain phase, some setback may take the hard-earned wind out of your sails. Although grief over a significant loss never completely ends, grieving for a child with special needs can be a particularly unpredictable and unfinished process.

How quickly your satisfaction with your child's progress can be snatched away. This week it happened with Ian. I went to pick him up, and he told me that he had fun at Mrs. Smith's and that he had an animal cookie for a treat. I was so pleased at how he volunteered that information and how much he volunteered. Then I hear the little girl behind us. "Guess what, Mom? I got a new toothbrush today. It's pink, and it's in my backpack. It's really cool." And on it went. All complete sentences and a real conversation. —Mo

I have peaceful moments, moments of insight and acceptance, moments even of gratefulness. But they are scattered moments, unpredictable in frequency and duration. I have as many moments of terror, guilt, [and] rage at the unknown, the uncontrollable. —Susan

Although your grief may be a constant undercurrent, you also experience positive feelings about your child's growth and development. This makes for a bittersweet mix. You can be thrilled and relieved about what your child can do and, at the same time, angry about what he or she can't do—and terrified that your little one will never be able to keep up or blend in with peers. This vacillation between grief and joy is common.

I literally start crying every time we get somewhere with Chris. To watch him work so hard on such little things as lifting his head while he's on his tummy. I know everything he does is such a challenge and every step is very hard earned for him. Sometimes, I feel so sad for him to have to struggle so hard. And yet every accomplishment—although it may be little to anyone else—is like chasing a star and catching it. —Angie

Some of life is positive, some negative—that's just the way it is. I don't see Caleb as a burden at all—he is a beautiful, sweet child who deserves every ounce of energy I can give him. But the complications from his prematurity are discouraging, upsetting, tiring, and ultimately isolate me from friends, relatives, and other new parents who cannot share my feelings. That's just the way it is. I deal with it, and that's my life. —Eva

I think I'm the most supportive and yet most critical of my son's development. When Conor reaches a milestone, my husband and I celebrate privately. When other people notice his accomplishments, we tend to play them down. I think it's because, as much as we want people to perceive Conor [to be] as normal as any other kid, at the same time we want them to realize how much harder everything is for him. —Laura

If you have multiple preemies with varying outcomes, this vacillation is especially inevitable. Your thrill over one child's progress is tempered by your worry about the other child's lack of progress.

Even when progress is distressingly slow, though, you can appreciate and admire your preemie's courageous struggle to move forward. If your little one had a difficult NICU course or has had many complications, you may feel especially grateful and relieved at every inch of growth. Any developmental progress gives you hope. Seeing progress also makes you want more, even though you know you might be setting yourself up for additional disappointment.

It's hard because, at this point, you increase your expectations. You go from having a healthy baby to the possibility of losing your child, so you deal with death, and after that you start over again, and then you're grateful for anything you get. Anything your child will do would be positive. And at that point for me, I said the hardest thing would be if my child would not recognize me as being his mom. That would be unbearable, I think. But as long as he recognizes me and he's a happy baby, that's all I want. That was months ago. Now, of course, I've increased my expectations and I want more. I keep expecting more as I see him develop and get better. So now, that would not be enough for me anymore. —Gallice

When grief is always there, staying in touch with your emotions can seem an overwhelming assignment. But it's an assignment with many rewards. Staying in touch with your emotions frees your energy so that you can apply it to nurturing your child and yourself. In contrast, avoiding, covering up, or compensating for your pain consumes your energy and can result in withdrawal from, overprotectiveness toward, or irritation with your child. If you discount the painful realities or your feelings (or ignore other sources of difficulty in your life), you may see your child as your only source of stress, unfairly placing the burden of your unhappiness on his or her tiny head. This is a common dynamic in families that have a child with special needs. Recognize that it is healthy to admit the downside to raising such a child.

Oh, how hard and how tiring it is to raise special needs children. It's hard to worry about them all the time. It is so hard to watch them struggle. It's hard to see them in pain. It's not the same as having "normal" kids. I can't believe how easy it is to raise my full-termer. She has no special needs. It's a piece of cake. —Mo

Nothing can prepare you for the challenges of raising a preemie—medically, socially, educationally, financially. We have been faced with increasing problems with our son. His "normal" appearance hides his developmental delays, until he tries to speak. It is heart-wrenching to watch your child try to fit in, to let him experience life and not try to do everything for him, and to watch him suffer with anxiety about being different. —Alice

It's not just the stress of the preemie experience, it's the ongoing life with a disabled child. The stress of doctors' appointments, illnesses, hospitalizations, therapies, constant care. It's the medical bills piling up and the "we can't afford it." It's not knowing where our future is. It's the guilt of not being able to give any of our children all they need because one child needs so much. It's facing the full-time job of medical research, decisions, insurance issues. —Julie

When grief wells up, attend to it and do what you need to do to face it and cope. As you acknowledge and work through your feelings, you also regularly emerge with renewed, realistic hope. And when you need help and support, seek it out. (For more help with the grieving process, review Chapters 2 and 3.)

It is agony each time you go through a new diagnosis or get answers to another test. When you have to keep adjusting your vision over time—even ten, fifteen years down the road—this makes it even harder. The crash of your hopes is one reason labels are so difficult to accept. However, once you go through this acceptance, daily life is easier. —Allison

Now that Conor's disabilities have become more apparent, he's gone off to preschool and his therapies are no longer "under my control." I've been feeling worse and worse as time goes on. I have never really obsessed over Conor's problems like this. I used to point out his strong points to everyone. Now I seem to be dwelling on his difficulties. I went to a homeopathic doctor for a remedy, and it has helped a little. However, she's the one who pushed me to see a counselor. My first appointment is Friday. Wish me luck! —Laura

Grief Triggers

As time has gone on, I find that the grief resurfaces. Sure, I have reached an acceptance phase, but particularly around those milestones like birthdays, I feel real twinges in my heart. When I see my daughter doing things she should be doing (in my perfect world), it hurts. The pain is less each year, but I suspect it will never go away completely. —Joyce

My son's delays have become more obvious as he's gotten older. They've also become more obvious to me now that I have a full-term nine-month-old daughter to compare him to. Her milestones have been bittersweet for me. Some things she accomplishes were never really accomplished by Conor, so I end up celebrating for her yet mourning his losses. —Laura

Being around full-term, "typical" kids, that's hardest for me. Not extended family, I'm prepared for that. It's the strangers who have typical kids. It's rather hard to see a cute two-year-old effortlessly doing things my kids struggle to do. I know the boys are "challenged," but it's a real downer for me to realize exactly how "challenged/delayed" they are when it smacks you upside the face. —Ramona

If you're surrounded by triggers much of the time, you may feel your grief rising often. Triggers—events such as anniversaries, holidays, evaluations, milestones, setbacks, and comparisons that rekindle painful emotions—contribute to ongoing grief. It can be difficult to avoid them. However, if you can view triggers as catalysts to help you move through your grief, they don't have to be your foes. Take the opportunity they provide to feel your sorrow, anger, failure, guilt, disappointment, envy—whatever it is you're experiencing. As you acknowledge and unleash your feelings, you'll be better able to cope. You may also reach a point where you can start talking back to your triggers. When a holiday isn't what you'd dreamed, for instance, tell yourself that dreams change, and get on with creating new ones. When you take your child for a checkup or evaluation, remind yourself that test results merely describe reality, with no judgments attached. Recall that being different is *not* equivalent to being inferior. When milestones bring new disappointments, remind yourself that your grief is necessary as you adjust to new expectations. Remember that accepting your child's differences and challenges inspires him or her to do the same. When you are ready to talk back to a trigger, find the words that soothe and reassure you.

I hear so many people say, "I don't know how you do it" with Jacob's special needs. But I know what the alternative was. It's easy when you think that the alternative would be that we wouldn't have him at all. When things overwhelm me, I go back to the fact that Jacob shouldn't even have survived. My ultimate bargain was that he live. I can deal with just about anything after that. —Julie

Catastrophic Worries

Some parents of preemies find their imaginings for the future plagued by catastrophic worries. In the back of your mind, you may be picturing something you're not sure you could cope with. For example, when your one-year-old isn't yet sitting up, you may imagine an immobile, floppy toddler, a concept that might throw you into a panic. If your preschooler is oblivious to potty training, you may picture yourself changing diapers for a teenager, a daunting thought. Perhaps most intimidating is the question of who would take care of this child if something were to happen to you. Who could do it with as much love?

I have a lot of anger with that, that mixed bag of who do I want to sue, how am I going to support this child for the rest of my life. ... I want her to have the best care until she dies. That's one of the million worries. If we died tomorrow, who's going to give her the love that Sue and I give her? Who would love her? No one would be able to give this child the love—no one would have the time ... so that's something that really bothers me. —Charlie

It is important for you to face your fears and give them a reality check. Ask your health care providers how likely something is, and learn to talk back to catastrophic thoughts. Try to focus on what *is*, not what *might be*. Also contact parents of children with special needs similar to your child's. They will be happy to offer support; to share their approaches, insights, and coping mechanisms; and to give you a more balanced picture of what it's *really* like. (For more on this subject, check out "Coping with Feelings of Vulnerability" in Chapter 14.)

And remember, getting to the bottom of your grief can dissipate much of your anxiety, freeing you to focus your energies to deal with what is, instead of what might be.

• • •

Isolation

When your child has special needs, you'll naturally feel isolated from parents with "regular" kids. But your isolation doesn't necessarily end there. If your preemie's disabilities don't fit into the typical categories, you may feel unwelcome in that crowd as well. For instance, if your child has visual impairments but also some developmental delays associated with other complications, you may not have much in common with the parents of children whose visual impairment is their primary disability.

I found out about my "special needs" child when he was thirty-two months old. It created a real sense of isolation for me. I no longer fit into the preemie-parent group that escaped the travails unscathed. —Joyce

I do feel different from other parents and feel that Josh and Evan are different from other kids. We fall in between the handicapped and "normal" world. I guess I relate more to the special needs world, but most of those parents don't want me there. —Stephie

Although it can be challenging, it's very important to find a community of other parents with whom you can share and commiserate. This community is a place for venting feelings, finding out you're not alone, and sharing knowledge and suggestions. It's a place where your life feels "normal" and you don't have to explain so much, where you can be emotionally honest and at the same time learn more about coping during this journey you're on.

As a start to finding a community, turn to Appendix C: Resources and to the lists at the backs of other books. Reading and Internet electronic mailing list groups are also a way to feel a sense of community.

Being a loving, accepting parent does not always come naturally. ... Being depressed on occasion because your child is seriously ill/disabled is a valid reason. [To the moms like me,] I support you in your struggles and want you to know you're not alone. I think about you and your kids all the time. And although you may not feel very inspirational, you are an inspiration to me, just because you get up every day and look at your kids and love them and fight for them even when you don't feel like you can go on. —Eva

• • •

612

Guilt

I'll always feel the "what-ifs." Like what if I had not ignored the initial sensation of PROM with Emily? What if the extra few hours would have been enough to see if any drugs could have slowed/stopped labor? What if I'd had a C-section? Would she still have had brain damage? —Diana

I have fought for years to overcome a deep sense of guilt over Jacob, Clare, and Emily's early birth. Did I want too much? Did I tempt fate? I am still fighting a societal attitude that Jacob is less than desirable because of his disabilities. —Julie

Parental guilt in the face of a child's special needs has several sources. The most common is wondering about your contributions to the early delivery, which started a chain of events that led to your child's disabilities, delays, or medical complications. If you blame yourself at all for the early delivery, you will likely also blame yourself to some extent for your child's struggles.

Something in the lingering indications of their prematurity will always break the hearts of the parents of preemies. Logical or not, we failed to protect them, to enable them to be born whole and intact. So many of us are fierce when it comes to advocating for them, and I believe that fierceness stems from, in no small part, our sense of failure surrounding the circumstances of their birth. —Susan

Besides the events surrounding the pregnancy and delivery, you may torture yourself with questions. "Were there things I did (like exposing my little one to germs) or didn't do (like being unable to do kangaroo care in the NICU) that made things worse?" "Did I let others dissuade me from following my intuitions about pursuing certain types of care, evaluation, or treatment?" "Were early interventions available, but I didn't know my child needed them or qualified for them?" "Would it have made a difference if I'd known?" Pondering these questions can be very distressing for families, and especially guilt-provoking for the primary caregiver.

I believe that if I could have held Alex more, breast-fed him, positioned him, set his cannula correctly, and done some other things I really wanted to do [in the NICU], it would have made a difference for Alex—long after his time in the NICU. That I wanted to do these things then and was discouraged makes it harder when I learn over time that my desires were right on target. —Allison

When we came home, we just let the boys go crazy with that baby. And I've got that on videotape, and when I see it, I'm like, "Oh, my God, how could we have done that?" That's part of the guilt, of course. Everybody tells us that if the germs were in the house, it would have happened anyway, but we could have easily prevented that part of it. —Gallice

Although Logan did progress with his friends to the kindergarten at his pre-school, we underestimated or overlooked how he would feel at not being able to do the work. By the end of the year, he was having fits of sadness, wanting to go to heaven, wanting to "stab" himself because he was so "dumb." I cannot express what this did to me and my marriage. Logan only expressed these feelings to me, so naturally my husband said it was a game that Logan was playing with me. Eventually I took Logan to a therapist (which really strained my marriage), and after several sessions, she stated that Logan was figuring out that he was not at the same level of the others. Her words were, "Logan is realizing that he is different." After the age of two, he seemed relatively "normal" and was booted out of all the state programs, so he had never received any follow-up or assistance, and we did not know any better. —Megan

With Emily, I feel guilty that we didn't recognize the obvious signs of cerebral palsy earlier. I attribute this in part to our being first-time parents with her. Now as we watch Eric develop "typically," we are keenly aware of what he can do that she still doesn't do. —Diana

Mothers typically feel the most guilt. We are under the impression that we could, if we were good enough, make sure that only the best things happen to our children and that they get everything they need. Our protective instincts are so strong—perhaps we assume that we have the power to match. But of course, we don't.

•••

Still you may ask, "Why didn't I know something was amiss right away?" Unfortunately, good, comprehensive, long-term follow-up is very difficult to come by. "Why didn't I pay attention to the warnings of that one specialist?" Ignoring something you don't consider to be accurate or possible is normal. "Would a standard early-intervention program have made a difference?" Early intervention might not have changed your child's overall outcome. Early intervention can produce early gains, but if you provided a stimulating environment with ample opportunities for motor play, emotional interaction, and cognitive exploration at home, you did essentially what an early intervention program does. That's why your child may very well end up in exactly the same place with or without formal intervention. Even so, while intervention may not vastly improve your child's ultimate outcome, it can give you ideas for making your child's path smoother—and your child can benefit *whenever* you start.

Recognizing that you failed to provide your child with early, specialized interventions, such as for feeding or sensory issues, can feel devastating due to any difficult struggles you and your child may have endured. But you can only see what you see and know what you know. Without follow-up and support from the health care system, finding just the right specialist with the right key can be a daunting task, especially for an elusive or subtle problem. Also remember that new research and therapies are always coming down the pike and that knowledge about these issues is constantly evolving. If it took you a while to discover something, the reason might be because the information wasn't widely disseminated or available any earlier. Finally, whether you believe you tend to be too vigilant or not vigilant enough, don't blame yourself for not intervening with the right treatment sooner. If you err on the side of being especially vigilant, remember how persistent you were in your search for explanations and solutions. Knowledge isn't always handed to you on a silver platter. Often, there is a necessary process of discovery, both for you *and* the field. If you err on the side of being especially relaxed about your preemie's progress, remember that your desire to treat your child "normally" is an honorable endeavor and may have actually influenced your child's development in many positive ways.

You also need to remember that so much is unpredictable and out of your hands. It's hard to know which aspects of your child's outcome were inevitable and which could have been changed. Remember that your child's disabilities may have been set in motion before the early delivery and coincided with prematurity, but were not caused by it. In any case, for parents who have preemies, and especially those who have babies with special needs, a big part of parenting is accepting that you do not have the power to control and fix whatever ails your child. Most "regular" parents have the chance to adjust to this idea slowly over many, many years. For you, this loss of control is massive and arrives so early, making it much more difficult to face.

Another aspect of guilt is wondering whether your parenting style has caused or contributed to your child's problems. Parents know that they play a role in their child's emotional, physical, intellectual, and social development. If your child has very challenging or annoying behaviors, tendencies, or reactions that persist or worsen in spite of your efforts, you may harbor serious doubts about your parenting abilities and feel stumped about how to discover and provide the effective guidance your child needs. Some children bring so many challenges to the table that even the most well-meaning, insightful, nurturing, and resourceful parents can be tapped out.

Whether your child is overreactive or underreactive, it can be very difficult to figure out how to stop the vicious cycle. For instance, if your child has frequent meltdowns over a lot of little things, you may end up feeling shell-shocked, and your exasperation, impatience, and desperation only feed more meltdowns. Or if your infant is much happier when left alone and you know that your overtures will be rebuffed (perhaps emphatically so), you may feel so rejected or wary that you withdraw from your little one, reinforcing his or her reclusive tendencies. If you feel that you and your child are stuck in a dysfunctional rut or caught in a continuous, destructive loop, seek professional evaluations and assistance. Keep looking until you find a specialist who understands your perceptions of the situation and recognizes that your child (and family) has some significant issues that need to be evaluated and addressed. Also keep in mind that the solution is two pronged: get your child the help she or he needs, but also get the help *you* need to learn how to deal with the challenges your child presents. High-quality treatment is comprehensive, supporting everyone in the family.

While we are happy with the kids and the progress they've made, it can be so depressing knowing how far they have to go. Maybe all preemie parents should be given therapy!—although most of us would have declined, thinking we could handle it. There are days that I think about foster care for Alex, and he's not that bad! So, I wonder about the parents who have had less-promising outcomes than we have had. —Mo

If your child is alive because of aggressive medical intervention, this can be another source of guilt and regret. Whether you were involved in the decisions or not, you may regret that the medical team intervened—and that your child is bearing the costs. You may feel that you have only a tenuous hold on this child, that he or she shouldn't really be here. Is your child here to stay? You may wonder, "Should I have fought so hard to keep my little one here? Am I sorry that I did?" These questions can be incredibly painful to consider. You may have deep and persistent feelings of anxiety about your child's ultimate outcome and secretly wonder whether it might have been better if your little one had died peacefully. Know that these feelings arise from your *love* for this child.

I'm not sure how this is going to sound when I say it, but I mean, I love her and everything, but I'm still in this kind of limbo. I don't know how she's going to turn out. She could turn out fine. She could turn out to have major problems. There are so many things that could happen. Whereas if she had died, that's it. It would have been done with, and I wouldn't be in that uncertainty anymore. It would be something solid, whereas right now I'm still standing in the clouds. It's not like I want her to die. It's that I wish there was some stability here, where I'm actually going to be able to hit a point where I'm like, "Okay, the ground is not going to drop out from under my feet anymore. We're okay." But that's not going to happen for a couple of years yet. ... It's going to be a couple of years yet until I feel like, "Okay, I can breathe now." —Brooke

I am the mother of a little boy who shouldn't be here. He was conceived artificially, then his life was supported artificially during the 100 days that a normal child would have been ensconced in the womb. He endured and survived more medical intervention and physical torture than modern medicine would dare inflict on the sickest consenting adult. He endured and survived—scarred and fragile, his trunk, his lungs, his eyes, his neurological wiring all carry the marks of his battle. The chasm between him and his naturally conceived,

full-term, normally developing brother is deep. They literally come from differ-
ent worlds. I love him fiercely, my mother-bear instincts on full alert at every
moment, too late to protect, still trying to ward off danger. But I love a child
who shouldn't be here, and that burden will be with me always. —Susan

Finally, and perhaps most troublesome, you may find yourself thinking, "*This* is not what I was wishing for"—and feel guilty for resenting your child's extraordinary needs. You may feel particularly guilty if you struck a bargain that if your child lived, you wouldn't complain about the outcome. At that point, anything but death was acceptable to you. Now that you are facing the challenges of your child's life, you may feel guilty for feeling even the slightest bit frustrated or dissatisfied. Yet your emotions are normal reactions to the often-relentless caregiving tasks involved in raising a child with special needs. You are not a bad parent for feeling resentful. You can love your kids and still hate this life, including all the uncertainty it holds.

The hardest thing for me is to say outloud that what we are going through is
not okay. Does that mean I would have done anything differently? No way. I
love Lars, I love our life, and this is what I want to be doing. But I sure
wouldn't have picked it. —Kris

It's the everyday little stuff that wears you out. Remember when you felt like
all you did all day was change diapers and make formula? That's what this is
like. Tedious. It takes away from the joy. But don't dare express those thoughts
or you will be condemned. I'm supposed to be thrilled that they are alive. And
I am, but I wish things would move along a little quicker. I've often said that
I wish I could fast-forward to the end of this movie so I can sit back and
relax, knowing how it comes out. —Mo

Rather than hiding from the truth of your feelings, it can help to face them and name them. Doing so can enable you to deal with them and eventually to move on with the realization that what you do every day is extraordinary—and you're entitled to your feelings about that.

• • •

Anger

I have a very, very, very hard time looking at children who are Erin's age ... to see them running around in their little skirts and their little shoes and their bows ... and Erin doesn't do that. ... Erin can't, and she's kind of by herself. It's hard. It's very hard. ... My wife wants me to go into counseling for hating little five-year-old girls. But I don't hate little girls. I hate the fact that Erin's not able to walk around in patent leather shoes and a dress. It aggravates me and upsets me that other kids are normal.—Charlie

When your child has special needs, your anger may have many facets. You may resent parents who take their children for granted or who are irresponsible and shirk their parenting duties. You may resent kids who don't appreciate their abilities or whose behavior undermines their health. You may feel angry that this had to happen to you, to your family, and mostly, to your child. If your religious beliefs teach that a higher power plays a direct role in making children what they are, you may feel angry at that higher power. Or you may question that line of thinking and feel angry at those who insist that if you had been a better person, this wouldn't have happened.

I am so sick of hearing the idea that God answered their prayers and healed their babies. What does that say to the rest of us whose prayers weren't answered? I have heard enough from my husband's family about my so-called lack of faith, by their standards, and how that has contributed to Alex's poor progress. What that says to me is that Alex is a punishment. What ever happened to this "gift from God"? As much as I would like him "healed," just because it doesn't happen doesn't mean that I am less of a "Christian" or that I deserve to be punished and Alex is it. I have been told that God knew that I couldn't handle triplets and that's why Caleb died. So he gave me two special needs kids? Now, do I believe all this crap? No, but it still irks me. I don't believe it, and it still makes me mad, so I wonder how it must make a person feel who may be susceptible to this crap. More guilt?

I don't want to be accused of being anti-Christian. I'm not anti-anything except anti-clueless and anti-mean. —Mo

Besides the unfairness of it all, you may also feel aggravated by the social, medical, and educational systems that do not provide adequate resources to help you meet your child's complex needs. It can be supremely frustrating to have to spend so much time and energy negotiating your way to the services that should be easily available to you and your child. On top of that, you have to sort through which specialists and interventions will offer your child the most benefit. These tasks put your patience, perseverance, and dedication to the test. You may feel resentful if you aren't getting the help and support you expect from your partner or other close family members. At particularly trying moments, especially when you are under extreme stress, you may also resent your child.

Of course, you have every right to be angry about these issues, and more. The trick is to find ways to acknowledge and constructively express this anger. If you try to suppress your anger, it will come out in ways that are hurtful. Instead, use your anger to energize you toward finding solutions to the challenges you encounter. Also, stay mindful of other stresses in your life and try to minimize what you can. Raising your child is complicated enough. Keep the rest of your life as simple as possible. When you reduce your general stress level, you'll be less susceptible to reaching "anger overload." (For support dealing with anger and parenting, see "Your Personal Growth as a Parent" in Chapter 15.)

Finding Peace

I think that I am coming to terms with Stuart's unique gifts/challenges more and more (with lots of ground left to cover, though). This helps me have moments when I feel less panicked, pressured, afraid. —Susan

Although your grief about how your child's future is unfolding can be continuous and overpowering at times, achieving a firm sense of peace is possible. Peace comes from letting go of the need to control, accepting your own vulnerability, and finding ways to integrate raising a child with special needs into the bigger picture of your life. Here are some ideas that might help your adjustment and healing. (Also see Chapter 23, as well as "Perspectives on Parenting Your Preemie" in Chapter 15, and refer to Chapter 3 for more on moving through painful feelings.)

- Allow yourself to grieve. By giving yourself permission to feel the way you do about the fact that you and your child don't have a typical experience, you can find ways to move forward. Remember that just as your grief may be continuous, *so is your adjustment and healing.*

- Give yourself permission to protest the unfairness of all of this. Being angry, disappointed, and scared doesn't mean that you don't love and value your child. It just acknowledges that if you could have magically made it different, you would have. As it stands, you are the one who must learn to adjust and be a much different sort of parent.

- Talk to other parents of children with special needs, parents with whom you can identify, and parents who strive to adjust and prevail. You'll be inspired to emulate their tenacity, and you'll see that you are not alone in your worries, in your needs, or in your hopes for the future.

- Focus on being a *parent*, rather than a doctor or a therapist. Be the one who can focus on who your child *is*, not just what he or she does.

- Resist the notion that every move you make must follow a treatment plan. Remember that your touch, your voice, your focused attention, and your enjoyment are the most beneficial parts of any therapeutic regimen.

- Take the time and energy to face your anger, guilt, anxiety, sadness, and disappointment about your child's disabilities. If you hide from your negative feelings about those challenges, you may displace them onto your child. If you can work through those feelings, you may find it easier to see your child in a positive light.

- If you are feeling inadequate, remind yourself that you've had to learn how to care for your little one day by day. There's no handbook on how to raise a preemie, especially one as unique as yours. Trial and error by its very nature includes error. There's no shame in making mistakes, as long as you learn from them.

- Partner with your child's health care providers in his or her medical and developmental care, but never forget that you are the most knowledgeable about your child's strengths and weaknesses. Learn what you can from the professionals, but don't hesitate to teach *them* about your child. Think of yourself as the *team leader* of your child's care.

- Empower yourself by obtaining information about the challenges your child and family face. There are many good books out there, as well as a vast network on the Internet, full of information, experience, and resources that can help you get to the root of problems and discover solutions that work for you and your child.

- As you grieve, know that you can move forward with direction and purpose. Your hopes can shift into trusting that your child is a precious soul in spite of the challenges, living the life he or she was meant to live. Adopt a wondering attitude about the future.
- By all means, seek counseling for yourself and/or your family. Coming to terms with disabilities and living with a child with special needs can be very challenging. Expect your adjustment to be more difficult at certain points. You deserve to have the support you need, whenever you need it.

Over time, peace creeps up in many disguises. As you find more answers and solutions to the problems that crop up, you fear less and embrace more, learning to enjoy your child and to let go of the things you cannot control. When you're ready and able, you can look for and appreciate the positives about raising your differently-abled child. In general, you can go to places you perhaps never thought you could—places of calm, insight, wisdom, courage, compassion, and acceptance.

I really am normally a tolerant person, but I like order. That has gone by the wayside. I have learned to let go of some of the things I thought I needed to control. I can't control my children's outcomes. I am less uptight about what my children are and more in tune with who they are. So what if Alex has written over almost every wall in the house. At least he can. It does drive me somewhat crazy, but since I can't really do too much about it except hide the pens, we just live with it. Every couple of weeks I take a roller with primer and paint over the scribbles. At least the walls look clean then. And I once said that my kids would never write on the walls. —Mo

Each of my children has brought something new to my life. Each has taught me something special and different. With Molly, I learned not to judge all children by the same yardstick. We learned to be patient with her and to accept her on her terms. I found myself feeling pride and joy at her smaller accomplishments. We let her develop at her own pace and did not push her. —Renee

Tom and I are very positive people, so we always felt like we would all get through it as a family, and we'd be stronger for it, and we knew that Dylan particularly (but all of them, really) had a lot of lessons for all of us. And they showed it to us every day, and Dylan still does it. He still amazes us.
—Betsy

Perspective also brings peace. As you work through your grief over your child's disabilities and struggles, you can realize that your child isn't *less* than normal, he or she is just *different* from normal. As Betsy says, "So what if he learns things more slowly than other people? So what if he's a baby longer?"

I think my biggest worry was that he would not be able to know that we loved him. Somehow I equated brain damage with severe impairment. Now I think my concerns are more realistic. I have also learned that nothing is impossible if you keep at it. I know that it may be years before Stephen can look at me and say, "I love you, Mommy" in words. I hope he will learn to sign it, but even if we have to come up with a picture representation of "love," he will learn to let me know that. —Tracy

Along with different abilities, your child may have different priorities, different ways of experiencing the world, different interests, and different aptitudes. As you adjust, you learn to focus on the strengths, not the weaknesses. Whenever you are struggling, pause and look for those strengths—that is where you will find your child.

Stuart is a delight. He has taught me that different can be wonderful, that imperfect is okay, that sometimes the very best life can offer is hidden where we are least likely to look for it. Practically speaking, he is an incredible combination of delayed and advanced. I am learning the wonder of trying to see the world through his eyes. He seems to see things differently, to attune to different details, to think and process things differently. The world, as my husband says, isn't set up for different, but I am realizing that we need to approach different with more respect. —Susan

You can also learn the difference between trying to help your child thrive as a "normal" kid and helping your child thrive as an individual. As you learn to appreciate your child's spirit, you stop wishing that he or she could be different. Indeed, you can't imagine your child being any other way. You may always carry a remnant of sorrow about what might have been, but you can also reach a comfortable place where you can say, "I can be an admirable parent to this admirable child." Particularly if you have multiples, one of whom has special needs, you can let go of comparisons and pity and recognize the opportunity to celebrate uniqueness and cultivate strengths.

I don't want to say that I no longer fear what's waiting for us around a corner, as we are only beginning Alex's schooling and still have a long way to go. But I no longer wonder, "Will my child be normal?" because I know what normal is. It's what we have lived through for the last five and a half years—that's normal for us. And quite simply, I no longer am curious about what scars she may have in her brain. I already know who and what she is. I've let go of that image of the perfect baby—of who she was "supposed" to be when I imagined her while pregnant. In fact, I've forgotten what that image even was because it's been replaced by the beautiful reality of my daughter. —Kathie

As you expand your definition of "normal," "desirable," and "good," you also expand your horizons and appreciate things you never noticed before. You can enjoy your child and revel in the miracle of growth, from a perspective that many parents will never experience.

We do make a big deal about both boys' progress because, after all, they are big accomplishments for ones who started out so small. —Angela

Every day is a new experience. I never looked at the simple beauty of human movement or heard the complex music of human speech the way I do now that Jacob's come into our lives. Every small step forward is a major celebration. I would never tell you that life with a special needs child is not hard, but I can guarantee you that it is rewarding. —Julie

There isn't a day that goes by, not even the best of them, that I don't look at Stuart and thank God for all he is and ask God to forgive me for all he isn't. Conversely, though, that awareness is also a wonderful gift, as I see him struggle and triumph, as I celebrate him, love him, enjoy him, experience daily the wonder of him. I look at "normal" parents of "normal" children, and I don't believe that they could ever understand the awe that I have for my children. After nurturing Stuart literally from death's door into life, after minutes, hours, days, weeks, months of sweating by his bedside waiting to see if he would live or die, waiting at each juncture—Will he see? Will he hear? Will he sit, stand, walk, speak?—I could never take for granted a breath that he takes. He is truly a walking miracle, the strongest, most tenacious little boy there could ever be, and I've witnessed each triumph, each time he defied the odds and pressed forward, and I get to be his mom! —Susan

By seeing through to your child's spirit, you can uncover new truths. More than anything, you realize that love lets you see beyond the disabilities. It is your obligation as a parent to teach your child about love, but it is also your privilege to learn about love from your child. On its deepest level, parenting is a relationship between two souls—yours and your child's.

Intervening

Intervention and Advocacy

After your child has been evaluated and you've faced the news, you will set out to gather information and find the therapeutic approach and/or educational setting that will meet your child's special needs. Advocating for your child can be a hopeful act, for it helps you see what can be done to help your child, plugs you into a network of other parents of preemies (and parents of other kids who have similar issues), and provides the support of caring therapists and teachers. Hooking up with professionals who understand the disability, *but also appreciate the whole child,* can help you focus on *"my child,* who happens to have this condition" rather than on *"this condition,* which has stolen my child."

Alex was enrolled in the Early Intervention program right away. This was really beneficial, as an occupational therapist and teacher came to our house early on. We worked with Alex to strengthen his muscles. They provided encouragement, and they taught me about things like positioning and ways to hold and communicate with him. He was very weak the first year—he was still on oxygen, had mild (as yet undiagnosed) cerebral palsy, and unbeknownst to us also had a diaphragmatic hernia. I was terribly worried about him, and it really helped to talk with other people about him and feel like they were invested also. —Allison

The best thing that ever happened to Taylor and his eating was going to a speech therapist who specializes in motor speech disorders. We got in with her during a six-month stay on the East Coast. In six months she was able to do what four years of previous therapy had not been able to. She got him off the bottle [and] drinking from a cup—yes, I had a four- (almost five-) year-old still drinking from a bottle—and taking actual bites of solid food. When we returned to the West Coast, I insisted on a therapist who had been trained in her techniques. And within a year, Taylor was able to stop his feeding therapy all together—a day that I doubted would ever really come. —Tammy

Of course, these therapies, schools, and professionals may not simply fall into your lap: you may have to search for appropriate treatments and professionals who can collaborate with you. But if you find just one program that fits your child or one professional who understands, that can be all you need. Also know that you aren't the only parent of a preemie who is out there pounding the pavement.

When a school psychologist tells me that auditory processing disorder is the "diagnosis du jour" and that she doesn't know about preemie neurodevelopmental issues, I could just scream. It is true that no one taught me any of this stuff when I was in education school, but these folks can read just as well as I can, and isn't it the job of the school system to provide the training that they need to keep them up on the lastest "news" about their profession? Imagine what happens to kids who have parents who can't or won't advocate for them or parents who believe that the professionals know what they're doing and saying. ... Sooner or later these professionals will get it; they won't have a choice because the cohort of school-aged preemies is getting larger and larger every year. —Maeve

We have had a largely positive experience with the school to date, the value of which I don't for a second underestimate after [hearing about] so many others' struggles with the school systems. Much of our satisfaction with the school and its services to Stuart comes from the quality of the program and the people who comprise it. And there are some things that we have done which have helped create the foundation for our relationship with and experience within the school.

We chose not to let the school personnel conduct the evaluations required to deliver the diagnosis that entitles our son to services. There are two main reasons for this. Despite our satisfaction with the school, we remain aware that there are political and power-related undercurrents inevitable in our interactions with them. It was important to me to come to the table as a partner in determining what services were necessary and appropriate for my child. To do that, I needed to be in control of this information; I wanted to hire the professionals who assessed my son, and bring the information to the school personnel rather than allow them to tell me what they determined concerning his skills and abilities. ... Most of all, when we sat down with the team of professionals at the school, we'd had time to reflect upon and come to terms with the information we presented to them. We'd been able to discuss with the doctor and have a voice in what and how information was prepared for their consideration. We'd had time to develop an idea of the services we believed he needed, so that we had an idea of what we'd like to see constructed in his IEP [Individualized Education Plan].

Also, in our ongoing interactions with the school, we've worked hard to set a tone of respectful and balanced communication. We approach the educators working with our son with respect for their experience and abilities, believing that they will do their best for him. Then we remain active and involved, always assessing whether this is, in fact, the case. When we are disappointed, we choose our battles very carefully. I am always aware that the schools are being asked to meet the needs of a very large and very diverse group of children. They cannot be everything for everyone. I believe that our role as parents is to make sure that his educational experience is appropriate and caring, and to provide additional supports to him as necessary. I work hard to develop trust with his team, to help them understand that I don't have unreasonable expectations as to what they can provide, and that I will be active in supporting them and their efforts with him.

Some of the teachers and therapists working with him have dazzled us with the care and involvement they've shown my son. Others have been adequate. I try to draw as much from the former as possible, and to make sure they know the depth of our gratitude for the impact that they have on his potential. I try to accept and support the efforts of the latter, knowing that not

•••
627
Discovering Disabilities

everyone he encounters in the years of education ahead can be a superstar. Mostly, I try to make sure that no one working with him inflicts any harm upon him. So far, so early down this path, so good … But I worry—there are so many things still looming out there, so far to go … When I get too far down the path of future worry, I try to remind myself that I am building the parent advocate skills now that hopefully will serve me as needed then. And Stuart is developing into Stuart, more so every day … as he has since we left the NICU, moving almost imperceptibly, yet relentlessly, out of the sphere of my influence, into that of his own. —Susan

Intervention and Balance

I hate that they have to go to so much therapy instead of playing with friends, or just hanging out. So much of their life has been scheduled. —Stephie

One thing that I wish I had had the chance to do after his homecoming was enjoy Colin just for being baby Colin. The weeks slipped into months with countless doctors' appointments, follow-up, and therapy. To some extent, our lives still operate this way, although I try to reserve one day during the week for no appointments. —Angela

The physical therapist frustrates me a bit sometimes. She pushes pretty hard and is quick to notice if he's not doing something perfectly. I'm just thrilled that he can do the things he does. —Teresa

There's no doubt about it: intervention can be a time-consuming imposition. You may resent the intrusion into what you wish could be a simpler life, but for many preemies, a certain amount of intervention can provide the support they need to reach for their best. As you consider the options, try to strike a balance between pushing your child to excel in conventional ways and accepting your child's uniqueness.

Still, you may not feel sure about when to push and when to hold back, when to worry and when to relax. There are so many uncertainties about treatment and the future. There are no maps to follow, no guarantees to rely on. This can be unnerving. You may second-guess whatever course of action you choose. If the approach your child's caregivers or therapists take is different from yours, you may doubt your choices—and feelings of guilt or inadequacy may surface.

The murky gray fog I see when I try to look into the future [Stuart is almost four now] has left me chilled and disoriented. I don't know where to turn; the only thing I know for sure is that no one knows anything for sure. At the same time that I agonize over his future, I continually second-guess his current course of treatment. Is it the right course? Does he receive enough intervention? Does he get it from the right people? His critical (developmentally) third year will soon be over. Did we maximize it or waste an opportunity? Should I sell my house and hire a team of professionals to give him twelve hours a day of intervention while he still may be young enough to respond? If I just relax (ha!) and enjoy him, am I shortchanging his future by not being vigilant in my efforts to support him? I'm exhausted, and I haven't even addressed the questions about his physical health, lungs, intestines, eyesight. —Susan

When he began crawling, and sitting up, I felt I should let him get on with exploring a bit and stop interfering with his grip or bent leg, for example. If he was really looking at a toy or book, it seemed to me that this was more important than how he was doing it. But I felt guilty all the same. —Anne

One of the curses of preemie parenthood: the fishbowl doesn't necessarily stop once you leave the hospital. Even though everyone who we work with (except the nutritionist, and we choose not to see her) thinks that I am a goddess of motherhood, still sometimes I feel scrutinized and judged. —Kris

There are many approaches to intervention for your child. Some parents focus on how much their child grows intellectually, socially, emotionally, physically, and verbally. They encourage their child toward milestones and celebrate each accomplishment as a sign that their child is making progress. Still other parents focus on how much their child thrives as a person, believing that doing less is "more." They question whether maximum potential is worth it if they're so busy with therapy, stimulation, and appointments that they can't live their life or enjoy the time they have with their child.

Discovering Disabilities

Lars only gets one therapy, and there still isn't time to fit in everything we "should" be doing—I can't imagine how hard it would be with more therapies to balance. Of course, whatever we're "supposed" to do has to fit in with whatever we're doing anyway, since sanity is always my main goal. I am lucky to be working with people who understand and support that. —Kris

You may believe that your child will benefit from hours and hours of active intervention or that you owe it to your child to give that approach a trial run. If this is the case, try to figure out which aspects of your child's disabilities are remediable and which cannot be changed. Prioritize your child's problems to figure out which aspects you're willing to advocate and fight for. Then focus on the ones that will make an appreciable difference to his or her quality of life.

Even with intensive intervention, it's possible to find a balance between "therapy" mode and "hang-loose" mode. Whatever approach you decide on, try to keep an open mind and be ready to change directions if something isn't working. Parents sometimes feel that if therapy isn't working, doing it longer or harder will fix the situation. If you hate to be considered a quitter or if you are reluctant to ignore all the time, effort, and money you've already invested in an approach, it can be difficult to change direction or cut your losses. It can be especially difficult to stop if there are no other options.

This is where your parental intuition serves you well. In general, if you and your child feel good about what you are doing and pursuing, then it's likely you're on the right track. If you feel uneasy about the path you are on, ask yourself whether this intervention is making a *significant difference* for your child. Without this treatment, will your child most likely be rendered helpless at the playground, unable to communicate intelligibly, or incapable of learning how to read? With them, will your child likely be able to participate in physical activities, have a social life, or learn to read? Or are the gradations much smaller? Will these interventions merely turn a child who needs constant supervision into a child who needs *almost* constant supervision? What is important to you? Most of all, what is important to your child?

Strive not to make your child's development a "project"; instead, lean toward making it a natural, fun, child-driven process. Trust that, under the right conditions, your child wants to mature, learn, adjust, and reach toward growth and health. Listen to your child, and follow his or her lead. As a general rule of thumb, if your child looks forward to a certain therapy, intervention, class, or schooling (at least after a reasonable adjustment period), that means it feels good and right and is meeting your child's needs for growth and adjustment.

I would say each child's special needs and strengths need to be assessed individually and addressed within the most supportive and naturalistic environment available. Look at what you need the child to learn and what it will take to get the child there. What are their strengths? Teach to those, through those. What are their weakness? Which ones can be improved with practice or therapy and which ones do we need to work around? Some things can't be fixed—but there are often alternative ways to get to the same goal. …What I do know is this: if a child has "special needs" it means they need something more, not less. That is, they do not need a classroom where they are made to sit through a watered down version of the regular ed curriculum. They do need to get an early start, but they do not need to have their time wasted. They need to be challenged. They need to learn to enjoy working hard to meet challenges. The learning environment should be exciting and fun. —Shaina

Sadly, sometimes disease, disability, or genetics render growth very slow and certain milestones out of reach. Sometimes it's impossible to discover or put in place the "right" keys or conditions. Some children simply do not thrive. You may have to decide whether it is better to persist with a recommended intervention marked by repeated bouts of misery in the hope that eventually the benefit will outweigh the burden, or to eliminate the misery even if that means your child's progress may stall or even deteriorate. Only you and your partner can decide for yourselves, your child, and your family.

Whatever your child's prognosis, as you reach for balance, you can learn to step back and relinquish the notion that you must always intervene directly or aggressively to address every aspect of your child's development or condition. You can learn to trust the process and find peace in surrendering control over the outcome.

We faced new challenges when Stuart reached school age and beyond, yet, in one remarkable area, there came a sense of calm and relief that afforded me the ability to shift my focus from the treatment to the child—to enable me to

*become less researcher and more mother—to see my child, not his symptoms—
to relish his gifts and accept his challenges.*

*From approximately two to four years of age, none of the medical
professionals diagnosing and treating him could agree on a diagnosis
(expressive- receptive language disorder, PDD-NOS, Asperger's Syndrome,
high functioning autism ...). Professional consensus on a diagnosis has, in
fact, at nearly eight years old, still not been achieved. I didn't understand it
at the time, but hindsight shows so clearly that each discipline viewed his
development through confines of its own specialty. No one was able to look
at the totality of his prematurity—at its effect on the totality of him—to see
that it impacted his neurology, his vision, his lungs, his gross and fine motor
development, his endocrinology, his social, oral, and sensory experiences. ...
The totality of its impact is most likely not clear, even now.*

*What every professional did agree upon was that early intervention was
critical. That would be great news for parents eager to intervene on their
child's behalf, except for the fact that there is essentially no professional agreement as to what sort of early intervention is effective—on what is the best for
a particular child and his particular challenges. The staggering thing that was
communicated to us was that this child—a child we'd already seen through
any number of life-threatening conditions, a child who'd survived despite every
possible catastrophic fate lurking around each new day's corner, a child on
whose behalf we thought we triumphed when we left the NICU and brought
him HOME—needed help, the right help, and he needed it now. We were
responsible for deciding which of the plethora of options was right for him—
choose the right treatment and open the door to his future, choose unwisely and
face losing him yet again.*

*Once again, the option of just being a mom was lost to me. I began
researching as if my son's life depended on it, because, frankly, it seemed to
me that it did. I read every book and authority promising complete cure and
detailing how total vigilance enabled parents to rescue their child. Ultimately,
with the patience and guidance of a much calmer, more confident spouse, who
has a deep ability to quietly trust in his instinct and inner guidance, we tried
a little of this and a little of that. And we did more of what seemed balanced
and right, and less of what seemed expensive and hyped. We learned to look
at and listen to our son. To believe in our ability to sense what helped and
leave behind what did not. Slowly we learned that if we listened, he could*

guide us in guiding him. And most of all, I stopped believing that a miracle intervention existed that would erase the effects of his prematurity and deliver him back, unscathed, to us. Ever so slowly, I realized that his prematurity is part of who he is, on every level. In some ways a gift, in many ways a challenge, but mostly it just is ... he just is. And finally, I guess that is who we all are—the products of the blessings and the challenges that have graced and shackled every life—for who survives without suffering and loss, without care and a bit of inexplicable stardust that falls onto the path before us?

And so the calm that came my way came when he passed the age that the experts agreed was critical for early intervention. He moved beyond the point at which he could be saved. But he didn't stop moving. In fact, he moved and grew and changed, and continues to evolve into who he is. And I am finally starting to realize that the complete responsibility for just who that might be doesn't reside solely with me ... that he has some part of that path to chart all on his own, as do the events and circumstances of his life, and my own, that are beyond my influence. And that, so far down this path of terror and tragedy, of the unforeseen and the seemingly unbearable, there has come an unexpected blessing to me. It has allowed me to be—more so than most anything else that has occurred—just a mom of just a boy, whose life like so many others has been marked with risk, and loss, and reward, and love. A boy whose future is very much still open, possible, waiting for the direction of his own firm footprints on his own waiting-to-be-navigated path. —Susan

Points to Remember

- If your child has disabilities, you will need to grieve more layers of loss. When grief rises, attend to it, do what you need to do to face it and cope. By working through your feelings (rather than avoiding them), you can emerge with renewed but realistic hope.

- Take the time and energy to face your anger, guilt, anxiety, sadness, and disappointment about your child's disabilities. Hiding from them may cause you to displace your negative feelings about those challenges onto your child. If you can work through those feelings, you may find it easier to see your child in a positive light.

- Your grief may feel constant, and it may have many triggers. As you face your feelings, though, you can learn to talk back to your triggers in ways that reassure you and build your hope. As you grieve, your adjustment and healing are ongoing as well.

- Part of adjusting is learning that your child isn't *less* than normal, he or she is just *different* from normal. You can learn to accept your child for who he or she *is*, not just for what he or she can (or can't) accomplish.

- Rely on your intuitions and your child's signals when deciding about intervention. As you consider the options, try to strike a balance between pushing your child to excel, and accepting your child's uniqueness. In general, if you and your child feel good about whatever it is you are doing and pursuing, and if your child is thriving, growing, or content under those conditions, then it's likely you're on the right track.

- As you reach for balance, you can step back and relinquish the notion that you must intervene directly or aggressively to address every aspect of your child's condition. You can learn to trust the process and find peace in surrendering control over the outcome.

CHAPTER NINETEEN

Your Family

A baby's premature birth can present special challenges to family relationships. If your baby's other parent is your partner, you will be facing the crisis together, but often reacting and coping in different ways. If you have other children at home, you will be concerned about meeting their needs for attention, reassurance, and support. Your own siblings and parents will be concerned about you and your baby and affected themselves. Having a premature baby is a family affair.

This chapter looks both at maintaining your relationship with your partner and parenting your other children. Single parents are addressed in the section "Parents without Partners." You'll find information about dealing with other family members and friends in Chapter 20.

You and Your Partner

The birth of any new baby into a family naturally affects the relationship between the parents. The dynamics, pace, balance, and flow of the relationship change to accommodate new roles, new demands, new priorities, hormonal changes, and the inevitable sleep deprivation. These changes are often accompanied by conflict, but also growth.

When the baby's birth is a crisis, the changes accumulate and intensify. For many preemie parents, the stress of grieving and adjusting depletes both partners so much that they may find it difficult to share the load or provide emotional support to each other. If this baby grows into a child with special needs, it may be especially hard for the parents to find the energy to put into their relationship. But as partners alternate between isolation and intimacy, they can discover new ways of working together and being there for each other. As many couples can testify, weathering this tough patch can lead to strengthened feelings of closeness and teamwork.

Her birth brought us closer in the sense that we realize she is a part of both of us and we regard her as a miracle. I think that was one of the first times we were able to sit down and really tell each other what we felt. Not only that, but we were able to lean on each other. —*Jackie*

I think Neil's prematurity brought us closer together as a couple and a family. Leaning on each other as the only people who really understood what we were going through made a huge difference, and we went out of our way to be kind to each other. —*Tara*

The premature birth of a baby forces some couples to reevaluate their relationship. When the going gets rough, unresolved issues can reappear, and poor communication skills can exacerbate sore points. Many couples learn that what has worked for them in the past simply isn't enough during a crisis.

Our relationship was strange at this time because of the different ways that we each were coping with the crisis [baby in the NICU]. My husband to this day has never cried about the situation in front of me, but I know that he did a lot of crying when he would go home each night. My husband really wanted to stay strong for me, but I wish that he would have opened up a little more. It seemed like I cried constantly through the whole ordeal. —*Marina*

For others, the premature birth of a baby temporarily mends rifts. They unite during this crisis, but unfortunately, if they do not address their underlying problems, this "second honeymoon" doesn't last. As Cindy observes: "Our relationship was difficult immediately prior to becoming pregnant, but the premature birth drew Stan and me closer. Our emotional closeness lasted for a while, but has since degenerated—[for] lots of reasons not related to the birth, I think."

Some couples overcome their difficulties with effort and renewed commitment. For others, the crisis of their baby's early arrival becomes a catalyst that breaks up an already troubled or fragile relationship.

Whatever the health of your relationship before or after your preemie's birth, there are things you can do to make sure your relationship survives. In addition to simply caring about your partner, some of the ingredients to maintaining a rewarding, lasting partnership include

- Opening the door for feelings
- Being honest and sharing
- Accepting differences
- Managing conflict
- Relying on your commitment
- Negotiating sex and intimacy
- Getting the outside support you need

When you're grieving deeply or feeling extremely anxious, you may not have the energy or inclination to do what it takes to maintain your relationship. When you're consumed by the demands of parenting your hospitalized infant, adjusting to having a new baby at home, or meeting the special needs of your young child, you and your partner may just coast for the time being. But if neglecting your relationship builds walls of anger, blame, or rejection between you, it will only drain you further. The investment you make in keeping your partnership healthy throughout this crisis will reap many benefits for you, your partner, and your family.

Opening the Door for Feelings

Failing to allow your partner to express a wide range of emotions is a common stumbling block in intimate relationships. You may squirm when your partner feels angry, disappointed, anxious, frustrated, envious, sad, uncertain, dissatisfied, or afraid. You may consider certain emotions such as anger or envy to be dangerous or sinful. To you, difficult emotions may indicate personal weakness. Often, the feelings you find hard to tolerate in yourself, you will find hard to tolerate in your partner. Even "positive" feelings such as joy, excitement, or closeness can make you overwhelmed or uncomfortable.

Here are some reminders for letting feelings flow in your relationship:

- Be aware of the emotions—and their intensity—to which you are sensitive. Take your attitudes into account when your partner shows those emotions. If you can acknowledge, verbalize, and tolerate a wide range and intensity of emotions in yourself, you'll be better able to tolerate the same in your partner.
- Recognize that feelings are simply emotional reactions to situations. They are not behaviors. Behaviors can be destructive or unacceptable, and they are within our control. Feelings emerge naturally and, by themselves, only reflect your internal experience.
- Accept that feelings are an integral part of you. They are how you experience being alive. They are what energize you and guide you toward fulfillment, goodness, wisdom, and health. Anger can be your defense against injustice. Envy can inspire you to reach a goal. Disappointment can motivate you to improve a situation. Guilt can prompt you to examine your contributions to a difficult situation. Fear can show you what your limits are. *Feelings hold the lessons of your life.*
- Accept the uniqueness of your perspectives on and reactions to situations. It's okay for you and your partner to have different ways of reacting. Your way is neither the "correct" way nor the "best" way. Your way is simply *your way*.
- Recognize that you are each responsible for your own emotional reactions. If you take responsibility for your partner's (or anyone else's) emotions, this is an unhealthy, unnecessary burden and a sign of poor boundaries. Don't blame yourself for your partner's sadness, disappointment, or anger; likewise, don't blame your partner for your feelings. The statements "You make me so mad" or "You never let me do what I want" place power where it doesn't belong. It is far more accurate and empowering to say, "I feel mad when our plans are forgotten" or "I'm afraid to do what I want because we might disagree/because I might fail/because I might look stupid." Remind yourself: "That's how my partner feels. *This* is how *I* feel."
- Recognize that you are each responsible for your own emotion-driven behaviors. Don't take responsibility for your partner's tears, complaints, or outbursts, and don't blame your partner for yours. "Look what you made me do" is a poor excuse, and it implies that you are your

partner's puppet. When you hand over the responsibility for your actions, you also hand over your dignity and self-control. It is far more accurate to say, "This situation is so stressful for me that I'm feeling overwhelmed and just need to vent." You can vent without attacking and listen without trying to fix.

If either one of you is having difficulty making room in your relationship for feelings, you may find it helpful to share this book. For one thing, you will both benefit from seeing your emotional experiences validated in print. You can also provide your partner with insight into your emotional experiences by pointing out the sections that seem most relevant to you at the time. You'll rarely be on the same page, but through reading and talking, you can at least share your experiences. This sort of "checking in" with your partner can foster mutual support.

Being Honest and Sharing

Honesty means being in touch with your feelings so that you can be truthful with yourself. This allows you to talk openly with your partner about your feelings and experiences so that you can mutually support each other. Honesty within a relationship that makes room for feelings and has healthy interpersonal boundaries allows you to feel mutually comforted and work through your emotional burdens. Sharing can help you feel connected to each other.

> *Ray and I both tend to avoid emotional stuff. It makes for some interesting "cold war"–type arguments. But when it came to Stephen, we have talked about his NICU time and our feelings at the time of his birth.* —*Tracy*

> *If you're afraid, feeling guilty, whatever it is, talk it out. It really does help. And Jon and I found out that sometimes, one of us had feelings but was afraid of what the other would say, and the other had those feelings, too.* —*Ami*

Honesty and sharing are not always easy. Sometimes you may be unaware of your emotions or fear being rejected if you open up. These patterns might have originated earlier in your life. You may have learned to cover up the truth to avoid humiliation or have been shamed for being scared, shy, or needy. The consequences of expressing anger could have been grave. It can be difficult to unlearn old lessons.

You might try keeping a journal for your eyes only to practice getting in touch with your emotions. You might also simply tell your partner that you are embarrassed or uncomfortable with exposing many of your feelings and thoughts. There is nothing wrong with being shy or private—you can be honest about your reserved nature, and your partner should respect your way of dealing with your feelings. Even if you continue to keep much to yourself, remember that sharing also includes being a good listener and accepting your partner's feelings without trying to fix or ease them. Staying in touch with your own feelings can make it easier to be a good listener.

Sharing also applies to sharing caregiving responsibilities for your preemie. Mothers, especially those who have done the bulk of the hospital visiting, may be reluctant to leave their partner in charge of the baby after homecoming for even a short time. Work on recognizing that your partner can become just as competent as you are. Everyone benefits from sharing caregiving responsibilities.

My husband took Alex to therapy classes, as they were at night. It was really wonderful that he could be involved in this with Alex. I think that helped our three-way relationship quite a bit. Certainly, my husband felt involved and was pleased to be able to participate and be with Alex by himself. —Allison

Accepting Differences

This was very, very hard for our marriage. I deal with emotional stress head on, while he avoids. He really would have preferred not to visit our daughter in the NICU, and I couldn't get enough. I think he was afraid to get too close.

Now that Lauren is home, he still tries to avoid talking about the experience, his feelings, or the current situation. He wants to pretend it didn't happen. I, on the other hand, have become so involved that others have accused me of being obsessed with the issue. This has really put a strain on our marriage. The only thing that has helped is that we have talked about, and agreed to recognize, how each one of us deals with it. I am okay with his blissful denial, just as long as he is okay with my strong desire for more knowledge.

Our marriage has changed. Not just because we have a child, but because of the problems associated with her birth, and so on. I think our marriage will fare well, but this is new territory for both of us after ten years of fairly uneventful times. —Robin

Integrating my grieving and healing process with that of my spouse is an incredible, daunting process. It is as if we are locked in some sort of weird, disjointed dance, never knowing when we whirl around which of the faces we have forged in surviving these events the other will be wearing. —Susan

When confronted with the premature birth of their baby, each parent brings to the situation different perspectives on a number of issues, including grief, anxiety, bonding, being in control, and expressing emotions. Besides individual differences in temperament, personality, philosophies, and past experiences, you and your partner also are molded by different biological, genetic, and social influences. (For more on this subject, see Chapter 4, "Especially for Fathers.") Although you face the same overwhelming and jarring circumstances, you and your partner will probably react and cope differently. It is normal for you to have different perceptions of the situation and to express and manage your tumultuous feelings in different ways and at different paces.

Russ, his life went on. He went to work. The baby was still in the hospital. He'd help me take care of the other kids. My life was consumed with, "I don't have my baby at home, and I'm going to the hospital." Now, Russ went to the hospital quite often too, and on the weekends we would go together, but he would get frustrated that life wasn't getting back to normal. And it just doesn't. It doesn't at least until after the baby comes home, which can be a long time. —Vickie

My husband and I reacted very differently. He had trouble bonding and realizing the complete severity of what we were going through. Since he wasn't bonded to them, he worried about how I would react if something happened to them, rather than about them. It took him a long time to feel like they were ours and needed his love, too. —Stephie

I felt enormous disparity between how my husband managed crises and how I managed them. Because of our differences in coping and our differences in daily life (he was working full-time, I was mommying full-time), I felt terribly isolated with my rage and my pain. Being the more obsessive personality, I let myself linger in the swamp of desperate emotions and seek more and more information. I did feel hope, but because I was addicted to my son's medical chart and nurse's notes and spent hour upon hour by his bedside, I was in no way closeted from the truth not only about how my son's medical crisis affected him but how it affected everyone around him. My husband was much more fluid with his emotional journey, moving fairly quickly and comfortably from the shock, the despair, and the intense worrying when our son was at his most critical to hope, optimism, and enjoyment when he became more stable and became "just" a growing, adorable baby. —Maureen

The day that we brought [the baby] home, it was the only time and the first time that I saw my husband cry. And a big piece of it was that he knew he couldn't do any of that when I [or the baby] was in the hospital. I think that he was really worried about me and really worried about my state of mind. He knew that if I saw him get really down, that I was just going to really lose it. And I did then, for just a minute. I remember thinking, "Oh, my God, what's he upset about? Oh, my God, he's scared. Something must be wrong. We're taking this baby home to die"—which I knew wasn't true, but for a minute I got a little worried. But then I realized that this was Bill's way of believing it was done and feeling it. —Jaimee

Grieving partners tend to balance each other emotionally, and this can be another source of differences. It is common for partners to take on complementary roles, opposing viewpoints, and different emotions and intensities. For instance, if your partner does most of the worrying, this frees you to be the optimist. If you obsess about what the future might bring, this frees your partner to focus on the here and now. If your partner is fuming about something, you may put your anger on hold. Sometimes, being in opposite corners helps couples to cope: when one is feeling overwhelmed, the other can step in with support. As Marcia puts it, "I don't think he was as devastated by it as I was, so I just drew strength from him."

Up until delivery, I carried and cared for my son. After his birth, we switched roles. Medically, my husband was on top of everything. I was in shock; felt such guilt, anger, and disbelief, that I was not functioning. —Raquel

Erin was a year old, and they finally told Sue that she had cerebral palsy. So she called me, and tells me over the phone in a tearful voice that Erin has cerebral palsy. I wanted to cry, too, shaken up as I was. ... Yet when Sue starts crying, that right away strengthens me [because] one of us has got to be strong here. So I say, "Okay, it's all right. We knew something was wrong. We didn't know what it was." But my mind goes, "Why me? Why am I having a child with CP? I don't want a child with CP. I don't want a child who is sick all the time." —Charlie

But even when your differences are complementary, it's inevitable that, at times, your opposing viewpoints will feel less like being balanced, and more like being out of sync, which can make both of you feel isolated and misunderstood. So, to use the examples above, if you are the worrier, you might feel angry that you are worrying alone. Or if you are the optimist, you may be irritated by your partner's incessant anxieties. If you're the one who fumes, you may wonder if your partner even cares about the situation. You may lack the energy to try to understand your partner when you're struggling to keep your head above water, and it can be difficult to hold on to your familiar ways of supporting each other.

My fear for my daughter was huge, but my husband never doubted that she would be fine. I wonder now if this wasn't a coping mechanism—his denial that anything was wrong. It made me angry that he would not see or admit how precarious her situation was. Perhaps I was jealous of his faith, but mostly it made me feel alone with my doubts and fears. —Renee

My wife experiences far more anxiety and worry than I do. ... The time this caused the biggest problem was when my daughter wasn't gaining much weight. My wife was very upset and worried about it, and was mad at me for not being as concerned, and because she felt like I was discounting her concerns. —David

I am much more pessimistic than my wife, Kathy, is. I always felt that she either couldn't give a damn what was occurring at specific tough times or had a naive optimism leading her to think that nothing was too terribly wrong in the first place. She just isn't as much of a "worry wart" as I am. She is also no where near as technically oriented as I am—I am an electrical engineer and tend to want the numbers behind the magic. I felt like I had to force her to understand what the NICU jargon meant—things like blood oxygen saturation levels, respiration rate, heart rate, oxygen percentages, and liter pressure. She really just wanted to hold her boys and not have to stare at the statistics while doing so. In retrospect, I think hers was a much more sanity-retaining method, but that's just not the way I am. I would rather know what is going on, no matter how it makes me worry for knowing it, than to have artificial peace of mind. —Craig

In general, I tend to be the one who actively seeks out new information, finds things that might be wrong or that might help Neil, that type of thing. I then sort the wheat from the chaff and present the findings to Peter. Sometimes I really resent this, as I can end up overdosing on information, looking at Neil and always wondering what could be wrong. Every so often I go through massive funks, thoroughly depressed and raging at myself, at the world, at Peter, at everything. Peter tends to be more stable, more relaxed, calmer, and less susceptible to paranoia. When I go to him saying that 50 percent of very low birthweight babies are retarded and 75 percent are disabled, he's quick to point out that 50 and 25 percent aren't, that Neil's been doing so well thus far, that even if something is wrong, we'll still love him, and so on. It's a good balance, really, though sometimes I wish I could share my worries more. He's more than willing to listen to me talk, but just has no desire to do the research. —Tara

It has not been easy by any means, and there are times when we grow frustrated with each other's individual coping mechanisms. My husband is the eternal optimist, which I see as being in denial. I am very guarded, which my husband sees as doomsday prophecy. But you are forced to either deal with it as a team or fall divided. We believe our sons need us to be a parental unit. In both cases, the premature births of our sons has brought us closer together and strengthened our marriage. —Jen

It's important for couples to remember that each person is responsible for and has a right to his or her own reality, perceptions, feelings, and ways of coping. Expect differences. You will not always share the same vision. You can disagree and still have a harmonious relationship. Harmony comes from tolerating, accepting, and being unthreatened by differences.

Human beings grieve differently, and I am too close to it all to know if there is any rhyme or reason to the differences. In answering a survey for his twentieth high school reunion, my husband will not list Spencer in the section that asks, "Children: names, ages, sex"—an omission that hurts my heart. But for him, the loss is too painful, too private to have it "cataloged" for strangers' viewing. We are learning that surviving the series of events that has forever reordered our lives requires us to respect and honor the differences in expression and experience in one another that we can't understand. —Susan

It is also important to remember that in spite of your differences, you share much common ground, including many of the same goals and heartfelt desires for your baby. You may have different perspectives and emotions, and even different opinions, but you both want what is best for your baby. Despite your differences, you can balance each other and be allies and mutual advocates for your little one.

My husband and I decided to keep some normalcy in our lives while our son was in the NICU. We called every morning to get information on the night activities, all stats and data and any changes. In the beginning we went in once or twice a day. Then as he improved and got older, I went twice a day, but my husband started going less. At first I was hurt and furious at him, assuming that he didn't think it was important. This frightened me, as our relationship was very new to us, and I didn't know if this meant he would not be an involved father.

Then one day I realized that, for me, I was coping by going there twice a day, in the morning and at night, to feel connected, helpful, "there" for my son. And I was insisting that my husband should be coping the same way. But that was unfair. I realized that he didn't believe that his presence was as important as mine, that Gabe was doing really well with the nursing staff and me. And the hospital upset him, threw him into an emotional place very difficult for him. He was coping with his fears by trying to stay with his schoolwork, his tasks at home, by being strong for me when I was falling apart.

So he went about half as often as I did. But when he was there, he was encouraged to be a part of everything, and he did so enthusiastically. They noticed that he wasn't there as often but didn't seem to judge him, I think because they could tell just how supportive he was to me, and how in love he was with his son. I didn't need him to come to prove he loved Gabe and was committed to him as a parent. He had a different definition for what Gabe needed than I did, and a different way of coping.

I still wish he had believed he was more important then. But then when Gabe needed surgery, you couldn't have kept him away. He suddenly leaped to action—for me, for Gabe, as moral support to everyone there, hugging the nurses and being the positive energy we all needed in a stressful time. Once home, I was able to hold Gabe as much as I wanted because he was so busy washing diapers, pumping equipment, bottles, and blankets, double-checking oxygen equipment, and then holding and feeding Gabe so I could sleep or get out with a friend.

Mostly, we have to accept each other for what we do best, or not, and catch up each other's slack. And we have to constantly thank each other and be grateful and appreciative of what each other does. I could have hated him for not going to the NICU every day. But I chose to love him for who he is and accept his way of dealing. We have a very happy boy who loves both his parents and knows we both love him and enjoy him. We are different in our styles, in what catches our eye or is important or significant to us. That is fine and good. We balance each other out, and the road is smoother for it in the end, I think. —Maren

Managing Conflict

We were thrown into a panic and never really got out of it. As a couple, we tensed up and never really relaxed. —Mark

Besides the fact that you and your partner may react differently to this stressful situation, you can also experience distressing emotions that can make it doubly hard to be supportive of each other. Minor irritations can explode into all-out war. When you are aggravated with the world, it's easy to be aggravated with each other.

With all that sleep deprivation, you get crazy and you get angry at each other and you fight over stupid things. You're just nuts, you're not yourself, you

haven't slept in weeks. So we went through a tough period, and I wouldn't want to go through it again. —Mitch

Many couples buy into the myth that the less fighting, the better the relationship. However, the health of a relationship is measured not by the amount or type of conflict it contains, but by the constructive and creative *management* of the conflict that inevitably arises. Willingness to listen, to empathize, to be influenced by your partner's point of view, and to compromise are key skills. It's all about mutual respect. When you fight cleanly, staying together is more probable because you do less damage to each other.

Further, the health of your relationship does not necessarily depend on the neat resolution of every problem—some problems are ongoing. Accepting that some of your differences will be perpetual and approaching them with tolerance and humor can help your relationship survive.

In accepting conflict as healthy expression in a marriage, you also accept that anger can be the fuel for negotiating and solving problems. Let your anger show you what issues require attention, rather than using it to punish, criticize, or blame your partner. Deal with conflict constructively by making honest statements about how you feel or how the situation is affecting you, without attacking or finding fault with your partner. Compare, for instance, these two statements: "I get so mad when I have to wait a long time." "You make me so mad when you're late." Even said with the same tone and inflection, these two statements carry very different messages. The first one is a simple declaration of how the situation (being made to wait) affects you, and you're indicating that you take responsibility for your reaction. Your goal is simply to let your partner know how you feel or what you need. Once you've conveyed this information, you can step back with the understanding that because your relationship with your partner is a caring one, your partner will become more sensitive and respectful of your feelings and needs. In contrast, the second statement accuses your partner of wrongdoing and puts him or her on the defensive. Rather than making your partner your ally, it is likely to produce counteraccusations and conflict. You engage your partner in a power struggle with the goal of proving that you're right and your partner is wrong. That approach makes it a lot less likely that your needs and feelings will be respected.

Here are some other tips for managing conflict:

- Recognize the difference between expressing feelings and criticizing.

Expressing feelings involves making straightforward statements that reflect current reality and are easy to understand. Criticizing involves statements that tend to be exaggerated, unreasonable, and full of blame. They often dredge up past or separate issues. Red flags include words or phrases such as "always," "never," "Why did you do that?" or "This is just another example of ... " Criticizing is often explosive or sarcastic and has more to do with past experiences or inner turmoil than with the current situation.

- If you want your partner to be able to hear you and respond constructively, express your feelings instead of criticizing. Also, if your partner is expressing his or her feelings, don't read criticism into it or assume that it is veiled criticism. If you feel criticized, recognize that you are sensitive to feedback, even when it is couched as a constructive expression. Share your sensitivity so your partner knows to be gentle, and also learn to hear what she or he is telling you without polluting it with the critical thoughts that are going on in your own head.

- If your partner is criticizing, let the outburst run its course. It can be hard to step back, especially if you feel attacked, but responding in kind will only make things worse. Resist the urge to defend yourself or argue the point. After all, your partner is in no mood to listen. Wait until things calm down to talk it out. For now, *you* can be the supportive, sympathetic listener.

- Planned discussions—during quiet, private times—are a useful way to talk things out. Talking and listening are easier and far more productive without the mayhem, adversarial positions, intrusive emotions, and lack of focus that characterize most arguments. During a planned discussion, it's easier for both partners to express their feelings and accept the other's. Minor problems may resolve themselves after emotions are aired and acknowledged. Other problems may require additional negotiation or compromise.

- Don't make vague requests or expect your partner to read your mind. Let your partner know specifically what you need without accusations. This can be challenging because you may not be sure what you want. But by being as clear and precise as you can, you will be more likely to figure it out. For example, instead of saying, "You never listen to me," try a gentle, "I need you to put down your magazine" or "Can I finish making my point before you have your turn?" With this approach, you'll be more likely to get what you really need.

- Avoid trying to convince your partner that your position is right. Your partner needn't agree with you to hear and understand your message.
- One person's anger does not mean that another person is at fault.
- Don't use your children (even grown ones) as confidants. Doing so will undermine their trust in and respect for you.
- Make the commitment to change your destructive patterns of relating. For some couples, shouting matches or simmering silences are the only emotional communication they feel comfortable with. If this is your style, you may find it especially difficult to call a truce. Before you decide that there is no hope for the relationship, consider that you will take this style of relating with you into future relationships. If your current relationship has a strong foundation, instead consider learning to manage conflict with this partner.
- Recognize that you may hold on to destructive habits in spite of your best efforts to change because they are easy and familiar. Change can be scary and unsettling. Although you may be eager to adopt better ways, you'll need transition time, and you can expect things to get worse before they get better. It can take a lot of grit and practice, but once you get over the initial hump, you're well on your way.
- Address underlying emotions. If you notice that you are having a lot of big fights over little issues, you may want to sort out your own feelings. Often dissatisfaction, fear, and hurt hide behind anger. Are your needs for respect, closeness, and understanding being met in the relationship? State clearly what you'd like and ask how you can give in turn. Are you happy with your life? Try carving out time to pursue the things that inspire and refuel you. Or perhaps you need to identify your anger triggers and talk back to them. (See "Dealing with Parenting Anger" in Chapter 15.) Do you need to let off some steam? Try writing a letter, having a good cry, running around the block. Do you need encouragement? Coping with difficult situations can make you question your worth and competence. Tell your partner or a good friend that you need to hear what he or she likes about you. Think how much you would enjoy returning the favor. Explore the underlying feelings that are fueling your fights.

...

649
Your Family

- If hidden agendas, long-standing issues, or hostilities are sabotaging your efforts to have constructive arguments or planned discussions, professional counseling can help you unpack emotional baggage and change damaging patterns.

Remember, marriage is a process, a learning experience, and an adventure. There will be tough times and easy times. Marriage is less about romance and undying love, and more about commitment and respect. Our culture may place a premium on sustaining romantic love, but a partnership needn't continuously sizzle nor be effortless to be worthwhile. Marriage is a far more gritty—and durable—affair.

Relying on Your Commitment

No matter what your partnership was like before, working through a crisis can create distance between partners. You've lost many precious things, and it's normal to withdraw into yourself. Especially if you and your partner have weathered infertility and/or previous pregnancy crises, you may feel particularly fragile as a pair. If you fear being abandoned by your partner, either literally or emotionally, it may be easier for you to run away than to stick around and risk rejection. If that's the case, it's natural to use anger and blame to push your partner away. You both may be withdrawing to avoid conflict or because your differences seem like barriers between you. Continued anger and withdrawal can become a painfully vicious cycle.

To break this vicious cycle and restore peace, first understand that anger and withdrawal mask underlying feelings of hurt and fear. The antidote is to reassure your partner that you are committed to staying in the relationship. The next time you want to stop an exchange from escalating or pick up the pieces after an argument, try saying something like this: "I'm not going anywhere. Even though this is hard, I'm not leaving you." You needn't say anything mushy or speak of love. After all, "I love you" can ring false in the midst of hostilities. You can also lighten the mood by using humor effectively. Find the reassuring words and style that work for you.

Negotiating Sex and Intimacy

We may go for days and weeks existing side by side without facing each other just because we don't have the time to turn around. ... I'd like to tell you that

Hal and I have found the magic potion to keep our marriage going. We haven't. What we have done is agree that we're going through a hard time that isn't permanent. The overwhelming resentment I felt toward him for his ability to leave for work each day is lessening. He's understanding better that "Hey, hun, wanna?" is just another demand on my limited time and energy. We sneak in what rare moments we have and cherish those memories until the next time. —Julie

All postpartum couples must find a new sexual equilibrium. It's very natural and common for partners to be at opposite ends of the spectrum in terms of desire or energy. Although differences are normal, for some couples the gap is so great that one feels deprived and the other feels pressured. In general, it's important for partners to acknowledge their differences and for the more interested one *not* to take personally the other's lack of interest. Biochemistry, medications, emotional health, physical fitness, stress, sleep deprivation, the availability of time and privacy, as well as the hormones involved in ovulation, pregnancy, and breast-feeding all influence sexual appetite. The stress of having a new baby in the hospital or at home, or of raising a young child or a child with special needs can significantly reorder priorities and leave little energy for much else. Couples who struggled to conceive or who have experienced the death of a baby during pregnancy or infancy may struggle to feel sexual again. It's natural for these reproductive stresses to change the dynamics of a relationship. Couples must make adjustments even when pregnancy and delivery go smoothly.

Instead of focusing on reconnecting sexually, begin by focusing on regaining feelings of closeness to one another. First, reestablish the lines of communication. By discussing your feelings, worries, hopes, and dreams (or whatever is important to or interests you) *and* responding compassionately and affectionately to each other, you will warm up your connection and set the stage for reconnecting sexually. It's also important to reassure each other that you want to be together in many different ways. Spend time together without the expectation of sex.

Second, show affection in ways that don't involve sex. Hugs, flowers, phone calls, notes, cuddling, attentive listening, kind responses, and generously (without needing reminders and without expecting displays of gratitude) pitching in on chores, errands, and child care are just some of the many ways of showing affection. All of these gestures strengthen your bond. Be sure that your partner knows what's meaningful to you. If you or your partner feel uncomfortable with a particular display of affection, try to find another gesture that fits. Affection is something you both *give*, not something that you take from each other.

The same is true of sex. Most people need to warm up, feel open, and have the emotional and physical energy for sexual intimacy. You'll need time to recover some equilibrium. Try to stop feeling that you *should* be having sex. Focus instead on spending time together doing relaxing, nonsexual things you both enjoy. Also try "non-demand touch," which involves sensual contact without the expectation of sex. Connect affectionately in ways that don't drain you, and in time, you'll be more likely to *want* sexual intimacy with your partner.

Getting the Outside Support You Need

Most healthy intimate relationships exist within a network of support. Whether the sailing is smooth or rough, each partner benefits from having friendships and alliances outside the primary relationship. No one person can fulfill another completely or meet all his or her partner's needs for companionship, conversation, and sharing of interests.

> *I wish I had had more support (like this Internet list) during the first eighteen months after Khalila was home. That would have helped me—and therefore, the relationship. —Mary*

Unfortunately, when your baby is born early, some of the people you thought you could rely on may not be there for you. To fill that void, you may turn to your partner even more. Although this may work for a while, it can put tremendous pressure on your relationship. It's important that you gather supportive people around you, during your baby's hospitalization and after. Counseling is one form of outside support that can be extremely beneficial. Connecting with the parents of other preemies, building relationships with supportive health care providers, and cultivating acquaintances who can become good friends all help you build a broader support network. (Chapter 20 contains suggestions for expanding your support network.)

Can Our Relationship Survive?
Weathering Change and Crisis

Stress like that in a marriage can do nasty things. You can either let it tear you apart or work on letting it draw you together. So we decided we were going to make an effort. We decided to purposely be a support to each other. And then we also had our own friends who we could lean on. Our family was a big support. We couldn't have done it without the help of many different things. It's just too much. —Vickie

Marriage is not a rigid structure. You should be prepared for change: in your circumstances, in yourselves, and in your ways of relating, all of which can affect your journey as a couple. Some changes will be easy to adjust to; others will be more difficult. You will grow (or not grow) as individuals and as a couple in response. To put things in perspective, it can help to remember that many of life's trials are both normal and temporary, and each phase brings new joys as well as new challenges.

When our son was about a year old, it all hit the fan for a while. I understand that all first-time fathers go through the "I'm second place" syndrome for a while. I think it was a little more pronounced with a preemie because he did need a considerable amount of attention. Now that he's two and a half it's gotten easier. He's more able to interact with us and verbalize, rather than a constant guessing game. We've also managed to get into a better town, handle many of the financial worries, and reduce the overall stress in our lives. I think overall we're in a much better "place" emotionally that we were a year ago. —Hugh

When you're going through a tough phase, keep in mind that it's possible to get through this together. Certainly the premature birth of your baby is likely to shake up your relationship and to bring with it much change. There may be times when you feel further apart than together. This is okay. You can figure out how to get through challenging experiences, and in time, you and your partner can draw closer again with fresh perspectives, lessons learned, and restored vigor for your partnership. Meanwhile, you can rely on your commitment to seeing your relationship through.

• • •

Luckily, my husband and I have a very strong marriage, so it was able to come through without much harm. It was stressful to have to go back and forth to the hospital, and I think that took a toll on our emotional and physical closeness. Also, because I spent so much time at the hospital, I tended to get onto him about not being there. I realized, however, that we dealt with it in different ways. We were also careful to take time out for ourselves to talk, relax, go out, and so on. —Claire

After three years, I do feel that the experience in some ways has brought us closer together. But just being new parents has distanced us as well, as we've had to work to spend interactive time together. ... The times which were the hardest were when we differed in how we felt about something. The best example was when Khalila didn't gain an ounce between age nine and twelve months corrected. I was very worried and pushing for more help from the pediatrician. David was worried, but less so, and definitely less stressed about it. I felt alone, and he felt pressured. That was when we got couples counseling—with good results. —Mary

Steve compartmentalized not only the latest crisis but eased all the past struggles into one smooth path leading to the days ahead, while I sat, paralyzed, with unbearable sorrow, the blackest anger. It took a very long time before I had healed enough to find Steve on his path and for him to slow down and find me on mine. When we finally reconnected, again we were of the "us against the world" mind-set, yet we also had become increasingly aware of the fact that his perspective and his coping mechanisms were quite different than mine and would likely always be. Accepting that made it much simpler for us to know one another's needs and have fewer expectations that the other person would be the answer to our own struggles. Rather, we are likely now to plainly ask for what we need from each other. We in turn listen more to the responses and then seek answers together. It helps a lot that he's just a really, really nice man. —Maureen

As long as you trust and like each other, there is hope for your relationship. If you think your partnership would benefit from counseling, do it. Go alone if your partner won't join you. As you learn new ways to open the door to feelings, share experiences and viewpoints honestly, accept differences, be

•••

654

flexible in the roles you take on, manage conflict, and offer reassurance, all your relationships will benefit.

We just have too much stress in our lives. We have our first counseling session together tomorrow. I got Mat to agree, with the argument that we have to do what we have to do with Lars. It's not going to change any time soon, and wouldn't it be great if someone could help us learn to do it with less stress? —Kris

Be proud of the way you and your partner can weather change and crisis. Give yourself credit for the maturity and skill you show, even though you know you aren't perfect. Particularly if you have multiple or extreme stresses in your life, appreciate the fact that you are sticking together for better and for worse.

Since my husband and I came out intact as a couple after my son's death, I do feel that we are stronger as a couple. Now, because of all the stresses of having a sick premature baby in the hospital and a child at home, he and I can get tightly wound up and get snippy sometimes. But we already know how to let go of the unimportant stuff and just focus on our little family, and on each other. —Balbir

Over the years, we have often reflected on the cycles of our marriage. We have discovered that the best times are moments in time, that each cycle bottoms out, and that we survive the depths knowing that they will propel us upward once again. —Susan

The Importance of Being "In Like"

Our marriage has not only survived, but grown. We have always turned to each other for love and support. But the fairy tale is over. We were newly married and had such a bright future ahead of us. I walk around in anger because "this is not what I signed up for." I would say definitely that having a preemie ended the fairy tale. —Raquel

As the years pass, you may at times wistfully think of your courtship days and wonder where the "in-love" went. But recognize that intoxication generally doesn't last very long, whether you have a preemie or not. As the intoxication wears off, other things keep you together, among them a sense of duty and commitment, religious beliefs, mutual respect, shared interests and goals, your children, and a true liking for and willingness to tolerate each other. The feelings of being "in love" come and go in peaks and valleys that are different for each relationship. When you're weathering a crisis, sometimes the qualities you adore come to the surface and sometimes they are buried in grief. Remind yourself of those admirable qualities in your partner. Idealizing your partner is an element that keeps a couple revisiting feelings of being in love, but being constantly "in like" is a more realistic day-to-day goal. It's not intoxication that binds you. You stay together because you respect and like each other, even through life's realities. And for many couples, loss and grief are part of the reality.

You may worry, though, that you are more apart than you should be. Don't compare your life—and your relationship—to the all-consuming relationships portrayed in movies, books, and magazine articles. Those relationships are based on an addiction to becoming "one," not on a healthy commitment between two unique and separate individuals. It is your differences and your separateness that make your partnership interesting and growth-enhancing. Celebrate your interconnectedness *and* your individuality, as both contribute to the success of your relationship through thick and thin.

Savoring the Journey People often speak of keeping a relationship "on track," as if getting "off track" is something to avoid. But sometimes being off track is part of the package of sharing life with one another over the long haul. There will be detours on the road. Sometimes you'll get lost. There is wisdom in asking a good marriage counselor for directions.

Keep in mind that marriage is a *journey*, not a place. Any partnership includes bumps, detours, and delays, as well as smooth traveling. Looking at your relationship as a journey may make it easier to forge ahead through the changes to see what's around the next bend.

> *It's just one of those things where you say, "Okay, well, our time as a couple will come. Right now, this is what's more important." And even to this day, we still can't leave them. Dylan's still on his feeding tube. We can't leave them with just anybody—we can't do an overnight situation or anything like that.*

• • •

So, that's just become a reality, and something we've learned to accept, but it's
something that's going to change, too. So, we see the end in sight, and you
know it's not going to be a forever thing, so we'll be okay. —Betsy

Parents without Partners

If your relationship has been broken through estrangement, separation,
divorce, or death, or if you didn't have an established relationship during your
pregnancy, you may long for a partner—a coparent—to commiserate with.
The grief you feel over your baby's early birth could awaken feelings of
bereavement related to the disintegration or loss of your relationship, or to the
fact that you decided to have a baby alone. To add to your pain, others may
fail to offer you the support and sympathy you need, or you may sense the disapproval of those who seem uncomfortable with your situation.

Single parenthood, divorce, death of a spouse—these special topics are
beyond the scope of this book, so if any of these issues touch you, be sure to
obtain information and support from other resources, such as those recommended in Appendix C. Below are some ideas on coping with your status as it
relates to your child's prematurity.

- If you separate from or divorce your partner after suffering the stresses
  of a premature birth, you may feel anger or resentment toward your
  child for "breaking up" the relationship. Try to remember that it wasn't
  your child, but the *prematurity* that was a catalyst. Also remember that
  you had significant, unresolvable issues in your relationship that came to
  the fore or were made worse by the crisis you faced. In fact, your relationship with your baby's other parent can continue to be a source of
  difficulty, whether you struggle to share parenting or you are forced to
  take it on by yourself. Especially if you are faced with critical decisions
  about your baby, and as you learn to negotiate parenting your premature child, collaborating with an estranged partner can require much
  effort. A family counselor or mediator can be an excellent source of
  support for you.
- If you are widowed, you grieve for your partner and all the dreams you
  had for a future, and at the same time, you must deal with the emotional challenges of having a preemie and the prospects of raising this
  child without your partner. During your baby's hospitalization, you may

feel especially alone and bereft. After homecoming, you will acutely miss having your partner as a coparent during challenging times. You may long for your loved one's companionship, commiseration, and simple presence. While this child will always be a symbol of your enduring love, you may also feel burdened by your preemie's needs and condition. Allow yourself your mixed feelings—of joy and sorrow, gratitude and anger. You are entitled to them all.

- Whether you are separated, divorced, or widowed, it's especially important that you get the support you need, not only in your grieving for your baby's premature birth and perhaps special needs, but also to grieve for your partnership. Although your bereavements may feel irrevocably entwined, it's important that you deal with each separately, perhaps attending support groups to address each of your losses. To find other books to complement this one, look in Appendix C under "General Emotional Adjustment" and "Parenting Challenges" for recommendations. Counseling can be particularly helpful as you work through your losses and struggles. Also make sure you get the assistance and respite you need and deserve as a single parent.

- However you arrived at your single-parent status, try not to idealize what it would be like to have a partner during this ordeal. Isolation and feeling alone are common among all parents of preemies because each person reacts and copes differently to the situation. Having a partner doesn't necessarily make this journey easier. Some single parents quietly give thanks that they don't have to deal with the struggles and entanglements of an intimate relationship during this difficult time.

- It's important for preemie parents to seek out additional supportive relationships, whether or not they are in a committed partnership. (See Chapter 20 for suggestions.) Internet organizations (such as those listed in Appendix C: Resources) provide access to vast networks of preemie parents who give each other much-needed comfort and advice. To help you cope and adjust, rely on and talk to friends, extended family, and other support people.

As a parent without a partner, your journey is especially challenging, but as you carry on, this path will reveal your strengths and offer you some blessings.

Your Other Children

If you have other children, they too can be deeply affected by the arrival of a preemie sibling. Changes in their parents and in family routines are particularly difficult for younger children. Children who are old enough to appreciate the fact that this baby is their sibling may have their own set of worries about this little one's birth, hospitalization, homecoming, and growth.

This section looks at ways to

- Respond to your other children's needs for attention and reassurance
- Prepare your children for NICU visits and, later, for the baby's homecoming
- Ease the adjustments when you're finally all together at home

Sharing Your Time and Attention

My daughter is in school during the day, so I get to see the baby in the hospital every weekday. I do wish, though, that I could spend all day with my baby. It's hard to leave her, yet my older child needs me, too. —Balbir

Parenting your preemie along with your other children can present some difficult choices. During bed rest, hospitalization (your baby's and perhaps your own), and after homecoming, how do you balance your preemie's special needs with your other children's needs for parenting? It can sometimes seem impossible to get everything in balance, and with the upheaval, you may feel sad, guilty, and frustrated.

When I was put on bed rest, eventually we had to place Lindsay in a day care. Since I had been a stay-at-home mom, this was very difficult for all of us. It broke my heart and threw her into a situation that she was not prepared for. The guilt set in early and quickly. She hated it, and so did I.

Although I regret having had to place her in day care, I know it was the best choice at the time. Looking back, probably a better situation for her would have been to be in an in-home day care, but at that point in time, I didn't have the time or the resources to go shopping for day care. We chose the closest center to our home, which was less than five minutes away. ... Somehow it all worked out, but it certainly wasn't easy. You do what you

• • •

have to do in a crisis situation, and you hope that you're making the right decision. It doesn't erase the guilt, though. —BJ

I found it extremely difficult to have a child at home and *have a child in the NICU. While I desperately wanted to be with my baby at the NICU, I also had a little three-year-old who was already traumatized. ... I was so jealous of the moms in the NICU who could sit there all day by their baby's side. I was running around desperately trying to find a sitter for my three-year-old or running to the hospital for an hour during her preschool. —Andie*

My biggest regret about the whole hospital period and first year was that I abandoned Jessica. She was only two and a half when Vincent was born, but once he came along, there wasn't enough Mummy to go round. I didn't have the mental or emotional space to also look out for a healthy child—beyond essential care—when Vincent needed so much time and devotion.

We had a great teenage babysitter who came to the house to play with Jessica—to bake and do Play-Doh and all those things I couldn't do. And Gary has a wonderful relationship with Jess—they're really close. But Jessica and I missed out on a really important stage of her development, and we've never quite recovered. —Anne

When a new baby is born, it's normal for siblings to have to give up some of their parents' time and attention. As the new baby grows, though, the attention becomes more balanced. But with any preemie, especially one who is hospitalized for a long time or has special needs after homecoming, the return to "balance" takes much longer—or in some cases, never comes. A new baby's arrival often produces sibling rivalry. But as the parent of a preemie, you have special worries about juggling the complex needs of your baby with being there for your other children, who may often feel left out.

I really hoped that my daughter would not be jealous of Sean or dislike him. I was really worried that Emma might not accept her baby brother, with all the attention he needed, and all the time and energy I had to devote to him. —Ami

I feel my oldest had a very difficult time adjusting to the new baby. I think that was exacerbated by the fact that this new baby was the reason that her Mommy was away from her in some way for five months—if you count all the time I was on bed rest, in the hospital, or visiting the baby every night. —Andie

If I had to do it again, I would spend more time with Dane. I really shut him out of my life for those three months. By the time I came home from the NICU, I was too exhausted to give him my attention. It took years for me to realize how much he was kept on the outside. —Julie

If your preemie is not your first child, and like most parents, you had wondered how you could feel as much love and care for another child, you may feel especially challenged by the demand on your time and emotional energy. Your family will have to find a new equilibrium. Especially if your baby has ongoing special needs or if you have multiple babies, the balance may require repeated fine-tuning. It's likely to take time for everyone to adjust, and the road to finding and maintaining the new equilibrium may be bumpy. Whether your other children precede or follow your preemie in birth order, it is natural to compare the special care you have given your preemie and worry about short-changing your other kids.

Since Luke had reflux and was not willing to breast-feed, I did do a good fraction of looking after him, and there was a lot of that. So I think that my bond with Luke will be much better than with his brother, who I don't get much time with. He is being breast-fed, and so I never feed him, and given the demands that Luke places on us, he never gets my undivided attention. In some sense Luke's brother is being short-changed. —Marco

Max had a very difficult time right after I got home from the hospital, not because there was a new baby, but because of the separation that we went through when I was in the hospital [on bed rest]. He had a really tough time with that. He was a brand-new five-year-old and he had always been a very social kid, and all of a sudden, he wouldn't go to friends' houses, he wouldn't sleep at my mother's house any more, and when he did go to a friend's house, he insisted that the mother be in the same room with them. He wouldn't even play if she went into the kitchen. She had to be in the same room. That was very difficult for him for probably a year. And he still is very leary. He doesn't want to be gone from me for more than a day or two at the most. —Jaimee

For James, who was very much mom's boy, [having a premature baby brother] has created a major upheaval in his world. Not only does Stephen take up the lion's share of my time and attention, but his chronic illness creates uncertainty in James's life that is hard for him. He still never knows when he comes home from school whether he'll find Mom and Stephen gone to the hospital. James is a kid who thrives on routine, so for him this is really hard. I have tried to give him warning when Stephen might be getting ill, but this is not always possible. I also try to make some time (by letting Dad or Sean handle Stephen) to do things with James, or just to be available. In spite of this, James is now being treated for clinical depression. —Tracy

Here are some tips for managing your other children's needs when you feel your attention is stretched to the limit:

- Remember that having a premature baby in the family is stressful for everyone. It's natural for your other children to be stressed—and it's not your fault.
- If you feel that your other children are showing more stress or problematic behaviors than seems normal for the situation, ask your pediatrician to make a referral to a therapist who specializes in working with children.
- Identify your priorities and make them clear to those around you so you get the support you need. When you feel pulled in too many directions, remind yourself (and others) what your priorities are for now. Say no to all the other stuff. It can wait.
- Managing your preemie's needs plus the day-to-day needs of your other children can be very challenging. When you are emotionally stressed and drained, it can be especially difficult to be a responsive parent. Know and honor your limitations—and keep in mind that you'll be better able to nurture your children when you take care of your own physical and emotional needs. Hold onto the idea that, over time, the demands on you will ease and you'll have more resources to go around. It can also bolster your morale to pause and appreciate the joy your children can bring you during this difficult passage. Set aside time for simply enjoying them.
- Recognize that you may need to find other sources of support for your children. Although you and your partner have likely been the only adults your kids depend on, now may be the time to include others.

This doesn't mean you're inadequate; it just means that you cannot meet everyone's needs all the time. In addition to friends and family, recruit the support of your children's teachers and other caregivers by keeping them abreast of developments at home.

- Remember that children need quantity time, not just quality time. They need you to just be there, hanging out, listening, being with them. It's the little stuff that counts. Don't feel you have to "make it up" to them by going special places or buying new toys. This is a time to keep things simple. Time spent playing cards, talking over breakfast, chatting in the car on errands, reading stories, or snuggling in bed can be far more comforting than major outings or new trinkets. Give yourself credit for doing these "little" things. They are what will make the biggest impact on your children.

- Children find comfort in routines. Especially during a family crisis, keep up as many old routines as possible; if you must institute some changes, establish new routines. Strive for simplicity and consistency. Even if you must be hospitalized, try to create as much of a "home life" there as your condition will allow.

- If you have more than one other child, set aside special one-on-one times. Each child will benefit from being the sole focus of your attention, especially when your attention is in short supply. Even if you simply run an errand, read a story, or make dinner together, this special "alone" time with you can be extra comforting to each child.

My husband and I tried to keep things as normal as possible for my older child. I'm still home when she returns from school. Her dad takes her to school every morning, and she gets to visit her friend for play dates like she always did. ... I asked my daughter how she was doing because I feared neglecting her needs in the midst of the chaos. She said, "I'm not worried because I know the baby's going to be fine." I said I wanted to know how she was doing, with me and dad being so busy. She said, "I know you love me and play with me and give me attention, so I'm fine." That's how I knew she was okay.
—Balbir

Offering Reassurances

> *It was very confusing for my five-year-old. Mommy was pregnant one day and not the next, but there was no baby when Mommy came home.* —Cynthia

> *We were so caught up in our own turmoil that we never gave him [our other son] a thought. We needed someone to nudge us and say that he was also going through this.* —Julie

When you're on bed rest, when your preemie is in the hospital, and even after homecoming, your other children will have concerns about what is happening and why. They may feel scared, confused, and left out and will need reassurance more than anything else.

Here are some tips for spreading calm:

- Be available to listen. Hear the concerns behind your children's words, questions, and behavior. Let them know that their reactions are normal. When you can, reassure them that these difficulties are temporary—and that all your children are important to you.
- Remember that children can imagine frightening scenarios when they aren't told the truth. The reality is usually more tolerable than what they have invented. So speak honestly with your children and answer questions simply, in ways that quell their fears. For instance, tell them that this new baby was born too early, and that's why she or he is so sick. Assure them that big, strong kids like them can handle germs— they won't need to be in intensive care like the baby.
- Children sometimes misinterpret even the most carefully crafted explanations and come up with some pretty scary ideas. For instance, they may assume that your baby will always need machines to help him breathe or that your little one will always have wires attached to her chest. Emphasize the temporary nature of these interventions. If your baby does come home with medical equipment, continue to orient your child and focus on the baby behind the machinery.
- Children sometimes project their own feelings onto the baby, assuming, for instance, that the baby is very bored in the NICU, is very lonely and misses Mommy and Daddy, or is scared of all the strange people who are hovering around. Reassure your children that most of the time your

baby just sleeps in order to grow big and strong and that all those nurses and doctors are giving your baby lots of special care. Show them the family photographs and other mementos that will stay at your baby's bedside. It can help to have your children visit the NICU so that they can see their tiny sibling for themselves and appreciate that little person's struggles. Visits also open opportunities for answering questions and offering reassurances. (For more on this, turn to the "Visiting the NICU" section of this chapter.)

- If you observe changes in your children's behavior, try to figure out what worries they might be dwelling on. If they can't find the words to express their worries or don't want to upset or burden you, their behavior may reflect their concerns. Reassure them that you welcome their questions and want them to share their worries with you. Then listen intently, helping them to articulate their thoughts and feelings, and assure them that your family can get through this time.

- Remember that young children are self-centered in their concerns. Not only do they worry about who will be available to take care of them, but they may also wonder if they are to blame for your feelings and actions. You can explain to them that you are crying or upset because the baby is very sick. You can remind your older children that the baby has to stay in the hospital and needs you to be there—and that's why you have to spend so much time at the NICU. Reassure them that you miss them while you're away.

- Encourage your children to express all their feelings, positive and negative, about this new baby. For example, it's typical for children to feel ambivalent about having a new baby brother or sister, so if they're "glad" the baby can't come home, see this as a sign that they're worried about what a new baby means for them. It's natural for them to feel confused and left out upon the birth of a sibling. It's even okay for them to be mad at the baby for taking your attention away from them.

- When children learn that "their baby" has to stay in the hospital, they may have a lot of questions about why the baby can't come home. They may even be angry with you for disappointing them. Give them room to express whatever they're feeling, empathize with them, and agree that this situation is hard on everyone. Remind them that the baby is a member of the family even though he or she can't yet come home, and then talk about how your child can visit the hospital and get to know the baby there. You can also explain that the NICU is just a temporary home-away-from-home and that the baby needs to stay in the hospital only until he or she is strong enough to come home.

- Recognize that young children often believe that their thoughts or actions are powerful enough to make things happen. If your child wished that the baby would hurry up and be born when you were on bed rest, she may feel responsible for the premature birth. If your child harbored any resentment toward the baby, he may fear that his thoughts made the baby get sick or might make the baby die. Your child may feel horribly guilty and unable to admit his or her presumed role in your baby's condition. Provide assurances that your baby's situation is nobody's fault and that your child's thoughts and wishes are not powerful enough to cause harm to the baby. Age-appropriate medical explanations of the baby's condition and treatments may help assuage feelings of self-blame. Find children's books about preemie siblings that talk about hospitalization, homecoming, and feelings. Read your children's favorites to them as often as they request. (See "Books for Children" in Appendix C.) When your child understands some of the physiology behind why some babies are born early or that these tiny babies' lungs aren't yet ready for air and their tummies aren't yet ready for food, she or he won't feel so responsible for your baby's struggles.
- Encourage your children to verbalize their feelings. Empathize and accept their feelings without trying to change or fix them. When you're available to listen and understand, this can be very comforting for your children. You can also teach them to express their feelings in other constructive ways besides talking, such as physical or creative activities that don't hurt anyone or anything. By encouraging them to identify and "unload" their feelings, you're helping them cope. This will make it less likely that they'll act out in annoying or destructive ways.
- Be a good role model. Acknowledging and verbalizing your own feelings should make it easier to encourage your children to do the same. It's also easier to deal effectively with an emoting child if you aren't trying to bury your own emotions at the same time. You needn't share your most overwhelming emotions and private thoughts, but you can be open when you're having a hard day and explain why.

• • •
666

- Tell your children's teachers and other caregivers about what is going on with the new sibling. This will enable them to be more sensitive to your children's emotional condition and provide the extra reassurance and guidance they may need.
- Make a baby book for your children, with photographs and keepsakes of their little sibling. They'll be able to turn to this special book when you're away at the hospital, and it can also be a catalyst for conversations and questions. Along a similar vein, work together to make a "big sister" or "big brother" book for your baby's incubator. Items such as these can help your other kids build a bond with their new little brother or sister.

We've got two other children. I wish that at the time we just would have been able to tell them that the baby was so sick, and that we might lose him, and that Mommy and Daddy were very scared for the baby. But we didn't want to worry them. We were so scared we didn't even know what to tell them. We didn't know what to think ourselves. So at that point we hid the truth from them and just avoided talking about all those issues with them. We were gone all day and so nervous, and they didn't get a chance to know why. That was not fair to them.

I realize, now, that was a big mistake because kids understand lots of things and they would've understood what they could. We should have faced the issue with them. Now they know that their baby was born early, too early, and he was very sick. They know that he almost died. They know they have to be very careful with germs, which I'm not proud about, but the word germs comes out of their mouths a lot. And they know that our baby is different. He needs more time to learn things. I think they need to know, maybe not everything, but they need to know part of it. —Gallice

Visiting the NICU

Cody (two years old) had been able to come up to the hospital before, but he was a little intimidated and overwhelmed by the whole experience. We took him into the "family room," but still, the babies had wires and hooks and tubes. It was ugly to look at, and he was thinking, "My gosh, this isn't a baby, it's a machine." —Pam

The thought of bringing your other children, especially young ones, to the NICU can be overwhelming. How will you manage them while you're trying to visit your baby? Won't they be scared by what they see? How can you help them build a relationship with their little sibling when there are so many barriers?

There are many things you can do to make a NICU visit a positive experience for your other children. Visiting can help them feel more connected, more involved, and less helpless—and can reassure them that their baby sibling is getting tender care in the hospital.

Here are some tips for preparing your other children for NICU visits and for handling the visits:

- Before you go, prepare your kids for the visit. Explain that there are lots of sights and sounds in the NICU that may seem strange at first, but that it's the safest place for the baby to be. Also explain what the baby looks like and that she needs all her energy for growing so she sleeps a lot. Say that because the baby is very tiny, he needs tiny touches and tiny whispers.
- Arrange for another adult to go with you and your children on the NICU visit so that you can attend to your infant while you're there. Your helper can give your older children the supervision and breaks they need based on their attention spans, interests, and abilities. Aim to make visits to the NICU meaningful for everyone.
- Before taking your older children to the NICU, practice the hand-washing and gowning procedures and any other routines they'll face so that they'll know what to expect when they visit the baby.
- Beforehand, explain what all the equipment is that surrounds your little one. Describe it in reassuring language, such as, "This one helps the baby breathe." Use photos you've taken or pictures from books.
- On the first visit or on other special occasions, plan a gift exchange, where your other children bring small tokens to the baby and receive a small token "from" the baby. You can also have your children exchange photos, cards, and messages with the baby, with you acting as translator. Exchanges such as these help build kinship bonds.

One thing she's happy with is our weekly family visit to the hospital. We all go see the baby, then my husband goes to the "family room" and plays with or reads to my older child while I visit the baby. Then we swap places, and I spend time with my older child while he visits the baby. My daughter likes these visits a lot, and both our children get one-on-one time with us. —Balbir

Beth and Cassie, my daughters, were all grins when they finally got to see their brother, they really saw how small and fragile Geoffrey was firsthand. Finally, was their opportunity to hold him on that visit, and they loved it. In fact they did not want to leave, although the nurses were pushing us out. Then we went back for another visit there was the fight over who got to hold him first. I must admit to being very proud of both of them that day. —Shaw

Preparing Siblings for Your Preemie's Homecoming

As your preemie's discharge approaches, your other children may wonder what this will mean for them. They may be concerned about the arrival home of this tiny baby, who has already taken so much of your attention. Will their needs suffer even more? On the other hand, they may look forward to this homecoming, hoping that things will get back to normal. They can't realize that life won't be returning to the way it used to be. There will be another adjustment period, as your family settles into a "new" normal.

Here are some tips for preparing your children for their sibling's homecoming:

- Sit down with them and talk about what will happen when your preemie comes home, explaining that the baby will at times require special care and disrupt routines. Outlining realistic expectations and letting them air their complaints or reservations reassures them that their viewpoints matter, while encouraging them to adjust and be flexible. Emphasize how important you believe it is to keep the lines of communication open and remind them that you are always willing to listen to their concerns. Younger children often simply need reassurance that Mommy and Daddy will be there, and that they are loved and important. Older children need this too, but they also benefit from being involved in figuring out how the household can make adjustments to accommodate the new baby. When they can contribute ideas and assistance, they become more invested in cooperating and carrying out solutions.
- Answer your children's questions about the baby's homecoming and

offer reassurances. Provide information that is appropriate to each child's age. Listen carefully to your children's questions and try to detect underlying concerns. For instance, say your child asks, "Why is the baby coming home now?" You could launch into a discussion of gestational age and due dates or medical indicators of readiness. But your child may actually be looking for the answer to a more delicate question: "We have no incubator or monitors or nurses at home; can we take good care of him?" Frame your answers to reassure your child about the baby's health and your continued availability.

- Involve your children in preparations for their new sibling's homecoming. They can help you set up the nursery and gather and organize supplies. As homecoming approaches, have them plan a simple celebration and perhaps decorate the house with balloons or handmade signs. Let yourself get caught up in their excitement and optimism.

- Get out your older children's baby books or photo albums and talk about how babies need soothing care. Remind them that just as you gave them this gentle, loving care, so will you care for the new baby. Tell them you'll teach them how they can help you. Practice with baby dolls how to be gentle, quiet, and considerate. Reinforce your lessons by having have them teach *you* how to hold, feed, diaper, dress, and soothe the baby. Play and have fun with these lessons—be a bumbling know-nothing! If your baby is coming home with medical equipment, fashion small replicas of tubes and wires (ask your NICU nurses for salvaged leftovers) for the baby doll, not because your children will be doing any caregiving, but so that they can express and master any concerns they might have.

- As the projected discharge week draws closer and seems probable, mark it on a calendar to make it more concrete. In the meantime, jot down some of your baby's special milestones on the calendar to show your little one's progress toward the big day. If the discharge date gets delayed, explain how the doctors want the baby to grow a little stronger and though you're disappointed, you can be patient too.

After Homecoming

When we got home, the [older] boys were really wild and crazy, and it was hard to hold them away from the baby. Probably they did get too close to him.

• • •

But we wanted to make it a normal life as soon as he got home and not consider him as a sick baby. Now we would do things differently. Now I would really put him in quarantine if I had to. —Gallice

Just as you may experience some emotional turmoil and adjustment when your preemie comes home, so might your other children. Now that family life seems to be getting back on track, they might feel freer to express any feelings they've been holding in. Just as you thought things would be getting easier, they may, in fact, get harder. This can be aggravating and disappointing.

Here are some tips for coping with the new challenges that can crop up when you bring your preemie home:

- It is a natural part of the adjustment process for your other children to begin acting out or to escalate their acting-out behaviors. Just as you and your preemie may be extra fussy the first couple of weeks at home, your other children may be, too. They may feel guilty for needing more of your attention or for being angry with the baby for consuming so much of everyone's time. But as you and your baby settle in, you'll be able to help your other kids settle in as well.
- Figuring out how this new baby fits into the family will take time and practice. Expect the biggest adjustments to take a few weeks, with additional rough spots along the way.
- Any family with growing children must make constant adjustments to the changing and developing needs of its members. You may need some professional support and guidance because of the special stresses and possible complications you're dealing with.
- Because you have other children, you've already established a parenting style—and you may want your new baby to fit right into it. As siblings fawn over the new baby, you may resist your protective urges to say, "No, don't touch." Yet you don't want to have to worry about communicable diseases and overstimulation of the baby. Though you may even be tempted to override your protective urges and turn away when you become anxious, that can pose real dangers to your baby. It's important to find a balance between your baby's very real needs for protection from germs and overstimulation and your need for your baby to "fit in" to your family life. Most of all, you want to be able to relax your vigilance in your own home.

- Let yourself depend on extended family and friends to support both you and your other children. You do not have to be the sole caregiver for your infant or for your other children. You can ask for some help taking care of your preemie so that you can spend uninterrupted time with your other children, and vice versa.
- Give your family as much "hanging-out" time as possible during this readjustment period by keeping your lives simple. Take advantage of the opportunities for unstructured quantity time. Children also find comfort in the small blocks of quality time that are built into the everyday routine, as that's when they can count on getting your full attention.
- Don't feel that you have to protect your other children from the realities you and your preemie must face. If you must make repeated doctors' visits or attend regular therapy sessions, take your other children with you occasionally. This takes the mystery out of your preemie's treatments, gives them compassion for their sibling, and creates family unity. Answer their questions as honestly as you can. Respect their curiosity and also their feelings about whatever medical or developmental hurdles your preemie faces.
- As your preemie gets integrated into the family and as your other children grow and mature, their perspectives will change—and new questions may crop up. In general, when you make your preemie's special history or current needs a topic for continued open discussion, your children should have fewer unnecessary fears and faulty conclusions.
- Particularly if your preemie has visible evidence of special needs, educate your children's friends so that they are not afraid of your preemie or cruel to your children about their special sibling. Children often tease out of fear or unfamiliarity. Matter-of-fact explanations and respect for their need to know can help ease tension and make your children's friends feel more comfortable around your special baby.
- At times, it can feel like an impossible task to meet the needs of all of your children. Remind yourself that your kids will survive those times when you are overwhelmed or depleted. Give them credit for their resilience, and take the time to notice that your children can also be a source of pride, comfort, and humor. As you recover your parenting reserves, your renewed care and attention will add to their resilience and reserves.

- Appreciate how your children come together in ways that benefit them all. Many parents report that their other children are benefiting from having a sibling who needs special care, and their preemie's development benefits from these sibling relationships. Look beyond the horizon. In the long run, it will all be worth it!

I took Mackenzie in for show and tell at kindergarten for both boys. One day a neighbor boy came over and said that Mackenzie looked ugly with her oxygen on. That was it—all it took for me to get started. I then decided it was time for children around the boys to understand their plight and what was going on with Mackenzie. I showed them all about prematurity (on their level) and her feeding tube and oxygen. They soaked it in and began to love Mackenzie. (The teacher thought I was crazy!) —Dianne

As Vincent grows up, I realize that one of the best things you can give a disabled child, if not the absolute best thing, is a sibling or two. Jessica is a fantastic friend and support to Vincent, and it really comforts me to think they'll always have each other (with luck). —Anne

Gregoire and Jeremy are more aware of children with disabilities. They don't look at it as being [strange]—it's part of their world. They're not shocked by it. It's good. It has helped them. They know that some children are different, some children can be sick. They know that children can die ... and [that] they are lucky they are healthy. And that children with disabilities can have a nice life and do nice things. They know there is hope and happiness with these children. —Gallice

Points to Remember

- Expect your relationship with your partner to be stressed by the premature birth of your baby. Change and conflict are inevitable, but if you face and manage the issues as they come up, your relationship can endure.

- Accept the differences between you and your partner in how you each navigate the emotional terrain. It's natural for each of you to react and cope differently, and also to balance and support each other when you feel overwhelmed at different times and by different things.

- Opening the door for feelings, listening without trying to fix, and giving each other the space you need can strengthen your relationship. Sometimes, partners can be alone together.

- Reassure each other that even as you drift apart during or after a crisis, you can come together again. Romantic love and passion may come and go, but your commitment to stay together through thick and thin is the most durable aspect of your relationship.

- If you are both determined that your relationship will survive, it probably will. If you think couples counseling might help, try it.

- If you are without a partner, know that having a partner doesn't necessarily make this journey easier. Whether you are in a committed relationship or not, seek out support from others. Having friends and other supportive people to talk to and rely on can be key to your healing.

- If you have other children, they need your support in adjusting to the arrival of their preemie sibling(s). Balancing the needs of all your children can be challenging. Get whatever caregiving help you need, particularly during hospitalizations.

- This is a time to keep things simple. Time spent playing cards, talking over breakfast, chatting in the car on errands, reading stories, or snuggling in bed with your children can be far more comforting than major outings or new trinkets.

- Encourage your children to ask questions and express their feelings. Answer reassuringly and listen openly. Just having you listen and empathize can be very comforting for your children.

CHAPTER TWENTY

Your Support Network and the Outside World

When you're in the midst of a crisis, you are isolated, mentally and physically, from the rest of the world. If your pregnancy requires strict bed rest and monitoring, you may be confined to your house or even the hospital for many weeks. After your baby's birth, you may spend weeks or months in the NICU. While immersed in this crisis, you tend to ignore everything else. The outside world can seem really distant, even strange.

Although you physically leave the NICU every day, emotionally and mentally, it's where you reside. Inevitably, on your forays outside you'll encounter others for whom this crisis is foreign. You'll see strangers on the street going about their business. You'll talk with family members or friends who try to be sensitive and helpful, but who don't understand how disjointed you feel. It may seem obscene that the rest of the world continues to function as if nothing is wrong—how can everything just keep on going when you are so preoccupied with your baby's fragility and uncertain future?

After your baby comes home, you might feel removed from your relatives, friends, and neighbors who also have babies. They don't have to endure long and stressful feedings or arrange for assessments and therapies. They don't need to avoid overstimulating their babies or fear germ-filled environments. They don't have to carefully calculate when they need to pump or when medications are due. You may vaguely recall being that carefree once, a very long time ago. A lifetime ago.

In addition to your day-to-day differences, people around you aren't relating to you or what you're going through. Your friends and relatives may not know what to think or expect. They may have no clue what a preemie looks like or needs, and they probably don't understand all the medical and emotional implications of your baby's early birth.

One of the only times I ever tried to talk to someone about my grief, I shared a little with an employee who[m] I had worked closely with and considered a friend. She told me that it was really time for me to stop thinking about it all and to do something constructive. She said I'd be better off doing something like that than wallowing in my grief and feeling sorry for myself. I'll always remember that because it had been so hard for me to say anything, and I felt like she was chastising me. I look back and realize now how isolated I felt from anything or anyone who could help. —Susan

People who haven't been through it, they don't understand it. I know they don't. You can describe it, you can show them videos. But they don't have the emotion of not being able to take that baby home. They don't have the stress of, every time the phone rings, is that the doctor? They don't have the fears of all the things that can go wrong. Most of the world thinks that a preemie is just a small baby, and they don't think about immature lungs, the trauma of brain bleeds, the possibility of cerebral palsy, NEC [necrotizing enterocolitis] with their intestines. There are so many preemie problems that are so typical, and most people are not aware of this. Even friends and family who've been through it with us, they just don't really understand. —Vickie

Although you may feel isolated, connections to other people can sustain you and your partner during difficult times. Still, several factors will affect your ability to find and take in the support that's available. They include
- Your current emotional condition
- How your extended family manages crisis
- How much your expectations of family and friends differ from the reality of their responses to your baby's birth
- The flexibility of your relationships, household, and work situation

- Your opportunities to network with other parents of preemies

This chapter explores these issues and provides some suggestions for enlisting the support of your extended family and friends, and dealing effectively with the outside world.

The Importance of Support Networks

When parents-to-be are expecting a baby, a network of support surrounds them. There are relatives who join the parents in planning for and welcoming this new member of the family. There are friends, some of whom may be having babies around the same time. And there are new friendships formed on the common ground of pregnancy and parenthood. This supportive social network creates a nurturing environment for new parents, bolstering their hopes and soothing their worries. It's helpful to be surrounded by others who understand what you're going through, others who have paved the way for you, and others who are willing to be involved with you on your terms.

Naturally, all parents find that some people are more supportive or understanding than others. But when your pregnancy ends with the premature delivery of a fragile infant, part of your social network may scatter. Unable to comprehend all that's involved, not knowing how to help, feeling sad and helpless themselves, some friends and relatives may be unable to figure out how to continue nurturing you.

To make matters more confusing, you may have contradictory needs, wanting to be treated both "normally" *and* with special sensitivity to your situation. You need people to say, "Congratulations. This must be so hard." Few people will know that you need this kind of acknowledgment. Still, when people express only sympathy, you notice the missing congratulations—and vice versa. If they try to reassure you with stories of "amazing" preemies, you may feel that they are naive and unaware of what you and your preemie are going through.

We needed support, not sympathy. Many people told us they were sorry that T. J. had been born. What they meant was that they were sorry he had been born prematurely, *but that's not the way it came out. —Claire*

People didn't know if they should say "Congratulations." People just didn't know what to say. My response was always, "Come over and meet him." And after people met him, they would ask, "How is Yoni doing today?" People don't want to say the wrong thing, but saying nothing is also painful. —Micki

There were a lot of things that people said and did that pissed me off in the beginning, but that just came from ignorance. There were those who congratulated me, when the kids were forty-eight hours old, when the word spread that we had twins. Now, they didn't know any better, so I just took their congratulations and I said very little except to those who we were very close to. But congratulating me? "Let me ask you a question, idiot" was what I would think to myself. "What are you congratulating me for? Yeah, I had twins, but they're on their death beds right now." But you can't say that to somebody because they don't know any better. All they know is that you had twins. Do they know that they're twenty-six weeks? They don't know that. But everybody would say that, "Oh, mazel tov, mazel tov! That's great!" What's great? My kids are dying right now. What do you know? I was very angry with people, but I didn't say anything. —Mitch

The response I got tired of was "Things are going to be okay. Everything is going to work out and going to be fine." Or "I knew somebody who had a one-pounder, and the baby's fine, they're sixteen years old now." They always knew somebody who had a smaller baby or a sicker baby, and that baby's perfectly fine now. But you never know with a preemie. You don't. And nobody can tell you that it is going to be okay. The doctors won't even tell you that, so how can somebody who doesn't even know what's going on tell you that? —Vickie

You can feel undermined if others misunderstand when you try to explain your loss or if they minimize what you're going through. Even when some of your friends and relatives *are* sensitive and empathic, you may no longer feel nurtured. Instead, you may feel summarily ejected from the "club" of new parents and newborns—and you have a gaping hole where your old hopes and dreams used to be. You've missed out on the expected rites of passage into parenthood. You may not even know of anyone else who has gone through this experience before you. Unsure of where you fit, who your peers are, or where you're going, it's not surprising that you feel adrift and alienated.

One of the worst parts about having my baby in the NICU was not being able to show him off. I wanted everyone to see my beautiful son. Unfortunately, I couldn't carry him around and show him to everyone. It was hard on us, but we found ways to cope: we took lots of pictures, invited our friends to come and see him, and kept mementos like hand/footprints, hand molds, and so on. —Claire

Something that I still battle with is not having the "normal," scheduled baby showers and being able to show Alison off once she finally came home. Many of our closer friends came up to see her at the hospital—through the window—but it was just not the same. —Stacy

It can be a struggle to create a network of people who can really understand what you're dealing with and appreciate what you're going through. Having friends and relatives who are sincerely willing to stay with you and learn along with you can be a tremendous comfort. Lisa says, "I knew if I was going to break down, they would help me pick up the pieces. I couldn't have done this without them."

It's really difficult to talk to people who don't understand. And the second time, we didn't have the energy to go through it with anybody else. You just get so tired of hearing responses that mean nothing, and you stop talking to people who don't know what you're going through. So my life this second time consisted of people who I knew I wanted to hear from or talk to. I started to just surround myself with people who could support me and encourage me, as opposed to people who were just saying things to make themselves feel better. —Vickie

When James was in hospital, and it was day fifty-five or so, and we were just waiting, waiting, waiting, waiting, I felt like I couldn't go on. I couldn't take one more day. My sister-in-law rang and asked how I was doing, and I started to cry. I told her how I felt, and she cried too. Now there was no way on earth that she could have understood exactly how I felt, but she cried too anyway. She knew what pain was, and she heard it in my voice and in my words and in my tears, and she cared enough about me to share my pain. And it was kind of nice to think that this person at the other end of the phone, whose life was nothing like mine, thought that my pain was reasonable enough to share it. It made me feel less alone for those ten minutes or so. —*Leanne*

We had many visitors. I realize now how blind we were to how my son appeared to our friends and family. Many came to the NICU as we proudly showed off our cute little son. We were very aware of how serious his medical condition was. We knew the incubator, wires, and tubes were scary to see. ... For us, the NICU was a fact of life; for our friends, it was a rare glimpse into a horror they never wanted to have as a part of their own lives. And yet they came to support us. —*Laura*

Connecting with Other Parents of Preemies

I had a support person from the hospital, a former preemie parent of [babies born at the same gestational age as mine]. It helped immensely to see her healthy, "big" children. Other parents I met on the unit were also my lifeline. I became really good friends with a mom of a baby who was born twelve days before Josh and Evan. She was our foreshadower for events to come, which I think made our stay psychologically easier to cope with. —*Stephie*

There were not really any support groups for parents of preemies at the time that Stef was born, but I did connect with other parents in the NICU. You can't really help but connect—no one else understands what you're going through like the parent of another preemie. —*Janet*

The other parents in the NICU were the greatest source of strength for us. These parents were of such diverse backgrounds, the only thing we possibly could have in common were our children. We encouraged each other. Gave updates on progress and setbacks. Comforted each other. And occasionally mourned for each other. —*Laura*

In addition to friends and family who are truly supportive, it can be immensely helpful for you to find people who *know* what you're going through without any coaching. What you are looking for is a "club" whose membership speaks the same language as you and shares a perspective similar to yours. You want to be able to talk to parents to whom you don't have to explain yourself quite so much. Belonging to a group where you can tap into the healing power of shared experience can be greatly beneficial. Naturally, this network is made up of other parents of premature babies.

As you feel your way around other parents of preemies, you may be concerned about how much their situations vary from yours. Yet there are many basic experiences on which you can relate: early pregnancy complications, struggles with bed rest and drugs, deliveries filled with fear and dread, gestational age in weeks and days, birthweight in grams, growth patterns, kinds and lengths of medical interventions, lengthy hospital stays, ongoing worries about medical fragility, developmental delay, or disability. Additionally, other preemie parents can appreciate the significance of simple developmental milestones: news that your baby is smiling, turning to your voice, or tracking objects. When you share these small but very significant triumphs, your baby gets the standing ovation he or she deserves. You can't talk to "regular" parents about this stuff.

Unfortunately, sharing experiences can also lead to complicated comparisons and rivalries. You may find yourself feeling competitive about whose baby was born the earliest, whose baby was vented the longest, or who suffered more—as if a medal were being handed out for "Bravery in the Face of the Most Terrible Situation." The opposite can be true as well: you may hesitate to talk about your good fortune at having a baby who was born later or heavier than another parent's, or hide your relief that your toddler appears to be free of any lingering effects of prematurity. In fact, some parents of preemies find themselves wondering if their experience really "counts." What is so important to remember is that the details of others' pregnancies, deliveries, NICU courses, and outcomes don't matter—it's the feelings about your experiences that count. Listen to the hopes lost, the grief and fears and struggles, and the dreams re-created. That's where you'll find common ground with other parents of preemies.

I may not have had the exact same feelings as someone else, but I have certainly had my share of feelings that made me uncomfortable, even shocked me. Lots of feelings that I certainly wished I never had and I was ashamed to admit to others. That is what allows me to connect with and empathize with the feelings preemie parents express, even if I haven't felt the particular feeling expressed. For me, shame is the most destructive emotion, and bringing our nightmares out into the light of day often takes the power out of them. —Kris

• • •

All parents of preemies feel upset, sad, and scared. To whatever degree your baby has been affected by prematurity, you have losses to grieve. As you begin to assess the damage and face your emotions, connect with other parents of preemies who are doing the same. All of you have faced adversity and are struggling to figure out how to adjust to new realities, how to live with uncertain futures, how to dare to hope, how to make meaning, and how to forge new parenting identities. Around these shared emotional issues, you'll find much-needed support from other parents of preemies.

Finding Support Groups

A support group can offer you the commiseration, advice, reassurance, and encouragement of other parents who have "been there." A well-run group is a safe place to voice your deepest thoughts, biggest fears, and true feelings about your situation, giving you an avenue to work through your emotions and move forward.

To find a support group or network of preemie parents, ask your NICU nurses or the social worker at the hospital or call a mental health agency. Look in community bulletins and newspapers, or ask a national support organization for a list of local support groups. Or you can surf the World Wide Web and find a "preemie parent list" where you can correspond with other parents of preemies. (See Appendix C for recommendations.) If you are too shy or overwhelmed to make inquiries, ask someone else to gather information for you. A good friend would likely be pleased to assist you with this.

If there is no support group at your hospital, you might convince a sympathetic health care provider to start one or to sponsor your efforts. A local college or university department of social work, nursing, psychology, or psychiatry might be interested in developing a program. It never hurts to ask. If you live in a sparsely populated area or if being part of a group doesn't appeal to you, ask your doctor or midwife to put you in touch with another preemie parent. If you have Internet access, you can hook up privately one-on-one with parents of preemies who you meet through a list or join a group that will pair you with another parent who can be your mentor. (See Appendix C for recommended Internet sites.) However you make the connection, another preemie parent can be a lifeline, both while your baby is in the NICU and after.

In the NICU, I was able to get to know a mom of another preemie very well. If she hadn't been in there for the first two to three weeks that Alison was, I do not think that I would have made it. —Stacy

It was so helpful to me to finally hear from some other parents that their child was going through the same things that mine was!! Until a week ago, I was about to check myself into counseling because I was on the verge of a break-down! I had almost no hope of future schooling for my child because I had run into so, so many roadblocks. Now I am pushing to have him evaluated by an occupational therapist for sensory integration dysfunction. ... Just knowing that this is common to preemies has helped me see my child in a whole new light. And now I am in a new fight to get him—and others like him—the help that they so deserve. —Ashley

Stay aware of your unique needs for support. As Vickie points out, "Just because a support group was wonderful for me the first time, it really wasn't the second time. I'm not saying I didn't need it, but I couldn't take listening to somebody else tell their story. I had too much going on with myself. I couldn't handle it emotionally." Accept where you are and find the kind of support that fits you.

Social Support for Fathers

It's hard for me because men don't really talk about it. When I talk to men, they just kind of skim over it and try to get on to the next subject. So at times it's kind of hard because I don't really have a "best" friend to confide in. I have a lot of friends, but I'm sure Janet's friends ask her, "How are you doing? How are you doing?" But men just don't do that. My brother sent me a nice card, but you just don't speak about it. That's just the way we were raised. —Tim

Some people will avoid talking to you or your partner about your baby's difficulties. If you're a father, you may wonder if others avoid the topic because they assume men have no feelings about the situation and so there's nothing to discuss. Many men are frustrated by the expectation that they should remain in control of or suppress their feelings, no matter how intense.

I think we fathers are often overlooked and dismissed. It is so easy for people to not want to get into the "heavy stuff" of parenting a preemie [with the dad]. Any dismissal [of his emotional struggles], I think, can be misinterpreted by the father as his having done something wrong or broken some social taboo. —Ed

On the other hand, if someone brings up the subject of your baby's struggle, you may feel self-conscious, unprepared, or unsure of how much to open up. You may feel as if the person is watching to see how you react. If you do cry or talk openly about your feelings, you may find that others are uncomfortable or judgmental. Worrying about how others perceive you doesn't make sharing or intimacy easy.

Some dads don't feel the need to talk about what they're going through. This may be what you're accustomed to. Or you may just not feel like sharing the intimate details of your emotional life or expect to find someone you're comfortable leaning on. It may not even occur to you that talking to someone might help.

I don't recall turning to someone to talk to them. I wasn't looking for support. Maybe guys are like that. I wasn't looking to lean on someone else. It sounds like a very macho thing to say, but I suspect that this is probably what was going on. I expected to be leaned on and not to have anyone to lean on myself. But I didn't think about it at the time. I just didn't think I needed to lean on anybody. Who was I going to tell something to? —Mitch

What holds many fathers back is the feeling that their baby's birth, their grief, and their fears are not appropriate topics of conversation, especially with their male friends. Many men feel more comfortable turning to women friends for emotional support. But by not confiding in your male friends and fellow preemie dads, you miss the sense of brotherhood and common ground that connecting with other men can provide. Having the courage to share your experiences and emotions may draw some of them out of their shells. Try opening up when you're working or playing side-by-side, which can be easier than talking face-to-face. You may be risking rejection, but the potential rewards are richer friendships, deeper affection, and mutual respect.

Men's groups and fathers' groups are excellent places to connect with others. As you brave the poorly charted emotional landscape of male relationships, keep in mind that the more comfortable you become with your own emotions, the more comfortable you'll feel around others, whatever their reaction. Additionally, you may feel more comfortable talking about what happened, rather than how it felt. Find the avenues of sharing that work best for you. (See Chapter 4: "Especially for Fathers," for more on men and coping.)

If I can talk to someone about something, have a seat, get a soda, and take the phone off the hook, without reservation, talking about the experience is helpful to me. But it's got to be someone you trust and who cares about you above their needs. Especially for dads. ... Fortunately I had the [Internet] list to speak my piece at times, people whom I still trust a great deal. They didn't seem to mind if it was heavy, and at times seemed to "reinforce" or "reward" open and honest expressions of the shared difficulties, as well as the unique. —Ed

You can experience your feelings in other contexts as well. Try writing in a journal, sorting through photographs, reading books and other materials, or simply setting aside time to be alone with your thoughts. Physical activity, such as hiking in restful places, or creative expressions, such as making something for your baby, can also help.

There is another kind of social support for fathers that is immensely helpful—assistance with the everyday chores and errands. After the premature birth of your baby, you may feel overwhelmed by the demands on your time and energy. There simply aren't enough hours in the day to fix everything that can actually be fixed. It is a relief to have others step in and do some of the more mundane chores that normally fall to you. This kind of assistance shores you up, reduces the pressure, builds your morale, and lets you know that others care. This assistance feels so supportive because it is an aspect of the nurturing that every new parent needs.

We were renting our home, and the front yard was a mess. The lawn was getting long, there were spider webs and stuff left over from the fall and winter. It wasn't really bad, it just needed attention, and it was the easiest thing to put off, but it was also the thing that was apparent every day when I pulled up in the driveway. Since we would go see Buddy on Wednesdays and Saturdays, and I tried very hard not to work on Sundays, the lawn just kept getting worse and worse.

Well, one Saturday we headed up to the hospital, and Buddy was probably either recovering from a surgery or getting ready for one. It was that time in his stay when his intestines were having a real hard time. We wanted to stay as long as we could, but we knew we had to get home to pick up our daughter, and there were things to do around the house.

When we arrived home, things looked very different. The lawn was mowed, the leaves were raked and piled, even the shrubs were trimmed. There were things done that I wouldn't have thought to do, even if Buddy hadn't been in the hospital. And I had no idea who did it. I suspect I do now, but I'll likely never be sure. When I saw it, I cried. Huge sobs of relief and gratitude. Not because it was a confirmation of all I couldn't do, but because someone had finally done something I really needed. I didn't need dinners and lunches or extensions on assignments. I needed my home and my family to be "unaffected." I needed something normal-looking. I needed not to have to ask or beg for help. I was asking for help with everything: school, church, bills, employers, hospital staff. Someone looked, found a need, organized it, and did it. All I could do was just say thanks.

And I could go in the house and relax and not feel guilty because I wanted to catch five minutes of a baseball game or play with my daughter, and it would be at least two weeks before it "had" to be done again. It freed me not only for that day, but for days to come. Since it was done anonymously, there also wasn't anyone I owed anything to either. No one to "pay back." It meant everything to me. I was given time to take care of me without some task pounding on the door demanding my attention. —Ed

Relationships with Your Extended Family

Pregnancy and birth naturally affect the new parents' extended family, including their parents, their siblings, and other important family members. At first, the role your family plays may be the role of onlooker. Those who do get involved may ask questions, make comments, and offer advice—and some will be more supportive and understanding than others. Initially, your baby's needs and your own needs are paramount, but inevitably, you'll also have to confront the needs of your relatives.

It has been especially difficult trying to explain things to people and make them understand. Especially my husband's mother. It's hard enough to deal with ignorance in general, let alone in a family member with whom you have to deal constantly. —Lisa

I remember focusing in on my mother's concerns, and [I] kept reassuring her that everything would be okay and that I was fine, while ignoring my own feelings. —Rosa

They were just so scared, which is understandable, but I was scared, and I didn't want to have to comfort somebody else. I mean, I needed to be comforted. I was the injured party there, not them. Well, they were, too, but not as close. I felt like some people were able to grieve more privately and didn't show it to me so that it became my burden, too. —Stephie

As your family reorganizes to include this new baby, their response to you and your little one can be very important. You may feel especially sensitive to the reactions of any family member with whom you have a close or meaningful relationship.

My sister-in-law does not call at all. She had her own full-term baby a few months after I did. I would figure we would have lots to talk about and share. Maybe it's me, because they weren't really there for me, that I hold it against them. I know it isn't good, but I can't help it. —Rosa

My youngest sister had her first baby four months before I had Tyler. I was so angry with her after Ty arrived. And jealous!! Wow, was I jealous. I had been to see her after she gave birth to Megan, and of course, there were congratulations, presents, and so on. With Ty, there was nothing. I know that my sister picked up on my feelings because she stopped calling and didn't visit any more. … She stayed away because she didn't know how to act with me. She loved me but couldn't possibly understand what I was going through. She felt her presence was just a very painful reminder to me, and she was in fact very right. —Kristy

I needed a lot of support from my family. I needed them to love and adore this child as much as I did. I needed them to reassure me that I was capable of taking care of a special needs child. I got all of this and more and am very grateful for them. —Claire

This section focuses on understanding and dealing with your extended family and offers tips for enlisting their support.

High Hopes ... Derailed

Part of preparation for childbirth is envisioning how your new baby will become part of your extended family. You may imagine leaning on family for advice and support or commiserating with them about "normal" newborn antics. But when your baby arrives early, these expectations are derailed. It may have been impossible, logistically and emotionally, to include your parents or other family members in the delivery and in those first days after birth. Instead of being able to pass your new baby to eager arms, you can at best only lead relatives to your baby's bedside— and they may be filled with shock and grief, instead of congratulations and delight. At this time, when you're most in need of your relatives' support, some of them may be unable to give it to you. You may even have to bear their feelings of helplessness, anger, and blame.

Family Coping

After your baby's early arrival, certain relatives will align themselves with you, providing nurturing support, while others will be too uncomfortable to face the whole situation. Common reactions include disappointment or even anger at you for your inability to keep this from happening; rejection of your grief in an attempt to hide from their own; and minimization of your experience in an effort to make you or themselves feel better. Any of these reactions can leave you feeling undermined and isolated.

I have to say I wish that my father-in-law knew what it was like to have a preemie. Because before my son came home from the hospital, he basically yelled at me and told me that I shouldn't be going to the hospital every day to see my son since the hospital was about an hour and a half away. That since we were paying the nurses good money in the hospital to take care of him, I shouldn't have wanted to be up there every second that I could. I should be taking care of my other son and my husband. Basically stuff like that. All I could think was that he didn't know what it was like to have to ask permission to hold your own son. To ask when you could hold him. To have to ask if you could feed him or even just change a diaper. To wonder if your son was really going to be all right. —Miranda

My husband's brother and his wife had a full-term baby just two weeks before our preemie was born. They called regularly to tell us how lucky we were that our son was not home with us, waking us up at night and having to be taken care of twenty-four hours a day. This whole thing made me feel very defensive and unsupported. We were being told that they were unlucky for having a healthy ten-pound full-term son and we were lucky for having a three-pound preemie with a vent and a feeding tube. Other in-laws were constantly telling us how difficult things were for this other family, while everything was supposedly great with us. —Terri

During your time in the NICU, whether your relatives react with composure or unsteadiness can depend on their comfort level with crisis. Some may be able to thoughtfully inquire and listen supportively while you talk about your baby and your feelings. Others may probe for details about the medical situation, but be uninterested in hearing about your emotional state. Or they may dodge the topic entirely in order to avoid your pain or their own anxiety. Some might not understand the complexity of what your baby faces—and it's common for confused relatives to ask questions repeatedly or to focus on just one aspect of your child's condition. Providing constant updates can be exhausting for you, especially if you know that the information isn't sinking in.

Homecoming presents another challenge. You may be very hurt if your relatives seem intimidated by or afraid of your infant or if they act differently with your baby than they do with the other little cousins or grandchildren. Some of your relatives may be ready to act as if everything is back to "normal." They may not feel the need to wash their hands anymore, or they might scoff if you refuse to attend a family event where your little one would be passed from person to person. In their disregard for your concerns, these relatives may be trying to send you the message that your child should be treated just like all the other kids in the family—even if it's evident that your little one has special requirements. You want your child to fit in, but you also want certain accommodations made. It's a tough balancing act, and finding family members who are able to support you becomes even more important.

I remember being scared of anyone else holding her for fear that she would "catch" something and that she would land back in the hospital. Bringing the baby home and trying to keep her germ free when everyone wants to touch/see/hold the baby—it was a difficult time for us. Excuse my language, but I got tired of being the "bitch" all the time and "having" to give reasons for trying to keep as many germs away from Alison as possible. She was also very sensitive and got overstimulated very easily. People just did not understand this. —Stacy

If your child has ongoing special needs, your relatives' unresponsiveness may leave you feeling bereft and alone or ashamed. Often, family members will try to force a "normal" situation or provide you with "advice" that doesn't fit your circumstances. They may anxiously ask if your child has reached some milestone that has particular significance for *them*—but that may have nothing to do with your reality with your preemie.

The biggest frustration is family. They keep talking as if this is a minor delay and that he is going to take off talking any day. They say things like, "Well, the other boys will teach him now that he's home more," and "The other kids didn't talk much until they were older, but once they started, look out." As if he is just taking his time about it. I have tried explaining to them that Stephen is different and that he will have to use other ways to communicate. I don't know whether to be furious or frightened. My worry is how they are going to react when this finally sinks in, and also, if it never does, how much frustration will they cause Stephen if they try to "make him talk" for things. —Tracy

My in-laws tend to test Conor all the time—give him obstacles, not respect his limitations. My sister and sister-in-law tend to compare their toddlers to him—they claim his problems are normal toddler behavior, which they are not. Because he looks "normal," people have a hard time dealing with his personality, which I believe is due in large part to his disabilities. —Laura

We gave them information to take away so they could understand more about cerebral palsy. My mother-in-law brought it all back and let me know that their only advice was that we had better watch out that we don't become too overprotective. I could have knocked her head off. Where do they come up with these things? I don't need or want her advice. Quiet support would be nice. —Lissa

Just as each parent learns to cope with the birth of a preemie, so too do the members of the extended family. If your relatives tune in to your needs and to those of your child, you will be comforted by their support. But when those who mean so much to you disappoint you, it's difficult to accept. If you feel you're not getting the support you want and need, here are some suggestions of things you might try:

- You and your closest relatives may share similar kinds of disappointments and worries about your preemie. If you can talk about feelings with each other, you may discover you have much in common. Remember the healing power of shared experience.
- Recognize that it's common for family members to hold back investing emotionally in a baby who may die or be "abnormal." Give them time to adjust their expectations and to get to know your baby as an individual.
- Make it clear that you don't expect or want your family members to "fix" your feelings. Let them know that you just need them to listen without criticizing, minimizing, or lecturing you.
- Know that family members may be earnest in their desire to help, but naive about the situation or about how to assist or support you. Educate them and give them feedback on what you need. Thank them when they say or do something helpful. Let them know when they make a remark or gesture that's hurtful. If they truly want to be supportive, they'll appreciate your letting them know they are on the right track or your direction on how they can be more helpful.
- Be open and honest with family members about the situation, your emotions, their role, and your baby's condition. If you need to confront them, be gentle, but avoid trying to protect their feelings. If they are embarrassed, angered, or saddened by your observations or suggestions, let them be. It's better that they deal with frank feedback about their unhelpful behavior than that you suffer silently.

• • •

- If family and friends call regularly for updates, consider leaving an outgoing message on your voice mail with whatever information you choose to share. This way, you don't have to repeat every detail for each caller.
- Share your knowledge about what your baby needs. Teach family members how to interact with your baby in ways that will help your little one stay calm. Share information sources with them. Include them in NICU rounds, follow-up visits, or therapy appointments so that they can learn more about your baby's special needs.
- If you are receiving unwelcome advice or if family members disregard your attempts to inform them about your baby's needs, emphasize to them that preterm babies are not just "little full-term babies." If they are insulted that you don't consider them to be parenting "experts," let them know that you welcome their efforts to join you in learning how to parent a preemie or a baby with special needs. Invite their partnership in navigating this new territory. Also keep in mind that *all* parents have to put up with advice and direction that they don't find helpful. It's not just a "preemie" thing.
- You deserve to get what you need. If your family members cannot be supportive, find other sources of support—from friends, other parents, and professional counseling. Don't rely on family members who are unreliable.

Grandparents Grieve, Too

Of all your relatives, your parents—your baby's grandparents—probably have the deepest emotional investment in your baby. Not only are they concerned about their dear new grandchild, but they may also find it very difficult to see their adult child in such pain. They may even seem to worry more about you than about the baby, which can feel uncomfortable when you're so focused on your little one. Try to recognize the "double sorrow" they feel.

Your baby's grandparents may be able to move past this pain, learn about their preemie grandchild, and fully support you both. Or they may continue to struggle with the situation. Unable to fully understand or accept their preemie grandchild's special beginning, they may not know how to support you while *you* adjust.

Just as you face losses and adjustments with the birth and growth of

Parenting Your Premature Baby and Child

your preemie, so, too, do your baby's grandparents. Naturally, this crisis can challenge your relationship with them.

> *Grandparents, they were a mixed blessing. Our parents visited at least weekly, probably more often. They were very involved, but sometimes I was having a hard enough time holding myself together that I couldn't be there for them. Both our moms are worriers by nature, and they would have this look in their eye or a question that would want to send me over the edge. I couldn't console their worries, and sometimes they seemed to worry about things I wasn't, and then it made me feel nuts.* —Stephie

Coping Styles During a major crisis, some grandparents are skilled at coping with their grief and tuning in to the needs of their adult children. But even if your parents have a good sense of what you might need, they may hold back, reluctant to intrude during a time of crisis for you and your partner. Others are more easily overcome by what is happening around them. They may urge you to move on because it's difficult for them to listen to how much you hurt. If they don't seem to be interested in details about your baby or if they question your decisions, you may feel betrayed by them at a time when you need them the most.

> *The grandparents were concerned and supportive, but distant as well (both physically and emotionally). They too wanted to believe that everything would turn out all right. We have had more support from them now with cerebral palsy issues that we did during the preemie experience itself.* —Diana

> *I had started to talk to my mother about it and about how angry I was and all these feelings. And she said, "Just don't think about that. Just think about how well he's doing." Okay. I can't just turn these feelings off. But then I just stopped telling her about those feelings because I didn't want to have to justify myself. She didn't know. She meant well, but she didn't know what I was going through. No one did.* —Marcia

Distance, misunderstanding, and discomfort are particularly difficult to accept with your own parents. It's hard to let go of the childhood notion that your parents automatically know what kind of help and support you need. But there is no grandparenting manual that tells them what they should do, just as you had no instructions to help you with your abrupt entry into parenting your preemie. They may be feeling overwhelmed, just as you are. Unsure of how to offer sensitive support, they may hesitate to say the words you long to hear.

Yet even if your parents are overwhelmed, angry, or frightened, your need for them to respond to you, to help you cope with your feelings, doesn't go away. Sometimes what they can give doesn't match what you need. In such cases, it's normal to feel disappointed by any lack of support. You want to be able to rely on them, at least on one of them. When you can, it feels priceless.

> *From the very first day, my father called me at the NICU every day while Sarah was listed as critical. When she was upgraded, he called at least twice a week to get progress reports. What meant the most to me about that was that he called me during the middle of the day knowing I was alone at the hospital. He knew Stan was working and that I needed the support. I guess someday I'll have to tell him. —Cindy*

Here are some tips for enlisting your parents' support:

- Start by assuming that your baby's grandparents have your best interests at heart.
- Accept their efforts to support you, even if they're clumsy.
- Remember that your baby's grandparents cannot read your mind. You need to tell them what you need, what helps, and what doesn't. If talking to them about this is too difficult, write an encouraging letter; your positive expectations can break unsupportive patterns.
- Tell your baby's grandparents that you appreciate the people in your life who can listen without trying to fix and who can accept your feelings without trying to minimize them or talk you out of them. Let them know that you need to surround yourself with people who can support your efforts in meeting your baby's unique needs. If they can hear and understand this, they'll want to be that kind of person. If the indirect approach doesn't work, then phrase your statements in a more straightforward way. Say, for example, "I need you to listen without trying to fix." (Also see the suggestions in the "Boundaries" section that follows.)
- Although seeing you upset and anxious can be difficult for your parents, hiding your sadness and anger benefits neither you nor your baby. Trust

your parents to take care of themselves. You have enough to do. You might suggest they read Appendix B or consider sharing this chapter with them.

Sometimes, facing a crisis as a family brings out the strength and resiliency in everyone. Turning to your parents for comfort, leaning on them for strength, borrowing their hope and their toughness can bring all of you closer. When they help in ways that you need, understand that just being with you means so much, and celebrate your baby's birth and milestones without minimizing the challenges, they are giving you gifts that strengthen your relationship.

My father-in-law is a big, brusque man. He was very uncomfortable with little babies and never even held his own children when they were infants. He came to visit one day when my son was two months old, two pounds and off the respirator. I gave him a gown and rocking chair, swaddled my son, and handed the baby over to him. He was extremely reluctant. But once he was holding him, he commented that the baby felt heavier than he thought he would. They rocked. When the fifteen minutes were up and I took my son back, my father-in-law was surprised that the time had gone by so quickly. Now almost two years later, I still see a special bond between them. —Laura

Boundaries Under even the best of circumstances, new parents struggle with how much input they want from the grandparents. Having a baby who requires special care can heighten your sensitivity to advice—and your desire for your parents' respect. Many parents of preemies find themselves dealing with grandparents who remain too distant—or who move in too close.

When grandparents pull back too far, you may feel abandoned or rejected. But pulling back is one way grandparents try to manage overwhelming feelings of fear and loss of control. They may keep their distance because they fear the pain of bonding with a baby who may die. Unfortunately, the cost of this distancing from you and your baby can be tremendous.

I have never been able to share a lot with my parents. Even when James was in hospital, my parents' view seemed to be and still is, "You deal with this, and then he'll come home and we'll forget that it ever happened." I decided that if strangers [on the Internet list] could think my feelings worthy enough to share, then surely my parents could as well, right? Wrong. My mum read [something I wrote about my feelings], and halfway through she looked at me and asked, "Did you write this?" "Yes, mum, I wrote it." She continued to read, finished, and put it down without comment. My sister read it as well, finished, and put it down without comment. I didn't even bother to show my dad. And that, as they say, was that. —Leanne

On seeing his grandson, my father told me I should have terminated the pregnancy when I had the chance. Not understanding how he could feel that way, I told my father to look at him—to me, he was a beautiful miracle. And his reply was, "Yes, just look at him!" My father came to visit the NICU a few times. He never could look at my son. He simply spoke to me as if there were no baby. He said he was concerned for me and my well-being. He said he didn't want me to suffer. What he could never realize was that he caused me more suffering by feeling the way he did—by not loving and accepting my son. It was extremely painful to be treated this way by both of my parents. I had not had wonderful childhood experiences with them, but we had cordial relationships. I guess in the back of my mind, I thought my parents might come through for me when I really needed them. I felt completely abandoned. —Laura

On the other end of the spectrum, grandparents who move in too close may be trying to take control to soothe their own feelings of anxiety and panic. They may react more intensely than you do, not leaving room for *your* emotions and needs. They may behave in ways that are intrusive, questioning your decisions or your style in the nursery or, later, at home. They may focus on themselves—visiting when it's convenient for them but not for the baby or you, horning in on the precious private moments you have with your baby, holding your fragile infant when your arms are aching to do that, and generally disregarding the baby's needs as well as yours. You may find yourself feeling that they are trying to relieve you of your job as parent.

While I have a very close relationship with my family, they almost drove me crazy while my daughter was in the hospital. I realized their intentions were good and they loved her too, but their constant scrutiny was unbearable at times. —Kimberly

Some grandparents who move in too close are overcompensating. If they live far away or if they are trying really hard to be helpful but just don't know how, they may attempt to make it up to you by hovering. They might grill you nightly about your baby's health. They may ask too frequently if their grandchild is rolling, scooting, walking, or talking "yet." They may not hear your replies, forgetting, discounting, or exaggerating what you've told them. All of this can leave you feeling very frustrated and drained.

Finding a happy balance between getting your needs met and dealing with the needs of your parents can be challenging. Maintaining healthy boundaries can take a lot of work and practice, especially if this has been a long-standing issue between you. The payoff is well worth the effort, though.

Here are some suggestions for building a healthy relationship with your baby's grandparents:

- You may feel keenly that it is you, the parents, who need support in this crisis, but try to recognize that grandparents need support as well. Clearly, they should lean on someone besides you, but acknowledging that this experience is hard for them too can strengthen your relationship.
- Remind yourself that your parents are responsible for their own actions and reactions, their perceptions and viewpoints. It's not your job to change them. You have the power and responsibility to change only yourself.
- Your parents' feelings belong to them, just as yours belong to you. It's not your job to protect them from reality or from their own pain.
- Just as you don't want your parents to "fix" your feelings, remember that you're not responsible for fixing theirs.
- Neither side needs to "give in" to solve a disagreement. You can each agree to respect the other's viewpoint.
- Stay clear about who the parents are and who the grandparents are in this situation. Each has a special role to play in this baby's life. Generally, the parents' place is center stage, with the proud grandparents watching and praising from the wings. Coaching should be minimal and on request, and not synonymous with taking charge, second-guessing, ordering, or pushing.
- Recognize that your feelings and perceptions are your own: others don't necessarily share them. The tendency to project your own

emotions and perceptions onto others is normal, but it can cause trouble. If you are feeling inadequate as a parent or embarrassed by your baby's frailty, remind yourself that others may not share those opinions of you or your baby. You may be hypersensitive to awkward silences, furrowed brows, or less-than-supportive comments, but don't assume that others are sending you negative messages. Just because you feel guilty, don't assume that others blame you. Just because you feel inadequate, don't assume that others perceive you as such. Just because you're feeling that you let them down, don't assume that others are disappointed in you or your baby. In a similar vein, if others really *do* blame you, criticize you, or accuse you of letting them down, don't assume that they are correct. Although you need to own up to your responsibilities, you needn't take on negative labels that others unfairly place on you. Your baby's premature birth and ongoing special needs are *not* your fault.

- Practice being assertive. Set limits on overbearing grandparents and stick to them. If you and your parents have a history of conflict, you may choose to keep them at a distance during your most vulnerable times. Tell them that, if they accept you and your family as you are, they can join you on this journey—but you will not tolerate them fighting against you. You need allies, not enemies.

- On the other hand, keep an open invitation for distant grandparents you'd like to see get more involved. To draw them in closer, make specific requests for help and support that tap their talents. If your dad is an artist or a skilled craftsman, ask for a drawing or a special item to commemorate your baby's birth. If your mother-in-law weaves, knits, or sews, ask her to make a special wall hanging. Invite them to share their favorite recipes or enlist their organizational skills. Making special requests for help lets your reluctant parents know that you value their strengths and may compel them to make a meaningful contribution This suggestion can work well with overbearing grandparents too, tapping their talents to redirect their involvement. Increased or more appropriate involvement can lessen grandparents' feelings of helplessness and strengthen their connection with you and your baby.

Friends and Others

The best thing that others gave us was the gift of listening without trying to "relate" or "understand." Just listening is very difficult for the listener but so good for the talker. ... And food. Definitely food. —Kris

It's natural and healthy to seek out the support and company of friends when you have a baby. Especially at first, you may try to figure out which of your friends can comprehend what you're experiencing. Which friends will really listen and *want* to understand? Which friends will shy away or ignore the significance of what has happened to you and your baby? Which friends will comfort you, and which ones will be insensitive to the painful feelings you're wrestling with?

I don't think it is possible to have a premature baby and not have some feelings of guilt. After all, you let down your own baby! And this makes you very sensitive to comments from other people. I guess the big thing to tell the world is, don't say things like, "I guess you shouldn't have done this or that after all." Try and focus on what the mother did right. —Linda

Sharing Information with Others

When you first tell friends, coworkers, and acquaintances about your baby's preterm birth, you may not know how much detail to share. Some parents of preemies are willing to talk to anybody who will listen and be supportive. If you feel this way, talking about what happened and what is going on day-to-day probably helps you to feel connected to others and less alone. As long as you can find sensitive listeners, you'll feel supported and understood.

Other parents are hesitant to share because they worry about how this information will affect their friends and their friendships. If you feel this way, you may long to talk with your friends about how you feel and what is happening, but worry whether that's the wisest thing to do.

After your baby's discharge, friends who failed to understand your feelings about the birth and the NICU stay may expect you to put it all behind you. If you hesitate to join in a playgroup with full-term babies (either out of fear for your baby's health or concern about your own reaction to being around full-term babies), these friends may be exasperated rather than supportive. You may long to be treated normally while at the same time wanting recognition of your special circumstances. If your baby has ongoing special needs or if you're raising one or more survivors from a multiple birth, you must tolerate your friends' reactions toward these painful issues, even as you struggle with your own intense and mixed feelings.

Everyone acts like they should feel sorry for us ... when in reality they should be celebrating with us. On the other hand, we get a lot of grief from friends who don't understand why we aren't very active socially and why we keep Nicholas away from them most of the time. —Sterling

Lots of friends and acquaintances are of the opinion that I should "get over it already," that she is almost one year and that all of that is "behind me," that she is "not a preemie any more." These things really bother me, and I usually harshly explain that "No, all is not well. My ten and a half-month-old doesn't sit on her own yet, doesn't crawl yet, and is nowhere near walking." I also ask if they think it's normal for an infant to be getting physical therapy. —Deb

I guess I'm frustrated the most because I get the line that I worry too much and she'll turn out okay. I get mad that people don't understand she has permanent brain damage and that her future is still uncertain. And I do get angry when people think I'm being pessimistic, because I think I am anything but that. I call myself an optimistic realist. I truly hope Alex turns out "normal," and who knows, perhaps she is only dyslexic and she'll learn to overcome. But she is still so young to know anything about her future. And then someone will feed me the line that all parents worry about their kids' future. And I'll counter that they are fearing the unknown while I'm dealing with a known issue, so it's not the same type of worry. (sigh) Perhaps it is the same, as I still fear the unknown, too. —Kathie

It appalls me that people think we should get over a very traumatic event that put our lives and our children's lives in very real danger. My son almost died so many times. Every day [we] are reminded of how fragile they really are. Every day we wonder what hurdle is waiting around the corner for them. —Laura

If you tend to be private by nature, you may consider your baby's struggles an intensely personal matter and prefer to limit the amount of information you give to those other than your closest supporters. Perhaps you can't bear the thought of crying in front of someone else, or you don't want others to see you get angry and agitated. It might be difficult for you to find a safe, contained way to discharge your feelings of sadness and anger, and to talk them through with friends.

We have lost a lot of friends due to our "preeminess." They don't understand that we have two special needs kids, and frankly, I'm sick of explaining our situation. They usually think that I could fix it if I wanted to. I can't fix what's wrong with my kids. If I could, I would. This is who they are. I find that I want to hang out with special ed parents or preemie parents who understand. —Mo

Whatever your situation, you may not be able to muster the energy to talk about your baby's daily ups and downs, especially during difficult periods. When your baby is in the midst of a crisis, it may be easier to keep your distance from friends and inquiring others.

Still, finding at least one supportive friend who can listen to you talk about your baby's progress—the ups, downs, good and bad—can be extremely therapeutic. Having just one person who merely *listens* and allows you to feel what you feel without having to apologize or explain will make a huge difference in how you cope.

It can be hard to find that "perfect listener"—someone who understands the medical jargon, realizes how serious this all is, and appreciates the small bits of progress that you celebrate. It takes a special friend to share your joy *and* make room for your pain. If there is no one in your circle of friends who can fill this bill, you may be able to find a supportive relative or turn an understanding acquaintance into a good friend.

Here are some suggestions for eliciting support from friends or close relatives:

- Have realistic expectations. You probably won't be able to get complete understanding from any one friend or family member. Different people may be better at supporting you through different aspects of your journey. Some may be better at listening or they might energize, comfort, or entertain you with their simple presence. Others may be better at doing practical things for you, such as housekeeping chores, car maintenance, or running errands.

- Remember that friends will take their cues from you. If you hide your grief, they'll assume that you're doing just fine. If they sense your withdrawal, they'll leave you alone, thinking that's what you want. Assume that your friends *want* to know how to support you. Let them know what you need. Tell them, write to them, or give them this book to read.

- When you try to help others understand and they reject what you tell them, their rejection doesn't mean that *you're* off base. What you are describing is real, even if they're unable to grasp it.

- Assume that those who make insensitive remarks are not being malicious. If your baby is extremely small or sick, for instance, some people may wonder aloud whether it wouldn't be a blessing for this baby to die. Although it's inappropriate for them to make such remarks and painful for you to hear them, their comments are really a show of concern for your baby's suffering and your suffering.

- When friends tell you stories about other preemies, they aren't trying to minimize your worries or deepen your hopelessness. They're simply trying to reassure you that you're not alone. When the stories are about "miracles," they're trying to build your hope. (For suggestions for dealing with information like this, see "Dealing with Others' Comments" later in this section.)

- If friends resist your directions on germ control once your baby comes home, try making official-looking signs to post in conspicuous places (even if it means posting a note on your baby!). Friends may be more likely to follow written instructions, you'll have to give fewer verbal reminders, and you'll be less likely to be accused of nagging.

- When friends question your priorities or your vigilance, remind them that you've been through such an incredible experience and learned so much that you can't help but be changed. This may help them see that your actions are about your life, not about second-guessing how they should live theirs. Also accept that the differences between you may cause you and certain friends to drift apart. This is only natural and a part of personal growth.

- If you sense that your friends are hesitating to say anything to you because they can't find the words, encourage them to use the first words that come to mind. Those words are usually the most honest and heartfelt. Your friends may be afraid to ask questions about your baby's medical or developmental condition because they fear bringing up a painful issue or using words that are offensive. (This may be particularly true when the subject is disabilities.) Open up the lines of communication by encouraging your friends not to worry about finding the "right" words. Tell them that you know their intent is sincere, and to use whatever words come to mind so that you can talk together. You can then suggest more accurate or appropriate terms.

- Remember that you are allowed to retreat and nurture yourself even if others want to have contact with you. Ask your partner or an understanding friend to be a buffer between you and others when you need to be alone.
- Learn to ask for help. Good friends will appreciate you asking or giving them ideas for supporting you. Remember that you do not need to justify what you need. (For more on this subject, see "Reaching Out for Help" at the end of this chapter.)
- If you're having difficulty verbalizing or even identifying what you need, give yourself the gift of consulting with a counselor who can help you identify what will help you. Then you'll know what to ask for from others.
- Consider that you may need more help than friends can give. If you're having trouble finding someone who is willing to listen, consider joining a support group for parents of preemies where you can vent, discuss your feelings, and find others who genuinely understand. Many NICUs have these groups, or they can suggest a mentor family who has already gone through this experience and is willing to help others in similar situations. If you have Internet access, there are several excellent parent groups that you can join. Finding a professional therapist who specializes in perinatal crisis can also provide an outlet for talking about what you're feeling and going through. Writing in a journal is another therapeutic outlet. For recommendations and more information on sources of support, turn to Appendix C in the back of this book, and see "Professional Counseling" and "Journaling" in Chapter 3.

In time, some of your friends will come around and understand more about your child's special start. If your child continues to have special needs, they will slowly realize that you are on a different path and they'll make accommodations. As time passes, you may feel more connected to—and better understood by—others.

Finding Your Place in the Parent Network

After your baby comes home, you'll encounter other parents who have infants. When parents get together, the discussion inevitably seems to turn to the grittier aspects of pregnancy and parenthood. It's natural to compare your experiences, hopes, and fears; it's a part of the initiation into the community of parents. But when you can't join in, you may feel isolated and misunderstood, hanging back when other parents tell their "war stories" about pregnancy, delivery, and early parenting. Most parents also love detailing their baby's characteristics and development. You wonder what these other parents would think if you told them that you only gained fifteen pounds during your pregnancy because you delivered many weeks too early. You hesitate to tell them that you can't remember the first time you saw your baby. You don't want to reveal your baby's medical complications or how hard pumping and breast-feeding has been. It's so hard to know what to say, how much to share, and how to explain what's going on, especially if you're dealing with uncertainties. Mostly, you expect that they won't be able to relate to your experience because you certainly can't relate to theirs. These feelings of isolation can make your challenges seem more difficult.

> *Our friends and coworkers were supportive, concerned, and polite at the time, but it's always been easy for them to "forget" that Emily has cerebral palsy now and come out with insensitive comments. It's been difficult to have friends (or acquaintances) with children born years after Emily be excited about their children reaching milestones (walking, toilet training, and so on) and say something like, "But of course Emily must have been doing that for a long time now ... ," and then for us to mumble something about how she's not yet.*
> —Diana

> *My husband and I spend most of our time with the kids. It's just too hard to arrange child care and then be around people who don't have a clue. We have a*

couple of friends who understand Alex and deal with him. Last summer we spent ten days at their house. Their kids are really accepting, too. But otherwise people just shy away. I read somewhere somebody said that it's okay to watch A Christmas Carol *and see Tiny Tim on TV, but it's another matter entirely to have Tiny Tim at your dinner table. Or banging his head against your wall, whatever the case may be. You can insert your own ethnic or religious occasion to fit the situation, but you get the idea.* —Mo

You may also hang back to protect other parents, and yourself. You may censor what you tell others because you don't want to hurt them, scare them, or highlight your differences. You may avoid sharing stories in an effort to protect yourself from stunned silence or well-meaning but inappropriate or superficial advice. And perhaps inevitably, you may feel quite inferior or set apart when you compare your experience with theirs.

I hear things like, "If I had a special needs child I would. ... " You don't know what you would do! I didn't know what I would do until I had one. t is not something you can truly prepare for. You can try, but until it happens you don't know how you would react. —Mo

I did experience and continue to experience many different emotions, such as feeling different from other families with full-term babies and feeling overwhelmed and very jealous about the twin issue. I continue to compare babies I see. —Rosa

I like being around full-term children. It helps me see what Conor is doing well and not so well. It's the parents of the full-term kids who usually bother me. —Laura

Remind yourself that until you tell others your story, you don't really know whether they can relate to you. Letting them know what you're going through allows those who have been there to step forward. When you reveal yourself, some people will run away, certainly, but others who have been where you are may share with you their own journeys. Many parents of preemies are pleasantly surprised by the support that comes from the most unlikely places. And by letting others—those who have been there and those who haven't—

• • •

know some of what you're feeling, you give them the chance to support you more effectively. It takes courage and stamina, but it can be rewarding to reach out when you need to.

Educating Others

I used to not explain and found that people would look at him as though he was defective. I found this to be more painful than to have them know why he is delayed and nonverbal. —Tracy

I used to think being a mom meant walking with your baby in a stroller in a mall. I soon found out that was not an easy task, especially with nine-month-old twins who looked newborn. Lots of people stopped me, and not momentarily, sometimes for a half an hour. I never lied about their age. I was proud of it. —Stephie

Many parents feel a strong personal desire to educate others about prematurity after their child's birth and NICU stay. You may do this for many reasons: to instill understanding, dispel misconceptions, avoid awkward silences, or elucidate the developmental challenges many preemies face. With every small bit of information you relay to others about what it's like to have a premature baby, your goal is to stamp out ignorance and establish an environment in which future parents of preemies will feel less alone and be less misunderstood.

Although your desire to educate others about your child and about prematurity in general may be intense, it's your prerogative to decide that you just can't explain right now or that you want to scale back your efforts to educate others. You're under no obligation to keep others informed or enlightened. In each situation, do what feels right or best for you.

As a somewhat reserved person with people I don't know well, I struggled with this after Jonathon was born. I felt like I had to explain, as I suddenly was no longer pregnant. But I found it difficult to talk about it without crying and just felt really awkward, especially in the beginning when he was still critically ill. Instead of accepting congratulations, we felt the need to explain. While in the scheme of life, this awkwardness wasn't a huge deal, it was one more thing signifying a loss of normalcy. —Tami

• • •

Right now the "issue" is development. Alison is doing great with fine motor and mental development, but not so well with gross motor. We keep trying to reassure ourselves that every child is different. It is hard for me still when other parents find out that Alison is not crawling yet. For us, it is easier at this point to joke about it than to explain the preemie story. We just say that she rolls to where she wants to go (which is very true!!) and that she is too chubby to be able to push her belly off the ground. —Stacy

For me, wanting to explain things is not because I'm making excuses for Gabriel or lowering expectations or needing a label. For me, it is because I want other people to understand how exhilarating and special and important these moments are for him, and for me—to have them "get it" and share with me how overjoyed I am at those moments of being "just one of the kids." —Maren

Dealing with Others' Comments

There were all these stupid people who would offer moronic comments about, "Oh, yeah, this one was premature, and that one was premature." But most of the time these idiots would be talking about somebody who was born at thirty-seven weeks, kids who had very few issues. "Oh yeah, my neighbor was premature." I'd think, "You don't know shit. Don't say anything to me!" There's no need to answer, but at first I would answer to these people, "What are you going to say if I tell you my kid had a test to see if his brain was bleeding? Are you going to stop talking? I don't think your little neighbor had this kind of problem." People who didn't know anything would say dumb things. —Mitch

When I had to report her birth for insurance purposes, a woman in employee services says, "Wow, you're so lucky. My baby was like ten pounds!" And I'm [thinking] like, I'm in hell. I'm lucky? Yeh. I'd rather be in hell for six hours pushing that baby out than be in hell for, like, the next two to three years, while I'm waiting to see how my daughter turns out. —Brooke

Especially if your baby was born very early or is very small or delayed, you will inevitably hear comments or advice from others that may bear no relation to your reality. While your baby is hospitalized, people's attempts to be comforting or encouraging can be both painful and aggravating. After discharge, especially during infancy, if your little one has any discrepancies between her age and her size, or between how old she looks and how old she behaves, people will be curious. Clearly, you can't control how others see your baby, but you can choose how to perceive and react to any stares or comments they may make.

We don't try to hide it. We say, "Oh, and this is Dylan, and he looks funny because he's got a tube stuck on his face." Little kids will come up and go "What's that?" and I'll just explain to them exactly what it is, and then they're okay with it. If they never get that, and if they never ask those questions, and if their parents say, "Oh, honey, don't go near that one"—you know what I mean?—or "Be careful" ... [We want to] surround ourselves with people who will be accepting of [disability] and learn about it. —Betsy

Our friends had a full-term boy the day after Kate was born [prematurely]. For two years, every time we got together with our friends or spoke to them on the phone, it was a constant onslaught of "amazing baby" stories. Their son was quite an amazing and bright little guy, but the level of competitiveness and pride his parents showed was overwhelming, particularly when I had a child who seemed to be writing her own developmental book, and I was just along for the ride.

I knew as soon as I heard their voice on the phone that I was about to hear how Kyle was walking, talking, doing calculus, negotiating a corporate takeover, validating cold fusion physics, establishing a lasting peace in the Middle East—"whatever"—and that was partly how I dealt with it. When I heard their voice, I simply conjured up some totally improbably thing he was doing (like discovering a cure for AIDS), and it made me laugh (inside). I realized they couldn't help themselves, that no amount of explaining about prematurity was going to "sink" in, and it wasn't worth my breath. They didn't mean to be thick or hurtful. They were just so filled with their own experience and their own pride it just "blinded" them to how hurtful their comments could be.

I realized on some level that I just needed to stop allowing myself to feel irked by their competitiveness, I didn't feel in my heart that their son was better or smarter, and I shouldn't allow the crowing or the barbs to make me feel otherwise.

•••
708

As a final footnote, after two years of being left in his dust, Kate decided that she was going to potty-train herself. When my friends discovered that, despite months of extreme pressure on their part, their son wasn't trained and Katie was asking to go to the potty, you'd have thought she'd discovered how to turn lead into gold, they were so shocked and jealous beyond belief. ... I'd like to tell you that I wasn't secretly smug, but it would be a bold-faced lie. In fact, nine years later, just remembering the look on their faces makes me smile.

You could try telling your friends about the long-range implications of prematurity, talk to them about the findings of the major studies, but it would likely be like trying to teach pigs to sing—it wastes your time ... and annoys the pig. —Sheila

To help yourself deal with the unthinking or cruel comments others can sometimes make, try some of these suggestions:

- Give people the benefit of the doubt. Assume that they are not being intentionally hurtful, but that they are simply ignorant, overly blunt, or unsure of what to say. View others' questions as simple curiosity or concern. Just as you try to make sense of the world around you and try to offer helpful advice, so do others. Interpret others' comments benevolently. Jaimee recalls, "I may have snapped at one friend, 'You can't give advice because you don't know!' But we all give advice about things we don't know."

- Pay attention only to comments that ring true or strike a nerve. You don't have to take every comment you hear to heart. Kathy observes, "You learn to tune out stupid statements. Just because someone says something doesn't make it so."

- If you feel embarrassed, inadequate, guilty, or angry in response to others' comments, recognize that *you are already harboring those feelings*. Stares and comments can't *make* you feel bad. Those comments simply stir up your own very painful emotions. Let the comment or stare remind you to face your feelings and take some time to try to work through them.

- Recognize that the more you are struggling with feelings about your baby's prematurity, the more sensitive and private you may feel. Even if no one pays much attention to you when you're out in public with your baby, you may still feel as if all eyes are on you and your little one. When others make harmless or even considerate inquiries, you may believe it's "none of their business" and feel insulted or invaded. As time passes and you feel more at peace, though, you'll become more relaxed around others' questions, and even their stares.

- If your child looks "different," see others' curiosity as an opportunity to help them get past appearances. Your ease and openness about your child with others will encourage them in their efforts to get to know your child for who he or she is, not just what he or she looks like.
- Figure out comfortable responses to others' questions and comments. To avoid more questions, some parents just give their child's adjusted age rather than his or her chronological age. If your baby looks and acts like a three-month-old, you can just say, "She's three months old." Or if you say, "She's six months old," and someone responds, "She's so tiny," you can simply reply, "Yes, she is." You don't owe anyone more information than you feel like sharing.
- You may decide on one set of answers for strangers, another set for acquaintances, and another set for potential friends. It's perfectly fine to have differing levels of disclosure for different levels of intimacy.

• • •

When our son died, my husband and I had several people in our lives offer their condolences for our loss. They went on to say they could understand because they had lost a very beloved dog or cat or some type of pet or another. It was very interesting how my husband's reaction to this was totally divergent from mine. To say this type of condolence caused a "Richter scale" reaction in him is about as nice as I can put it. I, on the other hand, was deeply honored that someone cared enough about me to reopen a deep emotional wound in their life and share their compassionate empathy with me. It wasn't about the fact that the "source" of that pain was a dog or a cat. The person didn't have a dog or cat relationship with that animal. They had deep, long-lasting love and companionship that was suddenly lost. My husband and I had as close to the "same" experience as two separate humans could have, yet ... the result in our own lives could not possibly have been more different. From that moment on, I realized that it's never about the "incident," it's about the "footprint" left in your life. —Sheila

Dealing with Other Women's Pregnancies

Over time I was able to tame my jealous rage into a woeful sort of envy. The sight of any pregnant woman made me unbearably sad, and I worked with several. I couldn't understand how they could possibly complain about the aches and pains of a state I felt I would never achieve again. I had to hold myself back from accosting perfect strangers on the street to tell them not to take a single moment of their own personal miracles for granted. —Susan

A good friend of mine just told me she is pregnant, and I feel bad because I am not happy for her. I hope that as time goes on I'll be able to deal with these feelings in a better way. —Rosa

Before the premature birth of your baby, like most expectant mothers, you probably enjoyed the company of other pregnant women: comparing belly sizes, pregnancy symptoms, due dates, or nursery themes. But after delivering your preemie, you may be surprised to feel a flurry of intense emotions when you encounter a pregnant woman, even one you knew before the birth of your baby. Instead of feeling linked to these women by maternal camaraderie, they can stir up feelings of envy, anger, inadequacy, and yearning. You may feel forlorn watching someone else walk the path that you had expected to take yourself. Your pain may be especially sharp if you haven't yet reached your premature child's due date.

In particular, you may be reluctant to speak with a pregnant woman about your experience because you don't want to frighten her unnecessarily. And if you try to warn her, you know that this woman may well ignore any anxiety you arouse. She will probably dismiss your experience with the observation that there must have been something wrong with *your* pregnancy, that *you* must have missed a warning signal or not followed your doctor's guidelines—and that's why what happened to *you* won't happen to *her*. You know her response because you used to have thoughts like these yourself—feeling in charge, having faith, being blissfully naive. Newly wise, you may want to shake her, warn her that bad things happen to good mothers, that a lot is beyond our control, that premature delivery can happen to *anyone*. Secretly, shamefully you might wish that terrible fate on her. Most of all, you want her to appreciate where she is and to be grateful for her good fortune. And you may fervently wish that you could return to that time of innocence, when you too assumed your high hopes would come true.

Feeling lonely, inadequate, angry, envious, and bereft when you encounter a pregnant woman is normal and understandable. Recognizing why you're swamped with painful emotion can help you cope. Particular circumstances and encounters can especially heighten your feelings of isolation and grief. Among these special challenges are

- Watching friends whose pregnancies pass your "gestational delivery date" and continue on
- Encountering someone whose due date is close to yours
- Watching pregnant women enjoying the milestones, such as shopping for maternity clothes, preparing the nursery, having a baby shower, taking maternity leave at the time they'd planned
- Noticing a pregnant woman's preoccupation with her changing body— when your figure might not have changed much because you delivered so early
- Listening to a woman talk about her birth plan and being reminded of what might have been for you
- Knowing a woman who is ignoring doctor's orders during a high-risk pregnancy, especially if everything turns out fine
- Hearing a woman bemoan a "long" pregnancy and share the "woes" of the end of the last trimester—maybe even saying that she wishes this baby would come early

When you encounter these triggers to your sorrow or anger, take it as an opportunity to work through those feelings. Instead of banishing them, name them, express them, talk about them, write about them. Over time you'll lessen their power to provoke painful emotions.

Here are some other thoughts and suggestions for coping with the pregnancies you see all around you:

- Acknowledge that your pregnancy and birth experience was different, but don't consider it inferior to the "textbook" version of pregnancy and birth.
- Find points in common with other pregnant women. No matter how difficult your pregnancy or how early your delivery, you may have thoughts, feelings, and experiences (such as morning sickness, recovery from childbirth, or adjustment to parenthood) in common with other mothers.

- Consider your experiences and lessons learned worth sharing.
- Recognize that your feelings of envy, aggravation, and longing are natural. Give yourself permission to have your feelings.
- If you sense that a pregnant woman is purposely avoiding you, interpret this as a testament to how powerful your experience seems to her. Knowing she can't disregard or minimize your experience, she avoids it. Give her the gift of space.
- Likewise, give yourself permission to maintain distance from pregnant women for as long as you feel it's necessary.

If a relative, friend, or coworker is pregnant and keeping your distance may be unrealistic or insensitive, consider these options:
- Discuss your feelings with this woman and explore ways for both of you to be comfortable for the remainder of her pregnancy. For instance, you might explain why it's too difficult for you to attend her shower or that you're concerned about alarming her by answering her questions about your pregnancy. If this woman is someone close to you, make the accommodation a shared effort.
- Remind yourself that she has the right to revel in her pregnancy and her happiness. If she tells you about her experience, you can let yourself feel some measure of happiness for her without relinquishing your own reality. You don't have to join her in reveling in it, but after all, you can appreciate her good fortune.
- Consider that sharing your experience with another woman can be legitimate and significant—you may alert her to the importance of knowing the warning signs of preterm labor. Share your original belief that you would carry your baby to term—and explain the difficulty of coping with the sudden and unexpected nature of preterm delivery.
- Consider showing the woman this chapter.
- If you are at work, focus on the tasks at hand. You are not obligated to talk about her pregnancy, or yours.
- Realize that no matter how much you explain, someone who is having an uneventful pregnancy may not fully understand. Take care of your needs, and let her worry about taking care of her own.

Someday, you'll likely be able to talk normally with pregnant women again. You may even be able to listen to a joyous birth story and realize how far you've come and how much you've grown that you can share others' triumphs without dwelling on your own sorrow. In fact, you may be able to listen to a "normal" birth story with hopes for the next time. (See Chapters 21 and 22 for more on this subject.)

Work and Home

Even when you're dealing with pregnancy complications, your baby's hospitalization, adjustment to homecoming, or some other crisis or transition, the practical, logistical aspects of work and home inevitably intrude. Having a premature baby can complicate your decisions and responsibilities around employment and your household. This section looks at negotiating parental leave with your employer, making the decision on whether to work outside the home or stay at home with your preemie, and suggestions for prioritizing and getting help with running your household.

Negotiating with Your Employer

> *That was the great thing about my company. The nurses told me that some parents had lost jobs because they had to make a choice between going to work and coming to the hospital. With my company, any time I'd talk to them, they'd say, "Tim, don't worry about it. Do what you have to do, and when you get back to work, you get back to work." —Tim*

Both mothers and fathers have important jobs to do in the NICU, and these may conflict at times with the jobs their employers pay them to do. Some workplaces have difficulty appreciating the value and importance of focusing on family needs. Others are generous and accommodating. But even with a supportive boss and coworkers, you may have felt pressured to complete work during bed rest or after delivery, or feel guilty for leaving your coworkers to clean up the mess left by your abrupt departure. Or if you work for yourself or in a field that demands more predictability or consistency, your job may not easily accommodate your family's needs. For dads, the unpredictability of mom's bed rest, delivery, and the baby's hospitalization can mean needing to leave work unexpectedly or frequently. If you are paid by the hour or are running out of personal and vacation time, although you may be able to keep

Parenting Your Premature Baby and Child

your job by taking time off without pay, you may feel extremely stressed by this loss of income at a time when your bills are mounting.

You might also worry about *when* to take your parental leave, especially if you're the mother. If you take a leave of absence while your baby is hospitalized, then you won't be able to be home when your baby is discharged. If you work while your baby is in the NICU, you're adding stress at a time when you're also struggling to adjust to the NICU, pump breast milk, get to know your tiny preemie, and recover from labor and delivery as well as any pregnancy complications.

To negotiate more flexibility at work, try these approaches:

- Tell your supervisor (preferably in writing) about the needs of your family at this time. Emphasize that you want to be a responsible employee, and that is why you're keeping them abreast of the stresses you face.

- Point out that by taking more time for family, you can be a better worker when you're there, instead of being distracted or worried. Knowing that your employer recognizes how important it is for you to care for your sick infant makes you feel valued as a person and can boost your loyalty to the company.

- Propose a plan for covering your responsibilities. If you think you can handle it, you might propose doing some projects at home. Consider the possibility of arranging a flexible job-sharing plan with someone you know or finding a temporary employee who you can help train.

- Ask for the specific times off that you need. You should be able to apply unused sick time to family leave. Some companies have a policy of letting employees donate sick time to a coworker in need; tap into that pool or suggest that the employer/employees create one. In addition, many fathers (as well as mothers) have access to family leave—find out what the laws are and check your employer's policies. You may also be able to arrange for flextime or job sharing so that you can work the hours that suit your situation at this time. You and your partner might consider taking your family leave at different times, so that there's at least one parent at home for your baby.

- If your work involves shifts, you and your partner may decide that working opposite shifts is more comfortable than leaving your preemie in day care or with a sitter. Or you may try working from home.

Work had always been my priority, but now my daughter Lauren is. Her needs come before anything else. Working from home has helped tremendously, but I have no set hours. I work around Lauren. Early mornings, nap time, and late at night. I still find it funny when I am on the phone and Lauren lets out screaming, and the attorneys that I am speaking with are caught off guard—and there are very few times when attorneys do not know what to say. Nothing is the same as before. It is different. You just adjust every detail of your life.
—Shanda

Finding that magic balance between work and family is a challenge for most parents. When you are overwhelmed by what's going on at home, it can be difficult to concentrate at work. Tim puts it this way: "The challenge is that I'm not allowed to make a mistake, and that's really hard right now. My bosses are fair, keeping everything in mind. But sometimes they lose sight of family being a priority. Sometimes they forget or give me a look of disapproval."

For most parents of preemies, the first few months are the most difficult. As time goes on, you find more time and energy for work. If you're in a bind in the early months, turn to your relatives and friends for practical and emotional help. If your child has ongoing special needs that disrupt your work or sleep, this can be especially taxing and you need to employ long-term strategies to find a reasonable balance.

Employment and Identity

When you have a premature baby, your decisions about working outside the home or parenting full-time may be especially loaded. On the one hand, you may value the way you feel at work. Your job provides a familiar routine and a sense of mastery. On the other hand, you value being with your baby. Deciding whether to work outside the home or to be a full-time parent is a personal choice, one you have to base on what's best for you, your children, and your family.

Returning to Work Having a preemie can change your personal goals—or change how you'll go about reaching your goals. Finding or holding on to your occupational, professional, employed self is often both challenging and critical to your personal identity and overall development. If you do not feel that you or your baby are best off with you as the full-time caregiver, remember that working outside the home can be an anchor that helps you feel competent and grounded. Choosing to work outside the home does not make you any less loving, nurturing, attuned, or effective a parent to your little one.

I was an idealist when I decided that I wanted to have children. I was captivated with the idea of having children without giving much thought at that point to the practicality of raising them. Jack was much more realistic about what raising them would entail. From our earliest discussions about parenting, he insisted that we could not bring children into the world and then leave them in day care ten hours a day. What worked best in our circumstances was for him to be the at-home parent.

I was grateful to have a husband willing to make this level of commitment to his (future) children, but I also had some trepidation. My biggest fear is that they would always prefer him, that they would cry for daddy when they were hurt or sick, that they would prefer daddy over mommy when they craved comfort and affection. [But my] fears about having a stay-at-home dad were unfounded. I've had the privilege of watching my husband evolve into a marvelous father. ... I am convinced daily that their lives will be all the richer for it. And they still need me. They call to me, cling to me, seek comfort from me, as they do their father. They have, in my opinion, the enviable experience of having a deeply connected, richly layered relationship with both of their parents, both of whom are entwined in their daily lives. We didn't "switch roles." We don't have a homemaker/breadwinner arrangement. We've had the incredible opportunity to construct an arrangement that allows our children to move easily and often from the guidance of one parent to another. —Susan

If you find yourself eager to go back to work, recognize that your work has tremendous meaning to you. The stimulation, networking, accomplishments, and creative outlet your job provides may help you heal and thrive. A nourishing job can be a respite from the more difficult parts of your life. Rather than considering yourself "selfish," see your ambitions as a healthy sign that you can emerge from the chaos of preemie parenthood and regain your drive and direction around personal or career goals. Just because you have a preemie doesn't mean your world has to revolve around that fact forever. Even when your baby or child has extraordinary needs, you can be a working parent *and* be a fully attentive and engaged parent to your little one. Whether you work outside the home for financial reasons or because it feeds your soul, remind yourself that doing so can help you to be a better mother or father to your precious child.

Recognize that juggling work and family is a complex task, and that your decision making is likely to evolve over time. You don't have to decide your entire future today. Make interim plans, and change your goals to fit.

I think that I always knew that I would return to working after the babies were born. But when I went on bed rest, I obviously had to stop working immediately, and it seemed impossible to me to go back when the girls were born—I was too preoccupied and the medical situation was too uncertain.

What ended up happening was that I gradually started to work again, and I was able to manage the transitions a little bit at a time. Early on, because we had developmental follow-up visits and pulmonology appointments, working much wasn't practical. It was sort of a relief to have a good reason not to work more at that time since at first, I didn't really want to be away from them. As time has gone on and their needs have become more typical, it's been easier to separate (for my work and their school). By the time I started working a full day, I was really comfortable with our sitter, and had developed a rhythm with mothering, pumping, and working. ...

But the feeling of being in the wrong place when I'm at work is still strong—and the need to get work done when I'm at home interferes with my parenting. I'm often torn even though I really love what I do professionally. —Rikki

When you work outside the home, it's natural to feel pulled between two deeply felt needs. You can love your child and also love your work. Figure out ways to feel fulfilled in both your parenting and work roles so that you don't feel cheated or negligent in either. Pick your priorities and find the compromises that let you reach for a healthy balance that feels best for you and your family. (For more on this, see "Fine-Tuning the Balance between Parenting and Career" later in this chapter. For support around enlisting other caregivers, see "Finding Caregivers You Can Trust" in Chapter 12.)

Staying Home

We had already decided that I would stay at home no matter what happened. In fact, I don't ever remember discussing any other option with Susan. ...

Stuart's prematurity and the loss of his twin twisted my life around three ways from Sunday, but it didn't affect the role I was to play. —Jack

Before Charlotte, I had a complicated pregnancy that ended in the death of my first daughter at full term, so it's difficult to tease out what led to my decision to stay home after Charlotte was born three months early. It's all tangled up together. But her prematurity and NICU experience are central to my decision, and probably on their own would have led me to change my plans. This experience changed my priorities. —Kate

During pregnancy, many moms and some dads plan to scale back or quit their jobs to stay home after their baby arrives. Many other parents intend to return to their jobs after parental leave, but a premature birth often changes plans. It's only natural that your baby's prematurity casts a new light on how you see the balance between work and family.

There are a number of reasons that may compel you to be a stay-at-home parent after your preemie's birth.

- You might decide that staying home full time is the best choice because of your preemie's increased vulnerability to infection, ongoing special needs, or your own reluctance to leave your preemie in the care of another.

- When you add up all the expenses of working outside the home, including transportation, wardrobe, meals, child care, taxes, and payroll deductions, you may discover that you would be left with only a fraction of your salary. You may well decide that the money your work would bring in is not worth the price you and your family would pay in increased stress or risk.

- Even if working outside the home would be financially lucrative, there is still the challenge of balancing your child's needs with your job responsibilities. You may decide that you're not up for an intense juggling act, and that staying home, especially during your preemie's formative years, is the best option.

- You may struggle to find quality day care. Like any parent, you know that you want the best care for your little one, with a warm and conscientious caregiver. If you're in a bind and leave your baby in a situation that you don't feel good about, you're bound to grieve, and your grief may take the form of depression or anger at the workplace that requires this separation. This situation isn't good for the baby, you, or your company.

- Even if affordable, high-quality day care is available, you might feel that your hands-on, daily nurturing is essential to your baby's development and your family's happiness. After what you've been through, staying at home with your baby can feel like a healing thing for you to do.

In addition to a priorities shift, Dave and I also felt that, as a practical matter, Charlotte was at risk for developmental delays and might receive early intervention services, so it would be optimal for one of us to stay home and foster her growth and development—it just felt right to us. Dave can make more money with his job than I've been able to recently, so it was a practical decision for me to stay home. We don't have a lot of money but we have made it work. I also wanted to stay home for emotional reasons—I was more attached to wanting to be with her full time. —Kate

Adjusting to Staying Home If you've quit working outside the home to be a full-time parent, your decision may trigger a personal crisis. Your role will suddenly shift, not just to being a stay-at-home parent to this baby, but also to no longer being engaged in your work, as before. Whether you decide to scale back your hours or quit entirely, you have to adjust to the fact that you're on a different career track. Even if you eagerly embrace your new role, you may still miss that other part of your life and struggle with your changing identity. Here are some tips for adjusting to your role as a stay-at-home parent.

- Change how you think about your productivity. If you are used to judging your productivity by how much money you bring in, by your accomplishments on the job, or by the esteem of your colleagues, staying home might feel utterly unproductive at first glance. But if you figure out how much it would cost to hire someone to do all you do at home, know that this is the amount of money you are saving for your family. If you make a list of everything you do in a day or a week, you can see how much managing, organizing, balancing, mediating, guiding, and budgeting you do. The accolades of little smiles and sloppy kisses are priceless. Feel your own pride as you look at the home and family life you've created.

- Maintain some sense of professional or occupational identity. Depending on your field, volunteer work, occasional consulting, and temporary, seasonal, or part-time work are some ways to keep a toe in the workforce. Attending a workshop or training session, or reading relevant books and articles can keep you up-to-date. Think of yourself as being on an extended sabbatical. You needn't have a job to feel connected to your career or work interests.
- Identify your losses. If you feel compelled to leave your job because it simply can't accommodate your family's needs or if you're obligated to stay home because your baby's needs are so high, it may seem like your baby's premature birth has swept away your vision for your own future. This can entail an enormous loss, which you must grieve in order to be able to come to terms with and embrace your new role.
- Face your feelings. Many parents struggle with feeling resentful, unimportant, unproductive, and unfulfilled as they adjust to staying at home. You might also feel that what's being demanded of you as a parent is more than you can give. When you can honestly identify and face these struggles, you can find ways to manage and cope. And if you continue to struggle and get to a point where, for you, the challenges far outweigh the joys, you'll know that you've got to create a better situation—for yourself and your family. Your yearnings can keep you focused on what you want your life to be like.

I have always been very career-oriented, and [after having] my babies, in particular Charlotte, I still feel excited about working outside of the home, but I have felt that I can take a pause, and it will all be okay. I'll probably be a better parent and a better professional. I have this child, and I want to be home with her during these early years, and I'll return to the working world as she begins her formal education.

I am inclined to second-guess myself a lot, but this is something that has felt like a sacred decision and one that fills me with certainty. I have always been a strong feminist and believed that women can have and deserve the careers they want to have. They can balance them with family. So can men, for that matter. I also feel that as a society we tend to devalue the domestic sphere and child raising in general. But I don't feel as though I am "just" home with my little daughter. I've made a valuable choice. Also, [instead of] judging myself based on what I "do," lately I think more about who I am; what I do is just part of that. I am many things and life ebbs and flows in various stages. —Kate

Well I guess since I didn't want to have kids in the first place, you could say I've struggled mightily with adjusting to my role as parent. Especially, with all that we've been through with Stuart, his twin, and now Justin.

Having the intestinal fortitude to not scream at the baby who's been screaming at you (with an earache) for the past three hours. Having the patience to finish changing one really dirty, stinking diaper while your other child is throwing up on the rug with the flu. Having the imagination and thoughtfulness to pack a snack, a drink, an extra binky, two spoons, and wet wipes in the cooler before you leave the house—even though you're already four minutes late for your pediatrician appointment. These are all important adjustments that you must make in order to survive any given day. Perhaps the hardest thing I've encountered so far, is that this stay-at-home-parent job is one that requires my presence seven days a week, twenty-four hours a day. It just never ends. I mean, you really understand the term "going postal."

Having children is the hardest job I've ever had in my life. I've worked as a plumber and crawled under houses coming face to face with rats while trying to fix a water leak. I've actually dug four-foot-deep ditches in ten degree cold. I've broken up concrete roads with a jackhammer during a summer that topped out at 110 degrees. AND I've been married for twenty-one years. None of those jobs are as hard as raising children. In fact, I've always said that if the members of the U.S. House of Representatives and the U.S. Senate ALL had to stay at home and raise children for six months, stay-at-home parents would receive tax breaks that would make Microsoft jealous.

I guess having kids was never meant to be an easy task. It's never boring and always rewarding. It's not just a job, it's an adventure. —Jack

Fine-Tuning the Balance between Parenting and Career

If only there were more hours in the day ... sometimes I wonder if we'd be better off as a family if I quit work to stay at home but I know I'd go crazy and drive everyone else nuts in the meantime ... but something has to give. How do other working parents find time to get help for their kids? Trying to schedule a psychologist's appointment that both of us can attend with Curtis while there's child care for Ellie is a nightmare! —Melissa

I do find that I'm the sort of person who needs to be working—I'd be a terrible stay-at-home-mom, I think. But I have to say that juggling mothering and working is really, really hard. I often feel guilty about the hours that I work, and the only reason that I can sustain this structure is because of our sitter and my husband who round out the caregiving team. —Rikki

All parents struggle at times to balance parenting and career. Whether you've returned to your job or are staying home, if you feel ambivalent about your decision, remember that it does not have to be an all-or-nothing choice.

Take some time to think through what both your career and your parenting role mean to you. For example, is your job, career, or schooling an obligation or a calling? What are the most meaningful and rewarding elements of your job or career goals? Similarly, identify the parenting tasks and experiences that are most meaningful and rewarding to you and your child. What are the family experiences that you consider most important or precious?

Next, consider the ways you can pursue the important aspects of your work and hold on to the most meaningful and rewarding elements of your parenting role. For example, you can stay informed and find ways to be connected to your career, or gradually or eventually get back into the workforce as your child's needs change. When you are working, putting your child in the care of someone you trust is a way to fulfill your responsibility as a nurturing parent. Feeling comfortable with your child care arrangement can be key to your peace of mind.

Mostly of course, we do what circumstances require us to do. But I am deeply grateful for my husband's foresight in insisting that we arrange our lives so that we could be the full-time caregivers to our child, because by the time we [brought Stuart home], handing him over to someone else seemed inconceivable. To whom could I possibly entrust this responsibility? I barely trusted us.

If you talked to people who know us, friends and family, most all of them would tell you that we are good parents, but most all of them would tell you that we are overprotective parents. I believe that is our privilege as parents

who've lost a child and seen a second through more than a few life-threatening
challenges. Nothing else will occur on our watch, if we can prevent it. ...
I'm thankful that when I am at work, the person caring for my sons is someone
who shares that perspective, someone who might be just a little too careful, but
is someone on guard. I couldn't ask that of a day care provider, but, because
of what we have weathered together, I don't have to ask that of their dad.
—Susan

Whether you choose to be a parent who stays home or a parent who
works outside the home, the crux of the matter is not what you decide, but
how you came to your decision and how you balance your priorities with it.
Whether working outside the home or staying home feels imperative, you can
appreciate that caring for your little one is an honorable and valuable
endeavor and modify your career path to suit that need. Whether that modifi-
cation is slight or significant, let obtaining balance be your guide. Be clear
about your feelings, motives, and priorities. Remember that you can attend to
your child's needs as well as your own development as an individual. Cultivate
feelings of worth based on who you are, not what you do, and strive to ensure
the quality of your family life, your inner life, and your life's work.

A lot of friends have disagreed with my decision to be a stay-at-home mom, to
give Zack an edge since his start in life certainly didn't give him one. I feel that
a lot of my friends don't respect me for this choice. I have two master's degrees,
and I am sure that many people see my life now as a "waste," but I couldn't
be happier with my choice.—Terri

It's okay to modify your goals over time. You might have planned to
return to work after a parental leave, but reconsider, and instead you decide to
leave the workforce. Or you might have imagined staying home as a full-time
parent, but later realized that you need the respite or stimulation of your work
environment to rejuvenate your parenting. Whatever you decide, it's also okay
to plan for your employment status to be a temporary phase or to reconsider
after a few months or years. The bottom line is identifying what fulfills you.
Find the balance that helps you feel your best and fine-tune it as you and your
baby grow and change.

• • •

Hindsight—being the wonderful tool that it is—allows me to see that the path I've chosen [being a stay-at-home dad] has been terribly costly, but infinitely fulfilling. To be truthful, before we had children I felt like I was "spinning my wheels." I wasn't going anywhere or heading toward anything worthwhile. I was having fun traveling, vacationing, and playing through life, but there was no value in what I was doing in my job. There was nothing to "go off to war for." There were no dragons to slay. There were no giants to kill. ...

[Now] I feel like I'm making a difference by shaping two young lives. I want to teach them to be patient. To be compassionate. To be someone who works hard and treats others as they wish to be treated. To be someone who stands up for what's right when everyone else around you wants to take the easy way out. That's [what] I needed in my life. By the way, I learn something new from Stuart and Justin every day. They're the best teachers I've ever had—and that's saying something. —Jack

Running the Household

We did not need condolences nearly as much as we need real, practical help. Having a premature baby is an enormous drain on a family's resources. I have remembered this when trying to help other parents. Do they need financial help? Can I clean house? Can I bring food? Most of all, can I babysit other children? Can I visit the hospital and hold the baby? —Renee

Whether you work in the home or out, you must find ways to take care of the chores and errands that make a house a home. Whether you're trying to juggle the responsibilities of a job, a preemie who is still hospitalized or has special needs, other children who need tending, the mounting piles of insurance paperwork, or the dust bunnies multiplying in every corner, keeping the household running often means asking for some help.

If you pride yourself on your independence or shy away from asking others for assistance, reaching out will be especially difficult. But remember that your family and friends are probably eager to know what they can do to give you some practical support. Helping you can make them feel less helpless. They may, in fact, ask you what they can do to assist you.

We found that people (those we knew and even those we barely or didn't know) felt a strong need to help us in some way. And we needed help. From helping us finish packing and moving to bringing us meals or taking me to the store (I wasn't allowed to drive), we asked for help. It made them feel like they contributed, and it helped us out in many ways. —Cindy

To make the most of those offers of help, list all the chores and errands and responsibilities that need to be taken care of. Include all those things you've been planning to get to, but just can't seem to fit in: things like big grocery-shopping trips, going to the post office, calling the insurance company, organizing bills, doing laundry, vacuuming, washing floors, or cooking meals. List things that you really need to have done and also things that will just help you feel as if your life isn't falling apart. Don't forget about mowing the lawn, shoveling snow, cleaning the kitty litter box, or walking the dog. When people ask you what they can do to help, show them the list and let them choose. If they offer to do something that isn't on the list, consider accepting their offer if it strikes you as something that could help you out.

Your primary responsibility at this time is to devote your energy to being with your baby, whether in the hospital or at home, and to be with your family. Allow your social network to support you so that you can tend to your priorities.

A good friend of mine recently gave birth to premature twins, and I desperately wanted to do for her all that had not been done for me. It included many things, but also I wanted to reassure her that she had done a fine job bringing two beautiful babies into the world. I also felt it was important to continue helping in the weeks and months after the birth, when life can really get difficult just as friends and family fade away. —Renee

Reaching Out for Help Asking for help, especially practical help, can be difficult for some people. Making a list is often the first step—but being able to present that list to others can be challenging. For many people, being *emotionally* able to ask for help is the real stumbling block.

If you recognize that it's hard for you to ask for help, to hand over some of your obligations to others, or to enlist professional support, take a moment to think about where this resistance comes from. Perhaps you measure your

Parenting Your Premature Baby and Child

competence in terms of your ability to manage on your own or with minimal support. It can be difficult to give up control in yet another area when you seem to have lost so much control already.

If you can identify your roadblocks to reaching out for support, you'll be better able to surmount them and get what you need. If you're afraid of appearing weak, acknowledge the courage it takes to recognize your limits. When crisis pushes you beyond your limits, you haven't become incapable, you've become swamped with more than anyone should have to handle alone. If you fear things won't be done "right," entertain the possibility that your helpers may do some things even better than you do, especially if you assign tasks according to others' talents and strengths. If you're worried about giving up control, remind yourself that you're delegating to regain control. If you're worried about imposing on others, recall how rewarding it feels to give and be of service. Everybody needs different kinds of help at different times. Your time is now. Reflect on what you need the most, then figure out who can provide it and how to ask for it.

Points to Remember

- Dealing with the outside world in the midst of your crisis can seem jarring and surreal.
- Depend on close friends and family to support you emotionally, but remember that the people who care about you may struggle with how to be most helpful.
- Other parents of premature babies can be the most consistently supportive and soothing group of people to talk with. Search for them through hospital networks, local support groups, and on the Internet. However you make the connection with them, parents of preemies can be your lifeline.
- Your own parents are also grieving—both for your pain and over their precious grandchild's struggle. Making special requests that tap their talents and strengths compels reluctant grandparents to make a meaningful contribution and redirects the involvement of overbearing grandparents. Asking them for help also ameliorates grandparents' feelings of helplessness and strengthens their connection with you and your baby.

- Friends and family may try to minimize or dismiss your concerns, or they may be so distressed themselves that there's no room for *your* feelings. Don't expect those who were distant before to suddenly be attentive and set limits with those who move in too close.
- Extended-family members and friends often stumble when trying to be empathic and supportive. Assume that even their clumsiest attempts are well-meaning. If you have the energy, let them know how you feel and what you think you need from them. Remind them that just listening really helps. Your closest friends *want* to know how to support you.
- Talking to strangers or acquaintances about your experience can be surprisingly therapeutic if they are able to listen—or draining and aggravating if they are set on giving inappropriate advice. If you don't want to explain your preemie's situation, don't feel that you must. If you do want to educate others, decide how much to divulge in each situation.
- You may feel different from other parents for a long time. This is normal, not a sign that something is wrong with you. But as your preemie grows and you come to terms with your experiences, you'll find common threads and ways to connect with other parents.
- Seeing pregnant women may bring on a twinge of envy or sadness. Keep distant from those touchy situations as long as you need to and enlist the support of those who understand your vulnerability.
- Figure out ways to feel fulfilled in your role as parent and in your job so that you don't feel cheated or negligent in either. Pick your priorities and find the compromises that fit. Whatever your situation, strive for a healthy balance between job and parenting.
- Juggling work, household, other children, and your preemie's special needs can be a challenge. Allow your social network to support you so that you can tend to your priorities. If you work outside the home, negotiate for flexibility in your job.

CHAPTER TWENTY-ONE

Considering Another Pregnancy

After the premature birth of a baby, most parents wrestle with whether—and if so, when—to get pregnant again. Like so many aspects of being a parent of a preemie, it's normal to have mixed feelings. One day you may vow never to get pregnant again, and the next you may long to give birth to another child. These back-and-forth feelings can happen whether you originally envisioned a larger family or planned on your preemie being your last baby.

Whatever your situation, many issues and emotions can enter into your decision about a subsequent pregnancy. This chapter looks at the decision-making process, as well as some ideas about obtaining vigilant prenatal care and suitable childbirth education. Chapter 22 addresses coping during a subsequent pregnancy (high risk or not) and what happens after delivery, whether your new baby is full-term or preterm.

Should We Try Again?

The decision to have another baby ... it wasn't "normal." It was met with a lot of fear instead of joy. It was also met with a lot of medical technology—in testing to make sure that the problems I had then were not an underlying problem that would affect and hinder another pregnancy. —Donna

The question of whether to have another child is often complicated for many couples, but when anxiety or risk factors compound the decision, the choice is neither easy nor stress-free. If you have struggled with infertility, if one or more of your babies died, or if you have your hands full raising multiples or a child with special needs, the pregnancy decision becomes particularly complex. You may recognize that there can be many joys to raising an only child or the number you already have, or you may feel that you should quit while you're ahead. You also feel particularly vulnerable to misfortune, now that you *know* it can happen to you. Even if the odds of another preterm birth are slim, you may not want to risk it.

There was about an 80 percent chance that everything would be fine. ... Somehow that 20 percent chance that it wouldn't sticks in your mind because you don't want to see your baby behind glass being poked and prodded.
—*Donna*

Trying again is scary. I asked the doctor, "What's the chance of this happening again?" and he said, "About as infinitesimal as its happening the first time." ... It's very scary. Very scary. And you know, until this happened to me, I didn't think that it happened to people who had good prenatal care and took care of themselves. I thought it was reserved for the drug addicts, alcoholics, generalized abusers. ... When you know what kinds of things can go wrong, there isn't any certainty. I don't think I'll go through another pregnancy joyful. I'll go through another pregnancy terrified. —Micki

To be honest, the thought of having another preemie has almost made me decide to get my tubes tied. The doctors have no way of knowing if my chances of having another preemie are higher than normal or not, but the thought of even going there again terrifies me. I can't imagine riding that roller coaster again. —Sterling

In contrast, many mothers sense that for them, another pregnancy is the healing thing to do. A new pregnancy may be full of positive meaning. If you're wrestling with feelings of loss or failure over your last pregnancy, a new pregnancy can bolster your hope for the future. If you want to experience having a healthy full-term newborn, trying again is a renewed effort to achieve that goal. Holding on to hope and imagining your success can boost your confidence.

Getting pregnant again was almost an insane obsession. I had a void that needed to be filled. It was terrifying being pregnant, but I had to. I had to prove to myself that I could do it, and I had to prove that I didn't have an incompetent cervix. I needed answers. I had to prove that my body could do this because I was still angry at my cervix, even though it hadn't done anything wrong. I needed to heal all these wounds. I needed to hold my baby when it was born. I needed to be able to take my baby home with me after it was born. I needed to be able to buy clothes for my baby because I knew it was going to live. I needed to be able to have a normal, healthy experience to make some emotional healing. —Stephie

I was very much in love with the idea of being pregnant. Maybe it was because I wanted that perfect pregnancy very much, or maybe it was that I just needed to prove to myself that I wasn't a failure as a woman. Maybe it was just because after losing our last baby, I wanted so badly to have the chance to hold a baby again. Maybe in a way I thought it would make the feelings of loss go away, or maybe I had just fallen in love with him already. All I know is I was ecstatic, scared, worried, happy—all in one. —Angie

I miss being pregnant. I hadn't gotten to that uncomfortable stage yet. I had just started to enjoy it. I was starting to feel her kicking me and stuff. It was kinda cool. ... I don't really feel so much like a failure any more, but the next time I get pregnant, which isn't going to happen for a long time, I want to do it right. I want to have the baby at nine months. That's one of the things I really want to do ... and then I want to be able to hold my baby right after. —Brooke

I want to have another baby just so that I can make up for what I missed. —Rosa

Not every parent has such clarity about whether or not to embark on another pregnancy. For many parents, any hopeful, eager, and happy feelings about another pregnancy are tempered by anxiety. A subsequent pregnancy can be a healing thing to do, but it can also be a challenging prospect. You may hesitate.

If you're vacillating about this decision, you may simply need more time to come to some resolution. Over time, the decision may become more obvious to you.

> *Jon and I have discussed the possibility of having another baby in a few years, when Sean is bigger and has hopefully outgrown some of his illnesses. I'm just afraid that something will go wrong with that pregnancy too. So, we've decided that before we try to have another baby, I'm seeing a gynecologist to make sure there is nothing wrong with my body that may have caused Sean to be born early. If there is, I'm having my tubes tied. I don't want to take a chance on having another baby and have it come earlier than Sean did, have more problems, or die. —Ami*

> *We want another baby and of course are worried because I will be classified as high risk automatically. We want a normal pregnancy this time—not another case of placenta trouble. I will take more time for the pregnancy— take more time to relax, not put myself under stress, monitor my blood pressure, take more calcium (it might help blood circulation in the placenta), keep educating myself. —Sara*

If you've struggled with infertility, the death of more than one baby, or more than one preterm delivery, you may wonder, "How many times can I go through this before giving up?" Don't try to answer that unanswerable question. Instead, ask yourself if you want to try *one more time*. Whatever your answer, that's what you need to know.

Of course, not every couple makes a purposeful decision about a subsequent pregnancy. You may conceive when you weren't planning to. Or you may feel ambivalent: either conception happens, or it doesn't. As Vickie discovered, the passage of time can help you forget the trauma, and you may simply be less careful about birth control:

> *We decided, after going through all the things we'd been through with my son, that we just couldn't go through it again. It was too much. It wasn't just the pregnancy, it wasn't just the NICU experience, it wasn't just that whole first*

year afterwards, it was all of it combined—it was too much. But after my son and daughter were five, six, seven years old, it was nagging on me that this was it, I'm never going to have any more. ...

This is it? I really wished we had more kids. But we could never come together on that. Well, one night we did. It was funny, because the next day, we were like, "This is not *a good idea, because we could really be in for it." When you get past it, for us by seven and a half years, you think that you can get through it and it wasn't that bad—*if *you don't think about it. When you really start to think about it, you remember how bad it was.*

Anyway, sure enough, I was pregnant. And I thought, okay, all right, this is a good thing. Now remember, I did have a daughter who went full term after they had said it wouldn't easily be done, so it's very likely that I could do that again. So we just kept to the really positive side of things. [But this baby was born premature, too.]

So now I'm not having any more babies. I can't go through it again. It's too much. I got a lovely third baby out of it. ... If I had known, no, I never would have gone through it. I never would have. But when you get that baby and you see that baby and you realize that, okay, it's worth it. Everything I've gone through is worth it. ... We knew that this pregnancy would be a risk. We just hoped it wouldn't be as bad as it was. But I'm glad now we went through it because now I have a wonderful little baby. He's so cute. —Vickie

For many couples, the decision about whether to have another baby is complicated, and there is no clearly right way to go. Vickie is living proof that there are potential benefits and risks either way. The best you can do is take into account that each path has its own rewards and figure out which risks you're willing to take. Then follow your heart.

Exploration and Discussion

If you're considering another pregnancy, you're bound to have questions for your doctor, and perhaps for a perinatologist—an obstetrician specializing in maternal-fetal health. Your most burning question may be, "How likely is it that I'll delivery early again?" If unpredictable or unusual pregnancy complications caused your previous baby's early birth, your doctor or midwife may consider it a "fluke" that probably won't happen again. Likewise, if your early delivery was the result of a predictable condition or event that is unlikely to recur or that is responsive to treatment, your health care providers may reassure you that you'll likely go to term this time. You may be certain in your own mind that your shortened pregnancy was the result of carrying multiples or another cause that you'll probably be able to manage or avoid this time with monitoring and vigilance.

For some causes of preterm delivery, such as placental abruption or preterm premature rupture of membranes, the low risks of recurrence might feel manageable. If you had placenta previa or a systemic complication such as preeclampsia or gestational diabetes, though, you may be more concerned about a recurrence. And if your premature delivery came about because of your own life-threatening illness, even if the risk of recurrence is low, that small risk may seem too high.

I do not want to go through this again, but I would very much like to have another child. Family members think I'm crazy for even considering it, so I feel like I would not have much support if things did go wrong again. —Terri

Unfortunately, in about 50 percent of cases, the cause of premature birth remains a mystery. If your preterm delivery is unexplained, you may feel unnerved by the uncertainty surrounding your level of risk or unclear about what measures you can take to prevent recurrence.

There are tests you can take before becoming pregnant and monitoring that can be done during a subsequent pregnancy so that your doctor can assess risks. Of course, nobody can give you guarantees, but whether the cause of your preterm delivery was determined or not, you can make informed decisions by asking questions and gathering information.

Learning about risk factors and signs of complications and, when possible, finding out the reasons behind your baby's premature delivery can give you a sense of mastery. Even though you couldn't control what happened, you can at least try to understand it. And if you have hopes for a future pregnancy, you can hold on to some optimism that what caused the problems the first time can be prevented or at least mitigated in a subsequent pregnancy.

Oh, do we ever want another baby!!! It is a very emotional topic for my husband and me knowing the risks. There seem to be many bridges to cross before it can become a reality (lots of research, trying to lose weight, lower my blood pressure, and eat better). I think that this issue is one of the reasons that I still have a tough time dealing with what happened the first time around. I am very scared of what could happen the second time. —Stacy

Making Decisions with Your Partner

My husband does not want to risk going through this again and feels the strain of the demands of parenthood. I have never had a strong need to have more than one child, but I am still open to the idea. My obstetrician said that the fact that this happened is just random chance, and there is a good chance I could have a normal pregnancy. So I am going to wait and see what it is like to parent a two-year-old, three-year-old, and so on, before asking my husband again about it. But if he doesn't want to, I won't push. —Mary

It's common for couples to feel uncertain about embarking on another pregnancy. One way a couple can express this uncertainty is for each partner to take an opposing position. You may even switch positions occasionally, trying on the opposing point of view. Because having each other's support during a subsequent pregnancy is so important, you're wise to wait until you both agree before taking the leap.

What if you're ready and your partner isn't? When you are at odds with each other over this decision, here are some ways to communicate about it.

- Instead of trying to talk your partner into agreeing to embark on another pregnancy, try listening. By encouraging your partner to talk about feelings and fears, you may be able to provide the support he or she needs to feel ready.
- By listening, you may also discover that you share many similar thoughts and feelings. This sense of common ground can be reassuring evidence that you agree more than you disagree.
- Remember that you each have a different perspective on the previous pregnancy. If you're the mother, you probably have feelings of vulnerability and failure that center on your body's ability to carry a pregnancy to term. If you're the father, you may have special fears about the mother's health and safety, especially if she almost lost her life last time. Sharing your perspectives can give you insight on ways to better support each other through this decision about another pregnancy.

- Be patient. You can't force someone to adjust or work through feelings. Simply easing off and reducing the pressure may give your partner the space he or she needs to move toward another pregnancy.
- Be aware that the more obsessed you are with getting pregnant, the more your partner may resist. By consciously putting the issue on hold, you may enable your spouse to feel more open to another pregnancy.

If you find yourself obsessed with getting pregnant, how can you stop focusing solely on this goal? Try putting your thoughts in a journal. By unloading them, you may reduce their obsessive quality. Attending to your emotional needs is another way to reduce obsession. In fact, your obsession may be serving to distract you from painful feelings of grief. Try to set aside time to work through your feelings about your baby's prematurity, hospitalization, and any ongoing challenges. Dwell on your memories about the pregnancy, delivery, and your baby's NICU stay. Facing your feelings can help you feel less desperate to move on to another pregnancy.

Also recognize that a new pregnancy will not fix the one that ended prematurely, nor will it erase your need to grieve. Another pregnancy can be part of your healing, but it won't banish persistent feelings of failure, guilt, or sadness. Working through your grief is the fundamental tonic that will bring you lasting peace and happiness.

Deciding against Another Pregnancy

I was so affected with the whole process of having him that I immediately had my tubes tied four months later to ensure never going through that again!
—Dawn

If you find yourself thinking that you cannot bear any more sorrow, risk, or tension, this can signal that you're becoming ready to move away from the reproductive phase of your life.

You may conclude that you're destined to have complicated pregnancies and not want to revisit that ordeal. Even if medical judgment points toward success, your intuition may tell you that your outcome won't match the statistical tables.

I don't do well with pregnancies, and I definitely would never take a chance of going through what I went through. I know logically that I have only a slight, slight risk, and the chances are better than good that I could have a totally normal pregnancy next time, but there is absolutely no way. I will never go through that again. —Jaimee

I never got pregnant again and did not attempt to do so. In fact, I avoided it like the plague! I had no desire to ever go through that again. I sought counsel from some of the premier high-risk ob-gyns in this part of the country, and after they looked at my records, they told me that they could not guarantee me a full-term birth the next time, but they would try to make it easier for me. After much discussion with my hubby, we decided that because I was having other medical problems and because my pregnancy was so traumatic, I would not be getting pregnant again. I was interested in adoption, but he wasn't. I would have liked for Stef to have a sibling or two, but life does not always work out the way you would like it to. I felt fortunate just to have her. —Janet

The thought of spending time and emotional energy thinking about getting pregnant when you could be devoting your attention to the child you've already been given may be overwhelming. You may decide that your energies are best devoted to the precious child, or children, you already have.

We may decide that not getting pregnant again is the best route for us. We are not decided fully yet, but knowing how some preemies' outcomes are much worse than my son's, that is something I could not deal with. … I don't want another sick baby to take away from my time with Zackary. … I don't want to miss a milestone with Zackary because I was lying in a hospital on my left side and forcing fluids. —Terri

We decided not to have another baby after Vincent. We thought we'd had a narrow escape and didn't want to press our luck. An even bigger concern for me was not wanting to take anything from the time and energy I had to care for Vincent. [Plus] Jessica was only two when Vincent was born, and she certainly missed out in the year that followed and to a lesser degree his second year. —Anne

• • •

737

Considering Another Pregnancy

It can be very difficult to give up your dreams. You may grieve deeply. After all, you're giving up the possibility, however remote, of experiencing the many exciting and sweet moments that pregnancy and babies can bring.

I'm really sad we didn't have a third child. Sometimes I even feel that there's someone missing from our family unit. Now that I'm too old to have another baby, I wish we'd not been so afraid to try again. Of course, the possibility of having an extremely premature baby remains terrifying. It's so hard to make these decisions and live with them. —Anne

Even though the decision to forego pregnancy can feel difficult and sad, it can be the right decision for you. Whatever your situation, it's natural to feel sorrow when you know you'll never again carry life within you. Shed the tears you need to. In time, as you mourn, this loss will become easier to bear. Particularly if you must quit trying before you're ready or if quitting seems difficult to bear, do something to honor the babies that might have been. You might, for example, want to make or buy a baby blanket, a stuffed animal, or an article of baby clothing. Doing things like this can be quite comforting. In general, do what you need to do to cope with your feelings of grief, and eventually you can accept that you're heading in a new direction. Over time, you start envisioning the many different ways in which life can be fulfilling.

Also recognize that although you may be unable or unwilling to undertake another pregnancy, you can still indulge your nurturing urges. There are many children in the world who can use the guidance of responsible, caring adults. Whether you adopt, volunteer at a children's hospital, become involved in developing social policy that favors children, or simply extend a helping hand or warm smiles to the kids in your neighborhood, you can feel the rewards that come with nurturing little ones.

Reconsidering Your "Ideal" Family Size

Most parents think about how many children they'd like to raise. While some parents hold a tentative vision, others vividly picture their ideal family, whether it includes one child or five. When facing unexpected financial, logistical, or medical realities, however, many parents find they must revise their dreams. A particularly active or high-need child can modify that vision. And struggles with infertility, high-risk pregnancies, multiple losses, or multiple babies can alter the best-laid plans.

The bottom line is, the more vulnerable or overwhelmed you feel, the more likely it is that you'll be inclined to hold back. You may feel like running for cover instead of risking more heartache or taking on more than you can handle. At the same time, you may feel so blessed with what you have that you don't feel the need or desire to push your luck again. Whatever your situation, you'll ultimately let go of what might have been and come to terms with the number of children you are raising.

Deciding to Try Again

The decision to attempt another pregnancy may come about after much detailed discussion with your partner and doctors, or arise intuitively, based on a sense of optimism. The related question then becomes when to take the plunge.

When to Try Again

Many factors play a part in the timing decision. There may be reasons for waiting, as well as reasons for diving right in. Certainly, waiting until the mother has recovered her health gives the pregnancy the best chance of succeeding. Here are some other reasons for waiting:

- You (and your doctors) may need time to uncover what went wrong in the previous pregnancy, so that you can be better prepared next time.
- You may need time to feel more settled in as a parent to your preemie, including developing a degree of competence and comfort managing your preemie's health issues or ongoing special needs.
- You may be working through strong emotions around your baby's early birth and feel that embarking on another pregnancy now would add too much to your turmoil. Waiting may help you be calmer during the next pregnancy.
- You may need time to gather your courage to try again. If the doctors are telling you there is a certain probability that you will have problems with your next pregnancy, you may need time to switch your focus to the probability that you *won't* have problems.
- You may believe you'll be able to enjoy a new baby more after you've had time to recover emotionally from your previous experience.

- Your partner may need time to warm up to the idea of another pregnancy.
- You may have envisioned your children spaced several years apart, so you might not feel a sense urgency about another pregnancy.

On the other hand, some factors may encourage you to dive right in:
- Your "biological clock" is ticking, and you believe that waiting until you "feel better" is unrealistic or could expose you or your unborn baby to additional risk factors.
- You want your children spaced close together.
- You've found an obstetrician who will be especially supportive and vigilant in terms of prenatal care, giving you the courage you need to go ahead.
- You believe that you are managing your fear or anxiety as well as you ever will, so now is as good a time as later.
- If infertility is an issue, you have the sense that you should start trying sooner rather than later. You're acutely aware, in any case, that with infertility you don't have a whole lot of control over "when."
- You are eagerly optimistic, believing that another pregnancy is a chance to recapture some of your lost dreams and that having another baby can give you the positive childbirth experience you long for.
- Your partner is eager to try again and will be supportive of you during this time.

Others, including your doctor, may have opinions about the timing of another pregnancy, but the decision belongs to you and your partner. As you decide, you can weigh and balance the information you gather, your doctor's advice, and your unique physical, emotional, medical, and logistical factors. Deciding for yourself can also help you repair the sense of control over your life that dissolved when your baby was born prematurely.

Here are some of the many factors you'll need to weigh to make the decision that's right for you:
- Ask your doctor questions about what went wrong and what you can do to increase your chances of carrying your baby to term in your next pregnancy.
- Educate yourself about the advantages and disadvantages of postponing pregnancy.

• • •

- Figure out which of the pros and cons apply to your situation, and then decide which ones are the most important to you.
- Consider the balance of your physical and emotional needs.
- Talk to other parents of preemies about their decisions and experiences. Look for books and articles to read. Listening to other perspectives can shed light on what's right for you. (See the section "Health, Pregnancy, Fertility" in Appendix C.)
- You don't have to decide today when (or even whether) to get pregnant. As you mull over the possibilities, you'll find the answer when you're ready. Take it a month at a time. Avoid the pressure to get pregnant by a specific date.
- Your decision making can rely on both rational thought and emotion. Weigh your options and listen to your heart and your intuition.
- Even if you know that waiting is the right decision in your situation, recognize that it can be frustrating. Likewise, even if you feel as ready as you're ever going to be, forging ahead can make you anxious. These feelings are natural and don't necessarily indicate that you should change your decision.
- Whether it occurs sooner or later, another pregnancy can have a healing effect. Take all the time you need.

We had planned before we first got pregnant that we wanted to have our children close together. We would have the first and then not do anything to prevent another, and we stuck to that plan ... and I knew that if we waited, I would be too scared to try again. —Mindy

It took almost eight years to think about trying again. My husband was as scared as I was, maybe more. Before my first child, I never thought about the possibility of having a problem pregnancy. I never thought about what would happen if I couldn't work through the ninth month. Now I had to consider what could happen to my family if we lost half our income, even temporarily. We were also not ready emotionally to face the possibility of repeating the first experience, being now more fully aware of the risks. Further, we found we were happy with a single child and were concerned that we would be "pushing our luck" to risk another pregnancy. —Shaina

•••

Coping with Others' Reactions

What I didn't expect was that my mom would be furious with me—she was so worried. The pregnancy was termed high risk from the start, and I think everyone but Joe thought I was nuts. —Mindy

If you do decide to take the plunge, you may find that some people disapprove. If your previous pregnancy was complicated or if you've struggled with infertility, friends and relatives may express surprise that you're going to try again. If fertility treatments put you at risk for a multiple pregnancy or if you have a history of high-risk pregnancies or definite risk factors for preterm delivery, others may consider your decision "reckless."

It helps to remember that these folks are expressing concern for you and cringe to see you open the door to possible heartache. You can respond to their concerns by saying that you are hopeful about bringing home a healthy baby, and heartache is a risk you're willing to take. You can also mention that you're informed about your risks and plan to be proactive in doing everything you possibly can to ensure a positive outcome. Additionally, you can point out that you're far more concerned for your precious baby's well-being than they could ever imagine! You know that maintaining your own good health is paramount because you want to raise this child. Remind them that you'd appreciate their encouragement and best wishes or prayers during this time.

Prenatal Care

If you decide to attempt another pregnancy, you'll have many worries and questions as you go along. Your pregnancy may go forward without a hitch, or it could take a detour and head for trouble. Whatever your status, it's reasonable for you to demand and receive vigilant and sensitive prenatal care during any subsequent pregnancy.

Working with Your Health Care Providers

If you're considered low risk during this new pregnancy, your health care providers may minimize the concern you feel when you become pregnant and simply encourage you to be optimistic. They may feel uncomfortable with your anxiety or ignore your vestiges of grief. There may be times during this pregnancy when even *you* might feel uncomfortable with the intensity of your emotions.

Whether you are high risk or low risk, it's normal to feel anxious and vulnerable. You'll want to take into account everything you've learned from previous pregnancies to maximize your chances for a healthy baby. To get the reassurance you need, you may want more monitoring than usual. Even if your pregnancy is in no apparent danger, it's natural to want more checkups and to pay more attention to any symptoms.

Here are some ideas for working with your doctor or midwife during a subsequent pregnancy:

- Don't apologize for how you feel. Your feelings make sense, and you are entitled to them. If you think it would help, ask for a referral to a counselor who is knowledgeable about the emotional aspects of childbearing losses, complicated pregnancies, and supporting parents of preemies. You needn't change or deny your feelings to be a "good" patient.
- Surround yourself with emotionally supportive people besides just your obstetric caregivers. Get in touch with other moms who are going through a post-preemie pregnancy. Continue to read books that help you deal with your grief or anxiety. Find friends with whom you can talk about your feelings. Keep a journal. Any of these measures can alleviate the pressure on your doctor or midwife to be your main source of support. (For more on the emotional aspects of a subsequent pregnancy, see Chapter 22.)
- Try to empathize with your health care providers. If you are being followed by a obstetric practice for high-risk pregnancies, you may encounter caregivers who are accustomed to dealing with anxious pregnant mothers. But if your caregivers aren't accustomed to working with medically low-risk moms who feel "high risk," they may find their relationship with you challenging and more complicated than their usual experiences. Your doctor or midwife may feel uneasy and unsure about how to support you; medical training in obstetrics doesn't always include a thorough education on the emotional aspects. To clear the air and build a foundation for a more comfortable partnership with your caregiver, talk openly about your anxiety and need for reassurance.
- Be in charge of your medical care. Empower yourself by acquiring information on pregnancy in general, your medical history and risk

factors, prenatal care, and any other topics that worry you. Accurate information is always an antidote to fear. You may also find that the more you know, the more in control you feel. Practice good prenatal care and educate yourself about the signs and symptoms of problems that could pose a threat to your baby and your pregnancy. Educate yourself about prenatal tests: what they indicate and how they are done. If it helps you to read every book and article you can find on high-risk pregnancy, do it. It's not morbid, it's mastery.

• Don't expect your health care providers to read your mind. Just because you're anxious doesn't mean that they'll know what you need and give it to you. Tell them what's on your mind. Ask for what you need, including information, reassurance, more visits, more monitoring, more or fewer tests. When you tell them what you want and need, your caregivers can be more sensitive and accommodating, even if they can't provide all the answers and make all the promises you desire.

• Recognize that your health care providers cannot always read your body, either. **If you're concerned about any symptoms or sensations, you must let them know that your condition feels worrisome and explicitly request further evaluation and examination to get answers or reassurances. You are your baby's best advocate.** If you ever have concerns that you feel shouldn't wait until office hours, **don't hesitate to call.** Obstetric health care providers expect calls at all hours and would rather head off disaster than have to deal with a full-blown crisis in the morning or after the weekend. Anxiety can be an alarm that draws your attention to imminent danger, and vigilance can sometimes avert trouble. Not every pregnancy complication or preterm delivery can be prevented, *but you can sure try.*

• Make appointments with those in the practice whom you find supportive. You don't have to "get to know" everyone. Should you end up with an unfamiliar doctor with a less-than-comforting bedside manner during delivery, you can still be surrounded by other supportive advocates you bring along, including your partner, a close friend, and a doula (a woman who provides information and emotional/physical support before, during, and after childbirth). If it's important to you to have a particular doctor for this delivery, talk to him or her about your feelings—your favorite doctor may be able to accommodate your request. If you would like more time to talk during appointments, ask the receptionist to budget extra time for you or to schedule your appointments during less hectic hours.

- If you decide to give your health care providers feedback, couch it in terms of what *you* need in this pregnancy (or needed in the earlier one). After all, you can't speak for every parent of a preemie, but you can say what would help (or would have helped) you. For example, "I need(ed) this" rather than "You should do (should have done) this." When you state your needs rather than issuing orders, your doctor or midwife will feel less defensive and more likely to take your suggestions to heart. As a result, you may get more of the support and understanding you need, and you'll increase their sensitivity to all parents of preemies.

You deserve to have a compassionate doctor or midwife who attends to your anxieties, respects your feelings, and works with you for a healthy pregnancy and a healthy baby. Caregivers who brush aside your concerns may increase your worry and make you feel less in control. A dedicated caregiver should be willing to accommodate your needs, displaying how committed he or she is to you and your baby.

It helps when doctors think one step ahead of the symptoms they are seeing or hearing about from their patients. What helps is compassionate care, the kindness, the understanding. Even if things go a different way than expected, having a doctor you can talk to and feel in partnership with, that you can question directly and offer your own insight as a woman, a mother, a patient, both medically and emotionally, means a great deal. I can think back and believe in my heart that my doctors cared for me, they cared for my unborn babies, they grieved along with me when things did not go well, rejoiced by my bedside when they did. That comforts me, and it's one of the things that has and continues to help me cope. —Maureen

Because you have delivered prematurely, you deserve to have the level of care you feel comfortable with, even if the same risk factors are no longer present. You can procure the care of high-risk specialists, whether or not you fit a high-risk profile. If your insurance won't cover ongoing specialized care, you can see a specialist for a second opinion, on a consultation basis with your regular obstetrical caregiver, or intermittently throughout your pregnancy.

Prenatal Diagnostic Testing

In this age of modern medicine, we often assume that the more technology we employ, the better the outcome. With prenatal care, however, it's important to remember that while some tests can improve the outcome, others simply indicate it. Testing can be especially useful when it shows how well the baby is faring in the womb or when it looks for conditions that can be remedied (e.g., hormone levels, amniotic fluid levels, high blood pressure, poor weight gain, infection, gestational diabetes). Treatment for remediable conditions or prompt delivery when a baby is showing signs of distress in the womb often improves outcome.

In contrast, prenatal tests that screen for or diagnose genetic or developmental problems in the baby vary widely in their ability to improve the outcome. If there's nothing that can or will be done if a test indicates potential problems or if having more information won't support you psychologically, then the test may be useless, even detrimental, to you and your baby.

I blamed my "need to control" for many of the problems with my first pregnancy, and I was trying desperately to learn from my experiences and do things differently this time. My doctor held the opinion that I should only have the amnio if I would choose to terminate the pregnancy if it showed [abnormalities]. If I was going to carry this baby to term no matter what the result, he felt there was no reason to subject him to the risks of the amnio procedure. He pointed out that I, of all people, should know that odds don't have a lot of meaning since I had defied so many of them. He was fond of saying that for each individual, the "odds" are 100 percent or 0. —Susan

Whether to do prenatal genetic or developmental testing on your baby is an intensely personal choice. Your decision may be simple and straightforward or belabored and complicated as you try to find the right balance between technology and letting nature take its course. Even if a test is highly recommended in your case, you can decide against it. Even if you have zero risk factors, you can decide you want a particular test. As with all your decisions, discuss with your doctor any test's level of risk and balance the risks against the benefits.

Whether prenatal genetic or developmental testing will have emotional benefits to you is a personal judgment call. If you have a constellation of worries, prenatal diagnostic testing can offer some measure of reassurance— or it may simply stir up your anxieties with its invasiveness and the wait-and-see nature of test results. When you're trying to carry a baby to term, the thought of taking a sample of placental tissue or amniotic fluid may seem too risky. Testing can also undermine your already shaky feelings of confidence or hopes for a positive future. You may simply want to avoid the life-and-death decisions that unfavorable test results could prompt, let come what may, and wait for the more complete information that is available after your baby is born.

You may also recall that mothers have been having healthy babies for centuries without prenatal genetic or developmental testing. Your protective feelings may be accompanied by a degree of fatalism—that this baby's fate is already sealed and there isn't anything you can or should do about it. Some mothers just hope for the best and accept the rest. (For more on coping with worry, see "High Anxiety" in Chapter 22.)

You can agree to some tests and not others. Or you can authorize preliminary blood tests or ultrasounds, and if those results are unfavorable, then decide whether to do a retest, get a second opinion, or proceed to more invasive testing. (If an alpha-fetaprotein [AFP] test is required by your state, remember that unfavorable results are often false alarms.) If you decide to forgo some or all diagnostic prenatal tests, you should be able to discuss your concerns with your health care providers, make an informed decision, and your doctor or midwife should support you. If your health care providers pressure you, recognize that they are simply trying to ensure that you receive state-of-the-art medical care. After all, they want what's best for you and your baby. And what's best is for you to make an informed decision about what tests you and your baby will have, in light of your own needs.

Childbirth Education

If you've never experienced a term delivery, you may feel woefully unprepared. With preterm delivery, you didn't have a chance to finish the childbirth education course—in fact, your preemie may have been born before you could attend even one class. If you've had a full-term pregnancy in the past and attended childbirth classes at that time, you may feel the need for a

• • •
747
Considering Another Pregnancy

refresher course with this pregnancy.

Especially if all you know is prematurity, you may hesitate to attend a class for "regular" parents because the naivete of other pregnant women may be emotionally hard for you to deal with. You may not want to frighten them with your history, or you may simply feel that you don't fit in with this group. You likely need more facts and reassurance about the labor process or want to delve into all your options with regard to childbirth setting, medications, interventions, activity during labor, and positions during delivery. Having been through a delivery marked by loss of control, you may feel driven to gather information that could increase your control this time.

Try calling local hospitals and birthing centers to see if they offer any specialized childbirth classes or if any of their instructors would consider creating a small class for parents pregnant again after a preterm delivery. If you know other parents in the same situation, perhaps you can organize a group and look for an instructor together. Even private meetings with a doula or midwife can help to answer your questions and prepare you for what you hope will be a joyful term delivery. You may also find small support groups for expectant mothers through local agencies, hospitals, or birthing centers, or even on the Internet. Internet support groups, in particular, can be quite specialized and provide tremendous encouragement and information for parents. (See "Internet" in Appendix C.)

Points to Remember

- Deciding whether and when to attempt another pregnancy after experiencing a preterm birth can be difficult. You may face intense and mixed feelings about the decision.
- Enlist the assistance of your physicians and other specialists in the process of decision making. Give yourself time to research all your questions, wonder about all the "what- ifs," and play out possible scenarios.
- Share your hopes and fears with your partner and give each other the space and support needed to come together on decisions about a subsequent pregnancy. Even when you hold opposing opinions about how to proceed, recognize how much common ground you actually share.
- If you decide against another pregnancy, allow yourself to mourn the loss of an imagined future with an additional child. At the same time, remember how much you appreciate the child(ren) and family that you have now. You can enjoy your family size as it is.
- If you become pregnant again, you're likely to need the sensitive attention of your physicians. Be sure to let them know what you need and don't hesitate to inform them of concerns you have throughout your pregnancy. Getting information from them, as well as their reassurance, can help you cope with your worries.
- If you become pregnant, prepare yourself for a range of reactions from other people. Some may respond with surprise or fear; others may act as if it's no big deal. Remind yourself that their reactions reflect their concern for you, as well as their own fears or denial.
- Use what you learned from the premature birth to arm yourself with information, to be sensitive to the nuances of this pregnancy, and to get the medical attention and support you need. Ask your questions, discuss your concerns, and plan as best you can for a smooth pregnancy and delivery with your obstetric caregivers and childbirth educators.
- Be open, honest, and flexible with your health care providers. Form a partnership in which you work together to give your next baby the best possible start.

• • •

749

CHAPTER TWENTY-TWO

Coping during a Post-Preemie Pregnancy

You research, you drive yourself nuts trying to ensure that everything will work out just fine ... but there is so much concentration on what could happen that the stress level is phenomenal, and you can't really express your feelings to many people ... even to your husband at times. How can you explain that you are panicked even though things appear to be fine right now? You know things can turn in a matter of hours from just fine to "Your baby is in distress, and we're taking her now." That thought is always with you the entire second pregnancy. —Donna

> *I think the subsequent high-risk pregnancy was scarier than the one that resulted in a preemie. ... Knowledge may be power, but it's also frightening. With the first one we were "hoping for twenty-eight weeks, happy with thirty, but would have really liked to get to thirty-two weeks." Afterwards, having seen the results of other pregancies that ended at these times and later, I wasn't willing to settle for anything less than thirty-six to thirty-seven weeks! —Melissa*

Having a pregnancy that ends prematurely naturally colors subsequent pregnancies. Pregnancy complications and preterm delivery aren't just abstract concepts to you. Your special sensitivity can make you feel especially grateful for the miracle of gestation and birth. You appreciate every moment. And yet, for most parents, especially mothers, a post-preemie pregnancy is also a time of uneasiness.

High Anxiety

During a post-preemie pregnancy, many mothers vacillate between hope and fear. The balance you strike between those two extremes can depend on your general outlook on life, your risk factors, or even where you are in your pregnancy. If the probability of preterm delivery is remote, you may sense that everything will be okay or feel that you are bound to have a trouble-free pregnancy this time. But if you are at the other end of the spectrum, you may feel doomed, dreading that problems similar to those in your earlier pregnancy will crop up or wondering if you are incapable of carrying a baby to term. If there's a real chance that this pregnancy will end early, you'll likely feel very vulnerable and scared. If your life was in danger in a previous pregnancy, your partner will be especially worried as well.

It was true. I really was pregnant. To say that I was euphoric would be a gross understatement. Completely unaware of the cataclysmic range of emotional turmoil I was embarking on, I spent the first few weeks of my pregnancy in a state of pure bliss. I didn't believe anything could go wrong this time since everything was totally different than the last time, but everyone around me was terrified. I wanted my husband to do and feel all the stereotypical expecting-dad things, but he was paralyzed with fear. I was angry with him until my doctor sat me down and said, "Susan, you will never know how many nights Jack thought he was going to have to leave this hospital not only without the boys but without you." He told me that Jack had a very healthy fear, and I needed to let him have the time to work through it. It seems remarkable to me now that I couldn't see that, but initially I was living in fairy-tale land. It didn't last long, but I am so glad that I had those weeks. —Susan

Once it was clear that Emily had brain damage, I truly felt fear during pregnancy with Eric, and with this pregnancy again, that the child would be born early and also suffer from a permanent disability. I fear the lack of control we have over our bodies and our inability to stop premature labor. —Diana

•••
752
Parenting Your Premature Baby and Child

I was disappointed in my reaction to the pregnancy. I had always imagined that if and when I did become pregnant again I would be delighted and all the fears would magically disappear. Instead, I was terrified. I imagined all the things that could go wrong and searched the literature for information on every twitch. —Shaina

If you know what caused your earlier preterm birth, you may be able to avoid those risk factors. Armed with knowledge about general risk factors and the signs of trouble, you can increase the chances of you and your medical team being able to stave off complications, contractions, or premature delivery. Feeling some sense of control over your fate can bolster your hope and optimism. On the other hand, you may be all too aware that even if you take good care of yourself, you can still deliver prematurely. Even if this pregnancy continues to go smoothly and you know intellectually that everything is likely to turn out fine, convincing yourself *emotionally* can be difficult. And if your risk factors remain or reappear as this pregnancy progresses, you may find it impossible to relax, as if you shouldn't dare to expect this pregnancy to go to term. You may experience flashbacks that fill you with dread, and you wonder how you will manage another premature birth and baby.

Even as you approach your due date, you may worry, as most parents do, about how you will manage another child. If your preemie has ongoing special needs, there will be an extra urgency to your anxiety.

As we drew close to the due date, I began to panic. My son was getting sicker, and we were scheduling surgery for him for after the baby came. He was also becoming more difficult to handle—a typical toddler. How on earth was I going to be able to handle two kids? What was I thinking? —Laura

To top it off, whereas your first post-preemie pregnancy can be anxious enough, a second post-preemie pregnancy can be even more worrisome. If all of your pregnancies have ended early, you may feel there's no way around another premature delivery. But even if your first subsequent pregnancy turns out fine, you may worry that you're tempting fate with this next attempt. You may be surprised at the intensity of your worries and flashbacks, feeling that, as a seasoned survivor, you should be calmer than you are this time around.

I am now pregnant again [for the second time since the preterm delivery] and have found myself worrying even more than I did during my previous pregnancy. My doctors are especially concerned that my cervix will open early, and I am frightened. I fear losing this, my last, baby. I even more fear delivering a baby with problems. I have quit jogging, and I am visiting my OB frequently. Although I take what steps I can to ensure a healthy pregnancy, I also wonder if my actions will make a difference. I secretly suspect that what will happen will happen, despite my precautions. I am almost obsessively afraid of delivering a special-needs baby and ironically, I worry that my fear will actually cause it to happen. I am certain this is all somehow related to my feelings before and after Molly's [premature] birth. —Renee

During any subsequent pregnancy, it is normal and natural to feel vulnerable and anxious much of the time. But feeling *extremely* vulnerable and *always* anxious that something could go wrong at any moment is cause for concern. If you (or your partner) are feeling overwhelmed or immobilized, or if you are having trouble in your relationships or in your ability to get through the day, it is essential that you get an evaluation and treatment for your distress. Untreated clinical depression or anxiety can pose risks to your pregnancy or your baby because of the physical havoc it wreaks on your body, plus it impairs your ability to take care of yourself and exercise good judgement. You, and therefore your baby, can benefit from the support and strategies a knowledgeable counselor can offer. (For support and suggestions, see "Professional Counseling" and "Getting to the Bottom of Your Grief" in Chapter 3.)

Managing Fear

For mothers in particular, the anxiety and sense of vulnerability can be difficult to bear. Although you may find it impossible to eliminate your fears, you *can* learn to manage them, to lessen their impact on the quality of your experience. Here are some ideas that may help:

- *Recognize the emotional source of your fears.* You are anxious because you feel vulnerable, not because there is something wrong with you. You feel vulnerable because you are personally acquainted with imperfect pregnancy and you can no longer trust that only good things happen to good people.

- *Know that it's normal for those who have had a preterm birth to feel anxious and vulnerable during subsequent pregnancies.* If your fears outweigh your optimism, it can be a comfort to know that this is normal and natural. In fact, recognizing that you're vulnerable is a healthy step toward coming to terms with your childbearing losses. Try to accept your vulnerability and learn to balance your anxiety with optimism for the future.

- *Acknowledge that many pregnant women worry.* Even women who have had uneventful pregnancies may wonder if this one will follow suit. Chalk up at least some of your fears to how normal you really are.

- *Separate real fears from imagined ones.* Minimize the fears that lurk only in your mind and pay attention to the ones that surface in response to physical symptoms, test results, your doctor's concerns, or your own strong intuitions.

- *Know that your fears are remnants of past experience, not predictors of future events.* Feeling vulnerable does *not* mean that something terrible is going to happen.

- *Recognize that your anxieties and thoughts by themselves do not have the power to harm your pregnancy or your baby.* Thoughts don't cause things to happen.

- *Ask your health care providers for information.* Talk with your health care team about the sorts of precautions you need to take, how to monitor your symptoms, and how to take the best care of yourself and your unborn baby. Don't make assumptions about what you must or must not do without first discussing it with your doctor or midwife. Let information, not anxiety, be your guide.

- *Practice preventive medicine and be proactive in arranging for monitoring or testing.* Taking the initiative helps you feel in control. Instead of waiting for trouble to blindside you, stay aware of your body and its physical sensations. If you notice any signs of preterm labor or change in your condition that relates to any risk factors or if your intuition tells you something isn't quite right, call your health care provider and get the monitoring or testing you need to check them out. Blood and urine testing, blood pressure monitoring, ultrasound checks, additional monitoring of uterine contractions or cervical changes, and fetal monitoring can all keep you informed about the status of your pregnancy and unborn baby. (For more about testing, see "Prenatal Diagnostic Testing" in Chapter 21.)

- *If you have certain superstitions, you can abide by them if this calms you, poses no threat to you or your baby, and doesn't interfere with your life.* Recognize that giving in to superstitions doesn't actually protect you. If you are feeling continually compelled to engage in or avoid certain behaviors or thoughts, this is a sign of serious anxiety that needs prompt attention.

- *Try relaxation techniques.* To find respite from worry, see the "Relaxation" section in Chapter 6 for things you can do to help you feel calmer.
- *Reduce your stress in other ways.* Give up nonessential responsibilities and set aside time for leisure. Engage in pastimes you enjoy and do whatever nurtures you.
- *Use positive imagery to redirect anxious thoughts and envision a hopeful future.* Imagine your belly ripe with the later stages of pregnancy. Imagine feeling the strong movement of your growing baby in your womb. Imagine holding your plump newborn after delivery. Although imagery cannot guarantee a term birth, it can calm you substantially, give you a break from your worries and reinforce your hopes for the future.
- *Talk about your fears.* Talking about your fears brings them out into the daylight where you can examine them—and either put them into perspective or act on them. Exposing your fears can lessen their power to scare you and run your life. Enlist people who can listen sympathetically, with whom you feel free to talk out your fears and perhaps reach some sort of resolution. Openly discussing your fears with your health care providers can help you get the kind of monitoring you want and deserve.
- *Write about your feelings and worries.* Like talking, writing can be therapeutic. Putting your fears on paper moves them from inside to outside, and the process can help you clarify your anxiety. Don't censor your thoughts and feelings. Instead, face them and deal with them. You might also try writing a letter to fate, Mother Nature, your higher power, God, or your unborn baby, expressing your fears *and* your hopes, especially your wish to give this baby a healthy start. By doing this, you can mobilize your ability to face whatever it is that scares you. Or, express your fears artistically as a way of exposing and releasing them. Keeping a journal, letters, or artwork can help you cope with roller-coaster emotions, and they will become treasured keepsakes, no matter what the outcome of this pregnancy.
- *Find out more about what scares you.* One way to master fears is through

knowledge. The more you learn about a scary topic, the less power it will have to worry you. You may think that learning about the possibilities might heighten your anxieties, but the facts may be far less frightening than what you are imagining. With data in hand, you can feel more knowledgeable and in control. Seek out facts about pregnancy, preterm labor, and your specific condition. Your doctor or midwife can be an excellent source of information, and perhaps reassurance. Ask questions, no matter how silly you may think they are. You have a right to know. Information empowers you; ignorance can make you a victim. If the information is reassuring but not calming your anxiety, or if the information is indeed frightening and you're having difficulty managing your fear, seek additional support and strategies for coping.

- *Recognize that you can't control everything.* Remind yourself that no matter how closely you monitor yourself, some things are simply out of your hands. Recognizing that you cannot be completely in charge of what happens with this pregnancy or baby can allow you to relax a bit—and perhaps simply to trust that things will go as they are meant to.
- *Recognize that you deserve emotional support at this time.* Facing unknowns takes much courage. You may need—and are entitled to—a great deal of emotional support to get through this experience. Seeing a qualified counselor who can help you air and manage your feelings can help you find some calm in this emotional storm. You deserve to find some relief and enjoy what you can during this precious time.

In general, the key to managing fears is facing them. Telling yourself to put the specter of preterm delivery out of your mind may very well make your obsession with it stronger. Instead, talking or writing about your worries—and examining and investigating what you fear—helps you manage your anxiety. Many times you can counter anxiety with factual information and careful attention to what's actually going on with your pregnancy. Stay out of your imagination and tune in to reality. Managing your fears may not completely eliminate your anxiety, but it can diminish the shadow cast over your pregnancy. (For more ideas on managing fear, see "Moving through Vulnerability and Fear" in Chapter 3, "Balancing Hopes and Fears" in Chapter 10, "Coping with Feelings of Vulnerability" in Chapter 14, and "Managing Heightened Vigilance" in Chapter 17.)

Also recognize the gift your preterm pregnancy gave you—a greater appreciation for your ability to carry and bear life. Even in the throes of high anxiety, try to revel in the miracle.

My first pregnancy was planned, but it was a "bother" to me in the beginning. I don't want to say I resented the baby, but I wished my first pregnancy away. I couldn't wait until the due date so I could resume my active life. ... Then to have her come so early and so small and vulnerable shook me to the core. How could I have wished away her warmth and comfort in my protective body? My second pregnancy, I didn't care. I would endure anything for this baby if only she would go to term. ... [A] small price to pay for a wonderfully healthy full-term girl that I enjoy today! I relished every move, every ache, every stretch mark I earned in that second pregnancy. —Donna

Facing and Managing Other Painful Feelings

While fear is the most salient feeling for many post-preemie mothers, you may experience other negative feelings with this new pregnancy. You may feel angry or disappointed that you can't have your innocence back so that you can enjoy the pregnancy experience. You may feel isolated if well-meaning friends and relatives encourage you to "just relax" or to "think positively." Their dismissive attitude makes you keep your fears to yourself and deprives you of much needed support.

If your pregnancy is identified as high risk at any point, in addition to feeling terrified, you may feel frustrated. Haven't you already paid your dues? Guilt, failure, or a sense of responsibility can arise as you wonder whether you have unwittingly contributed to the complications.

Even if you can envision making it to term this time, you may grieve anew that you were unable to carry your preemie to term as well. Ironically, carrying this new baby longer than you carried your premature baby can renew feelings of guilt around not providing the benefits of a longer pregnancy to your preemie.

Part of me feels a little like it's not going to be fair to Daniel and Shayna to have a healthy baby—that they're going to have a sibling who got what they didn't get. If the baby is born on time, I think I might actually feel bad for Daniel and Shayna. —Debbie

I am currently pregnant. The stress is incredible, along with the guilt I have now that I am carrying this baby so much longer than I could Casey. I can't help but wonder how sorry I will feel for Casey when this baby is able to do things so much easier than Casey is.—Kelly

To manage these painful feelings, first recognize that it is normal to continue to grieve your losses surrounding your preterm pregnancy and your premature baby. As part of this grief, you may still harbor feelings of anger, failure, guilt, and sadness. Although you may fear that your grief could harm your new pregnancy or baby, in fact, continuing to grieve will enhance your ability to accept what happened and to look to the future with hope. Facing and working through your pain can free you to more fully enjoy this pregnancy and invest in the baby you are now carrying. Try to use this pregnancy as a doorway to your feelings and as an opportunity to achieve yet another level of important grief work.

Also recognize that while painful feelings are a normal part of subsequent pregnancy, so are positive feelings, such as relief, wonder, and joy.

Getting Past Significant Milestones

Once I hit the twenty-nine-week mark and passed Emily's "birth day," on the next morning I was relieved, but only cautiously so. —Diana

Depending on when your premature baby was delivered, you may feel that if you can make it past a certain point, you can relax a little. During any subsequent pregnancy, you can expect your anxiety to intensify at around the time in gestation when you first encountered serious problems, and again around the time you delivered your preemie. You may find yourself breathing sighs of increasing relief as you make it through successive weeks without encountering trouble. You may also become an expert on fetal growth, each week marking off the developmental milestones that your baby has reached. When you pass your preemie's gestational age at birth, you may find yourself looking at pictures of your baby in the NICU—and realizing with amazement that your unborn child now looks just like that inside you. On the other hand, it can be a bit unnerving to be able to describe exactly what your unborn baby looks like and can do at this stage of pregnancy.

Coping during a Post-Preemie Pregnancy

Being pregnant the second time, with Ilyssa, was so, so scary. Because I knew everything. I knew how big she was every single week. Like, okay, if she's born now, this is how big she is, this is what her odds are, this is what could happen to her, this is how long she'd be in the NICU. It was like, I don't need to know all that. This is just way, way, way too much information. —Stephie

As your baby grows and passes developmental milestones, you may find yourself reaching emotional milestones, where your anxiety diminishes and your optimism grows. The stage of earliest viability is significant, and next is viability with a high probability of a good outcome. Then there's an early delivery that probably won't require invasive life support, and most joyous of all, a timely delivery where you and your baby needn't be separated from each other at all.

There is a huge part of you that never lets go of that worry until you pass each magical milestone of the pregnancy. I know I was "fine" on paper my entire second pregnancy, but I secretly counted down to "viability." Then I was counting down to "Okay, the lungs should be doing well enough now to not have to worry about that." I was watching all the statistics lower on the possible negative outcomes if the baby came early again. —Donna

If this pregnancy is uneventful or if you've been at risk but make it to thirty-six weeks, you may begin to feel some guarded optimism. As your due date approaches, you may be surprised to hear yourself complaining about the discomforts of a big belly or exclaiming how you want this to be "over, already!" These are the very feelings that you may have raged against when you heard them from other pregnant women! You might feel sheepish—after all, you *are* so grateful for a full-term pregnancy. How normal, how wonderful it is to be part of the world of pregnant women who can complain about being large and uncomfortable, wishing to deliver sooner rather than later.

When I became pregnant again two years later, I worried about another premature delivery. As I approached the twenty-eighth week, I was afraid to move or exert myself in any way! I began to breathe easier as each subsequent week passed. By the time I reached the thirty-second week, I began to feel overdue, and I tortured myself the rest of the pregnancy! My second daughter was born four hours and fifteen minutes after *my due date.* —*Renee*

The hardest part was after the crisis was over and I was off bed rest and Brethine [terbutaline] and the baby still didn't come! The docs kept saying "any day," and the baby just didn't get the message. I got huge, my feet swelled, I got sick of waiting, I didn't like being full term! I was soooo uncomfortable. ... And it was very emotionally challenging to shift my thinking from never expecting to make it to even thirty-six weeks to watching weeks thirty-six, thirty-seven, thirty-eight, and thirty-nine pass without a baby. Once again I had to accept that someone instead of me was in charge and that things happen that I can't control. I'm a control freak, and both of my pregnancies and life as a parent have taught me to let up some. —*Melissa*

Coping with a High-Risk Pregnancy and Bed Rest

Now [with this third pregnancy] I'm really high risk. I've reached the twenty-six-week point and expect to be on complete bed rest in one week or so. There is still no certainty surrounding the why *of my premature labors. This time around, I had a cerclage [cervical stitch] put in, just in case. I have already stopped lifting/carrying the children, which has been hard to do with two non-ambulatory kids.* —*Diana*

As if you haven't been through enough, you may be facing another high-risk pregnancy. Whether you were taken by surprise or knew there was a very good chance of problems recurring, you may feel very discouraged to find that you just *can't* "do it right." Rather than turning against yourself, recognize that your baby needs you to work *with* your body, even though you may wish you could trade it in for a different one. Now that you know what "high-risk pregnancy" and "premature baby" can really mean, it's especially important to surround yourself with people who understand and are supportive.

It seemed really strange to me to be placed on bed rest at thirty-four weeks with my daughter after my experience with my son, where they kept telling me, "We're just trying to get you to thirty-four weeks." It was like I got to a goal and someone moved the goalposts! I realize that what they really want in all pregnancies is to get everyone to thirty-seven-plus weeks, but it was difficult for me to take the risks seriously since my thirty-weeker had done so well. Having Internet friends who were going through the same thing and who understood my joy and fear was wonderful. They encouraged me and reminded me of the ultimate goal ... a healthy baby we could bring home without a side trip to the NICU. —Melissa

If your health care provider prescribes bed rest, it can be a real challenge. This section contains some ideas for dealing with the limits bed rest imposes. Many suggestions also apply to high-risk pregnancies in general and to coping with partial bed rest or activity restrictions.

A note about bed rest: If you're told you only need to be on partial bed rest, you may think that perhaps total bed rest would be even better for your baby. However, unless it's necessary, total bed rest is not especially good for your body and can create more problems than it solves. Imposing more restrictions on yourself than your doctor recommends can actually backfire—do talk specifically with your doctor about what "restricted activity" and "bed rest" mean in your situation. If you're on partial bed rest, move around as much as you feel comfortable with. It can be good for you physically and emotionally. In fact, weight-bearing activity is tremendously beneficial, so if your doctor recommends it, you'll be doing yourself a favor by complying, both during your pregnancy and during your recovery. (Refer to Judith Maloni's research on the effects of bed rest on mother and baby in the "Internet" section of Appendix C.) Vickie had this to say about her partial bed rest: "It wasn't strict bed rest. I was glad for that. I could let myself do a little bit, like get a bagel and then go back and lie down instead of feeling *so* restricted. A little bit of freedom helped my morale more than anything."

Managing the Uncertainties

There are numerous complications that can put a pregnancy at risk. One of the most frustrating and frightening aspects of coping with a high-risk pregnancy is that physicians often can predict very little about how a pregnancy will progress and may offer precious few reliable strategies for heading off trouble. It's natural to wish that your doctor could reassure you, could predict what will happen next, and could tell you exactly what to do to prevent a preterm delivery. When you encounter trouble in a subsequent pregnancy, you're faced head on with uncertainty—again. It's agonizing to realize that, no matter how much you researched, discussed, and thought about your options and then chose your strategies, you might have another preemie. It's frightening to realize that your status could change at any time. Your fears for your baby, yourself, and your family's future can feel immobilizing.

Despite the lack of guarantees, most physicians will recommend intervention strategies to address the risks you face. You many need to keep close tabs on your blood pressure and lab values. You may be advised to go on bed rest, although there is some debate about the benefits and risks. *Ask your doctor or midwife about the latest research on bed rest and other interventions and how they apply to you.*

In any case, complications or preterm labor contractions do not necessarily doom you to deliver a tiny, fragile baby. Many highly monitored pregnancies produce healthy term babies. With heightened vigilance and treatments, you may well carry your little one close to term.

And it may also help to remember that preterm delivery does not necessarily doom a baby to a struggle in the NICU. The closer you get to term, the more robust your baby can be. As long as it's safe for your baby to stay inside your body, every day is another precious day of growing and developing. As you turn the corner past twenty-five weeks, then twenty-seven, thirty, and thirty-two, your baby's chances of surviving and having a healthy, bright future improve dramatically. (For more on coping with anxiety, see "Managing Fear" earlier in this chapter.)

Overcoming Feelings of Failure

If you are experiencing complications or facing a high-risk pregnancy, you may wonder why other pregnant women can sail through pregnancy and stay active without threatening their own or their unborn baby's life. You may ask, "Why me?" and wonder what you've done to deserve this.

Fight feelings of failure by recognizing that with treatment, you're doing something right by taking steps to keep your baby safe and inside you. Instead of berating yourself for being unable to predict, prevent, or cure problems in your pregnancy, remind yourself that even medical science doesn't have all the answers, so how can you be expected to? All you can do is your best—to get through each hour and each day, controlling what you can and letting go of the rest. If you feel worthless for getting "nothing" done, remember, *you are growing a baby*. This is your most important job. If that is all you accomplish in a day, that's plenty.

If you knew you were taking some risks in becoming pregnant again, it can be difficult and disappointing when you encounter problems, but perhaps not devastating. The risks in this subsequent pregnancy may be fairly significant or rather low. Armed with experience and information, you may feel better equipped than last time to handle what may come. If you and your physician can monitor and manage the symptoms, you may progress further in this subsequent pregnancy and deliver a baby later in gestation—or perhaps one who is not even preterm. But if having preemies seems to be your lot in life, adjusting your expectations can help you cope.

> *It is only because of the continuing problems with subsequent premature labor that I have stayed in such close contact with preemie-dom. And yet, since all of our children so far have been born prematurely, our expectations were shifted rapidly, and neither of us dwells too much anymore on the "Why me?" of it all. —Diana*

If you entered this subsequent pregnancy with the expectation that your risks were low but developed problems nonetheless, you may feel damaged—unable to have a simple pregnancy or easily carry a baby to term. These feelings of failure may run deep and can be hard to move past. If you feel this way, talk with your doctor about the possible reasons for your recurring complications. Ask for insight and reassurance that you are not a failure as a woman or as a mother.

Subduing Helplessness during Bed Rest

When you're an independent adult, it's hard to be suddenly dependent on the assistance of others to accomplish the simplest things. You're used to being active, able to do what you want and get what you need for yourself, as well as your family. Asking someone else to do the laundry; fix a meal; get that magazine, the mail, or the phone can feel awkward—especially if, except for the pregnancy complications that landed you in bed, you're healthy. Even when you're in the hospital, it's easy to feel that you're imposing or too demanding. Like many women, you may be more comfortable with being the primary caregiver, not the primary care receiver.

To deal with this unfamiliar situation, it can help to reframe things:

- *First, you* do *deserve to have every need met.* You're not selfish. That box of tissues is a need, not a frivolous desire. You deserve to have whatever adds to your comfort, anything you would naturally do for yourself.
- *Second, your family, colleagues, and your true friends are eager to help you.* People get great satisfaction out of helping others through hard times. Don't deny them this opportunity to contribute to your baby's safe arrival.
- *Third, lighten your partner's load by accepting all offers of help.* Whatever others can do for you are things your partner won't have to take care of.
- *Finally, recognize that when others do something for you, they are also doing it for your baby.* Taking care of yourself is intertwined with taking care of your baby. Accepting practical and emotional support is the best thing you can do for *both* of you.

Maintaining Your Primary Relationship

Getting through a high-risk pregnancy and bed rest is definitely something you cannot do alone. To make it through, you must have an involved and emotionally supportive partner. That partner may be the baby's father; your significant other; or if you're a single mom, a relative, close friend, or someone you hire. Enlist your partner's support by acknowledging that his or her assistance directly contributes to your baby's health and growth, as well as helping you do your part. If you're hospitalized, knowing that your partner is covering for you at home can be a significant load off your mind. And when you're feeling discouraged, frustrated, aggravated, or distressed by your condition, your partner's encouragement and praise is a salve that can soothe or energize you.

Unfortunately, while you'd give anything to be up and about, your partner, overloaded with responsibilities, would probably give anything to spend a few days in bed. Even in the best of partnerships, this envy can give rise to conflict.

Try to approach bed rest as a team effort. Bed rest is not something you've invented to enslave your partner. It's something you're both doing to promote your baby's well-being. For you, bed rest means confinement; for your partner, bed rest means more responsibilities. At times you may feel sorry that your partner has the worse end of the deal, but he or she may feel the same way about you. Talking openly about the situation can reassure the other that you don't mind rising to the occasion and fulfilling your important role, and it allows you to express your gratitude for your partner's sacrifice. Just as your partner can encourage you when you're feeling low, you can let your dear one know that the time, effort, and energy that he or she is putting forth are indispensable contributions to your infant's future.

Especially if your partner is also the coparent, making the baby real can build confidence and eagerness to help. Let your partner feel the baby move, and buy or borrow a doppler (ask your health care provider) so that you can listen together to your baby's world. Promoting your partner's bond with the baby also cements your unity with your bed rest ally.

Being able to count on other people to support you can also help your relationship, because it relieves your partner of carrying all the responsibilities alone.

> *I think we did a great job. Before I became pregnant, we discussed all the "what if"'s and made sure we had full support from our families (mostly mine since his weren't in a position to drop everything and come help). Friends and family made a huge difference. ... We had several friends who were "on call" to help with our older child if needed. —Melissa*

If your partner is having difficulty supporting you in your bed rest, definitely enlist outside help. If this difficulty stems from problems in your relationship, you'll eventually need to attend to these, but you may put that off during this high-stress period. Still you can encourage your partner to talk about his or her feelings or possible resentments toward you or the baby. Ask your partner about fears regarding the risks to you and/or the baby. Naturally, many partners don't want to talk about difficulties or share their negative feelings because they don't want to burden the mother any further. It can be particularly important for your partner to have outside support—a friend or counselor to confide in.

Finally, do what you must to take care of yourself and your unborn child. The dynamics between you and your partner will only become more stressful if you deliver prematurely. Enlist the outside support you need to guard your health and to help you carry your pregnancy as long as you can.

Parenting during a High-Risk Pregnancy

Along with the concerns you may have about maintaining your relationship with your partner, you may also worry about how your high-risk pregnancy will affect your other children. How will you manage to care for them if you're instructed to reduce your activity, stop lifting them, or even stay in bed? What if you have a child with special needs or a very dependent little one? Activity restrictions can be especially frustrating in these situations. You may also wonder how your children will adjust to your restrictions. If you're hospitalized, how will they adjust to your absences? How will they react to your anxiety or ill health?

For more on supporting your children during family crisis, turn to "Your Other Children" in Chapter 19. Much of the information there applies during a high-risk pregnancy as well.

Child Care and Staying Connected If you're at home on bed rest with a toddler or young children, you will probably need to engage others to help you care for your youngsters. If your children are older, you can expect them to become more independent. If you are hospitalized, your physical distance from your children and your emotional preoccupation with this difficult pregnancy can leave you feeling disconnected from your life and torn about where you should be and which of your children needs you more.

There are several ways in which you can lay low and still take care of your other children. If your little one is now in day care or preschool, it may feel best to keep him or her there, especially since maintaining a familiar routine can be a comfort to him or her. Or you may want the simplicity and convenience of in-home child care instead. If your child is unaccustomed to having other caregivers, try to ensure that the situation you set up is consistent and reliable to give your child a sense of stability and security. Consider having a neighborhood high-school student or a family member come over to the house regularly. When your child develops an attachment to a substitute caregiver, your relief may be marred by mixed feelings. If you're used to feeling like the center of your child's world, you may feel sad about sharing the spotlight. Recognize that your child's contentment is a sign of healthy adjustment, and pat yourself on the back for enlisting a caregiver who can nurture your child so well. Remember that you are *still* at the center of your child's world.

Though your activity is restricted, you can still be deeply involved with your family, but in different sorts of ways. Talk with your daughter about the project she's working on for the science fair or with your son about packing for an overnight playdate. Your younger children can color by your bedside and tell you what they're thinking. Encourage your child(ren) to relate their adventures at school, the playground, a friend's house, or on their hike. They will appreciate having such an eager—and captive—audience. Work hard to communicate with and maintain your emotional connection to your child(ren), especially if hospitalization puts physical distance between you.

> *[When I was put on hospital bed rest] we came into that hospital room, took down the pictures, and put up our own, including pictures of [two-year-old] Tommy, and we had some of his toys there and books and videos, and [ate] dinner together every night in that room. We tried to make it like a second home, so that he would feel comfortable climbing up into bed with me and reading a book or watching a video or taking a nap. We felt like that was something we had to do in order to stay healthy as a family. —Betsy*

Managing on Your Own Even if you have child care, you will probably still be at home alone with your little one for part of the day. There will be times when you'll want your child close to you—but not all youngsters can be content simply snuggling in bed for hours. Try "nesting" together—bringing pillows, blankets, and activities for your child into your bed or arranging them on the floor nearby. Some children love to be read to. Playing hide-and-go-seek with small toys in the "wilderness" of the bedcovers can offer imaginary fun and adventure. It's important to set limits on sharing your space, though, based on your child's natural activity level as well as your own energy level and medically mandated restrictions. Enforcing limits can be easier when you remind yourself (and explain to your child) that they won't last forever.

If you have resisted employing strategies such as videos or television to entertain your child, this might be a time to relax those standards. Most important right now is that the two of you make it through the days. You can watch with your child, which is always a good strategy with TV viewing. During this period, give yourself permission to make do in whatever ways work. These measures are only temporary. See Appendix C: Resources (under "Health, Pregnancy, Fertility") for the titles of books on high-risk pregnancy.

•••

These contain many practical suggestions for what to do with children when your activities are restricted.

Balancing Conflicting Needs Most mothers wrestle with balancing the needs of the child on the "inside" and the child on the "outside." It's easy to stand firm with choices that are a matter of life or death, but most choices during bed rest or high-risk pregnancy aren't that clear-cut. It's hard to know how to measure the importance of each child's needs or how to weigh the consequences of your actions on the inside child compared with their restrictive effects on the outside child.

If you have any feelings of ambivalence about the pregnancy or the restrictions it's placing on you, you may consider your commitment to your outside child clearer and more pressing, yet feel guilty for even considering possibly compromising the inside child. If you view your commitment to your inside child as more critical right now, that decision can seem unfair to the child who sits before you. You may feel trapped in a no-win situation where your compromises make you feel as if you're shortchanging *all* your children.

Broadening your definition of what it means to be a "good" mother may help you cope with this situation. Recognize that you can be invested in all your children and that you can concentrate on meeting their most important needs throughout this journey. Talk with your doctor about the specific risk factors you face. Speak openly about the demands on you and your body, and brainstorm ways to manage your restrictions and balance all your children's needs. The more information you have, the more tailored your decisions will be. Also keep in mind that your outside child is resilient enough to thrive under less-than-ideal conditions. Your restrictions can also give your children an opportunity for growth. Even very young children can feel proud of handling more responsibility and contributing to the family in times of great need.

You may also feel sad about losing these last months with your older child, recognizing that your pregnancy is already drawing on your physical and emotional resources in a way that isn't typical before delivery. Although it's unusual for sibling rivalry to appear this soon, competing needs are a natural way of life for brothers and sisters. If your son or daughter seems to resent the baby that is growing inside you, encourage the expression of his or her feelings and empathize: "I know this is hard on you—it's hard on all of us." By making room for any negative feelings to surface, you allow the

Coping during a Post-Preemie Pregnancy

positive feelings to come forward as well. By taking "special care" of the baby, you show your child that in your family, when someone needs special care, he or she gets it. This is comforting knowledge for a child.

Children's Emotional Needs If your activities are moderately restricted and you must visit the doctor frequently, even young children are likely to notice that you're a bit distracted and preoccupied. If you've been placed on bed rest at home, the change will be more obvious. Your children may worry or feel angry that you're unable to do what you used to do for and with them. Young children need to know why mommy can't do what she usually does, otherwise their imaginations can cook up scary ideas. Explain the situation so that your children understand that your limitations are not ominous or a rejection of them.

Because very young children do not have a clear sense of time, your bed rest may seem interminable to them. They may even assume you'll be this way "forever." Use a calendar or other visual aid to point out the holidays, seasons, and significant events that are likely to take place during your confinement and talk to them about the temporary nature of the situation. Focus on what you can still do with them and offer activities and contact that are consistent with the parameters of your bed rest. Your partner's extra attention and time, especially doing the more vigorous activities with your child(ren), can alleviate much of the impact of your restrictions. If you also don't feel well, explain to them that your body needs to rest so that you can stay as healthy as possible until the baby is born.

If you have children who are old enough to understand your previous premature delivery and the NICU stay, they may be very worried. Keep them in the loop, providing them with basic, accurate, age-appropriate information. Respond to their questions reassuringly by also addressing common underlying fears. Remember that information empowers. For your children as well as for you, having information can make the difference between being overwhelmed by anxiety and being able to cope.

Pay close attention to your children's questions and try not to flood them with too much information at once. Children are likely to ask questions, listen to the answers, go off to play or do something else, and then return later with more questions. Respect their pace. Consult with a mental health care professional specializing in children if you're unsure how to talk with your children about difficult topics. Request suggestions that are age appropriate and can meet your children's various needs.

...

Also remember that your ability to listen empathetically is just as important to your children's emotional coping as anything you say. Just as you need to have your worries heard and validated, so do your children. Older children are more likely to verbalize what they're worried about and to tell you that they're upset or angry. Younger children are more likely to test limits, have meltdowns, and express conflict in their pretend play when they're feeling uneasy or frustrated. So listen to their words—and pay attention to their behaviors. Remember that during this time, children need honest information; they also need reassurance that you're okay and that you love them more than ever. If you find that hearing or responding to their concerns frightens or saddens you, be sure to get support for yourself as well.

Tending to Your Emotional Needs during Bed Rest

Besides your partner and child(ren), you may also have concerns about your own well-being during this subsequent pregnancy. Your health care providers and others around you will probably focus on your physical health because it directly affects the baby, but your emotional health can be just as important to your overall well-being. After all, when your emotional needs are being met, you're more likely to recognize and take care of your physical needs. Unfortunately, the rigors of high-risk pregnancy intervention don't help your emotional condition, as bed rest can make you feel isolated, drugs can have side effects, and hospitalization can make you miserable. Knowing how to confront these challenges can help you physically *and* emotionally.

For moms on bed rest, the most common difficulties revolve around boredom, isolation, giving up control of responsibilities, and keeping spirits up. By doing what you can to deal with these factors, you'll enhance your ability to cope.

Gracefully Giving Up Control If you're on bed rest or restricted activity, you won't be able to do everything you've always done to run your household or conduct your job-related business. You'll need to become accustomed to chores and assignments being done another way—not necessarily your way. You may cringe at the thought of ill-sorted laundry resulting in muddy whites or an inefficiently run project. If you're hospitalized, you may shudder to imagine what your home or your work looks like without you there to manage it.

Try to look honestly at your desire for control of the household or your job. Recognize that it may have a lot to do with trying to regain control over your pregnancy. It's your pregnancy that you *really* wish you could control, after all. You may unconsciously think that if you could restore control over the other parts of your life, you would feel more like yourself. It can be difficult and aggravating to adjust to restrictions. Understanding the source of your struggle against letting go can help you reign in your impulse to stay in control of all that you survey.

Here are more tips for gracefully ceding control:

- *Identify what really matters to you and what doesn't.* Let go of the things that don't really matter to you. For the things that do matter, try to express your preferences as concerns, not demands.
- *Negotiate priorities.* Make a list of household and family priorities with your partner and job priorities with your boss. Negotiate which ones you can still be in charge of, as director and guide.
- *Give your helpers the benefit of the doubt.* They may surprise you with their eagerness and ability to take over what you let go of.
- *Be creative and change your perspective.* Wear only dark clothing, and develop the attitude, "So what if my underwear isn't blinding white?" Imagine the project at work being done in new ways that might reveal new discoveries for you or others.
- *Acknowledge that this situation is tough.* Admit that it's difficult to be confined to bed and unable to do things the way you like. Concede that sometimes you're anxious, bored, and crabby. Who wouldn't be?
- *Express your gratitude to your helpers.* It's only human nature to want to do more for people who are appreciative. Don't underestimate the importance of a simple "please" or "thank you."
- *Remember that this is temporary.* By letting go and not sweating the small stuff, you will prevail.

Being placed on bed rest was a signal that I once again wasn't in charge of my life and needed to slow down. Unfortunately, it was the second time in three years that I'd had to go on bed rest a few days before final exams for my students. But the lesson I learned in the first pregnancy was that my department could get by without me and that the students would take their exams and pass and that someone else could do some or all of my work and the world wouldn't come crashing down! —Melissa

Fighting Boredom Before you entered the world of high-risk pregnancy, you may have led a life so full, so busy, and so hectic that you'd occasionally fantasize about spending a few weeks in bed. Given the chance, you'd surround yourself with good reading, beloved projects, and all those movies you missed that are now out on video or DVD. But when you *must* stay in bed for weeks upon weeks because you're trying to carry a baby to term, this restriction is an anxiety-provoking requirement, not a peaceful luxury. Reclining on your left side or tilted back can render many activities too challenging, and all the reading and projects and movies can feel trivial rather than compelling. Without your varied routine and trips outside, it's easy for boredom to set in.

Especially for the times in your day when you don't have a child to entertain, consider these suggestions as ways of combating boredom:

- *Establish a routine that works for you.* Meals, naps, show times, visits with friends, or your child's rhythms can provide structure that can make the hours go by faster. If you must take medication, for example, you may find yourself saying, "Oh, is three hours up already?" Weekly doctor appointments can also be concrete evidence that time is passing. If a routine doesn't develop naturally, it can help to establish one.

- *Vary your activities each day.* Doing one thing all day can become tedious, and it promotes boredom. Without some variety, you're likely to lose interest. Do your best to find something different to look forward to each day.

- *Focus on organizational tasks.* It can be very difficult to find time in a busy life to complete all those organizational projects you'd like to accomplish. These might be just the tasks to keep you occupied now. Consider organizing your recipe box, putting your photographs in albums and labeling each photo, catching up on the baby books, or restoring order to your address book. If you're at home, you might tackle the filing cabinet, kitchen cupboards, linen closet, bathroom cabinets, or bureau drawers (enlisting someone who thrives on order to deliver the contents to you so that you can sort through and organize them). Remember, only do this if it appeals to you, not because you think you "should"!

- *Pick and choose your favorite household chores.* If you find satisfaction and a sense of calm in taking care of household chores, you can try doing some of these jobs from your bed: going through the mail, clipping coupons, balancing the checkbook, and if you're at home, sorting socks and mending clothes. Limit yourself to the chores you really *enjoy* doing and willingly take a break from the rest.

- *Rent or borrow a laptop computer.* A computer you can use from your bed gives you access to e-mail and the World Wide Web.
- *Keep your mind active.* If you enjoy brainteasers and puzzles, bookstores offer many activity books.
- *Change your surroundings.* If you can, set up shop in a different room of the house each week.
- *Expand your TV horizons.* If you find daytime TV depressing (after the initial fascination wears off), record good evening programming to watch during the day. Public television always offers quality programming.
- *Read.* Read books on subjects you've always been intrigued by but never had the time to learn about. Catch up on those magazines that you've been holding on to in hopes of reading someday. Enlist a friend who enjoys going to the library or the video store to keep you stocked with interesting reading and movies.
- *Rediscover daydreaming.* Look through old yearbooks, photo albums, or letters and let yourself be transported back in time. Peruse those "coffee table" books that you've had forever but never taken the time to enjoy. Fantasize about what you'd do if you won the lottery. Plan your ideal trip around the world. Design and decorate your dream house or garden. The possibilities are limited only by your imagination.

If you find yourself unable to look forward to doing anything, keep in mind that the sensory deprivation that occurs with bed rest can cause a sort of lethargy or low-level depression. Lack of physical activity can reinforce fatigue and boredom, perpetuating a vicious cycle. To combat depression, consider spending part of the day reclining outside or ask your doctor for physical, occupational, or massage therapy. This kind of stimulation can perk you up a bit—and it can be good for your overall health.

Resisting Isolation Loneliness may be your biggest hurdle, especially if you're an extrovert who thrives on lots of contact with others. Even if you have children at home with you, bed rest can feel extremely isolating. If you have been hospitalized with complications, you may feel very alone, even if caregivers are constantly in and out of your hospital room.

Again, remind yourself that this situation is temporary. At the same time, honor your need to connect with others. Try some of these suggestions:

- *Use the phone to stay in touch with friends and family.* If you worry about imposing on their time, make phone dates so that you feel assured that they've set aside the time to talk with you. If, on the other hand, you're enjoying the peace and quiet of bed rest, limit the number or length of phone calls you're willing to receive (or make).

- *Stay in touch with your partner.* Even though no sex is allowed, you can still be affectionate.
- *Invite others to visit you.* You may not feel like much of a hostess, but your visitors know that they're visiting someone who is bed- or couch-bound. You can be a lively conversationalist even in your pajamas.
- *Start a club.* If you have one or more friends who share your passion for gardening books, mysteries, or Hepburn/Tracy movies, you can form a book club or a movie club. The reading or watching assignments related to the club will give purpose to your days, and you'll be participating in discussions about topics that interest you.
- *Make use of electronic connections.* A laptop computer will give you access to a whole world of others who know what your experience is like. Make use of e-mail and the chat rooms and bed-rest support groups on the World Wide Web. See Appendix C: Resources for contact numbers for Sidelines (an international bed-rest support organization that provides phone contacts for bed-resting women) and links to Internet mailing lists for mothers on bed rest.
- *Stay in touch with others like you in your community.* Ask your health care providers to hook you up with other moms in your community who are on bed rest. Especially if your doctors are part of a high-risk obstetric practice, there are bound to be others they can refer you to.

If you become concerned that you're feeling more and more isolated, recognize that the lethargy of bed rest may be setting in. You may be slipping into the doldrums in spite of your attempts to prevent this. If so, you might try forcing yourself to reach out more to counteract bed rest–induced depression. Or ask your partner to help you arrange some social contacts. You may find it less of a hurdle to receive a call than to initiate one.

Keeping Your Spirits Up Keeping your spirits up is central to your emotional health and your ability to cope with extended bed rest. The topics covered in the previous three sections are some of the keys to boosting your morale. Here are some more general tips for keeping your spirits up:

- *Surround yourself with supportive people.* Bed rest is a huge job. The appreciation of people who recognize the challenge you face can boost your morale and feelings of accomplishment.

- *Don't feel obligated to be productive.* Don't make oppressive to-do lists or feel that you must get a lot done during all this supposed "free" time. Friends may ask, "So, what are you doing to keep busy?" Remember that just maintaining your pregnancy and just getting through each day is a momentous achievement. Every additional day in your womb is an immeasurable gift to your baby.

- *Talk to others who have been on bed rest before.* Ask your doctor or midwife to hook you up with others who can share their tips with you—and who can remind you that "this, too, shall pass." It can encourage you when you hear perspectives that in hindsight it was such a short time, and so very worth it.

- *If it's safe, counteract the physical deterioration that can accompany prolonged bed rest.* Doing what physical activity you can often boosts morale. Unfortunately, the only way to prevent sore, stiff, or atrophying muscles is by engaging in weight-bearing activities, such as walking. Ask your doctor or midwife for specific guidelines as to whether and how you can do any weight-bearing activities. If this is inadvisable for you, doing some bed-centered activities can still be beneficial. Ask your doctor or midwife to recommend safe exercises you can do in bed—exercises that won't propel you into labor or complications. Do them as long as they don't increase your anxiety about uterine contractions or other problems.

- *Read books about pregnancy and fetal development.* Focusing on your baby's progress—his or her continuing growth and development—can give you a sense that this period of your life is moving along as well.

- *Get answers from your health care providers.* Don't spend bed rest stewing over unasked questions and worries that may not be real. Ask your health care providers about the concerns you have and keep asking until you get the answers you need. Knowledge can be a real spirit-lifter.

- *Don't do things that raise your anxiety level.* If you're not on total bed rest, you and/or your partner may be asked if you want an NICU tour for high-risk pregnancy patients. Pass this up if all it will do is make you more anxious, even if you're planning to deliver in an unfamiliar hospital. If, on the other hand, you feel it would be helpful to take a tour or occasionally meet with a neonatologist, ask your doctor to arrange it.

- *Try to define the length of your bed rest.* If you can count down the days until your bed rest officially ends—which may be as soon as three weeks before your due date—your restrictions may not seem so interminable, and it will be easier to keep your spirits up. Also ask your doctor to estimate the gestational age at which your baby might not need intensive care after birth.
- *Call your doctor with important concerns.* Remember that you can call your doctor at any time, day or night.
- *Stay optimistic.* Allow yourself to hope and imagine that your baby will be okay. Pessimism drains energy, hope, and peace of mind. Optimism is free, and its benefits are priceless.
- *Nestle with a baby blanket or other baby things.* You may consider surrounding yourself with baby things too optimistic, but if it gives you hope or comfort, do it.

Some moms concede that, with adequate support, there can be some positive aspects to bed rest. After all, you get to experience and appreciate the nurturing care and support of others. Unfortunately, the positives are tainted by the fear that comes along with bed rest. But if bed rest, monitoring, and frequent doctor visits help you to bring your pregnancy to term, there is no question that you'll be pleased you did these things. When you look back on this period, the happy ending will have made it all worthwhile.

Birth and Afterward

The hospital where I delivered all of my kids has two maternity wings, the east, very old, where all the problem pregnancies stay (close to the operating rooms) and the west, newly constructed and decorated, where all the happy, healthy babies are born. Of course, I had spent all my time in the east wing and was greatly looking forward to being a "regular" mom in the west wing this time. However, when I checked in, the west wing was full, and they put me in the east wing. The poor, startled admitting nurse probably still doesn't understand to this day why a hugely pregnant woman wept incoherently when she took her into her room. I was sure it was an omen, that I belonged in the east wing because my baby was not going to be okay. —Susan

If you make it close to term or at least "out of the woods," just when you expected to be infused with joyous anticipation, you may be wracked with anxiety and grief. Whether you waited six months or six years to get pregnant again, your sadness or regret over your earlier preterm delivery may intensify as this due date approaches. You may be surprised at how many flashbacks this labor and delivery can induce. It's normal and inevitable that you will compare your experiences. You have a high investment in getting what you want this time. Emotions—both positive and negative—may overlay all that happens.

When Joy Mixes with Sadness

There is much joy around giving birth, but delivery can also trigger sadness for new mothers. There are the fluctuating hormones, the sleep deprivation, and the demands of caring for a newborn. Naturally, there is also a sense of loss and a literal emptiness surrounding your physical and psychological separation from the baby you carried inside you. You may also have some grief over the birth itself. Perhaps unplanned interventions were necessary or you were separated from your baby for a while. All of these sources of sadness are a part of *normal* postpartum recovery.

Although these losses pale in comparison to the losses you experienced in your preterm delivery, be sure to allow yourself to feel this pain, too. Particularly if your labor and delivery again did not go as you had hoped and planned, your disappointments may take you back to the preterm birth, and you may grieve anew. If you must be separated from your baby, it won't matter that it's just for fifteen minutes this time, instead of for days, weeks, or months. The ache of not being able to hold your baby right after birth doesn't diminish, even as you appreciate being able to room-in and snuggle. You can cherish the wonder of having a healthy newborn while still being sad that you didn't have a dream delivery. This is normal. It doesn't mean that you'll be carrying a huge package of grieving again. It just means that there are some aspects of this birth that saddened or disappointed you.

It is also quite normal for this birth to act as a catalyst to stir up your residual grief over your preemie's early arrival. Take advantage of the opportunity to do more grief work. It's natural for the joys of this experience to mingle with the despair of deliveries past. Allow any grief to flow. Doing so will free you to enjoy your new baby to the fullest.

Indeed, there is so much to celebrate. Just making it closer to term is a triumph. If this time you have the delivery you'd always wished for, revel in that joy. Let your positive experiences contribute to your continued healing.

> *My daughter arrived two weeks late. She was delivered vaginally in the most glorious experience of my life. The entire labor and delivery was relaxed and private. I have never felt such joy as the moment I pushed her out and they laid her body on my chest. I breast-fed her immediately. She was a "squishy" baby—a normal, chubby little baby with lots and lots of fleshy folds. Each of my children was brought to me in a miraculous way. Each child is cherished and special in their own way. Having two children is a challenge, but easier than I ever imagined. —Laura*

Revisiting What Might Have Been

For many mothers, mingled with the joy of this new birth is the continued longing for what might have been the last time. Delivering and holding this baby in your arms can bring you to another level of realization of everything you missed before. This birth may remind you again of the preterm delivery—and you may blame yourself anew.

> *The main time I experienced flashbacks was when I was in labor with my daughter. I should have expected it, but I didn't. I thought having a healthy, full-term baby would erase my pain. Instead, I was at the same hospital, and panicking. ... I was so, so terrified and remembering things that were coming back to me, memories flooding and flooding. ... So here, two and a half years later, I was walking at the same hospital in labor, and I just started crying— as hard as the first time. It was just so unfair that Josh and Evan had to suffer and this new baby probably wouldn't have to. Why should they have suffered? —Stephie*

The flip side to pondering what might have been in your previous delivery is how blessed you are to have this full-term baby after giving birth to a preemie. You know what might have been had this baby been born early as well. You're acutely aware of the dangers, uncertainties, and heartache that you've managed to sidestep this time. You remember your devastation when your preemie was in the NICU, and your basketload of regrets. This time, there is no "if only" or "Why *my* baby?" Instead, you can say, "There but for

Coping during a Post-Preemie Pregnancy

the grace of God/fate/Mother Nature/the Universe go I." Because of what you've been through, you feel deeply grateful to deliver a baby you can hold and take home very soon.

I was so happy to get to have a normal pregnancy and a full-term baby. It didn't in any way detract from the enormous love and feeling I have for Stuart. The emotions are very different. I fought so hard for Stuart, and he fought so hard to live, that we have a bond that is different, and special, and that will always bind us together in a unique, wonderful way. But my heart is entwined with Justin in another powerful, but very different way. His birth, his being, healed me in some fashion—not completely, by a long shot, but he soothed some critical wounded part of me. I can't express what it meant to get to be a normal mommy, to have natural childbirth, do all the regular, normal things without sorrow and despair coloring each moment. But it is that sorrow and despair that enable me to appreciate it all to the degree that I did and do. In some ways, I wouldn't trade it away because I value the heightened sensitivity I have to the blessings in my life. But of course, I'd give it up in a heartbeat to have my little boy Spencer in my arms. This is all contradictory, I know, but my emotions aren't logical, they just are. —Susan

Complications with a Full-Term Birth

If your full-term newborn has unexpected difficulties during delivery or after birth, your first response may be surprise and disbelief. You know, intellectually, that even full-term babies can have problems, but you didn't dare imagine that this could happen to *you* (just as you never imagined the earlier preterm birth). As a veteran of the NICU, you may feel a sense of weariness if your full-term newborn is sent there to be monitored or for assistance with breathing difficulties, infection, or glucose levels. You never imagined that *you* would have one of those giant babies on the open warmer. If your newborn must spend some time in the NICU, you'll need to call upon the coping strategies you learned with your preemie. Ask questions and be active. You *can* get through this again.

Homecoming

Going home with your new full-term baby is such a triumph. Even so, you may have mixed feelings as they wheel you to discharge. Acutely sensitive to the fact that some of the people crossing the hospital's threshold may be visiting their fragile babies in the NICU, you may long to tell them that you have walked in their shoes. You may see yourself in their plodding movements and preoccupied gaze. At the same time, you want to revel in the normalcy of leaving without fuss and fanfare. Allow yourself the joy of an uncomplicated discharge. There will be other times to think about other parents of preemies and to give them support.

Just as you will inevitably compare your deliveries, you will also compare homecomings and newborn periods. If you assume that having a full-term, healthy baby will be an easy, joyous existence, you may be surprised when you encounter difficulties or your own mixed emotions. If your preemie has ongoing special needs, balancing those needs with your new baby's can be a challenge. You may find your experiences tinged with regret, and your attentions spread too thinly.

I was in for one big surprise when I brought Justin home. It was hard! Prior to his birth, when reading parenting magazines ... that talked about the stress and difficulties concerning parenting a newborn, I really (privately) scoffed at them. I thought that, having survived what I had survived, having a healthy pregnancy and a healthy newborn would be a piece of cake. But it was hard. Physically and emotionally we went through a real adjustment period. I was back at work after two weeks, which, again, I didn't think would be difficult after my previous challenges, but it was difficult—very! I really underestimated all of this, so it came as quite a shock. It was certainly a different kind of hard, and the reality of my other experiences didn't negate this one.
—Susan

I definitely got more depressed after my full-term daughter was born nineteen months after Conor's birth. Having a new, healthy baby made me mourn for what could have been with my son. We missed out on so many simple pleasures. I missed out on his infancy, and now I feel like hers is slipping by too quickly. Instead of rejoicing in her amazing milestones, I mourn all that Conor never had. A new baby is supposed to be the center of attention. Not in our home. Baby's needs always come second to my son's. I feel guilty that they are both being cheated. —Laura

•••
781
Coping during a Post-Preemie Pregnancy

You may so look forward to focusing on the joy of this new baby that you may try to gloss over any difficulties. As you naturally compare newborn experiences, you may try to suppress your sorrow. Recognize, though, that stifling your emotions will make it impossible to feel any of them fully. Permit yourself to feel the full range and intensity of your painful emotions, and you'll open yourself up to the happy ones. If you have nagging concerns about your feelings or your bonding to your new baby, find a counselor who is experienced in supporting preemie or grieving parents. Mothering an infant is such a precious and fleeting time. You deserve to enjoy and experience this period to the fullest, warts and all. Doing so will benefit you and your baby.

Another Preemie

I really thought that I could carry my second daughter to term, seeing as how my doctor could not find any reason for my water breaking [too early] with my first daughter. When I delivered my second daughter a week earlier than my first, this was devastating to me and my husband. We could not believe that it was happening again. —Suzy

For me, it was weird. I'm dreaming this again. I remember standing outside the window and thinking, "It's just not happening." And then I'd say, "God, I'll never swear for the rest of my life. If this baby comes, let it be healthy." I'd give up whatever, just to have this baby survive. I couldn't do it again, you know? And I knew my wife was going to be just completely devastated. This time Sue asked if they could bring Erin to her before she would leave, in case anything happened. So when they got her stabilized, they brought her in the little bubble container, and Sue got to reach in and touch her hand. —Charlie

After having a premature baby, perhaps your greatest fear is that it might happen again. Delivering at around the same gestational age, or even earlier than before, can be devastating. You may wonder if it's a sign of deeper problems or of your inadequacy as a parent. Your feelings of guilt and failure may know no bounds. You may fear that you cannot survive this ordeal yet again. But you're probably more resilient than you think. You've shown your mettle before, and you can gather your strength and courage to prevail this time as well.

I'll admit the memories resurfaced a little when I became pregnant again with Levi. However, since we didn't consider me high risk, the memories were fleeting. Now, though, I'm angry that I've had to endure this twice. Even though Jonah is fine and Levi appears to be on the road to a normal life, I still get upset sometimes that I missed out on the wonderful birthing experience I had with Elijah, my first son. —Jen

They sewed me up, and I just remember lying there, thinking, "I can't believe it happened again. I just can't believe it happened again" and trying to remember the courage that I had gotten after already going through the experience. Having gone through it once, I think you acquire certain knowledge and a certain understanding of things, to be able to get through it a little easier, but then the emotional part is still as strong as ever.

Of course, having a C-section now, I knew things were going to be so much different. It wasn't until the next day that I saw him. We went into the unit together, and I just looked at him and he was very small and very skinny and hooked up to ... I was comparing the two. This time it wasn't so much seeing things for the first time ... it was a little more familiar. But I got right up to him, and they had the plastic over the open warmer, and he's got the CPAP and he's all hooked up to everything, and I just think, "How am I going to go through this again?" And then they told me he's younger than I thought. And I'm thinking, "This could be a whole different story, a whole different outcome." I just didn't even know what to think at that point. —Vickie

Coping the Second (or More) Time Around

If you deliver prematurely again, try to find some comfort in these observations:

- Even if you deliver as early or earlier than you did last time, every baby is different. It is entirely possible that this baby will have a smoother hospital course, fewer complications, a faster homecoming, and an easier infancy than your earlier preemie did. Have hope.
- If you deliver later than last time but still prematurely, you may be amazed at what a difference an extra week or month can make for a baby. In general, a slightly premature baby has fewer difficulties and struggles than a moderately premature baby; likewise, a moderately premature baby will likely have an easier time than a severely premature newborn. This means you may have fewer anxieties and

disappointments with your new preemie. Diana talks about her second preterm delivery, which was a lot different than her first because baby Eric was only slightly premature:

One of the moments I'll always remember occurred about an hour after Eric's birth. After I had been stitched up from some mild lacerations, all the doctors and nurses had left to go to lunch, and my husband left the room to find some food for himself. Eric and I were alone, he wrapped in a blanket and cuddling on my chest. I looked around the room, realized we were alone, and felt very out of sorts. Shouldn't someone be here? A nurse? A doctor? Are you sure he's still okay? Is it normal for a mother and a newborn to be left alone, unattended?! It was the first time that things felt completely different between my two birthing experiences. —Diana

The NICU, Again

I never, ever thought that I would ever see the inside of the NICU again. And now I'm going through the whole rigmarole again. Two babies born by emergency cesareans. Two babies that I never got to see after they were born. And two babies who have had to fight for their lives. And two babies who I never got to enjoy being babies because I was/am so scared that I would/will lose them. —Jo

As you approach the NICU roller coaster for another go-around, you are at an advantage. You may feel more comfortable this time negotiating your way around the unit and becoming a member of your baby's health care team. You may feel better able to ask questions and request what you need. You may feel more parental, more confident, and more knowledgeable about the technology and interventions. Because of this, you may wonder if your previous NICU experiences can protect you from serious emotional pain this time. But although you may handle this experience differently, and feel more educated and prepared for what you're going to see and go through, you can't be more prepared *emotionally*.

My second time through the NICU unhinged me like Dorothy's house in the Wizard of Oz. Neither of my "visits" to the NICU were significant by some

standards, but I apparently am very sensitive about the loss of "normal."
—Sheila

Just because you've been through the NICU experience once doesn't mean you're safe this time from the powerful emotions this experience raises. In fact, you may feel doubly disappointed and more weary, and you may get less support from family and friends than you did the last time. You may have similar worries, and you have to cope with a wide range of painful feelings. You have to again face your anger, your sadness, your guilt, your anxiety—whatever you're feeling this time. You are on another, separate journey, and you are just as entitled to your emotions along the way as you were in your earlier journey. It's also important to remember how important the support of others—especially other parents of preemies—can be to your coping, even though you're a "veteran" this time.

Going down there, I had the strength to do it because I'd done it before. It wasn't so traumatic. But this time I wasn't sure what kind of road it was going to be. I was not so readily willing to have people help me through it. I don't know if it was because I felt like I'd been through it and I should be strong enough to go through it again, but I didn't connect up with anybody. I really kept myself at bay, almost like I didn't want to believe it or I didn't want to make it real. Almost like I didn't want to talk about it. In fact, this is how queer it was—I remember calling friends and family saying, "He's doing great. Everything's going fine." People would call us: "How's he doing?" "He's doing great."

And finally I remember Russ and I sitting here saying, "Why are we acting like this is nothing? Why are we telling people that it's not a big deal when it is, you know? I mean, we've got a baby who was born way before he should have been born. We don't know what's going to happen." How can I describe it? I think it was our own defenses. We made light of it because we didn't want to feel the pain of it this time. So we talked about how we needed to talk more about what was really going on, what was happening. You know, the fear of the transfusion, the fear of the problems, like he was having reflux so bad it was causing the [apnea] spells, and all these things that were going on. At any time, something could take a bad turn, and were we even prepared for that? And I don't think we were. We really relied on the [belief] that things were just going to be okay and we were just going to glide through it without really feeling it.

So Russ and I decided we really needed to talk more about what was actually happening instead of just saying, "Oh, he's fine." So when people would ask, even though they didn't want to hear, we would tell them, "Well, he had a setback today and this is the problem, and this is what's going on." But it's amazing because even then, people didn't really want to hear that. They just want you to say that everything's okay because they don't really know how to deal with it. So then we found ourselves talking to people in a way to protect them instead of us. —*Vickie*

Just because you have some experience negotiating the NICU doesn't mean it's not a big deal to have another baby in the unit. But you can use your abilities and experience to your advantage. Rely on your knowledge that you *can* survive this ordeal. Apply the skills you acquired the first time around regarding facing your feelings, coping, and getting what you need. You can be assertive about your desire to nurture your little one in the NICU. As an experienced parent of a NICU preemie, you have a lot to offer your new baby.

Points to Remember

- A subsequent pregnancy after a premature birth is bound to be filled with anxiety. It's natural to worry whether you will have an uncomplicated pregnancy, labor, and delivery. Your fears are balanced with the hope that you and your new baby will avoid the NICU this time.
- Remember that feelings of anxiety are not premonitions of disaster. Your fears do not predict the future, nor do they cause it.
- Let yourself fully examine your anxiety so that you can also revel in the joy that you feel. Denying your worries can numb all your feelings.
- Information is an antidote to anxiety. Talk with your health care providers about the sorts of precautions you need to take, how to monitor your symptoms, and how to take the best care of yourself and your unborn baby. Don't make assumptions about what you must or must not do before discussing it with your doctor. Let information, instead of anxiety, be your guide.

- As you approach your due date, let yourself complain about those last-trimester aches and pains, just like all the other very pregnant women. You've earned the right.
- If your pregnancy doesn't go smoothly, it does not automatically mean that you will have another preemie. Many complicated pregnancies end at term, with a healthy baby.
- Coping during a high-risk pregnancy can mean activity restrictions, bed rest, hospitalization, and frequent doctors' visits for monitoring. You may feel frustrated and disappointed to have to go through all of this again, when you long so much for a "normal" pregnancy.
- A complicated pregnancy is even more complicated when you have other children to consider. Enlist practical and emotional support rom others.
- If you must be on bed rest, keeping your spirits up can be key to coping. Find ways to fight boredom and stay connected with others. Remember that you deserve to have your needs met and that you are accepting assistance on behalf of the baby you are carrying.
- The birth of your post-preemie baby may be an intensely emotional time. It is natural for some grief to accompany your joy.
- The events that you had imagined—labor and delivery, rooming-in, and homecoming—may not be as you planned. Give yourself permission to feel any disappointment, even though you know how lucky you really are.
- Adjustment to a new baby is challenging, even when everything is going really well. You are entitled to have the support and assistance you need.
- If this baby arrives prematurely, you may worry how you can possibly survive another NICU journey and raise another preemie. Rest assured that you come to this NICU stay armed with more confidence and information—and with a clear identity as a parent. All of these will serve you well. You will survive.

Parenting Your Premature Baby and Child

CHAPTER TWENTY-THREE

Healing and
Moving On

Some things happen before they should: Early winter storms that bury tender, green shoots; shiny wonder gone from an adolescent's eyes; alarmingly pink-skinned babies born before their lungs can sustain their breath.

My sons were born too soon ... yanked out of the womb ... shy of the time they needed to develop thick enough skin, strong enough lungs, stable enough internal organs to thrive in this world. Even our advanced medical technology could not save the older, the larger, the sicker of the two—sick only because my body was unable to maintain a safe harbor for him, for his brother. But technology did save his brother, slowly, haltingly, and at a terrible price.

Babies should catch their first glimpses of the world from the protective arms of their parents, not pinned to a board, warmed by a light, and covered with Saran Wrap. There is a terrible toll exacted for extreme prematurity—a toll paid by much-too-tender babies who are pierced and poked, intubated and artificially paralyzed, babies who aren't held, or stroked, or nursed at birth. There is a cost beyond measure that is witnessed by helpless, terrified parents who can only pray and hope, wonder and worry—parents full of guilt, parents who can't protect, parents who pledge fervent, unspoken promises, who make deals, bargains, pleas, as regularly as breath comes and goes.

How cold I must be to remember it so starkly, so vividly, so as it was. When my three-year-old wriggles, giggles, and tickles with me on the floor, how can I not soften the memories, peer back through a haze of gratitude for this incredible child, for this little person, so delicate, yet with the strength and persistence to defy the cruelty of his birth.

But there are lingering reminders, subtle differences between my son and his younger, full-term brother, between my son and his three-year-old peers, differences that remind me daily of the battle he fought, the battle he fights. Language comes slowly to him, comes stiffly from him. Sensory difficulties interfere with his ability to feed himself, to tolerate textures. And his scars ... oh, his scars.

I am unable to adequately articulate the fierce protectiveness I feel toward this child. Daily I am humbled by the strength, the sheer grit he has shown, continues to show. And I love him with a depth and passion previously unknown, unimaginable to me. —Susan

The journey that accompanies your baby's premature birth is one that you probably never imagined taking. Such a journey often begins abruptly, raising more questions than answers. Early on, and perhaps many times over the months and years that follow, you may wonder whether you can ever heal from the grief and recover from the trauma of this journey. Others may admonish you to let it go, and you may secretly wonder, "Will I ever get over this experience?"

Just when I think I've done okay, something happens and I realize I've still got far to go. Our daughter, Hannah, really has done remarkably well. Even so, I still feel traumatized to some extent by the experience. —Stephanie

Like any difficult significant life event, having and raising a premature baby is not something that you simply get over. Instead, it's only natural that prematurity continues to touch your life in many ways, directly and indirectly, obviously and subtly. You may wonder how you can ever move on when you're still so affected by this experience.

Moving on doesn't mean forgetting or becoming emotionally hardened. Moving on means

- Being able to remember without falling apart
- Letting go of what might have been
- Going forward in spite of uncertainty
- Finding meaning and treasure in adversity
- Finding a balance between vulnerability and hope
- Appreciating your own resilience
- Embracing your own personal growth

These are all hallmarks of healing.

This final chapter holds some thoughts and words of encouragement about adjusting, healing, and moving on.

Remembering

After you have a premature baby, you may wish that you could erase those memories because remembering is so painful. But if you can let yourself remember your experience, dwell on it, and really *feel* it, you can actually come to value your experience—not for the pain and suffering it caused, but for what you've learned, how you've grown, and the good that you've harvested because of it. Eventually you'll be able to say, "You know what? I *got* something from that."

Early on, when your grief takes center stage, you may notice only the negative effects of your baby's premature birth. But after a time, even if you've been shaken to your core, as you work through your painful emotions you can begin to feel a mending taking place. Gradually, you can let go of your pain while holding on to and savoring your personal growth. This transformation can positively affect your life.

Taking these positive effects with you on your journey, you will begin to integrate prematurity into your life. Being the parent of a preemie becomes but one facet of who you are. Instead of trying to put the entire ordeal behind you, you come to value where you've been and embrace all of your experiences and emotions, the joy and the sorrow. When you embrace the full journey, your life feels enriched, and you can feel more whole. Indeed, as you heal, you may notice that your joy takes on a brilliance and complexity that sets your life apart from the everyday. You owe this brilliance to where you've been—and to where you're headed.

I really do understand my blessings. I am still aware of my pain. I am learning to be happy and sad at the same time. It is incredible. It is a relief. I will endure. —Susan

Still, for months or years after your baby's birth, you may have moments of intense sadness, anger, fear, or regret. In particular, you may be deeply affected by other losses in your life, as well as by outside events that hit close to home. These may include other premature births and, particularly, the deaths of children in your community. Events that reactivate your original trauma are opportunities for you to work through deeper layers of your grief and to reach for more healing.

As time goes on and my boys grow, my perspective shifts and changes. I'm better able to compartmentalize my emotions and prevent the sorrow from those years ago from tainting the pure pleasure I feel now in having witnessed my once–critically ill preemies become funny and smart and beautiful children. It can still be difficult, though, to separate then and now. When I see an ambulance with its lights turning and siren blaring racing down the road, I instantly bite my lip and have to hide my panic. I wonder if the passenger is like my little one when he was tiny and had to be raced back to the NICU for a second course. But then I look over and see him thoughtfully doing his alphabet puzzle, and the anxiety eases. —Maureen

Nathan wasn't one of my son's close friends, but his death has hit me so hard. I keep thinking of his mother leaving the hospital with empty arms and going home to an empty bed, forever. ... I grieve for Nathan and his family, I grieve for me and James, and I grieve for anyone and everyone else who has felt the pain of a sick child as well. Nathan's death has been almost like a turning point. It seems so awful, but that one event has opened up places inside me that have been dark for years, five and a half years to be exact. There seems to be so much now that's bursting, demanding to be written or spoken, and I'm surprising myself with how I'm coping with it all. It's difficult when an idea or a feeling emerges. I feel that I have to put pen to paper to remain calm. It's very odd. But each time I write, part of me heals just that little bit more. At times I almost feel still, peaceful ... not very often, perhaps only once or twice, but it feels good to know that I can reach that place. —Leanne

• • •

You may also be strongly affected by childbearing joys in your life, as well as by the childbearing joys of others. You may wistfully wish that your preemie could have been a full-term baby like your subsequent child, or the old jealousy may stir when you hear of another parent's ease with childbirth. These situations may prompt your grief to rise up, giving you the chance to work through yet another layer. As you continue to heal, you'll be able to reach for the joy without being overcome by grief.

I still feel jealousy sometimes. But it is so hard to put it into words because I think we push that away as a "bad" feeling. But it is so normal, so understandable. I tend to understand it as part of my grieving process, and then move away from the jealousy/anger/resentment place and move under that to the real sadness and loss that fuels the jealousy.

And I am feeling the jealousy less often, and being grateful more often, and not needing to compare so much because my boy is my angel and I couldn't want anything but what we have right now—so much love. —Maren

You'll find evidence of your healing when you can look back and remember without feeling overwhelmed. Instead of an unrelenting flood of emotion, you feel only a small stream or perhaps just a trickle. *Looking back* no longer means *going back.* You can remember your baby's birth, hospitalization, and homecoming with more emphasis on and appreciation of the positive than the negative. You can survive other reminders—women whose bellies are ripe with pregnancy, newborn babes in arms, news of another premature baby's being born—with a sigh instead of a gasp. You can survive anniversaries, and your baby's birth date becomes more clearly a celebration and a time to recognize your joy.

It wasn't until everybody started singing "Happy Birthday" that I just lost it. I just couldn't believe it was a whole year that had passed. Tom and I just looked at each other, but here they were, eating cake, smashing their fingers in it. —Betsy

Conor's going to be four in two weeks. We had an early birthday party for him this weekend. It was a wonderful day. But even so, I had to hug him, smell him, and cry because I'll never get over what we've faced and what we continue to face. —Laura

You can call me Susan "yo-yo," but I have been feeling much more integrated of late. Not less sad, but still more happy, and overall more peaceful. It is amazing to me that this sense has stayed with me even today, the eve of the [fifth] birthday of the twins. —Susan

I get more emotional around Charlie's birthday because I know it was a much harder place to get to. ... Around his birthday I say, "Oh, my God, look at him. He makes me laugh and he's so funny. He's so wonderful and cute." I love him so much, and I can't help but think that I really almost didn't have him. —Jaimee

It's hard to believe those scrawny, tiny, funny-looking babies I had seven years ago today are now rambunctious, maddening, hyperactive, lovable, robust seven-year-olds. I only had one bad dream in the days leading up to this last birthday, so that's a great improvement over the previous years. And in the dream, it wasn't me having the preemie; it was the woman in the next bed. Whatever would Freud say? —Joyce

Whatever your catalysts, there will be times over the years when you will still cry, yell, or wonder wistfully about what might have been. As you continue your journey, you will continue to grieve, but also to heal—at your own pace, along your unique path.

From my own experience I can tell you that the blues can still find me, the guilt can still creep up when I'm not looking, and the sense of responsibility is constantly present. Even some of the old fears surface and try to drag me under. Parts of these emotions are attributable to being a preemie parent, parts are simply because of being a parent, period. —Maureen

I still have fears, but I try to see it as something I have learned to cope with. In the beginning I could not talk about it without crying—the first second I opened my mouth—and now I can talk about it almost without crying. I guess you heal. No matter what you have to deal with, your life continues and you go through a healing process. —Gallice

Moving On but Not Forgetting

When the boys were over four years old, I was visiting the unit and taking part in a parent training. All the parents were talking about how hard it was to make the transition to breast-feeding their babies at home. I listened and didn't cognitively think anything about it. I have long gotten over the fact that I couldn't breast-feed Josh and Evan. Well, that night my right breast started hurting, and then the next morning I did a breast exam, and milk came out! I freaked out and was even checked by the doctor, who confirmed that I had had a psychosomatic reaction to being on the unit again and talking about breast-feeding. Weird, huh? Even when we think we are cognitively over things, our body isn't! It remembers! —Stephie

James starts preschool (four-year-old kindergarten) tomorrow, his first tentative steps into the "big school" system. My boy looked at me and said, "Remember, mummy, I'm only a little bloke. I might need you to stay. What if I get sad?" Those words knocked me flat—"Remember, I'm only a little bloke." How could I ever forget? Will I ever forget? ... He's only been my baby for four years. I want some more time. I'm not ready to hand him over yet. ... He's mine, we survived together. ... He held onto my finger when his hand was too small to reach around it all the way, and tomorrow I put his hand into another's. ... I can't. I don't want to. ... "Remember, mummy, I'm only a little bloke." Oh, but I will. —Leanne

As you come to terms with what happened, you can heal and move on, not because you forget about your experience, but because you can live with it. You can live with it because you've felt your grief, releasing it—and in turn, it releases you. Even though you may still have remnants of grief, you can achieve a feeling of peace. It happened, and you'll always be sad about it, but you can live with it.

As you release your grief and happiness begins to predominate, your memories become bittersweet and your reactions are softer and easier to bear. And looking back, you can see evidence that all along, you were going to prevail.

I can't say that, for me, there's any one revelation of peace and acceptance. We're thrown into accepting what we never thought we could and allowed to experience what we sometimes doubted we would each and every day. And I think the peace has been there from day one. It continues to help me climb those stairs. —Julie

Over time, as your memories and reactions soften, you also change how you talk to others about what happened. When prematurity is such a big focus in your life, you may feel that nothing short of the whole story will do. But as you adjust and acquire perspective, you become more selective about how much and with whom you share the details. You can value your journey privately, without the urge to tell everyone your story. It can be liberating to be able to say simply, "Yes, she's small" and leave it at that. And when you do share your story, it isn't a draining or heart-wrenching ordeal. You can talk more matter-of-factly about your child's premature birth, hospitalization, and development.

You may also notice a change in your reaction to the observations of your child's health care providers or follow-up team. At first, you may feel flustered, unsure of what to say to these people. When professionals are scrutinizing you and your child, you may feel exposed and inadequate, and you may discount your own observations. Over time, though, you will come to appreciate and trust what *you* know about your child. Gaining this confidence is more evidence of your emotional healing.

The turning point is very clear for me. It came when we went through a second round of developmental testing when Lars was around twenty-one months old. I disagreed with some of the results, but instead of getting angry, I realized that no one else knows Lars like I do, and I don't need anyone else to tell me that he's okay. Wow. It was around that time that I finally began to have a deep sense of his wellness. Strangely enough, his bout with respiratory syncytial virus (RSV) just increased my confidence in his basic health instead of bouncing me back into "sick baby" mode. —Kris

• • •
796

Letting Go of What Might Have Been

There are some times when I think about it. But I don't cry because they were born premature. I cry because Jacob has special needs. But it doesn't happen very often anymore. It used to happen so often when things were up in the air.
—*Julie*

As you grieve, you can let go of idealized images of what should have, could have, or would have been—and realize that all deliveries have their disappointments, all new parents have their struggles, and all babies have their imperfections and temperamental idiosyncrasies. With time and experience, you can come to appreciate your parenthood and your little one's presence. The circumstances of your baby's arrival and early months fade into the background, and you focus on what you have, instead of on what you missed.

I had had such a picture in my mind my entire life, it seems, of how happy I would be when I finally had a baby. I can remember thinking this as a very young child. And how great the moment when you first met your baby would be. Well, of course, with a preemie it was far from the moment I had waited for all my life. Since Bronwen's birth I have been struggling with feelings of being cheated, being angry that I didn't get the birth I had planned, angry at what my baby had to go through, and on and on.

I have been getting a little bit better with this kind of thing lately, but today something wonderful happened. I had a moment where I looked at Bronwen and I realized that I do have all those things I was hoping for so long ago. It was a perfect moment. I saw her and thought, "Isn't my baby wonderful? I love being a mom!" and none of those other feelings were there to mar the moment. Of course, I have thought those exact same things before, but today it was different because there were no negatives coming up behind, like, "Yes, but maybe it could have been better!"

My dreams have come true, just not exactly when I thought they would.
—*Nola*

You also learn to appreciate your child's unique mix of strengths and challenges. Instead of wondering who your child would have been if he or she had been born at term, you can focus on who your child is now.

•••
797
Healing and Moving On

In so many ways I think Macy's most amazing qualities somehow may have resulted from her preemie-ness and/or the battle that it required her to wage. I will always wonder what she would have been like if she had been full term, but I cannot imagine her being any smarter or funnier or more energetic or more athletic or more anything that is desirable in a child. My view as her mother is of course clouded, but I think she is just the cat's meow. I can truly, honestly say she might have been different had she been full term, but she couldn't possibly have been "better" than she is. —Christi

If your preemie is disabled or has ongoing medical problems, you will always wish that things could be easier for her or him, but as time passes, this wish will take up less and less space in your life or in your relationship with your child. Instead of expending energy thinking about what didn't happen and doesn't exist, you learn to embrace reality. In fact, your child may inspire you the most, by his or her ability to accept what can seem to you to be entirely unacceptable.

So many times people comment on my positive attitude, and I want to scream, "What choice do I have?" This is how it was and is, and nothing can change that. Stephen has fought and fought to come as far as he has and still has more fights ahead. His example is what keeps me going. He deserves a mommy who can laugh and smile with him. Who will play and be silly. Who will always be there to help him and support him. I do cry in my time late at night, after all the others are in bed. [But] my positive attitude is a shield of sorts. It lets me get through the day with my miracle and return his joy, smile for smile. —Tracy

Moving On in the Face of Uncertainties

Clare's and Emily's issues are pretty much gone. We're still on the lookout for learning problems, but they're doing great in school so far. Jacob's problems are severe and eternal. It's not a matter of integrating his premature birth but more his disabilities into our lives. When I look at Jacob, I no longer say, "He's a preemie" but rather, "He's a little boy with multiple handicaps." And we're still floundering with issues of disabilities. No one person can take our hands and lead us to the right decisions for Jacob. Our intense love for Jacob gets us through each day. —Julie

• • •

If you're raising a child whose future is still uncertain or looks challenging, you may wonder how you can move on when you don't know where you're going. Although you may not know exactly how your child will develop, you do know how she or he is today, and you can probably guess where your child is headed tomorrow and perhaps next week. Staying focused on current realities can help you cope.

Unfortunately, even the current realities are not always clear. Doctors don't yet grasp all of the ongoing effects of prematurity, and they can't always give you definitive answers. But as you learn to trust your intuitions and find health care professionals and teachers you can collaborate with, you can know what is knowable, and you can move forward, rather than being stuck. Just as your child's growth will unfold over a lifetime, perhaps in unexpected ways, the same is true for your coming to terms with your child's special needs.

I remember the "turning point" very clearly. It was just this past summer. After our trip to Denver, when Stephen was so much healthier and able to do more, I felt as though we had gotten over the hump in his care, so to speak. Even this winter, when he did have a brief return to his illness, I felt that it was a temporary setback, and not part of a permanent pattern.

Oddly enough, it was the [respiratory specialists] in Denver who also helped me be more at peace with the idea that he will likely have long-term delays and possible mental disabilities. They were the first who would actually look me in the eye and tell me that Stephen might be mildly retarded. All the others have talked around it. It was hearing it straight out that allowed me to begin to assimilate it and learn to adjust my life to it. Until then, the most frustrating thing has been that "delay" implies a lag that will be made up. I kept waiting for Stephen to "catch up." Now that it has been put into terms implying a permanent situation, I can deal with it as part of life and not wait for an ending that won't come. —Tracy

I am in the process of finding a sense of peace about raising a special needs child. Yet I am completely at peace with the child. We have a quiet snuggle each morning when I wake him up for preschool, and the weight of him in my arms, against my chest, the flutter of his eyelashes as he struggles awake, his breathing, yawning, stretching—they are miraculous to me again and again. I am in awe of this little being in my life. —Susan

• • •

Talking to Your Growing Child about the NICU

My daughter likes to see pictures from when she was in the hospital. She gets really upset if she doesn't see my hand there or something of mine right by her. She's like, "Why weren't you there, mommy?" "I couldn't be. I'm sorry!" Those times hit me pretty hard—not being able to help it. —Marcia

It's normal for children to be curious about their birth and infancy. They want to know how they arrived and how their parents reacted. When they see photographs or tiny baby clohes, they want to hear the stories behind them.

You will want to be able to talk to your growing preemie about his or her birth and NICU stay. These experiences shouldn't be a secret or something to be tiptoed around. Your child deserves to hear about those special beginnings. However, you might worry about frightening your child or about your own feelings spilling out.

Even if you have been acknowledging and working through your feelings over time, you may still feel emotional when your little one asks questions about the past. Use your child's curiosity to advance your own healing. If you're feeling overwhelmed at the prospect of talking to your child about his or her birth, first try writing down your story as if you were telling it to your child. Be sure to include anecdotes about the pregnancy, delivery, and hospitalization and include how it felt—how exciting, how scary it was—and also how much hope and love you felt. Writing down your story without censoring the information or your emotions gives you the opportunity to organize your thoughts and consider how to talk to your child. Getting your feelings out on paper, especially your guilt and regret, can help you share this story calmly with your child and without falling apart.

When you do talk with your child, be honest, open, age appropriate, and reassuring. Answer questions directly with minimal detail; your child can ask for more details when he or she wants them. As your child gets older and more sophisticated, you can add layers of detail to the story when questions arise.

Answering questions in a comforting manner helps keep your child from being troubled by what you tell her or him. Reassure your daughter that the doctors and nurses took very good care of her and that you visited whenever you could. Explain that she slept most of the time (rather than lying awake, missing you) because she was so busy growing big and strong. If you're looking at photographs with your son, reassure him that all that equipment helped the nurses take care of him and helped him grow. Explain that most of the wires were just stuck to him with tape, and that if the doctors or nurses needed to do more, they gave him medicine so that it didn't hurt. Let your twins know that your sadness about that time isn't because you are sad about having had them, but because it was so hard to have to leave them in the hospital. Of course, you wanted to hold them and bring them home right away, but you couldn't! And how happy you were when they did come home! Remember always to convey the deep joy you feel about having your little one(s) in your family.

Also reassure your child that it was nobody's fault that he or she was born early. If you tell your child that she came early because she "wanted to" or because she was "ready to get out and see the world," she may feel responsible for her early birth and guilty about scaring you or causing her own problems. Instead, you can say that there must have been reasons that she was meant to be born earlier rather than later.

In general, describing your child's early experiences with a measure of pride ("You did so well!") and nonchalance ("You sailed through surgery!") encourages your child to take those NICU experiences or complications in stride. Try to avoid relating your horror or heart-wrenching emotions. As Sheila observes, "It seems that both Kate and Kayla [Kate's friend, also a preemie] are very comfortable with their unique journeys, scars and all."

Finding Meaning in Your Journey

When you can find meaning in your journey, you can feel less victimized by what has happened to you and your little one. You can see a deeper purpose, and you don't feel so much that you've been randomly chosen or that you suffered needlessly.

One way to find meaning is through understanding what has happened and why. Gathering information and answers can help you feel a sense of mastery over what occurred. Even if no one can tell you why this happened medically, the more you learn, the better you can put together an account that makes sense to you and that you can live with.

There's also a spiritual side to finding meaning. Over the years, as you look at the big picture, you may acquire a sense of purpose—you may conclude that you endured these experiences for a reason that has to do with the path you and your child were meant to take. The twists of fate can seem less cruel and arbitrary when you feel a sense of destiny or higher purpose.

Finding spiritual meaning in your journey can be an important part of integrating your experiences into your life. You may find meaning through certain philosophies or religious beliefs about life and fate. You can also find meaning in the good that arises from your experiences, including your deepened appreciation for parenthood, resilience, and personal growth.

> *I'm very energetic. I'm very impatient. I'm a doer and a mover, and I like to get things done. With Erin, my life has come to a complete skid. With the boys [it's], "Hey, let's go upstairs and watch TV," and [snaps fingers] we're there. But with Erin you've got to get her out of her wheelchair, and when you get upstairs, you've got to strap her into some apparatus—it's a whole process. To go anywhere with her, to do anything with her, to go to a movie, anything, it's a slow, slow, tedious process. With my wife, who's the most patient, loving person you could ever meet, it's no big deal for her—she adapted. This is something that I think God wanted to give her the day she was born. It was like, "This woman here, she could raise a child with cerebral palsy." So when she got older, she got a child with cerebral palsy. Me, he probably said, "This boy needs to settle down. We need to slow him down a little bit, so let's give him this child too, and he can develop into a person who can slow down, by being with her." —Charlie*

Finding Treasure in Adversity

> *Here's my cousin having one [healthy child] after another. The worst is that they just don't realize how blessed they are. They take it all for granted. And in that weird little way, I think that perhaps there is a little bright side to having a preemie because no one else but a preemie parent will understand the amazing joy I feel when James does such a simple thing as smile at me. —Teresa*

Most parents eventually find a treasure or something positive that comes out of this ordeal. As time passes and your grief softens, you begin to take stock. You may take solace in what you've learned from your child or how you've grown through this experience. Your perspective may change, and you may have a greater appreciation for the little things. You may find yourself giving thanks that the situation wasn't worse. You may undertake new, meaningful pursuits, perhaps advocating for premature babies or supporting other parents of preemies.

> *When I've talked to people who've been through it, I know exactly what they've been through. You know you can help someone like no one else can. That's very rewarding.* —Vickie

> *The university recruited a doctor who is well known for his work with children who have pervasive developmental disorder (PDD), autism, and the like. He is putting together a committee of medical people, therapists, school people, and parents to work on developing a community-based center to provide services to the children and their families. I am excited that he asked me to participate. I am hoping this effort might help me develop the sense of doing something with all that we went through, just as I have found writing [about my experiences for this book] so helpful.* —Susan

> *Although this experience was one of the worst of my life, it changed the way I practice medicine. I know how parents feel. I can share with them that I have gone through the same ordeal and that I know how scared and frustrated they are. My patience with parents and their oftentimes endless questions has increased. I make it a point to talk to every parent whenever there is a chance, and I try to be sensitive to their fears and needs. Our daughter's prematurity might not have made me a better person, but it most certainly has made me a better physician.* —Christoph

Uncovering meaning or silver linings is something others cannot (and should not) do for you. It's up to you to find your own way through this part of the journey. If others are offering you their insights or pointing out your "blessings in disguise," you can gently inform them that you appreciate their attempts to help but that this is something you must discover for yourself, in your own time.

Anything good that you've extracted from this experience certainly doesn't make your child's premature birth something you would wish for, given a choice. Still, recognizing anything positive from this experience can help you come to terms with it. Finding special meaning in the ordeals you and your child have been through allows you to integrate them into your life in a way that adds value.

Some might think I had a dream lifestyle—no kids, some money, the ability to come and go as I pleased. But there was a problem. My relationship with Susan was less than rock solid. I felt like we were husband and wife, but that we were just roommates much of the time. I did my thing. She did hers. And sometimes we did stuff together. It's as if we were two pieces of bread with no peanut butter to really hold us together.

I needed the peanut butter. I just didn't realize that the peanut butter would show up in the form of children. —Jack

• • •

Weaving Treasures into Your Tapestry

When you begin to grieve and adjust to your baby's premature birth, you take the coarse, unwieldy threads of your feelings, identity, and relationships, and you reluctantly begin weaving them into your tapestry. At first, up close, all you see are the cruel knots, the unconventional colors, and the messy, uneven pattern—and you are repelled. You may wish you could do the rough parts differently, or cover them, or remove them. But after a while, you can take a step back, see your tapestry as a whole, and appreciate how those rough spots fit into the big picture. They're complicated and show the struggle, but they make your tapestry richer and more interesting, and you are pleased with the overall effect. By accepting those parts, you aren't denying the pain, betraying the difficult realities, or relinquishing the need to continue adjusting. But part of healing and moving on is allowing the threads to have their place and acknowledging their value to your tapestry. Instead of turning away from the rough patches, you treasure them. From this comes peace.

• • •

After much reflection I find that I do not feel like I am in a different place now than I was two years ago, than I was six years ago. What is different is that I have stopped trying to escape this place and begun to understand, accept that this is the place in which I am now and forever rooted. At first, then for years, everything for me was about the shock and denial that I could be the mother of a dead son, that I could be the mother of a surviving son who might not be normal, a son who might be marked differently but as indelibly as I was from the experiences we survived. My efforts to understand this reality, to organize it, to label it, to change it, to control it, were all born from a drive to escape the place I found myself in. I never expected to be in that place, so surely I could find a way to make sure my stop there was a brief one. But the place grew in me, and I grew in it, and finally I could see that separating me from it was fantasy.

The thing—finally—is, I have what I have. I am the mother of a dead son, a different son, a dear son. I have three very different boys who root me differently to the very same place. A certain kind of sorrow will always filter my experiences, as will a certain sort of appreciation, a depth of experience and understanding I could not have gained any other way. All of which I'd still give anything to have been able to avoid, but the gifts of which I can finally begin to embrace along with the pain.

Every day in some way I miss Spencer, the wonder of what might have been, the unanswered questions, the aching over the missing space in every aspect of our family. Every day in some way I marvel at Stuart; I am continually catapulted between the heights of pride and appreciation for who he is, what he has survived and accomplished, and the depths of fear for the unknowns in his future, the hurts yet to come. Every day in some way I am healed by Justin, so transparent in his adoration, his heart so kind, so open. There is something hard and raw about living this gamut of loss, grace, fear, hope, wonder, risk, awe. But there is something also, something powerful and peaceful, about looking it all full in the face and sitting down squarely in the middle of this place. —Susan

• • •

Vulnerability, Appreciation, and Hope

*We all have our hurts, our losses, our isolations. If we don't have them now or haven't had them in the past, we can rest assured that they are coming. One of the biggest ways that I am different than I was, one of the challenges I now face daily, is learning to live effectively and fully with that knowledge.
—Susan*

Over time, you can learn to accept and cope with feelings of vulnerability to life's adversities. You protect yourself when it's possible and adopt philosophies about why bad things happen. All of this can help you let go of what you can't control and focus on what you can.

You can even come to value this sense of vulnerability because it keeps you in touch with your child and with your own emotional landscape. With vulnerability come awe and appreciation.

I guess one thing that I've hung on to, to try and make sense of this, is just—appreciation. I've been reading a lot of philosophical stuff over the past few years about appreciation. I just try to appreciate the fact that my husband and I have a beautiful daughter who is small but healthy! I have just tried to keep the perspective of being thankful that Hannah's challenges are (hopefully!) only temporary—that she does not have a permanent disability. —Stephanie

It's very easy for me to see how bad things could be. ... Even with Emily's cerebral palsy, it's always possible to compare her with children who have much more severe cases and be grateful—again, relatively. —Diana

Having a premature baby has made me grateful for even the tiniest things. I realized how thankful I was for modern medicine and for all of those people who had decided to become doctors and nurses. I was thankful for every gram T. J. gained and every breath he took. It really made me grateful for the little things. —Claire

I know I would have loved them if they were full term, but I don't know if I would be in awe or so appreciative of them. They are my heroes; they showed me that miracles are possible. That's a gift too priceless for words. —Stephie

•••

Even though you may maintain a sense of vulnerability, you learn to balance your fears with hopes. As your grief subsides, you become more open to optimism—and you find encouragement in unexpected places. If your preemie is struggling with delays or disabilities, you learn how to attend to even the smallest rays of hope.

When Macy was about a year old, I had a bittersweet experience while looking at some photos of my husband's family. I came across one of him as an infant, and it looked so much like Macy at the same age that I just burst into tears. Peter found me there still crying much later and asked with alarm what was wrong. When I was finally able to talk, I blubbered "and she looks just like you did." He was confused, and then bemused—"Why is that something to cry about?" But he never did understand why it made me so emotional. Somehow seeing the physical similarities told me that she might not be scarred forever by her "preemie-ness," that she just might be okay after all. It was one of those odd healing moments. —Christi

There have been many turning points. I look at them more like stair steps instead of corners because each small turning point takes us further upward (and some downward). When I saw Jacob yawn and stretch like a normal baby at two months old, I finally truly believed he'd live. Watching Clare and Emily grow up. Learn to walk, talk, make friends. Their first day off to school. The first time Jacob laughed out loud, said "I wan cook," yelled "Go Bulls!" during the playoffs, his hero worship of Michael Jordan. Watching Clare and Emily in the classroom, seeing the spectacular drawings they do, listening to them explain the world in their own voices.

Stepping down when Jacob had his first seizure and being thrown into a whole new world of worries. Watching him balance on his own for the first time, only to throw himself off balance by clapping so hard for himself. Looking at the pure joy on his face the first time he rode a bike; the pure terror as he realizes he's slipping into another seizure; and the satisfaction, after babbling the same phrase over and over, when we finally get it. Our despair as we watched him waste away in just a few weeks and have to finally make the decision to place a G-tube, and our thrill when he finally breaks thirty pounds at six and a half years old. My angels as flower girls in my friend's wedding, watching them walk down the aisle hand in hand and having my breath taken away by their unbelievable beauty. Holding each of my children's hands and marveling at the perfection and grace of movement in a hand whose palm used to be the size of my thumbnail. —Julie

Resilience

I've had people at work who say, "If it were me in your situation, I couldn't have done that. To come back to work and just turn it off and go to work and then go home and deal with your problems at home, and then come back to work, turn it off, do your work." They just respected the strength I had, to do that. It was very hard to do, and yet I just did it. —Charlie

You and your family may have been through more than you ever imagined you could survive. With each blow, each scare, and each disappointment, you might have wondered whether you'd be able to get up again and move forward. At first, you might have decided that you *had* to get up for your baby's sake. As time passes, though, you may begin to see that you get up again and again because you *want to,* because you are resilient and stronger than you ever believed possible. Resilience doesn't mean not feeling. It doesn't mean not crying or never getting angry. It means having the internal where-withal to take a deep breath and get back up again—holding tight to whomever or whatever helps you to feel strong and steady. Resilience means seeing yourself as able to bend when necessary, to hang in there, to adapt, and to bounce back. Resilience is knowing that you can survive what you must. But resilience is not just getting through, it's also becoming vibrant again, perhaps even more so than before.

They don't show that many signs of their prematurity. It's just their past and our past. We certainly went through a long trauma. It was a tough experience, and knowing what all is involved with it, it's pretty impressive we went through it and came out in good shape. —Mitch

Out of the rubble came "I." Just a mom who loves her kids, wants to do the best she can, and deals with all these "oxymoronic medical conditions" with oxymoronic emotions. There isn't a set way or a formula for me, though there seems to be a pattern of rebounding. I try to take my emotional cues from the

• • •

boys. If they can laugh and smile and joke about this, then so can I, even if it's "fake it till you make it" there in the beginning. —Ramona

The cashier said, "Oh, you have the pendant I always wanted (a necklace symbol of mother and child). You only have one child?" I told her I have two, then showed her my "mother rings." Then she asked why I have three rings. When I explained remembering the one I lost, she exclaimed, "Oh, my son means so much to me. I could never survive such a loss. I don't know how you did it. I could never do it." From a great calm distance, I told her that I have learned that we do, we survive what we have to. She didn't believe, but saying the truth to a stranger was a comfort, a validation. —Susan

As time passes, life can get easier. Even in the NICU, you can settle in to your parenting role and routine. After homecoming, you and your baby can really come into your own. Over time, outcomes become clearer, and if necessary, you adjust to any special needs. If you are still in the early months or years of your journey, hold on to the hope that it can get more manageable. Know that you'll be able to dust yourself off and that your resilience will shine on. If you hear about outcomes that discourage you, remember that if you do end up traveling that path, your resilience will carry you through.

As my preemies get older, the good does greatly outweigh the bad. When they were infants, life was hard. From feeding issues to sleep deprivation to sensory overload to follow-up clinics to not meeting milestones, it was all so frustrating. When they were toddlers, I was dealing with watching Clare and Emily take off, leaving Jacob behind, and coming to grips with exactly how handicapped Jacob was. When they were kindergartners, I was worrying about learning issues for Clare and Emily and navigating the nightmare of a special ed system with Jacob. Things are finally settling in. I love to watch Clare and Emily play with their friends and know that no one has a hint of their early beginnings. Jacob is coming into his own with a wonderful school situation. He's the healthiest he's ever been and is thriving despite his multiple handicaps. —Julie

Personal Growth and Adaptation

Having a premature baby, there are a lot of obstacles, there are a lot of things that are going to happen, there's just so much you and your child are going to go through. It's going to make you stronger, even if the outcome is not a favorable one. ... I've learned so much from this experience. —Betsy

We all do what we have to do. Over the last three and a half years, I have been exposed to many things (prematurity, cerebral palsy) about which I knew nothing before, and circumstances forced us to learn. While I wouldn't wish these experiences on anyone, I know that I am a more patient and compassionate person today because of what we've been through. —Diana

Now I know what it's really like to juggle. At work, I'm juggling clients, but no one's going to die if I screw up. When a big client would come in, I'd worry, but there's no worrying anymore because nobody's going to die. I might get fired or something, but that's it. It takes the pressure off. —Charlie

I guess that my perception of what I considered "fine" five years ago has certainly changed dramatically. Back then, fine would have meant having a couple of stiches after my tiring but natural birth of a rather large but healthy full-term baby who is grazing at my breast as I lovingly gaze into the eyes of my husband! Today, "fine" means that my baby has survived another day, Tyrell [my first child] hasn't decided to leave home, and I'm still in one piece and still have a partner!!! —Jo

There were times when I worried that we'd never make it where we are today or times when I just couldn't see far enough into the future to imagine it. I have two beautiful daughters about to enter middle school and puberty. Even their typical pre-teen theatrics can bring a smile to my face. I have my miracle son who brings me joy every day in his unconditional love and in his zest for life.

I am not the person I was before Jacob, Clare, and Emily were born. I'm richer, I'm fearful, I'm overprotective, I'm fulfilled, I'm amazed, I'm accepting, I'm grieving, I'm intense, I'm grateful, I'm a better person, all because of three tiny babies. —Julie

• • •

Personal growth can be a significant part of the treasure you find in adversity. With hindsight, you may see that you've undergone a personal transformation of sorts. Of course, you knew that you felt "different" as soon as your baby was born, but early on, you may have assumed (or at least hoped) that you would return to "normal." Little did you know that the changes this experience made in you would be permanent. As you begin to recognize and accept these signs of personal growth, you reach for a new normal—and see your growth as another treasure you can reap from your experiences.

> *I think I came through pretty good. I know that I surprised myself. I came through having a little more faith in what I am capable of. If someone had told me beforehand that this was something that I would have made it through, I wouldn't have believed it. I would not have thought that I would have been able to do it. I would've said, "Oh, that's not me. I cannot do that. I will lose my mind and not be able to handle it." And I really think I handled it fairly well, and I think that it has done something permanently to a piece of my self-confidence, so that was a positive thing. —Jaimee*

> *What I now believe is a big miracle is that my daughter has helped me to change. I'm so much more open to people based on their terms or abilities or situations—not mine. And I can now become completely overwhelmed with pride and joy and appreciation when my daughter accomplishes most anything! —Karen*

Because of what you've been through with your preemie, you may be a more compassionate person and a more conscious parent. You may feel more resilient, strong, confident, and assertive. You may be more in touch with your feelings and better balanced emotionally. You may also recognize and accept your limitations, asking for help when you need it, because you know that asking for help takes more courage than going it alone. You may reorder your priorities, changing your ideas about what it means to be a successful person, balance work and family, and incorporate your children into your life. You may revise your beliefs about life to help you cope with the twists and turns of fate.

> *How has a premature birth changed my life? Oh, my. One, I learned how to ask for help. Sounds like such a simple thing. Stan and I are very independent*

people. It was not an easy lesson. Two, I am thankful for the small things. My daughter chatters constantly. Waking up to her crying means that she's breathing. She is trying to learn how to wink. Those things are pure joy for me. Three, I do not say, "I can hardly wait until she ... " I enjoy each and every moment as it is. It all passes too quickly. And four, I reach out to those who may need a smile or an encouraging word. I used to be too busy. Not now. —Cindy

Peter probably would have been an involved dad anyway, but as I found the NICU removing more and more of my faith in my ability to be a good mother, it was simultaneously instilling confidence in Peter! He probably does half the caregiving now, from which we all benefit. His priorities changed dramatically, I think. Having a baby who weighs less than two pounds can do that to you! But he went from thinking that work was one of the most important aspects of his life to realizing that his family is what really matters. He's turned down promotions since Neil's birth, and since he wants to be home with us more, he works from home. —Tara

It was not until about two and a half months into Lauren's hospital stay that my priorities changed. ... Lauren needed me so much more than anyone at work ever would. And no one was going to die if I did not answer my work line, respond to e-mails, or issue settlement checks. My daughter was a different matter. Things were life and death. From that point forward, I've done my best for my company, but I always put Lauren first. —Shanda

I'm more positive about everything the children do. Everything has such a big meaning to me now. Everything they say, everything they do. If they do something wrong, it doesn't count as much anymore. I see the positive side of things more. I'm grateful we can be a tight-knit family. —Gallice

This pregnancy and birth were a real eye opener. I felt compassion for every woman who ever gave birth. My relationship with my husband has also deepened and grown. —Ruby

It's made our family stronger. I also don't dwell on the small stuff. I've seen the rough part of life. I've seen what these children have had to go through, and I think that in the day-to-day situations it's going to work itself out. It's not a life-threatening thing. If it's fixable, it's okay. —Betsy

I think that my experience has really helped emphasize to me that every child is an individual. I find myself looking at others through a "different light" now and asking myself, "I wonder what they have had to go through to get to where they are now?" —Stacy

Your personal growth is also reflected in your developing identity. After your baby's birth, as you immerse yourself in meeting your little one's significant needs, the focus of your parental identity is likely to be on your child's prematurity. As your baby grows and as your grief softens, preemie parenthood can become less central to your view of yourself. You can integrate the "preemie" part of your experience into your larger parental identity, so that doesn't take more than its fair share of energy. This experience, and the lessons it has taught you about yourself as a parent and as a person, weaves together who you used to be with who you are becoming. As you are healing, you are integrating your experiences into your identity, and into the tapestry of your life.

I don't think you will ever get over the fact that your baby came early. In time, you accept your situation and grow from it. One thing for sure, you're never the same again, which is good, I think. —Kathy

I don't think you ever feel like "yourself" again. Too much has changed. ... If given the choice, I certainly would not ask for a premature baby; however, I think I'm a much better person now. I think I'm stronger and happier. I never appreciated the small things in life. Now I cherish almost every moment. —Laura

I don't think I'll ever be myself again because a part of me passed away with Dominique. But I'm a much better person now than I ever was. —Rosa

Seeing Your Transformation as Healing

Many parents talk about how their premature babies amaze them. "They are so strong," parents say. "They are such survivors, such fighters." You may remember witnessing your own baby's determination, fighting with all he or she had.

Remember, too, that *you* made it through something you couldn't even have imagined before it happened—and you survived, putting up a determined fight. Total bed rest? Magnesium sulfate? Juggling the needs of older children and unborn ones? Splitting time between all the competing demands of work, school, home, partner, and a struggling baby in the NICU? You've done all this and more: knowing and loving your tiny baby and growing child; wishing you could take his or her place; making unfathomable decisions; wishing and hoping while living with uncertainty.

But after a year, two years, or twenty, you may worry about how much you are still affected by the traumas and losses of having a premature baby. Despite the joy you take in your child, you may worry about the strong feelings that occasionally well up, and wonder if this experience has irreparably damaged something in you.

Parents who have uncomplicated pregnancies and term deliveries often say with a chuckle, "I'll never be the same again," but this may feel like an understatement to the parent of a premature baby. Not only will you never be the same again, you have been utterly transformed. Your journey is following an uncharted path—one that seems longer and marked by more twists and turns than the paths most other parents follow. You are *so* different now. The unease you feel comes in part from your struggle to figure out who this new you is, how you fit into the world you used to inhabit, and how you want to move forward.

When you are struggling, pause for a moment and look back—at your baby's premature birth and at all that has passed since then. Marvel at yourself. Think about who you were before this pregnancy, this child. Can you remember? Think about what you have learned about yourself. Reflect on the knowledge that you now possess, the lessons that transformed you into the person you are today. Most parents can detail their preemie's developmental steps, small and large. Have you given yourself the chance to really appreciate your *own* metamorphosis?

At times you may feel like the walking wounded; at other times, you may feel more robust, recognizing and valuing your own development. This mix of feelings is not just the result of the premature birth, but of your personal journey.

As you move through your life's journey, there are many opportunities to pause, look back, and take stock. Imagine yourself looking out over the path you have traveled, your vantage point high above the road you've climbed. You can see the many twists and turns, even the obstacles that you overcame—and those that stopped you cold. Though you are still traveling and will continue to travel for the rest of your life, you can appreciate the beauty and complexity of your path. You are a seasoned explorer, skilled with your compass and adept with your map. The terrain has become familiar to navigate, and you remain oriented even when you come across new or similar obstacles.

Feeling "better" (which for me means feeling in control) came when I realized that I didn't have to let the preemie experience, the emotional discoveries, and even the pain, fade away.

That I could find peace even with maintaining a heightened sense of what motherhood means to me based on what I had been through, what my children had been through. That I actually was forever different as a person because of our family journey and that it was okay, even years later, to still know the hurt intimately, still live with the ache, still feel my breath catch in my throat when I told our stories. That moving on and watching my sons grow into fine, strong children didn't mean that you "got over it," or that their early arrivals and immense struggles no longer counted. That the past blended into the present, which offered a glimpse of the future. That the journey doesn't always begin with tomorrow, that there doesn't have to be a disconnection to the anguish in order to seek and find and feel and believe the joy.

Surviving my sons' premature births means simply that—that I continue to wake each day wanting the best for them, wanting to protect them, wanting to give them the gift of a loving home and a loving heart, wanting to watch them soar. Surviving it means embracing it. —Maureen

Take some time and think about the way things used to be—the way *you* used to be. Think some more about what this experience has given you.

The journey is ongoing. The road you are on continues to be different from the one you had planned to take. The parent you've become is different from the one you imagined. But different is not the same as damaged. Different doesn't mean that you haven't recovered from the premature birth. Different means that you are transformed. And that's exactly as it should be.

We spent New Year's at the beach. It was a peaceful few days, and James and I enjoyed a couple of amazing hours together in the water jumping over or running away from the waves. I say amazing [because] it seems that amongst all that sand and water there was another step in my journey, one that James and I took together.

James loves to run away from the waves. He teases them and laughs at them, but the minute the water reaches his toes he usually turns tail and runs.

This particular day he decided that he didn't want to run away. So my little boy and I stood in the water and let the waves crash around us. When James was frightened and the water seemed to be getting too deep, I lifted him up as he jumped high and I held him over my head, away from the water, and calmed his fears.

It was odd to be in this water as it rushed in toward the shore and then ran out again, trying to pull us with it. It made me think of childbirth, the contractions like waves rising and falling—an odd connection, perhaps, but it seemed quite right that I was able to lift James out of the water and hold him away from the waves when he was afraid. Being able to protect him in this way and make him feel safe, [being] able to be beside him and do something for him when I hadn't been able to protect him all those years ago.

It was so healing those couple of hours, watching James move through the water, running and chasing and then standing close as we challenged the ocean together, and together we won.

And the journey continues. Thanks for wanting to share it with me.
—Leanne

A Note to Caregivers

While you may find your job incredibly rewarding, it can also be incredibly distressing. Working with sick and struggling infants can be discouraging and emotionally depleting. Watching their suffering can be painful. Some babies die or have chronic problems, and you grieve for them and their families. You will witness many mothers and fathers with broken hearts. But you will also witness joy, triumph, and growth—emotional growth in the parents and physical/developmental progress for the babies. In recognition of the inspiring as well as challenging and draining aspects of your job, we offer the following tips for supporting parents and taking care of yourself, in ways that honor their needs as well as your own. Some of these points are more applicable to NICU settings while others are broader, encompassing maternity, NICU, and follow-up care. Take what seems useful and find the balance that works for you. Also check out Chapter 7 for more insight and suggestions for building collaborative relationships with parents.

Supporting Parents ...

Consider "family-centered care" to be so much more than just a protocol or set of techniques. It is a positive attitude that welcomes parents into the NICU as full partners in taking care of their baby. It is a philosophy that provides a respectful, collaborative environment where everyone recognizes that the baby is part of a family and that the family is part of the health care team. A fervent mission is to reinforce the relationship between parents and their babies by honoring their central roles in caregiving and decision making, and supporting them in nurturing their babies and making the most appropriate decisions. Consider developing and posting your "unit philosophy" so that parents will know from the start that you believe their presence in the NICU is important, you regard them as members of their baby's health care team, and you respect their observations and contributions. Make sure that all of your NICU staff members are on board by providing them with the education that they need to understand and implement the unit's philosophy, a forum to discuss their questions and concerns, and adequate staffing and encouragement to give them the support they need.

Recognize that you are the host and also the guest. Family-centered care recognizes the power that families possess in determining their own paths and eliminates the power differential that exists between them and medical staff. In order to truly collaborate with families, you must hold the attitude that you are the host *and* you are the guest. So for instance, when you go to the bedside of a baby, you are the host because the baby is in your unit; you are the one with the expert medical knowledge; you are the one who invites the parents to become members of the health care team; you are the one who guides them through their NICU course. But at the same time you are also the guest: You are in their "family space" in the unit; you are brought into their family crisis to be a trusted consultant; when you connect with the parents and their infant, you become a guest family member; you walk with them on their personal and family journeys. As the host, you have much to teach families; as the guest, you will learn so much from them as well. Feel the honor in both of these roles.

Provide developmentally supportive care for babies *and* parents. In the NICU, providing developmentally supportive care is central to implementing a family-centered care philosophy. Developmentally supportive care promotes health and development in babies because it is sensitive, responsive, appropriate, and individualized. When you provide developmentally supportive care to babies, in effect you are also providing one important component of developmentally supportive care to the parents, because it reflects, affirms, and accommodates parents' natural urges to nurture and protect their babies from the harsh or overwhelming aspects of intensive care. This fosters their growing competence, confidence, and bond with their little one. Developmentally supportive care also mandates close physical contact between baby and parent, often through touch, kangaroo care, and feeding at the breast, with precious few circumstances getting in the way. Incidentally, when your unit provides the education, resources, staffing, and support you and your colleagues need to carry out family-centered care, that means that you're getting developmentally supportive care for yourself, which promotes your health and growth as a professional. (For more on developmentally supportive care see "The Growth of Developmentally Supportive Care" in Chapter 7; for information on developmentally supportive care for caregivers, see " … And Taking Care of Yourself" later in this appendix.)

Help parents gather together all the parts of their story. Because delivery, early days in the NICU, and medical crises are usually chaotic and traumatic times, most parents will have gaps in their memories and knowledge about what happened, both to the mother and the baby. Parents benefit from going over the details of the labor, delivery, and NICU care with the attending nurses, obstetricians, and neonatologists. Asking, "What happened?" and "Why?" is a way for parents to reclaim memories and satisfy their need to know. Remember that their questions are not meant to second-guess or attack, but to fill in the gaps. When a parent can create a coherent narrative, it is profoundly healing.

Address feelings first. Before you talk to parents about the medical issues, acknowledge the emotional issues. Sit down and ask parents, "How are you doing with all this? What does this feel like for you? What are your concerns?" Help them to verbalize their feelings and help to normalize them, for example, "I can see how disappointing this is for you—many parents feel this way." Stay with them and give them both the attention and space they need. By being emotionally available and inviting them to express and share their experiences with you, you've begun to develop a relationship. Building a rapport with you helps parents negotiate the emotional terrain, which in turn

• • •

helps them listen and absorb information when you talk about the medical terrain. With emotions out on the table, when you start discussing the medical facts, issues, and options, you will probably find that parents are more able to fully participate in these difficult conversations. Any time you can really be with the parents, walk the emotional journey with them. Ultimately, it will make your job easier. You'll be a more effective supporter and teacher, and parents will see you as their ally and teammate, which makes for a trusting, collaborative relationship. Your collaborative and emotionally supportive relationship with the parents is in the best interests of the baby who is in your care.

Expect a variety of emotional responses from parents, including detachment, anxiety, anger, sadness, vigilance, and depression. Adjusting to a baby's premature birth, hospitalization, and outcome is a process, and parents can experience a wide range of intense and often contradictory feelings. Each parent brings with them a personality, temperament, and baggage that will affect how they cope. Respect differences, and remember that you only know a small bit of their larger emotional stories.

Show parents their baby. When you introduce new parents to the NICU, before you point out the equipment and technology and lay of the land, first take the time to introduce them to their baby. Ignore the tubes and wires and talk about the baby first, as a person instead of a medical case. Point out the "normal things"—the soft ears, downy hair, long torso, tiny fingers, and facial features. Address issues of the baby's comfort such as warmth, positioning, pain control, and shielding from harsh lights and noise. Tell them about the importance of parental touch. Talk about the ways that tiny babies show how they know their parents, such as changes in heart and respiratory rates and turning toward voice, touch, and smell. Make sure that you know about developmentally supportive care and reading babies' signs of distress and relaxation, and start teaching the parents about how they too can learn to read these cues and respond to their baby's need for comfort.

Show parents you care about them. Parents won't care what you know until they know you care. Tell them that you are glad to be attending to their baby and, while you know it's not the same as being the parent, you'll do your best. This reassures them that you aren't trying to commandeer their parenting role, but you are invested in their child, and will take good care of their little one.

Encourage parents to enjoy their baby, but elaborate on what

you mean by that. Many parents are in agony, and the suggestion that they enjoy this baby can infuriate them. First tell them that you know this is a difficult time for them, full of uncertainties, fears, and other painful feelings. Reassure them that you are here to support them through this turmoil. Then gently express your hope that they can remember that in spite of the difficulties, their baby is a precious little one, growing and changing before their very eyes, and there is so much for them to witness and marvel at. Encourage them to enjoy what they can about the baby, because this will give them respite from the harder parts of the NICU journey.

Consider writing notes to the parents in the form of a "diary from their baby." The idea of baby diaries was developed at Simpson Maternity Hospital in Edinburgh, Scotland, when the nurses began leaving messages and notes for the next nurse coming on shift. They began sharing these "diary entries" with parents who were delighted and comforted by these little notes "from" their babies. As one mother in this book says, "It made me giggle and made me cry. ... It really helped with the bonding process and helped us accept this wee scrap of fighting life as our son." Of course, some nurses will feel more comfortable and confident doing this than others will. And not all parents will be open to this lighthearted touch. But for many others, it will give a much-needed break from the grind of having a sick preemie, and they will treasure their diaries. Diaries are also powerful, cherished mementos for parents of babies who die. (See Chapter 8 for more on baby diaries.)

Accommodate parents' needs to be involved with their baby. Instead of expecting parents to adjust to the constraints of the NICU, try to make your NICU accommodate parents. Tell parents that their presence, touch, observations, advocacy for, and parenting of their babies are valued. Encourage their participation in the baby's care, making room for them to do as much as possible, and involve them as members of the health care team. This partnership with you helps them exercise their parenting abilities and promotes feelings of competence and confidence. Obtain their consent for *everything* but emergency procedures and treatments. This reminds them that you know that this is *their* baby and demonstrates your respect for their role as primary nurturers and decision makers, which supports them as they come into their own as confident parents of this child. More importantly, when their consent is required, they become their child's primary advocate and protector, which facilitates bonding with their infant. Recognize the importance of "firsts" and the parents' desires to be there whenever possible to witness and participate in milestones. Reassure them that you share a common goal: to get their baby healthy enough so she or he can go home.

Keep parents informed during their baby's roller-coaster course. Parents benefit from knowing the whole story—the good, the bad, and the uncertain. If their infant's prognosis is poor or uncertain, they have a right to know that not every baby comes out of the NICU unscathed. You can tell them this without extinguishing their hopes. Still, when a baby has a major complication or setback, telling parents can be very difficult. Bad news is hard for them to hear and some parents may not seem to absorb it. And sometimes, what you consider a minor setback in their baby's course can feel monumental and devastating to the parents. You may feel like you want to spare them by not fully disclosing the details. Unfortunately, keeping parents in the dark robs them of their ability to master reality and reinforces unreasonable expectations. Keeping information from parents also creates barriers between them and their baby, and spawns anger and mistrust toward their baby's caregivers. The parents may even question your motives and assume you are trying to protect yourself, not them. In any case, withholding information from them does *not* protect them. Instead of worrying about how parents will react when they hear bad news, plan on helping them face the situation *and* their emotions. It's your job to support them, *not* hide the truth from them.

Instead of walking away from parents, walk with them. You serve parents best, and your job is made easier in the long run, if you can speak honestly and openly *and then support them as they face painful feelings head on.* This is how you can *walk with them.* It may also help to remember that because knowledge is empowering, it is far easier for parents to cope with the grief they feel when facing bad news or uncertainties from the outset than to cope with the confusion, disappointment, and disempowerment bred by half-truths and cover-ups. Most importantly, when parents are fully informed, they can be fully present and involved with what's going on, which in turn enables them to integrate what is happening to them and to their baby. Parents may encounter some painful situations, and you may be tempted to protect them from being overwhelmed or scared. But sometimes the truth *is* overwhelming and scary. If you're having concerns, remind yourself that by sharing information about their baby you are drawing parents into the circle of caregivers, which in and of itself provides comfort and instills confidence and courage.

Accommodate parents' unique and changing needs for information—and help them stay focused on their baby. Although your goal is to keep parents fully informed, you must be responsive to what "fully informed" means to each parent. Some parents just want to know what is going on with their baby right now, while others also want to know every etiological detail you know and every future possibility you might surmise. Some parents want to be spared all the "gory details" and just given the big picture, while others want a crash course in neonatology. Some parents just want the most basic information at first, adding layers of knowledge over time, while others want it all right away. So rather than loading up parents with standard information, take into account what the parents really want to know, their biggest concerns, and their readiness to absorb facts and advice. Say to parents, "Let's talk about what's going on so you can figure out what you want to know," and then follow their lead. Parents will be grateful for your responsiveness to their style of information gathering and mastery. And when parents are overwhelmed with information, you can help them narrow their focus. For instance, you can disclose all the risks of a treatment *and* be more specific about what that may realistically mean for *their* child. You can refer parents to the research *and* help them interpret the implications for *their* infant. You can help them cope with "bad news" by acknowledging their feelings and answering their questions. Also, always keep in mind that when you are sharing information, you're not giving a report, *you are building rapport.*

Be honest about uncertain or grim prognoses. One of the hardest answers to give a parent is "I don't know." However, parents would rather hear that than your guesses and opinions presented as facts or guarantees. You can acknowledge the uncertainties of the future, but be honest in saying that this child has a lot to overcome. There is a huge difference between saying, "Your child will never be able to ... " and "I've never seen a child with these sorts of complications be able to ... " Parents will appreciate this show of sensitivity and integrity. While it can be painful for parents to discover that medical technology cannot always predict or cure, your honesty creates a bond that will benefit all of you. Perhaps harder than "I don't know" is "There's nothing more to do but comfort care." If it looks like the baby is turning away from the path that leads toward home, keep parents abreast. Parents benefit from being included when goals change. Knowing that their baby is dying allows parents to make the most of the time that's left and to make plans that are meaningful to them. Likewise, if the baby has catastrophic problems that require long-term hospitalization or that may become permanent or chronic, parents need to be informed as soon as possible so they can adjust their expectations. When you are honest with parents their hopes don't disappear, they gradually change direction.

Be a decision collaborator and sometimes a decision leader. When a baby's prognosis is certain and the treatment plan is clear, be a decision leader. For instance, when the baby's survival is virtually certain and the standard interventions are in order, you can bring the parents on board by informing them about what is happening and why these treatments are in the best interests of their child. Likewise, when the baby's death is virtually certain and comfort care is the best option, you can bring the parents on board by informing them about what is happening and why these treatments are in the best interests of their child. But when the prognosis is uncertain or if experimental treatments are an option, be a decision collaborator. Bring the parents on board by explaining the options, risks, benefits, and outcomes, and inviting them to be central partners in the decision-making process to determine what is in the best interests of their child.

Slow down and listen to parents. Most of us need to become better at slowing down and listening. This means giving parents information and then being able to sit quietly and patiently with them. Encourage questions and then stick around to give parents time to formulate those questions, express what's on their minds, and note anything that is still unclear to them. Open the door to questions that the parents may be having trouble formulating and normalize this process by saying something like, "It takes time for parents to form questions. Do you have things on your mind that you want to talk about, even if you're not sure if it'll make sense?" Be comfortable with silence, as parents need time to think, ask, and respond. Validate how difficult their baby's hospitalization must be for them and ask them, "How are you doing with all this?" Consider tape-recording these meetings (see below), so parents can have the opportunity to listen again when they feel less overwhelmed or shocked by the information. Also be present and available for follow-up chats in person, by phone, or by e-mail. By being accessible, going at the parents' pace, and providing audiotapes, you increase the likelihood of them absorbing information from you.

• • •

Audiotape your conversations and give parents a copy.
Although there is a new movement to audiotape care conferences and give
tapes to the parents, many caregivers are wary. But there are many benefits. If
parents can listen to a tape repeatedly, they are more likely to absorb what you
say. By sharing the tape with relatives, they can be spared daily grilling by concerned family members and friends. If you agree that parents don't always
remember what they are told, audiotapes can be a remedy. If you are worried
that audiotapes will only encourage parents to obsess, remember that they can
and will obsess even without a tape. The audiotape can ground them in
reality, and in fact, you might encourage them to listen to the information as
many times as they need. When parents have access to audiotapes, they can
be more informed, be more satisfied with professional-parent communication,
and have a better working relationship with you—which as you know, reduces
the chance of lawsuits being filed against you. If you behave in a responsible,
professional, ethical manner, you have nothing to hide, and a tape cannot be
effectively used against you.

 Accept the parents' right to cry at their baby's bedside. Tears
don't hurt babies, and parents often benefit from shedding tears in their baby's
presence. Give parents their space and privacy when they cry, because your
presence, touch, or words may convey the message to "calm down and dry
your tears." If one parent's tears lead to another's, accept that floodgates will
open sometimes in the NICU. If your unit culture respects a range of expression by parents, this is a sign that you are providing an emotionally healthy
and supportive place. Another healthy sign is that limits are set. If a parent is
losing control and behaving in ways that intimidate or endanger anyone or
anything, they will benefit from your gentle intervention to help them calm
down or to lead them to a place where they can vent without restraint.
When your instinct tells you that things are getting out of hand, trust it and
act quickly and decisively.

 **If a parent is venting anger toward you, don't take it person-
ally.** Even if the parent personalizes the attack, remember that it's *the situation*
that deserves those charges. If you can listen and *acknowledge their anger*, this can
help diffuse it. Validate their attendant feelings of powerlessness, confusion,
shock, and fear. Agree with them that this situation holds many disappointments and uncertainties, and that it can be really hard to deal with.
Acknowledging and validating their painful feelings shows them that you are

an ally, not the enemy. It also shows them that they can feel angry and not lose your support.

Avoid judging parents. It is tempting to make snap judgements when parents behave in ways you consider inappropriate, especially toward their babies. But you don't know their whole story, their background, or the hurdles they experience. For parents who live far from the hospital or who are without transportation, funds, babysitters for older children, strong social support, or emotional resources, spending a lot of time with their baby can be more than they can manage. Negotiating the maze of continued medical and developmental follow-up may be unduly burdensome. Even if you don't respect lifestyle choices such as drug abuse, know that their lives are way more chaotic than you'll ever know and having a sick baby might be just a drop in the bucket, rather than the center of their existence. Parents do the best they can, and while that may not seem adequate, it's still their best. Judgement is a poison; empathy is a salve—for them as well as for you.

Deal with difficult parents. Every parent comes to the unit with a unique personal history of stress or loss or difficulty adjusting. First assume that any interpersonal challenges you're seeing are a result of the trauma of having a premature infant. If everything you've tried to do to support a parent seems ineffective, call for a psychiatric consultation and collaborate with your affiliated mental health care providers who are knowledgeable about both perinatal stress and psychological dynamics. When a parent needs support above and beyond what your best efforts can supply, recognize their limitations, don't take their criticisms to heart, and rely on the staff who can work best with these folks.

Give parents the benefit of the doubt. Recognize that even though many parents become overwhelmed at some point or may seem bumbling or incompetent, they do have a life outside the NICU or preemie parenthood where most likely they can function very well. Try to see them as competent people who need time to find emotional equilibrium and learn the ropes in this unfamiliar, often scary situation.

Make referrals. Parents can benefit from support or assistance beyond what you offer, so refer them to resources and get other agencies involved. Most parents would benefit from a support group or psychological counseling. Getting additional assistance outside the NICU will help them get back on their feet, as well as give you peace of mind and the ability to let go, especially with particularly needy parents. If services are lacking in your area, church groups, Internet groups, and national organizations can be important resources. Let parents know that there is a network out there of other parents of preemies. They deserve the benefits to be gained by plugging into it.

Show cultural sensitivity. Nowadays, diversity is the norm. Whether you work in a large metropolitan area or a small village, remain open-minded and become culturally aware.

Even if the parents look, act, or talk like you, do not assume that they feel like you or think like you.

Remember that some people have a basic fear or distrust of authority figures. Whether they hail from foreign countries ruled by corrupt or brutal regimes or from the oppressive inner cities of your region, some parents will not automatically look to you for help and support. You can earn their respect and trust, but it may take extra time and effort.

Always ask parents about their religious and spiritual beliefs. Ask about their rituals for celebrating life, dealing with crisis, and if the baby dies, for honoring the dead. Seek clarification from other family members or cultural and religious agencies.

Encourage the supportive presence of many family members. Remember that loud displays of weeping are considered normal and appropriate in many cultures.

Look beyond language barriers and relate to the person. When using a translator, maintain the most common usage and keep your words to a minimum. This reduces the chances of filtering, mistranslation, or confusion. Be aware of the importance of nonverbal communication. Touch and eye contact are more appropriate in some cultures than others.

Even when English is the common language, choose your words sensitively. For example, you might want to stay away from the phrase "quality of life" because a family may feel as though you're judging them and their baby, implying that they are incapable of providing a quality life for this child. Instead, talk about "suffering." And rather than wondering if parents distrust you because you are from different cultures, ask, "Are you worried that there are medical treatments we aren't offering you?" This gives families a chance to air their concerns and get reassurance.

Your best credentials are your warmth and sincerity.

Honor the journey that parents are on. Instead of trying to get parents to make the "right" decisions or helping them cope "the right way," remember that your job is to *walk with them on their journey*. Recognize that while you have much to teach parents, they have much to teach you as well. And how well you listen is more important than what you say. You can shine a light on the options and be a sounding board, but ultimately, you must let them go down the path they feel drawn to.

When a Baby Is Dying or after a Baby Dies

Most hospitals have protocols in place for dealing with families whose baby is dying or has died. However, don't rely on the protocol to be "the absolute right way" to manage every situation. Don't assume that the protocol will suit the needs of every parent. Don't assume that what's right for one family (or for you) is right for another. Don't consider marching through a protocol as the key to providing support to grieving parents. The key to providing support is *forming a warm connection with parents*, including

- Being present with the parents
- Listening and accepting their expression of feelings without trying to fix them
- Being sensitive and responsive to their emotional, physical, and spiritual needs
- Informing them of their options and recognizing that their first decisions may change
- Letting parents know that you will be checking in with them every couple of hours to assess their changing needs and desires
- Giving them the time they need to make the most of their opportunities to have contact with their dying baby or their baby's body
- Encouraging and answering their questions
- Showing tenderness and respect for their baby and later, their baby's body
- Taking into account that this is an exhausting and traumatic time for parents. For example, some parents may find it most helpful to be given time to absorb the shock of their baby's death and warm up to the idea of having contact with their infant's body, instead of having the baby thrust upon them

Perhaps most important of all, instead of persuading parents to buy into a certain protocol, *encourage them to do what is best for themselves.* The goal of encouraging parents to be with their dying baby or their baby's body should be that parents have as little regret as possible about how they handled the opportunity to spend time with their little one. No parent should have to regret a lack of contact; likewise, no parent should have to regret the contact imposed on them. The parents who are reluctant to have contact with their baby can be encouraged but not coerced.

To walk this fine line between encouragement and coercion with reluctant parents, it is imperative that you yourself not be overly invested in a particular outcome. Keep in mind that every parent in this situation is on his or her own journey. Your job is to walk with parents on their journeys and not to try to force them to take one path or another. Encourage parents to follow their intuitions and their hearts. Some parents will intuitively know without much encouragement from you that contact with their baby is something they need and want. Others need a chance to talk about their reservations, ask questions, and get reassurance. For example, is it scary to be with a dying baby? How will death come? What will death look like? Is it morbid to spend time with the body after death? Others will know that contact is something they do not want. Others need to hear that some parents decline, but that many others find it comforting and helpful to see how normal their baby looks without tubes and wires, and to do nurturing things such as cuddling and dressing their baby, and after death, bathing their baby's body. Ask them to tell you what are the best ways to support them as they meet death.

The benefits of any supportive protocol come out of the heartfelt connection between you and the parent. Build a warm and responsive rapport with parents. Practice good communication skills and informed consent, giving parents options and time to keep their options open and make these important decisions. Encourage them to follow their hearts. *Walk with them on their unique journeys.*

Parents won't remember what you said.
Parents won't remember what you did.

They'll remember how they were affected by your presence.
They'll remember *how* you said what you said.

• • •

829

A Note to Caregivers

They'll remember *how* you did what you did.

They'll remember how well you listened

and how they felt supported, understood, and accepted by you.

... and Taking Care of Yourself

One of the most important parts of being an effective caregiver is giving care to yourself. By nurturing yourself first and foremost, you can approach your patients or clients from a place that is centered and healthy. This in turn will better enable you to encourage them on their own journeys toward balance and health.

Acknowledge your own feelings of sorrow. If you form meaningful relationships with the babies and families you care for, then when tragedy strikes or difficulties arise, it can be sad for you too. Even their discharge home can bring mixed feelings of happiness and sorrow. If you try to deaden your grief, you'll also dampen your ability to feel joy, satisfaction, and accomplishment. Additionally, you'll find it more difficult to tolerate painful feelings in the parents you deal with. It may help you to keep a journal where you can process some of your feelings by writing. Psychosocial rounds are another way for staff to get together to discuss challenging parents, babies, or situations; to talk about emotional coping; and to provide support to each other. Find outlets away from the NICU whereby you can process your own emotions and tensions.

Face your own past losses. Since your work encompasses loss and sorrow, it may dredge up unresolved grief from your past. It is important for you to acknowledge all of your past losses, big and small, and give yourself permission to experience all your emotions and thoughts about them in a safe and private place. Some of your emotions may seem unacceptable to you, but if you have them, you are entitled to them. Find ways to work through your feelings by talking to others, writing, exercise, meditation, creating art, joining support groups, or getting professional counseling. If you can free yourself from the past, you can deal more effectively with the present. (See Chapters 3 and 4 for more on grief and recovery.)

Get your emotional needs met outside the NICU, so that you can become close to parents because they need it, not because *you* need it. This also frees you to be able to truly support and encourage parents. If your emotional bank account is full, you can make meaningful withdrawals without draining yourself or your family.

Find ways to add energy and health to your life. Good nutrition and exercise feed your body and spirit, and can help you weather the demands of your job. Lighten your life by finding the humor or absurdity in things, especially those things that annoy you. Leave your job at work. Trust that the families and babies are in the kind and capable hands of your peers. You do important work, but to do your best, you must make time for play. You need time away to recharge your batteries.

Allow yourself to cry. For many people, crying can be a valuable coping tool. If this is true for you, once you accept its value, it will feel less embarrassing. Still, if your culture or the unit culture frowns upon emotional displays, you will feel pressure to stifle your tears. The trick is to try to find a balance that works for you and the families you work with. For instance, be careful not to express your emotions in ways that put parents in a position where they feel *they* have to take care of *you*. Shedding some soft tears in front of parents may be appropriate and appreciated whereas sobbing usually is not. If you feel you are losing control, excuse yourself, with reassurances that you'll return soon. Find ways to calm down or a place away from the NICU (such as the chapel, where no one would think twice if they saw or heard you) where you can shed your tears.

Start an open relationship with each parent, as if the slate is wiped clean. Do what you need for yourself so that you don't shut down because the last parent was difficult or even if your first impression is poor. Give them the benefit of the doubt and let yourself be emotionally available.

Find a healthy balance in your relationships with parents. Get close to families, but also set limits and boundaries. Don't take on all their problems. You can care about them without taking care of things for them. Find a balance between involvement and detachment. Involvement can allow you to be empathetic and supportive; detachment can protect you from others' emotional intensity. Remember that both extremes—caring too deeply or not caring much at all—when chronic, are ineffective and unprofessional. Caring too deeply and becoming enmeshed can lead to burnout and clinical depression. Not caring and remaining aloof leads to numbness and detachment. A supportive and professional relationship with families includes a balance between and within the two extremes. Balance also includes showing your humanness and honoring your unique, heartfelt style of supporting parents.

Maintain your own emotional balance. If you are sensitive and empathetic, it is normal for you to be affected by the profound emotions expressed by parents. However, you need to be able to empathize without taking on the intensity of others' feelings. When parents are having a hard time and you're starting to feel overwhelmed or over-involved, affirm your boundaries by reminding yourself that you are most helpful when you remember that the pain is natural and belongs to them. Repeat this mantra to yourself: "This is their baby and their journey. I help them by walking with them, not for them." Refer parents to specific support people or organizations; trust them to find their own solutions in their own time. Talk with coworkers and others about your feelings—you are likely to discover that you are not alone, and that others have found ways to keep from becoming emotionally submerged.

Have realistic expectations for your work with families. Do not expect yourself to make a significantly positive impact on every family you work with. Some families will be easier, more rewarding, or a better personality fit for you to work with than others, and that's okay. Also, remember the ripple effect—that by helping just one family, you've made a difference that stretches to many other lives, the way a drop of water makes ripples that fan out.

Have realistic expectations for your work with babies. Remember that you do not have the power to know all the answers. No one is perfect, and everyone makes some errors in judgment and mistakes in care. If you had a crystal ball that told you the information you needed and every correct move to make, you'd use it, because you want the best for your patients. But since you don't have a crystal ball, you cannot expect yourself to always have the answers or to never err. Some babies' conditions are so complicated or bewildering, and some babies are born only to die or to be significantly impaired, in spite of your best efforts. While letting yourself off the hook can be difficult, if you learn from your experiences, then your trials and errors are not in vain. Also learn from the babies and families you work with. While you have much to teach them, recognize that they have much to teach you too.

Understand the emotional aspects of parenting a preemie in the NICU. Part of taking care of yourself is making sure you have the knowledge and skills to do what you need to do every day in your dealings with struggling and distraught parents. If you don't understand the dynamics or don't have the skills to interact effectively and supportively with parents, you'll continually feel inadequate, drained, and demoralized—the recipe for burn out. Having resources you can rely on—including informational materials, supportive consultants, and colleagues—can boost your competence and replenish your emotional reserve. Push for developmentally supportive care for babies and their parents in your NICU, as this integral part of family-centered care and philosophy will make your job easier and more rewarding.

Push for developmentally supportive care for caregivers in your NICU. Ask your hospital to improve your unit by funding efforts to support staff by providing the time and resources to attend in-services, seminars, and conferences that deal with family-centered care and the emotional aspects of parenting in the NICU. Advocate for the establishment of NICU psychosocial rounds and perinatal mortality rounds, which should be facilitated by an outside professional who is knowledgeable about the emotional aspects of perinatal crisis and adjustment and tuned into the needs of families and staff. (The Schwartz Center specializes in helping hospitals set up rounds like these—for more information on their model, go to www.theschwartzcenter.org/rounds.asp) These rounds can be a place where you and your colleagues can share your experiences, gather insight and ideas for ways of working with parents, talk openly, and alleviate some of the stress of being with sick babies and their grieving families. Also recognize that some staff members have a natural gift for working with dying babies and their families, and they should be considered important resources to all of us.

Know when it's time to move on. If you are feeling burned out, exhausted, depressed, depleted, overwhelmed, or waning interest in the welfare of others, take heed. You may be ready for a significant leave of absence or moving on to new challenges. It can be hard to quit. You may resist this need because of finances, guilt, or feelings of inadequacy. But there is no shame in acknowledging that this job is no longer right for you. You have changed and grown, given and given. Perhaps it's time to seek another path, one that doesn't involve the aspects of your job that you can no longer tolerate. Listen to your needs. Find ways to continue to use your signature strengths. Do what makes you happy, not what makes you miserable.

Being an effective caregiver doesn't involve changing the world. Just plant seeds of hope and encouragement. In other words, don't try to "fix"

• • •

or erase others' difficulties or emotional pain. You may have the answers for your own life, but don't assume or insist that those will work well for others. People need to feel, recover, learn, move on, and live at their own pace, in their own way. In your role as caregiver, planting seeds means being a good listener and encouraging each person to find their own path. For instance, by giving a teen mother extra nurturing, you have planted seeds of encouragement that can germinate when the time is right in that girl's life. By showing faith in a mother who has little confidence, listening to a dad talk about his childhood, or encouraging befuddled parents to read their babies' cues, you have planted seeds of comfort and assurance that they can draw strength from. If you need closure, it may help you to follow up with families. NICU reunions; follow-up clinics; communication with social workers, pediatricians, and occupational, speech, and physical therapists can provide this opportunity. Whether you seek follow-up or not, trust that you do make a difference simply by planting seeds of hope and encouragement.

A Note to Friends and Relatives

One of life's most intensely rewarding experiences is the birth of a baby. When pregnancy is confirmed, you imagine what lies ahead with eager antic- ipation. Your body (or your partner's body) will blossom with life. The kicks will grow stronger, the hiccups so precious. You will take your time to choose just the right name. You will meet other expectant parents in childbirth class, compare notes and complaints, and make plans for your labor. There's plenty of time until your baby is ready to be born.

You imagine others making plans too. Friends may give you a baby shower. Employers may pencil in parental leave, and family members may prepare to take time off to help during the early weeks after the baby is born. Your nest will be ready, and near your due date, you'll feel eager to hold your baby in your arms. When the time comes, you will welcome labor contrac- tions and review your plans, nervous but expectant. You'll grab your bag, packed with everything that you want and need during delivery.

You imagine entering your softly decorated birthing room and laboring (or helping your partner labor) with the encouragement of supportive care- givers. Soon you are welcoming an adorable, squalling, healthy baby who is ready to nuzzle at the breast and gaze attentively into your adoring eyes. In a day or so, you'll go home to admiring friends and relatives who will coo at your beautiful newborn and congratulate you on your achievement. Just as you had hoped, your dreams will come true.

Unless they don't.

Imagine
>the unimaginable.

Imagine
>the countdown to your due date taking on an urgency that could be a matter of life and death.

Imagine
>all you have read about pregnancy and infancy becoming useless, and everything you believe about what to expect becoming irrelevant.

Imagine
>the uncertainty and confusion, the fear and dread that replaces happy anticipation.

Imagine
>feeling your unborn baby kick and move—knowing how each day inside matters and hoping for a week, a day, an hour.

Imagine
>enduring a medical crisis during a time that is meant to be challenging, but still smooth and natural.

Imagine
>bracing yourself for the worst, during a time that is supposed to be filled with the best.

Imagine
>the losses. Imagine being robbed of the final months of pregnancy— that time of preparation, adjustment, and delicious anticipation.

Imagine
>missing the birth you had planned, losing forever those first precious moments after delivery.

Imagine
>your tiny, unfinished baby—perhaps blue and unresponsive—whisked away by strangers in scrubs.

Imagine
>being left with empty arms and an aching heart.

Imagine
>facing an overwhelming, unfamiliar, and frightening landscape—a foreign land—where humming machines loom over tiny babies.

Imagine

struggling to learn the new language of newborn intensive care, not comprehending what is happening.

Imagine

a flood of questions filling your mind, along with the terror of asking them and hearing the answers.

Imagine

wanting to hope, being afraid to hope, longing to know what the future holds.

Imagine

wanting to protect your baby from pain and suffering in the NICU, knowing that your womb or your arms are far gentler than the embrace of warming beds and ventilators.

Imagine

aching to nurse a baby who is far too young or sick to suckle.

Imagine

longing to caress and cuddle, fearing that your touch will hurt.

Imagine

holding your baby for the first time and realizing that your voice and touch are comforting.

Imagine

going home without your new baby, to an unfinished nursery and a life turned upside down.

Imagine

an uncertain future stretching before you, perhaps filled with doctors and evaluations and therapists.

Imagine

watching your baby's breathing and not taking it for granted.

Imagine

measuring your baby's feedings in milliliters and weight gain by the ounce.

Imagine

having to work so hard to help your baby grow and develop, and wanting so much to attain a sense of normalcy.

Imagine

feeling all alone, searching for a way to convey this experience to the people who care about you.

Imagine

being faced with an unexpected path, a journey that is so very different from the one you had planned.

• • •

837

A Note to Friends and Relatives

Needless to say, parents can be deeply emotionally affected by the premature birth of their baby. Your general sensitivity to that fact, in and of itself, will be a great support to them. You will find many insights into the experience of having a premature baby throughout this book. Chapter 20 is especially pertinent to your relationship with a preemie parent.

More specifically, here are some pointers for you to remember in your efforts to be supportive.

- Like most pregnant parents, your loved ones probably looked forward to an uncomplicated, joyful delivery. They eagerly anticipated meeting and snuggling their newborn. They daydreamed about leaving the hospital with a baby nestled in their arms and going home to hear, "Congratulations!" But when the baby is born early, all of their expectations come crashing down. They are faced with a different reality—empty arms and aching hearts. The future is uncertain and while there is hope, there is also great fear. They must hand over their baby to the foreign, confusing world of the NICU, invasive treatments, and frightening medical complications. They may feel helpless as they watch their infant struggle, unable to protect and nurture it the way they wish they could. Mothers in particular may feel a sense of guilt over their perceived failure to have a healthy, full-term pregnancy. Both parents may struggle in their own unique ways to figure out how to parent their newborn in an intensive-care setting. And they will grieve deeply for what might have been.
- Understand that yes, life goes on, and *at the same time*, they grieve. They won't get over it, they will get *through* it. In the meantime, they need friends who will walk with them instead of pushing too fast or pulling them along before they are ready. Adjust your expectations to recognize that grief is a long, complicated, but ultimately fruitful process.
- Parents often feel isolated from friends and relatives who don't understand how they feel. While you'll never truly know how they feel, you *can* understand and empathize with how painful and complicated this is for them. On the one hand, their precious baby has arrived and there is some joy to that—indeed, most parents appreciate flowers, gifts, and cards (personal, heartfelt cards are best rather than regular congratulatory ones with pictures of full-term, healthy babies on the front) to acknowledge that the baby has arrived, regardless of what the outcome

might be. But at the same time, their little one is hospitalized and separated from them, and there is devastation about that. **Help them to welcome their new little one to the world, but at the same time, acknowledge how difficult this is for them**. Don't wait until you're sure the baby is okay before reaching out to them. Parents appreciate your consistent support from the start.

- Don't avoid them just because you don't know what to say. Your quiet presence can be a comfort. They need someone who can listen and accept their emotions, someone who won't try to make them feel better or "fix" them. They also need you to not let your own uncertainty or anxiety bleed into conversations with them. You can tell them that you don't know what to say, but you want to hear whatever they want to tell you. Resist the temptation to encourage them to buck up or snap out of it or look on the bright side. Unless they ask you to, avoid telling them every story you ever heard about that two-pound preemie who is now six feet tall. On the other hand, avoid ruminating out loud about how much their tiny baby is struggling or how many complications must be lurking ahead. Just listen.

- Give special attention to the boundary between you and the parents. Even if you are a grandparent or close family friend, do not volunteer your opinions about their preemie's care, the doctor's competence, decisions about therapies or isolation, or their spouse's behaviors and reactions unless invited to do so. Ask questions gently, and make yourself available. Listen, but do not second-guess. You can expect the boundaries to become more relaxed as they become acclimated to their situation and get more and more comfortable with themselves as parents to this baby.

- It is possible that for now, the parents will find it too difficult to be around other healthy bouncing babies in the family or your circle of friends. Ask them about this, and if this is the case, be their advocate or "spokesperson" by encouraging other family members and friends to be mindful of their need to avoid painful reminders of the early parenting and babyhood they have lost, or their need to avoid the distressing contrast between full-term babies and their preterm baby(ies). In these ways, by acknowledging and validating their feelings and being their advocate, you can be a tremendously reassuring and supportive presence

•••

839

A Note to Friends and Relatives

in their lives. Your respect can give them room to adjust and heal.

- Recognize that it is healthy for them to talk about their baby. Dwelling on their hopes *and* sorrows is an important way of coping. If you can tolerate and acknowledge the unexpected mixture of wishes and fears, you can offer them the valuable opportunity to voice previously unspoken worries. By visiting their baby in the hospital or looking at photos or videotapes, you can offer your reassurance that their little one is beautiful, even if his or her appearance is shocking or frightening at first. By meeting and "getting to know" this baby, you also affirm that this baby is part of their family—despite the difficult beginnings or ongoing struggles. This simple recognition can be immensely supportive to parents.

- You can also offer to help them with some of the mundane chores of daily life. Being with and worrying about their baby may consume most of their time and energy. Even though their baby is in the hospital, parents usually find it almost impossible to "keep up" with responsibilities such as housework and paying bills. The emotional drain on the family can be tremendous, and tasks that used to seem simple can appear gargantuan. If you can offer to prepare some meals, do some laundry, take care of pets, vacuum some rugs, or run some errands, you can be tremendously helpful. If asking, "How can I help?" is met with blank stares or polite refusal, be specific—"Can I drop off lasagna for you Wednesday night?"

- If the parents have other children, your offers to babysit or spend time with the kids mean a lot. Especially if the baby is in the NICU for an extended period of time or comes home with long-term special needs, your ongoing involvement can relieve some of the parents' worries about their other children getting enough care and attention.

- Parents also want to be able to spend time with their other children—or have some time for themselves. If the parents consider you to be a potential babysitter for their preemie, learn CPR so that you can be a skilled caregiver. By becoming skilled, you acknowledge the realities of this baby's needs, and you can offer respite care that parents can accept with greater confidence.

- If they seem to need some distance from you for a time, respect that too. Sometimes, the effort of explaining their baby's medical issues and their own emotional response is simply too much to handle. Be sensitive to their needs and let them know that you will try to find a comfortable balance between keeping in touch and being involved. Sometimes, they may need to talk and sometimes all they may need is lasagna.

- Recognize that parenting a preemie is a long process that doesn't end when the baby is out of the woods medically or when the baby is discharged from the hospital. Even after their infant comes home, parents may still have many fears and worries about physical, intellectual, and emotional well-being. Because preterm birth presents many long-term risk factors for health and development, their baby will probably be more prone to infections, illness, and disability. The parents may need your support and advocacy around these issues. You can back them up when they want others to wash hands and stay away when sick. You can advocate for their protective instincts. Again, acknowledge and validate their anxieties—don't belittle or patronize or warn them against being "overprotective." Just understand that learning how to parent a preemie is *different*. Preemies are not just babies that happen to be extra little. Most preemies have a whole host of special needs, especially at first, and the parents must learn to become a special kind of parent. You can be a tremendous help to them by learning what they and their baby need, and respecting the limits they set. You too can become a special kind of grandparent/aunt/uncle/cousin/friend.

- Remember that you needn't be the parents' sole source of support. In fact, it is better for them if they have multiple sources they can turn to. If you think they might benefit from counseling, ask the hospital social worker to get more involved or to make a referral to a specialist or a support group. Most parents find it comforting to associate with other parents who are dealing with or have managed to get through this experience. If they have access to the Internet, there is an online support group for parents of premature babies called Preemie-L at www.preemie-l.org. Books can be valuable resources too (see Appendix C).

Special thanks to Dianne Maroney for granting us permission to use the concept of "Imagine" to describe the preemie-parent experience.
For more on her idea, go to www.premature-infant.com/Articleimagine.html.

• • •

841

A Note to Friends and Relatives

Resources

Books

These are books we've discovered, read, recommended to others, and in many cases, used ourselves. They all offer additional advice, wisdom, and encouragement in a variety of areas which you may encounter on your journey of parenting your preemie. When reading any book (including this one!), embrace what you find helpful, and pass by whatever isn't. This is not an exhaustive list—keep your eyes and ears open for other books that offer you support, insights, and solutions. And if you like a particular author, look into other books they may have written.

Books for Parents of Preemies

While most of these books give a nod to the emotional elements, they mainly focus on the medical and caregiving issues you face with your preemie. Some focus on the time in the NICU; others focus on what you need to know after homecoming; some deal with both.

Bradford, N. *Your Premature Baby: 0 – 5 Years.* Westport, Conn.: Firefly Books, 2003.

Garcia-Prats, J. A. and S. S. Hornfischer. *What to Do When Your Baby Is Premature: A Parent's Handbook for Coping with High-Risk Pregnancy and Caring for the Preterm Infant.* New York: Times Books, 2000.

Harrison, H. with A. Kositsky. *The Premature Baby Book: A Parents' Guide to Coping and Caring in the First Years.* New York: St. Martin's Press, 1983. (A classic, the first big book for parents of preemies that invited them into the NICU and encouraged them to be an informed advocate for their babies.)

Klein, A. H. and J. A. Ganon. *Caring for Your Premature Baby: A Complete Resource for Parents.* New York: HarperCollins, 1998.

Linden, D. W., E. T. Paroli, and M. W. Doron. *Preemies: The Essential Guide for Parents of Premature Babies.* New York: PocketBooks, 2000.

Luddinton-Hoe, S. M. and S. K. Golant. *Kangaroo Care: The Best You Can Do to Help Your Preterm Infant.* New York: Bantam Doubleday Dell, 1993. (The classic that illuminates the origins, practice, and profound benefits of skin-to-skin contact between preemies and parents.)

Madden, S. L. *The Preemie Parents' Companion: The Essential Guide to Caring for Your Premature Baby in the Hospital, at Home, and through the First Years.* Cambridge: Harvard Common Press, 2000.

Manginello, F. P. and T. F. Digeronimo. *Your Premature Baby: Everything You Need to Know about the Childbirth, Treatment, and Parenting of Premature Infants.* Rev. ed. New York: John Wiley and Sons, 1998.

Resta, B. *Believe in Katie Lynn.* Nashville: Eggman Publishing, 1995. (A children's picture book—beautifully illustrated, heartfelt story about the powers of developmentally supportive care in the NICU. See also under "Books for Children.")

Sears, W., R. Sears, J. Sears, and M. Sears. *The Premature Baby Book: Everything You Need to Know about Your Premature Baby from Birth to Age One.* Boston: Little, Brown and Company, 2004. (Taking care of your preemie, with an emphasis on "attachment parenting" and the responsive practices that strengthen your relationship with your baby.)

Tracy, A. E., D. I. Maroney, et. al. *Your Premature Baby and Child: Helpful Answers and Advice for Parents.* New York: Berkley, 1999. (A complete handbook on taking care of your preemie after hospital discharge.)

Zaichkin, J. *Newborn Intensive Care: What Every Parent Needs to Know.* Petaluma, Calif.: NICU Ink, 1996. (A big and thorough book detailing physical and developmental conditions associated with prematurity and medical treatments in the NICU.)

For Bereaved Parents

Barney, A. *Stolen Joy: Healing after Infertility and Infant Loss.* Baltimore: Icarus Books, 1993. (Poetry written by the author, who is grieving after her newborn's death. Gets to the heart of a mother's grief.)

Chethik, N. *FatherLoss: How Sons of All Ages Come to Terms with the Deaths of Their Dads.* New York: Hyperion, 2001. (Beautiful, lucid exploration and accounts of men's experiences with grief. Written for men, about men, by a man. Affirming. See also under "General Emotional Adjustment.")

Davis, D. L. *Empty Cradle, Broken Heart: Surviving the Death of Your Baby.* Rev. ed. Golden, Colo.: Fulcrum, 1996. (A gentle, comprehensive book that focuses on the emotional aspects of grieving, coping and healing after the death of a baby.)

Housden, M. *Hannah's Gift: Lessons from a Life Fully Lived.* New York: Bantam, 2002. (A mom shares the transformative lessons she received during her three-year-old daughter's last year of life. Shows how joy and sorrow intertwine when a child is dying.)

Loizeaux, W. *Anna: A Daughter's Life.* New York: Arcade Publishing, 1993. (Parenting a baby through multiple hospitalizations, surgeries, and procedures; coping with death and grief.)

Mehren, E. *After the Darkest Hour the Sun Will Shine Again: A Parent's Guide to Coping with the Loss of a Child.* New York: Simon and Schuster, 1997. (Comfortingly written by a preemie parent, author of *Born Too Soon*, which is listed in "Medical Ethics.")

Nuland, S. B. *How We Die: Reflections on Life's Final Chapter*. New York: Knopf, 1993. (A strangely comforting book demystifying the physical realities of dying and death.)

Staudacher, C. *Men and Grief: A Guide for Men Surviving the Death of a Loved One*. Oakland, Calif.: New Harbinger Publications, 1991. (Examines the ways men grieve; encourages men to face feelings.)

Medical Ethics

These books support the parent's right to be involved in medical life-and-death decision making for their newborns, as well as the idea that some fates are worse than death. Many of them are beautifully written personal accounts that can offer you affirmation and reassurance around these heart-wrenching decisions.

Alecson, D. *Lost Lullaby*. Berkeley: University of California Press, 1995. (A personal account: medical ethics and parental rights to decline medical intervention for a baby whose prognosis is grim.)

Anspach, R. R. *Deciding Who Lives: Fateful Choices in the Intensive Care Nursery*. Berkeley: University of California Press, 1997. (Medical ethics and decision making in the NICU.)

Belkin, L. *First Do No Harm*. New York: Simon and Schuster, 1993. (Medical ethics and decision making.)

Butler, M. *Born to Die?* Dublin: Marino Books, 1995. (A mother's personal account: making difficult medical decisions; overcoming ambivalent feelings toward her baby whose prognosis is poor.)

Davis, D. L. *Fly Away Home: For Bereaved Parents Who Turned Away from Aggressive Medical Intervention for Their Critically Ill Child*. Omaha: Centering, 2000. (A gentle, affirming book about making and living with the profound decision to refuse aggressive medical intervention for the terminally ill child. Includes a reassuring chapter on parenting the dying child.)

Davis, D. L. *Loving and Letting Go: For Bereaved Parents Who Turned Away from Aggressive Medical Intervention for Their Critically Ill Newborn.* Rev. ed. Omaha: Centering, 2002. (A gentle, affirming book about making and living with the agonizing and heartfelt decision to refuse aggressive medical intervention in the NICU.)

Dubler, N. and D. Nimmons. *Ethics On Call: Taking Charge of Life-and-Death Choices in Today's Health Care System.* New York: Vintage Books, 1993. (Medical ethics and decision making. Chapters on newborns and children.)

Ellenchild Pinch, W. J. *When the Bough Breaks: Parental Perceptions of Ethical Decision-Making in NICU.* Lanham, Md.: University Press of America, 2002. (Written as an academic textbook, parents' experiences in the NICU and beyond.)

Kay, R. *Saul.* New York: St. Martin's Press, 2000. (A memoir based on the author's own experiences with her son, who was born extremely prematurely and died four months later. She wrote the book from her baby's point of view—which is why it's listed as fiction by the publisher—about their experiences in a British neonatal intensive care unit. While it gives emotional depictions of infant and parent suffering in the NICU, it is also surprisingly comforting in terms of helping the reader see the hope, purpose, meaning, and love that prevails. Because the author imagines and showcases the baby's experience and acceptance of the NICU roller coaster and the medical decisions made, the book can be very reassuring if you are harboring any doubts, whatever your decision or the outcome. Ultimately, it offers the healing perspective that your baby's NICU experience was part of his or her unique and ultimately spiritual path.)

Kuebelbeck, A. *Waiting with Gabriel: A Story of Cherishing a Baby's Brief Life.* Chicago: Loyola Press, 2002. (A beautiful book and personal account of the life-and-death decision-making process with a critically ill newborn. It covers medical ethics, prenatal diagnosis, heart-wrenching decision making before and after birth, letting nature take its course as the way to give a baby the best quality of life; parenting, bonding, grieving.)

Lantos, J. D. *The Lazarus Case: Life-and-Death Issues in Neonatal Intensive Care.* Baltimore: Johns Hopkins University Press, 2001. (A composite malpractice case that illustrates the ambiguities, misunderstandings and responsibilities in life-and-death decision making in the NICU.)

Lyon, J. *Playing God in the Nursery.* New York: W. W. Norton, 1985. (Medical ethics and decision making in the NICU.)

Mehren, E. *Born Too Soon: The Story of Emily, Our Premature Baby.* New York: Doubleday, 1991. (Parenting a premature baby in the NICU; the joys and challenges of the roller coaster; dealing with doctors, nurses, and hospital policies; medical ethics and advocating for their baby's best interests; decision making and letting nature take its course. A story of hope, courage, and love.)

General Emotional Adjustment

These books deal more generally with your emotional needs around personal growth, spiritual searching, and your relationships. They support your awareness of your authentic self, and encourage you to reach for emotional health and balance. We've also included a popular women's magazine, because it addresses the search for fulfillment and meaning and encourages you to tap into your own power. For more support around emotional adjustment, also check out the books under "Personal Stories."

Emotional Health, Personal Growth, and Authentic Living

Beck, M. *Finding Your Own North Star: Claiming the Life You Were Meant to Live.* New York: Three Rivers Press, 2002. (How to reconnect with your essential self and regain the capacity to steer your own course toward happiness and fulfillment of your life's true purpose. One of the best "personal coaching" books.)

Boss, P. *Ambiguous Loss: Learning to Live with Unresolved Grief.* Cambridge: Harvard University Press, 1999. (Puts you in touch with the losses that are difficult to identify and mourn, and shows you how to find meaning and peace.)

Chethik, N. *FatherLoss: How Sons of All Ages Come to Terms with the Deaths of Their Dads.* New York: Hyperion, 2001. (Even though this book focuses on men's experiences with grieving the death of a father, it offers supportive insight into how dads of premature babies react and cope with their losses. See also under "For Bereaved Parents.")

Goldbart, S. and D. Wallin. *Mapping the Terrain of the Heart: Passion, Tenderness and the Capacity to Love*. Northvale, N. J.: Jason Aronson, Inc., 2001. (Psychodynamic approach, looking at how to form a healthy, fulfilling emotional connection and stay in a lifelong romantic relationship. Written primarily for a professional audience.)

Goleman, D. *Emotional Intelligence*. New York: Bantam, 1995. (The classic that identifies and describes emotional intelligence, a key to living a successful and fulfilling life.)

Hernandez-Hacker, P. and C. Ringo. *Early Passage: A Journal for Parents of Premies*. Petaluma, Calif.: NICU Ink, 2001. (A beautiful book for journaling, constructed specifically for parents of premature babies, with inspiring, comforting messages scattered throughout the pages.)

Krasnow, I. *Surrendering to Motherhood: Losing Your Mind, Finding Your Soul*. New York: Miramax, 1998. (If you can overlook the author's ease in childbearing and focus on the more personal, developmental journey, this book is a gem about shifting your point of view toward the relative values of and balance between motherhood and career. In fact, a turning point for her was her first-born's time in a pediatric intensive care unit when he was a toddler, an experience whose telling will resonate with preemie parents. It explores the soul-searching evaluation of priorities experienced by many mothers (including the author, an exquisitely entertaining and honest storyteller) and the discovery that you can reorganize your life, focus on motherhood, and find personal fulfillment therein, ultimately realizing that it can actually be satisfying to let your career slow down or be put on hold. This book can inspire you to relax and enjoy the chaos and charm of parenting babies and young children, and stop feeling like you're "missing out.")

Krasnow, I. *Surrendering to Yourself: You Are Your Own Soulmate*. New York: Miramax, 2003. (In the author's wonderful style of personal narrative woven with interviews of others, this book offers inspiring examples of the struggles and successes of personal growth and discovery, inspiring you to listen to the deepest part of yourself, follow your passions, and live the life you were meant to live.)

Levoy, G. M. *Callings: Finding and Following an Authentic Life.* New York: Three Rivers Press, 1998. (Listening to the healthiest, most essential part of yourself, following your dreams and passions, and finding fulfillment. Full of encouragement and inspiring personal stories.)

Martin, T. L. and K. J. Doka. *Men Don't Cry, Women Do: Transcending Gender Stereotypes of Grief.* New York: Brunner-Routledge, 1999. (Written for professionals; focuses on instrumental and intuitive grieving styles.)

McClure, V. *The Path of Parenting: Twelve Principles to Guide Your Journey.* Novato, Calif.: New World Library, 1999. (A gentle, supportive book on becoming a conscious parent. The twelve principles get to the heart of what's important. Also listed under "Parenting Style and Caregiving.")

Moran, V. *Fit from Within: 101 Simple Secrets to Change Your Body and Your Life—Starting Today and Lasting Forever.* Chicago: Contemporary Books, 2002. (A nurturing, encouraging, empowering book on having a healthy relationship with food and your body.)

Ruiz, D. M. *The Four Agreements: A Practical Guide to Personal Freedom.* San Rafael, Calif.: Amber-Allen Publishing, 1997. (Four simple but empowering principles to help you live your life with love and freedom from unnecessary suffering.)

Seligman, M. E. P. *Authentic Happiness: Using the New Positive Psychology to Realize Your Potential for Lasting Fulfillment.* New York: The Free Press, 2002. (The value of focusing on your signature strengths and optimism; insightful chapters on love and raising children.)

Seligman, M. E. P. *Learned Optimism: How to Change Your Mind and Your Life.* New York: PocketBooks, 1998. (A companion book to M. E. P. Seligman's *The Optimistic Child* (listed under "Supporting Your Preemie's Development"), gives you tools you need to be resilient, especially in the face of adversity.)

Siegel, D. and M. M. Hartzell. *Parenting from the Inside Out: How a Deeper Self-Understanding Can Help You Raise Children Who Thrive.* New York: Jeremy P. Tarcher, 2003. (Fascinating book that helps you understand your own tendencies and how to build the kind of relationship with your child that helps him or her become compassionate and resilient. See also under "Supporting Your Preemie's Development" and "Parenting Style and Caregiving.")

Winfrey, O., ed. *O, The Oprah Magazine.* (Contains many supportive, insightful articles that can help you live your life to the fullest, with emotional intelligence and spiritual awareness.)

Marriage

These books give honest and realistic descriptions of marriage and offer the comfort of knowing that you are not alone when you're wondering about the state of your partnership. (For improving marriage, see "Relationship Skills.")

Coleman, J. *Imperfect Harmony: How to Stay Married for the Sake of Your Children and Still Be Happy.* New York: St. Martin's Press, 2003. (Insightful and supportive, this book offers alternatives to the devastation of divorce. It presents a realistic look at marriage, encourages you to let go of idealized images and unrealistic expectations, and suggests constructive ways to think about your relationship, your past, your needs, your abilities, and your pursuit of happiness.)

If you're wondering, "Is this it?" or "What if?" these next books are for you:

Krasnow, I. *Surrendering to Marriage: Husbands, Wives, and Other Imperfections.* New York: Hyperion, 2001. (Through the author's own experiences and interviews of others, she explores the unspoken truths about what it's really like to be married—to build a life with another person who is ultimately so different from you, to be attracted to someone else, to consider parting—and all the challenge, reward, and compromise marriage entails.)

Viorst, J. *Grown-Up Marriage: What We Know, Wish We Had Known, and Still Need to Know about Being Married.* New York: The Free Press, 2003. (The author's observations and interviews encourage you to ground your expectations, endure the ebbs and flows of long-term relationships, and let go of the notion that the grass is greener on the other side.)

Divorce

Allison, S. *Conscious Divorce: Ending a Marriage with Integrity, A Practical and Spiritual Guide for Moving On.* New York: Three Rivers Press, 2001. (Begins with helping you get in touch with your intuition and what you really want, and then walks you through the ways to transform an unhealthy marriage into a healthy divorce.)

Ford, D. *Spiritual Divorce: Divorce as a Catalyst for an Extraordinary Life.* San Francisco: HarperSanFrancisco, 2001. (Empowering whether you're already divorced, in the process, or contemplating it—how to transform the breakdown of your relationship into an opportunity for personal growth, spiritual enlightenment, and emotional renewal.)

Widowhood

Feinberg, L. S. *I'm Grieving as Fast as I Can: How Young Widows and Widowers Can Cope and Heal.* Far Hills, N.J.: New Horizon Press, 1994.

Relationship Skills

Gottman, J. M. and J. DeClaire. *The Relationship Cure: A Five-Step Guide for Building Better Connections with Family, Friends, and Lovers.* New York: Crown Publishers, 2001. (Focuses on forging and maintaining healthy relationships.)

Gottman, J. M. and N. Silver. *The Seven Principles for Making Marriage Work: A Practical Guide from the Country's Foremost Relationship Expert.* New York: Crown Publishers, 1999. (Focuses on how successful marriages work and the ways of relating that build and maintain a healthy relationship.)

Heitler, S. *The Power of Two: Secrets to a Strong and Loving Marriage.* Oakland, Calif.: New Harbinger Publications, 1997. (Focuses on the communication skills that make marriage a supportive and rewarding partnership for both people—how to talk, how to listen, how to have constructive discussions, and how to deal with differences, anger, decision making, and conflict resolution. Rich in details and examples.)

Coping with Uncertainty and Difficult Circumstances; Spirituality

DeBecker, G. *Protecting the Gift: Keeping Children and Teenagers Safe (and Parents Sane)*. New York: Random House, 1999. (Encourages parents to examine their fears in light of the facts and to listen to and trust their intuitions about the safety or danger of particular situations as they arise.)

Jeffers, S. *Embracing Uncertainty: Breakthrough Methods for Achieving Peace of Mind When Facing the Unknown*. New York: St. Martin's Press, 2003. (How to let go of the outcome and trust the process when you are facing change or entering uncharted territory; accepting your destiny, finding treasures in adversity, following your intuition, finding meaning and purpose.)

Katie, B. *Loving What Is: Four Questions That Can Change Your Life*. New York: Harmony Books, 2002. (How to accept reality and live with it in peace. If this approach works for you, it may help you come to terms with the disappointing aspects of delivering and parenting your preemie.)

Remen, R. N. *Kitchen Table Wisdom: Stories That Heal*. New York: Riverhead Books, 1996. (A book of touching true stories that can inspire you to find treasure in adversity.)

Shelton, M. M. *Guidance from the Darkness: The Transforming Power of the Divine Feminine in Difficult Times*. New York: Jeremy P. Tarcher, 2000. (Spirituality; finding meaning in adversity; supportively encourages you to listen to your heart, trust the process, and let go of trying to control the outcome. Inspiring.)

Zukav, G. *The Seat of the Soul*. New York: Simon and Schuster, 1989. (Spiritual searching, meaning of life, basic truths.)

Personal Stories

All of these books are beautifully written by gifted writers, and while they may bring you to tears, they are healing to read. Besides making you feel less alone, these books are honestly written, filled with perspectives and insights that can help you cope with your own struggles. While not all of these books deal specifically with prematurity, they all carry childbearing and parenting themes that you may be dealing with and grieving over, and many come with the recommendation of other parents of preemies. Keep in mind that even if the details of your situation differ from the author's, the theme of "personal growth" can be meaningful to you. This is not an exhaustive list, so if reading this kind of book helps, we encourage you to find other personal stories that speak to you.

Barsuhn, R. *Growing Sophia: The Story of a Premature Birth.* St. Paul: deRuyter-Nelson Publications, 1996. (The roller coaster of birth, NICU, and homecoming.)

Beck, M. *Expecting Adam: A True Story of Birth, Rebirth, and Everyday Magic.* New York: Times Books, 1999. (Prenatal diagnosis, coming to terms with a child's disability, and learning to find treasures in differences from "the norm.")

Berstein, J. *Loving Rachael: A Family's Journey from Grief.* Pittsburgh: Coyne and Chenoweth, 1988. (Coming to terms with a baby's unfolding disabilities.)

Brunner, S. H. *Perfect Vision: A Mother's Experience with Childhood Cancer.* Fuquay-Varina, N. C.: Research Triangle, 1996. (Coping with raising a child with chronic illness and unknown prognosis.)

Gill, B. *Changed by a Child: Companion Notes for Parents of a Child with a Disability.* New York: Doubleday, 1998. (A mom describes her own journey, giving reassurance and guidance to readers along the way.)

Keller, H. *The Story of My Life.* Reissue Edition. New York: Bantam Classics, 1991. (The inspiring story of Helen Keller's triumph in spite of her disabilities and the brilliant instruction, discipline, and support of her teacher, Anne Sullivan, whose high expectations and refusal to pity Helen spurred her to emerge from her dark, silent prison and find her way in the world.)

Kephart, B. *A Slant of Sun: One Child's Courage.* New York: W. W. Norton, 1998. (Becoming a special kind of parent to a child who is "different," dealing with diagnoses of autism and pervasive developmental disorder.)

Seroussi, K. *Unraveling the Mystery of Autism and Pervasive Developmental Disorder: A Mother's Story of Research and Recovery.* New York: Simon and Schuster, 2000. (Explores the controversial link between autism and food cravings/sensitivities, but the other focus is on how this mother followed her instincts and became her child's best advocate and detective. See also under "Parenting Challenges.")

Westby, J. *They Will Know They Are Loved: A Family's Life with Premature Twins.* New York: Kirk House Publishing, 2002. (A father's memoir. Honest, heartfelt, focuses on his baby boys' early birth and his relationships with them as well as with his wife.)

Woodwell, W. H. *Coming to Term: A Father's Story of Birth, Loss, and Survival.* Jackson, Miss.: University of Mississippi Press, 2001. (A dad's account of HELLP syndrome, extremely premature delivery, death of one twin, the NICU experience.)

Zimmermann, S. *Grief Dancers: A Journey into the Depths of the Soul.* Golden, Colo.: Nemo Press, 1996. (Coming to terms with her child's disabilities.)

Collections of Personal Stories
Some of these collections are written by the parents themselves and put together by an editor; others are written by an author and based on observations and interviews with parents or health care providers. All of these books sensitively present a wide variety of situations and outcomes within the focus.

Brown, A. B. and K. R. McPherson, eds. *The Reality of Breastfeeding: Reflections by Contemporary Women.* Westport, Conn.: Bergin and Garvey, 1998. (Moving and entertaining short essays by moms, speaking honestly and opening about breast-feeding struggles, wonders, disappointments, and triumphs. A wide range of experiences and outcomes and all the attendant tears, joy, frustration and relief. See also under "Breast-Feeding.")

Humes, E. *Baby E.R.: The Heroic Doctors and Nurses Who Perform Medicine's Tiniest Miracles.* New York: Simon and Schuster, 2000. (Stories from the front lines in the NICU, real and varied.)

Kennedy, N. J . and D. Pegher. *Baby Hands and Baby Feet: Poems and Drawings from the Nursery.* Petaluma, Calif.: NICU Ink, 1995. (Written by nurses, touching emotional and visual snapshots. Rich and affirming for health care providers, and a window into the NICU for uninitiated friends and relatives.)

Marsh, J. D. B., ed. *From the Heart: On Being the Mother of a Child with Special Needs.* Bethesda, Md.: Woodbine House, 1995. (Mothers in a variety of situations talk about coping emotionally with the challenges that arise—organized according to themes such as "Being Heard," "Life Amplified," and "Healing.")

McCarty, R., ed. *You Are Not Alone: 20 Stories of Hope, Heroism, Heartache, and Healing as Told by the Parents of Children Treated in the NICU.* South Weymouth, Mass.: Children's Medical Ventures, 1998.

Meyer, D. J., ed. *Uncommon Fathers: Reflections on Raising a Child with a Disability.* Bethesda, Md.: Woodbine House, 1995. (The companion book to Marsh's book *From the Heart*. Fathers in a variety of situations talk about coping emotionally with the challenges that arise.)

Naseef, R. *Special Children, Challenged Parents: The Struggles and Rewards of Raising a Child with a Disability.* Baltimore: Brookes Publishing, 2001 (Insightful, supportive, practical, comprehensive guide based on the author's personal experiences with his son who has autism, as well as interviews with other parents of children with disabilities. See also under "Parenting Challenges.")

Powell K. A. and K. Wilson, eds. *Living Miracles: Stories of Hope from Parents of Premature Babies.* New York: St. Martin's Press, 2000. (Inspirational stories from parents whose preemies survived; a variety of outcomes are represented.)

Simons, R. *After the Tears: Parents Talk about Raising a Child with a Disability.* New York: Harcourt-Brace, 1987. (Reinforces that this child is precious and you will survive.)

Smith, T. *Miracle Birth Stories of Very Premature Babies: Little Thumbs Up!* Westport, Conn.: Bergin and Garvey, 1999. (Based on interviews, detailed accounts of parents' experiences with their preemies' early arrivals and hospitalizations.)

Sullivan, T. *Special Parent, Special Child: Parents of Children with Disabilities Share Their Trials, Triumphs, and Hard-Won Wisdom.* New York: G. P. Putnam's Sons, 1995. (Interviews with parents who have learned to reframe their initial discouragement and have come to see disability as a small part of who their child is.)

Breast-Feeding

All these books support, encourage, and advocate for breast-feeding, and it wouldn't hurt to have more than one on hand.

Brown, A. B. and K. R. McPherson, eds. *The Reality of Breastfeeding: Reflections by Contemporary Women.* Westport, Conn.: Bergin and Garvey, 1998. (Moving and entertaining short essays by moms, speaking honestly and openly about breast-feeding struggles, wonders, disappointments, and triumphs. A wide range of experiences and outcomes, and all the attendant tears, joy, frustration, and relief. Also listed under "Collections of Personal Stories.")

Bumgarner, N. J. *Mothering Your Nursing Toddler.* Schaumburg, Ill.: La Leche League International, 2000. (Supportive and encouraging, promotes the idea of child-led weaning and the benefits of continuing to breast-feed beyond the first year.)

Mohrbacher, N. and J. Stock. *The Breastfeeding Answer Book.* Rev. ed. Schaumburg, Ill.: La Leche League International, 1997. (Written for health care providers, so it tends to be dry and clinical, but it's packed full of data and information, including a comprehensive chapter on prematurity.)

Neifert, M. *Dr. Mom's Guide to Breastfeeding.* New York: Penguin, 1998. (A comprehensive, supportive guide; excellent chapters on problems and on preemies.)

Newman, J. and T. Pitman. *The Ultimate Breastfeeding Book of Answers: The Most Comprehensive Problem-Solution Guide to Breastfeeding from the Foremost Breastfeeding Expert in North America.* Roseville, Calif.: Prima Publishing, 2000. (This big book is full of information and support for breast-feeding, advocating and uncovering myths—especially when it comes to preemies. It also has an excellent, encouraging chapter on tips for "when baby refuses the breast.")

Sears, W. and M. Sears. *The Breastfeeding Book: Everything You Need to Know about Nursing Your Child*. Boston: Little, Brown and Company, 2000.

Parenting Books

These are not your typical "how-to" parenting books. Rather than telling parents what they should do, these books guide you toward positive, healthful action while empowering you to figure out solutions that will work for you and your children. They recognize that every parent and every child is unique, and suggest different ways of thinking about, coping with, and handling your most important, complicated, and creative role—that of parent. They consider the emotional as well as the physical/biological components of development, behavior, and parent-child interaction. Recognizing that your needs and your child's needs are sometimes at odds, these books are flexible and empathic, and encourage you to find the balance that's right for you. By acknowledging the importance of uncovering underlying problems, they are able to offer useful guidance and ideas to help you find real solutions that can work for you and your child.

We've included our favorite books that explain ways to support your child's development, that help you think about your parenting style, that explore positive approaches to discipline, and that address the more challenging aspects of parenting, whether you have a "high-need" child, a child with disabilities, or a child who simply marches to the beat of a different drummer.)

Supporting Your Preemie's Development

Well-written and informative, these books offer insights into the connections between a child's development and the brain, inborn temperament, and relationships with caregivers. Filled with guidance and support, these books can help you foster your preemie's development and identify the real sources of difficulties, enabling you to find real and holistic solutions that strengthen your relationship with your child.

Eliot, L. *What's Going on in There? How the Brain and Mind Develop in the First Five Years of Life*. New York: Bantam, 2000. (A comprehensive overview of current scientific knowledge about infant and early childhood brain development, with a focus on how you, the parent, can affect this complex process. Detailed, scientific, yet accessible.)

Greenspan, S. with N. B. Lewis, *Building Healthy Minds: The Six Experiences That Create Intelligence and Emotional Growth in Babies and Young Children*. Cambridge, Mass.: Perseus Books, 1999. (Shows parents how to nurture a rewarding relationship with their infant and use their baby's budding abilities to build on their emotional and cognitive development. The case studies are especially helpful in pointing out ways to relate with babies who have sensitivities and weaknesses by building on their strengths. Also listed under "Parenting Style and Caregiving.")

Gottman, J. *The Heart of Parenting: Raising an Emotionally Intelligent Child*. New York: Simon and Schuster, 1997. (See also under "Parenting Style and Caregiving.")

Sears, W. and M. Sears with E. Pantley. *The Successful Child: What Parents Can Do to Help Kids Turn out Well*. Boston: Little, Brown and Company, 2002.

Seligman, M. E. P. *The Optimistic Child: A Proven Program to Safeguard Children against Depression and Build Lifelong Resilience*. New York: HarperPerennial, 1996. (See also under "Parenting Challenges.")

Siegel, D. and M. M. Hartzell. *Parenting from the Inside Out: How a Deeper Self-Understanding Can Help You Raise Children Who Thrive*. New York: Jeremy P. Tarcher, 2003. (Fascinating book that draws the connection between brain development, attachment, and interpersonal relationships. Helps you understand your own tendencies and how to build the kind of relationship with your child that helps him or her become compassionate and resilient. See also under "Parenting Style and Caregiving" and "Emotional Health, Personal Growth, and Authentic Living.")

Stern, D. *Diary of a Baby: What Your Child Sees, Feels, and Experiences*. New York: Basic Books, 1992. (This fascinating book is the imaginary diary of a child from the age of six weeks to four years, based on the latest infant development and brain research.)

• • •

Developmental Challenges

Berk, L. *Awakening Children's Minds: How Parents and Teachers Can Make a Difference.* New York: Oxford University Press, 2001. (Also listed under "Parenting Challenges.")

Greene, R. W. *The Explosive Child: A New Approach for Understanding and Parenting Easily Frustrated, "Chronically Inflexible" Children.* New York: HarperCollins, 1998. (Also listed under "Parenting Challenges.")

Greenspan, S. I. *The Challenging Child: Understanding, Raising, and Enjoying the Five "Difficult" Types of Children.* Reading, Mass.: Addison-Wesley, 1995. (Also listed under "Parenting Challenges.")

Koplewicz, H. S. *It's Nobody's Fault: New Hope and Help for Difficult Children.* New York: Times Books, 1996. (Also listed under "Parenting Challenges.")

Kranowitz, C. S. *The Out-of-Sync Child: Recognizing and Coping with Sensory Integration Dysfunction.* New York: Perigree, 1998. (Also listed under "Parenting Challenges.")

Kurcinka, M. S. *Raising Your Spirited Child: A Guide for Parents Whose Child Is More Intense, Sensitive, Perceptive, Persistent, Energetic.* New York: HarperPerennial, 1992. (Also listed under "Parenting Challenges.")

Levine, M. *A Mind at a Time: America's Top Learning Expert Shows How Every Child Can Succeed.* New York: Simon and Schuster, 2002. (Explains how the eight neurodevelopmental systems evolve, interact, and contribute to a child's success in school. Advocates for identifying and teaching to a child's strengths.)

Sears, W. and M. Sears. *Parenting the Fussy Baby and High-Need Child: Everything You Need to Know—From Birth to Age Five.* Boston: Little, Brown and Company, 1996. (Also listed under "Parenting Style and Caregiving.")

Sears, W. and L. Thompson. *The A.D.D. Book: New Understandings, New Approaches to Parenting Your Child.* Boston: Little, Brown and Company, 1998. (Also listed under "Parenting Challenges.")

Parenting Style and Caregiving

Brazelton, T. B. and S. I. Greenspan. *The Irreducible Needs of the Child: What Every Child Must Have to Grow, Learn, and Flourish.* Cambridge, Mass: Perseus Books, 2000. (Written more for professionals and policymakers, this book is full of Dr. Brazelton's and Dr. Greenspan's accumulated experience, research, and wisdom.)

Brazelton, T. B. and J. D. Sparrow. *Touchpoints: Both Volumes of the Nation's Most Trusted Guide to the First Six Years of Life.* Cambridge, Mass.: Perseus, 2002. (Originally in two volumes: birth to age three and ages three to six. Explores the developmental strides, growth spurts, and typical regressions that babies and children experience to help parents understand and empathize with their child's ups and downs, progress and setbacks.)

Davis, L. and J. Keyser. *Becoming the Parent You Want to Be: A Sourcebook of Strategies for the First Five Years.* New York: Broadway Books, 1997. (A warm, open-minded book that offers lots of ideas, suggestions, and encourages you to figure out what's best for you and your child.)

Douglas, A. *The Mother of All Baby Books: The Ultimate Guide to Your Baby's First Year.* Indianapolis, Ind.: Hungry Minds, 2002. (Down-to-earth and informative, this book tackles topics that are off-limits to many other baby books, such as prematurity. You can pick up this "mainstream baby book" and get support for the postpartum, breast-feeding, sleeping, equipment and routine baby care issues that you have in common with full-term parents *and* also feel acknowledged and accounted for in the special sections devoted to prematurity issues.)

Gottman, J. *The Heart of Parenting: Raising an Emotionally Intelligent Child.* New York: Simon and Schuster, 1997. (Teaches and supports parents in how to honor feelings and approach parenting and discipline in emotionally healthy ways, which is what makes parents most effective. Also listed under "Supporting Your Preemie's Development.")

Greenspan, S. with N. B. Lewis, *Building Healthy Minds: The Six Experiences That Create Intelligence and Emotional Growth in Babies and Young Children.* Cambridge, Mass.: Perseus Books, 1999. (Also under "Supporting Your Preemie's Development.")

Klaus, M. H., J. H. Kennell, and P. H. Klaus. *Bonding: Building the Foundations of Secure Attachment and Independence.* Reading, Mass.: Addison-Wesley, 1995. (A supportive book that reassures and encourages parents in their efforts to form a bond with their infant. Includes an excellent chapter on prematurity.)

McClure, V. *Infant Massage: A Handbook for Loving Parents.* New York: Bantam Books, 2000. (Teaches the advantages and techniques of infant massage.)

McClure, V. *The Path of Parenting: Twelve Principles to Guide Your Journey.* Novato, Calif.: New World Library, 1999. (A gentle, easy-to-read, practical book that focuses on parents and examines emotionally healthy principles that can ground your parenting in the conscious decisions you make about how you want to live your life and what kind of relationship you want with your child through the years. See also under "General Emotional Adjustment.")

McKay, M., ed., et al. *When Anger Hurts Your Kids: A Parent's Guide.* New York: MJF Books, 1996. (A practical, supportive book that offers ways to identify and talk back to anger triggers, enabling parents to be more effective.)

Pantley, E. *The No-Cry Sleep Solution: Gentle Ways to Help Your Baby Sleep through the Night.* New York: McGraw-Hill/Contemporary Books, 2002. (Work *with* your baby toward good sleep habits. Presents a variety of solutions so you can chose what works best for you and your baby. Endorsed by William Sears, pediatrician and author of *Nighttime Parenting.*)

Rose, L. *Learning to Love: The Developing Relationships between Mother, Father, and Baby During the First Year.* Camberwell, Victoria: Acer Press, 2000. (Ideas and support for attuning to, interacting with, and connecting with your baby.)

Rosenfeld, A. *Hyper-Parenting: Are You Hurting Your Child by Trying Too Hard?* New York: St. Martin's Press, 2000. (Examines the tendency for parents to strive to raise perfect kids in perfect ways and encourages them to relax, enjoy, simplify, do what feels right, trust their abilities, and accept imperfection—in the children and themselves.)

Samalin, N. *Loving without Spoiling and 100 Other Timeless Tips for Raising Terrific Kids.* Chicago: Contemporary Books, 2003. (A nice overview of responsive, nurturing parenting.)

Sears, W. *Nighttime Parenting: How to Get Your Baby and Child to Sleep.* Rev. ed. New York: Plume, 1999. (Encourages parents to be as responsive to a baby's needs at night as they are during the day and shows the advantages and how-tos of cosleeping.)

Sears, W. and M. Sears. *The Attachment Parenting Book: A Commonsense Guide to Understanding and Nurturing Your Baby.* Boston: Little, Brown and Company, 2001. (The definitive guide to attachment parenting, an approach that emphasizes responding to your child's needs, figuring out what works best for both of you, and strengthening the connection between you and your child from infancy onward. Excellent section on the benefits of attachment parenting for preemies and their parents.)

Sears, W. and M. Sears. *The Baby Book: Everything You Need to Know about Your Baby from Birth to Age Two.* Boston: Little, Brown and Company, 2003. (Responsive parenting; informative supportive chapter on "Babywearing: The Art and Science of Carrying Your Baby.")

Sears, W. and M. Sears. *Parenting the Fussy Baby and High-Need Child: Everything You Need to Know—From Birth to Age Five.* Boston: Little, Brown and Company, 1996. (A supportive book, encouraging parents to become attuned to their high-need baby or child. Also listed under "Developmental Challenges.")

Siegel, D. and M. M. Hartzell. *Parenting from the Inside Out: How a Deeper Self-Understanding Can Help You Raise Children Who Thrive.* New York: Jeremy P. Tarcher, 2003. (See under "Supporting Your Preemie's Development" and "Emotional Health, Personal Growth, and Authentic Living.")

Small, M. *Our Babies, Ourselves: How Biology and Culture Shape the Way We Parent.* New York: Anchor Books, 1998. (Looks at parenting and nurturing across cultures, thereby encouraging parents to question the culturally ingrained practices that don't work or feel right and to reach for ones that do.)

Thevenin, T. *The Family Bed: An Age-Old Concept in Child Rearing*. Wayne, N.J.: Avery, 1987. (Looks at sleeping practices across the ages and cultures, and opens the mind toward the idea of having a family bed.)

Discipline

Brazelton, T. B. and J. Sparrow. *Discipline: The Brazelton Way*. Cambridge, Mass.: Perseus Publishing, 2003. (Concise, practical, empathic.)

Faber, A. and E. Mazlish. *Siblings without Rivalry: How to Help Your Children Live Together So You Can Live Too*. Expanded ed. New York: Avon, 1998. (Full of practical examples; teaches parents how to view sibling relationships realistically and how to cultivate healthy relationships between your kids.)

Kurcinka, M. S. *Kids, Parents and Power Struggles: Winning for a Lifetime*. New York: HarperCollins, 2000. (How to use "emotion coaching" to build a warm, nurturing, effective relationship with your child.)

Nelson, J. *Positive Discipline: The Classic Guide for Parents and Teachers to Help Children to Develop Self-Discipline, Responsibility, Cooperation, and Problem-Solving Skills*. Rev. ed. New York: Ballantine, 1996. (Offering many pearls of wisdom, this warm, practical book shows parents and other caregivers how to look for the underlying needs that aren't being met when children misbehave. Reframes "discipline" as gentle and firm guidance and encouragement that makes children feel better, which naturally and intrinsically motivates them to behave better.)

Samalin, N. and M. M. Jablow. *Loving Your Child Is Not Enough: Positive Discipline That Works*. New York: Penguin, 1998. (Another book that focuses on solving underlying problems and reframing discipline in positive ways.)

Parenting Challenges

Berk, L. *Awakening Children's Minds: How Parents and Teachers Can Make a Difference*. New York: Oxford University Press, 2001. (Academic but insightful and instructive with plenty of examples, this book highlights principles of child development, the overall importance of early childhood education, and how to structure home and school environments. Supportive and informative chapter on children with disabilities, focusing on ADHD. Also listed under "Developmental Challenges.")

Bryan, E. M. *Twins, Triplets, and More: Their Nature, Development, and Care.* New York: St. Martin's Press, 1998. (Addresses many unique parenting concerns, including managing the logistics, emotional coping, bonding, disability, death, and selective reduction.)

Greene, R. W. *The Explosive Child: A New Approach for Understanding and Parenting Easily Frustrated, "Chronically Inflexible" Children.* New York: Harper-Collins, 1998. (How to reclaim your sanity—and your child. Excellent guide that looks at parenting a child with challenging temperamental qualities who has frequent "meltdowns" and doesn't respond to typical or even skillful parenting. Offers insights into what's going on with the child's brain chemistry and physiology, with suggestions for repairing and strengthening your relationship with your child and teaching him or her self-regulation. Also listed under "Developmental Challenges.")

Greenspan, S. I. *The Challenging Child: Understanding, Raising, and Enjoying the Five "Difficult" Types of Children.* Reading, Mass.: Addison-Wesley, 1995. (An insightful, supportive guide to acquiring a unique parenting style that suits your child's unique personality and needs. Also listed under "Developmental Challenges.")

Greenspan, S. I., and R. Weider. *The Child with Special Needs: Encouraging Intellectual and Emotional Growth.* Cambridge, Mass.: Perseus Press, 1998. (How to enlist your child's strengths to help him overcome weaknesses. Also listed under "Developmental Challenges.")

Harwell, J. *Ready-to-Use Tools and Materials for Remediating Specific Learning Disabilities.* West Nyack, N.Y.: The Center for Applied Research in Education, 1995.

Koplewicz, H. S. *It's Nobody's Fault: New Hope and Help for Difficult Children.* New York: Times Books, 1996. (Looks at the biochemical basis for children who present with challenging behaviors—the brain-behavior connection. Also listed under "Developmental Challenges.")

Kranowitz, C. S. *The Out-of-Sync Child: Recognizing and Coping with Sensory Integration Dysfunction*. New York: Perigree, 1998. (For parents of kids who are under- or overwhelmed by sensory stimulation, the classic book on sensory integration dysfunction. Also listed under "Developmental Challenges.")

Kurcinka, M. S. *Raising Your Spirited Child: A Guide for Parents Whose Child Is More Intense, Sensitive, Perceptive, Persistent, Energetic*. New York: HarperPerennial, 1992. (How to work with, not against, your child's inborn temperament and enjoy him or her. Also listed under "Developmental Challenges.")

Lavin, J. L. *Special Kids Need Special Parents: A Resource for Parents of Children with Special Needs*. New York: Berkley, 2001. (A practical and supportive book that covers emotional issues, family dynamics, and behavioral challenges, as well as advocating for your child in medical settings and at school, and dealing with pain and mobility issues.)

Miller, N. B. *Nobody's Perfect: Living and Growing with Children Who Have Special Needs*. Baltimore: Paul H. Brookes Publishing Company, 1994. (A warm, supportive book that identifies and describes four overlapping processes of adaptation to parenting a child with any kind of special needs, helping parents make sense of their unique experiences.)

Miller, N. B. and C. C. Sammons. *Everybody's Different: Understanding and Changing Our Reactions to Disabilities*. Baltimore: Paul H. Brookes Publishing Company, 1994.

Naseef, R. *Special Children, Challenged Parents: The Struggles and Rewards of Raising a Child with a Disability*. Baltimore: Paul H. Brookes Publishing Company, 2001. (Focuses on the emotions and grieving process of parents struggling to accept and raise a child with special needs. Supportive, insightful guide to coping and balancing needs. Great for fathers. See also under "Collections of Personal Stories.")

Noel, B. and A. Klein. *The Single Parent Resource*. Beverly Hills, Calif.: Champion Pr Ltd, 1998.

Pruitt, D. B., ed. *Your Child: What Every Parent Needs to Know about Childhood Development from Birth to Preadolescence—What's Normal, What's Not and When to Seek Help.* New York: HarperCollins, 1998. (A general guide that can help you differentiate between normal developmental struggles and difficulties that call for professional intervention.)

Rothbart, B. *Multiple Blessings: From Pregnancy through Childhood, A Guide for Parents of Twins, Triplets, or More.* New York: Hearst Books, 1994.

Sears, W. and L. Thompson. *The A.D.D. Book: New Understandings, New Approaches to Parenting Your Child.* Boston: Little, Brown and Company, 1998. (A supportive, informative book that looks at the neurological basis for Attention Deficit Disorder, examines the child's positive traits, and offers suggestions for alternative treatments, including neurofeedback, that build on the child's strengths, instead of relying solely on drug therapies. (Also listed under "Developmental Challenges.")

Segal, M. *In Time and with Love: Caring for the Special Needs Baby.* Rev. ed. New York: Newmarket Press, 2001. (Gentle, supportive, affirming.)

Seligman, M. E. P. *The Optimistic Child: A Proven Program to Safeguard Children against Depression and Build Lifelong Resilience.* New York: HarperPerennial, 1996. (Guiding your child toward holding an optimistic view of life, people, and events, which fortifies the ability to bounce back from disappointment, frustration, rejection, discouragement, and misfortune—and find authentic happiness. See Seligman's other books in "General Emotional Adjustment.")

Seroussi, K. *Unraveling the Mystery of Autism and Pervasive Developmental Disorder: A Mother's Story of Research and Recovery.* New York: Simon and Schuster, 2000. (Explores the link between autism and food cravings/sensitivities. A story of advocating for your child. See also under "Personal Stories.")

Trozzi, M. and Massimini, K. *Talking With Children about Loss: Words, Strategies, and Wisdom to Help Children Cope with Death, Divorce, and Other Difficult Times.* New York: Perigree, 1999. (Sensitive, helpful guide. Includes an example about preemie twins and how to talk to the child who survived about the one who died in infancy.)

School Advocacy

Siegel, L. *The Complete IEP Guide: How to Advocate for Your Special Ed Child.* Berkeley, Calif.: Nolo Press, 2001.

Wright, P. W. D. and P. D. Wright. *Wrightslaw: From Emotions to Advocacy—The Special Education Survival Guide.* Hartfield, Va.: Harbor House Law Press, 2001.

Books for Children

Collins, P. L. *Waiting for Baby Joe.* Niles, Ill.: Albert Whitman and Company, 1990. (Explores the emotions families feel when their baby is born prematurely and they have to wait for the baby to get better and come home.)

Lafferty, L. and N. Flood. *Born Early: A Premature Baby Story.* Minneapolis: Fairview, 1998. (Shows the NICU, explains medical procedures, simply written and illustrated with gentle photographs. Covers birth to homecoming.)

Murphy-Melas, E., D. Tate, and W. Troyer. *Watching Bradley Grow: A Story about Premature Birth.* Atlanta, Ga.. Longstreet Press, 1996. (Deals with feeling left out when you can't visit the baby in the hospital, and your parents are spending a lot of time there.)

Resta, B. *Believe in Katie Lynn.* Nashville: Eggman Publishing, 1995. (A beautifully illustrated, heartfelt story about a baby in the NICU; good explanation of a special beginning to show your growing preemie or your other children. See also under "Books for Parents of Preemies.")

Health, Pregnancy, Fertility

Alcaniz, L. *Waiting for Bebé: A Pregnancy Guide for Latinas.* New York: One World/Ballentine, 2003. (Available in Spanish and English.)

Chism, D. M. *The High-Risk Pregnancy Sourcebook: Everything You Need to Know.* Los Angeles: Lowell House, 1997. (Looks at risk factors, complications, and what you can do to have the best chance for a healthy baby.)

Douglas, A. and J. R. Sussman, *Trying Again: A Guide to Pregnancy after Miscarriage, Stillbirth, and Infant Loss*. Dallas: Taylor Trade Publishing, 2000. (A thorough, supportive book detailing pregnancy, testing, complications, and coping for anxious parents.)

Douglas, A. and J. R. Sussman. *The Unofficial Guide to Having a Baby*. New York: MacMillan, 1999. (An empowering book packed full of information to help you make sound decisions during pregnancy.)

Dunwold, A. and D. G. Sanford. *Postpartum Survival Guide*. Oakland, Calif.: New Harbinger, 1994. (Examines postpartum reactions with suggestions on how to cope.)

Kleiman, K. and V. D. Raskin, *This Isn't What I Expected: Overcoming Postpartum Depression*. New York: Bantam, 1994. (Compassionate and supportive, provides a comprehensive description of postpartum depression, treatments, and advice around this misunderstood and often misdiagnosed condition.)

Luke, B. *Every Pregnant Woman's Guide to Preventing Premature Birth: A Program for Reducing the Sixty Proven Risks That Can Lead to Prematurity*. New York: Times Books, 1995. (Looks at risk factors and what you can do about them.)

McIntyre, A. *The Complete Woman's Herbal: A Manual of Healing Herbs and Nutrition for Personal Well-Being and Family Care*. New York: Henry Holt, 1995.

Moran, V. *Fit from Within: 101 Simple Secrets to Change Your Body and Your Life— Starting Today and Lasting Forever*. Chicago: Contemporary Books, 2002. (A nurturing, encouraging, empowering book on having a healthy relationship with food and your body.)

Murkoff, H., A. Eisenberg, and S. Hathaway, *What to Expect When You're Expecting*. New York: Workman Publishing, 2002. (Newly updated, packed with information.)

Peoples, D. and H. R. Ferguson. *Experiencing Infertility: An Essential Resource.* New York: W. W. Norton, 1998. (Focuses on emotions as well as practical matters such as seeking treatment, adoption. Written in easy-to-read question-and-answer style.)

Rothman, B. K. *The Tentative Pregnancy: Prenatal Diagnosis and the Future of Motherhood.* New York: Penguin Books, 1986. (Takes a look at what prenatal diagnostic testing can mean for parents who may hesitate to invest in a baby until the tests come back "normal," or who must now face decisions they never imagined.)

Salzer, L. P. *Surviving Infertility: A Compassionate Guide through the Emotional Crisis of Infertility.* New York: HarperPerennial, 1991. (Supportive; focuses mostly on the emotional aspects and coping strategies.)

Sears, W. and M. Sears. *The Pregnancy Book: Month by Month, Everything You Need to Know from America's Baby Experts.* Boston: Little, Brown and Company, 1997. (Comprehensive and supportive.)

The Staff of RESOLVE with Diane Aronson, Executive Director. *Resolving Infertility: Understanding the Options and Choosing Solutions When You Want to Have a Baby.* New York: HarperCollins, 1999. (Informative, focuses on treatment options.)

Tracy, A. E. and R. H. Schwarz. *The Pregnancy Bed Rest Book: A Survival Guide for Expectant Mothers and Their Families.* New York: Berkley Publishing Group, 2001. (Practical tips and emotional support.)

Videos

The March of Dimes is developing a program, including videos, to offer comprehensive support to parents in the NICU. Contact The March of Dimes Resource Center (See "Resource Organizations" below.)

Parents on the Threshold: You Are Not Alone, produced by the Colorado Collective for Medical Decisions (CCMD) and Nickel's Worth Productions in 1999, a 30-minute videotape that supports parents who face life-and-death decisions in the NICU. To obtain an order form, contact Nickel's Worth Productions at NickelTV@aol.com. See Appendix D for more on the video and CCMD's Neonatal Guidelines.

Special Beginnings introduces families to the NICU with an overview of care and validation of emotions that parents experience. Contact the Centering Corporation (See "Resource Organizations" below.)

Resource Organizations

These organizations publish a variety of supportive books and materials for parents experiencing crisis during pregnancy or after delivery, including bed rest, prematurity, raising a child with special needs (including difficulty feeding), and death of a baby. Some also distribute resources from other publishers, including books for parents, siblings, NICU baby books. Contact them to order catalogs or to explain your special needs.

A Place to Remember
Publisher and distributor:
deRuyter-Nelson Publications, Inc.
1885 University Avenue, Suite 110,
Saint Paul, MN
(800) 631-0973
www.APlaceToRemember.com

Brookes Publishing
P.O. Box 10624, Baltimore, MD
21285-0624
(800) 638-3775 | Fax: (410) 337-8539
www.brookespublishing.com

Centering Corporation
Publisher and distributor
P.O. Box 4600, Omaha, NE 68134
(402) 553-1200
www.centering.org

Children's Medical Ventures
Products developed specifically for preemies and NICU care providers
www.childmed.com/

The March of Dimes
Resource center and developer of the NICU Family Support Program for hospitals nationwide
(888) MODIMES
www.marchofdimes.com

Woodbine House
Special Needs Collection
Books for Parents, Professionals, and Children
(800) 843-7323
www.woodbinehouse.com

Internet

The quantity and variety of Web sites and Listservs on the Internet are endless. Listed are some central sites providing links to many other sites that you can look into to meet your needs for information, ideas, and support. As always, use your judgement, and look for Web sites that are legitimate and reliable sources of information and comfort, or Listservs that are well-run communities of mutual respect, sharing, and support.

Community

www.preemie-l.org

Parents of Premature Babies

Preemie-L ("L" stands for "list")

The premier Listserv for parents of premature babies, a virtual community sharing ideas, information, and support. In addition to participation in the discussion groups, parents can request that they be put in touch with another family whose situation is similar to theirs and whose preemies are now older. Parents have volunteered, and been trained to be mentors. Check out their links to other resources, including *The Early Edition* newsletter, Recommended Booklist, and Selected Resources.

www.prematurity.org

Premature Baby – Premature Child

Provides articles, resources and support from parents and doctors for parents of children born prematurely. This site includes a mailing list, information on parenting your premature child, the long-term impacts of prematurity, the special needs of children, celebrating and coping with prematurity, an e-mail support group, and an Internet forum.

www.preemie-hearts.com

Home of Preemie Purple Hearts, beautiful blown-glass pendant/pins for parents and others who journey with prematurity. "An outward sign of unity among a special group of people ... the Heart can be with you when you feel alone, remind you there are hundreds of others who keep you in their hearts."

www.thepreemieplace.org/

The Preemie Place

A smaller board for parents of premature children.

Emotional Support

www.parentingyourprematurebaby.com

> Parenting Your Premature Baby and Child: The Emotional Journey
> Short articles written by Davis and Stein (authors of this book) and
> some links to other preemie and parenting sites

http://members.aol.com/KBone91/tbone.html

> T-Bone's Survival Tips for New Preemie Parents

www.premature-infant.com

> Parenting in the NICU and Beyond
> A resource for parents of preemies and for health care professionals
> by Dianne Maroney, a former NICU nurse, coauthor of *Your Premature
> Baby and Child*, and mother of a preemie.

Fathers

www.jeffslife.net

> Heartfelt, beautifully written essays by writer Jeff Stimpson, father of
> Alex (preemie) and Ned.

Breast-Feeding

www.lalecheleague.org

> La Leche League International

Multiples

www.mostonline.org/

> Mothers of Supertwins Online

www.groups.yahoo.com/group/specpar/join

> SPECPAR (for parents of multiples where one or more of the children
> has special needs)

www.synspectrum.com/multiplicity.html

> Multiplicity: The Special Challenges of Parenting Twins and More
> Loss, Prematurity and Special Needs
> Designed and maintained by Elizabeth A. Pector, M.D., a family
> practitioner and parent to a surviving preemie twin.

NICU and Medical Information

www.pediatrics.wisc.edu/childrenshosp/parents_of_preemies/

> Answers to commonly asked questions; Web site developed by Jane E.
> Brazy, M.D., neonatologist. Available in Spanish and English.

www.hhs.gov/ocr/hipaa

U.S. Department of Health and Human Services

Office for Civil Rights – HIPAA Medical Privacy Rules –

National Standards

This government Web site provides information about laws regarding medical records and getting access to them.

Family-Centered Care

www.familycenteredcare.org

The Institute for Family-Centered Care, a nonprofit organization, provides essential leadership to advance the understanding and practice of family-centered care. The Institute serves as a central resource for both family members and members of the health care field, providing information, education, training, and networking.

www.theschwartzcenter.org

The Kenneth B. Schwartz Center

Promotes collaborative and healing relationships between families and caregivers. Provides consultation and a model of hospital rounds that supports and builds community for health care providers.

101 Merrimac Street, Suite 603

Boston, MA 02114-2792

(617) 724-4746

Resource Listings for Preemie Parents

http://members.aol.com/MarAim/preemie.htm

Resources for Parents of Preemies

www.prematurity.org/preemiepgs.html

http://kingproductions.com/babylink.htm

Tommy's Cybernursery Preemie Web

Daddy's Link Library, comprehensive listing of Internet sites

www.storknet.com/cubbies/index.html

Storknet.com

Comprehensive pregnancy and parenting site, including special topics such as neonatal intensive care and pregnancy/infant loss support.

www.pregnancy.org/topics.php

> Pregnancy.org: Preconception, Pregnancy, and Parenting
> Comprehensive site and community, topics include preemies, infertility, grief and loss, special needs, twins and multiples; run by parents who've been there.

www.sidelines.org

> Sidelines provides emotional support and practical suggestions during pregnancy bed rest.

http://fpb.cwru.edu/bedrest/

> From Judith Maloni, RN, Ph.D. regarding the latest medical information about pregnancy bed rest.

Feeding Issues

www.members.iinet.net.au/~scarffam/serve/cache/1.html

> Support group for G-tube, NG-tube, J-tube and GJ-tube users and their caregivers. Members range from parents trying to make the decision to have a tube placed in their children to those who are veterans.

www.network54.com/Hide/Forum/109925

> GERD Word: A board for parents of children with reflux

www.feedingcenter.org/discussion.html

> Center for Pediatric Feeding and Swallowing Disorders

www.health.groups.yahoo.com/group/feeding/

> The feeding group on Yahoo

http://hometown.aol.com/Lmwill262/

> Small Wonders – Preemie Place
> Preemie-related issues, particularly "Feeding and Preemies."

Postpartum Depression

www.depressionafterdelivery.com/

> Depression After Delivery

www.postpartum.net/

> Postpartum Depression International

Childbearing Losses

www.climb-support.org

> CLIMB: Center for Loss in Multiple Birth
> Provides support by and for parents of twins, triplets, or higher multiple birth children who have experienced one or more of their children's deaths during pregnancy, at birth, in infancy, or in childhood.

http://health.groups.yahoo.com/group/elimbo/

LIMBO Loss in Multiple Birth Outreach

www.plida.org/

PLIDA Pregnancy Loss and Infant Death Alliance

A nationwide, collective community of professionals and bereaved parents that promotes awareness, advocacy, parent support, and resources for grieving parents and their families.

www.nationalshareoffice.com

SHARE Pregnancy and Infant Loss Support

Provides a national list of parent support groups and other resources

(800) 821-6819

www.resolve.org/main/national/index.jsp?name=home

RESOLVE The National Infertility Association

A nationwide network of chapters providing education, advocacy, and support.

Family Medical Leave Laws

www.dol.gov/esa/whd/fmla/

U.S. Department of Labor Web site that provides compliance assistance for the Family Medical Leave Act (FMLA)

Education Advocacy

www.wrightslaw.com/

Accurate, up-to-date information about special education law and advocacy for children with disabilities.

www.allkindsofminds.org/

A nonprofit institute for understanding differences in learning. This is a comprehensive Web site for families, educators, and clinicians.

www.ideapractices.org

The Individuals with Disabilities Education Act Web site will provide you with information on the laws that govern early intervention and special education services.

www.ldanatl.org

Learning Disabilities Association

Resources and information on learning disabilities, including ADD.

www.copaa.net/

The Council of Parent Attorneys and Advocates

Tools and information for effective advocacy.

Children with Special Needs

www.geocities.com/heartland/plains/8950

> The Cerebral Palsy Network
>
> Parents improving the lives of their children who have CP.

www.oneaddplace.com

> One ADD Place
>
> Resources on attention deficit disorder, including links to online support.

www.our-kids.org

> Our Kids: Devoted to Raising Special Kids with Special Needs
>
> An e-mail support group for parents, caregivers, and others who are working with children with physical and/or mental disabilities and delays.

www.childrensdisabilities.info

> Children's disabilities information.

http://childrenwithspecialneeds.com/ipw-web/bulletin/bb/index.php

> Community for families of children with special needs.

http://groups.yahoo.com/group/KidPower/

> Kid Power: A board for parents of children with mild CP.

www.childdevelopmentnet.com/clinical/general/milestonesa.html#3

> A resource for developmental milestones.

www.eparent.com

> Exceptional parent magazine.

www.familyvillage.wisc.edu

> Family Village is a huge Web site with a wealth of parenting and disability information.

www.rarediseases.org

> The National Organization for Rare Disorders (NORD)

www.cheshire-med.com/forums/cldforum.html

> Chronic lung disease forum. This is really designed for adults but is a great resource for those with pulmonary issues.

www.nichcy.org

> NICHY is the National Information Center for Children and Youth with Disabilities. English and Spanish.

www.tash.org/

TASH is an international association of people with disabilities, their family members, other advocates, and professionals fighting for a society in which inclusion of all people in all aspects of society is the norm.

www.bridges4kids.org/HelpForKids-US.html

Bridges for Kids: "Building partnerships between families, schools, and communities"

A nonprofit parent organization providing a comprehensive list of resource and referral centers for parents looking for any kind of help for children from birth through transition to adult life.

www.yellowpagesforkids.com/

Yellow Pages for Kids with Disabilities

www.normemma.com/

Professional Development on Disability and Non-Coercive Practices

www.specialchild.com/bulletin.html

Special Child: lists equipment for sale/giveaway, and items wanted.

Financial and Health Care Access Assistance

www.familyvoices.org

Family Voices is a national organization devoted to helping families with their health care and insurance concerns.

www.challengedamerica.com

Challenged America: offers grants up to $500 for equipment purchase.

www.dcrf.com

Disabled Children's Relief Fund

Offers assistance to obtain medical care and equipment for disabled children.

www.npath.org/

Patient Travel

You can call twenty-four hours a day, seven days a week:

(800) 296-1217

www.miracleflights.org

Miracle flights for kids—free flights for medical care on commercial and private planes.

www.angelflight.com

Angel Flight—offers free flights for medical care.

Neonatal Guidelines
for Parents and Health Care Professionals

The Colorado Collective
for Medical Decisions

The Colorado Collective for Medical Decisions (CCMD) was a group of concerned health care professionals, parents, and community members across Colorado who worked together over the course of about five years (1994 to 1999) in order to create community-based guidelines that addressed medical care and end-of-life decision making. To address the medical care of critically ill newborns, CCMD created the Neonatal Guidelines and Neonatal Video Parents on the Threshold: You Are Not Alone. Our goal in developing community-based guidelines was to serve the following purposes:

- To promote open community discussion around difficult NICU medical/ ethical issues in the hope that these medical resources and technology will be used wisely and humanely

- To encourage and enhance the dialogue between the parents and health care professionals during this difficult, heart-wrenching time

- To empower physicians to be decision leaders when a baby's prognosis is clear, whether poor or favorable

- To facilitate collaborative decision making between health care providers and the parents of critically ill newborns for whom the prognosis is unclear

- To support parents emotionally, whatever decision they make for their babies

- To remind outsiders that they must be fully informed about the specific medical realities before voicing an opinion about treatment choices or attempting to represent the best interests of any infant

CCMD Neonatal Guidelines

Modern medical technology achieves many good and important goals. A primary goal of neonatal intensive care is to help sick infants become healthy children.

To use technology wisely, we must acknowledge its limitations. For some infants, the burdens of treatment outweigh the benefits.

Parents must be fully informed about the risks, benefits, outcomes, and uncertainties of aggressive medical intervention for their individual baby. Whether an infant lives or dies, it is the parents who ultimately live with the result.

When the prognosis is clear, health care providers should be decision leaders.

When the prognosis is unclear (or becomes unclear), health care providers should work collaboratively with parents as decisions are made about an infant's care.

When aggressive intervention is withheld or withdrawn, comfort care should be provided.

When aggressive intervention is pursued for an infant whose outcome is uncertain, physicians should discuss with parents the specific burdens of treatment and how benefits and outcomes remain speculative.

For all NICU infants, regular and timely care conferences between parents and health care teams are an integral part of providing appropriate treatment. Follow-up care should be provided to all families.

Please copy and distribute CCMD guidelines.
CCMD Neonatal Videotape
Parents on the Threshold: You Are Not Alone was designed to support parents and enhance parent-professional communication when a newborn infant has a poor or uncertain prognosis.

CCMD Guidelines featured as written text in the video:

Infants who are likely to survive should be given appropriate medical care even if they have mental or physical limitations.

Infants who are extremely unlikely to survive infancy due to extreme prematurity should receive comfort care instead of aggressive life-sustaining interventions.

Infants who are extremely unlikely to survive infancy due to a lethal birth defect should receive comfort care instead of aggressive life-sustaining interventions.

Infants for whom survival offers only a short lifetime filled with significant suffering should receive comfort care instead of life-sustaining interventions.

When the outcome of aggressive medical care for an infant is uncertain, the family should be provided with comprehensive information about outcomes.

When the outcome of aggressive medical care for an infant is uncertain, decisions about life-sustaining interventions should be made jointly by the family and medical team.

To obtain copies of the CCMD neonatal videotape, please contact Nickel's Worth Productions, NickelTV@aol.com; (303) 825-5555 for other information; ParentingYourPrematureBaby.com for questions, concerns, and feedback.

• • •

Each video includes written materials that describe the video's intended uses, offer guidance for providing support to parents and involving them in decision making, plus the CCMD Neonatal Guidelines for medical decision making in the NICU.

Index

F

Failure: dying baby and, 368; fathers' feelings of, 96; feelings of, in NICU, 64; grief and, 41; moving through feelings of, 62–65, 763–64

Faith, questioning your, 91–92

Family, 635–74; in coping, 688–92; extended, 672, 686–98; ideal size of, 738–39; other children in, 659–73; partner relationship in, 635–56; single parents in, 657–58

Family-centered care in the NICU, 193, 200

Family leave, 715

Family therapy in handling grief, 85

Father(s): assistance with everyday chores and errands, 685–86; in avoiding grief, 103–4; dying baby and, 393–95; in early delivery, 134, 148–50; feelings of, 62, 95–116, 640–46; negotiating with employer, 714–16; pregnancy complications and, 120, 121; pride and, 96; as protector, 105; separation from baby and, 138; social support for, 683–86

FatherLoss (Chethik), 102

Fatigue, 176–79; grief and, 34–35

Fear(s): about future, 44–45; anger and, 248–49; early delivery and, 132–33; effect on relationships, 638; facing, 249; getting in touch with, 107–9; hopes and, 332–39; of inadequacy, as caregiver, 433–35; management of, 76–81, 211; in post-preemie pregnancy, 754–58; pride and, 28–29; voicing, 47, 756

Feeding: for multiple babies, 310–11; in the NICU, 295–311; oral difficulties in, 540–46. *See also* Bottle-feeding; Breast-feeding; Diet; Dieting

Feelings: acceptance of, 27, 36, 64–65, 606–20; difference between being and, 27; expression of, by other children, 665; identifying your, 27; managing painful, in high-risk pregnancy, 758–59; mixed, about premature baby, 441–42; between partners, 637–39; sorting through, 47; talking about, 28. *See also specific*

Focus, shifting of, in delivery, 134–35

Food sensitivities, 450, 532

Forgetting, moving on, but not, 795–96

Forgiveness, asking for, 75–76

Formula feeding, 296–98; decision making on, 296–98. *See also* Bottle-feeding

Fourth trimester, 160

Friends in support network, 699–714

Frustration, feelings of, in fathers, 96

Full-term birth, complications with, 780

Funerals, 382

Future: fears about, 44–45; hopes for, 55, 514–15

G

Gastroesophageal reflux, 563

Gender, grief and, 97–115

Genetic contributions, guilt and, 361

Genetic testing, 746–47

Gestational diabetes, 734

Giftedness, 524

Gorski, Peter, 584

Grandparents, grief of, 692–98

Greenspan, Stanley, 493

Grief: anticipatory, 35, 366; avoidance of, 80–81, 103–4; counseling in handling, 84–89; couples and, 112–15; on death of baby, 360–72; disabilities and, 604–11; feelings of, 37–45; gender and, 97–115; getting to bottom of, 81–92; of grandparents, 692–98; having patience with, 427–28; letting flow, 46–47; physical symptoms of, 34–35; as process, 28–45; realistic expectations for, 47–48; relationships and, 637, 642; revisiting, 35; styles of, 51–52, 104–7; suppressing, 46; triggers for, 609–11; tube feeding and, 543; understanding, 34–36, 620–25

Grievers: blended, 100; dissonant, 100–101; instrumental, 99–100, 114; intuitive, 99; types of male, 102–3

Group therapy for PTSD, 79

Growth charts, 537–38

G-tube, 542, 546

Guarantees, lack of, in NICU, 40

Guilt: dying baby and, 361–62, 368; effect on relationships, 638; grief and, 41; letting go of, 72–76, 351–54; moving through, 69–76; over disabilities, 613–18

H

Hanging-out time, 672

Harmony in relationship, 644–45

Healing: after death of baby, 382–85; coping and, 45–56, 789–816; seeing transformation as, 814–16; time and, 35

Health care providers: dashing of hopes by, 336–37; feeling displaced by, 253–56; parent as member of, 205, 206–7; partnering with, 202–6, 621; for premature baby, 200–8; in prenatal care, 742–46

Health insurance, in paying for counseling, 87

Heart palpitations, grief and, 34–35

Help: reaching out for, 726–27. *See also* Support; Support network

Helplessness: during bed rest, 764–65. *See also* Powerlessness

Hemorrhoids, 174

Herb therapy, 186

High-risk pregnancy: balancing needs in, 769–70; boredom in, 773–74; child care during, 767–68; emotions and, 63; feelings of failure in, 763–64; finding obstetric practice specializing in, 743; identification of, 117–18; isolation in, 774–75; other children's emotional needs in, 770–71; painful feelings in, 758–59; parenting during, 767–71; significant milestones in, 759–61; uncertainties in, 762–63

High-tech emergency delivery, 41

Hindmilk, 164–65

Hobbies, renewing, 64

Holding, positions for, 440

Home, staying, 431–55, 718–22

Homecoming, 421–28; anger on, 66–67, 434; bonding and, 281; dropping emotional guard on, 425–27; by dying baby, 377–78; emotional fallout and, 423–28; extended family and, 689–90; feelings on, 43; with full-term baby, 780–82; having patience with grief on, 427–28; by other premature babies, 445; preparing siblings for, 669–70; reorientation of baby on, 436–37; siblings post, 670–73; of surviving babies, 366. *See also* Discharge

Home health care agency, use of, in baby's discharge, 413

Homeopathy, 87, 186

Honesty between partners, 639–40

Hope, 806–8; on birth of new baby, 7, 9–10; change of direction in, 338–39; dashing of, by health care team, 336–37; denial and, 24–25; derailing of high, 688; despair and, 123; fears and, 332–39; holding on to, for the future, 55, 338

Hospital, transferring back to local, 400–1

Household, running, 725–27

Humor, grief and, 54

Hyperactivity, 524

Hypnotherapy, 186

I

Identity, employment and, 716–25

Imagery, relaxation and, 184

Immersion, 83–84

Inadequacy, guilt and, 71

Incompetence, feelings of, 62–65

Infant behavioral states, 312–13

Infant massage, 292–93

Infertility, 63, 730, 732

Information, 208–23; benefits of, 209–12; challenges of, 212–13; limits on, in NICU, 222–23; sharing, with others, 699–704; sharing about children in the NICU, 342; sources of, 213–15

Information overload, 216–18

Informed consent, 224–25

Inner searching, 506

Instrumental grievers, 99–100, 114

Interpersonal conflicts, 218–19

Interpersonal support, responding to, 113

Interventions: anger and, 617; disabilities and, 625–33; regrets about, 388; second thoughts on refusing, 388–91

Intimacy between partners, 650–52

Intuitive grievers, 99

Isolation: disabilities and, 612; dying baby and, 368; grief and, 43, 52; in high-risk pregnancy, 774–75; need for support and, 675–77

J

Jealousy, feelings of, on bed rest, 66

Journaling, 27, 49–51, 64, 68, 75, 87, 89–90, 148, 640, 685, 703, 736, 743, 756

Joy, mix of sadness with, 778–79

K

Kangaroo care, 226, 287–92; arrangements for, 291–92; benefits of, 289–90; breast-feeding and, 304; for dying baby, 373, 377; emotions in, 290–91

Keepsakes: death of baby and, 372, 378–80; feelings and, 83

Kennell, John, 493

Klaus, Marshall and Phyllis, 493

Knowledge: as empowering, 64; in mastering your fears, 27, 756–57

L

Labels: assigning negative, 510, 511–13; understanding, 563–65

Lactation consultant, 163

La Leche League, 165

Language therapy, 526

Laughter, relaxation and, 185

LeShan, Eda, 493

Let down reflex, 163

Letting go, 77, 797–98; in parenting, 498–99, 504, 506–7; perspective on, 391–94

Liberation from NICU restrictions, 432–33

Life-and-death decisions in the NICU, 347–54

Light sleep, 313

Listening: finding perfect listener in, 701; to other children, 664, 670

Lochia, 172

Longing, grief and, 45

Long-term care, decisions on, in the NICU, 354–55

Losses on premature birth, 30–33

M

Male grievers, types of, 102–3

Martin, Terry, 99

Massage, 87, 186

Mastery, NICU and, 210

Mastitis, 167–68

Medical barriers, negotiating, in the NICU, 249–53

Medical complications: dealing with, 244–45, 412–13; discharge and, 403–4

Medical equipment, discharge with or without, 408–13

Medical intervention, need for, 515

Medical opinions, dealing with differing, 322–23

Medical procedures, parent presence at, 227

Medical records, requesting, 27

Medical staff, communication with, 215–16

Medications: for postpartum depression, 159–60; for PTSD, 79; side effects of, 119

Medicine, expectations of modern, 13

Meditation, 87, 186

Memorial services, 382

•••

P

Notes

Notes

Notes

Notes

SHARING THE GIFT OF COMFORT

A special note from the authors

There are a great number of books available that focus on a premature baby's medical conditions, developmental diagnoses, treatments and procedures, and that guide caregiving tasks. *Parenting Your Premature Baby and Child: The Emotional Journey* focuses on the emotional aspects of parenting your premature baby, from your first encounter with pregnancy complications, during your baby's delivery and through hospitalization, after discharge and homecoming, and into infancy and early childhood. The purpose of this book is to offer comfort, empathy, support, and empowerment. Rather than telling parents what to do, it walks alongside parents on their journey, encouraging them to figure out what is best for themselves and their baby.

In this country one of every ten babies is born prematurely. If this book has helped you and you would like to share the comfort it has brought you by donating copies of it to health care providers, hospitals, or support organizations, please let us know. Fulcrum Publishing is happy to provide a substantial discount for multiple copies. For details, please contact Jessica Dyer at 1-800-992-2908 or via e-mail at jessica@fulcrum-books.com and ask about making a donation of *Parenting Your Premature Baby and Child*.

—*Debbie & Mara*

Fulcrum Publishing